2001–02

MILLER

GAAP

FINANCIAL STATEMENT DISCLOSURES MANUAL

GEORGE GEORGIADES, CPA

Aspen Law & Business
A Division of Aspen Publishers, Inc.
Gaithersburg New York
(Formerly published by Harcourt Professional Publishing)

A Division of Aspen Publishers, Inc.
A Wolters Kluwer Company
www.aspenpublishers.com

Portions of this work were published in previous editions.

Printed in the United States of America
1 2 3 4 5 6 7 8 9 0

ISBN 0-7355-2501-3

About Aspen Law & Business

Aspen Law & Business is a leading publisher of authoritative treatises, practice manuals, services, and journals for accountants, auditors, attorneys, environmental compliance professionals, financial and tax advisors, corporate and bank directors, and other business professionals. Our mission is to provide practical solution-based how-to information keyed to the latest regulatory, legislative, and judicial developments.

We offer publications in the areas of accounting and auditing; banking and finance; bankruptcy; business and commercial law; construction law; corporate law; environmental compliance; pensions, benefits, and labor; insurance law; securities; taxation; intellectual property; government and administrative law; real estate law; matrimonial and family law; environmental and health law; international law; legal practice and litigation; and criminal law.

Other books in the Aspen Law & Business accounting and auditing library include:

Accounting Irregularities and Financial Fraud
Audit Committees: A Guide for Directors, Management, and Consultants
Construction Accounting Deskbook
CPA's Guide to Developing Effective Business Plans
CPA's Guide to Effective Engagement Letters
CPA's Guide to E-Business
Federal Government Contractor's Manual
How to Manage Your Accounting Practice
Medical Practice Management Handbook
Miller Audit Procedures
Miller Compilations and Reviews
Miller European Accounting Guide
Miller GAAP Guide
Miller GAAP Practice Manual
Miller GAAS Guide
Miller GAAS Practice Manual
Miller Governmental GAAP Guide
Miller International Accounting Standards Guide
Miller Local Government Audits
Miller Not-for-Profit Organization Audits
Miller Not-for-Profit Reporting
Miller Single Audits
Professional's Guide to Value Pricing

ASPEN LAW & BUSINESS
A Division of Aspen Publishers, Inc.
A Wolters Kluwer Company
www.aspenpublishers.com

SUBSCRIPTION NOTICE

This Aspen Law & Business product is updated on a periodic basis with supplements to reflect important changes in the subject matter. If you purchased this product directly from Aspen Law & Business, we have already recorded your subscription for the update service.

If, however, you purchased this product from a bookstore and wish to receive future updates and revised or related volumes billed separately with a 30-day examination review, please contact our Customer Service Department at 1-800-234-1660 or send your name, company name (if applicable), address, and the title of the product to:

ASPEN LAW & BUSINESS
A Division of Aspen Publishers, Inc.
7201 McKinney Circle
Frederick, MD 21704

Our Peer Review Policy

Thank you for ordering the 2001–02 *Miller GAAP Financial Statement Disclosures Manual*. Each year we bring you the best accounting and auditing reference guides available. To confirm the technical accuracy and quality control of our materials, Aspen Law and Business (formerly Harcourt Professional Publishing) voluntarily submitted to a peer review of our publishing system and our publications (see the Peer Review Statement on the following page).

In addition to peer review, our publications undergo strict technical and content reviews by qualified practitioners. This ensures that our books and electronic workpapers meet "real-world" standards and applicability.

Our publications are reviewed every step of the way—from conception to production—to ensure that we bring you the finest guides on the market.

Updated annually, peer reviewed, technically accurate, convenient, and practical—the 2001–02 *Miller GAAP Financial Statement Disclosures Manual* shows our commitment to creating books and electronic workpapers you can trust.

May 26, 2000

Board of Directors
Aspen Publishers, Inc.

We have reviewed the system of quality control for the development and maintenance of MILLER GAAP FINANCIAL STATEMENT DISCLOSURES MANUAL: 2001 EDITION (materials) of Aspen Publishers, Inc. (the Company) (formerly materials of Harcourt, Inc.) in effect for the year ended April 30, 2000, and the resultant materials in effect at April 30, 2000, in order to determine whether the materials are reliable aids to assist users in conforming with those professional standards the materials purport to encompass. The design of the system, and compliance with it, are the responsibilities of the company. Our responsibility is to express an opinion on the design of the system, and the company's compliance with that system based on our review. Our review did not cover the development and maintenance of the continuing education programs included in the materials.

Our review was conducted in accordance with the standards for reviews of quality control materials established by the peer review committee of the SEC practice section of the AICPA Division for CPA Firms. In performing our review, we have given consideration to the following general characteristics of a system of quality control. A company's system for the development and maintenance of quality control materials encompasses its organizational structure and the policies and procedures established to provide the users of its materials with reasonable assurance that the quality control materials are reliable aids to assist them in conforming with professional standards in conducting their accounting, auditing, and attest practices. The extent of a company's quality control policies and procedures for the development and maintenance of quality control materials and the manner in which they are implemented will depend upon a variety of factors, such as the size and organizational structure of the company and the nature of the materials provided to users. Variance in individual performance and professional interpretation affects the degree of compliance with prescribed quality control policies and procedures. Therefore, adherence to all policies and procedures in every case may not be possible.

Our review and tests were limited to the system of quality control for the development and maintenance of the aforementioned materials of Aspen Publishers, Inc. (formerly materials of Harcourt, Inc.) and to the materials themselves and did not extend to the application of these materials by users of the materials nor to the policies and procedures of individual users.

In our opinion, the system of quality control for the development and maintenance of the quality control materials of Aspen Publishers, Inc. (formerly materials of Harcourt, Inc.) was suitably designed and was being complied with during the year ended April 30, 2000 to provide users of the materials with reasonable assurance that the materials are reliable aids to assist them in conforming with those professional standards the materials purport to encompass. Also, in our opinion, the quality control materials referred to above are reliable aids at April 30, 2000.

CALDWELL, BECKER, DERVIN, PETRICK & CO., LLP.
CALDWELL, BECKER, DERVIN, PETRICK & CO., L. L. P.

20750 Ventura Boulevard, Suite 140 • Woodland Hills, CA 91364
(818) 704-1040 • (323) 873-1040 • FAX (818) 704-5536

About the GAAP Hierarchy

The meaning of the term *generally accepted accounting principles* (GAAP) has varied over time. Originally, GAAP referred to accounting policies and procedures that were widely used in practice. As standard-setting bodies and professional organizations became more involved in recommending preferred practices, the term came to refer more to the pronouncements issued by particular accounting bodies. Today, many different series of authoritative literature exist, some of which are still in effect but are no longer being issued, like APB Opinions and AICPA Accounting Research Bulletins. Others—such as FASB Statements—continue to be issued by accounting organizations.

To better organize and clarify what is meant by GAAP, SAS-69 (The Meaning of "Present Fairly in Conformity with Generally Accepted Accounting Principles") established what is commonly referred to as the GAAP hierarchy. The purpose of the hierarchy is to instruct financial statement preparers, auditors, and users of financial statements concerning the relative priority of the different sources of GAAP used by auditors to judge the fairness of presentation in financial statements. Though the GAAP hierarchy appears in the professional auditing literature, its impact goes beyond its importance to auditors: Preparers, users, and others interested in financial statements must understand the sources of GAAP that underlie those statements.

SAS-69 defines the *GAAP hierarchy* by outlining four categories of established accounting principles. Because these sources of accounting principles arose over five decades and were promulgated by different groups, some conflicts exist among them. The four categories of GAAP correspond to these principles' relative authoritativeness. Higher categories carry more weight and must be followed when conflicts arise. When two or more sources of GAAP within a given level of the hierarchy disagree on a particular transaction, the approach that better portrays the substance of the transaction should be followed.

In addition to these four levels, the GAAP hierarchy recognizes other types of accounting literature that may be useful in resolving financial reporting problems when issues have not been covered in established sources of GAAP.

The figure on the following page displays the four levels of established principles that are supported by authoritative accounting literature, as well as the additional sources of GAAP, and the corresponding Miller coverage.

GAAP Hierarchy	Miller Coverage
LEVEL A*	
• FASB Statements of Financial Accounting Standards (FAS)	2001 *Miller GAAP Guide*
• FASB Interpretations (FIN)	2001 *Miller GAAP Guide*
• APB Opinions (APB)	2001 *Miller GAAP Guide*
• Accounting Research Bulletins (ARB)	2001 *Miller GAAP Guide*
LEVEL B*	
• FASB Technical Bulletins (FTB)	2001 *Miller GAAP Practice Manual*
• AICPA Industry Audit and Accounting Guides	2001 Miller Engagement Series
• AICPA Statements of Position (SOP)	2001 *Miller GAAP Practice Manual*
LEVEL C*	
• Consensus Positions of the Emerging Issues Task Force (EITF)	2001 *Miller GAAP Practice Manual*
• AICPA AcSEC Practice Bulletins (PB)	2001 *Miller GAAP Practice Manual*
LEVEL D*	
• AICPA Accounting Interpretations (AIN)	2001 *Miller GAAP Practice Manual*
• FASB Implementation Guides (FIG)	2001 *Miller GAAP Practice Manual*
• SEC and FASB Staff Positions (Topic Ds)	2001 *Miller GAAP Practice Manual*
• Industry practices widely recognized and prevalent	2001 *Miller GAAP Practice Manual*

* All four levels are covered monthly in the *Miller GAAP Update Service.*

Other Accounting Literature

- FASB Concepts Statements (CON)
- APB Statements
- AICPA Issues Papers
- International Accounting Standards Committee Statements (2001 *Miller International Accounting Standards*)
- GASB Statements, Interpretations, and Technical Bulletins (2001 *Miller Governmental GAAP Guide*)
- Pronouncements of other professional associations and regulatory bodies
- AICPA Technical Practice Aids
- Accounting textbooks, handbooks, and articles

Contents

Part I—Special Financial Statement Topics and Disclosures

Preface

The 2001–02 *Miller GAAP Financial Statement Disclosures Manual* is current through the issuance of the following pronouncements:

- FASB Statement No. 140 (Accounting for Transfers and Servicing of Financial Assets and Extinguishments of Liabilities)
- FASB Interpretation No. 44 (Accounting for Certain Transactions Involving Stock Compensation—An Interpretation of APB Opinion No. 25)
- EITF Issue No. 00-27 (Application of EITF Issue No. 98-5, *Accounting for Convertible Securities with Beneficial Conversion Features or Contingently Adjustable Conversion Ratios,* to Certain Convertible Instruments)

The 2001–02 *Miller GAAP Financial Statement Disclosures Manual* provides a complete, quick, and valuable reference source for financial statement disclosures. Specifically, the *Manual*:

- Provides over 850 examples of realistic sample footnote disclosures to assist in the preparation of financial statements for an audit, a review, or a compilation engagement.
- Facilitates compliance with authoritative pronouncements by integrating, in each chapter, the specific disclosure requirements with the sample footnotes.
- Provides sample disclosures that are technically sound, understandable, and comprehensive and that cover a variety of scenarios, from the most common to the most unusual.
- Incorporates all currently effective pronouncements, including those that cover areas of unusual difficulty, such as financial instruments, income taxes, pensions, accounting changes, and going concern.

All of the sample disclosures in the 2001–02 *Miller GAAP Financial Statement Disclosures Manual* are included on the accompanying CD-ROM. Therefore, once you've identified the disclosure suited to your specific needs, you can simply select it from the CD-ROM, place it into your financial statements, then modify it as necessary.

The *Manual* is divided into four major parts. Part I, Special Financial Statement Topics and Disclosures, covers major financial accounting and reporting topics. The chapters in Part II, Balance Sheet, are arranged in the order in which the major assets, liabilities, and equity captions ordinarily appear in a balance sheet. For example, assets and liabilities are discussed first in general, then cash and cash equivalents, and so on. Part III, Income Statement, covers the specific elements of "results of operations" that are required to be presented separately under GAAP. Part IV, Statement of Cash Flows, discusses the presentation of specific types of transactions in cash flow statements, alternative formats for presenting the statements, and the disclosure of noncash transactions.

The book is designed for ease of use. You can locate information based either on the disclosure topic or on the disclosure's location in the financial statement. In addition, each chapter is composed as a stand-alone chapter, providing you with all the information you'll need on a specific topic. Each chapter consists of the following parts:

1. **Executive Summary.** This summary provides a clear and concise discussion of the specific financial statement topic or standard.
2. **Authoritative Literature.** This section provides a complete listing of the relevant authoritative pronouncements so that you can access the authoritative information quickly and easily.
3. **Disclosure Requirements.** This section provides a detailed listing of the disclosure requirements mandated by GAAP.
4. **Examples of Financial Statement Disclosures.** This section contains specific examples of disclosures that cover different situations, circumstances, assumptions, and so on. Unless specifically indicated, the examples provided assume that the most recent financial statements presented are for the year ended December 31, 2000.

The *Manual* also includes a financial statement disclosures checklist that provides a centralized resource of the required and recommended GAAP disclosures currently in use. It is designed to assist the user in determining whether the required financial statement disclosures have been made.

The author and publisher welcome comments, suggestions, and recommendations to improve this *Manual*. These will be considered for incorporation in future revisions of the *Manual*. Please send your comments to:

Anita Rosepka, Managing Editor
Aspen Law & Business
1185 Avenue of the Americas
New York, NY 10036

Acknowledgments

Thanks are due to the staff of Aspen Publishers, Inc. and especially to Anita Rosepka, Managing Editor, for her constructive input and diligent efforts in producing the *Manual* and to Jennifer Crane for her patience in bringing this edition to press. The author and publisher also thank Kendall G. Merkley, CPA, of Corbin & Wertz for his review and comments on the *Manual* as this year's revision got under way. Also, I thank my fiancée, Caroline Seliga, CPA, for her continuous support and encouragement, and particularly for her assistance in compiling the specific examples of financial statement disclosures.

George Georgiades
Laguna Niguel, California

About the Author

George Georgiades, CPA, has more than 20 years of experience in public accounting, including seven years as an audit senior manager with a major international accounting firm. He currently has his own firm and consults exclusively with CPA firms on technical accounting, auditing, and financial statement disclosure issues. In writing this *Manual,* Mr. Georgiades has capitalized on the extensive experience he has gained from association with clients and with international, national, regional, and local accounting firms. He has been personally involved in more than 600 audit engagements and related financial statements of both small, closely held companies and large, publicly held enterprises. He has personally conducted more than 50 peer reviews, consulting reviews, and inspections. He also brings to the *Manual* extensive hands-on experience in performing independent technical reviews of financial statements.

Mr. Georgiades is also the author of *Miller Audit Procedures, Miller GAAS Practice Manual,* and the *Miller GAAS Update Service.* He is a member of the American Institute of Certified Public Accountants and the California Society of Certified Public Accountants.

Part I—
Special Financial Statement Topics and Disclosures

CHAPTER 1
ACCOUNTING CHANGES

CONTENTS

EXECUTIVE SUMMARY

Accounting changes are broadly classified into three categories:

1. Changes in an accounting principle
2. Changes in an accounting estimate
3. Changes in the reporting entity

Corrections of errors in previously issued financial statements are not accounting changes, but they are covered in the same accounting literature because of their similarity.

Promulgated generally accepted accounting principles (GAAP) identify three accounting methods to account for accounting changes and corrections of errors: (1) current and prospective method, (2) cumulative effect method, and (3) retroactive restatement method. These methods are not alternatives—the authoritative literature is specific concerning which method is to be used for each type of accounting change or correction of error.

Accounting Changes

Common changes in accounting principles include the following:

1. Changing the method of pricing inventory (e.g., changing from LIFO to FIFO or from FIFO to LIFO)
2. Changing the method of depreciating previously recorded assets (e.g., changing from a straight-line method to an accelerated method or from an accelerated method to a straight-line method)
3. Changing the method of accounting for long-term construction-type contracts
4. Adopting a new accounting principle

A change in an accounting estimate usually is the result of new events, changing conditions, more experience, or additional information, any of which requires previous estimates to be revised. Estimates are necessary in determining depreciation and amortization of long-lived assets, uncollectible receivables, provisions for warranty, and a multitude of other items involved in preparing financial statements.

A change in the reporting entity takes place when the following occurs:

1. Presenting consolidated or combined financial statements in place of statements of individual companies

2. Changing specific subsidiaries comprising the group of companies for which consolidated financial statements are presented
3. Changing the companies included in combined financial statements

Correction of Errors

Errors that are discovered in financial statements subsequent to their issuance are reported as prior-period adjustments. Errors result from mistakes in mathematics and in the application of an accounting principle or from misjudgment in the use of facts. Although correcting an error and changing an estimate are similar and are sometimes confused, they are different in that a change in estimate is based on new (revised) information that was not previously available. A change from an unacceptable accounting principle to a generally accepted one is considered an error correction for financial reporting purposes.

Authoritative Literature

APB-9	Reporting the Results of Operations
APB-16	Business Combinations
APB-20	Accounting Changes
FAS-3	Reporting Accounting Changes in Interim Financial Statements
FAS-63	Financial Reporting by Broadcasters
FAS-73	Reporting a Change in Accounting for Railroad Track Structures
FAS-111	Rescission of FASB Statement No. 32 and Technical Corrections
FIN-1	Accounting Changes Related to the Cost of Inventory
FIN-20	Reporting Accounting Changes under AICPA Statements of Position

DISCLOSURE REQUIREMENTS

Change in Accounting Estimate

1. For an accounting-estimate change that affects several future periods (e.g., change in service lives of depreciable assets, actuarial assumptions affecting pension costs), disclosure should

include the effect on income before extraordinary items and net income (and on related per share amounts when presented) of the current period (APB-20, par. 33).

2. For an accounting-estimate change made each period in the ordinary course of accounting for items such as uncollectible accounts or inventory obsolescence, disclosure should be made of the effect, if material, on income before extraordinary items and net income (and on related per share amounts when presented) (APB-20, par. 33).

Change in Accounting Principle

1. For an accounting-principle change that is made in the year in which the change occurs, the following disclosures should be made (APB-20, par. 17):
   a. The nature of the change in accounting principle
   b. The justification for the change in accounting, including a clear explanation of why the newly adopted accounting principle is preferable
   c. The effect of the change on income before extraordinary items and net income (and related per share amounts when presented)
2. For an accounting-principle change that is accounted for as a cumulative effect adjustment, the following disclosures should be made (APB-20, pars. 19–26):
   a. The amount of the cumulative effect should be shown as a separate item in the income statement between the captions "extraordinary items" and "net income" along with the related tax effect (and related per share amounts when presented)
   b. The effect of adopting the new accounting principle on income before extraordinary items and on net income (and on related per share amounts when presented) for the period in which the change occurs
   c. Pro forma amounts of income before extraordinary items and net income (and related per share amounts when presented) should be shown on the face of the income statements for all periods presented as if the newly adopted accounting principle had been applied during all periods affected
   d. If the pro forma amounts cannot be computed or reasonably estimated for individual prior periods, but the cumulative effect on retained earnings at the beginning of the period of change can be determined, the reason for not showing the pro forma amounts by periods should be disclosed

e. If the amount of the cumulative effects of an accounting-principle change on retained earnings at the beginning of the period of change cannot be computed (generally limited to a change from the FIFO inventory method to LIFO), the following disclosures should be made:

— The effect of the change on the results of operations (and on related per share amounts when presented) for the period of change

— The reason for omitting (i) accounting for the cumulative effect and (ii) disclosures of pro forma amounts for prior years

3. For an accounting-principle change that is reported by restating prior years' financial statements, the following disclosures should be made (APB-20, par. 28):

    a. The nature of and justification for a change in accounting principle

    b. The effect of the change on income before extraordinary items and net income (and on related per share amounts when presented) for all periods presented

4. The following disclosures should be made for a change in the method of depreciation, depletion, or amortization for newly acquired assets while a different method continues to be used for assets of that class acquired in previous years (APB-20, par. 24):

    a. Description of the nature of the change in method

    b. The effect of the change in method on income before extraordinary items and net income (and on related per share amounts when presented) for the year in which the change in method occurred

5. If an accounting change is not considered material for the period in which the change occurs, but it is reasonably certain that the change will have a material effect on financial statements of subsequent years, appropriate disclosures should be made whenever the financial statements of the year of change are presented (APB-20, par. 38).

Change in Reporting Entity

1. The following disclosures should be made for a reporting-entity change for the period in which the change has occurred (APB-20, par. 35):

    a. A description of the nature of the change

    b. A description of the reason for the change

c. The effect of the change on income before extraordinary items and net income (and on related per share amounts when presented) for all periods presented

Prior-Period Adjustments (Correction of Errors)

1. The following disclosures should be made for errors discovered in previously issued financial statements (disclosures required only for the year in which the error is discovered) (APB-20, par. 37; APB-9, par. 26):
   a. The nature of the error
   b. The effect of the correction of the error on income before extraordinary items and net income (and related per share amounts when presented) in the period of correction
   c. The amount of income tax applicable to each prior-period adjustment
2. If the effect of an error is presented in single-period financial statements, the effect (gross and net of tax) on the opening balance of retained earnings and on net income (and on related per share amounts when presented) of the preceding year should be disclosed (APB-9, par. 26).
3. If the effect of an error is presented in comparative financial statements, the effect should be presented as an adjustment to the opening balance of retained earnings and by restating prior-period financial statements affected by the error (APB-9, par. 18).

EXAMPLES OF FINANCIAL STATEMENT DISCLOSURES

The following sample disclosures are available on the accompanying disc.

Change in Accounting Estimate

Example 1–1: Change in Depreciable Lives of Property and Equipment—General

It is the Company's policy to periodically review the estimated useful lives of its fixed assets. This review during 2000 indicated that actual lives for certain asset categories generally were longer than the useful lives used for depreciation purposes in the Company's financial statements. As a result, the Company revised the estimated useful lives of certain categories of property, principally machinery and equipment, retroactive to January 1, 2000. The effect of this change in estimate was to reduce 2000 depreciation expense by $100,000 and increase 2000 net income by $60,000.

Example 1–2: Change in Depreciable Lives of Property and Equipment—Specific Reference Made to Average Depreciation Lives

Effective January 1, 2000, the Company changed its estimates of the useful lives of certain machinery and equipment at its manufacturing plant. The plant's asset depreciation lives that previously averaged ten years were increased to an average of 15 years, while those that previously averaged six to eight years were increased to an average of ten years. The Company made these changes to better reflect the estimated periods during which such assets will remain in service. This change had the effect of reducing depreciation expense by $250,000 and increasing net income by $120,000 in 2000.

Example 1–3: Change in Both Estimated Lives and Capitalization Policy—Specific Reference Made to Estimated Lives

Traditionally, the Company has deferred certain costs associated with the acquisition of new customer accounts and amortized the costs over their estimated useful lives. For costs incurred after January 1, 1999, the estimated useful life of these costs was extended from one year to three years, thereby reducing amortization in 1999 by $180,000 and increasing 1999 net income by $100,000. In 2000, the Company conformed its treatment of other customer acquisition costs that had been previously expensed so that customer acquisition costs are consistently capitalized and amortized over three years. The effect of this change in accounting estimate in 2000 was to reduce amortization in 2000 by $150,000 and increase 2000 net income by $90,000.

Example 1–4: Change in Accounting Principle Inseparable from Change in Accounting Estimate—The Change Is Accounted for as a Change in Accounting Estimate

Prior to October 1, 2000, production and tooling costs were charged to cost of sales based on the estimated average unit cost for Projects A, B, C, and D (the Projects) which, in the aggregate, consist of 100,000 lead-rubber bearings. Effective October 1, 2000, the Company changed its accounting for cost of sales on the Projects from the average cost basis to the specific-unit cost basis. This change to the specific-unit costing method for the Projects was made in recognition of production rates, existing order base, and length of time required to achieve project deliveries, and, therefore, the resultant increased difficulty, which became apparent in the fourth quarter of 2000, in making the estimates necessary under the average cost basis method. Because the effect of this change in accounting principle was inseparable from the effect of the change in accounting estimate, the change was accounted for as a change in estimate. As a result, the Company recorded a noncash pretax charge to operations of $500,000 in the fourth quarter of 2000. The effect of the charge was to decrease 2000 net income by $300,000.

Change in Accounting Principle

Example 1–5: Change in Method of Applying Overhead to Inventory—Cumulative Effect of the Change on Prior Years Is Recorded in the Current Year

Historically, the Company used a single overhead rate in valuing the ending inventory, which had been determined by comparing the total manufacturing overhead expenses for the year with total direct labor costs for the year. In 2000 the Company performed an extensive study to precisely determine the manufacturing overhead to be applied to specific product lines. As a result, effective January 1, 2000, the Company changed its method of applying overhead to inventory to more closely reflect the results of this study.

The Company believes that the change in the application of this accounting principle is preferable because it provides a better determination of overhead costs in inventory and, therefore, improves the matching of production costs with related revenues in reporting its operating results. In accordance with generally accepted accounting principles, the cumulative effect of the change for the periods prior to January 1, 2000, totaling $500,000, after reduction of income taxes of $300,000, has been recorded in the 2000 income statement. The effect of the change on the current year's net income before cumulative effect of a change in accounting principles is not material.

Pro forma net income for 1999 is $850,000, assuming the new accounting principle was applied retroactively.

Note: The following table illustrates the cumulative effect of the change as shown at the bottom of the Company's income statement (assume the Company's year-end is December 31 and the latest year presented is 2000).

	2000	*1999*
Earnings before cumulative effect of a change in accounting principle	$925,000	$730,000
Cumulative effect to January 1, 2000, of changing overhead recorded in inventory	500,000	-0-
Net earnings	$1,425,000	$730,000

Example 1–6: Change from LIFO to Average Cost Method for Valuing Inventory—Effect on Prior Years Is Determinable and Financial Statements for Prior Periods Retroactively Restated

Effective January 1, 2000, the Company changed its basis of valuing inventories from the last-in, first-out (LIFO) method to the average cost method. In 1999 and prior years, the cost of substantially all inventories was determined using the LIFO method. The Company believes that the average cost method of inventory valuation provides a more meaningful presentation of its financial position since this method reflects more recent costs in the balance sheet. Under the current economic environment of low inflation and an expected reduction in inventories and lower production costs, the Company believes that the average cost method also results in a better matching of current costs with current revenues.

The effect of the change in accounting principle was to increase 2000 net income by $450,000. The change has been applied to prior years by retroactively restating the financial statements presented for 1999. The effect of the restatement was to increase retained earnings as of January 1, 1999, by $1,350,000. The restatement decreased 1999 net income by $305,000.

Note: The following table illustrates the retroactive application of the change as shown on the face of the Company's statement of retained earnings or statement of stockholders' equity (assume the Company's year-end is December 31 and the latest year presented is 2000).

	2000	*1999*
Retained earnings at beginning of year, as previously reported	$4,725,000	$2,750,000
Cumulative effect on prior years of retroactive restatement for accounting change	-0-	1,350,000
Retained earnings at beginning of year, as restated	4,725,000	4,100,000
Net income	700,000	625,000
Retained earnings at end of year	$5,425,000	$4,725,000

Example 1–7: Change from FIFO to LIFO Method for Valuing Inventory—Effect on Prior Years Is Not Determinable

Effective January 1, 2000, the Company changed its method of valuing a significant component of its inventory from the first-in, first-out (FIFO) method to the last-in, first-out (LIFO) method. Management believes the LIFO method results in a better matching of current costs with current revenues and minimizes the effect of price level changes on inventory valuations. The cumulative effect of this accounting change for years prior to 2000 is not reasonably determinable, nor are the pro forma effects of retroactive application of the LIFO method to prior years. The effect of the change in 2000 was to decrease net income by $800,000.

Example 1–8: Change in Depreciation Method for Newly Acquired Assets

For financial statement purposes, the Company changed to the straight-line method of depreciation effective January 1, 2000, for all newly acquired property and equipment. Assets acquired before the effective date of the change continue to be depreciated principally by accelerated methods. The Company believes the new straight-line depreciation method will more accurately reflect its financial results by better matching costs of new property over the useful lives of these assets. In addition, the new depreciation method more closely conforms with that prevalent in the industry. The effect of the change was not material to the 2000 financial results of operations.

Example 1–9: Change in Pension Assumptions and Amortization Period of Prior Service Costs

In 2000, the Company reduced the amortization period of prior service costs from ten years to six years, and changed its assumption relating to investment return from 8% to 5% for all its employee benefit plans. The effect of these changes was to decrease net income for 2000 by $123,000.

Example 1–10: Change in Method of Accounting for Major Maintenance and Repairs Costs

Effective January 1, 2000, the Company changed its method of accounting for the cost of maintenance and repairs incurred in connection with major maintenance shutdown programs at all its manufacturing plants. These major maintenance costs, which result in plant shutdowns for approximately four to eight weeks, comprise principally amounts paid to third parties for materials, contract services, and other related items. Under the new method, major maintenance costs on projects exceeding $100,000 are capitalized when incurred and then charged against income over the period benefited by the major maintenance shutdown program, usually three years. Prior to this change in accounting method, major maintenance costs relating to plant shutdowns were charged against income when incurred.

The Company believes that the new method of accounting is preferable in that it provides for a better matching of major maintenance costs with future revenues. The Company's management believes that the investment in such major maintenance and repair costs enhances the reliability and performance of its manufacturing plants and, therefore, economically benefits future periods.

The cumulative effect of this accounting change for years prior to 2000, which is shown separately in the income statement for 2000, resulted in a benefit of $2 million after related income taxes of $800,000. Excluding the cumulative effect, this change increased net income for 2000 by $400,000.

Pro forma net income for 1999 is $1,800,000, assuming the accounting change was applied retroactively.

Note: The following table illustrates the cumulative effect of the change as shown at the bottom of the Company's income statement (assume the Company's year-end is December 31 and the latest year presented is 2000).

	2000	*1999*
Income before cumulative effect of change in accounting principle	$1,825,000	$1,630,000
Cumulative effect of change in accounting principle	2,000,000	-0-
Net income	$3,825,000	$1,630,000

Example 1–11: Change from the Completed Contract Method to the Percentage-of-Completion Method of Accounting

Effective January 1, 2000, the Company changed its method of accounting for long-term contracts from the completed contract method to the percentage-of-completion method. The Company believes that the new method more accurately reflects periodic results of operations and conforms to revenue recognition practices predominant in the industry. The effect of this change was to increase 2000 net income by $600,000. The change has been applied to prior years by retroactively restating the financial statements presented for 1999. The effect of the restatement was to increase retained earnings as of January 1, 1999, by $1,000,000. The restatement decreased 1999 net income by $305,000.

Note: The following table illustrates the retroactive application of the change as shown on the face of the Company's statement of retained earnings or statement of stockholders' equity (assume the Company's year-end is December 31 and the latest year presented is 2000).

	2000	*1999*
Retained earnings at beginning of year, as previously reported	$4,400,000	$2,900,000
Cumulative effect on prior years of retroactive restatement for accounting change	-0-	1,000,000
Retained earnings at beginning of year, as restated	4,400,000	3,900,000
Net income	650,000	500,000
Retained earnings at end of year	$5,050,000	$4,400,000

Example 1–12: Change in Accounting Method for Start-Up Activities

In April 1998, the American Institute of Certified Public Accountants issued Statement of Position 98-5 (Reporting on the Costs of Start-Up Activities), which requires that such costs, as broadly defined in the Statement, be expensed as incurred. The Statement is effective for years beginning after December 15, 1998, and the initial application must be reported as the cumulative effect of a change in accounting principle. The Company adopted the new Statement in 1999, which resulted in the recording of a cumulative effect of a change in accounting principle of $1,400,000 ($0.26 per share), net of the applicable income tax benefit. This charge represents the unamortized portion of previously capitalized organization, start-up, pre-operating and integrated logistics services contract implementation costs primarily incurred as a part of the Company's expansion activities, and long-term contract activity from 1996 through 1998. The Company believes that the ongoing application of this Statement will not have a material adverse effect on the Company's financial position, results of operations, or cash flows.

Example 1–13: Change in Reporting Period for Subsidiary from Fiscal Year to Calendar Year—The Parent Company's Reporting Period Is a Calendar Year Ending December 31

Effective January 1, 2000, the Parent Company changed the reporting period of its majority-owned subsidiary XYZ, Inc. from a fiscal year ending November 30 to a calendar year ending December 31. The results of operations of XYZ, Inc. during the period between the end of the 1999 fiscal year and the beginning of the new calendar year (the stub period) amounted to a net income of $350,000. This amount was credited to retained earnings to avoid reporting more than 12 months results of operations in one year. Accordingly, the 2000 consolidated operations include the results for XYZ, Inc. beginning January 1, 2000. The cash activity for the stub period is included in "Other cash activities—stub period, XYZ, Inc." in the Consolidated Statements of Cash Flows.

Example 1–14: Change to Equity Method from Cost Method of Accounting for Investment

During 2000, the Company bought an additional 25% interest in Bodair Co., thereby increasing its holdings to 40%. As a result, the Company changed its method of accounting for this investment from the cost method to the equity method. Under the cost method, the investment is recorded at cost and dividends are treated as income when received. Under the equity method, the Company records its proportionate share of the earnings or losses of Bodair Co. The effect of the change was to increase 2000 net income by $437,000 ($.23 per share). The financial statements for 1999 have been restated for the change, which resulted in an increase of net income for 1999 of $211,000 ($.12 per share). Retained earnings as of the beginning of 1999 has been increased by $589,000 for the effect of retroactive application of the new method.

Example 1–15: Change from Cash Basis to Accrual Basis of Accounting

In previous years, the Company prepared its financial statements on a cash basis of accounting. In 2000, the financial statements have been prepared on the accrual basis of accounting, in conformity with generally accepted accounting principles. Management also believes that the accrual basis of accounting more accurately reflects the Company's financial position and results of operations. The effect of this change was to increase net income for 2000 by $375,000. The financial statements for 1999 have been retroactively restated for the change, which resulted in a decrease of net income for 1999 of $125,000. Retained earnings has been increased by $150,000 as of January 1, 1999, for the effect of retroactive application of the new basis of accounting, as follows:

	Increase (Decrease) in Retained Earnings as of January 1, 1999
Adjustment to record accounts receivable	$500,000
Adjustment to record prepaid expenses and other assets	25,000
Adjustment to record accounts payable	(125,000)
Adjustment to record deferred revenue	(150,000)
Adjustment to record related deferred tax liability on items above	(100,000)
Net increase in retained earnings as of January 1, 1999	$150,000

Example 1–16: Adoption of New FASB Statement in the Current Year—Prior Year Financial Statements Not Restated

In 2000, the Company adopted Financial Accounting Standards Board Statement No. [*number*] [(*title*)], which requires [*describe briefly the requirements of the new standard*]. The effect of this change was to [*increase/decrease*] 2000 income before extraordinary items and 2000 net income by $[*amount*]. Financial statements for 1999 have not been restated, and the cumulative effect of the change, totaling $[*amount*], is shown as a one time [*credit/charge*] to income in the 2000 income statement.

Example 1–17: Adoption of New FASB Statement in the Current Year—Prior Year Financial Statements Restated

In 2000, the Company adopted Financial Accounting Standards Board Statement No. [*number*] [(*title*)], which requires [*describe briefly the requirements of the new standard*]. The effect of this change was to [*increase/decrease*] 2000 income before extraordinary items and 2000 net income by $[*amount*]. The financial statements for 1999 have been retroactively restated for the change, which resulted in an [*increase/decrease*] in income before extraordinary items and net income for 1999 of $[*amount*]. Retained earnings as of January 1, 1999, has been adjusted for the effect of retroactive application of the new Statement.

Example 1–18: Adoption of New FASB Statement in the Current Year—No Material Effect on the Financial Statements

In 2000, the Company adopted Financial Accounting Standards Board Statement No. [*number*] [(*title*)], which requires [*describe briefly the requirements of the new standard*]. There was no material impact on the Company's results of operations or financial condition upon adoption of the new Statement.

Example 1–19: New FASB Statement to Be Adopted in the Future

In December 2000, the Financial Accounting Standards Board (FASB) issued Statement No. [*number*] [(*title*)], which requires [*describe briefly the requirements of the new standard*]. The new standard is effective for the year ending December 31, 2001.

The adoption of the new Statement is not expected to have a material effect on the Company's financial position, results of operations, or cash flows.

Or:

The Company is currently evaluating the effect that implementation of the new standard will have on its financial position, results of operations, and cash flows.

Change in Reporting Entity

Example 1–20: Financial Statements Currently Consolidated to Include the Accounts of a Previously Unconsolidated Affiliate

Effective January 1, 2000, the Company began to consolidate into its financial statements the accounts of XYZ Corporation, formerly an unconsolidated affiliate. XYZ Corporation, which primarily manufactures medical equipment, is a venture between the Company and ABC Company of Ohio. The consolidation occurred as a result of revisions of the Stockholders' Agreement between the Company and ABC Company of Ohio. Financial data presented for previous years have not been restated to reflect the consolidation of XYZ Corporation. The consolidation is not material to financial position or results of operations for the periods presented and had no effect on previously reported net income, which included XYZ Corporation on an equity basis.

Example 1–21: Financial Statements Currently Include on the Equity Basis of Accounting the Accounts of a Previously Consolidated Business

On January 1, 2000, the Company transferred its medical equipment business segment and contributed certain assets and liabilities, totalling $15 million and $4 million, respectively, to a joint venture named Hope Enterprises (a partnership). The Company's equity interest in the joint venture is 35%. As a result, the 1999 income statement, which included the accounts of the medical equipment business segment on a consolidated basis, has been restated to reflect adjustment of line items for revenue and costs applicable to the medical equipment business segment transferred to the joint venture and to reflect the losses of this business on the equity basis of accounting.

Prior-Period Adjustments (Correction of Errors)

Example 1–22: Correction of Error in Comparative Financial Statements—Error Relates to a Year Not Presented in the Comparative Financial Statements

Retained earnings as of January 1, 1999, has been reduced by $125,000, net of income tax effect of $75,000, to correct an error made in 1998 [*or a prior year*] by including in inventory certain costs totalling $200,000 that should have been expensed to conform with generally accepted accounting principles. The error had no effect on net income for 1999.

Note: The following table illustrates the correction of error as shown on the face of the Company's statement of retained earnings or statement of stockholders' equity (assume the Company's year-end is December 31 and the error relates to 1998 or a prior year).

	2000	*1999*
Retained earnings at beginning of year, as previously reported	$3,125,000	$2,625,000
Prior period adjustment—Error in capitalizing certain inventory costs that should have been expensed in 1998 (or a prior year)	-0-	(125,000)
Retained earnings at beginning of year, as restated	3,125,000	2,500,000
Net income	700,000	625,000
Retained earnings at end of year	$3,825,000	$3,125,000

Example 1–23: Correction of Error in Comparative Financial Statements—Error Relates to First Year Presented in the Comparative Financial Statements

During 2000, the Company discovered that its previously issued 1999 financial statements excluded from property and equipment and debt certain lease obligations that were classified at that time as operating leases, and they should have been classified as capital leases to conform with generally accepted accounting principles. The accompanying financial statements for 1999 have been restated to reflect the recording and classification of these lease arrangements as capital leases. The effect of the restatement was to increase net income for 1999 by $50,000, net of related income tax of $30,000.

Note: The following table illustrates the correction of error as shown on the face of the Company's statement of retained earnings or statement of stockholders' equity (assume the Company's year-end is December 31 and the error relates to 1999). Similar to the presentation below, the balance sheet, the income statement, and the statement of cash flows should clearly indicate in the 1999 columns the word "Restated."

	2000	*1999 (Restated)*
Retained earnings at beginning of year	$4,725,000	$4,100,000
Net income, as restated for 1999	700,000	625,000
Retained earnings at end of year	$5,425,000	$4,725,000

Example 1–24: Correction of Error in Single Year Financial Statements—Error Relates to Immediately Preceding Year

The Company's financial statements as of December 31, 1999, contained the following errors: (1) overstatement of accounts receivable by $150,000, (2) understatement of accounts payable by $200,000, and (3) understatement of accrued expenses by $50,000. Retained earnings as of January 1, 2000, has been reduced by $275,000 to correct the aggregate effect of the errors of $400,000, net of their related income tax effect of $125,000. Had the errors not been made, net income for 1999 would have been decreased by $200,000, net of income tax of $100,000.

> **Note:** The following table illustrates the correction of error as shown on the face of the Company's statement of retained earnings or statement of stockholders' equity (assume the Company's year-end is December 31 and the error relates to 1999).

	2000
Retained earnings at beginning of year, as previously reported	$3,500,000
Prior period adjustment—See Note [X]	(275,000)
Retained earnings at beginning of year, as restated	3,225,000
Net income	500,000
Retained earnings at end of year	$3,725,000

CHAPTER 2
ACCOUNTING POLICIES

CONTENTS

EXECUTIVE SUMMARY

Accounting policies are important considerations in understanding the content of financial statements. Professional standards require the disclosure of significant accounting policies as an integral part of financial statements when the statements are intended to present financial position, cash flows, or results of operations in conformity with generally accepted accounting principles (GAAP). An accounting policy is significant if it materially affects the determination of financial position, cash flows, or results of operations.

The preferable presentation of disclosing accounting policies is stated in the first note of the financial statements, under the caption "Summary of Significant Accounting Policies" or "Significant Accounting Policies." However, professional standards do recognize the need for flexibility in the matter of formats. Accounting-policies disclosures need not duplicate information presented elsewhere in the financial statements. Therefore, in some instances the accounting-policies note may refer to information that will be found in another note.

Generally, the "Summary of Significant Accounting Policies" note deals with policies and not with numbers. For example, a company may disclose in its Summary note the inventory cost method used (e.g., FIFO) and indicate in a separate note the dollar breakdown of raw materials, work-in-process, and finished goods.

Authoritative pronouncements often require an entity to disclose a specific accounting policy. Following are examples of areas of accounting for which policies are specifically required to be disclosed:

- Basis of consolidation
- Depreciation methods
- Inventory methods
- Amortization of intangibles
- Pension plans
- Cash and cash equivalents
- Recognition of profit on long-term construction contracts
- Recognition of revenue from franchising and leasing operations

Authoritative Literature

APB-22	Disclosure of Accounting Policies
FAS-95	Statement of Cash Flows
SOP 94-6	Disclosure of Certain Significant Risks and Uncertainties

DISCLOSURE REQUIREMENTS

A company should disclose a description of its significant accounting policies, particularly principles and methods that involve any of the following (APB-22, pars. 8–15):

1. A selection from existing acceptable alternatives
2. The areas peculiar to a specific industry in which the entity functions
3. Unusual and innovative applications of GAAP

In addition, GAAP requires disclosures about the nature of an entity's operations and the use of estimates to prepare financial statements, which are typically included in the first note to the financial statements relating to significant accounting policies. These disclosure requirements are discussed in detail in Chapter 9, "Contingencies, Risks, Uncertainties, and Concentrations."

EXAMPLES OF FINANCIAL STATEMENT DISCLOSURES

The following are examples of the nature of information frequently disclosed in the "Summary of Significant Accounting Policies," the first note to the financial statements. The following sample disclosures are available on the accompanying disc.

Accounting Period

Example 2–1: Calendar Year—Saturday Nearest December 31

The Company's accounting period ends on the Saturday nearest December 31. The 2000 and 1999 years ended on January 1, 2001, and January 2, 2000, respectively.

Example 2–2: Fiscal Year—52 or 53 Week Period

The Company's fiscal year is the 52 or 53 weeks ending on the last Saturday in July. The fiscal year ended July 31, 2000, comprised a 53-week year, and the fiscal year ended July 25, 1999, comprised a 52-week year.

Example 2–3: Change in Fiscal Year

During 2000, the Company changed its fiscal year from one ending on the last Sunday in April to one ending on the last Sunday in December. Accordingly, the Company's transition period that ended on December 26, 2000, includes the 35 weeks from April 26, 2000, to December 26, 2000, (Transition 2000). The Company's full fiscal years include either 52 or 53 weeks. Fiscal 2000 and 1999 each include 52 weeks.

The following are selected financial data for Transition 2000 and for the comparable 35-week period of the prior year:

	December 26, 2000 (35 weeks)	*December 27, 1999 (35 weeks)*
Net sales	$45,000,000	$40,000,000
Cost of goods sold	30,000,000	27,000,000
Gross profit	15,000,000	13,000,000
Selling and administrative expenses	10,000,000	9,000,000
Interest expense	1,000,000	1,000,000
Other income, net	500,000	800,000
Income before income taxes	4,500,000	3,800,000
Income tax expense	2,000,000	1,500,000
Net income	$ 2,500,000	$ 2,300,000

Accounts Receivable

Example 2–4: Allowance Method Used to Record Bad Debts

The Company uses the allowance method to account for uncollectible accounts receivable. Accounts receivable are presented net of an allowance for doubtful accounts of $425,000 and $365,000 at December 31, 2000, and December 31, 1999, respectively.

Example 2–5: Allowance Method Used to Record Bad Debts Is Specifically Described

The Company provides an allowance for doubtful accounts equal to the estimated uncollectible amounts. The Company's estimate is based on historical collection experience and a review of the current status of trade accounts receivable. It is reasonably possible that the Company's estimate of the allowance for doubtful accounts will change. Accounts receivable are presented net of an allowance for doubtful accounts of $940,000 and $790,000 at December 31, 2000, and December 31, 1999, respectively.

Example 2–6: Direct Write-Off Method Used to Record Bad Debts

The Company has elected to record bad debts using the direct write-off method. Generally accepted accounting principles require that the allowance method be used to recognize bad debts; however, the effect of using the direct write-off method is not materially different from the results that would have been obtained under the allowance method.

Example 2–7: Unbilled Receivables

Unbilled receivables represent revenue earned in the current period but not billed to the customer until future dates, usually within one month.

Example 2–8: Long-Term Accounts Receivable

The Company finances certain sales to Latin American customers over two to three years. At December 31, 2000, and December 31, 1999, the Company had long-term accounts receivable outstanding of approximately $3,500,000 and $2,300,000, respectively, relating to these sales, which are included in other assets. As of December 31, 2000, the Company has not experienced any significant change in these receivables; however, the economic and currency related uncertainties in these countries may increase the likelihood of nonpayment. As a result, the Company increased its bad debt reserve at December 31, 2000.

Example 2–9: Classification of Accounts Receivable with Credit Balances

Accounts receivable with credit balances have been included as a current liability in "Accounts payable" in the accompanying Balance Sheet.

Advertising Costs

Example 2–10: Advertising Costs Are Expensed as Incurred

Advertising and sales promotion costs are expensed as incurred. Advertising expense totaled $295,000 for 2000 and $270,000 for 1999.

Example 2–11: Advertising Costs Are Expensed the First Time the Advertising Takes Place

Production costs of future media advertising are expensed the first time the advertising takes place. Advertising expense totaled $457,000 for 2000 and $393,000 for 1999.

Example 2–12: Direct-Response Advertising Costs Are Capitalized and Amortized

Direct-response advertising costs, consisting primarily of catalog book production, printing, and postage costs, are capitalized and amortized over the expected life of the catalog, not to exceed six months. Direct response advertising costs reported as prepaid assets are $275,000 and $350,000 at December 31, 2000, and December 31, 1999, respectively. Total advertising expenses were $1,900,000 in 2000 and $1,600,000 in 1999.

Example 2–13: Certain Advertising Costs Are Expensed the First Time the Advertising Takes Place and Direct-Response Advertising Costs Are Capitalized

The Company expenses the production costs of advertising the first time the advertising takes place, except for direct-response advertising, which is capitalized and amortized over its expected period of future benefits. Direct-response advertising consists primarily of magazine advertisements that include order coupons for the Company's products. The capitalized costs of the advertising are amortized over the six-month period following the publication of the magazine in which it appears.

> **Note:** Example 2–13 assumes that the details of advertising costs expensed and capitalized are disclosed in a separate note to the financial statements. See Chapter 3, "Advertising Costs," for such an illustration.

Business Combinations

Example 2–14: General Policy for Accounting for Business Combinations, Allocation of Purchase Price, and Acquisition Contingencies

The Company assesses each business combination to determine whether the pooling-of-interests or the purchase method of accounting is appropriate. For those business combinations accounted for under the pooling-of-interests method, the financial statements are combined with those of the Company at their historical amounts, and, if material, all periods presented are restated as if the combination occurred on the first day of the earliest year presented. For those acquisitions accounted for using the purchase method of accounting, the Company allocates the cost of the acquired business to the assets acquired and the liabilities assumed based on estimates of fair values thereof. These estimates are revised during the allocation period as necessary when, and if, information regarding contingencies becomes available to define and quantify assets acquired and liabilities assumed. The allocation period varies but does not exceed one year. To the extent contingencies such as preacquisition environmental matters, litigation, and related legal fees are resolved or settled during the allocation period, such items are included in the revised allocation of the purchase price. After the allocation period, the effect of changes in such contingencies is included in results of operations in the periods in which the adjustments are determined.

In certain business combinations, the Company agrees to pay additional amounts to sellers contingent upon achievement by the acquired businesses of certain negotiated goals, such as targeted revenue levels. Contingent payments, when incurred, are recorded as purchase price adjustments or compensation expense, as appropriate, based on the nature of each contingent payment.

Example 2–15: Pooling-of-Interests

On July 1, 2000, the Company completed a business combination with ZYZ Corporation, which is a provider of integrated multi-service access products. The combination was a stock-for-stock merger that was accounted for as a "pooling-of-interests." In connection with the merger, the Company issued 3,000,000 shares of common stock and assumed 700,000 stock options and 250,000 warrants in exchange for all the outstanding stock, options, and warrants of XYZ Corporation. Accordingly, the Company's historical financial statements for 2000 and 1999 have been restated to include the accounts of ZYZ Corporation as if the companies had combined at the beginning of the first period presented.

There were no significant transactions between the Company and XYZ Corporation before the combination and no adjustments were necessary to conform XYZ Corporation's accounting policies.

Example 2–16: Purchase Method

On May 23, 2000, the Company acquired XYZ Corporation, which was involved in the development of surgical specialty products. The acquisition, which was accomplished through the issuance of preferred stock, was accounted for under the purchase method of accounting and, accordingly, the results of operations have been included in the Company's consolidated financial statements since the date of acquisition. The purchase price of approximately $16,000,000 was allocated to the individual assets acquired and liabilities assumed based upon their respective fair values at the date of acquisition (see Note [X]). The transaction resulted in cost in excess of net assets acquired of approximately $4,000,000, of which $2,500,000 was allocated to in-process research and development and was subsequently written off.

Capitalization of Interest

Example 2–17: Capitalization of Interest Costs on Borrowings

The Company capitalizes interest cost on borrowings incurred during the new construction or upgrade of qualifying assets. Capitalized interest is added to the cost of the underlying assets and is amortized over the useful lives of the assets. For 2000 and 1999, the Company capitalized $450,000 and $525,000 of interest, respectively, in connection with various capital expansion projects.

Cash Equivalents

Example 2–18: Types of Cash Equivalents Specifically Identified

Cash and cash equivalents consist primarily of cash on deposit, certificates of deposit, money market accounts, and investment grade commercial paper that are readily convertible into cash and purchased with original maturities of three months or less.

Example 2–19: Types of Cash Equivalents Described in General Terms

The Company considers deposits that can be redeemed on demand and investments that have original maturities of less than three months, when purchased, to be cash equivalents. As of December 31, 2000, the Company's cash and cash equivalents were deposited primarily in three financial institutions.

Comprehensive Income

Example 2–20: Components of Other Comprehensive Income Disclosed

Comprehensive income consists of net income and other gains and losses affecting shareholders' equity that, under generally accepted accounting principles, are excluded from net income. For the Company, such items consist primarily of unrealized gains and losses on marketable equity investments and foreign currency translation gains and losses. The changes in the components of other comprehensive income (loss) are as follows:

	Years Ended December 31			
	2000		*1999*	
	Pre-Tax Amount	*Tax Expense (Credit)*	*Pre-Tax Amount*	*Tax Expense (Credit)*
Unrealized gain on securities	$650,000	$225,000	$725,000	$265,000
Foreign currency translation adjustments	90,000	31,000	(35,000)	(13,000)
Total other comprehensive income	$740,000	$256,000	$690,000	$252,000

Concentrations of Credit and Other Risks

For examples of financial statement disclosures, see Chapter 9, "Contingencies, Risks, Uncertainties, and Concentrations."

Consolidation Policy

Example 2–21: Consolidation Policy Specifically Described

The accompanying consolidated financial statements include the accounts of the Company and its majority-owned subsidiary partnerships and corporations, after elimination of all material intercompany accounts, transactions, and profits. Investments in unconsolidated subsidiaries representing ownership of at least 20%, but less than 50%, are accounted for under the equity method. Nonmarketable investments in which the Company has less than 20% ownership and in which it does not have the ability to exercise significant influence over the investee are initially recorded at cost and periodically reviewed for impairment.

Example 2–22: Combined Financial Statements

The financial statements of ABC, Inc. and ZYZ Corp. are combined because each company is owned beneficially by identical shareholders. All significant intercompany accounts and transactions have been eliminated in the combination.

Note: For additional examples of disclosures relating to consolidated and combined financial statements, see Chapter 8, "Consolidated and Combined Financial Statements."

Contingencies

Example 2–23: General Accounting Policy for Contingencies

Certain conditions may exist as of the date the financial statements are issued, which may result in a loss to the Company but which will only be resolved when one or more future events occur or fail to occur. The Company's management and its legal counsel assess such contingent liabilities, and such assessment inherently involves an exercise of judgment. In assessing loss contingencies related to legal proceedings that are pending against the Company or unasserted claims that may result in such proceedings, the Company's legal counsel evaluates the perceived merits of any legal proceedings or unasserted claims as well as the perceived merits of the amount of relief sought or expected to be sought therein.

If the assessment of a contingency indicates that it is probable that a material loss has been incurred and the amount of the liability can be estimated, then the estimated liability would be accrued in the Company's financial statements. If the assessment indicates that a potentially material loss contingency is not probable but is reasonably possible, or is probable but cannot be estimated, then the nature of the contingent liability, together with an estimate of the range of possible loss if determinable and material, would be disclosed.

Loss contingencies considered remote are generally not disclosed unless they involve guarantees, in which case the nature of the guarantee would be disclosed.

Deferred Revenue

Example 2–24: Amounts Billed in Advance

The Company recognizes revenues as earned. Amounts billed in advance of the period in which service is rendered are recorded as a liability under "Deferred revenue."

Earnings Per Share

Example 2–25: Basic and Diluted Net Earnings per Share

Basic net earnings (loss) per common share is computed by dividing net earnings (loss) applicable to common shareholders by the weighted-average number of common shares outstanding during the period. Diluted net earnings (loss) per common share is determined using the weighted-average number of common shares outstanding during the period, adjusted for the dilutive effect of common stock equivalents, consisting of shares that might be issued upon exercise of common stock options. In periods where losses are reported, the weighted-average number of common shares outstanding excludes common stock equivalents, because their inclusion would be anti-dilutive.

Environmental Costs

Example 2–26: Environmental Expenditures Expensed or Capitalized

Costs related to environmental remediation are charged to expense. Other environmental costs are also charged to expense unless they increase the value of the property and/or provide future economic benefits, in which event they are capitalized. Liabilities are recognized when the expenditures are considered probable and can be reasonably estimated. Measurement of liabilities is based on currently enacted laws and regulations, existing technology, and undiscounted site-specific costs. Generally, such recognition coincides with the Company's commitment to a formal plan of action.

Example 2–27: Accruals for Environmental Matters Exclude Claims for Recoveries

Accruals for environmental matters are recorded when it is probable that a liability has been incurred and the amount of the liability can be reasonably estimated, or if an amount is likely to fall within a range and no amount within that range can be determined to be the better estimate, the minimum amount of the range is recorded. Accruals for environmental matters exclude claims for recoveries from insurance carriers and other third parties until it is probable that such recoveries will be realized.

Estimates

Example 2–28: General Note Regarding Estimates Inherent in the Financial Statements

Preparing the Company's financial statements in conformity with generally accepted accounting principles requires management to make estimates and assumptions that affect reported amounts of assets and liabilities and disclosure of contingent assets and liabilities at the date of the financial statements and the reported amounts of revenues and expenses during the reporting period. Actual results could differ from those estimates.

Example 2–29: Significant Estimates Relating to Specific Financial Statement Accounts and Transactions Are Identified

The financial statements include some amounts that are based on management's best estimates and judgments. The most significant estimates relate to allowance for uncollectible accounts receivable, inventory obsolescence, depreciation, intangible asset valuations and useful lives, employee benefit plans, environmental accruals, taxes, contingencies, and costs to complete long-term contracts. These estimates may be adjusted as more current information becomes available, and any adjustment could be significant.

Financial Instruments

Example 2–30: Fair Value of Financial Instruments Approximate Carrying Amount

The Company's financial instruments are cash and cash equivalents, accounts receivable, accounts payable, notes payable, and long-term debt. The recorded values of cash and cash equivalents, accounts receivable, and accounts payable approximate their fair values based on their short-term nature. The recorded values of notes payable and long-term debt approximate their fair values, as interest approximates market rates.

Example 2–31: Fair Value of Financial Instruments Is Based on Quoted Market Prices or Pricing Models

Fair values of long-term investments, long-term debt, interest rate derivatives, currency forward contracts, and currency options are based on quoted market prices or pricing models using prevailing financial market information as of December 31, 2000.

Example 2–32: Fair Value of Financial Instruments Is Based on Management's Estimates

The fair value of current assets and liabilities approximate carrying value, due to the short-term nature of these items. There is no quoted market value for the Senior Secured Notes; however, management estimates that, based on current market conditions, such Notes have a fair value of approximately 45% to 55% of the face value of such

Notes. Fair value of such financial instruments is not necessarily representative of the amount that could be realized or settled.

Example 2–33: Fair Value of Long-Term Debt Is Estimated Based on Current Rates and Terms Offered to the Company

The fair value of the Company's long-term debt is estimated based on the current rates offered to the Company for debt of similar terms and maturities. Under this method, the Company's fair value of long-term debt was not significantly different from the carrying value at December 31, 2000.

Example 2–34: Fair Value of Notes Receivable Based on Discounted Cash Flows

The fair value of notes receivable, which is based on discounted cash flows using current interest rates, approximates the carrying value at December 31, 2000.

Example 2–35: Interest Rate Swap Agreements—Prior to Adoption of FASB Statement No. 133 (Accounting for Derivative Instruments and Hedging Activities)

The Company enters into interest rate swap agreements to manage exposure to fluctuations in interest rates. The interest rate swap agreements lock in the underlying U.S. treasury security rate and convert a portion of the commercial paper from a floating rate obligation to a fixed rate obligation. The fair value of interest rate swap agreements is based on market prices. The fair value represents the estimated amount the Company would receive/pay to terminate the agreements, taking into consideration current interest rates. The fair value of the interest rate swap agreements is not recognized in the financial statements because the agreements are accounted for as hedges.

The cash differentials paid or received on interest rate swap agreements are accrued and recognized as adjustments to interest expense or interest income. Gains and losses realized upon the settlement of these agreements are deferred and either amortized to interest expense over a period relevant to the agreement if the underlying hedged instrument remains outstanding, or recognized immediately if the underlying hedged instrument is settled and the swap agreement is terminated.

Cash flows related to interest rate swap agreements are classified as "Operating activities" in the Consolidated Statements of Cash Flows.

Example 2–36: Foreign Exchange Forward Contracts—Prior to Adoption of FAS-133

The Company enters into foreign exchange forward contracts as part of managing its exposure to fluctuations in foreign currency. The Company does not speculate on interest or foreign currency exchange rates. Foreign currency agreements are accounted for under the fair value method. Gains and losses on contracts designated as hedges of intercompany transactions that are permanent in nature are accrued as exchange rates change and are recognized in stockholders' equity as foreign currency translation adjustments. Gains and losses on contracts that are not permanent in nature or are not designated as hedges are accrued as exchange rates change and are recognized in income. Gains and losses on contracts designated as hedges of identifiable foreign currency firm commitments are deferred and included in the measurement of the related foreign currency transaction.

Cash flows related to foreign exchange forward contracts are classified as operating activities in the Consolidated Statements of Cash Flows.

Example 2–37: Commodity Futures Contracts—Prior to Adoption of FAS-133

The Company enters into commodity futures contracts to hedge its exposure to price fluctuations for certain raw material purchases. Gains and losses on these hedge contracts are deferred and included in the measurement of the related transaction.

Example 2–38: Off-Balance Sheet Financial Instruments—Prior to Adoption of FAS-133

The Company utilizes various off-balance sheet financial instruments to manage market risks associated with fluctuations in certain interest rates and foreign currency exchange rates. It is the Company's policy to use derivative financial instruments to protect against market risks arising in the normal course of business. Company policies prohibit the use of derivative instruments for the sole purpose of trading for profit on price fluctuations or to enter into contracts that intentionally increase the Company's underlying exposure. The criteria the Company uses for designating an instrument as a hedge include the instrument's effectiveness in risk reduction and direct matching of the financial instrument to the underlying transaction. Gains and losses on currency forward and option contracts that are intended to hedge an identifiable firm commitment are deferred and included in the measurement of the underlying transaction. Gains and losses on hedges of anticipated revenue transactions are deferred until such time as the underlying transactions are recognized, or recognized immediately if the transaction is terminated earlier than initially anticipated. Gains and losses on any instruments not meeting the above criteria are recognized in income in the current period. Subsequent gains or losses on the related financial instrument are recognized in income in each period until the instrument matures, is terminated or is sold. Income or expense on swaps is accrued as an adjustment to the yield of the related investments or debt hedged by the instrument. Cash flows associated with derivative transactions are reported as arising from operating activities in the Consolidated Statements of Cash Flows.

Example 2–39: Derivative Instruments and Hedging Activities—After Adoption of FAS-133

The Company has adopted Financial Accounting Standards Board Statement No. 133 (Accounting for Derivative Instruments and Hedging Activities), which requires that all derivative instruments be recorded on the balance sheet at fair value. On the date derivative contracts are entered into, the Company designates the derivative as either (i) a hedge of the fair value of a recognized asset or liability or of an unrecognized firm commitment (fair value hedge), (ii) a hedge of a forecasted transaction or of the variability of cash flows to be received or paid related to a recognized asset or liability (cash flow hedge), or (iii) a hedge of a net investment in a foreign operation (net investment hedge).

Changes in the fair value of derivatives are recorded each period in current earnings or other comprehensive income, depending on whether a derivative is designated as part of a hedge transaction and, if it is, depending on the type of hedge transaction. For fair value hedge transactions, changes in fair value of the derivative instrument are generally offset in the income statement by changes in the fair value of the item being hedged. For cash flow hedge transactions, changes in the fair value of the derivative instrument are reported in other comprehensive income. For net investment hedge transactions, changes in the fair value are recorded as a component of the foreign currency translation account, which is also included in other comprehensive income. The gains and losses on cash flow hedge transactions that are reported in other comprehensive income are reclassified to earnings in the periods in which earnings are impacted by the variability of the cash flows of the hedged item. The ineffective portions of all hedges are recognized in current period earnings.

The adoption of FAS-133 did not have a material effect on the Company's primary financial statements but did reduce comprehensive income by $100,000 in the accompanying Consolidated Statement of Shareholders' Equity.

Foreign Operations

Example 2–40: Company's Future Operations Are Dependent on Foreign Operations

The Company's future operations and earnings will depend on the results of the Company's operations in [*name of foreign country*]. There can be no assurance that the Company will be able to successfully conduct such operations, and a failure to do so would have a material adverse effect on the Company's financial position, results of operations, and cash flows. Also, the success of the Company's operations will be subject to numerous contingencies, some of which are beyond management's control. These contingencies include general and regional economic conditions, prices for the Company's products, competition, and changes in regulation. Because the Company is dependent on international operations, specifically those in [*name of foreign country*], the Company will be subject to various additional political, economic, and other uncertainties. Among other risks, the Company's operations will be subject to the risks of restrictions on transfer of funds; export duties, quotas and embargoes; domestic and international customs and tariffs; changing taxation policies; foreign exchange restrictions; and political conditions and governmental regulations.

Example 2–41: Foreign Currency Adjustments—Functional Currency Is the Foreign Country's Local Currency

The financial position and operating results of substantially all foreign operations are consolidated using the local currencies of the countries in which the Company operates as the functional currency. Local currency assets and liabilities are translated at the rates of exchange on the balance sheet date, and local currency revenues and expenses are translated at average rates of exchange during the period. The resulting translation adjustments are recorded directly into a separate component of shareholders' equity.

Example 2–42: Foreign Currency Adjustments—Functional Currency Is the U.S. Dollar

The Company's functional currency for all operations worldwide is the U.S. dollar. Nonmonetary assets and liabilities are translated at historical rates and monetary assets and liabilities are translated at exchange rates in effect at the end of the year. Income statement accounts are translated at average rates for the year. Gains and losses from translation of foreign currency financial statements into U.S.

dollars are included in current results of operations. Gains and losses resulting from foreign currency transactions are also included in current results of operations.

Example 2–43: Foreign Currency Adjustments—Certain Assets and Liabilities Are Remeasured at Current Exchange Rates and Others Are Remeasured at Historical Rates

The U.S. dollar is the "functional currency" of the Company's worldwide continuing operations. All foreign currency asset and liability amounts are remeasured into U.S. dollars at end-of-period exchange rates, except for inventories, prepaid expenses and property, plant and equipment, which are remeasured at historical rates. Foreign currency income and expenses are remeasured at average exchange rates in effect during the year, except for expenses related to balance sheet amounts remeasured at historical exchange rates. Exchange gains and losses arising from remeasurement of foreign currency-denominated monetary assets and liabilities are included in income in the period in which they occur.

Going Concern Issues

Example 2–44: Company's Successful Operations Are Dependent on Those of Its Parent

The Company has historically relied on its parent company to meet its cash flow requirements. The parent has cash available in the amount of approximately $83,000 as of December 31, 2000, and a working capital deficit of $80 million. The Senior Secured Notes in the amount of $65 million have been reclassified because the Company's parent company does not currently have sufficient funds to make the next interest payment (in the approximate amount of $6 million) due in May 2001. Failure by the parent to make such payment could allow the holders of the Notes to declare all amounts outstanding immediately due and payable. The Company and its parent will need additional funds to meet the development and exploratory obligations until sufficient cash flows are generated from anticipated production to sustain operations and to fund future development and exploration obligations.

The parent plans to generate the additional cash needed through the sale or financing of its domestic assets held for sale and the completion of additional equity, debt, or joint venture transactions. There is no assurance, however, that the parent will be able to sell or finance its assets held for sale or to complete other transactions in the future at commercially reasonable terms, if at all, or that the Company will be able to meet its future contractual obligations.

Impairment of Long-Lived Assets

Example 2–45: Impairment Evaluation Policy Described—No Impairment Exists

Long-lived assets consist primarily of property and equipment, excess of cost over net assets of acquired businesses, and other intangible assets. The recoverability of long-lived assets is evaluated at the operating unit level by an analysis of operating results and consideration of other significant events or changes in the business environment. If an operating unit has indications of impairment, such as current operating losses, the Company will evaluate whether impairment exists on the basis of undiscounted expected future cash flows from operations before interest for the remaining amortization period. If impairment exists, the carrying amount of the long-lived assets is reduced to its estimated fair value, less any costs associated with the final settlement. As of December 31, 2000, and December 31, 1999, there was no impairment of the Company's long-lived assets.

Example 2–46: Impairment Evaluation Policy Described—Impairment Exists

Long-lived assets are reviewed whenever indicators of impairment are present and the undiscounted cash flows are not sufficient to recover the related asset carrying amount. At December 31, 1999, intangible assets included the excess of the investment in ABC over the fair market of the net assets acquired of approximately $4 million. The intangible assets were reviewed during 2000, in light of the Company's acquisition of XYZ Corp. and the resultant closure of one of ABC's manufacturing plants. This review indicated that the ABC intangible assets were impaired, as determined based on the projected cash flows from ABC over the next three years. The cash flow projections take into effect the net sales and expenses expected from ABC products, as well as maintaining its current manufacturing capabilities. Consequently, the carrying value of the ABC goodwill and other long-lived assets totaling $2 million and $1.5 million, respectively, were written off as a component of operating expenses during 2000.

Income Taxes

Example 2–47: C Corporation

Deferred tax assets and liabilities are recognized for the future tax consequences attributable to differences between the financial statement carrying amounts of existing assets and liabilities and their respective tax bases. Deferred tax assets, including tax loss and credit carryforwards, and liabilities are measured using enacted tax rates expected to apply to taxable income in the years in which those temporary differences are expected to be recovered or settled. The effect on deferred tax assets and liabilities of a change in tax rates is recognized in income in the period that includes the enactment date. Deferred income tax expense represents the change during the period in the deferred tax assets and deferred tax liabilities. The components of the deferred tax assets and liabilities are individually classified as current and non-current based on their characteristics. Deferred tax assets are reduced by a valuation allowance when, in the opinion of management, it is more likely than not that some portion or all of the deferred tax assets will not be realized.

Example 2–48: S Corporation

The Company, with the consent of its stockholders, has elected under the Internal Revenue Code to be taxed as an S Corporation. The stockholders of an S Corporation are taxed on their proportionate share of the Company's taxable income. Therefore, no provision or liability for federal income taxes has been included in the financial statements. Certain specific deductions and credits flow through the Company to its stockholders.

This election is valid for [*State*]; however, [*State*] law requires a minimum tax of [*amount*]% on State taxable income. Therefore, a provision and a related liability have been included in the financial statements for [*State*] income taxes.

Example 2–49: Limited Liability Company

As a limited liability company, the Company's taxable income or loss is allocated to members in accordance with their respective percentage ownership. Therefore, no provision or liability for income taxes has been included in the financial statements.

Example 2–50: Partnership

The Partnership is not a taxpaying entity for federal or state income tax purposes; accordingly, a provision for income taxes has not been recorded in the accompanying financial statements. Partnership income or losses are reflected in the partners' individual or corporate income tax returns in accordance with their ownership percentages.

Example 2–51: Proprietorship

The Proprietorship is not a taxpaying entity for federal or state income tax purposes; accordingly, a provision for income taxes has not been recorded in the accompanying financial statements. Federal and state income taxes of the proprietor are computed on [*his/her*] total income from all sources.

Example 2–52: Taxes Provided on Undistributed Earnings of Foreign Subsidiaries

The Company's practice is to provide U.S. Federal taxes on undistributed earnings of the Company's non-U.S. sales and service subsidiaries.

Example 2–53: Taxes Not Provided on Undistributed Earnings of Foreign Subsidiaries

A provision has not been made at December 31, 2000, for U.S. or additional foreign withholding taxes on approximately $10 million of undistributed earnings of foreign subsidiaries because it is the present intention of management to reinvest the undistributed earnings indefinitely in foreign operations. Generally, such earnings become subject to U.S. tax upon the remittance of dividends and under certain other circumstances. It is not practicable to estimate the amount of deferred tax liability on such undistributed earnings.

Example 2–54: Realization of the Deferred Income Tax Asset Is Dependent on Generating Future Taxable Income

Deferred tax assets are reduced by a valuation allowance when, in the opinion of management, it is more likely than not that some portion or all of the deferred tax assets will not be realized. Realization of the deferred income tax asset is dependent on generating sufficient taxable income in future years. Although realization is not assured, management believes it is more likely than not that all of the deferred income tax asset will be realized. The amount of the deferred income tax asset considered realizable, however, could be reduced in the near term if estimates of future taxable income are reduced.

Example 2–55: Tax Credits Accounted for on the Flow-Through Method

Tax credits, grants, and other allowances are accounted for in the period earned (the flow-through method).

Example 2–56: Tax Credits Accounted for on the Deferral Method

Investment tax credits are deferred and included in income as a reduction of income tax expense over the estimated useful lives of the assets that gave rise to the credits.

Example 2–57: Tax Credits Accounted for on the Cost Reduction Method

Investment tax credits are accounted for as decreases of the bases of the assets that gave rise to the credits. The credits are included in income through a reduction of the amount of depreciation expense, which would otherwise be charged to operations, over the estimated useful lives of the assets that gave rise to the credits.

Example 2–58: Company Has Substantial Net Operating Loss Carryforwards and a Valuation Allowance Is Recorded

The Company recognizes the amount of taxes payable or refundable for the current year and recognizes deferred tax liabilities and assets for the expected future tax consequences of events and transactions that have been recognized in the Company's financial statements or tax returns. The Company currently has substantial net operating loss carryforwards. The Company has recorded a 100% valuation allowance against net deferred tax assets due to uncertainty of their ultimate realization.

Example 2–59: Subchapter S Status Terminated

Before January 1, 2000, the Company had operated as a C corporation. Effective January 1, 2000, the stockholders of the Company elected to be taxed under Subchapter S of the Internal Revenue Code. During such period, federal income taxes were the responsibility of the Company's stockholders as were certain state income taxes. As of the effective date of the election, the Company was responsible for Federal built-in-gain taxes to the extent applicable. Accordingly, the consolidated statement of operations for the year ended December 31, 2000, provides for such taxes. The S corporation election terminated in connection with the consummation of the initial public offering of the Company's common stock on October 10, 2000.

Example 2–60: Conversion from Cash Basis to Accrual Basis for Tax Purposes Results in a Deferred Tax Liability

In the current year, the Company converted from a cash basis to an accrual basis for tax purposes in conjunction with its conversion to a

C corporation. Due to temporary differences in recognition of revenue and expenses, income for financial reporting purposes exceeded income for income tax purposes. The conversion to an accrual basis along with these temporary differences resulted in the recognition of a net deferred tax liability, and a corresponding one-time charge to expense, of $3.5 million as of December 31, 2000.

Example 2–61: Subsidiary Files a Consolidated Federal Income Tax Return with Its Parent

The Company files a consolidated federal income tax return with its parent company, but files a separate state income tax return. In accordance with the intercorporate tax allocation policy, the Company pays to or receives from the parent company amounts equivalent to federal income tax charges or credits based on separate company taxable income or loss using the statutory rates.

Intangible Assets

Example 2–62: Goodwill

Goodwill represents the purchase price and transaction costs associated with business acquisitions in excess of the estimated fair value of the net assets of these businesses. Goodwill is amortized on a straight-line basis over a period ranging from 25 to 40 years commencing on the dates of the respective acquisitions. Accumulated amortization was $[*amount*] at December 31, 2000, and $[*amount*] at December 31, 1999.

The carrying value and useful lives of goodwill [*and other intangible assets*] are based on management's current assessment of recoverability. Management periodically evaluates whether certain circumstances may affect the estimated useful lives or the recoverability of the unamortized balance of goodwill [*or other intangible assets*] using both objective and subjective factors. Objective factors include management's best estimates of projected future earnings and cash flows and analysis of recent sales and earnings trends. Subjective factors include competitive analysis and the Company's strategic focus.

Example 2–63: Additional Goodwill Resulting from Future Contingent Payments

The initial purchase price in excess of the fair value of identifiable net assets acquired (goodwill) of XYZ Corp. is being amortized on a straight-line basis over 15 years. Additional goodwill resulting from future contingent purchase price payments earned will be amortized on a straight-line basis over the remaining life of the original 15-year period. The earnout agreement provides for contingent payments, not to exceed $1,500,000, payable in cash or the Company's stock, based on the profitability of XYZ Corp. over a four year period from the acquisition date.

Example 2–64: Negative Goodwill

The Company purchased its subsidiary, DEF Corp., at a cost that was below the fair value of the subsidiary's net assets at the date of acquisition. The difference, negative goodwill, represents the unallocated portion of the excess of net assets acquired over cost of the subsidiary and is being amortized on the straight line basis over 25 years.

Example 2–65: Patent Costs

Patent costs include direct costs of obtaining the patents. Costs for new patents are capitalized and amortized over the estimated useful life of the patent, generally five years, using the straight-line method. The cost of patents in process is not amortized until issuance. In the event of a patent being superseded, the unamortized costs are written off immediately.

Accumulated amortization relating to patents was approximately $300,000 at December 31, 2000, and $275,000 at December 31, 1999.

Example 2–66: Subscription Lists

Subscription lists are recorded at purchase cost. Amortization is computed based on a straight-line basis or the percentage of nonrenewing original subscribers.

Example 2–67: Deferred Financing Costs

Costs incurred in connection with the issuance of notes and debentures and the execution of revolving credit agreements are deferred and amortized using the effective interest method over the life of such issues and agreements.

Example 2–68: Organization Costs

Organization costs, including legal fees, are expensed as incurred. Organization costs charged to operations totaled $23,000 for 2000 and $12,000 for 1999.

Example 2–69: Other Intangible Assets—Customer Lists, Covenants Not to Compete, and Other Intangibles

Other intangible assets consist primarily of customer lists, covenants not to compete, licenses, permits, and contracts. *Other intangible assets* are recorded at cost and amortized on a straight-line basis. Customer lists are generally amortized over five to seven years. Covenants not to compete are amortized over the term of the covenant agreement, which is generally three to five years. Licenses, permits, and contracts are amortized over the shorter of the definitive terms of the related agreements or 40 years. Accumulated amortization was $[*amount*] at December 31, 2000, and $[*amount*] at December 31, 1999.

Example 2–70: Review of Carrying Value of Intangible Assets—No Impairment

Management periodically reviews the carrying value of acquired intangible assets to determine whether an impairment may exist. The Company considers relevant cash flow and profitability information, including estimated future operating results, trends, and other available information, in assessing whether the carrying value of intangible assets can be recovered. If it is determined that the carrying value of intangible assets will not be recovered from the undiscounted future cash flows of the acquired business, the carrying value of such intangible assets would be considered impaired and reduced by a charge to operations in the amount of the impairment. An impairment charge is measured as any deficiency in the amount of estimated undiscounted future cash flows of the acquired business available to recover the carrying value related to the intangible assets. Based on this assessment there was no impairment at December 31, 2000.

Example 2–71: Carrying Value of Long-Lived Assets Is Impaired

The Company assesses potential impairments of its long-lived assets when evidence exists that events or changes in circumstances have made recovery of the asset's carrying value unlikely. An impairment loss would be recognized when the sum of the expected future net cash flows is less than the carrying amount of the asset. During 2000, the Company implemented a restructuring plan that included a number of cost reduction actions and operational improvements (see Note [*X*]). As a result of this plan, impairment losses of $1,850,000 were recorded for certain of the Company's long-lived assets.

Inventory

Example 2–72: Inventories Accounted for under FIFO

Inventories are stated at the lower of cost (first-in, first-out basis) or market (net realizable value).

Example 2–73: Inventories Accounted for under LIFO

Inventories are stated at the lower of cost or market. Cost is determined by the last-in, first-out (LIFO) method for all inventories. Market value for raw materials is based on replacement cost and for work-in-process and finished goods on net realizable value.

Example 2–74: Inventory Stated at Standard Cost—Due Consideration Given to Obsolescence and Inventory Levels in Evaluating Net Realizable Value

Inventories are stated at the lower of cost or market. Cost is determined on a standard cost basis that approximates the first-in, first-out (FIFO) method. Market is determined based on net realizable value. Appropriate consideration is given to obsolescence, excessive levels, deterioration, and other factors in evaluating net realizable value.

Example 2–75: Inventories Accounted for under LIFO and FIFO

Inventories, consisting of manufactured products and merchandise for resale, are stated at the lower of cost or market. Manufactured products include the costs of materials, labor, and manufacturing overhead. Inventories accounted for using the last-in, first-out (LIFO) method approximated 60% and 65% of total inventory as of year-end 2000 and 1999, respectively. Remaining inventories are generally determined using the first-in, first-out (FIFO) cost method. For detailed inventory information, see Note [*X*].

Example 2–76: Inventory Valuation Includes Provision for Obsolescence

Inventories are stated at the lower of cost (FIFO) or market, including provisions for obsolescence commensurate with known or estimated exposures. Inventories are shown net of a valuation reserve of $450,000 at December 31, 2000, and $300,000 at December 31, 1999.

Example 2–77: Inventory Note Describes Accounting Policy for New Products

Inventories are stated at the lower of cost (determined by the first-in, first-out method) or market (net realizable value). Costs associated with the manufacture of a new product are charged to engineering, research and development expense as incurred until the product is proven through testing and acceptance by the customer.

Example 2–78: Inventory Note Addresses Risk Exposure to Technological Change

Inventories are stated at the lower of cost (FIFO) or market. Inventories consist primarily of components and subassemblies and finished products held for sale. Rapid technological change and new product introductions and enhancements could result in excess or obsolete inventory. To minimize this risk, the Company evaluates inventory levels and expected usage on a periodic basis and records adjustments as required.

Investments

Example 2–79: Short-Term Investments

As part of its cash management program, the Company from time to time maintains a portfolio of marketable investment securities. The securities have an investment grade and a term to earliest maturity generally of less than one year and include tax exempt securities and certificates of deposit. These securities are carried at cost, which approximates market.

Example 2–80: Held-to-Maturity, Trading, and Available-for-Sale Marketable Securities

The Company classifies its debt and marketable equity securities into held-to-maturity, trading, or available-for-sale categories. Debt securities are classified as held-to-maturity when the Company has the positive intent and ability to hold the securities to maturity. Debt securities for which the Company does not have the intent or ability to hold to maturity are classified as available for sale. Held-to-maturity securities are recorded as either short-term or long-term on the balance sheet based on contractual maturity date and are stated at amortized cost. Marketable securities that are bought and held principally for the purpose of selling them in the near term are classified as trading securities and are reported at fair value, with unrealized gains and losses recognized in earnings. Debt and marketable equity securities not classified as held-to-maturity or as trading are classified as available-for-sale and are carried at fair market value, with the unrealized gains and losses, net of tax, included in the determination of comprehensive income and reported in shareholders' equity.

The fair value of substantially all securities is determined by quoted market prices. The estimated fair value of securities for which there are no quoted market prices is based on similar types of securities that are traded in the market. Gains or losses on securities sold are based on the specific identification method.

Example 2–81: Reverse Repurchase Agreements

Securities purchased under agreements to resell (reverse repurchase agreements) result from transactions that are collateralized by negotiable securities and are carried at the amounts at which the securities will subsequently be resold. It is the policy of the Company not to take possession of securities purchased under agreements to resell. At December 31, 2000, and December 31, 1999, agreements to resell securities in the amount of $1,300,000 with a three-day maturity and $3,200,000 with a 14-day maturity were outstanding, respectively.

Life Insurance

Example 2–82: Life Insurance Policies Net of Policy Loans

The Company's investment in corporate owned life insurance policies is recorded net of policy loans in "Other assets" in the Balance Sheets. The net life insurance expense, including interest expense, is included in "Administrative and general expenses" in the Statements of Operations.

Nature of Operations

Example 2–83: Company Describes Its Primary Products

The Company designs, manufactures, markets, and services test systems and related software, and backplanes and associated connectors. The Company's top five products are (1) semiconductor test systems, (2) backplane connection systems, (3) circuit-board test systems, (4) telecommunications test systems, and (5) software test systems.

Example 2–84: Company Describes the Types of Customers It Has

The Company is a leading global developer, manufacturer, and distributor of hand tools, power tools, tool storage products, shop equipment, under-hood diagnostics equipment, under-car equipment, emissions and safety equipment, collision repair equipment, vehicle service information, and business management systems and services. The Corporation's customers include professional automotive technicians, shop owners, franchised service centers, national accounts, original equipment manufacturers, and industrial tool and equipment users worldwide.

Example 2–85: Company Describes U.S. Geographic Locations Where It Operates

The Company is a leading designer and manufacturer of open-architecture, standard embedded computer components that system designers can easily use to create a custom solution specific to the user's unique application. The Company has operations in New York, New Mexico, Minnesota, North Carolina, and California. The Company's product lines include CPU boards, general purpose input/output modules, avionics interface modules and analyzers, interconnection and expansion units, telemetry boards, data acquisition software, and industrial computer systems and enclosures.

Example 2–86: Company Indicates That Its Operations Are Vulnerable to Changes in Trends and Customer Demand

The Company is a nationwide specialty retailer of fashionable and contemporary apparel and accessory items designed for consumers with a young, active lifestyle. The Company's success is largely dependent on its ability to gauge the fashion tastes of its customers and to provide merchandise that satisfies customer demand. The Company's failure to anticipate, identify, or react to changes in fashion trends could adversely affect its results of operations.

Example 2–87: Company's Operations Are Substantially in Foreign Countries

Substantially all of the Company's products are manufactured in the Dominican Republic, Mexico (under the Maquiladora program), Switzerland, Ireland, and Slovakia. These foreign operations represent captive manufacturing facilities of the Company. The Company's operations are subject to various political, economic, and other risks and uncertainties inherent in the countries in which the Company operates. Among other risks, the Company's operations are subject to the risks of restrictions on transfer of funds; export duties, quotas, and embargoes; domestic and international customs and tariffs; changing taxation policies; foreign exchange restrictions; and political conditions and governmental regulations.

Example 2–88: Company Specifies Percentage of Net Sales Relating to Foreign Operations

Sales to customers outside the United States approximated 35% of net sales in 2000 and 25 % of net sales in 1999.

New Accounting Pronouncement

Example 2–89: Future Adoption of New Accounting Pronouncement

FAS-133 (Accounting for Derivative Instruments and Hedging Activities), as amended by FAS-137 (Accounting for Derivative Instruments and Hedging Activities—Deferral of the Effective Date of FASB Statement No. 133) and FAS-138 (Accounting for Certain Derivative Instruments and Certain Hedging Activities), establishes accounting and reporting standards for derivative financial instruments and for hedging activities related to those instruments, as well as other hedging activities. This Statement requires an entity to recognize all derivatives as either assets or liabilities in the statement of financial position and measure those instruments at fair value. The Company is required to adopt the new Statement in 2001. The Company is currently evaluating the effect that implementation of the new standard will have on its results of operations and financial position.

Example 2–90: Change in Accounting Method for Start-Up Activities

In April 1998, the American Institute of Certified Public Accountants issued Statement of Position 98-5 (Reporting on the Costs of Start-Up Activities), which requires that such costs, as broadly defined in SOP 98-5, be expensed as incurred. The Statement is effective for years beginning after December 15, 1998, and the initial application must be reported as the cumulative effect of a change in accounting principle. The Company adopted SOP 98-5 in 1999, which resulted in the recording of a cumulative effect of a change in accounting principle of $400,000 ($0.06 per share), net of the applicable income tax benefit. This charge represents the unamortized portion of previously capitalized organization, start-up, pre-operating, and integrated logistics services contract implementation costs primarily incurred as a part of the Company's expansion activities and long-term contract activity from 1996 to 1998. The Company believes that the ongoing application of this Statement will not have a material adverse effect on the Company's financial position, results of operations, or cash flows.

Example 2–91: FASB Interpretation No. 44 of APB-25 Relating to Transactions Involving Stock Compensation

In March 2000, FASB issued Interpretation No. 44 (FIN-44) (Accounting for Certain Transactions Involving Stock Compensation—an Interpretation of APB Opinion No. 25). This Interpretation clarifies (1) the definition of "employee" for purposes of applying APB Opinion No. 25 (Accounting for Stock Issued to Employees), (2) the criteria for determining whether a plan qualifies as a noncompensatory plan, (3) the accounting consequence of various modifications to the terms of a previously fixed stock option or award, and (4) the accounting for an exchange of stock compensation awards in a business combination. This Interpretation is effective July 1, 2000, but certain conclusions in this Interpretation cover specific events that occur after either December 15, 1998, or January 12, 2000. The Company believes that FIN-44 will not have a material effect on the consolidated financial position or results of our operations.

Pension and Other Employee Benefit Plans

Example 2–92: Defined Benefit Pension Plans

The Company has two defined benefit retirement plans that cover substantially all of its employees. Defined benefit plans for salaried employees provide benefits based on employees' years of service and five-year final overall base compensation. Defined benefit plans for hourly paid employees, including those covered by multi-employer pension plans under collective bargaining agreements, generally provide benefits of stated amounts for specified periods of service. The Company's policy is to fund, at a minimum, amounts as are necessary on an actuarial basis to provide assets sufficient to meet the benefits to be paid to plan members in accordance with the requirements of the Employee Retirement Income Security Act of 1974 (ERISA). Assets of the plans are administered by an independent trustee and are invested principally in fixed income securities, equity securities, and real estate.

Example 2–93: Defined Contribution Plan

Certain employees are covered by defined contribution plans. The Corporation's contributions to these plans are based on a percentage of employee compensation or employee contributions. These plans are funded on a current basis.

Example 2–94: Profit-Sharing Plan

The Company has a profit-sharing plan covering most employees with more than two years of service. The Company contributes 5% of earnings before income taxes to the Plan.

Example 2–95: Salary Reduction Plan

The Company has a defined contribution, salary-reduction plan that covers all its employees after one year of service. Employees may contribute up to 15% of their salary to the plan and the Company makes a matching contribution of 50%, up to 3% of compensation.

Example 2–96: Postretirement Benefits Other Than Pensions

The Company provides certain postretirement medical, dental, and life insurance benefits principally to most employees. The Company uses the corridor approach in the valuation of postretirement benefits. The corridor approach defers all actuarial gains and losses resulting from variances between actual results and economic estimates or actuarial assumptions. Amortization occurs when the net gains and losses exceed 10% of the accumulated postretirement benefit obligation at the beginning of the year. The amount in excess of the corridor is amortized over the average remaining service period to retirement date of active plan participants or, for retired participants, the average remaining life expectancy.

Property and Equipment and Depreciation Methods

Example 2–97: Basis for Recording Fixed Assets, Lives, and Depreciation Methods

Property and equipment are recorded at cost. Expenditures for major additions and improvements are capitalized, and minor replacements, maintenance, and repairs are charged to expense as incurred. When property and equipment are retired or otherwise disposed of, the cost and accumulated depreciation are removed from the accounts and any resulting gain or loss is included in the results of operations for the respective period. Depreciation is provided over the estimated useful lives of the related assets using the straight-line method for financial statement purposes. The Company uses other depreciation methods (generally accelerated) for tax purposes where appropriate. The estimated useful lives for significant property and equipment categories are as follows:

Vehicles	3 to 10 years
Machinery and equipment	3 to 20 years
Commercial containers	8 to 12 years
Buildings and improvements	10 to 40 years

Example 2–98: Amortization of Leasehold Improvements

Amortization of leasehold improvements is computed using the straight-line method over the shorter of the remaining lease term or the estimated useful lives of the improvements.

Example 2–99: Assets Held under Capital Leases

Assets held under capital leases are recorded at the lower of the net present value of the minimum lease payments or the fair value of the leased asset at the inception of the lease. Amortization expense is computed using the straight-line method over the shorter of the estimated useful lives of the assets or the period of the related lease.

Example 2–100: Construction in Progress and Estimated Cost to Complete Construction of New Facility

The Company is constructing a new facility scheduled to be completed in 2002. As of December 31, 2000, the Company incurred and capitalized in Construction in Progress $1,600,000. The estimated cost to be incurred in 2001 and 2002 to complete construction of the facility is approximately $12 million.

Example 2–101: Review of Carrying Value of Property and Equipment for Impairment—No Impairment

The Company reviews the carrying value of property, plant, and equipment for impairment whenever events and circumstances indicate that the carrying value of an asset may not be recoverable from the estimated future cash flows expected to result from its use and eventual disposition. In cases where undiscounted expected future cash flows are less than the carrying value, an impairment loss is recognized equal to an amount by which the carrying value exceeds the fair value of assets. The factors considered by management in performing this assessment include current operating results, trends and prospects, and the effects of obsolescence, demand, competition, and other economic factors. Based on this assessment there was no impairment at December 31, 2000.

Reclassifications

Example 2–102: Items Reclassified Not Specifically Identified

Certain reclassifications have been made to the prior years' financial statements to conform to the current year presentation. These reclassifications had no effect on previously reported results of operations or retained earnings.

Example 2–103: Items Reclassified Specifically Identified

In the current year, the Company separately classified goodwill in the Balance Sheets and has included stock based compensation as selling, general and administrative expense in the Statements of Operations. For comparative purposes, amounts in the prior years have been reclassified to conform to current year presentations.

Rent Obligation

Example 2–104: Operating Lease Contains Provisions for Future Rent Increases

The Company has entered into operating lease agreements for its corporate office and warehouses, some of which contain provisions for future rent increases or periods in which rent payments are reduced (abated). In accordance with generally accepted accounting principles, the Company records monthly rent expense equal to the total of the payments due over the lease term, divided by the number of months of the lease term. The difference between rent expense recorded and the amount paid is credited or charged to "Deferred rent obligation," which is reflected as a separate line item in the accompanying Balance Sheet.

Reorganization and Re-Incorporation

Example 2–105: Re-Incorporation in a New State

The Company originally was organized under the laws of the state of New York on June 1, 1988 and was subsequently reincorporated under the laws of the state of Georgia on November 12, 1999. The name of the company was changed to DEF, Inc. from ABC Corp. on October 15, 2000. In connection with the re-incorporation of the Company in November 1999, as approved by the stockholders, the number of authorized shares of the Company's common stock was increased to one hundred million (100,000,000) and each share of common stock was assigned a par value of $.01. The shares outstanding and all other references to shares of common stock reported have been restated to give effect to the re-incorporation.

Example 2–106: Conversion from a Limited Liability Company to a C Corporation

The Company, formerly ABC LLC, converted from a limited liability company to a C corporation on January 1, 2000. To effect the conversion, the Company formed a new corporation and transferred all of the assets and liabilities into the newly formed entity. The new corporation, XYZ, Inc., simultaneously issued 10,000,000 shares of common stock, with a par value of $0.01 per share, and 15,000,000 shares of Series A redeemable preferred stock in exchange for each existing member's respective percentage ownership interest in ABC LLC. The exchange has been recorded at the Company's historical carrying values on the date of conversion.

Upon conversion to a C corporation on January 1, 2000, the Company recorded a net deferred tax asset of $450,000, computed based on the difference between the book and tax bases of its assets and liabilities as of that date.

Example 2–107: Emergence from Bankruptcy

Upon emergence from its Chapter 11 proceedings in April 2000, the Company adopted "fresh-start" reporting in accordance with AICPA Statement of Position No. 90-7 (Financial Reporting by Entities in Reorganization Under the Bankruptcy Code), as of March 31, 2000. The Company's emergence from these proceedings resulted in a new reporting entity with no retained earnings or accumulated deficit as of March 31, 2000. Accordingly, the Company's financial information shown for periods prior to March 31, 2000, is not comparable to consolidated financial statements presented on or subsequent to March 31, 2000.

The Bankruptcy Court confirmed the Company's plan of reorganization. The confirmed plan provided for the following:

Secured Debt—The Company's $[*amount*] of secured debt (secured by a first mortgage lien on a building located in Nashville, Tennessee) was exchanged for $[*amount*] in cash and a $[*amount*] secured note, payable in annual installments of $[*amount*] commencing on July 1, 2001, through June 30, 2004, with interest at 13% per annum, with the balance due on July 1, 2005.

Priority Tax Claims—Payroll and withholding taxes of $[*amount*] are payable in equal annual installments commencing on July 1, 2001, through July 1, 2006, with interest at 11% per annum.

Senior Debt—The holders of approximately $[*amount*] of senior subordinated secured notes received the following instruments in exchange for their notes: (a) $[*amount*] in new senior secured debt, payable in annual installments of $[*amount*] commencing March 1, 2001, through March 1, 2004, with interest at 12% per annum, secured by first liens on certain property, plants, and equipment, with the balance due on March 1, 2005; (b) $[*amount*] of subordinated debt with interest at 14% per annum due in equal annual installments commencing on October 1, 2001, through October 1, 2007, secured by second liens on certain property, plant, and equipment; and (c) [*percent*]% of the new issue of outstanding voting common stock of the Company.

Trade and Other Miscellaneous Claims—The holders of approximately $[*amount*] of trade and other miscellaneous claims received the following for their claims: (a) $[*amount*] in senior secured debt, payable in annual installments of $[*amount*] commencing March 1, 2001, through March 1, 2004, with interest at 12% per annum, secured by first liens on certain property, plants, and equipment, with the balance due on March 1, 2005; (b) $[*amount*] of subordinated debt, payable in equal annual installments commencing October 1, 2001, through October 1, 2006, with interest at 14% per annum; and (c) [*percent*]% of the new issue of outstanding voting common stock of the Company.

Subordinated Debentures—The holders of approximately $[*amount*] of subordinated unsecured debt received, in exchange for the debentures, [*percent*]% of the new issue outstanding voting common stock of the Company.

Preferred Stock—The holders of [*number*] shares of preferred stock received [*percent*]% of the outstanding voting common stock of the new issue of the Company in exchange for their preferred stock.

Common Stock—The holders of approximately [*number*] outstanding shares of the Company's existing common stock received, in exchange for their shares, [*percent*]% of the new outstanding voting common stock of the Company.

Example 2–108: Petition for Relief under Chapter 11

On February 13, 2000, ABC Company (the Debtor) filed petitions for relief under Chapter 11 of the federal bankruptcy laws in the United

States Bankruptcy Court for the Western District of Tennessee. Under Chapter 11, certain claims against the Debtor in existence prior to the filing of the petitions for relief under the federal bankruptcy laws are stayed while the Debtor continues business operations as Debtor-in-possession. These claims are reflected in the December 31, 2000, Balance Sheet as "Liabilities subject to compromise." Additional claims (liabilities subject to compromise) may arise subsequent to the filing date resulting from rejection of executory contracts, including leases, and from the determination by the court (or agreed to by parties in interest) of allowed claims for contingencies and other disputed amounts. Claims secured against the Debtor's assets (secured claims) also are stayed, although the holders of such claims have the right to move the court for relief from the stay. Secured claims are secured primarily by liens on the Debtor's property, plant, and equipment.

The Debtor received approval from the Bankruptcy Court to pay or otherwise honor certain of its prepetition obligations, including employee wages and product warranties. The Debtor has determined that there is insufficient collateral to cover the interest portion of scheduled payments on its prepetition debt obligations. Contractual interest on those obligations amounts to $[*amount*], which is $[*amount*] in excess of reported interest expense; therefore, the Debtor has discontinued accruing interest on these obligations.

Research and Development Costs

Example 2–109: Research and Development Costs Expensed

Research, development, and engineering costs are expensed in the year incurred. For 2000 these costs were $2,050,000 and for 1999 they were $1,100,000.

Example 2–110: Product Development Costs Deferred

The Company defers certain costs related to the preliminary activities associated with the manufacture of its products, which the Company has determined have future economic benefit. These costs are then expensed in the period in which the initial shipment of the related product is made. Management periodically reviews and revises, when necessary, its estimate of the future benefit of these costs and expenses them if it is deemed there no longer is a future benefit. At December 31, 2000, and December 31, 1999, product development costs capitalized totaled $611,000 and $523,000, respectively.

Example 2–111: Capitalized Costs of Computer Software to Be Sold, Leased, or Otherwise Marketed

Research and development costs are charged to expense as incurred. However, the costs incurred for the development of computer software that will be sold, leased, or otherwise marketed are capitalized when technological feasibility has been established. These capitalized costs are subject to an ongoing assessment of recoverability based on anticipated future revenues and changes in hardware and software technologies. Costs that are capitalized include direct labor and related overhead.

Amortization of capitalized software development costs begins when the product is available for general release. Amortization is provided on a product-by-product basis on either the straight-line method over periods not exceeding two years or the sales ratio method. Unamortized capitalized software development costs determined to be in excess of net realizable value of the product are expensed immediately.

Restricted Funds

Example 2–112: Restricted Funds Held by Trustees

Restricted funds held by trustees of $1,300,000 and $900,000 at December 31, 2000 and 1999, respectively, are included in other noncurrent assets and consist principally of funds deposited in connection with plant closure obligations, insurance escrow deposits, and amounts held for new plant and other construction arising from industrial revenue financing. These amounts are principally invested in fixed income securities of federal, state, and local governmental entities and financial institutions. The Company considers such trustee-restricted investments to be held to maturity. At December 31, 2000, and December 31, 1999, the aggregate fair value of these investments approximates their amortized costs, and substantially all of these investments mature within one year.

Example 2–113: Investments Restricted for Construction Financing

Restricted investments consist of U.S. governmental obligations with maturities of more than one year. These investments are carried at fair value and are restricted as to withdrawal for construction financing. Restricted investments are held in the Company's name and custodied with two major financial institutions.

Example 2–114: Restricted Cash Included in Other Non-Current Assets

At December 31, 2000, other non-current assets included restricted cash of $1,200,000 pledged to support a bank credit facility. At December 31, 1999, restricted cash balances of $2,450,000 represented amounts pledged to support bank guarantees issued on several large construction contracts.

Revenue Recognition

Example 2–115: Sales Recorded When Products Are Shipped, with Appropriate Provisions for Discounts and Returns

Sales are recorded when products are shipped to customers. Provisions for discounts and rebates to customers, estimated returns and allowances, and other adjustments are provided for in the same period the related sales are recorded. In instances where products are configured to customer requirements, revenue is recorded upon the successful completion of the Company's final test procedures.

Example 2–116: Revenue from Service Contracts

The Company recognizes revenue on service contracts ratably over applicable contract periods or as services are performed. Amounts billed and collected before the services are performed are included in deferred revenues.

Example 2–117: Contract Revenue Recognized on the Percentage-of-Completion Method

The Company recognizes engineering and construction contract revenues using the percentage-of-completion method, based primarily on contract costs incurred to date compared with total estimated contract costs. Customer-furnished materials, labor, and equipment, and in certain cases subcontractor materials, labor, and equipment, are included in revenues and cost of revenues when management believes that the company is responsible for the ultimate acceptability of the project. Contracts are segmented between types of services, such as engineering and construction, and accordingly, gross margin related to each activity is recognized as those separate services are rendered.

Changes to total estimated contract costs or losses, if any, are recognized in the period in which they are determined. Claims against customers are recognized as revenue upon settlement. Revenues recognized in excess of amounts billed are classified as current assets under contract work in progress. Amounts billed to clients in excess of revenues recognized to date are classified as current liabilities under advance billings on contracts.

Changes in project performance and conditions, estimated profitability, and final contract settlements may result in future revisions to construction contract costs and revenue.

Example 2–118: Right of Return and Price Protection Exist

Product revenue is generally recognized upon shipment to the customer. The Company grants certain distributors limited rights of return and price protection on unsold products. Product revenue on shipments to distributors that have rights of return and price protection is recognized upon shipment by the distributor.

Example 2–119: Deferral of Certain Revenue and Gross Margins

Product sales are generally recognized upon shipment of product. However, the Company defers recognition of revenues and gross margin from sales to stocking distributors until such distributors resell the related products to their customers. The Company has deferred recognition of gross margin amounting to $4,000,000 and $3,500,000 as of December 31, 2000, and December 31, 1999, respectively.

Example 2–120: Warranty Contract Revenue

Warranty contract fees are recognized as revenues ratably over the life of the contract and the contract costs are expensed as incurred.

Example 2–121: Membership Fee Income

Revenue from membership fees is recognized at the end of the membership period (upon the expiration of the refund offer), because membership fees are fully refundable during the entire membership period.

Example 2–122: Revenue from Sales-Type and Operating Leases

Revenue from sales-type leases (primarily with terms of 60 months or greater) is recognized as a "sale" upon shipment in an amount equal to the present value of the minimum rental payments under the fixed non-cancelable lease term. The deferred finance charges applicable to these leases are recognized over the terms of the leases using the effective interest method.

The Company also leases equipment to customers under long-term operating leases (primarily leases with terms of 36 to 54 months), which are generally non-cancelable. Rental revenues are recognized as earned over the term of the lease.

Example 2–123: Revenue Relating to Consignment Method Sales

Revenues are recognized at the time the circuit boards are shipped to the customer, for both turnkey and consignment method sales. Under the consignment method, original equipment manufacturers provide the Company with the electronic components to be assembled, and the Company recognizes revenue only on the labor used to assemble the product.

Example 2–124: Income on Loans

Income on all loans is recognized on the interest method. Accrual of interest income is suspended at the earlier of the time at which collection of an account becomes doubtful or the account becomes 90 days delinquent. Interest income on impaired loans is recognized either as cash is collected or on a cost-recovery basis as conditions warrant.

Example 2–125: Revenue Recognition from Grants

The Company receives employment and research grants from various non-U.S. governmental agencies, and the grants are recognized in earnings in the period in which the related expenditures are incurred. Capital grants for the acquisition of equipment are recorded as reductions of the related equipment cost and reduce future depreciation expense.

Self-Insurance

Example 2–126: Self-Insured Claims Liability

The Company is primarily self-insured, up to certain limits, for automobile and general liability, workers' compensation, and employee group health claims. Operations are charged with the cost of claims reported and an estimate of claims incurred but not reported. A liability for unpaid claims and the associated claim expenses, including incurred but not reported losses, is actuarially determined and reflected in the balance sheet as an accrued liability. The self-insured claims liability includes incurred but not reported losses of $1,500,000 and $1,745,000 at December 31, 2000, and December 31, 1999, respectively. The determination of such claims and expenses and the appropriateness of the related liability is continually reviewed and updated.

Example 2–127: Self-Insured Health Plan Supplemented by Stop Loss Insurance

The Company has a self-insured health plan for all its employees. The Company has purchased stop loss insurance to supplement the health plan, which will reimburse the Company for individual claims in excess of $50,000 annually or aggregate claims exceeding $1,000,000 annually.

Shareholders' Equity

Example 2–128: Stock Split

In June 2000, the board of directors approved a three-for-two stock split of the Corporation's common stock effected in the form of a 100% stock dividend, which was distributed on September 10, 2000, to shareholders of record on August 20, 2000. Shareholders' equity, common stock, and stock option activity for all periods presented have been restated to give retroactive recognition to the stock split. In addition, all references in the financial statements and notes to financial statements, to weighted average number of shares, per share amounts, and market prices of the Company's common stock have been restated to give retroactive recognition to the stock split.

Example 2–129: Stock Repurchase Program

In January 2000, the Company's Board of Directors approved a stock repurchase program whereby up to 3 million shares of common stock may be purchased from time to time at the discretion of management. As of December 31, 2000, the Company had purchased 1,900,000 shares at a total cost of $28,500,000. The repurchased shares are held as treasury stock and are available for general corporate purposes.

Example 2–130: Treasury Shares

Common stock held in the Company's treasury has been recorded at cost.

Stock Option Plans

Example 2–131: Accounting Requirements of FAS-123 Have Not Been Adopted for Employee Stock Options

Financial Accounting Standards Board Statement No. 123 (Accounting for Stock-Based Compensation) encourages, but does not require, companies to record compensation cost for stock-based employee compensation plans based on the fair value of options granted. The Company has elected to continue to account for stock-based compensation using the intrinsic value method prescribed in Accounting Principles Board Opinion No. 25 (Accounting for Stock Issued to Employees) and related interpretations and to provide additional disclosures with respect to the pro forma effects of adoption had the Company recorded compensation expense as provided in FAS-123 (see Note [*X*]).

In accordance with APB-25, compensation cost for stock options is recognized in income based on the excess, if any, of the quoted market price of the stock at the grant date of the award or other measurement date over the amount an employee must pay to acquire the stock. Generally, the exercise price for stock options granted to employees equals or exceeds the fair market value of the Company's common stock at the date of grant, thereby resulting in no recognition of compensation expense by the Company.

Example 2–132: Accounting Requirements of FAS-123 Have Been Adopted for Employee Stock Options

The Company has adopted the fair value based method of accounting prescribed in Financial Accounting Standards Board Statement No. 123 (Accounting for Stock-Based Compensation) for its employee stock option plans.

Warranty Costs

Example 2–133: Accrual for Warranty Costs Is Made in the Period in Which the Revenue Is Recognized

The Company provides product warranties for specific product lines and accrues for estimated future warranty costs in the period in which the revenue is recognized.

Example 2–134: Accrual for Warranty Costs Is Made When Such Costs Become Probable

Provision for estimated warranty costs is made in the period in which such costs become probable and is periodically adjusted to reflect actual experience.

Example 2–135: Product Warranty Policy and Period Described

The Company warrants its products against defects in design, materials, and workmanship generally for three to five years. A provision for estimated future costs relating to warranty expense is recorded when products are shipped.

Example 2–136: Warranty Costs Are Subject to Significant Estimates

The Company's warranty accruals are based on the Company's best estimates of product failure rates and unit costs to repair. However, the Company is continually releasing new and ever-more complex and technologically advanced products. As a result, it is at least reasonably possible that product could be released with certain unknown quality and/or design problems. Such an occurrence could result in materially higher than expected warranty and related costs, which could have a materially adverse effect on the Company's results of operations and financial condition in the near term.

CHAPTER 3
ADVERTISING COSTS

CONTENTS

EXECUTIVE SUMMARY

In most cases, the costs of advertising should be expensed as incurred or the first time the advertisement occurs. However, there are two exceptions to this general rule:

1. Certain direct-response advertising costs should be capitalized and amortized over the period during which the future benefits or sales are expected to be received. For direct-response advertising where (a) it can be shown that customers responded to a specific advertisement, and (b) there is a probable future economic benefit, only the following two types of costs should be capitalized:
   - —Incremental direct costs incurred in transactions with independent third parties (e.g., idea development, writing advertising copy, artwork, printing, magazine space, and mailing).
   - —Payroll and payroll-related costs for employees who are directly associated with the direct-response advertising activ-

ities. Items such as administrative costs, rent, and depreciation should not be included in the capitalized advertising costs.

2. Expenditures for advertising costs that are made subsequent to recognizing revenues related to those costs should be capitalized and charged to expense when the related revenues are recognized. For example, some entities assume an obligation to reimburse their customers for some or all of the customers' advertising costs (cooperative advertising). Generally, revenues related to the transactions creating those obligations are earned and recognized before the expenditures are made. Those obligations should be accrued and the advertising costs expensed when the related revenues are recognized.

An entity should periodically assess the realizability of the advertising costs that remain capitalized by comparing the carrying amounts, on a cost-pool-by-cost-pool basis, to the probable remaining future net revenues expected to result directly from such advertising. If the carrying amounts exceed the remaining future net revenues, the excess should be reported as advertising expense of the current period.

Authoritative Literature

SOP 93-7	Reporting on Advertising Costs
EITF 99-17	Accounting for Advertising Barter Transactions
PB-13	Direct-Response Advertising and Probable Future Benefits

DISCLOSURE REQUIREMENTS

The financial statements should include the following disclosures about advertising costs:

1. For direct-response advertising (SOP 93-7, par. 49):
   a. A description of the direct-response advertising reported as assets, if any
   b. The accounting policy being followed
   c. The amortization period
2. For non-direct response advertising costs, whether such costs are expensed as incurred or the first time the advertising takes place (SOP 93-7, par. 49)

3. The total amount charged to advertising expense for each income statement presented, with separate disclosure of amounts, if any, representing a writedown to net realizable value (SOP 93-7, par. 49)
4. The total amount of advertising costs reported as assets in each balance sheet presented (SOP 93-7, par. 49)
5. The amount of revenue and expense recognized from advertising barter transactions for each income statement period presented (EITF 99-17). Entities providing advertising in barter transactions that do not qualify for recognition at fair value under EITF 99-17 should disclose for each income statement presented the volume and type of advertising provided and received, such as the number of equivalent pages, number of minutes, or the overall percentage of advertising volume.

EXAMPLES OF FINANCIAL STATEMENT DISCLOSURES

The following sample disclosures are available on the accompanying disc.

Example 3–1: Advertising Costs Are Expensed as Incurred

Advertising costs are expensed as incurred. Advertising expense totaled $477,000 for 2000 and $392,000 for 1999.

Example 3–2: Advertising Costs Are Expensed the First Time the Advertising Takes Place

Production costs of future media advertising are expensed the first time the advertising takes place. Advertising expense totaled $532,000 for 2000 and $410,000 for 1999.

Example 3–3: Direct-Response Advertising Costs Are Capitalized

Direct response advertising costs, consisting primarily of catalog book production, printing, and postage costs, are capitalized and amortized over the expected life of the catalog, not to exceed six months. Direct response advertising costs reported as "Prepaid assets" are $275,000 and $350,000 at December 31, 2000, and December 31, 1999, respectively. Total advertising expenses were $1,900,000 and $1,600,000 in 2000 and 1999, respectively.

Example 3–4: Certain Advertising Costs Are Expensed the First Time the Advertising Takes Place, and Direct-Response Advertising Costs Are Capitalized and Written Down to Net Realizable Value

The Company expenses the production costs of advertising the first time the advertising takes place, except for direct-response advertising, which is capitalized and amortized over its expected period of future benefits.

Direct-response advertising consists primarily of magazine advertisements that include order coupons for the Company's products. The capitalized costs of the advertising are amortized over the six-month period following the publication of the magazine in which it appears.

At December 31, 2000, and December 31, 1999, capitalized direct-response advertising costs of $570,000 and $612,000, respectively, were included in "Other assets" in the accompanying Balance Sheets. Advertising expense was $5,264,000 in 2000, including $432,000 for amounts written down to net realizable value related to certain capitalized direct-response advertising costs. Advertising expense was $6,079,000 in 1999.

Example 3–5: Advertising Barter Transactions

In 2000 and 1999, the Company entered into barter agreements whereby it delivered $1,165,000 and $1,059,000, respectively, of its inventory in exchange for future advertising credits and other items. The credits, which expire in November 2001, are valued at the lower of the Company's cost or market value of the inventory transferred. The Company has recorded barter credits of $115,000 and $236,000 in "Prepaid expenses and other current assets" at December 31, 2000, and December 31, 1999, respectively. At December 31, 2000, and December 31, 1999, "Other noncurrent assets" include $279,000 and $323,000, respectively, of such credits. Under the terms of the barter agreements, the Company is required to pay cash equal to a negotiated amount of the bartered advertising, or other items, and use the barter credits to pay the balance. These credits are charged to expense as they are used. During the years ended December 31, 2000, and December 31, 1999, approximately $1,080,000 and $751,000, respectively, were charged to expense for barter credits used.

The Company assesses the recoverability of barter credits periodically. Factors considered in evaluating the recoverability include management's plans with respect to advertising and other expenditures for which barter credits can be used. Any impairment losses are charged to operations as they are determinable. During the years ended December 31, 2000, and December 31, 1999, the Company charged $250,000 and $425,000, respectively, to operations for such impairment losses.

CHAPTER 4
BUSINESS COMBINATIONS

CONTENTS

EXECUTIVE SUMMARY

A *business combination* occurs when two or more entities combine to form a single entity. An *asset combination* results when one company acquires the assets of one or more other companies, or when a new company is formed to acquire the assets of two or more existing companies. An *acquisition of stock combination* occurs when one company acquires more than 50% of the outstanding voting common stock of one or more target companies, or when a new company is formed to acquire controlling interest in the outstanding voting common stock of two or more target companies.

There are two basic methods of accounting for combining two or more businesses into one entity: (1) the purchase method and (2) the pooling-of-interests method. The method used depends on the attributes of the combining companies, how the combination is accomplished, and whether certain planned transactions exist. The pooling method is required when certain criteria regarding the nature of the consideration given and the circumstances of the exchange are met. If the pooling criteria are not met, the purchase method of accounting must be used to record the combination. The primary difference between the two methods is that the purchase method views the combination as an acquisition of one company by the other, and the pooling-of-interests method treats the combination as a uniting of ownership interests.

Under the purchase method of accounting, the purchase price should be allocated to the assets acquired and the liabilities assumed as follows:

1. Assets and liabilities should be recorded at their fair values as of the acquisition date.
2. If the cost of the acquired company exceeds the sum of the amounts assigned to the assets and liabilities acquired, the excess should be recorded as goodwill.

3. If the values assigned to the assets acquired and liabilities assumed exceed the cost of the acquired company, the amounts assigned to the noncurrent assets acquired, other than long-term investments in marketable securities, should be reduced by a proportionate part of the excess. After the noncurrent assets have been reduced to zero, any excess of assigned values over cost of the acquired company should be recorded as negative goodwill.

In a pooling-of-interests combination, the combined entity reports the assets and liabilities of the target company at the book values previously reported by the combining entities. In a pooling transaction, only voting common stock may be given as consideration, and it is recorded in an amount equal to the net book value of the combined assets and liabilities; therefore, no goodwill is recorded in a pooling transaction. The operating statements for pooling-of-interests combinations are combined for the full year in the year of the combination regardless of the specific date the pooling occurs. Comparative prior years' financial statements are restated retroactively to reflect the pooled status.

FASB Outstanding Exposure Draft

As this book goes to press, the FASB has an outstanding exposure draft of a Statement of Financial Accounting Standards (Business Combinations and Intangible Assets) that may have an important effect on accounting for intangible assets. The primary effects of the exposure draft would be that the pooling-of-interests method of accounting for business combinations would no longer be allowed, and intangible assets (including goodwill) would be subject to a maximum life of 20 years rather than 40 years as is current practice. The requirement that intangible assets older than the 20-year maximum be amortized could be overcome if the asset clearly is expected to generate identifiable cash flows beyond that time, and either the asset is exchangeable or control over the future economic benefits is obtained through contractual or other legal rights. In these circumstances, the intangible asset would not be amortized until its life is determined to be finite.

Following are some of the more important conclusions that have been reached or confirmed in recent FASB deliberations:

- Goodwill should be recognized initially as an asset because it meets the definition of an asset in CON-6 (Recognition and Measurement in Financial Statements of Business Enterprises).
- Goodwill should be measured initially as the excess of the cost of the acquired enterprise over the sum of the amounts assigned to identifiable assets acquired less liabilities assumed.

- An identifiable intangible asset should be recognized separately if it is separable or if control over the future economic benefits of the asset is obtained through contractual or other legal rights.
- The scope of the project will include purchased intangibles but not internally developed intangibles.

The practitioner should be alert to the issuance of a final pronouncement that would affect the guidance provided in this chapter.

Authoritative Literature

ARB-43	Chapter 1A, Rules Adopted by Membership
ARB-51	Consolidated Financial Statements
APB-16	Business Combinations
FAS-10	Extension of "Grandfather" Provisions for Business Combinations
FAS-38	Accounting for Preacquisition Contingencies of Purchased Enterprises
FAS-72	Accounting for Certain Acquisitions of Banking or Thrift Institutions
FAS-79	Elimination of Certain Disclosures for Business Combinations by Nonpublic Enterprises
FAS-87	Employers' Accounting for Pensions
FAS-106	Employers' Accounting for Postretirement Benefits Other Than Pensions
FAS-109	Accounting for Income Taxes
FAS-111	Rescission of FASB Statement No. 32 and Technical Corrections
FAS-121	Accounting for the Impairment of Long-Lived Assets and for Long-Lived Assets to Be Disposed Of
FIN-4	Applicability of FASB Statement No. 2 to Business Combinations Accounted for by the Purchase Method
FIN-9	Applying APB Opinions No. 16 and 17 When a Savings and Loan Association or a Similar Institution Is Acquired in a Business Combination Accounted for by the Purchase Method
FTB 85-5	Issues Relating to Accounting for Business Combinations

DISCLOSURE REQUIREMENTS

Purchase Method

1. The acquiring company should make the following disclosures in its financial statements for the period a business combination accounted for by the purchase method occurs (combining several minor acquisitions for disclosure purposes is acceptable) (APB-16, par. 95):
   a. Name and brief description of the acquired enterprise
   b. Method of accounting for the combination (i.e., the purchase method)
   c. Period for which results of operations of the acquisition are included in the acquiring company's income statement (usually starts at the date of acquisition)
   d. Cost of the acquired enterprise and, if applicable, the number of shares of stock issued or issuable, including the amount assigned to the issued and issuable shares
   e. Description of the plan for amortization of acquired goodwill, including the amortization method and period
   f. Other pertinent information such as contingent payments, options, or other commitments
2. For research and development assets acquired in a business combination accounted for as a purchase that have no alternative future use, disclosure should be made of the portion of the purchase price that has been allocated to research and development and charged to expense at the date of consummation of the business combination (FIN-4, par. 5).
3. Consideration that is issued or issuable at the end of a contingency period or that is held in escrow should be disclosed (APB-16, par. 78).
4. The following supplemental information should be disclosed in the notes to the financial statements of an acquiring company that is publicly held (optional for nonpublic companies) in the year of acquisition (APB-16, par. 96; FAS-79, par. 6):
   a. Results of operations for the current period as though the companies had combined at the beginning of the period, unless the acquisition was at or near the beginning of the period
   b. If comparative statements are presented, results of operations for the immediately preceding period as though the companies had combined at the beginning of that period
   c. On a pro forma basis, at a minimum, revenue, income before extraordinary items, net income, and earnings per share amounts

5. If preacquisition contingencies (for business combinations accounted for as a purchase) are not allocated as required by Financial Accounting Standards Board Statement No. 38 (Accounting for Preacquisition Contingencies of Purchased Enterprises), the amount and nature of adjustments determined after December 15, 1980, should be disclosed (FAS-38, pars. 6 and 10).

6. The following disclosures should be made if a combined entity plans to incur costs from exiting an activity of an acquired entity, involuntarily terminating employees of an acquired entity, or relocating employees of an acquired entity and the activities of the acquired entity that will not be continued are significant to the combined entity's revenues or operating results or the cost recognized from those activities as of the consummation date are material to the combined entity (EITF 95-3, par. 13a-b):

   a. For the period in which a purchase business combination occurs:

      — When the plans to exit an activity or involuntarily terminate or relocate employees of the acquired entity are not final as of the balance sheet date, a description of any unresolved issues, the types of additional liabilities that may result in an adjustment to the purchase price allocation, and how any adjustment will be reported

      — A description of the type and amount of liabilities assumed in the purchase price allocation for costs to exit an activity or involuntarily terminate or relocate employees

      — A description of the major actions that make up the plan to exit an activity or involuntarily terminate or relocate employees of an acquired entity

      — A description of activities of the acquired entity that will not be continued, including the method of disposition, and the anticipated date of completion and description of employee groups to be terminated or relocated

   b. For all periods presented subsequent to the acquisition date in which a purchase business combination occurred, until a plan to exit an activity or involuntarily terminate or relocate employees of an acquired entity is fully executed:

      — A description of the type and amount of exit costs, involuntary employee termination costs, and relocation costs paid and charged against the liability

      — The amount of any adjustments to the liability account and whether the corresponding entry was an adjustment of the costs of the acquired entity or included in the determination of net income for the period

Pooling-of-Interests Method

1. The combined enterprise should disclose in its financial statements that a combination accounted for by the pooling-of-interests method has occurred during the period, including the basis of current presentation and restatements of prior periods. In addition, the combined company should disclose the following for the period in which the business combination occurs (APB-16, pars. 56 and 64):
   a. Name and brief description of the companies combined
   b. Method of accounting for the combination (i.e., the pooling-of-interests method)
   c. Description and number of shares of stock issued to effect the combination
   d. Details of the results of operations for each separate company, prior to the date of combination, that are included in the current combined net income
   e. Description of the nature of adjustments of net assets of the combining companies to adopt the same accounting policies and of the effects of the changes on net income reported previously by the separate enterprises and now presented in comparative financial statements
   f. If any of the combining companies changed their fiscal year as a result of the combination, details of any increase or decrease in retained earnings as a result of the change (At a minimum, the details should include revenue, expenses, extraordinary items, net income, and other changes in stockholders' equity for the period that are excluded from the reported results of operations)
   g. Revenue and earnings previously reported by the acquiring company (the company that issues the stock to effect the combination) reconciled with the amounts shown in the combined financial statements
   h. The nature of and effects on earnings per share of nonrecurring intercompany transactions involving long-term assets and liabilities that were not eliminated from current period income
2. If a transaction expected to be treated as a pooling has been initiated, and a portion of the stock has been acquired, but the pooling is not consummated at the date of the financial statements, the investor should disclose combined results of operations of all prior periods and the entire current period as they will be reported if the combination is later accounted for as a pooling (APB-16, par. 62).

3. Information should be disclosed in notes to financial statements, on a pro forma basis, for a proposed business combination (to be accounted for as a pooling-of-interests) that is given to stockholders of combining enterprises (APB-16, par. 64).
4. Any plan of combination that has been initiated but not consummated at a balance sheet date must be disclosed fully, including the effects of the plan on combined operations and any changes in accounting methods (APB-16, par. 65).

EXAMPLES OF FINANCIAL STATEMENT DISCLOSURES

The following sample disclosures are available on the accompanying disc. For examples of financial statement disclosures relating to consolidated and combined financial statements, see Chapter 8, "Consolidated and Combined Financial Statements."

Purchase Method

Example 4–1: Stock Purchase Business Combination

In August 2000, the Company completed the purchase of MBK, Inc., a privately held manufacturer of industrial computer systems and enclosures, by acquiring all of the outstanding capital stock of MBK, Inc. for a total purchase price of $24 million. The acquisition was accounted for using the purchase method of accounting and, accordingly, MBK, Inc.'s results of operations have been included in the consolidated financial statements since the date of acquisition. The source of funds for the acquisition was a combination of the Company's available cash and advances totaling $10 million under its existing credit facility.

The following table presents the allocation of the acquisition cost, including professional fees and other related acquisition costs, to the assets acquired and liabilities assumed:

Cash and cash equivalents	$ 1,000,000
Accounts receivable	4,000,000
Inventories	7,000,000
Other current assets	3,000,000
Property, plant, and equipment	6,000,000
Goodwill	10,000,000
Other noncurrent assets	5,000,000
Total assets	$ 36,000,000

Amounts payable to banks and long-term debt due within one year	$ (4,000,000)
Other current liabilities	(5,000,000)
Long-term accrued liabilities	(1,000,000)
Long-term debt	(2,000,000)
Total liabilities	$(12,000,000)
Total acquisition cost	$ 24,000,000

The allocation of the purchase price is based on preliminary data and could change when final valuation information is obtained.

The following (unaudited) pro forma consolidated results of operations have been prepared as if the acquisition of MBK, Inc. had occurred at January 1, 1999:

	December 31, 2000	*December 31, 1999*
Sales	$79,000,000	$64,000,000
Net income	8,200,000	3,600,000
Net income per share—Basic	1.86	0.82
Net income per share—Diluted	1.58	0.70

The pro forma information is presented for informational purposes only and is not necessarily indicative of the results of operations that actually would have been achieved had the acquisitions been consummated as of that time, nor is it intended to be a projection of future results.

> **Note:** If the pro forma effects are not material, the pro forma information presented above should be replaced with the following: "The pro forma effects of the MBK, Inc. acquisition on the Company's Consolidated Financial Statements were not material."

Example 4–2: Asset Purchase Business Combination Includes Contingent Cash Payment

In October 2000, the Company purchased the Golden Spider brand from Zeelo Co. for $9,500,000 in cash. Under the terms of the agreement, the Company purchased the Golden Spider name, accounts and notes receivable, and tooling, and assumed certain liabilities. The company also incurred $500,000 of direct, acquisition-related costs, which were capitalized as part of the purchase price. The Company may also be required to pay a single contingent cash payment of up to $4,000,000 based on the cumulative net sales of the acquired business during the three-year period January 1, 2001, through December 31, 2003.

The acquisition was recorded using the purchase method of accounting. Accordingly, the purchase price has been allocated to the assets acquired and liabilities assumed based on the estimated fair values at the date of acquisition. The excess of purchase price over the estimated fair values of the net assets acquired, totaling $3,200,000, has been recorded as goodwill and will be amortized on the straight-line method over ten years. The operating results of this acquisition are included in the Company's Consolidated Results of Operations from the date of acquisition.

The following table presents the allocation of the purchase price, including related acquisition costs, to the assets and liabilities acquired:

Accounts and notes receivable	$5,000,000
Tooling equipment	1,900,000
Goodwill	3,200,000
Accounts payable	(600,000)
Total purchase price	$9,500,000

Example 4–3: Pro Forma Results of Operations Are Not Presented Because the Acquired Company Is a Development Stage Company and Results of Operations Are Not Significant

In November 2000, the Company acquired MSX, Inc., a company that is a provider of audio and video capabilities to the personal computer market. The Company completed the acquisition by issuing or reserving for future issuance an aggregate of 2,500,000 shares of common stock, with 1,200,000 of these shares reserved for stock options and employee retention arrangements. The acquisition was accounted for using the purchase method with a purchase price of $17 million. In connection with the acquisition, the Company recorded $5 million of unearned compensation related to employee retention arrangements, which will be charged to operating expenses, primarily research and development, over the next 26 months.

Pro forma results of operations for the MSX, Inc. acquisition have not been presented, because MSX, Inc. is a development stage company and results of operations to date have been insignificant.

Example 4–4: Exchange of Investment Accounted for on the Equity Method for a Majority Ownership in an Unrelated Entity

On October 15, 2000, the Company exchanged its 45% interest in Eagle, Co. for 91% of the common stock of Boiler, Co. On that same date, pursuant to a "split-up" of Eagle, Co. structured for tax purposes as a tax-free reorganization under Internal Revenue Code Section 355, Boiler, Co. received 100% of the machining operations of Eagle, Co. The Company has accounted for this transaction under the purchase method of accounting. Accordingly, the carrying value of the Company's equity investment in Eagle, Co., totaling $8,000,000 at October 15, 2000, was treated as the purchase price for accounting purposes. The assets acquired by Boiler, Co. included substantially all of the real estate and equipment owned by Eagle, Co. in Cleveland, Ohio and used in the machining and boiler assembly operations and certain other assets and liabilities.

Example 4–5: Exercise of Conversion Option on Preferred Stock Results in Consolidation of Investment Previously Accounted for on the Cost Basis

Prior to 2000, the Company accounted for its investment in the preferred stock of Oslo, Inc. on the cost basis. Effective October 1, 2000, the Company exercised its conversion option on its 500,000 shares of Series A 4% Participating Convertible Preferred Stock and as a result is now the record holder of 2,000,000 shares (89%) of the voting stock of Oslo, Inc. The conversion was accounted for using the purchase method of accounting; accordingly, the consolidated results of the Company include the results of Oslo, Inc. since the date of the conversion. Oslo, Inc. is a leading supplier of laboratory instruments and related products.

The unaudited pro forma information that follows was prepared assuming that the conversion had taken place January 1, 1999. In preparing the pro forma financial information, various assumptions were made; therefore, the Company does not imply that the future results will be indicative of the following pro forma information:

	December 31, 2000	*December 31, 1999*
Sales	$65,000,000	$52,000,000
Net income	6,200,000	2,600,000
Net income per share—Basic	1.16	0.81
Net income per share—Diluted	1.02	0.75

The Company received, prior to the conversion, and recognized as income in 2000 $1,200,000 in Preferred Stock cash dividends from Oslo, Inc.

Example 4–6: Amount Initially Assigned to Goodwill Subsequently Revised

In October 1999, the Company acquired XDEG, Inc., a leading provider of health care information products. The Company issued

3,000,000 shares of common stock and 700,000 common stock options, with a total fair value of $35,000,000, in exchange for all outstanding shares of XDEG, Inc. The Company accounted for the acquisition using the purchase method of accounting for business combinations. The purchase price and costs associated with the acquisition exceeded the preliminary estimated fair value of net assets acquired by $10,200,000, which was preliminarily assigned to goodwill.

During 2000, the Company completed the valuation of the intangible assets acquired in the XDEG, Inc. transaction. Pursuant to the valuation, the Company expensed $4,400,000 of the excess purchase price representing purchased in-process technology that previously had been assigned to goodwill. In management's judgment, this amount reflects the amount the Company would reasonably expect to pay an unrelated party for each project included in the technology. The value of in-process research and development of $4,400,000 represented approximately 37% of the purchase price and was determined by estimating the costs to develop the purchased technology into commercially viable products, then estimating the resulting net cash flows from each project that was incomplete at the acquisition date, and discounting the resulting net cash flows to their present value. The $4,400,000 charge is included as a component of "Other charges" in the accompanying Consolidated Statements of Operations for the year ended December 31, 2000. Based on the final valuation, the remaining excess purchase price of $5,800,000 was assigned to existing technologies, trade names, and goodwill. The pro forma effects of the XDEG, Inc. acquisition on the consolidated financial statements were not material.

Example 4–7: Additional Purchase Price Payments Subsequently Made for Achieving Specified Levels of Profitability

During 2000 the Company paid $13 million to the former owners of businesses acquired in previous years. These payments resulted from the acquired businesses having achieved specified levels of profitability during designated periods subsequent to the acquisition. These payments were recorded as additional goodwill and are being amortized over the remainder of the original 30 year amortization period.

Example 4–8: Business Combination Pending Government and Shareholder Approval

In November 2000, the Company signed a definitive agreement to purchase ESY, Inc., a provider of programmable switches. Under the terms of the agreement, between 2,500,000 and 3,000,000 shares of the Company's common stock will be exchanged for all of the outstanding shares and options of ESY, Inc. The agreement is subject to the receipt of certain government approvals and the approval of ESY, Inc.'s shareholders. The deal is expected to be consummated in the first or second quarter of 2001. The Company expects to account for the acquisition using the purchase method of accounting for business combinations. The historical operations of ESY, Inc. are not expected to be material to the financial position or results of operations of the Company.

Example 4–9: Certain Assets Acquired in Business Combination Will Be Sold and Are Classified as Assets Held for Sale

Effective July 1, 2000, the Company completed the acquisition of The Basly Group for approximately $38 million, including the assumption of approximately $16 million of debt. The Basly Group, based in Michigan, is a major supplier of automotive interior systems. The acquisition was accounted for as a purchase. The excess of the purchase price over the estimated fair value of the acquired net assets, which approximated $8 million, was recorded as goodwill. The Basly Group's results have been included in the Company's consolidated financial statements from the date of acquisition. The purchase was initially financed with commercial paper and it is anticipated that a portion will subsequently be financed with long-term debt. Pro forma results of operations to reflect this acquisition have not been presented because the Company believes such information would not be meaningful given the planned restructuring activities and sale of non-core businesses, as described below.

As part of The Basly Group acquisition, the Company recorded a restructuring reserve of $4 million. The reserve was established for anticipated costs associated with consolidating certain of The Basly Group's manufacturing, engineering, and administrative operations with existing capacity of the Company. The majority of the reserve was attributable to expected employee severance and termination benefit costs and plant closure costs. The restructuring activities are expected to be completed by the end of 2001.

Certain businesses acquired in The Basly Group purchase have been classified as net assets held for sale in the Consolidated Statement of Financial Position at December 31, 2000. At the date of acquisition, the Company identified several operations of The Basly Group that were outside of the Company's core businesses and, as such, will be sold. The net assets of the businesses were valued at fair value less estimated costs to sell, including cash flows during the holding period. The Company expects to complete the sale of these businesses in 2001. The operating results of the businesses to be sold, which were not material for 2000, have been excluded from the Company's consolidated operating results.

Example 4–10: Adjustments Made to Previously Determined Values of Assets Acquired in Business Combination

On September 1, 1999, the Company acquired the stock of Sibik, Ltd. for $27,000,000, which includes costs of acquisition. The acquisition was accounted for as a purchase; accordingly, the Company's Consolidated Results of Operations and Cash Flows include the results of operations of Sibik, Ltd. since the date of acquisition.

Because Sibik, Ltd. was acquired late in 1999 and was a complex operation, it required a comprehensive review of asset values and liabilities and a significant part of the evaluation had to take into consideration the integration of Sibik, Ltd. The final assessment of asset values, restructuring the manufacturing and marketing organization, and making other necessary changes was not completed until the third quarter of 2000. The determination of the final fair values resulted in adjustments, made in 2000, consisting of changes from initially determined values as of September 1, 1999, as follows:

Increase in goodwill	$ 1,300,000
Increase in property and equipment	2,100,000
Increase in other assets	400,000
Decrease in inventory	(2,800,000)
Decrease in accounts receivable	(1,000,000)

Example 4–11: Multiple Business Acquisitions

In August 2000, the Company acquired 9,000,000 shares of Class A voting common stock of Lillo, Inc., a leading automotive parts manufacturer, in a private sale. Such shares, which were valued at $35 million, represent an approximately 37% economic interest and 76% voting interest in Lillo, Inc. After the purchase price was applied to the fair value of assets acquired and liabilities assumed, goodwill of approximately $6 million was generated and will be amortized over 30 years.

In July 2000, the Company acquired the Ferno brand and related brand assets from ABC Company. The purchase price consisted of 600,000 shares ($6,200,000) of the Company's common stock, $3,300,000 in cash, $3,500,000 in notes and assumption of net liabilities of $4,000,000. Total consideration, including transaction costs of approximately $250,000, was $17,000,000. The excess of the purchase price over the estimated fair value of assets acquired approximated $2,000,000 and is being amortized over 30 years. In connection with the acquisition, the Company entered into employment agreements with five employees for terms expiring June 2005.

In May 2000, the Company purchased from XYZ Co. the "Stars" product line and related manufacturing equipment for approximately $7 million in cash. The excess of the purchase price over the estimated fair value of assets acquired approximated $3 million and is being amortized over 20 years.

In April 1998, the Company acquired 80% of the issued and outstanding capital stock of JALIL, Inc., a manufacturer of automotive components, for approximately $8 million (net of cash acquired). During June 1999 and 2000, the Company increased its investment by an additional 4% each year. Under the purchase and sale agreements, the Company has the option to acquire, and in certain circumstances, may be required to acquire, the remaining 12% of common stock at prices set forth in the agreements.

The foregoing acquisitions have been recorded under the purchase method of accounting and, accordingly, the results of the acquired businesses are included in the Consolidated Financial Statements since the date of acquisition. The following unaudited pro forma consolidated results of operations have been prepared as if the foregoing acquisitions had occurred as of January 1, 1999, and therefore include an estimate of incremental operating expenses, interest expense, amortization of goodwill, and income tax expense:

	December 31, 2000	*December 31, 1999*
Sales	$39,000,000	$32,000,000
Net income	4,200,000	1,600,000
Net income per share—Basic	1.06	0.62
Net income per share—Diluted	.98	0.53

Pooling-of-Interests Transactions

Example 4–12: Financial Statements Retroactively Restated as a Result of Merger

On November 15, 2000, the Company consummated a merger with PBC, Ltd., accounted for as a pooling of interests (the PBC Merger) and, accordingly, the accompanying Consolidated Financial Statements have been restated to include the accounts and operations of PBC, Ltd. for all periods presented. Under the terms of the PBC Merger, the Company issued 0.736 of a share of its common stock for each share of PBC, Ltd.'s outstanding common stock. Prior to the PBC Merger, the Company owned approximately 2.4% of PBC, Ltd.'s outstanding shares, which were canceled on the effective date of the PBC Merger. The PBC Merger increased the Company's outstanding shares of common stock by approximately 22,000,000 shares, and the Company assumed PBC Ltd.'s stock options equivalent to approximately 3,100,000 underlying shares of the Company's common stock.

The Consolidated Balance Sheets at December 31, 2000, and December 31, 1999 reflect the combining of (a) the Company (DHI Services) prior to consummation of the PBC Merger and (b) PBC, Ltd. as of those dates. Combined and separate results of operations for the year ended December 31, 1999, and the nine months ended September 30, 2000 (the closest interim period to the date the merger was consummated) of DHI Services and PBC, Ltd. for the restated periods are as follows:

	DHI Services	*PBC, Ltd.*	*Combined*
Nine months ended September 30, 2000:			
Operating revenues	$92,000,000	$6,500,000	$98,500,000
Income (loss) from continuing operations before income taxes	(1,700,000)	500,000	(1,200,000)
Net income (loss)	(1,200,000)	300,000	(900,000)
Year ended December 31, 1999:			
Operating revenues	$90,000,000	$6,000,000	$96,000,000
Income (loss) from continuing operations before income taxes	(1,000,000)	200,000	(800,000)
Net income (loss)	(800,000)	100,000	(700,000)

Prior to November 15, 2000, the Company and PBC, Ltd. entered into certain transactions for the purchase and sale of products in the normal course of business. These intercompany transactions have been eliminated in the accompanying financial statements.

Note: The following table illustrates the adjustment made in the Consolidated Statement of Stockholders' Equity for the PBC Merger described above.

	Common Stock	*Additional Paid-in Capital*	*Retained Earnings*
Balances at December 31, 1998, as previously reported	$400,000	$7,000,000	$6,000,000
Pooling of interests adjustments—PBC merger	300,000	1,500,000	1,100,000
Balances at December 31, 1998, as restated	700,000	8,500,000	7,100,000
Net income (loss)	-0-	-0-	(700,000)
Balances at December 31, 1999	700,000	8,500,000	6,400,000
Net income (loss)	-0-	-0-	(1,300,000)
Balances at December 31, 2000	$700,000	$8,500,000	$5,100,000

Example 4–13: Pooling-of-Interests Transaction Results in Significant Charges Incurred in Current Period and to Be Incurred in Future Periods

In connection with the PBC Merger, the Company incurred significant charges in 2000. Additionally, the Company expects to incur additional costs throughout 2001 that are transitional in nature and not accruable until incurred or committed. The table below reflects the amounts charged to merger costs related to the PBC Merger, as well as merger costs expected to be incurred in future periods for the respective transactions:

	Charges in 2000	*Charges Expected in Future Periods*
Transaction or deal costs, primarily professional fees and filing fees	$ 800,000	$-0-
Employee severance, separation, and transitional costs	2,300,000	1,200,000
Restructuring charges relating to the consolidation and relocation of operations, and the transition and implementation of information systems	900,000	400,000
Estimated loss on the sale of:		
Duplicate facilities and related leasehold improvements	200,000	-0-
Duplicate revenue producing assets	100,000	-0-
	Charges in 2000	*Charges Expected in Future Periods*
Provision for the abandonment of:		
Revenue producing assets	300,000	-0-
Other assets, consisting primarily of computer hardware and software costs that have no future value	150,000	-0-
Total	$4,750,000	$1,600,000

Included in the charges above are estimates for anticipated losses related to the sales of assets. These anticipated losses have been estimated based on the Company's assessment of relevant facts and circumstances, including consideration of the various provisions of asset sale agreements. In certain instances, the asset sale agreements contain contingencies, the resolution of which are uncertain and could materially change the proceeds that the Company will ultimately receive. Accordingly, dependent upon actual future experience and the resolution of certain contingencies, the amount of losses ultimately recorded by the Company could materially differ from the amounts provided for by the Company.

Example 4–14: Pooling Involves Companies with Different Fiscal Years

On December 29, 2000, XYZ Co. completed a merger with TIX, Inc. in which TIX, Inc. became a wholly owned subsidiary of XYZ Co. The merger qualified as a tax free exchange and was accounted for as a pooling of interests. XYZ Co. issued 2,000,000 shares of common stock in exchange for all the outstanding capital stock of TIX, Inc. The financial statements have been restated to retroactively combine TIX, Inc.'s financial statements as if the pooling had occurred at the beginning of the earliest period presented, as of January 1, 1999.

Prior to the acquisition, TIX, Inc. used a fiscal year ending October 31. Subsequent to the pooling, TIX, Inc. changed its year-end to December 31 to conform with that of XYZ Co. The accompanying Consolidated Statements of Operations and Cash Flows for the year ended December 31, 1999, reflect the results of operations and cash flows for XYZ Co. for the year then ended combined with the statements of operations and cash flows for TIX, Inc. for its fiscal year ended October 31, 1999. The accompanying Consolidated Balance Sheet as of December 31, 1999, reflects the financial position of XYZ Co. on that date combined with the financial position of TIX, Inc. as of October 31, 1999.

As a result of XYZ Co. and TIX, Inc. having different fiscal years and the change in TIX, Inc.'s fiscal year, TIX, Inc.'s results of operations for the two-month period ended December 31, 1999, have been excluded from the reported results of operations and added to retained earnings at January 1, 2000. The total revenue and net income of TIX, Inc. for the two-month period ended December 31, 1999, were $6,000,000 and $500,000, respectively.

The following table presents a reconciliation of net sales and net income previously reported by the Company to those presented in the accompanying Consolidated Financial Statements [*this is part of the footnote*]:

	XYZ Co.	*TIX, Inc.*	*Combined*
Year ended December 31, 2000:			
Net sales	$36,000,000	$19,000,000	$55,000,000
Net income	1,200,000	500,000	1,700,000
Year ended December 31, 1999:			
Net sales	$32,000,000	$17,000,000	$49,000,000
Net income	600,000	100,000	700,000

Note: The following table illustrates the adjustment made in the Consolidated Statement of Stockholders' Equity to give effect to the TIX, Inc. acquisition described above.

	Common Stock	*Additional Paid-in Capital*	*Retained Earnings*
Balances at December 31, 1998, as previously reported	$600,000	$5,000,000	$4,000,000
Pooling of interests adjustments—TIX, Inc. acquisition	200,000	1,500,000	1,600,000
Balances at December 31, 1998, as restated	800,000	6,500,000	5,600,000
Net income (loss)	-0-	-0-	700,000
Balances at December 31, 1999	800,000	6,500,000	6,300,000
Adjustment to conform with pooled companies' fiscal year ends	-0-	-0-	500,000
Net income (loss)	-0-	-0-	1,700,000
Balances at December 31, 2000	$800,000	$6,500,000	$8,500,000

Example 4-15: Impairment and Asset Valuation Adjustments as a Result of Merger

As a result of the Company's merger with ABC Enterprises in October 1999, strategic review of operations, and organizational alignments, the Company reviewed the carrying values of related long-lived assets on a company-wide basis in 2000. These reviews included estimating remaining useful lives and cash flows and identifying assets to be abandoned. Where this review indicated impairment, discounted cash flows related to those assets were analyzed to determine the amount of the impairment. As a result of these reviews, the Company wrote off some assets and recognized impairments to the value of other assets, recording a combined charge of $3,200,000 ($1,900,000 after tax) in 2000. The impairments and write-offs primarily related to the Company's operations in southern California, duplicate or obsolete equipment, and certain non-operating plant and other assets.

CHAPTER 5
CHANGING PRICES

CONTENTS

EXECUTIVE SUMMARY

Financial statements prepared in conformity with generally accepted accounting principles (GAAP) are based on the assumption of a stable monetary unit. That is, the assumption is made that the monetary unit used to convert all financial statement items into a common denominator (i.e., dollars) does not vary sufficiently over time so that distortions in the financial statements are material. Also, financial statements prepared in conformity with GAAP are primarily historical-cost based (i.e., the characteristic of most financial statement items that is measured and presented is the historical cost of the item).

Over the years, two approaches have been proposed and procedures developed to compensate for changes in the monetary unit and in the value of assets and liabilities after their acquisition. The two approaches are current value accounting and general price-level accounting. Current value accounting substitutes a measure of current value for historical cost as the primary measurement upon which the elements of financial statements are based. General price-level accounting adheres to historical cost but substitutes a current value of the dollar for historical dollars through the use of price indexes. Neither current value accounting nor general price-level accounting is required at the present time. However, procedures are established in the accounting literature for enterprises that choose to develop either general price-level or current value financial statements.

Authoritative Literature

FAS-89 Financial Reporting and Changing Prices

DISCLOSURE REQUIREMENTS

The following are the disclosure requirements for companies that elect to disclose supplementary information on the effects of changing prices (the disclosures are currently voluntary):

1. For each of the five most recent years, disclosures should include (FAS-89, par. 7):
   a. Net sales and other operating revenues
   b. Income from continuing operations on a current cost basis
   c. Purchasing power gain or loss on net monetary items
   d. Increase or decrease in the current cost or lower recoverable amount of inventory and property, plant, and equipment, net of inflation
   e. The aggregate foreign currency translation adjustment on a current cost basis, if applicable
   f. Net assets at year-end on a current cost basis
   g. Income per common share from continuing operations on a current cost basis
   h. Cash dividends declared per common share
   i. Market price per common share at year-end
   j. The Consumer Price Index for all Urban Consumers (CPI-U) used for each year's current cost/constant purchasing power calculations
   k. If the Company has a significant foreign operation measured in a functional currency other than the U.S. dollar, disclosure should be made of whether adjustments to the current cost information to reflect the effects of general inflation are based on the U.S. general price level index or on a functional currency general price level index
2. In addition to the information above, if income from continuing operations on a current cost/constant purchasing power basis differs significantly from the income from continuing operations reported in the primary financial statements, the following additional information should be disclosed (FAS-89, pars. 11–13):
   a. Components of income from continuing operations for the current year on a current cost/constant purchasing power basis
   b. Separate amounts for the current cost or lower recoverable amount at the end of the current year of inventory and property, plant, and equipment

c. The increase or decrease in current cost or lower recoverable amount before and after adjusting for the effects of inflation of inventory and property, plant, and equipment for the current year

d. The principal types of information used to calculate the current cost of (1) inventory; (2) property, plant, and equipment; (3) cost of goods sold; and (4) depreciation, depletion, and amortization expense

e. Any differences between (1) the depreciation methods, estimates of useful lives, and salvage values of assets used for calculations of current cost/constant purchasing power depreciation and (2) the methods and estimates used for calculations of depreciation in the primary financial statements

3. For companies with mineral resource assets (other than oil and gas), such as metal ores or coal, the following additional disclosures are required (FAS-89, par. 14):

   a. Estimates of significant quantities of proved mineral reserves or proved and probable mineral reserves (whichever is used for cost amortization purposes) at the end of the year or at the most recent date during the year for which estimates can be made

   b. If the mineral reserves include deposits containing one or more significant mineral products, the estimated quantity, expressed in physical units or in percentages of reserves, of each mineral product that is recoverable in significant commercial quantities

   c. Quantities of each significant mineral produced during the year

   d. Quantity of significant proved, or proved and probable, mineral reserves purchased or sold in place during the year

   e. The average market price of each significant mineral product or, for mineral products transferred within the enterprise, the equivalent market price prior to use in a manufacturing process

4. When determining the quantities of mineral reserves to be reported in item 3, the following should be applied (FAS-89, par. 15):

   a. If consolidated financial statements are issued, 100% of the quantities attributable to the parent company and 100% of the quantities attributable to its consolidated subsidiaries (whether or not wholly owned) should be included

   b. If the company's financial statements include investments that are proportionately consolidated, the company's quantities should include its proportionate share of the investee's quantities

c. If the company's financial statements include investments that are accounted for by the equity method, the investee's quantities should not be included in the disclosures of the company's quantities; however, the company's share of the investee's quantities of reserves should be reported separately, if significant

EXAMPLE OF FINANCIAL STATEMENT DISCLOSURE

The following sample disclosure is available on the accompanying disc.

Example 5–1: Five-Year Comparison of Selected Financial Data Adjusted for the Effects of Changing Prices

The Company is voluntarily presenting certain historical cost/constant dollar information to indicate the effect of changes in the general price level on certain items that are shown in the primary financial statements based on dollar values determined as of the varying historical dates when the transactions occurred.

Revenues for 2000 are assumed to have occurred ratably in relation to the change in the Consumer Price Index during the year and are therefore already expressed in average 2000 dollars. The presentation also shows the gain from decline in purchasing power as a result of net amounts owed. All information shown is in terms of average 2000 dollars as measured by the Consumer Price Index for all Urban Consumers (CPI-U).

The preparation of these numbers requires the use of certain assumptions and estimates and these disclosures should, therefore, be viewed in that context and not necessarily as a precise indicator of the specific effect of changing prices on the Company's operating results or its financial position. Also, the Company's costs may not change in proportion to changes in the Consumer Price Index.

The following table presents a five year comparison of selected supplementary financial data adjusted for the effect of changes in the general price level.

	Year Ended December 31				
	2000	*1999*	*1998*	*1997*	*1996*
Revenues:					
Historical	$500,000	$450,000	$400,000	$350,000	$300,000
Constant dollar basis	$500,000	$461,000	$411,000	$361,000	$318,000
Income (loss) from continuing operations	$21,800	$15,300	$(5,100)	$(7,200)	$11,700
Gain from decline in purchasing power of net amounts owed	$10,000	$8,000	$9,000	$6,000	$7,000
Excess of increase in specific prices of inventory and property, plant, and equipment over increase in the general price level	$27,500	$23,000	$18,000	$19,000	$8,000
Foreign currency translation adjustment	$(1,400)	$(800)	$(500)	$(400)	$(600)
Net assets at end of year	$200,000	$160,000	$135,000	$120,000	$105,000
Per share information:					
Income (loss) from continuing operations	$2.75	$1.10	$(.24)	$(.70)	$.65
Cash dividends declared	$1.10	$1.00	$.95	$.90	$.87
Market price at year end	$51.50	$41.75	$33.20	$27.90	$25.70
Average consumer price index	314.7	306.9	298.4	289.1	272.4

CHAPTER 6
COMMITMENTS

CONTENTS

EXECUTIVE SUMMARY

Commitments typically involve uncompleted transactions or uncertainties that should be disclosed because of their effect on an entity's financial statements. Commitments include long-term contractual obligations with suppliers or customers for future purchases or sales at specified prices and sometimes at specified levels. The terms of commitments should be disclosed and a provision should be made in the financial statements for any material losses expected to be sustained. Generally accepted accounting principles (GAAP) require disclosure of commitments such as the following:

- To purchase or sell a material amount of inventory at a fixed price
- To restrict dividends
- To limit additional debt or reduce debt by a specified amount
- To enter into significant long-term leases
- To enter into a business combination
- To make material capital expenditures
- To issue shares of capital stock
- To maintain a certain level of working capital

Authoritative Literature

APB-16	Business Combinations
ARB-43	Chapter 3A, Current Assets and Current Liabilities
ARB-43	Chapter 4, Inventory Pricing
FAS-5	Accounting for Contingencies
FAS-13	Accounting for Leases
FAS-38	Accounting for Preacquisition Contingencies of Purchased Enterprises

FIN-14	Reasonable Estimation of the Amount of a Loss
FIN-34	Disclosure of Indirect Guarantees of Indebtedness of Others
SOP 94-6	Disclosure of Certain Significant Risks and Uncertainties

DISCLOSURE REQUIREMENTS

For large or unusual commitments, the financial statements should disclose (1) a description of the commitment, (2) the terms of the commitment, and (3) the amount of the commitment. Such disclosures apply to the following types of commitments:

- Unused letters of credit (FAS-5, par. 18)
- Obligation to reduce debt (FAS-5, par. 18)
- Obligation to maintain working capital (FAS-5, par. 18)
- Obligation to restrict dividends (FAS-5, par. 18)
- Commitments for major capital expenditures (FAS-5, par. 18)
- Assets pledged as security for loans (FAS-5, par. 18)
- Net losses on inventory purchase commitments (ARB-43, Ch. 4, par. 17)

EXAMPLES OF FINANCIAL STATEMENT DISCLOSURES

The following sample disclosures are available on the accompanying disc. For examples of disclosures of commitments in connection with lease arrangements, see Chapter 18, "Leases." For examples of disclosures of commitments in connection with unconditional purchase obligations, see Chapter 40, "Debt Obligations and Credit Arrangements."

Example 6–1: Royalty Commitments

The Company has entered into various license agreements whereby the Company may use certain characters and properties in conjunction with its products. Such license agreements call for royalties to be paid at 5% to 10% of net sales with minimum guarantees and advance payments. Additionally, under one such license, the Company has committed to spend 11% of related net sales, not to exceed $2,000,000, on advertising per year. Royalty expense under these agreements was $1,000,000 in 2000 and $900,000 in 1999. Future annual minimum royalty commitments as of December 31, 2000, are as follows:

2001	$ 1,200,000
2002	1,500,000
2003	1,800,000
2004	2,500,000
2005	3,000,000
Thereafter	9,000,000
	$19,000,000

Example 6–2: Milestone Payment Due upon First Product Approval

The Company is obligated to make a milestone payment to Intexts Corp. of $1,200,000 upon the approval of its first product by the FDA or the governing health authority of any other country. This fee can be offset against future royalty payments. In addition, the Company is obligated to pay royalties on its net sales revenue and a percentage of all revenues received from sublicenses relating to the XTS gene therapy technology. Failure to comply with the terms of the License Agreement with Intexts Corp. may cause its termination, which would have a materially adverse effect on the Company.

Example 6–3: License Fee Commitments under License Agreement

The Company entered into an agreement to license software to be incorporated into its data conferencing products. Under the agreement, the Company is obligated to pay annual minimum license fees, ranging from $150,000 to $350,000, through the year 2004 and the Company may cancel the agreement at any time, provided the Company has paid a minimum of $1,000,000 in connection with the agreement. As of December 31, 2000, the Company had paid $475,000 of the minimum license fees. In February 2001, the Company re-negotiated the terms of the contract and paid a lump sum figure of $195,000. Under the terms of this new contract, the Company has no further obligation regarding any fees associated with this licensed software.

Example 6–4: Purchase Contracts

In connection with the EFTX transaction in January 1999, EFTX and the Company entered into a manufacturing agreement whereby the Company committed to purchase minimum amounts of goods and services used in its normal operations during the first 48 months after the transaction. Future annual minimum purchases remaining under the agreement are $19 million and $22 million for 2001 and 2002, respectively. During 2000 and 1999, the Company's total purchases under the agreement were $17 million and $13 million, respectively.

Example 6–5: Firm Price Commitment Manufacturing and Supply Agreement

The Company entered into a firm price commitment manufacturing and supply agreement in connection with the acquisition of the F&D trademarks purchased in 2000. The agreement was entered into with the seller of the trademarks to obtain from the seller tools and other manufacturing resources of the seller for the manufacture of products, upon request by the Company. The manufacturing and supply agreement has created a firm commitment by the Company for a minimum of $4,500,000. A minimum payment of $500,000 on the agreement was due on December 31, 2000, with three additional payments of $400,000 and five additional payments of $560,000 to follow thereafter, through December 31, 2004, which is also the date on which the agreement terminates.

Example 6–6: Commitment to Reimburse Supplier for Certain Capital Additions in Connection with Production Agreements

The Company has production agreements, which expire in May 2007, with Elexix, Ltd. to produce certain specialized products for the Company. The agreements require the Company to reimburse Elexix, Ltd. over the terms of the agreements for specified facility additions, not to exceed $2,500,000, required to manufacture the products. Elexix, Ltd. retains title to the facility additions. Furthermore, if the Company terminates the agreements, it is obligated to pay Elexix, Ltd. for the remaining unreimbursed facility additions. The Company recorded expense of $675,000 and $620,000 under the agreements in 2000 and 1999, respectively. The remaining unreimbursed facility additions totaled $710,000 at December 31, 2000.

Example 6–7: Commitments to Allow Returns of Overstocked Inventory

The Company has agreements with distributor customers that, under certain conditions, allow for returns of overstocked inventory and provide protection against price reductions initiated by the Company. Allowances for these commitments are included in the consolidated balance sheets as reductions in trade accounts receivable. The Company adjusts sales to distributors through the use of allowance accounts based on historical experience. During 2000 and 1999, provisions for these commitments were recorded in the amounts of $3,700,000 and $3,200,000, respectively.

Example 6–8: Commitment to Sell Inventory at a Fixed Price

At December 31, 2000, the Company has an agreement with a customer to sell a specified minimum number of units of its Eglaze adhesive products over the next 30 months at a fixed price of $10,200,000. The fixed price is equal to approximately 5% above the aggregate selling price at current market prices.

Example 6–9: Obligations to Maintain Working Capital and Financial Ratios, Restrict Dividends and Capital Expenditures, and Borrow Money

The Company has a $10 million revolving bank line of credit that expires in August 2001. Advances under the line of credit bear interest at the bank's prime rate (8.5% at December 31, 2000) and are secured by inventories and accounts receivable. Under the terms of the line of credit agreement, the Company is required to maintain certain minimum working capital, net worth, profitability levels, and other specific financial ratios. In addition, the agreement prohibits the payment of cash dividends and contains certain restrictions on the Company's ability to borrow money or purchase assets or interests in other entities without the prior written consent of the bank. There were no borrowings under the line of credit at December 31, 2000.

Example 6–10: Commitment to Pay Certain Termination Benefits under Employment Agreements

As of December 31, 2000, the Company had entered into employment agreements with four employees. Under each of the four agreements, in the event employment is terminated (other than voluntarily by the employee or by the Company for cause or upon the death of the employee), the Company is committed to pay certain benefits, including specified monthly severance of not more than $25,000 per month. The benefits are to be paid from the date of termination through May 2004.

Example 6–11: Future Commitment for Minimum Salary Levels under Employment Contracts

The Company has employment agreements with its executive officers, the terms of which expire at various times through January

2001. Such agreements, which have been revised from time to time, provide for minimum salary levels, adjusted annually for cost-of-living changes, as well as for incentive bonuses that are payable if specified management goals are attained. The aggregate commitment for future salaries at December 31, 2000, excluding bonuses, was approximately $3,500,000.

Example 6–12: Commitments for Construction and Acquisition of Property and Equipment

At December 31, 2000, the Company had commitments of approximately $12,000,000 for construction and acquisition of property and equipment, all of which are expected to be incurred in 2001. Also, in connection with an expansion at the Company's manufacturing facility in Boise, Idaho, capital grants from the State totaling $2,500,000 have been approved, $1,000,000 of which had not been received as of December 31, 2000, and are contingent upon the Company spending approximately $6,000,000 for plant and equipment in Boise.

Example 6–13: Commitment to Maintain Liquid Funds to Secure an Obligation

The Company holds $400,000 in short-term U.S. government money market funds to secure a continuing contractual payment obligation of the Company arising from its acquisition of Axis, Ltd. As a result of this agreement, the Company has classified such funds and the interest earned thereon, totaling $416,000 at December 31, 2000, as "Restricted investments" under noncurrent assets on the accompanying Consolidated Balance Sheets.

Example 6–14: Commitment to Purchase Capital Stock under Stock Redemption Agreements

The Company has stock redemption agreements with two major stockholders for the purchase of a portion of the common stock from their estates at market value upon death. The Company's commitment under such arrangements, totaling $8,500,000 at December 31, 2000, is funded by life insurance policies owned by the Company.

Example 6–15: Commitment to Complete Business Acquisition

In December 2000, the Company announced that it had entered into a definitive agreement to acquire Akcent, Inc., whose products include remote access networking solutions for the small to medium enterprise market segment. The Company expects that the total cash required to complete the transaction will be approximately $13 million, which will be provided from borrowings on the Company's line of credit.

Example 6–16: Business Combination Includes Contingent Consideration

In connection with the acquisition of Calciose, Inc., the Stock Purchase Agreement mandates additional payments by the Company to the former stockholders of Calciose, Inc. The payments are contingent on the future earnings performance of Calciose, Inc. Any additional payments made, when the contingency is resolved, will be accounted for as additional costs of the acquired assets and amortized over the remaining life of the assets.

Example 6–17: Letters of Credit—Inventory

At December 31, 2000, and December 31, 1999, the Company has outstanding irrevocable letters of credit in the amount of $1,800,000 and $700,000, respectively. These letters of credit, which have terms from two months to one year, collateralize the Company's obligations to third parties for the purchase of inventory. The fair value of these letters of credit approximates contract values based on the nature of the fee arrangements with the issuing banks.

Example 6–18: Letters of Credit—Contracts and Debt Obligations

At December 31, 2000, standby letters of credit of approximately $2,400,000 have been issued under an agreement, expiring September 30, 2001. The letters are being maintained as security for performance and advances received on long-term contracts and as security for debt service payments under industrial revenue bond loan agreements. The agreement provides a maximum commitment for letters of credit of $3,500,000 and requires an annual commitment fee of $25,000.

Example 6–19: Letters of Credit—Self-Insurance Program

The Company has letters of credit of $22,000,000 outstanding at December 31, 2000. The letters are maintained to back the Company's self-insurance program.

Example 6–20: Letters of Credit—Operating Lease, the Terms of Which Have Not Been Finalized

At December 31, 2000, the Company is committed to enter into an operating lease for manufacturing and distribution facilities, the terms of which have not been finalized. In connection with this commitment, during 2000, the Company issued on its behalf irrevocable standby letters of credit in the amount of $6,500,000. Upon execution of the lease, the letters of credit will be canceled.

CHAPTER 7
COMPENSATED ABSENCES

CONTENTS

EXECUTIVE SUMMARY

A company must accrue a liability for employees' compensation for future absences (e.g., vacations, illnesses, holidays) if all of the following conditions are met:

1. The company's obligation relating to employees' rights to receive compensation for future absences is attributable to employee's services already rendered
2. The obligations relate to rights that eventually vest or accumulate
3. Payment of the compensation is probable
4. The amount can be reasonably estimated

If the first three conditions are met but the company cannot reasonably estimate the amount of the accrual, the reasons for not making the accrual should be disclosed in notes to the financial statements.

Authoritative Literature

FAS-43 Accounting for Compensated Absences

DISCLOSURE REQUIREMENTS

Liabilities must be appropriately accrued and reported for employees' compensation for future absences. If the entity has not accrued a liability for compensated absences because the amount cannot be reasonably estimated, that fact should be disclosed in notes to the financial statements (FAS-43, pars. 6, 7, and 15).

EXAMPLE OF FINANCIAL STATEMENT DISCLOSURE

The following sample disclosure is available on the accompanying disc.

Example 7–1: Company Has Not Accrued a Liability for Compensated Absences Because the Amount Cannot Be Reasonably Estimated

Employees of the Company are entitled to paid vacation and paid sick days depending on job classification, length of service, and other factors. At December 31, 2000, and December 31, 1999, the Company had approximately 1,200 employees. Of this total, approximately 1,000 are hourly employees and 200 are salaried employees. Approximately 98% of the Company's hourly employees and 37% of its salaried employees are represented by a number of labor unions. Each union contract contains different provisions for employee-compensated absences. It is not practicable for the Company to estimate the amount of compensation for future absences; accordingly, no liability for compensated absences has been recorded in the accompanying financial statements. The Company's policy is to recognize the costs of compensated absences when actually paid to employees.

CHAPTER 8
CONSOLIDATED AND COMBINED FINANCIAL STATEMENTS

CONTENTS

EXECUTIVE SUMMARY

Consolidated financial statements represent the financial position, results of operations, and cash flows of a parent and its subsidiaries as if the group were a single enterprise. They are prepared by combining all parent and subsidiary accounts and eliminating intercompany balances and transactions. Consolidated financial statements are presumed to present more meaningful information than separate financial statements and must be used in substantially all cases in which a parent directly or indirectly controls the majority voting interest (over 50%) of a subsidiary. Consolidated financial statements should not be used when (1) the parent's control of the subsidiary is temporary or (2) there is significant doubt concerning the parent's ability to control the subsidiary.

Consolidated financial statements usually are justified on the basis that one of the consolidating entities exercises control over the affiliated group. When there is no such control, combined financial statements may be used to accomplish the same results. For example, a group of companies controlled by an individual shareholder, or a group of unconsolidated subsidiaries that could otherwise not be consolidated, should utilize combined financial statements. Combined financial statements are prepared on the same basis as consolidated financial statements except that no company in the group has a controlling interest in the other.

Consolidated financial statements are prepared primarily for the benefit of creditors and shareholders. Minority interests in net income are deducted to arrive at consolidated net income. Minority interests are theoretically limited to the extent of their equity capital, however, and losses in excess of minority interest equity capital are charged against the majority interest. Subsequently, when the losses reverse, the majority interests should be credited with the amount of minority interest losses previously absorbed before credit is made to the minority interests.

If a parent's and a subsidiary's fiscal years differ by no more than about three months, it is ordinarily acceptable to consolidate the subsidiary using the subsidiary's financial statements for its fiscal year. However, in those circumstances, intervening events or transactions that materially affect the results of operations or financial position should be disclosed or otherwise recognized.

Authoritative Literature

ARB-43	Chapter 1A, Rules Adopted by Membership
	Chapter 2A, Comparative Financial Statements
ARB 51	Consolidated Financial Statements (as amended)
APB-16	Business Combinations

FAS-94	Consolidation of All Majority-Owned Subsidiaries
FAS-109	Accounting for Income Taxes
FAS-131	Disclosures about Segments of an Enterprise and Related Information
FIN-13	Consolidation of a Parent and Its Subsidiaries Having Different Balance Sheet Dates

DISCLOSURE REQUIREMENTS

Consolidated financial statements should disclose the following:

1. The consolidation policy followed by the company, such as the companies consolidated (ARB-51, par. 5; ARB-22, par. 13)
2. Material intercompany transactions and accounts, and any profits or losses on assets are eliminated (ARB-51, par. 6)
3. If the consolidated financial statements are prepared using the financial statements of a subsidiary that has a different year-end from the parent, disclosures should be made for intervening events that materially affect financial position or results of operations (ARB-51, par. 4; FAS-12, pars. 18–20; FIN-13)
4. If an entity is a member of a group that files a consolidated tax return, the entity should disclose the following in its separate financial statements (FAS-109, par. 49):
   a. Aggregate amount of current and deferred tax expense for each statement of operations presented
   b. Amounts of any tax related balances due to or from affiliated entities as of the date of each balance sheet presented
   c. The method used to allocate consolidated current and deferred tax expense to members of the group and the nature and effect of changes in that method during the years for which the disclosures in items a. and b. are presented
5. Summarized information about assets, liabilities, and results of operations relating to majority-owned subsidiaries that were unconsolidated in financial statements for fiscal years 1986 or 1987 but which are now consolidated based on FAS-94 (FAS-94, par. 14)

EXAMPLES OF FINANCIAL STATEMENT DISCLOSURES

The following sample disclosures are available on the accompanying disc.

Example 8–1: Consolidation Policy Specifically Described

The accompanying Consolidated Financial Statements include the accounts of the Company and its majority-owned subsidiary partnerships and corporations, after elimination of all material intercompany accounts, transactions, and profits. Investments in unconsolidated subsidiaries representing ownership of at least 20% but less than 50%, are accounted for under the equity method. Nonmarketable investments in which the Company has less than 20% ownership and in which it does not have the ability to exercise significant influence over the investee are initially recorded at cost and periodically reviewed for impairment.

Example 8–2: Consolidated Statements Include Subsidiaries with Different Year Ends (Parent Company Has a December Year-End)

The Consolidated Financial Statements include the accounts of the parent company and subsidiaries, after elimination of intercompany accounts and transactions. The accounts of certain subsidiaries are consolidated as of November 30 due to the time needed to consolidate these subsidiaries. No events occurred related to these subsidiaries in December 2000 and December 1999 that materially affected the financial position, results of operations, or cash flows.

Example 8–3: Change in Reporting Period for Subsidiary from Fiscal Year to Calendar Year—The Parent Company's Reporting Period Is a Calendar Year Ending December 31

Effective January 1, 2000, the Parent Company changed the reporting period of its majority-owned subsidiary XYZ, Inc. from a fiscal year ending November 30 to a calendar year ending December 31. The results of operations of XYZ, Inc. for the month of December 1999 (representing the period between the end of its 1999 fiscal year and the beginning of its new calendar year) amounted to a net income of $350,000. This amount was credited to "Retained earnings" to avoid reporting more than 12 months results of operations in one year. Accordingly, the 2000 consolidated operations include the results for XYZ, Inc. beginning January 1, 2000. The cash activity for the stub period is included in "Other cash activities—Stub period, XYZ, Inc." in the Consolidated Statements of Cash Flows.

Note: The following table illustrates the effect on retained earnings as a result of the change in year end of a subsidiary, as reflected in the Consolidated Statement of Stockholders' Equity.

	Common Stock	*Additional Paid-in Capital*	*Retained Earnings*	*Total*
Balances at December 31, 1998	$500,000	$1,000,000	$2,300,000	$3,800,000
Net income	-0-	-0-	800,000	800,000
Balances at December 31, 1999	500,000	1,000,000	3,100,000	4,600,000
Net income	-0-	-0-	1,000,000	1,000,000
Dividends	-0-	-0-	(600,000)	(600,000)
Net income for the month ended December 1999, due to the change in fiscal year-end of a subsidiary	-0-	-0-	350,000	350,000
Balances at December 31, 2000	$500,000	$1,000,000	$3,850,000	$5,350,000

Example 8–4: Certain Subsidiaries Are Not Consolidated

The Consolidated Financial Statements include the accounts of the Company and all majority-owned subsidiaries, except for certain insignificant subsidiaries, the investments in which are recorded under the cost method because of restrictions upon the transfer of earnings and other economic uncertainties. All significant intercompany accounts and transactions have been eliminated.

Example 8–5: Consolidated Financial Statements Include Less Than 50% Owned Entity

The Consolidated Financial Statements include the accounts of the parent company and its subsidiaries, including XYZ Corp. in which the parent company holds a minority interest. At December 31, 2000, the parent company owned 26% of XYZ Corp.'s capital stock, representing 78% voting control. All significant intercompany accounts and transactions have been eliminated.

Example 8–6: Change in Ownership in Previously Consolidated Subsidiary Results in Using the Equity Method of Accounting in the Current Period

In 1998, the Company formed a joint venture with Sycom, Inc. (the Sycom Joint Venture) for the manufacture, distribution, and marketing of leather furniture. The Company originally acquired a 51% interest in the Sycom Joint Venture for $4,000,000 and, accordingly, the joint venture's Financial Statements had been consolidated with the Company's Financial Statements from the acquisition date to December 31, 1999. Effective January 1, 2000, the Company sold a 5% interest in the Sycom Joint Venture for $350,000 reducing its interest to 46%. As a result, in 2000 the Company's investment in the Sycom Joint Venture is being accounted for using the equity method. The deconsolidation of the Sycom Joint Venture had an insignificant effect on the Company's consolidated total assets and net sales as of and for the year ended December 31, 2000.

Example 8–7: Financial Statements Currently Consolidated to Include the Accounts of a Previously Unconsolidated Affiliate

Effective January 1, 2000, the Company began to consolidate into its Financial Statements the accounts of XYZ Corporation, formerly an unconsolidated affiliate. XYZ Corporation, which primarily manufactures medical equipment, is a venture between the Company and ABC Company of Ohio. The consolidation occurred as a result of revisions of the Stockholders' Agreement between the Company and ABC Company of Ohio. Financial data presented for previous years have not been restated to reflect the consolidation of XYZ Corporation. The consolidation is not material to financial position or results of operations for the periods presented and had no effect on previously reported net income, which included XYZ Corporation on an equity basis.

Example 8–8: Consolidation of Newly Formed Entity That Has a Minority Interest

In October 2000, the Company contributed $2,765,000 in assets to a newly created partnership, Hope Enterprises, L.P. (the Partnership), in exchange for a 79% general partner interest in the Partnership. The contributed assets consisted of certain trademarks that are licensed to the Company pursuant to exclusive long-term license agreements, accounts receivable, property and equipment, and cash. In addition, an outside investor contributed $735,000 in cash to the Partnership in exchange for a 21% limited partner interest. For financial reporting purposes, the Partnership's assets and liabilities are consolidated with those of the Company and the outside investor's 21% interest in the Partnership is included in the Company's Financial Statements as minority interest.

Example 8–9: Presentation of Minority Interest in the Consolidated Financial Statements

Minority interest represents the minority stockholders' proportionate share of the equity of Nostars, Inc. At December 31, 2000 and December 31, 1999, the Company owned 22% of Nostars, Inc.'s capital stock, representing 75% voting control. The Company's 75% controlling interest requires that Nostars, Inc.'s operations be included in the Consolidated Financial Statements. The 78% equity interest of Nostars, Inc. that is not owned by the Company is shown as "Minority interest in consolidated subsidiary" in the 2000 and 1999 Consolidated Statement of Earnings and Consolidated Balance Sheet.

> **Note:** The following table illustrates the presentation of minority interest in the Consolidated Balance Sheets between the liabilities section and the stockholder's equity section. Whereas minority interests are insignificant and do not warrant a separate classification in the Consolidated Balance Sheets, some entities have disclosed minority interests among other liabilities.

	2000	*1999*
Total current liabilities	$15,000,000	$13,000,000
Long-term debt	6,000,000	5,000,000
Deferred income taxes	1,500,000	2,300,000
Minority interest in consolidated subsidiary	1,100,000	1,400,000
Stockholders' equity	7,600,000	6,900,000

> **Note:** The following table illustrates the presentation of minority interest in the Consolidated Statements of Operations as a component of "Other income (expense)."

	2000	*1999*
Net sales	$41,000,000	$37,000,000
Costs and expenses	39,000,000	34,000,000
Operating income	2,000,000	3,000,000
Other income (expense):		
Interest expense	(500,000)	(400,000)
Minority interest in income of subsidiary	(600,000)	(800,000)
Other—net	200,000	500,000
	(900,000)	(700,000)
Income before income taxes	1,100,000	2,300,000
Income taxes	(450,000)	(900,000)
Net income	$ 650,000	$ 1,400,000

Note: The following table illustrates the presentation of minority interest in the Consolidated Statements of Operations as a separate line item before "Net income."

	2000	*1999*
Net sales	$41,000,000	$37,000,000
Costs and expenses	39,000,000	34,000,000
Operating income	2,000,000	3,000,000
Other income (expense):		
Interest expense	(500,000)	(400,000)
Other—Net	200,000	500,000
	(300,000)	100,000
Income before income taxes and minority interest	1,700,000	3,100,000
Income taxes	(450,000)	(900,000)
Income before minority interest	1,250,000	2,200,000
Minority interest in income of subsidiary	(600,000)	(800,000)
Net income	$ 650,000	$ 1,400,000

Example 8–10: Parent Company to Spin-Off Previously Consolidated Subsidiary, Resulting in Restatement of Prior Year's Financial Statements

On August 5, 2000, the Company's Board of Directors approved a plan to spin-off the Company's wholly owned subsidiary, Citrom Specialties, Inc. (Citrom), to the Company's shareholders in the form of a tax free dividend. The Company has requested and received a ruling from the Internal Revenue Service that this distribution will not be taxable to the Company's shareholders.

The Company's investment in and the results of operations of Citrom are reflected in the Company's Consolidated Financial Statements on the equity method as Citrom is now a temporary investment that the Company anticipates distributing to its shareholders during the year 2001. Accordingly, the 1999 Financial Statements have been restated. As a part of the spin-off, approximately $3,000,000 of Citrom's indebtedness to the Company has been contributed as capital. Summary financial information of Citrom consists of the following:

	Year Ended December 31	
	2000	*1999*
Net sales	$33,000,000	$29,000,000
Costs and expenses	35,000,000	30,000,000
Loss before income taxes	(2,000,000)	(1,000,000)
Tax benefit allocated by the parent	250,000	200,000
Net loss	$ (1,750,000)	$ (800,000)

	As of December 31	
	2000	1999
Current assets	$12,000,000	$10,000,000
Fixed assets	2,000,000	1,500,000
Other assets	3,000,000	2,500,000
Total assets	$17,000,000	$14,000,000
Current liabilities	$11,000,000	$ 8,000,000
Long-term liabilities	4,000,000	3,800,000
Shareholders' equity	2,000,000	2,200,000
Total liabilities and shareholders' equity	$17,000,000	$14,000,000

Included in accounts receivable of the Company at December 31, 2000, and December 31, 1999, are net amounts due from Citrom of $650,000 and $475,000, respectively. During the years ended December 31, 2000, and December 31, 1999, the Company sold medical products and equipment to Citrom totaling $5,500,000 and $4,900,000, respectively.

Note: The following table shows the restatement of the Company's Financial Statements to reflect the spin-off of Citrom.

	Year Ended December 31	
	2000	1999
Consolidated Statements of Operations		
Net sales	$82,000,000	$76,000,000
Costs and expenses	87,000,000	73,000,000
Income (loss) before loss of non-consolidated subsidiary—Citrom	(5,000,000)	3,000,000
Loss of non-consolidated subsidiary—Citrom	(2,000,000)	(1,000,000)
Income (loss) before income taxes	(7,000,000)	2,000,000
Income taxes benefit (expense)	3,000,000	(800,000)
Net income (loss)	$ (4,000,000)	$1,200,000

	As of December 31	
	2000	1999
Consolidated Balance Sheets		
Total current assets	$45,000,000	$43,000,000
Other assets:		
Investment in non-consolidated subsidiary—Citrom	2,000,000	2,200,000

Example 8–11: Consolidated Financial Statements Include Nonhomogenous Operations

The Company's Consolidated Financial Statements include the accounts of Max Credit Corp., a wholly owned finance subsidiary. Business operations of this subsidiary consist primarily of financing certain customer obligations resulting from retail sales of home furnishings, accessories, and related other merchandise charged on credit cards. Summarized financial information of Max Credit Corp. are presented below.

	December 31	
	2000	*1999*
Balance Sheets		
Current assets, primarily accounts receivable	$4,500,000	$4,200,000
Property and equipment	400,000	350,000
Other assets	150,000	100,000
Total assets	$5,050,000	$4,650,000
Short-term debt	$1,000,000	$1,200,000
Accounts payable and accrued liabilities	700,000	650,000
Long-term debt	550,000	400,000
Stockholders' equity	2,800,000	2,400,000
Total liabilities and stockholders' equity	$5,050,000	$4,650,000

	Year Ended December 31	
	2000	*1999*
Income Statement		
Revenues	$6,000,000	$5,000,000
Costs and expenses	5,150,000	4,300,000
Income before income taxes	850,000	700,000
Income taxes	450,000	400,000
Net income	$ 400,000	$ 300,000

Example 8–12: Combined Financial Statements

The accompanying Combined Financial Statements include the accounts of the following entities, all of which are under common control and ownership:

Or:

The accompanying Combined Financial Statements include the accounts of the following entities because each entity is owned beneficially by identical shareholders:

Name of Entity	*Form of Entity*
Amishar, Inc.	Corporation
Sandust, L.P.	Partnership
Basin & Sons	Sole proprietorship

All significant intercompany profits, accounts, and transactions have been eliminated in the combination.

Note: The following table presents the individual components of equity if the combined entities have different ownership forms. This may be presented in the equity section on the face of the balance sheet or in a note to the financial statements.

	December 31	
	2000	*1999*
Equity		
Stockholders' equity	$1,200,000	$1,000,000
Partners' capital	600,000	700,000
Proprietor's capital	400,000	300,000
Total equity	$2,200,000	$2,000,000

Note: The following table presents the Statement of Changes in Equity accounts if the combined entities have different ownership forms.

	Amishar, Inc. (Corporation)			*Sandust, L.P. (Partnership)*	*Basin & Sons (Proprietorship)*
	Common Stock	*Additional Paid-in Capital*	*Retained Earnings*	*Partners' Capital*	*Proprietor's Capital*
Balances, December 31, 1998	$100,000	$400,000	$ 700,000	$600,000	$300,000
Net income			400,000	300,000	100,000
Cash dividends			(100,000)		
Partner's withdrawals				(200,000)	
Proprietor's withdrawals					(100,000)
Balances, December 31, 1999	100,000	400,000	1,000,000	700,000	300,000
Net income			400,000	300,000	400,000
Cash dividends			(200,000)		
Partners' withdrawals				(400,000)	
Proprietor's withdrawals					(300,000)
Balances, December 31, 2000	$100,000	$400,000	$1,200,000	$600,000	$400,000

CHAPTER 9
CONTINGENCIES, RISKS, UNCERTAINTIES, AND CONCENTRATIONS

CONTENTS

EXECUTIVE SUMMARY

Loss and Gain Contingencies

The following two conditions must be met for a loss contingency to be accrued as a charge to income and disclosed as of the date of the financial statements:

1. It is probable that, at the date of the financial statements, an asset has been impaired or a liability incurred.
2. The amount of loss can be reasonably estimated.

Disclosure is required for loss contingencies not meeting both those conditions if a reasonable possibility exists that a loss may have been incurred.

Gains from gain contingencies should *not* be credited to income because to do so might result in the recognition of income before it is realized. Gain contingencies, however, should be adequately disclosed in the notes to the financial statements, and care should be exercised in disclosing gain contingencies to avoid misleading implications as to the recognition of revenue prior to its realization.

As a general rule, disclosing loss contingencies that have a remote possibility of materializing is not required. However, loss contingencies that may occur as the result of a guarantee must be disclosed in the financial statements, even if they have a remote possibility of materializing.

Environmental Remediation Contingencies

Companies are subject to a wide range of federal, state, and local environmental laws and regulations. The accrual for environmental remediation liabilities should include incremental direct costs of the remediation effort and costs of compensation and benefits for employees to the extent an employee is expected to devote time directly to the remediation effort.

The measurement of the liability should include (a) the entity's allocable share of the liability for a specific site and (b) the entity's share of amounts related to the site that will not be paid by other potentially responsible parties or the government. The measurement of the liability should be based on the following:

1. Enacted laws and existing regulations and policies
2. Remediation technology that is expected to be approved to complete the remediation effort
3. The reporting entity's estimates of what it will cost to perform all elements of the remediation effort when they are expected to be performed

The measurement may be discounted to reflect the time value of money if the aggregate amount of the obligation and the amount and timing of cash payments for the obligation are fixed or reliably determinable.

Risks, Uncertainties, and Concentrations

Volatility and uncertainty in the business and economic environment result in the need to disclose information about the risks and uncertainties confronted by reporting entities. Generally accepted accounting principles (GAAP) require entities to disclose significant risks and uncertainties in the following areas:

1. *Nature of operations.* Disclosures concerning the nature of operations do not have to be quantified, and relative importance may be described by terms such as *predominantly, about equally,* and *major.*
2. *Use of estimates in the preparation of financial statements.* Financial statements should include an explanation that their preparation in conformity with GAAP requires the application of management's estimates.
3. *Certain significant estimates.* Disclosure regarding an estimate is required when both of the following conditions are met: (a) it is at least reasonably possible that the estimate of the effect on the financial statements of a condition, situation, or set of circumstances that existed at the date of the financial statements will change in the near term due to one or more future confirming events, and (b) the effect of the change would have a material effect on the financial statements.
4. *Current vulnerability due to certain concentrations.* Financial statements should disclose concentrations if all of the following conditions are met: (a) the concentration existed at the date of the financial statements, (b) the concentration makes the enterprise

vulnerable to the risk of a near-term severe impact, and (c) it is reasonably possible that the events that could cause the severe impact will occur in the near term.

Authoritative Literature

APB-16	Business Combinations
FAS-5	Accounting for Contingencies
FAS-16	Prior Period Adjustments
FAS-38	Accounting for Preacquisition Contingencies of Purchased Enterprises
FAS-87	Employers' Accounting for Pensions
FAS-109	Accounting for Income Taxes
FAS-112	Employers' Accounting for Postemployment Benefits
FIN-14	Reasonable Estimation of the Amount of a Loss
FIN-34	Disclosure of Indirect Guarantees of Indebtedness of Others
SOP 94-6	Disclosure of Certain Significant Risks and Uncertainties
SOP 96-1	Environmental Remediation Liabilities

DISCLOSURE REQUIREMENTS

Loss and Gain Contingencies

1. The nature and amount of an accrued loss contingency should be disclosed if (a) exposure to loss in excess of the amount accrued exists or (b) disclosure is necessary to keep the financial statements from being misleading (FAS-5, par. 9).
2. If no accrual is made for a loss contingency, or if an exposure to loss exists in excess of the amount accrued, the following disclosures should be made when there is at least a reasonable possibility that a loss or an additional loss may have been incurred (FAS-5, par. 10):
   a. The nature of the contingency
   b. An estimate of the possible loss or range of loss, or a statement that such an estimate cannot be made
3. For losses and loss contingencies that arise subsequent to the date of the financial statements, the following disclosures should be made when it is necessary to keep the financial statements from being misleading (FAS-5, par. 11):

a. The nature of the loss or loss contingency

b. An estimate of the amount or range of loss, or possible loss, or a statement that an estimate cannot be made

4. The following disclosures should be made for certain remote loss contingencies relating to guarantees made for outside parties (such as guarantees of indebtedness of others, obligations of commercial banks under stand-by letters of credit, and guarantees to repurchase receivables or other properties that have been sold or assigned) (FAS-5, par. 12):

   a. The nature of the loss contingency

   b. The nature and amount of the guarantee

   c. If subject to estimation, the value of any recovery from other outside parties that could be expected to result

5. Loss contingencies relating to guarantees (direct, indirect, written, or oral) made for outside parties, including the nature and amounts thereof, should be disclosed. Also, disclosure should include the value of any recovery that could be expected to result, if estimable (FAS-5, par. 12).

6. Adequate disclosures should be made for unasserted claims or assessments if it is considered probable that a claim will be asserted and there is a reasonable possibility that a loss will arise from the matter (FAS-5, par. 10).

7. Gain contingencies should be adequately disclosed, but care should be exercised to avoid misleading implications about the likelihood of realization (FAS-5, par. 17).

Environmental Remediation Contingencies

1. If accruals for environmental remediation loss contingencies have been recorded in the financial statements, the following information should be disclosed (SOP 96-1, pars. 7.11, 7.20):

   a. Whether the accrual for environmental remediation liabilities is measured on a discounted basis

   b. The nature and amount of the accrued loss contingency

   c. If any portion of the accrued obligation is discounted, the undiscounted amount of the obligation and the discount rate used

   d. If it is at least reasonably possible that the accrued obligation or any recognized asset for third-party recoveries will change within one year of the date of the financial statements and the effect is material, an indication that it is at least reasonably possible that a change in the estimate will occur in the near term

2. When environmental remediation loss contingencies have not been accrued, or when exposures exist in excess of the amounts accrued, the following information should be disclosed (SOP 96-1, par. 7.21):
   a. A description of the reasonably possible loss contingency and an estimate of the possible loss, or a statement to the effect that such an estimate cannot be made
   b. If it is at least reasonably possible that the estimated contingency will change within one year of the date of the financial statements and the effect is material, an indication that it is at least reasonably possible that a change in the estimate will occur in the near term
3. Entities are also *encouraged*, but not required, to disclose the following information (SOP 96-1, par. 7.22):
   a. The estimated time frame of disbursements for recorded amounts if expenditures are expected to continue over the long term
   b. The estimated time frame for realization of recognized probable recoveries, if realization is not expected in the near term
   c. The factors that cause the estimates to be sensitive to change with respect to (i) the accrued obligation, (ii) any recognized asset for third-party recoveries, or (iii) reasonably possible loss exposures, or disclosed gain contingencies
   d. If an estimate of the probable or reasonable possible loss or range of loss cannot be made, the reasons why it cannot be made
   e. If information about the reasonably possible loss or the recognized and additional reasonably possible loss for an environmental remediation obligation related to an individual site is relevant to an understanding of the financial position, cash flows, or results of operations of the entity, the following disclosures with respect to the site should be made:
      — The total amount accrued for the site
      — The nature of any reasonably possible loss contingency or additional loss, and an estimate of the possible loss or the fact that an estimate cannot be made and the reasons why it cannot be made
      — Whether other potentially responsible parties are involved and the entity's estimated share of the obligation
      — The status of regulatory proceedings
      — The estimated time frame for resolution of the contingency
4. If an environmental liability for a specific clean-up site is discounted because it meets the criteria for discounting in SOP

96-1 and the effect of discounting is material, the financial statements should disclose the undiscounted amounts of the liability and any related recovery and the discount rate used (SOP 96-1, par. 7.20).

Risks, Uncertainties, and Concentrations

1. The following disclosures are required regarding the nature of the entity's operations (SOP 94-6, par. 10):
   a. A description of the entity's major products or services
   b. The principal markets (e.g., industries and types of customers) for the entity's products or services
   c. The relative importance of each line of business, together with the basis for making that determination (e.g., based on sales, assets, earnings) (This information need not be quantified; instead, relative importance could be conveyed by using terms such as *predominantly, about equally,* or *major.)*
2. The financial statements or a footnote should include a general statement that the preparation of financial statements requires the use of estimates by management. The following disclosures are required regarding significant estimates used in the determination of the carrying amounts of assets or liabilities or in disclosure of gain or loss contingencies, if (i) it is at least reasonably possible that the effect on the financial statements of the estimates will change within one year of the date of the financial statements due to one or more future confirming events, and (ii) the effect of the change would be material to the financial statements (SOP 94-6, pars. 11 and 13–15):
   a. The nature of the estimate
   b. An indication that it is at least reasonably possible that a change in the estimate will occur in the near term
   c. The factors that cause the estimate to be sensitive to change (this disclosure is encouraged but not required)
   d. If the entity uses risk-reduction techniques to mitigate losses or the uncertainty that may result from future events and, as a result, determines that the criteria described above are not met, the disclosures in items a, b, and c are encouraged, but not required
3. The following disclosures about concentrations are required if (i) the concentration exists at the date of the financial statements, (ii) the concentration makes the entity vulnerable to the risk of a near-term severe effect, and (iii) it is at least reasonably possible that the events that could cause the severe effect will occur in the near term (SOP 94-6, pars. 21, 22, and 24):

a. Concentrations in the volume of business transacted with a particular customer, supplier, lender, grantor, or contributor (for purposes of this disclosure, it is always considered at least reasonably possible that any customer, grantor, or contributor will be lost in the near term)

b. Concentrations in revenue from particular products, services, or fund-raising events

c. Concentrations in the available sources of supply of materials, labor, or services, or of licenses or other rights used in the entity's operations

d. Concentrations in the market or geographic area in which the entity conducts its operations (for purposes of this disclosure, it is always considered at least reasonably possible that operations located outside an entity's home country will be disrupted in the near term)

e. For concentrations of labor subject to collective bargaining agreements, the percentage of the labor force covered by a collective bargaining agreement and the percentage of the labor force covered by a collective agreement that will expire within one year

f. For concentrations of operations located outside the entity's home country, the carrying amounts of net assets and the geographic areas in which they are located

EXAMPLES OF FINANCIAL STATEMENT DISCLOSURES

The following sample disclosures are available on the accompanying disc. For examples of disclosures of commitments, see Chapter 6, "Commitments." For examples of disclosures of contingencies in connection with unconditional purchase obligations, see Chapter 40, "Debt Obligations and Credit Arrangements."

Loss Contingencies

Example 9–1: General Accounting Policy for Contingencies Disclosed as Part of the Accounting Policies Note to the Financial Statements

Certain conditions may exist as of the date the Financial Statements are issued, which may result in a loss to the Company but which will only be resolved when one or more future events occur or fail to occur. The Company's management and its legal counsel assess such contingent liabilities, and such assessment inherently involves an exercise of judgment. In assessing loss contingencies related to legal proceedings that are pending against the Company or unasserted claims that may result in such proceedings, the Company's legal counsel evaluates the perceived merits of any legal proceedings or unasserted claims as well as the perceived merits of the amount of relief sought or expected to be sought therein.

If the assessment of a contingency indicates that it is probable that a material loss has been incurred and the amount of the liability can be estimated, then the estimated liability would be accrued in the Company's Financial Statements. If the assessment indicates that a potentially material loss contingency is not probable, but is reasonably possible, or is probable but cannot be estimated, then the nature of the contingent liability, together with an estimate of the range of possible loss if determinable and material, would be disclosed.

Loss contingencies considered remote are generally not disclosed unless they involve guarantees, in which case the nature of the guarantee would be disclosed.

Example 9–2: No Accrual Is Made for Litigation Because the Likelihood of a Material Adverse Outcome Is Remote

The Company is a defendant in a case entitled *Jones v. The Company,* which is in the United States District Court in the Northern District of California. The case arose from claims by Mrs. Jones, a former employee, that the Company had discriminated against her during her employment at the Company. The suit seeks damages totaling $1,500,000. The Company believes that the claims are without merit and intends to vigorously defend its position. The ultimate outcome of this litigation cannot presently be determined. However, in management's opinion, the likelihood of a material adverse outcome is remote. Accordingly, adjustments, if any, that might result from the resolution of this matter have not been reflected in the Financial Statements.

Example 9–3: No Accrual Is Made of Potential Liability Because Management Does Not Believe It Is Probable

A former employee of the Company has filed a workers' compensation claim related to injuries incurred in connection with the September 2000 fire at the Company's Temecula facility. In the claim, the employee is requesting payment of an additional 50% award of compensation, approximating $450,000, claiming the Company violated a State safety statute in connection with the occurrence of his injury. As of December 31, 2000, the Company has not recorded a provision for this matter as management intends to vigorously defend these allegations and believes the payment of the penalty is not probable.

The Company believes, however, that any liability it may incur would not have a material adverse effect on its financial condition or its results of operations.

Example 9–4: Accrual Is Made but Exposure Exists in Excess of Amount Accrued

The Company is a defendant in a lawsuit, filed by a former supplier of electronic components alleging breach of contract, which seeks damages totaling $750,000. The Company proposed a settlement in the amount of $500,000, based on the advice of the Company's legal counsel. Consequently, $500,000 was charged to operations in the accompanying 2000 financial statements. However, if the settlement offer is not accepted by the plaintiff and the case goes to trial, the amount of the ultimate loss to the Company, if any, may equal the entire amount of damages of $750,000 sought by the plaintiff.

Example 9–5: Unasserted Claim for Penalties Resulting from Contract Delays

In the ordinary course of business, the Company enters into contracts that provide for the assessment by the Company's customers of penalty charges for delays in the required production capability or completion of contracts. At December 31, 2000, the Company had not achieved the 50% production capacity specified in a major contract, which also provides for penalties of up to $1,500,000. The Company's management believes that failure to meet the contract's production capacity requirement was caused primarily by customer initiated changes and additional customer requirements after the placement of the order and has informed the customer of the delays caused thereby. No claims for penalties have been made by the customer, and although some uncertainty exists as to whether the final delivery date can be achieved, the Company believes it can fulfill all remaining contractual requirements so that ultimately no penalties will have to be paid.

Example 9–6: Unasserted Claim Relating to Product Defects

In September 2000, the Company announced that it will conduct an inspection program to eliminate a potential problem with an electrical component supplied to various manufacturers of microwave ovens. The ultimate cost of the repair will not be known until the inspection program is complete, which could have a material effect on the Company's financial condition and results of operations.

Example 9–7: Contingent Liability Resulting from Government Investigation

The Company is currently the subject of certain U.S. government investigations. If the Company is charged with wrongdoing as a result of any of these investigations, the Company could be suspended from bidding on or receiving awards of new government contracts pending the completion of legal proceedings. If convicted or found liable, the Company could be fined and debarred from new government contracting for a period generally not to exceed three years.

Example 9–8: Contingent Liability Relating to Businesses Sold

The Company is contingently liable for obligations totaling approximately $4,000,000 under Industrial Revenue Bond Agreements related to manufacturing plants of businesses that were sold. In November 2000, the Company was notified that an event of default relating to the nonpayment of $300,000 semi-annual interest installment due October 2000, by the purchaser of the businesses had occurred. The Company has agreed to loan $300,000 to the purchaser to cure the event of default.

Example 9–9: Contingent Liability Relating to Lease Termination

In September 2000, the Company notified the developer and landlord of its planned future headquarters in Paramount, California, that the Company intends to terminate the project. The Company had previously entered into a 15-year lease agreement for the new site. Although groundbreaking for the new site has not occurred, the Company anticipates that it will incur lease termination costs. The Company is not able to make a meaningful estimate of the amount or range of loss that could result from an unfavorable resolution of this matter. Consequently, the Company has not provided any accruals for lease termination costs in the Financial Statements.

Example 9–10: Contingent Liability Relating to Performance and Payment Bonds Issued by Sureties

The Company is contingently liable to sureties in respect of performance and payment bonds issued by the sureties in connection with certain contracts entered into by the Company in the normal course of business. The Company has agreed to indemnify the sureties for any payments made by them in respect of such bonds.

Example 9–11: Contingency Resulting from Default under Lease Agreements

The Company leases certain plant machinery and equipment at its manufacturing facility in Boise, Idaho. As a result of the Company's default under its debt obligations, as more fully discussed in Note [X] to the Financial Statements, the Company is in default under these lease agreements. As a result, the lessors have the right to require the Company to prepay the remaining future lease payments required under the lease agreements. Because the lease payments have been made and are expected to be made in a timely manner, the Company does not expect that the lessors will assert this right under these lease agreements.

Example 9–12: Lawsuit Settlement Amount Is Recorded at Present Value of Amount to Be Paid

In October 2000, the Company settled a legal action brought by a group of employees alleging certain discriminatory employment practices by the Company. Under the settlement, the Company has agreed to provide monetary relief in the amount of approximately $2,500,000, to be paid in installments over a five-year period. The present value of the cost of the settlement and estimated additional legal fees, totaling $1,900,000, have been included in results of operations for 2000. The current portion of the liability recorded is approximately $500,000 and the remaining $1,400,000 is classified as a noncurrent liability at December 31, 2000.

Example 9–13: Settlement of Claims Is Not Expected to Exceed Company's Insurance Coverage

Through December 31, 2000, claims valued at approximately $7,000,000 had been filed against the Company relating to product damage associated with the contamination of a formulated agricultural chemical. Management, based on consultation with its legal counsel, believes that the ultimate settlement of claims for this loss will not exceed its insurance coverage, which totals $15,000,000.

Example 9–14: Company Is without Insurance for Various Risks That Could Adversely Affect the Company's Financial Condition and Operations

Because of the state of the market for insurance in recent years, the Company, and many U.S. corporations, have been unable to obtain insurance for various risks at rates and on terms that they consider reasonable. Consequently, the Company is to a significant degree without insurance for various risks, including those associated with product liability. Although the Company has recorded estimated liabilities for uninsured risks to the extent permitted by generally accepted accounting principles, the absence of various insurance coverages represents a potential exposure for the Company. Therefore, the financial condition and net income of the Company in future periods could be adversely affected if uninsured losses in excess of amounts provided were to be incurred. The portion of liabilities for uninsured losses estimated to payable after one year is included in "Other noncurrent liabilities" in the accompanying Balance Sheets.

Example 9–15: Company Involved in Arbitration

The Company had been involved in an arbitration entitled *The Company v. ABC, Ltd.* The case was based on the Company's claims that ABC, Ltd. breached noncompetition provisions and other terms of a distribution agreement between the Company and ABC, Ltd.

In October 2000, the Company was informed that while it had won the case based on the merits of its claims, any recovery of damages was time barred under the terms of the original agreement between the two parties in the dispute. As a result, the Company was required to pay a portion of ABC, Ltd.'s fees and costs related to the arbitration, in the amount of $800,000. The Company expensed these fees and costs awarded to ABC, Ltd. in 2000. This payment completes the Company's involvement in the matter.

Example 9–16: Litigation Settlement Is Subject to a Confidentiality Agreement

In January 2000, Stuart Construction Co. (Stuart) filed suit against the Company alleging that the Company had failed to provide coated, welded pipe fittings and joints in accordance with contract specifications for a construction project in the Pacific Grove area. In November 2000, the parties involved agreed to settle the suit. The financial terms of the settlement are subject to a confidentiality agreement; however, the settlement will not have a material effect on the Company's financial condition or results of operations.

Example 9–17: Company Is Subject to Various Claims and Legal Proceedings in the Ordinary Course of Business That Are Not Considered Material

The Company is subject to various claims and legal proceedings covering a wide range of matters that arise in the ordinary course of its business activities, including product liability claims. Management believes that any liability that may ultimately result from the resolution of these matters will not have a material adverse effect on the financial condition or results of operations of the Company.

Example 9–18: Company Is in Dispute with Taxing Authority over a Tax Assessment

The Company is in dispute over a 1998 tax assessment, including penalties and interest, by the Ohio Department of Revenue and Taxation for the years 1993 through 1997 in the approximate amount of $9.5 million. The Company has filed written protests as to these assessments and will vigorously contest the asserted deficiencies through the administrative appeals process and, if necessary, litigation. The Company believes that adequate provision has been made in the financial statements for any liability.

Example 9–19: Company's Tax Returns Are under Examination by the IRS

The Internal Revenue Service (IRS) is currently examining the Company's tax returns for years 1997 through 1999. Management believes the ultimate resolution of this examination will not result in a material adverse effect to the Company's financial position or results of operations.

Example 9–20: IRS Has Completed Examination and Issued a Deficiency Notice—No Accrual Made

The Internal Revenue Service (IRS) has completed an examination of the federal income tax returns filed by the Company for the years ended December 31, 1997, and December 31, 1998. The IRS has proposed to disallow certain deductions taken by the Company in connection with an acquisition and has sent the Company a statutory notice of deficiency. The Company disagrees with the position of the IRS, intends to pursue its judicial remedies, and is confident that, upon final resolution of the issue, the proposed tax deficiencies will be substantially reduced. No provision has been made in the Financial Statements for the proposed additional taxes and interest because the ultimate liability cannot be reasonably estimated. Full loss of the contested deductions, plus interest costs through December 31, 2000, would result in a charge to net earnings of approximately $750,000.

Example 9–21: Settlement Reached with IRS about Proposed Adjustments—Accrual Made

The Internal Revenue Service (IRS) has proposed certain adjustments to the Company's federal tax returns for 1997 and 1998. The Company has entered into an agreement with the IRS concerning some of the proposed adjustments and has reached an informal understanding with the IRS regarding the others. The provision for current income taxes for 2000 include an additional $450,000 resulting from the settlement with the IRS. As of December 31, 2000, the Company has accrued the additional tax liability of $450,000, plus $92,000 for estimated interest due.

Gain Contingencies

Example 9–22: Amount of Claim Asserted in Litigation Is Not Specified in the Financial Statement Disclosure

In May 2000, the Company initiated a legal action against one of its suppliers alleging breach of contract, breach of warranty, and misrepresentation. Management believes, based on the advice of the Company's legal counsel, that the suit could result in a settlement or award by the court in favor of the Company. However, the ultimate outcome of the litigation cannot be determined and no amount has been recognized for possible collection of any claims asserted in the litigation.

Example 9–23: Amount of Claim Asserted in Litigation Is Specified in the Financial Statement Disclosure

On August 10, 2000, the Company filed suit against Able & Baker Co., its former management consultant and advisory firm. The complaint charges Able & Baker Co. with professional malpractice, negligent misrepresentation, breach of fiduciary duty, breach of contract, and fraud in connection with its advice and services regarding the Company's sale of Hope Enterprises. The complaint seeks $495,000 in compensatory damages, plus prejudgment interest and punitive damages. Able & Baker Co. has included in its answer to the complaint certain "unasserted counterclaims" for fees and expenses incurred by it. A trial date has not been set yet, and no estimate can be made of the amount of the settlement, if any, that will actually be received.

Example 9–24: Gain Not Recognized in the Financial Statements until Received

In December 2000, a federal court jury found that Dobatek, Inc. infringed on some of the Company's patents and awarded the Company $6,000,000 in damages. Dobatek, Inc. will be required to pay interest on the award amount and legal fees. Should Dobatek, Inc. appeal, the jury verdict or the amount of the damage award could be affected; therefore, the Company will not recognize any award amount in the Financial Statements until it is received.

Example 9–25: Litigation Settlement Results in Receipt of Award Amount and Gain Recognition

In March 2000, the Company settled its two year copyright infringement and trade secrets litigation with Britek, Inc. Under the terms of the settlement, Britek, Inc. paid the Company $6,500,000, which was received in full in May 2000, and the parties have dismissed all pending litigation. The Company recognized a pretax gain, net of related legal fees and other expenses, of $5,300,000 resulting from the settlement, which is included in "Other income" in the 2000 Consolidated Statement of Operations.

Example 9–26: Insurance Claim Proceeds Are Recorded as Deferred Gain until Final Settlement

In December 1999, the Company's Vista manufacturing plant in Detroit was extensively damaged as a result of a fire. A $3,000,000 pretax charge was recorded in 1999 for expected uninsured costs associated with the incident, including deductibles. In 2000, the Company received interim payments of $14,500,000 on its insurance claim. The Company is in discussions with its insurers as to additional insurance proceeds that the Company believes it is entitled to. Insurance proceeds received under the Company's property damage claim are being deferred pending final settlement of the claim. The Company expects to record a substantial non-recurring gain in 2001, representing the difference between the property insurance settlement on the plant and the carrying value of the plant at the time of the explosion. The amount of the gain will be dependent on final construction, clean-up expenditures, and the settlement reached with the Company's insurance carriers. As of December 31, 2000, $14,500,000 has been recorded as a deferred gain and is included in "Other liabilities" in the accompanying Balance Sheet.

Contingencies Relating to Business Combinations

Example 9–27: Business Combination Includes Contingent Consideration

On September 15, 2000, the Company acquired approximately 46% of the outstanding stock of Calciose, Inc., a leading manufacturer and distributor of medical diagnostic instruments. With this acquisition, the Company increased its ownership to approximately 90%. The Company paid $3,000,000 in cash and issued 450,000 shares of the Company's common stock with an approximate market value of

$4,950,000. The Stock Purchase Agreement contains additional payments contingent on the future earnings performance of Calciose, Inc. Any additional payments made, when the contingency is resolved, will be accounted for as additional costs of the acquired assets and amortized over the remaining life of the assets. Prior to this acquisition, the Company accounted for its investment in Calciose, Inc. using the equity method. The following unaudited pro forma consolidated results of operations for the years ended December 31, 2000, and December 31, 1999 are presented as if the acquisition had been made at the beginning of each year presented.

	Years Ended December 31	
	2000	*1999*
Net sales	$82,000,000	$75,000,000
Net earnings	$4,700,000	$3,200,000
Basic earnings per share	$1.10	$1.04

Example 9–28: Royalty Payments Relating to Business Acquisitions

In connection with certain acquisitions, the Company pays royalties (ranging from 3% to 10%) on revenues generated by the acquired businesses for periods expiring through 2009. Such contingent payments, when incurred, will be recorded as additional cost of the related acquisitions and amortized over the remaining amortization period. Royalty payments in 2000 and 1999 were $4,200,000 and $3,800,000, respectively.

Example 9–29: Company to Indemnify Prior Owners of Acquired Business for Certain Liabilities

As part of the Company's purchase of certain business operations of Mastol, Inc., the Company agreed to indemnify Mastol, Inc. for certain liabilities that may arise from events that occurred during Mastol's ownership. As this contingency is resolved and if additional consideration is paid, the amount of such payments will be recorded as additional cost of the acquired business and will increase the amount of goodwill recorded for this acquisition.

Environmental Remediation Contingencies

Example 9–30: Company Has Been Designated as a Potentially Responsible Party and Accrued Estimated Liability on an Undiscounted Basis

The Company has been designated as a potentially responsible party (PRP) by federal and state agencies with respect to certain sites with which the Company may have had direct or indirect involvement. Such designations are made regardless of the extent of the Company's involvement. These claims are in various stages of administrative or judicial proceedings and include demands for recovery of past governmental costs and for future investigations and remedial actions. In many cases, the dollar amounts of the claims have not been specified and, with respect to a number of the PRP claims, have been asserted against a number of other entities for the same cost recovery or other relief as was asserted against the Company. The Company accrues costs associated with environmental matters, on an undiscounted basis, when they become probable and reasonably estimable. As of December 31, 2000, and December 31, 1999, the Company has accrued $1,900,000 and $1,600,000, respectively, which represents its current estimate of the probable cleanup liabilities, including remediation and legal costs. This accrual does not reflect any possible future insurance recoveries but does reflect a reasonable estimate of cost-sharing at multiparty sites.

Although the Company's probable liabilities have been accrued for currently, hazardous substance cleanup expenditures generally are paid over an extended period of time, in some cases possibly more than 30 years. Annual cleanup expenditures during 2000 and 1999 were approximately $625,000 and $450,000, respectively.

Example 9–31: Accrual for Estimated Environmental Remediation Costs Has Been Discounted

The Company is involved in environmental remediation and ongoing compliance at several sites. At December 31, 2000, the Company estimated, based on engineering studies, total remediation and ongoing monitoring costs to be made in the future to be approximately $6,500,000, including the effects of inflation. Accordingly, the Company recorded a liability of approximately $4,000,000, which represents the net present value of the estimated future costs discounted at 6%. This is management's best estimate of these liabilities, although possible actual costs could range up to 50% higher. The Company has not anticipated any third party payments in arriving at these estimates.

Example 9–32: Company Has Not Been Designated as a Potentially Responsible Party but Accrued the Highest Amount in the Range of Potential Loss Because Likelihood of Loss Is Probable

As part of its environmental management program, the Company is involved in various environmental remediation activities. As sites are identified and assessed in this program, the Company determines potential environmental liability. Factors considered in assessing liability include, among others, the following: whether the

Company had been designated as a potentially responsible party, the number of other potentially responsible parties designated at the site, the stage of the proceedings, and available environmental technology. As of December 31, 2000, the Company had identified three sites requiring further investigation. However, the Company has not been designated as a potentially responsible party at any site.

Management has assessed the likelihood that a loss has been incurred at one of its sites as probable and, based on findings included in remediation reports and discussions with legal counsel, estimated the potential loss at December 31, 2000, to range from $1,500,000 to $2,500,000. As of December 31, 2000, $2,500,000 had been accrued and is included with "Other accrued liabilities" in the Consolidated Balance Sheets. Although the Company may have a right of contribution or reimbursement under insurance policies, amounts recoverable from other entities with respect to a particular site are not considered until recoveries are deemed probable. No assets for potential recoveries were established as of December 31, 2000.

Example 9–33: Company Has Not Been Designated as a Potentially Responsible Party but Accrued the Lowest Amount in the Range of Potential Loss Because Likelihood of Loss Is More Likely Than Remote but Not Probable

The Company assesses reasonably possible environmental liability relating to environmental remediation and ongoing compliance at several sites. Such liability is not probable but is more likely than remote. As of December 31, 2000, while the Company has not been designated as a potentially responsible party at any site, the amount of environmental liability identified that is reasonably possible is in the range of $2,000,000 to $5,500,000. As of December 31, 2000, the Company accrued $2,000,000 with respect to potential environmental liability. The Company does not expect to incur liabilities at the higher end of the range, based on the limited information currently available.

Example 9–34: Environmental Matter May Result in Increased Operating and Capital Costs to the Company

In 2000, the State of California made a determination that some of the cement materials stored at the Company's Riverside plant are a Type I waste and requested that the Company apply for a formal permit for an on-site landfill. The Company understands that similar notices were sent to other cement manufacturers in the State. The Company is protesting this determination through legal channels and has received a stay to allow it to demonstrate that current management practices pose no threat to the environment. The Company believes that the State's determination ultimately will be reversed or the Company will receive the needed permit or other adequate relief, such as an agreed order requiring certain additional waste management procedures that are less stringent than those generally required for Type I wastes. If the Company is not successful in this regard, however, like other cement producers in the State, the Riverside plant could incur substantially increased operating and capital costs.

Example 9–35: Accruals for Estimated Future Costs Relate to Divested Operations and Locations No Longer in Operation

The accompanying Consolidated Balance Sheets include accruals for the estimated future costs associated with certain environmental remediation activities related to the past use or disposal of hazardous materials. Substantially all such costs relate to divested operations and to facilities or locations that are no longer in operation. Due to a number of uncertainties, including uncertainty of timing, the scope of remediation, future technology, regulatory changes, and other factors, the ultimate remediation costs may exceed the amounts estimated. However, in the opinion of management, such additional costs are not expected to be material relative to consolidated liquidity, financial position, or future results of operations.

Risks, Uncertainties, and Concentrations

Nature of Operations

Example 9–36: Company Describes Its Primary Products

The Company designs, manufactures, markets, and services test systems and related software, and backplanes and associated connectors. The Company's top five products are semiconductor test systems, backplane connection systems, circuit-board test systems, telecommunications test systems, and software test systems.

Example 9–37: Company Describes the Types of Customers It Has

The Company is a leading global developer, manufacturer, and distributor of hand tools, power tools, tool storage products, shop equipment, under-hood diagnostics equipment, under-car equipment, emissions and safety equipment, collision repair equipment, vehicle service information, and business management systems and services. The Corporation's customers include professional automotive technicians, shop owners, franchised service centers, national accounts, original equipment manufacturers, and industrial tool and equipment users worldwide.

Example 9–38: Company Describes U.S. Geographic Locations Where It Operates

The Company is a leading designer and manufacturer of open-architecture, standard embedded computer components that system designers can easily utilize to create a custom solution specific to the user's unique application. The Company has operations in New York, New Mexico, Minnesota, North Carolina, and California. The Company's product lines include CPU boards, general purpose input/output modules, avionics interface modules and analyzers, interconnection and expansion units, telemetry boards, data acquisition software, and industrial computer systems and enclosures.

Example 9–39: Company Indicates That Its Operations Are Vulnerable to Changes in Trends and Customer Demand

The Company is a nationwide specialty retailer of fashionable and contemporary apparel and accessory items designed for consumers with a young, active lifestyle. The Company's success is largely dependent on its ability to gauge the fashion tastes of its customers and to provide merchandise that satisfies customer demand. The Company's failure to anticipate, identify, or react to changes in fashion trends could adversely affect its results of operations.

Example 9–40: Company's Operations Are Substantially in Foreign Countries

Substantially all of the Company's products are manufactured in the Dominican Republic, Mexico (under the Maquiladora program), Switzerland, Ireland, and Slovakia. These foreign operations represent captive manufacturing facilities of the Company. The Company's operations are subject to various political, economic, and other risks and uncertainties inherent in the countries in which the Company operates. Among other risks, the Company's operations are subject to the risks of restrictions on transfer of funds; export duties, quotas and embargoes; domestic and international customs and tariffs; changing taxation policies; foreign exchange restrictions; and political conditions and governmental regulations.

Example 9–41: Company Specifies Percentage of Net Sales Relating to Foreign Operations

Sales to customers outside the United States approximated 35% of net sales in 2000 and 25% of net sales in 1999.

Estimates

Example 9–42: General Note Regarding Estimates Inherent in the Financial Statements

The preparation of the Company's Financial Statements in conformity with generally accepted accounting principles, requires management to make estimates and assumptions that affect reported amounts of assets and liabilities and disclosure of contingent assets and liabilities at the date of the Financial Statements and the reported amounts of revenues and expenses during the reporting period. Actual results could differ from those estimates.

Example 9–43: Significant Estimates Relating to Specific Financial Statement Accounts and Transactions Are Identified

The Financial Statements include some amounts that are based on management's best estimates and judgments. The most significant estimates relate to allowance for uncollectible accounts receivable, inventory obsolescence, depreciation, intangible asset valuations and useful lives, employee benefit plans, environmental accruals, taxes, contingencies, and costs to complete long-term contracts. These estimates may be adjusted as more current information becomes available, and any adjustment could be significant.

Example 9–44: Significant Accounting Estimates—Inventory

The Company's provisions for inventory write-downs are based on the Company's best estimates of product sales prices and customer demand patterns, and its plans to transition its products. However, the Company operates in a highly competitive industry that is characterized by aggressive pricing practices, downward pressures on gross margins, and rapid technological advances. As a result of the industry's dynamic nature, it is at least reasonably possible that the estimates used by the Company to determine its provisions for inventory write-downs will be materially different from the actual amounts or results. These differences could result in materially higher than expected inventory provisions and related costs, which could have a materially adverse effect on the Company's results of operations and financial condition in the near term.

Example 9–45: Significant Accounting Estimates—Assets Held for Sale

In October 2000, in connection with its strategy to reduce debt, the Company decided to sell land and buildings formerly used by a discontinued manufacturing unit. As a result, the Company recorded a non-cash write-down of $1,400,000 to reflect these assets at their estimated fair value of $4,200,000, which is shown as "Assets held for sale" at December 31, 2000. The charge of $1,400,000 reflects the Company's best estimate of the amount anticipated to be realized on the disposition of the assets. This estimate is based on negotiations with potential buyers and independent parties familiar with valuations of this nature. The amount that the Company will ultimately realize could differ materially from the amount recorded in the Financial Statements.

Example 9–46: Significant Accounting Estimates—Deferred Tax Assets

Included in the accompanying Balance Sheets at December 31, 2000, and December 31, 1999 are deferred tax assets of $2,500,000 and $2,200,000, respectively, representing tax loss and credit carryforwards. Realization of that asset is dependent on the Company's ability to generate future taxable income. Management believes that it is more likely than not that forecasted taxable income will be sufficient to utilize the tax carryforwards before their expiration in 2008 and 2009 to fully recover the asset. However, there can be no assurance that the Company will meet its expectations of future income. As a result, the amount of the deferred tax assets considered realizable could be reduced in the near term if estimates of future taxable income are reduced. Such an occurrence could materially adversely affect the Company's results of operations and financial condition.

Example 9–47: Significant Accounting Estimates—Self-Insured Claims

The Company is primarily self-insured, up to certain limits, for automobile and general liability, workers' compensation, and employee group health claims. The Company has purchased stop loss insurance, which will reimburse the Company for individual claims in excess of $50,000 annually or aggregate claims exceeding $1,000,000 annually. Operations are charged with the cost of claims reported and an estimate of claims incurred but not reported. A liability for unpaid claims and the associated claim expenses, including incurred but not reported losses, is actuarially determined and reflected in the Balance Sheet as an accrued liability. Total expense under the program was approximately $3,200,000 and $2,900,000 in 2000 and 1999, respectively. The self-insured claims liability includes incurred but not reported losses of $1,500,000 and $1,745,000 at December 31, 2000, and December 31, 1999, respectively.

The determination of such claims and expenses and the appropriateness of the related liability is continually reviewed and updated. It is reasonably possible that the accrued estimated liability for self-insured claims may need to be revised in the near term.

Example 9–48: Significant Accounting Estimates—Accrued Liability for Product Warranties

The Company sells the majority of its products to customers along with unconditional repair or replacement warranties. The accompanying Financial Statements for 2000 and 1999 include a provision of $1,600,000 and $1,300,000, respectively, for estimated warranty claims based on the Company's experience of the amount of claims actually made. As of December 31, 2000, and December 31, 1999, the accrued liability for product warranty claims totaled $5,200,000 and $4,900,000, respectively. It is reasonably possible that the Company's estimate of the accrued product warranty claims will change in the near term.

Other Risks, Uncertainties, and Concentrations

Example 9–49: Company Describes the Risks of the Industry in Which It Operates and Potential Effect on the Company's Operations

The Company participates in a highly volatile industry that is characterized by rapid technological change, intense competitive pressure, and cyclical market patterns. The Company's results of operations are affected by a wide variety of factors, including general economic conditions, decreases in average selling prices over the life of any particular product, the timing of new product introductions (by the Company, its competitors, and others), the ability to manufacture sufficient quantities of a given product in a timely manner, the timely implementation of new manufacturing process technologies, the ability to safeguard patents and intellectual property from competitors, and the effect of new technologies resulting in rapid escalation of demand for some products in the face of equally steep decline in demand for others. Based on the factors noted herein, the Company may experience substantial period-to-period fluctuations in future operating results.

Example 9–50: Company Has Geographic Exposure to Catastrophe Losses

The Company has a geographic exposure to catastrophe losses in certain areas of the country. These catastrophes can be caused by various events, including hurricanes, windstorms, earthquakes, hail, severe winter weather, and fires, and the incidence and severity of catastrophes are inherently unpredictable. The extent of losses from a catastrophe is a function of both the total amount of insured exposure in the area affected by the event and the severity of the event. Most catastrophes are restricted to small geographic areas; however, hurricanes and earthquakes may produce significant damage in large, heavily populated areas. The Company generally seeks to reduce its exposure to catastrophes through individual risk selection and the purchase of catastrophe reinsurance.

Example 9–51: Company Requires No Collateral and Concentrations of Credit Risk Virtually Limited

Financial instruments that potentially subject the Company to concentrations of credit risk consist primarily of cash and cash equivalents and accounts receivable. The Company places its cash and cash equivalents with high quality financial institutions and limits the amount of credit exposure with any one institution. Concentrations of credit risk with respect to accounts receivable are limited because a large number of geographically diverse customers make up the Company's customer base, thus spreading the trade credit risk. At December 31, 2000, and December 31, 1999, no single group or customer represents greater than 10% of total accounts receivable. The Company controls credit risk through credit approvals, credit limits, and monitoring procedures. The Company performs credit evaluations of its commercial and industrial customers but generally does not require collateral to support accounts receivable.

Example 9–52: Company Requires Collateral and Has Concentrations in Accounts Receivable

The Company sells its products to distributors and original equipment manufacturers throughout the world. The Company performs ongoing credit evaluations of its customers' financial condition and, generally, requires collateral, such as letters of credit, whenever deemed necessary. At December 31, 2000, three customers, each of who accounted for more than 10% of the Company's accounts receivable, accounted for 58% of total accounts receivable in aggregate. At December 31, 1999, four customers, each of who accounted for more than 10% of the Company's accounts receivable, accounted for 52% of total accounts receivable in aggregate.

Example 9–53: Concentrations in Sales to Few Customers

In 2000, the two largest customers accounted for 30% and 21% of sales. In 1999, the three largest customers accounted for 32%, 19%, and 18% of sales.

Example 9–54: Concentrations in Sales to Foreign Customers

During 2000 and 1999, approximately 38% and 35%, respectively, of the Company's net sales were made to foreign customers. An adverse change in either economic conditions abroad or the Company's relationship with significant foreign distributors could negatively effect the volume of the Company's international sales and the Company's results of operations.

Example 9–55: Company Has Accounts Receivable and Contract Concentrations in Specific Industries

The majority of accounts receivable and all contract work in progress are from engineering and construction clients primarily concentrated in the steel and utility industries throughout the United States. The Company generally does not require collateral, but in most cases can place liens against the property, plant, or equipment constructed or terminate the contract if a material default occurs. The Company maintains adequate reserves for potential credit losses and such losses have been minimal and within management's estimates.

Example 9–56: Company Is Dependent on Few Major Suppliers

The Company is dependent on third-party equipment manufacturers, distributors, and dealers for all of its supply of communications equipment. In 2000 and 1999, products purchased from the Company's three largest suppliers accounted for approximately 51% and 65% of product purchases, respectively. The Company is dependent on the ability of its suppliers to provide products on a timely basis and on favorable pricing terms. The loss of certain principal suppliers or a significant reduction in product availability from principal suppliers could have a material adverse effect on the Company. The Company believes that its relationships with its suppliers are satisfactory; however, the Company has periodically experienced inadequate supply from certain handset manufacturers.

Example 9–57: Risks Associated with Concentrations in the Available Sources of Supply of Materials

Certain components and products that meet the Company's requirements are available only from a single supplier or a limited number of suppliers. The rapid rate of technological change and the necessity of developing and manufacturing products with short life cycles may intensify these risks. The inability to obtain components and products as required, or to develop alternative sources, if and as required in the future, could result in delays or reductions in product shipments, which in turn could have a material adverse effect on the Company's business, financial condition, and results of operations.

Example 9–58: Company Uses Parts and Materials That Are Subject to Industry-Wide Shortages Which Has Forced Suppliers to Allocate Available Quantities

The Company uses numerous suppliers of electronic components and other materials for its operations. Some components used by the Company have been subject to industry-wide shortages, and suppliers have been forced to allocate available quantities among their customers. The Company's inability to obtain any needed components during periods of allocation could cause delays in manufacturing and could adversely affect results of operations.

Example 9–59: Concentrations of Labor Subject to Collective Bargaining Agreement

At December 31, 2000, the Company had a total of approximately 1,200 employees. Of this total, approximately 1,000 are hourly workers and 200 are salaried. Approximately 98% of the Company's hourly employees and 37% of its salaried employees are represented by a union. The existing union agreement will expire in November 2001.

Example 9–60: Company Limits the Amount of Credit Exposure Through Diversification

The Company places its short-term investments in a variety of financial instruments and, by policy, limits the amount of credit exposure through diversification and by restricting its investments to highly rated securities.

Example 9–61: Cash in Excess of FDIC Insured Limits

The Company maintains its cash in bank deposit accounts which, at times, may exceed federally insured limits. Accounts are guaranteed by the Federal Deposit Insurance Corporation (FDIC) up to $100,000. At December 31, 2000, and December 31, 1999, the Company had approximately $1,250,000 and $1,155,000, respectively, in excess of FDIC insured limits. The Company has not experienced any losses in such accounts.

Guarantees

Example 9–62: Guarantee of Indebtedness of Related Entity

As of December 31, 2000, the Company is contingently liable as guarantor with respect to $5,400,000 of indebtedness of Ecaped, Inc., an entity that is owned by the Company's stockholders. No material loss is anticipated by reason of such guarantee.

Example 9–63: Loss Recorded as a Result of Guarantee of Indebtedness of an Affiliate

In 2000, the Company accrued a loss of $400,000 for a loan to an insolvent affiliate that was guaranteed by the Company.

Example 9–64: Guarantee of Indebtedness of Joint Venture Obligates Company to Advance Funds to the Joint Venture if Certain Loan Covenants Are Not Met

The Company holds a 25% ownership interest in Stellark, Inc., which has a $7,000,000 line of credit agreement (Agreement) with First Nations Bank. Under terms of the Agreement, the Company is obligated to advance to Stellark, Inc. a maximum of $2,500,000 if its working capital falls below $500,000 or its current ratio is less than 1. Any funds advanced under this Agreement are available to First Nations Bank. In addition, First Nations Bank may have claims against the Company in an amount not to exceed $2,000,000 of any unsatisfied required advances. At December 31, 2000, Stellark, Inc. was in compliance with the terms of the Agreement with First Nations Bank.

Example 9–65: Guarantee of Future Lease Payments

In March 2000, the Company sold The Red Shoe, Inc., a chain of 25 stores located throughout Ohio and Michigan. In connection with this sale, the Company has guaranteed that certain lease payments will be made by the purchasers. The amount of future lease payments guaranteed by the Company totaled $6,800,000 at December 31, 2000. The Company believes that the purchasers will be able to perform under their respective lease agreements and that no payments will be required and no losses incurred under such guarantees.

Example 9–66: Guaranteed Advance and Royalty Payments in Connection with New Joint Venture

In January 2000, the Company entered into a joint venture agreement with Sapiex Corp. creating a new limited liability company (LLC) in which the Company holds a 50% ownership interest. On December 1, 2000, the LLC entered into a license agreement expiring December 31, 2010, with an option for a five year automatic extension if the LLC pays the licensor $27,000,000 in royalties during the initial ten year period of the agreement. The license agreement includes guaranteed minimum royalty payments of $18,000,000 payable over the ten year initial term and $7,500,000 payable over the five year renewal period, if applicable. The Company is responsible for funding $8,000,000 of the $18,000,000 guaranteed royalty payments. The guarantee payments include a $3,000,000 advance, paid within 15 days after the agreements were executed, and ten minimum guaranteed installments of $1,500,000, due each January 30, starting in 2001 and ending 2010. The Company was responsible for funding $1,000,000 of the initial advance and is responsible for funding $500,000 of the first four and $750,000 of the next six of ten yearly installments.

CHAPTER 10
DEFERRED COMPENSATION ARRANGEMENTS

CONTENTS

EXECUTIVE SUMMARY

Deferred compensation contracts are accounted for individually on an accrual basis. Estimated amounts to be paid under a deferred compensation contract that is not equivalent to a pension plan or a postretirement health or welfare benefit plan should be accrued over the period of an employee's active employment from the time the contract is signed to the employee's full eligibility date. If elements of both current and future services are present, only the portion applicable to the current services is accrued.

If a deferred compensation contract contains benefits payable for the life of a beneficiary, the total liability is based on the beneficiary's life expectancy or on the estimated cost of an annuity contract that would provide sufficient funds to pay the required benefits. The total liability for deferred compensation contracts is determined by the terms of each individual contract. The amount of the periodic accrual, computed from the first day of the employment contract, must total no less than the then present value of the benefits provided for in the contract. The periodic accruals are made systematically over the active term of employment.

If individual deferred compensation contracts, as a group, are in substance a retirement plan, they should be accounted for in accordance with generally accepted accounting principles (GAAP) for pension plans as discussed in Chapter 21, "Pension Plans." Similarly, if individual deferred compensation contracts, as a group, are in substance a postretirement benefit plan other than pensions, they should be accounted for in accordance with GAAP for postretirement benefits as discussed in Chapter 23, "Postretirement Benefits Other Than Pensions."

Authoritative Literature

APB-12	Omnibus Opinion—1967 (Deferred Compensation Contracts)
FAS-106	Employers' Accounting for Postretirement Benefits Other Than Pensions

DISCLOSURE REQUIREMENTS

Authoritative pronouncements require no specific disclosures about deferred compensation contracts or arrangements. However, disclosures similar to those for pension plans and postretirement benefits are found in practice and are considered informative disclosures. The disclosure requirements for pension plans are discussed in Chapter 21, "Pension Plans," and the disclosure requirements for postretirement benefits other than pensions are discussed in Chapter 23, "Postretirement Benefits Other Than Pensions."

EXAMPLES OF FINANCIAL STATEMENT DISCLOSURES

The following sample disclosures are available on the accompanying disc.

Example 10–1: Present Value of Estimated Future Benefit Payments Are Being Accrued over the Service Period

In March 2000, the Company entered into a deferred compensation agreement with a key executive. The agreement provides for certain postretirement benefits, contingent on certain conditions, beginning in 2009 and payable over the remaining life of the executive and spouse. The Company accrues the present value of the estimated future benefit payments over the period from the date of the agreement to the retirement date. The Company recognized expense of $141,000 in 2000 and $102,000 in 1999 related to this agreement.

Example 10–2: Deferred Compensation Plan Is Funded by Life Insurance Contracts and Provides Guaranteed Interest Rate

The Company has a deferred compensation plan that permits management and highly compensated employees to defer portions of their compensation and earn a guaranteed interest rate on the deferred amounts. The salaries that have been deferred since the plan's inception have been accrued and the only expense, other than salaries, related to this plan is the interest on the deferred amounts. Interest expense during 2000 and 1999 includes $103,000 and $68,000, respectively, related to this plan. The Company has included in "Deferred employee benefits" $1,150,000 and $935,000 at December 31, 2000, and December 31, 1999, respectively, to reflect its liability under this plan. To fund this plan, the Company purchases corporate-owned whole-life insurance contracts on the related employees. The Company has included in "Other assets" $1,200,000 and $967,000 at December 31, 2000, and December 31, 1999, respectively, which represents cash surrender value of these policies.

Example 10–3: Deferred Compensation Obligation Is Accrued but Unfunded

The Company has two deferred compensation plans for management and highly compensated associates, whereby participants may defer base compensation and bonuses and earn interest on their deferred amounts. Under one plan, a participant may elect to defer a maximum of 100% of his or her compensation. Under another plan, a participant could elect to defer a minimum of 3% of his or her compensation. These deferred compensation plans are unfunded; therefore, benefits are paid from the general assets of the Company. The total of participant deferrals, which is reflected in long-term liabilities, was $823,000 and $554,000 at December 31, 2000, and December 31, 1999, respectively. The participant deferrals earn interest at a rate based on U.S. Government Treasury rates. The interest expense related to this plan was $65,000 in 2000 and $47,000 in 1999.

Example 10–4: Non-Plan Independent Consultant Stock Options

During the year ended December 31, 2000, the Company's Board of Directors approved the grant of stock options to an independent consultant to purchase an aggregate of 50,000 shares of its common stock. These options have an exercise price of $11.49 and as of December 31, 2000, none of these option shares were vested. As a result, the Company has recorded $215,000 in "Deferred compensation," which will be amortized to expense over the three-year vesting period of the options. For the year ended December 31, 2000, an amount of $36,000 has been amortized to expense. These options were not issued as part of any of the Company's registered Stock Option Plans.

Example 10–5: Restricted Stock Plan

The Company has a Restricted Stock Plan, covering 1,200,000 shares of common stock, whose purpose is to permit grants of shares, subject to restrictions, to key employees of the Company as a means of retaining and rewarding them for long-term performance and to increase their ownership in the Company. Shares awarded under the plan entitle the shareholder to all rights of common stock ownership except that the shares may not be sold, transferred, pledged, exchanged, or otherwise disposed of during the restriction period. The restriction period is determined by a committee that is appointed by the Board of Directors and the period may not exceed ten years. During 2000 and 1999, 95,000 shares and 83,000 shares, respectively, were granted with restriction periods of four to six years at market prices ranging from $13.125 to $18.475 in 2000 and $11.375 to $16.875 in 1999. The shares were recorded at the market value on the date of issuance as deferred compensation and the related amount is being amortized to operations over the respective vesting period. Compensation expense for the years ended December 31, 2000, and December 31, 1999, related to these shares of restricted stock was $375,000 and $290,000, respectively. At December 31, 2000, the weighted-average grant date fair value and weighted-average contractual life for outstanding shares of restricted stock was $15.03 and 5.2 years, respectively.

CHAPTER 11
DEVELOPMENT STAGE ENTERPRISES

CONTENTS

EXECUTIVE SUMMARY

A *development stage company* is one in which principal operations have not commenced or principal operations have generated an insignificant amount of revenue. A development stage company issues the same basic financial statements as any other enterprise, and such statements should be prepared in conformity with generally accepted accounting principles (GAAP). Accordingly, determining whether a particular cost should be charged to expense when incurred or should be capitalized or deferred should be based on the same accounting standards regardless of whether the enterprise incurring the cost is already operating or is in the development stage.

The financial statements of an entity that is in the development stage should be identified as those of a development stage company. In addition, the statements should include certain disclosures, including cumulative amounts of revenues, expenses, and cash flows from the entity's inception.

Authoritative Literature

FAS-7	Accounting and Reporting by Development Stage Enterprises
FIN-7	Applying FASB Statement No. 7 in Financial Statements of Established Operating Enterprises

DISCLOSURE REQUIREMENTS

The financial statements of development stage companies and related notes should include the following:

1. A balance sheet, including any cumulative net losses reported with a descriptive caption such as "deficit accumulated during the development stage" in the stockholders' equity section (FAS-7, par. 11)
2. An income statement showing (a) amounts of revenue and expenses for each period covered by the income statement and (b) cumulative amounts from the entity's inception (FAS-7, par. 11)
3. A statement of cash flows showing (a) the cash inflows and cash outflows for each period for which an income statement is presented and (b) cumulative amounts from the entity's inception (FAS-7, par. 11)
4. A statement of stockholders' equity showing the following from the entity's inception (FAS-7, par. 11):
   a. For each issuance, the date and number of shares of stock, warrants, rights, or other equity securities issued for cash and for other consideration
   b. For each issuance, the dollar amounts (per share or other equity unit, and in total) assigned to the consideration received for shares of stock, warrants, rights, or other equity securities (dollar amounts should be assigned to any noncash consideration received)
   c. For each issuance involving noncash consideration, the nature of the noncash consideration and the basis for assigning amounts
5. The financial statements should be identified as those of a development stage company and should include a description of the nature of the development stage activities in which the entity is engaged (FAS-7, par. 12)
6. For the first year the entity is no longer in the development stage, disclosure should be made that in prior years the entity had been in the development stage. (If financial statements for prior years are presented for comparative purposes, the cumulative amounts and other additional disclosures required by items 1–5 above need not be shown.) (FAS-7, pars. 12 and 13)

EXAMPLES OF FINANCIAL STATEMENT DISCLOSURES

The following sample disclosures are available on the accompanying disc.

Note: Examples 11–1 to 11–6 assume that the entity was formed on July 1, 1998, and that financial statements for the years ended December 31, 2000, and December 31, 1999, are presented. Note that the Statements of Operations, Statements of Stockholders' Equity, and Statements of Cash Flows must be from inception even though Comparative Financial Statements for 2000 and 1999 are presented. Details of other note disclosures (e.g., property and equipment, stock options, income taxes) are omitted because they are similar to other businesses.

Example 11–1: Balance Sheets of a Development Stage Enterprise

Prostech Corp.
(A Development Stage Enterprise)
Balance Sheets
December 31, 2000, and December 31, 1999

	December 31	
	2000	*1999*
Assets		
Current assets:		
Cash and equivalents	$74,353	$250,255
Total current assets	74,353	250,255
Property and equipment, net	2,111	2,439
Other assets	1,065	-0-
Total assets	$77,529	$252,694
Liabilities and Stockholders' Equity		
Current liabilities:		
Accounts payable and accrued liabilities	$68,824	$ 15,460
Total current liabilities	68,824	15,460
Stockholders' equity:		
Preferred Stock—$0.01 par value, 5,000,000 shares authorized, none issued at December 31, 2000, and December 31, 1999	-0-	-0-
Common Stock—$.001 par value, 40,000,000 shares authorized, 7,537,319 issued at December 31, 2000, and 5,979,528 at December 31, 1999	7,538	5,980
Additional paid-in capital	751,584	675,252
Note receivable for common stock issued	(7,242)	-0-
Deficit accumulated during development stage	(743,175)	(443,998)
Total stockholders' equity	8,705	237,234
Total liabilities and stockholders' equity	$77,529	$252,694

Example 11–2: Statements of Operations of a Development Stage Enterprise

Prostech Corp.
(A Development Stage Enterprise)
Statements of Operations
For the Years Ended December 31, 2000, and December 31, 1999, and the Period from July 1, 1998, (Inception) to December 31, 2000

	For the Years Ended December 31		*July 1, 1998, (Inception) to December 31, 2000*
	2000	*1999*	
Revenue	$193,500	$ -0-	$243,500
Costs and expenses:			
Cost of sales	-0-	-0-	-0-
Research and development	345,592	283,922	669,514
Selling, general, and administrative	151,315	174,472	345,787
Total costs and expenses	496,907	458,394	1,015,301
Loss from operations	(303,407)	(458,394)	(771,801)
Interest income	4,230	14,396	28,626
Net loss	$(299,177)	$(443,998)	$(743,175)

Example 11–3: Statements of Stockholders' Equity of a Development Stage Enterprise

Prostech Corp. (A Development Stage Enterprise)
Statements of Stockholders' Equity for the Period from July 1, 1998, (Inception) to December 31, 2000

	Common Stock					
	Number of Shares	*Amount*	*Additional Paid-in Capital*	*Note Receivable for Common Stock Issued*	*Deficit Accumulated during Development Stage*	*Total*
Issuance of Common Stock on July 1, 1998 for cash at $.12 per share	5,616,528	$5,617	$657,465	$ -0-	$ -0-	$663,082
Net loss July 1, 1998 to December 31, 1998	-0-	-0-	-0-	-0-	-0-	-0-
Balance at December 31, 1998	5,616,528	5,617	657,465	-0-	-0-	663,082
Distribution of Common Stock for services at $.05 per share	363,000	363	17,787	-0-	-0-	18,150
Net loss for 1999	-0-	-0-	-0-	-0-	(443,998)	(443,998)
Balance at December 31, 1999	5,979,528	5,980	675,252	-0-	(443,998)	237,234
Issuance of Common Stock for cash upon exercise of options at $.05 per share	1,410,000	1,410	69,090	-0-	-0-	70,500
Issuance of Common Stock for cash and note receivable at $.05 per share	147,791	148	7,242	(7,242)	-0-	148
Net loss for 2000	-0-	-0-	-0-	-0-	(299,177)	(299,177)
Balance at December 31, 2000	7,537,319	$7,538	$751,584	$(7,242)	$(743,175)	$ 8,705

Example 11–4: Statements of Cash Flows of a Development Stage Enterprise

Prostech Corp.
(A Development Stage Enterprise)
Statements of Cash Flows
For the Years Ended December 31, 2000, and December 31, 1999, and the Period from July 1, 1998, (Inception) to December 31, 2000

	For the Years Ended December 31		*July 1, 1998, (Inception) to December 31,*
	2000	*1999*	*2000*
Cash Flows from Operating Activities			
Net loss	$(299,177)	$(443,998)	$(743,175)
Adjustments to reconcile net loss to net cash used in operating activities:			
Depreciation	828	300	1,128
Non-cash distribution of common stock	-0-	18,150	18,150
Increase in accounts payable and accrued liabilities	53,364	15,460	68,824
Other, net	(1,065)	-0-	(1,065)
Net Cash Used in Operating Activities	(246,050)	(410,088)	(656,138)
Cash Flows from Investing Activities			
Purchase of property and equipment	(500)	(2,739)	(3,239)
Net Cash Used in Investing Activities	(500)	(2,739)	(3,239)
Cash Flows from Financing Activities			
Proceeds from issuance of common stock upon exercise of options	70,500	-0-	70,500
Proceeds from sale of common stock	148	-0-	663,230
Net Cash Provided by Financing Activities	70,648	-0-	733,730
Net Increase (Decrease) in Cash and Equivalents	(175,902)	(412,827)	74,353
Cash and Equivalents, Beginning of Period	250,255	663,082	-0-
Cash and Equivalents, End of Period	$ 74,353	$250,255	$ 74,353

Example 11–5: Description of Development Stage Operations

Prostech Corp. (Company) was incorporated on July 1, 1998, in Delaware. Shares of Common Stock of the Company totaling 5,616,528 shares were sold for a total cash consideration of $663,082.

The Company is a development stage entity and is primarily engaged in the development of pharmaceuticals to treat urological disorders. The initial focus of the Company's research and development efforts will be the generation of products for the treatment and diagnosis of prostate cancer. The production and marketing of the Company's products and its ongoing research and development activities will be subject to extensive regulation by numerous governmental authorities in the United States. Prior to marketing in the United States, any drug developed by the Company must undergo rigorous preclinical (animal) and clinical (human) testing and an extensive regulatory approval process implemented by the Food and Drug Administration (FDA) under the Food, Drug and Cosmetic Act. The Company has limited experience in conducting and managing the preclinical and clinical testing necessary to obtain regulatory approval. There can be no assurance that the Company will not encounter problems in clinical trials that will cause the Company or the FDA to delay or suspend clinical trials.

The Company's success will depend in part on its ability to obtain patents and product license rights, maintain trade secrets, and operate without infringing on the proprietary rights of others, both in the United States and other countries. There can be no assurance that patents issued to or licensed by the Company will not be challenged, invalidated, or circumvented, or that the rights granted thereunder will provide proprietary protection or competitive advantages to the Company.

For the year ended December 31, 2000, revenues of $193,500 were from a research agreement. The Company has no significant operating history and, from July 1, 1998, (inception) to December 31, 2000, has generated a net loss of $743,175. The accompanying financial statements for the year ended December 31, 2000, have been prepared assuming the Company will continue as a going concern. During the year 2001, management intends to raise additional debt and/or equity financing to fund future operations and to provide additional working capital. However, there is no assurance that such financing will be consummated or obtained in sufficient amounts necessary to meet the Company's needs.

The accompanying financial statements do not include any adjustments to reflect the possible future effects on the recoverability and classification of assets or the amounts and classifications of liabilities that may result from the possible inability of the Company to continue as a going concern.

Example 11–6: Disclosure That Company Was in the Development Stage in Prior Years

> **Note:** Example 11–6 assumes that the Company is considered an operating company in the year 2001 and that 2000 was the last year that the Company was in the development stage.

Prostech Corp. (Company) was incorporated on July 1, 1998, in Delaware and was in the development stage through December 31, 2000. The year 2001 is the first year during which the Company is considered an operating company and is no longer in the development stage.

CHAPTER 12
FINANCIAL INSTRUMENTS, DERIVATIVES, AND HEDGING ACTIVITIES

CONTENTS

EXECUTIVE SUMMARY

Financial Instruments

A *financial instrument* is defined as cash, evidence of an ownership interest in an entity, or a contract that meets the following criteria:

1. Imposes on one entity a contractual obligation (a) to deliver cash or another financial instrument to a second entity or (b) to exchange other financial instruments on potentially unfavorable terms with the second entity, and

2. Conveys to that second entity a contractual right (a) to receive cash or another financial instrument from the first entity or (b) to exchange other financial instruments on potentially favorable terms with the first entity.

Generally accepted accounting principles (GAAP) require all entities to disclose the fair value of their financial instruments and certain information relating to these financial instruments; however, certain disclosures are optional for nonpublic companies that (1) have total assets on the financial statement date of less than $100 million and (2) have no instrument that, in whole or in part, is accounted for as a derivative instrument.

When disclosing the fair value of financial instruments, both assets and liabilities that are recognized and not recognized in the balance sheet should be included, as long as it is practicable to estimate fair value. The fair value of a financial instrument is the amount at which the instrument could be exchanged in a current transaction between willing parties, other than in a forced or liquidation sale. If a quoted market price is available for a financial instrument, the fair value to be disclosed for that instrument is the product of the number of trading units of the instrument multiplied by that market price.

Disclosure of information about significant concentrations of credit risk from an individual counterparty or groups of counterparties for all financial instruments is also required.

Derivative Instruments and Hedging Activities

A *derivative instrument* is a financial instrument or other contract with all three of the following characteristics:

1. It has (a) one or more underlyings and (b) one or more notional amounts or payment provisions or both. An *underlying* is a specified interest rate, security price, commodity price, foreign exchange rate, index of prices or rates, or other variable. An underlying may be a price or rate of an asset or liability but is not the asset or liability itself. A *notional amount* is a number of currency units, shares, bushels, pounds, or other units specified in the contract.
2. It requires no initial net investment or an initial net investment that is smaller than would be required for other types of contracts that would be expected to have a similar response to changes in market factors.
3. Its terms permit or require net settlement, it can readily be settled net by a means outside the contract, or it provides for delivery of an asset that puts the recipient in a position not substantially different from net settlement.

GAAP require that all derivatives (both assets and liabilities) be recognized in the statement of financial position at fair value. Each derivative instrument is classified in one of the following four categories: (1) no hedge designation, (2) fair value hedge, (3) cash flow hedge, and (4) foreign currency hedge.

Gains and losses on derivative instruments are accounted for as follows:

1. *No hedge designation.* The gain or loss should be recognized currently in earnings.
2. *Fair value hedge.* The gain or loss should be recognized currently in earnings.
3. *Cash flow hedge.* The effective portion of the gain or loss (i.e., change in fair value) on a derivative designated as a cash flow hedge is reported in other comprehensive income (outside net income). The remaining gain or loss, if any, should be recognized currently in earnings. Amounts in accumulated other comprehensive income are reclassified into earnings (net income) in the same period in which the hedged forecasted transaction affects earnings.
4. *Foreign currency hedge.* The gain or loss should be accounted for as follows:
   a. The gain or loss on the hedging derivative or nonderivative instrument in a hedge of a foreign currency-denominated firm commitment and the offsetting loss or gain on the hedged firm commitment should be recognized currently in earnings in the same accounting period.
   b. The gain or loss on the hedging derivative instrument in a hedge of an available-for-sale security and the offsetting loss or gain on the hedged available-for-sale security should be recognized currently in earnings in the same accounting period.
   c. The effective portion of the gain or loss (i.e., change in fair value) on the hedging derivative instrument in a hedge of a forecasted foreign currency-denominated transaction should be reported as a component of other comprehensive income (outside net income) and reclassified into earnings in the same period or periods during which the hedged forecasted transaction affects earnings. The remaining gain or loss on the hedging instrument should be recognized currently in earnings.
   d. The gain or loss on the hedging derivative or nonderivative instrument in a hedge of a net investment in a foreign operation should be reported in other comprehensive income (outside net income) as part of the cumulative translation adjustment to the extent it is effective as a hedge.

Authoritative Literature

FAS-80	Accounting for Futures Contracts (superseded by FAS-133, which is effective for all fiscal quarters of fiscal years beginning after June 15, 2000)

FAS-105	Disclosure of Information about Financial Instruments with Off-Balance-Sheet Risk and Financial Instruments with Concentrations of Credit Risk (superseded by FAS-133, which is effective for all fiscal quarters of fiscal years beginning after June 15, 2000)
FAS-107	Disclosures about Fair Value of Financial Instruments (amended by FAS-133, which is effective for all fiscal quarters of fiscal years beginning after June 15, 2000)
FAS-119	Disclosure about Derivative Financial Instruments and Fair Value of Financial Instruments (superseded by FAS-133, which is effective for all fiscal quarters of fiscal years beginning after June 15, 2000)
FAS-126	Exemption from Certain Required Disclosures about Financial Instruments for Certain Nonpublic Entities
FAS-133	Accounting for Derivative Instruments and Hedging Activities (effective for all fiscal quarters of fiscal years beginning after June 15, 2000)
FAS-137	Accounting for Derivative Instruments and Hedging Activities—Deferral of the Effective Date of FASB Statement No. 133
FAS-138	Accounting for Certain Derivative Instruments and Certain Hedging Activities
FAS-140	Accounting for Transfers and Servicing of Financial Assets and Extinguishments of Liabilities
FIN-39	Offsetting of Amounts Related to Certain Contracts
FIN-41	Offsetting of Amounts Related to Certain Repurchase and Reverse Repurchase Agreements

DISCLOSURE REQUIREMENTS

In June 1998, the FASB issued Statement No. 133 (Accounting for Derivative Instruments and Hedging Activities). FAS-133 establishes accounting and reporting standards for derivative instruments and requires that an entity recognize all derivatives as either assets or liabilities in the statement of financial position and measure those instruments at fair value. FAS-133 was originally effective for all fiscal quarters of fiscal years beginning after June 15, 1999. Due to the complexity of FAS-133, the FASB issued, in June 1999, FAS-137 (Accounting for Derivative Instruments and Hedging Activities—Deferral of the Effective Date of FASB Statement No. 133), which delays the effective date of FAS-133 by one year. Therefore, FAS-133 is effective for all fiscal quarters of fiscal years beginning after June 15, 2000. In addition, in June 2000 FASB issued FAS-138 (Accounting for Certain

Derivative Instruments and Certain Hedging Activities), which amended FAS-133 to address a limited number of issues.

This section discusses the disclosure requirements in effect before and subsequent to the adoption of FAS-133, as amended by FAS-138.

Financial Instruments

Disclosure Requirements If FAS-133, as Amended by FAS-138, Has Not Been Adopted (Note: FAS-133 and FAS-138 are effective for all fiscal quarters of fiscal years beginning after June 15, 2000.)

1. For financial instruments with off-balance-sheet risk, the following disclosures should be made by category of financial instrument:
   a. The face or contract amount (or notional principal amount if there is no face or contract amount) (FAS-105, par. 17)
   b. The nature and terms of the financial instruments, including at a minimum a discussion of (i) the credit and market risk of those instruments, (ii) the cash requirements of those instruments, and (iii) the related accounting policy (FAS-105, par. 17)
   c. The disclosures required in items a and b above should (FAS-119, pars. 8 and 14):
      — Distinguish between financial instruments held or issued for trading purposes (including dealing and other trading activities measured at fair value with gains and losses recognized in earnings) and financial instruments held or issued for purposes other than trading
      — Include a description of the leverage features and their general effect on the credit and market risk, cash requirements, and related accounting policy
      — Be made for options and other derivatives that do not have off-balance-sheet risk
      — Be made by category of financial instrument (e.g., class of financial instrument, business activity, or risk), distinguishing between those held for trading purposes and those held for purposes other than trading
2. For financial instruments with off-balance-sheet credit risk, the following disclosures should be made (FAS-105, par. 18):
   a. The amount of accounting loss the entity would incur if any party to the financial instrument failed completely to perform according to the terms of the contract and the collateral or other security, if any, for the amount due proved to be of no value to the entity

b. The entity's policy of requiring collateral or other security to support financial instruments subject to credit risk

c. Information about the entity's access to that collateral or other security

d. The nature and a brief description of the collateral or other security supporting those financial instruments

3. Significant concentrations of credit risk arising from all financial instruments should be disclosed, including the following about each significant concentration (FAS-105, par. 20):

   a. Information about the activity, region, or economic characteristic that identifies the concentration

   b. The amount of accounting loss caused by credit risk the entity would incur if parties to the financial instruments that make up the concentration failed completely to perform according to the terms of the contract and the collateral or other security, if any, for the amount due proved to be of no value to the entity

   c. The entity's policy of requiring collateral or other security to support financial instruments subject to credit risk

   d. Information about the entity's access to the collateral or other security

   e. The nature and a brief description of the collateral or other security supporting those financial instruments

4. The following information about fair value of financial instruments should be disclosed either in the body of the financial statements or in the accompanying notes (These disclosures about the fair value of financial instruments are optional for an entity that meets *all* of the following criteria: (i) the entity is a nonpublic entity, (ii) the entity's total assets are less than $100 million on the date of the financial statements, and (iii) the entity has not held or issued any derivative financial instruments during the reporting period.) (FAS-107, pars. 10 and 14; FAS-119, par. 15):

   a. Fair value of financial instruments for which it is practicable to estimate fair value (For trade receivables and payables, no disclosure is required when the carrying amount approximates fair value). In connection with this item:

      —When disclosure is made in the accompanying notes, the fair value should be presented together with the related carrying amount in a form that makes it clear whether the fair value and carrying amount represent assets or liabilities and how the carrying amounts relate to what is reported in the balance sheet

      — Disclosure should be made in a single note or, if disclosed in more than a single note, one of the notes should include a summary table that contains the fair value and related carrying amounts and cross-references to the locations of the remaining disclosures

b. The methods and significant assumptions used to estimate the fair value of financial instruments (The disclosures should distinguish between financial instruments held or issued for trading purposes, including dealing and other trading activities measured at fair value with gains and losses recognized in earnings, and financial instruments held or issued for purposes other than trading.)

c. In disclosing the fair value of a derivative financial instrument, the entity should not (i) combine, aggregate, or net that fair value with the fair value of nonderivative financial instruments or (ii) net that fair value with the fair value of other derivative financial instruments, except to the extent that the offsetting of carrying amounts in the balance sheet is permitted

d. For financial instruments for which it is concluded that estimating fair value is not practicable, (i) information related to estimating the fair value of the financial instrument (such as the carrying amount, effective interest rate, and maturity) and (ii) the reasons why it is not practicable to estimate fair value

5. If the entity transfers financial instruments during the period and it is not practicable to estimate the fair values of the assets obtained or liabilities incurred in the transfer, the assets and liabilities should be described and the reasons why it is not practicable to estimate their fair value should be disclosed (FAS-140, par. 17).

Disclosure Requirements If FAS-133, as Amended by FAS-138, Has Been Adopted (Note: FAS-133 and FAS-138 are effective for all fiscal quarters of fiscal years beginning after June 15, 2000.)

1. Significant concentrations of credit risk arising from all financial instruments should be disclosed, including the following about each significant concentration (FAS-133, par. 531):

   a. Information about the activity, region, or economic characteristic that identifies the concentration

   b. The maximum amount of loss due to credit risk that, based on the gross fair value of the financial instrument, the entity would incur if parties to the financial instruments that make up the concentration failed completely to perform according to the terms of the contracts and the collateral or other security, if any, for the amount due proved to be of no value to the entity

c. The entity's policy of requiring collateral or other security to support financial instruments subject to credit risk

d. Information about the entity's access to the collateral or other security

e. The nature and a brief description of the collateral or other security supporting those financial instruments

f. The entity's policy of entering into master netting arrangements to mitigate the credit risk of financial instruments, information about the arrangements for which the entity is a party, and a brief description of the terms of those arrangements, including the extent to which they would reduce the entity's maximum amount of loss due to credit risk

2. The following information about fair value of financial instruments should be disclosed either in the body of the financial statements or in the accompanying notes (These disclosures about the fair value of financial instruments are optional for an entity that meets *all* of the following criteria: (i) the entity is a nonpublic entity, (ii) the entity's total assets are less than $100 million on the date of the financial statements, and (iii) the entity has not held or issued any derivative financial instruments during the reporting period.) (FAS-107, pars. 10 and 14; FAS-133, pars. 531 and 532):

   a. Fair value of financial instruments for which it is practicable to estimate fair value (For trade receivables and payables, no disclosure is required when the carrying amount approximates fair value.) In connection with this item:

      — When disclosure is made in the accompanying notes, the fair value should be presented together with the related carrying amount in a form that makes it clear whether the fair value and carrying amount represent assets or liabilities and how the carrying amounts relate to what is reported in the balance sheet

      — Disclosure should be made in a single note or, if disclosed in more than a single note, one of the notes should include a summary table that contains the fair value and related carrying amounts and cross-references to the locations of the remaining disclosures

   b. The methods and significant assumptions used to estimate the fair value of financial instruments

   c. In disclosing the fair value of a financial instrument, the entity should not net that fair value with the fair value of other financial instruments, except to the extent that the offsetting of carrying amounts in the balance sheet is permitted

   d. For financial instruments for which it is concluded that estimating fair value is not practicable, (i) information related to estimating the fair value of the financial instrument (such as the carrying amount, effective interest rate, and maturity) and (ii) the reasons why it is not practicable to estimate fair value

3. If the entity transfers financial instruments during the period and it is not practicable to estimate the fair values of the assets obtained or liabilities incurred in the transfer, the assets and liabilities should be described and the reasons why it is not practicable to estimate their fair value should be disclosed (FAS-140, par. 17).

Derivative Instruments and Hedging Activities

Disclosure Requirements If FAS-133, as Amended by FAS-138, Has Not Been Adopted (Note: FAS-133 and FAS-138 are effective for all fiscal quarters of fiscal years beginning after June 15, 2000.)

1. The following disclosures should be made, either in the body of the financial statements or in the accompanying notes, about derivative financial instruments held or issued for trading purposes (FAS-119, par. 10):
   a. The average fair value of those derivative financial instruments during the reporting period, presented together with the related fair value at the balance sheet date and distinguishing between those that are assets and those that are liabilities
   b. The net gains or losses (often referred to as *net trading revenues*) arising from trading activities during the reporting period disaggregated by class, business activity, risk, or other category that is consistent with the management of those activities and where those net trading gains or losses are reported in the income statement (If the disaggregation is other than by class, the entity also should describe for each category the classes of derivative financial instruments, other financial instruments, and nonfinancial assets and liabilities from which the net trading gains or losses arose.)
2. The following disclosures should be made about derivative financial instruments held or issued for purposes other than trading (FAS-119, par. 11):
   a. The entity's objectives for holding or issuing the instruments
   b. The context needed to understand the entity's objectives
   c. The entity's strategies for achieving those objectives, including the classes of derivative financial instruments used
   d. A description of how each class of derivative financial instrument is reported in the financial statements, including the policies for recognizing (or reasons for not recognizing)

and measuring the derivative financial instruments held or issued, and when recognized, where those instruments and related gains and losses are reported in the balance sheet and income statement

e. For derivative financial instruments that are held or issued and accounted for as hedges of anticipated transactions (both firm commitments and forecasted transactions for which there is no firm commitment), the following should be disclosed:

— A description of the anticipated transactions whose risks are hedged, including the period of time until the anticipated transactions are expected to occur

— A description of the classes of derivative financial instruments used to hedge the anticipated transactions

— The amount of hedging gains and losses explicitly deferred

— A description of the transactions or other events that result in the recognition in earnings of gains or losses deferred by hedge accounting

3. In disclosing the fair value of a derivative financial instrument, the entity should not (i) combine, aggregate, or net that fair value with the fair value of nonderivative financial instruments or (ii) net that fair value with the fair value of other derivative financial instruments, except to the extent that the offsetting of carrying amounts in the balance sheet is permitted (FAS-119, par. 15).

4. The following disclosures should be made for futures contracts that have been accounted for as hedges (FAS-80, par. 12):

   a. The nature of the assets, liabilities, firm commitments, or anticipated transactions that are hedged with futures contracts

   b. The method of accounting for the futures contracts

   c. The description of the events or transactions that result in recognition in income of changes in value of the futures contracts

Disclosure Requirements If FAS-133, as Amended by FAS-138, Has Been Adopted (Note: FAS-133 and FAS-138 are effective for all fiscal quarters of fiscal years beginning after June 15, 2000.)

1. The following disclosures should be made for all derivative instruments (and for nonderivative instruments designated and qualifying as hedging instruments) (FAS-133, par. 44):

   a. The entity's objectives for holding or issuing the instruments

   b. The context needed to understand the entity's objectives

c. The entity's strategies for achieving these objectives

d. The entity's risk management policy for each type of hedge, including a description of the items or transactions for which risks are hedged

e. For derivative instruments not designated as hedging instruments, the purpose of the derivative activity

f. The disclosures for items a through e above should distinguish between:

— Derivative instruments (and nonderivative instruments) designated as fair value hedging instruments

— Derivative instruments designated as cash flow hedging instruments

— Derivative instruments (and nonderivative instruments) designated as hedging instruments for hedges of the foreign currency exposure of a net investment in a foreign operation

— All other derivatives

2. The following disclosures should be made for derivative instruments designated and qualifying as fair value hedging instruments (as well as nonderivative instruments that may give rise to foreign currency transaction gains or losses) and for the related hedged items, for each reporting period for which a complete set of financial statements is presented (FAS-133, par. 45):

   a. The net gain or loss recognized in earnings during the reporting period representing (i) the amount of the hedges' ineffectiveness and (ii) the component of the derivative instruments' gain or loss, if any, excluded from the assessment of hedge effectiveness, and a description of where the net gain or loss is reported in the statement of income or other statement of financial performance

   b. The amount of net gain or loss recognized in earnings when a hedged firm commitment no longer qualifies as a fair value hedge

3. The following disclosures should be made for derivative instruments that have been designated and qualifying as cash flow hedging instruments and for the related hedged transactions (FAS-133, par. 45):

   a. The net gain or loss recognized in earnings during the reporting period representing (i) the amount of the hedges' ineffectiveness and (ii) the component of the derivative instruments' gain or loss, if any, excluded from the assessment of hedge effectiveness, and a description of where the net gain or loss is reported in the statement of income or other statement of financial performance

b. A description of the transactions or other events that will result in the reclassification into earnings of gains and losses that are reported in accumulated other comprehensive income, and the estimated net amount of the existing gains or losses at the reporting date that is expected to be reclassified into earnings within the next 12 months

c. The maximum length of time over which the entity is hedging its exposure to the variability in future cash flows for forecasted transactions excluding those forecasted transactions related to the payment of variable interest on existing financial instruments

d. The amount of gains and losses reclassified into earnings as a result of the discontinuance of cash flow hedges because it is probable that the original forecasted transactions will not occur

4. The following disclosure should be made for derivative instruments designated and qualifying as hedging instruments for hedges of the foreign currency exposure of a net investment in a foreign operation (as well as for nonderivative instruments that may give rise to foreign currency transaction gains or losses) (FAS-133, par. 45):

   a. The net amount of gains or losses included in the cumulative translation adjustment during the reporting period

5. The following disclosures should be made as part of reporting changes in the components of other comprehensive income (FAS-133, pars. 46 and 47):

   a. The net gain or loss on derivative instruments designated and qualifying as cash flow hedging instruments that are reported in comprehensive income should be displayed as a separate classification within other comprehensive income

   b. As part of the disclosures of accumulated other comprehensive income, the following should be disclosed separately:

      — The beginning and ending accumulated derivative gain or loss

      — The related net change associated with current-period hedging transactions

      — The net amount of any reclassification into earnings

EXAMPLES OF FINANCIAL STATEMENT DISCLOSURES

The following sample disclosures are available on the accompanying disc. For additional information, see the following chapters in this book:

- Chapter 2, "Accounting Policies," for related additional disclosures, including concentrations of credit risk
- Chapter 6, "Commitments," for related additional disclosures, including letters of credit
- Chapter 9, "Contingencies, Risks, Uncertainties, and Concentrations," for related additional disclosures, including concentrations of credit risk and financial guarantees
- Chapter 31, "Cash and Cash Equivalents," for related additional disclosures, including cash balances in excess of federally insured limits
- Chapter 32, "Accounts and Notes Receivable," for related additional disclosures, including concentrations of credit risk and transfers of accounts receivable under FAS-140

Illustrative Disclosures Prior to Adoption of FAS-133 (Examples 12–1 to 12–8)

Example 12–1: Disclosure of Issuance of FAS-133

FAS-133 (Accounting for Derivative Instruments and Hedging Activities), as amended by FAS-137 (Accounting for Derivative Instruments and Hedging Activities—Deferral of the Effective Date of FASB Statement No. 133) and FAS-138 (Accounting for Certain Derivative Instruments and Certain Hedging Activities), establishes accounting and reporting standards for derivative financial instruments and hedging activities related to those instruments as well as other hedging activities. This Statement requires that an entity recognize all derivatives as either assets or liabilities in the statement of financial position and measure those instruments at fair value. The Company is required to adopt the new Statement in 2001. The Company is currently evaluating the effect that implementation of the new standard will have on its results of operations and financial position.

Example 12–2: Disclosures about Fair Value of Financial Instruments by a Nonfinancial Entity

The Company uses the following methods and assumptions to estimate the fair value of each class of financial instruments for which it is practicable to estimate such value:

Cash and short-term investments—The carrying amount approximates fair value because of the short maturity of those instruments.

Accounts receivable—The carrying value of accounts receivable approximates fair value due to their short-term nature and historical collectibility.

Long-term investments—The fair values of some investments are estimated based on quoted market prices for those or similar investments. For other investments for which there are no quoted market prices, a reasonable estimate of fair value could not be made without incurring excessive costs. Additional information pertinent to the value of an unquoted investment is provided below.

Accounts payable—The carrying value of accounts payable approximates fair value due to the short-term nature of the obligations.

Long-term debt—The fair value of the Company's long-term debt is estimated based on the quoted market prices for the same or similar issues or on the current rates offered to the Company for debt of the same remaining maturities.

Foreign currency contracts—The fair value of foreign currency contracts (used for hedging purposes) is estimated by obtaining quotes from brokers.

The estimated fair values of the Company's financial instruments are as follows:

	2000		*1999*	
	Carrying Amount	*Fair Value*	*Carrying Amount*	*Fair Value*
Cash and short-term investments	$1,113,000	$1,113,000	$987,000	$987,000
Accounts receivable	3,218,000	3,218,000	2,946,000	2,946,000
Long-term investments for which it is:				
Practicable to estimate fair value	894,000	894,000	716,000	716,000
Not practicable to estimate fair value	477,000	-0-	412,000	-0-
Accounts payable	(1,171,000)	(1,171,000)	(1,342,000)	(1,342,000)
Long-term debt	(1,561,000)	(1,487,000)	(953,000)	(905,000)
Foreign currency contracts	102,000	102,000	91,000	91,000

It was not practicable to estimate the fair value of an investment representing 14% of the issued common stock of an untraded company; that investment is carried at its original cost of $477,000 and $412,000 at December 31, 2000, and December 31, 1999, respectively.

Pertinent financial information reported by the untraded company are as follows:

	2000	*1999*
Total assets	$9,818,000	$8,971,000
Stockholders' equity	$5,100,000	$4,539,000
Revenues	$14,676,000	$13,974,000
Net income	$561,000	$398,000

The Company determined estimated fair value amounts by using available market information and commonly accepted valuation methodologies. However, considerable judgment is required in interpreting market data to develop the estimates of fair value. Accordingly, the estimates presented herein are not necessarily indicative of the amounts that the Company or holders of the instruments could realize in a current market exchange. The use of different assumptions and/or estimation methodologies may have a material effect on the estimated fair values.

Example 12–3: Disclosures about Fair Value of Financial Instruments by a Financial Entity

The Company uses the following methods and assumptions to estimate the fair value of each class of financial instruments for which it is practicable to estimate such value:

Cash and short-term investments—For those short-term instruments, the carrying amount is a reasonable estimate of fair value.

Investment securities and trading account assets—For securities and derivative instruments held for trading purposes (which include bonds, interest rate futures, options, interest rate swaps, securities sold not owned, caps and floors, foreign currency contracts, and forward contracts) and marketable equity securities held for investment purposes, fair values are based on quoted market prices or dealer quotes. For other securities held as investments, fair value equals quoted market price, if available. If a quoted market price is not available, fair value is estimated using quoted market prices for similar securities.

Loan receivables—For certain homogeneous categories of loans, such as some residential mortgages, credit card receivables, and other consumer loans, fair value is estimated using the quoted market prices for securities backed by similar loans, adjusted for differences in loan characteristics. The fair value of other types of loans is estimated by discounting the future cash flows using the current rates at which similar loans would be made to borrowers with similar credit ratings and for the same remaining maturities.

Deposit liabilities—The fair value of demand deposits, savings accounts, and certain money market deposits is the amount payable on demand at the reporting date. The fair value of fixed-maturity certificates of deposit is estimated using the rates currently offered for deposits of similar remaining maturities.

Long-term debt—Rates currently available to the Company for debt with similar terms and remaining maturities are used to estimate fair value of existing debt.

Interest rate swap agreements—The fair value of interest rate swaps (used for hedging purposes) is the estimated amount that the Company would receive or pay to terminate the swap agreements at the reporting date, taking into account current interest rates and the current creditworthiness of the swap counterparties.

Commitments to extend credit, standby letters of credit, and financial guarantees written—The fair value of commitments is estimated using the fees currently charged to enter into similar agreements, taking into account remaining terms of the agreements and the present creditworthiness of the counterparties. For fixed-rate loan commitments, fair value also considers the difference between current levels of interest rates and the committed rates. The fair value of guarantees and letters of credit is based on fees currently charged for similar agreements or on the estimated cost to terminate them or otherwise settle the obligations with the counterparties at the reporting date.

The estimated fair values of the Company's financial instruments are as follows:

	2000		*1999*	
	Carrying Amount	*Fair Value*	*Carrying Amount*	*Fair Value*
Financial assets:				
Cash and short-term investments	$1,230,000	$1,230,000	$1,565000	$1,565,000
Trading account assets	2,341,000	2,341,000	2,978,000	2,978,000
Investment securities	5,033,000	5,033,000	5,622,000	5,622,000
Loans	10,236,000		9,253,000	
Less: allowance for loan losses	(632,000)	-0-	(581,000)	-0-
Loans, net of allowance	9,604,000	9,543,000	8,672,000	8,581,000

	2000		*1999*	
	Carrying Amount	*Fair Value*	*Carrying Amount*	*Fair Value*
Financial liabilities:				
Deposits	11,409,000	11,182,000	10,736,000	10,471,000
Securities sold not owned	618,000	618,000	563,000	563,000
Long-term debt	1,762,0000	1,744,000	1,382,000	1,371,000
Off-balance-sheet instruments:				
Interest rate swaps:				
In a net receivable position	1,075,000	1,043,000	1,123,000	1,094,000
In a net payable position	(1,100,000)	(1,125,000)	(1,178,000)	(1,152,000)
Commitments to extend credit	(5,608,000)	(5,532,000)	(4,923,000)	(4,892,000)
Standby letters of credit	(674,000)	(674,000)	(532,000)	(532,000)
Financial guarantees written	(418,000)	(410,000)	(323,000)	(307,000)

The Company determined the estimated fair value amounts by using available market information and commonly accepted valuation methodologies. However, considerable judgment is required in interpreting market data to develop the estimates of fair value. Accordingly, the estimates presented herein are not necessarily indicative of the amounts that the Company or holders of the instruments could realize in a current market exchange. The use of different assumptions and/or estimation methodologies may have a material effect on the estimated fair values.

Example 12–4: Concentration of Credit Risk Virtually Limited and Collateral Is Not Required

Financial instruments that potentially subject the Company to concentrations of credit risk consist primarily of cash and cash equivalents and accounts receivable. The Company places its cash and cash equivalents with high quality financial institutions and limits the amount of credit exposure with any one institution. Concentrations of credit risk with respect to accounts receivable are limited because a large number of geographically diverse customers make up the Company's customer base, thus spreading the trade credit risk. At December 31, 2000, and December 31, 1999, no single group or customer represents greater than 10% of total accounts receivable. The Company controls credit risk through credit approvals, credit limits, and monitoring procedures. The Company performs credit evaluations of its commercial and industrial customers but generally does not require collateral to support accounts receivable.

Example 12–5: Description of Objectives and Strategies for Holding and Issuing Derivatives

The Company uses derivative instruments to manage well-defined interest rate and foreign currency exposures. The Company does not use derivative instruments for speculative or trading purposes. The criteria used to determine if hedge accounting treatment is appropriate are (a) the designation of the hedge to an underlying exposure, (b) whether or not overall risk is being reduced, and (c) if there is a correlation between the value of the derivative instrument and the underlying obligation.

The Company has operations in a number of countries and has intercompany transactions among them and, as a result, is exposed to changes in foreign currency exchange rates. The Company manages most of these exposures on a consolidated basis, which allows netting certain exposures to take advantage of any natural offsets. To the extent the net exposures are hedged, forward contracts are used. Gains and losses on these foreign currency hedges are included in income in the period in which the exchange rates change. Gains and losses have not been material to the consolidated financial statements. At December 31, 2000, and December 31, 1999, the Company had outstanding foreign exchange forward contracts in Australian dollars and British pounds, maturing in up to 12 months for both years, totaling $11 million and $9 million, respectively.

In addition, the Company enters into interest rate swap agreements to manage interest costs and risks associated with changing interest rates. The differentials paid or received on interest rate agreements are accrued and recognized as adjustments to interest expense. Gains and losses realized upon settlement of these agreements are deferred and amortized to interest expense over a period relevant to the agreement if the underlying hedged instrument remains outstanding, or immediately if the underlying hedged instrument is settled. The Company has interest rate swap agreements in place to pay fixed interest rates in exchange for floating interest rate payments. At December 31, 2000, and December 31, 1999, the notional principal amount outstanding of these agreements was $4 million and $3 million, respectively.

The Company is exposed to credit losses in the event of non-performance by the counterparties to its interest rate swap and foreign exchange contracts. The Company does not anticipate non-performance by the counterparties. The Company does not obtain collateral or other security to support financial instruments subject to credit risk but monitors the credit standing of the counterparties and enters into agreements only with financial institution counterparties with a credit rating of "A" or better.

Example 12–6: Interest Rate Swap Agreements

The Company enters into interest rate swap agreements to manage interest rate exposure. The differential to be paid or received under these agreements is accrued consistent with the terms of the agreements and is recognized in interest expense over the term of the related debt using a method that approximates the effective interest method. The related amounts payable to or receivable from counterparties are included in other liabilities or assets. The fair value of the swap agreements and changes in the fair value as a result of changes in market interest rates are not recognized in the financial statements.

The Company has entered into interest rate swap agreements to reduce the effect of changes in interest rates on its floating rate long-term debt. At December 31, 2000, the Company had outstanding 2 interest rate swap agreements with commercial banks, having a total notional principal amount of $5 million. Those agreements effectively change the Company's interest rate exposure on its $2 million floating rate notes due 2004 to a fixed 11% and its $3 million floating rate notes due 2006 to a fixed 11.5%. The interest rate swap agreements mature at the time the related notes mature. The Company is exposed to credit loss in the event of nonperformance by the other parties to the interest rate swap agreements. However, the Company does not anticipate nonperformance by the counterparties.

Example 12–7: Foreign Exchange Contracts

The Company enters into foreign exchange contracts as a hedge against foreign accounts payable. Market value gains and losses are recognized, and the resulting credit or debit offsets foreign exchange gains or losses on those payables. At December 31, 2000, the Company had contracts maturing June 30, 2001, to purchase $12.9 million in foreign currency (18 million deutsche marks and 5 million Swiss francs at the spot rate on that date).

> **Note:** See Chapter 14, "Foreign Operations and Currency Translation," for additional examples of disclosures of foreign exchange contracts.

Example 12–8: Commodity Contracts

The Company is exposed to risk from fluctuating prices for steel used in the manufacture of its products. Some of this risk is hedged through commodity swaps executed over the counter with a commercial bank. The Company utilizes commodity swaps to effectively fix the price the Company will pay for steel, which is a principal component in the manufacturing process, over the life of the swap. Cost of products sold reflects the commodity cost including the effects of the commodity swaps. At December 31, 2000, and December 31, 1999, $8 million and $7 million, respectively, of commodity swaps were outstanding, maturing through December 31, 2002. The maturity of the contracts highly correlates to the actual purchases of the commodity. Under such contracts, the Company pays the counterparty at a fixed rate and receives from the counterparty a floating rate per pound of steel. Only the net differential is actually paid or received, and the amount is calculated based on the notional amounts under the contracts.

The use of such commodity swaps effectively protects the Company against an increase in the price of steel, to the extent of the notional amount under the contract. This also effectively prevents the Company from benefiting in the event of a decrease in the price of steel, to the extent of the notional amount under the contract. The fair value of commodity swaps at December 31, 2000, and December 31, 1999, was unfavorable, $400,000 and $650,000, respectively, based on dealer quotes. This fair value has not been recorded by the Company at December 31, 2000, and December 31, 1999, and will be reflected in the cost of the commodity as it is actually purchased.

Illustrative Disclosures Subsequent to Adoption of FAS-133 (Examples 12–9 to 12–17)

Example 12–9: Initial Application of FAS-133 Results in Transition Adjustment of Accumulated Other Comprehensive Income

Effective January 1, 2001, the Company adopted Financial Accounting Standards Board Statement No. 133 (Accounting for Derivative Instruments and Hedging Activities), as amended by FAS-138 (Accounting for Certain Derivative Instruments and Certain Hedging Activities), which requires that all derivative instruments be recorded on the balance sheet at fair value. On the date derivative contracts are entered into, the Company designates the derivative as either (a) a hedge of the fair value of a recognized asset or liability or of an unrecognized firm commitment (fair value hedge), (b) a hedge of a forecasted transaction or of the variability of cash flows to be received or paid related to a recognized asset or liability (cash flow hedge), or (c) a hedge of a net investment in a foreign operation (net investment hedge).

Changes in the fair value of derivatives are recorded each period in current earnings or other comprehensive income, depending on whether a derivative is designated as part of a hedge transaction and, if it is, depending on the type of hedge transaction. For fair value hedge transactions, changes in fair value of the derivative instrument are generally offset in the income statement by changes in the fair value of the item being hedged. For cash-flow hedge transactions, changes in the fair value of the derivative instrument are reported in other comprehensive income. For net investment hedge transactions, changes in the fair value are recorded as a component of the foreign currency translation account that is also included in other comprehensive income. The gains and losses on cash flow hedge transactions that are reported in other comprehensive income are reclassified to earnings in the periods in which earnings are effected by the variability of the cash flows of the hedged item. The ineffective portions of all hedges are recognized in current period earnings.

Upon initial application of FAS-133 in 2001, the Company recorded the fair value of the existing interest rate swap contracts on the Balance Sheet and a corresponding unrecognized gain of $42,000 as a cumulative effect adjustment of accumulated other comprehensive income. Of that amount, approximately $28,000 is expected to be transferred to earnings during 2002.

Example 12–10: Disclosures about Fair Value of Financial Instruments by a Nonfinancial Entity

The Company uses the following methods and assumptions to estimate the fair value of each class of financial instruments for which it is practicable to estimate such value:

Cash and short-term investments—The carrying amount approximates fair value because of the short maturity of those instruments.

Accounts receivable—The carrying value of accounts receivable approximates fair value due to their short-term nature and historical collectibility.

Long-term investments—The fair values of some investments are estimated based on quoted market prices for those or similar investments. For other investments for which there are no quoted market prices, a reasonable estimate of fair value could not be made without incurring excessive costs. Additional information pertinent to the value of an unquoted investment is provided below.

Accounts payable—The carrying value of accounts payable approximates fair value due to the short-term nature of the obligations.

Long-term debt—The fair value of the Company's long-term debt is estimated based on the quoted market prices for the same or similar issues or on the current rates offered to the Company for debt of the same remaining maturities.

Foreign currency contracts—The fair value of foreign currency contracts (used for hedging purposes) is estimated by obtaining quotes from brokers.

The estimated fair values of the Company's financial instruments are as follows:

	2000		*1999*	
	Carrying Amount	*Fair Value*	*Carrying Amount*	*Fair Value*
Cash and short-term investments	$1,113,000	$1,113,000	$987,000	$987,000
Accounts receivable	3,218,000	3,218,000	2,946,000	2,946,000
Long-term investments for which it is:				
Practicable to estimate fair value	894,000	894,000	716,000	716,000
Not practicable to estimate fair value	477,000	-0-	412,000	-0-
Accounts payable	(1,171,000)	(1,171,000)	(1,342,000)	(1,342,000)
Long-term debt	(1,561,000)	(1,487,000)	(953,000)	(905,000)
Foreign currency contracts	102,000	102,000	91,000	91,000

It was not practicable to estimate the fair value of an investment representing 14% of the issued common stock of an untraded company; that investment is carried at its original cost of $477,000 and $412,000 at December 31, 2000, and December 31, 1999, respectively. Pertinent financial information reported by the untraded company are as follows:

	2000	*1999*
Total assets	$9,818,000	$8,971,000
Stockholders' equity	$5,100,000	$4,539,000
Revenues	$14,676,000	$13,974,000
Net income	$561,000	$398,000

The company determined the estimated fair value amounts by using available market information and commonly accepted valuation methodologies. However, considerable judgment is required in interpreting market data to develop the estimates of fair value. Accordingly, the estimates presented herein are not necessarily indicative of the amounts that the Company or holders of the instruments could realize in a current market exchange. The use of different assumptions and/or estimation methodologies may have a material effect on the estimated fair values.

Example 12–11: Disclosures about Fair Value of Financial Instruments by a Financial Entity

The Company uses the following methods and assumptions to estimate the fair value of each class of financial instruments for which it is practicable to estimate such value:

Cash and short-term investments—For those short-term instruments, the carrying amount is a reasonable estimate of fair value.

Investment securities and trading account assets—For securities and derivative instruments held for trading purposes (which include bonds, interest rate futures, options, interest rate swaps, securities sold not owned, caps and floors, foreign currency contracts, and forward contracts) and marketable equity securities held for investment purposes, fair values are based on quoted market prices or dealer quotes. For other securities held as investments, fair value equals quoted market price, if available. If a quoted market price is not available, fair value is estimated using quoted market prices for similar securities.

Loan receivables—For certain homogeneous categories of loans, such as some residential mortgages, credit card receivables, and other consumer loans, fair value is estimated using the quoted market prices for securities backed by similar loans, adjusted for differences in loan characteristics. The fair value of other types of loans is estimated by discounting the future cash flows using the current rates at which similar loans would be made to borrowers with similar credit ratings and for the same remaining maturities.

Deposit liabilities—The fair value of demand deposits, savings accounts, and certain money market deposits is the amount payable on demand at the reporting date. The fair value of fixed-maturity certificates of deposit is estimated using the rates currently offered for deposits of similar remaining maturities.

Long-term debt—Rates currently available to the Company for debt with similar terms and remaining maturities are used to estimate fair value of existing debt.

Commitments to extend credit, standby letters of credit, and financial guarantees written—The fair value of commitments is estimated using the fees currently charged to enter into similar agreements, taking into account remaining terms of the agreements and the present creditworthiness of the counterparties. For fixed-rate loan commitments, fair value also considers the difference between current levels of interest rates and the committed rates. The fair value of guarantees and letters of credit is based on fees currently charged for similar agreements or on the estimated cost to terminate them or otherwise settle the obligations with the counterparties at the reporting date.

The estimated fair values of the Company's financial instruments are as follows:

	2000		*1999*	
	Carrying Amount	*Fair Value*	*Carrying Amount*	*Fair Value*
Financial assets:				
Cash and short-term investments	$1,230,000	$1,230,000	$1,565000	$1,565,000
Trading account assets	2,341,000	2,341,000	2,978,000	2,978,000
Investment securities	5,033,000	5,033,000	5,622,000	5,622,000
Loans	10,236,000	-0-	9,253,000	-0-
Less: allowance for loan losses	(632,000)	-0-	(581,000)	-0-
Loans, net of allowance	9,604,000	9,543,000	8,672,000	8,581,000
Financial liabilities:				
Deposits	11,409,000	11,182,000	10,736,000	10,471,000
Securities sold not owned	618,000	618,000	563,000	563,000
Long-term debt	1,762,0000	1,744,000	1,382,000	1,371,000
Off-balance-sheet instruments:				
Commitments to extend credit	(5,608,000)	(5,532,000)	(4,923,000)	(4,892,000)
Standby letters of credit	(674,000)	(674,000)	(532,000)	(532,000)
Financial guarantees written	(418,000)	(410,000)	(323,000)	(307,000)

The Company has determined the estimated fair value amounts by using available market information and commonly accepted valuation methodologies. However, considerable judgment is required in interpreting market data to develop the estimates of fair value. Accordingly, the estimates presented herein are not necessarily indicative of the amounts that the Company or holders of the instruments could realize in a current market exchange. The use of different assumptions and/or estimation methodologies may have a material effect on the estimated fair values.

Example 12–12: Concentration of Credit Risk Virtually Limited and Collateral Is Not Required

Financial instruments that potentially subject the Company to concentrations of credit risk consist primarily of cash and cash equivalents and accounts receivable. The Company places its cash and cash equivalents with high quality financial institutions and limits the amount of credit exposure with any one institution. Concentrations of credit risk with respect to accounts receivable are limited because a large number of geographically diverse customers make up the Company's customer base, thus spreading the trade credit risk. At December 31, 2000, and December 31, 1999, no single group or customer represents greater than 10% of total accounts receivable. The Company controls credit risk through credit approvals, credit limits, and monitoring procedures. The Company performs credit evaluations of its commercial and industrial customers but generally does not require collateral to support accounts receivable.

Example 12–13: Description of Objectives and Strategies for Holding and Issuing Derivatives

The Company holds and issues derivative financial instruments for the purpose of hedging the risks of certain identifiable and anticipated transactions. In general, the types of risks hedged are those relating to the variability of future earnings and cash flows caused by movements in foreign currency exchange rates and changes in commodity prices and interest rates. The Company documents its risk management strategy and hedge effectiveness at the inception of and during the term of each hedge. In hedging the transactions the Company, in the normal course of business, holds and/or issues the following types of derivatives:

Forward rate agreements—The purpose of this instrument is to hedge the fair value of firm purchase or sale commitments denominated in foreign currencies and of the net investments in foreign subsidiaries.

Interest rate swaps—The purpose of this instrument is to hedge the fair value of fixed-rate debt and cash flows of variable-rate financial assets.

Futures contracts—The purpose of this instrument is to hedge the fair value of microchips inventory.

Call and put options—The purpose of this instrument is to hedge the cash flows of forecasted sales or purchases of inventory.

The Company holds and issues such derivatives only for the purpose of hedging such risks, not for speculation. Generally, the Company enters into hedging relationships such that changes in the fair values or cash flows of items and transactions being hedged are expected to be offset by corresponding changes in the values of the derivatives. At December 31, 2000, hedging relationships exist for short-term investments, bond indebtedness, microchips inventory, firm foreign-currency-denominated purchase commitments, and anticipated purchases and sales of microchips inventory.

Derivatives that have been designated and qualify as cash flow hedging instruments are reported at fair value. The gain or loss on the effective portion of the hedge (i.e., change in fair value) is initially reported as a component of other comprehensive income. The remaining gain or loss, if any, is recognized currently in earnings. Amounts in accumulated other comprehensive income are reclassified into net income in the same period in which the hedged forecasted transaction affects earnings.

Example 12–14: Fair Value Hedging Instruments

During 2000 and 1999, the Company recognized net gains of $84,000 and $67,000, respectively, from derivative instruments designated and qualifying as fair value hedges. All hedges were highly effective; therefore, the gains, which are included in other income, are attributable to the portion of the change in the fair value of the derivative hedging instruments excluded from the assessment of the effectiveness of the hedges.

Also, during 2000, a previous hedge on a firm future foreign currency commitment no longer qualified as a fair value hedge, because the hedging relationship was no longer deemed to be highly effective. As a result, a loss of $39,000 was recognized in the 2000 Statement of Operations.

Example 12–15: Hedges Giving Rise to Foreign Currency Transaction Gains or Losses

The Company holds forward foreign currency contracts to hedge future license fees income as earned to be received in Japanese Yen. During 2000 and 1999, foreign currency gains of $57,000 and $43,000, respectively, are included in other income. The total amounts of such gains represent the portion of the change in the fair value of the forward contracts excluded from the assessment of the hedge's effectiveness.

> **Note:** See Chapter 14, "Foreign Operations and Currency Translation," for additional examples of disclosures of foreign exchange contracts.

Example 12–16: Cash Flow Hedging Instruments

During 2000 and 1999, the Company recognized net gains of $72,000 and $59,000, respectively, from cash flow hedges. All hedges were highly effective; therefore, the gains, which are included in other income, are attributable to the portion of the change in the fair value of the derivative hedging instruments excluded from the assessment of the effectiveness of the hedges. Cash flow hedges of forecasted transactions resulted in an aggregate credit balance of $97,000 remaining in accumulated other comprehensive income at December 31, 2000. The Company expects to transfer approximately $61,000 of that amount to earnings during 2001 when the forecasted transactions actually occur. All forecasted transactions currently being hedged are expected to occur by 2002. Also, during 2000, the Company transferred $41,000 to earnings from accumulated other comprehensive income because a forecasted transaction that was originally expected to occur was cancelled.

Example 12–17: Reporting Changes in the Components of Comprehensive Income

The following is an analysis of the changes in the net gain on cash flow hedging instruments included in accumulated other comprehensive income:

	2000	*1999*
Balance at beginning of year	$47,000	$43,000
Net gain for the year	21,000	16,000
Amount transferred to earnings	(15,000)	(12,000)
Balance at end of year	$53,000	$47,000

> **Note:** See Chapter 42, "Stockholders' Equity," and Chapter 48, "Comprehensive Income," for additional examples of disclosures of reporting changes in the components of comprehensive income.

CHAPTER 13
FINANCIAL STATEMENTS: COMPARATIVE

CONTENTS

EXECUTIVE SUMMARY

The presentation of comparative financial statements enhances the usefulness of annual and interim reports. Although not required, ordinarily it is desirable that financial statements of two or more periods be presented. Footnotes and explanations that appeared on the statements for the preceding years should be repeated, or at least referred to, in the comparative statements to the extent that they continue to be of significance.

It is necessary that prior-year figures shown for comparative purposes be comparable with those shown for the most recent period, or that any exceptions to comparability be clearly identified and described.

Authoritative Literature

ARB-43 Chapter 2A, Comparative Financial Statements

DISCLOSURE REQUIREMENTS

Reclassifications or other changes affecting comparability of financial statements presented should be disclosed (ARB-43, Ch. 2A, par. 3).

EXAMPLES OF FINANCIAL STATEMENT DISCLOSURES

The following sample disclosures are available on the accompanying disc. For information on disclosures of changes in accounting principles, changes in accounting estimates, changing in the reporting entity, and corrections of errors, see Chapter 1, "Accounting Changes."

Example 13–1: Reclassifications of a General Nature

Certain amounts in the prior periods presented have been reclassified to conform to the current period financial statement presentation. These reclassifications have no effect on previously reported net income.

Example 13–2: Reclassifications of a Specific Nature

Previously, the Company classified as sales revenue amounts charged on sales invoices for delivery of its products and related delivery expense was included in cost of sales. Commencing in 2000, the Company is classifying delivery revenue as a reduction of delivery expense. Prior net sales and cost of sales have been reclassified accordingly for comparative periods presented in the accompanying financial statements. This change in classification has no effect on previously reported net income.

CHAPTER 14
FOREIGN OPERATIONS AND CURRENCY TRANSLATION

CONTENTS

EXECUTIVE SUMMARY

There are two major areas of foreign operations: (1) translation of foreign currency financial statements for purposes of consolidation, combination, or reporting on the equity method and (2) accounting for and reporting foreign currency transactions.

Before an attempt is made to translate the records of a foreign operation, the records should be in conformity with generally accepted accounting principles (GAAP). In addition, if the foreign statements have any accounts stated in a currency other than their own, they must be converted into the foreign statement's currency before translation into U.S. dollars or any other reporting currency. In summary:

1. Assets, liabilities, and operations of an entity should be expressed in the functional currency of the entity. The functional currency of an entity is the currency of the primary economic environment in which the entity operates.
2. The current rate of exchange should be used to translate the assets and liabilities of a foreign entity from its functional currency into the reporting currency. The weighted average exchange rate for the period is used to translate revenue, expenses, and gains and losses of a foreign entity from its functional currency to the reporting currency. The current rate of exchange is used to translate changes in financial position other than those items found in the income statement, which are translated at the weighted average exchange rate for the period.
3. Gain or loss on the translation of foreign currency financial statements is not recognized in current net income but should be reported in other comprehensive income. If remeasurement from

the recording currency to the functional currency is necessary prior to translation, however, gain or loss on remeasurement is recognized in current net income.

4. The amounts accumulated in the translation adjustment component of stockholders' equity are realized on the sale or substantially complete liquidation of the investment in the foreign entity.
5. The financial statements of a foreign entity in a country that has had cumulative inflation of approximately 100% or more over a three-year period (highly inflationary) must be remeasured into the functional currency of the reporting entity.
6. Gains or losses from foreign currency transactions are recognized in current net income, except for:
   a. Gain or loss on a designated and effective economic hedge of a net investment in a foreign entity
   b. Gain or loss on certain long-term intercompany foreign currency transactions
   c. Gain or loss on a designated and effective economic hedge of a firm, identifiable, foreign currency commitment that meets certain conditions
7. Deferred taxes generally must be provided for the future tax effects of taxable foreign currency transactions and taxable transaction adjustments. However, deferred taxes should not be provided on unremitted earnings of a foreign subsidiary in certain instances.

Financial Accounting Standards Board Statement No. 52 (Foreign Currency Translation) is the primary source of GAAP for foreign operations and foreign currency translation. However, FAS-52 is amended by FAS-133 (Accounting for Derivative Instruments and Hedging Activities), which was initially effective for fiscal years beginning after June 15, 1999. FAS-137 (Accounting for Derivative Instruments and Hedging Activities—Deferral of the Effective Date of FASB Statement No. 133) amends FAS-133 by delaying its effective date by one year so that the Statement's new effective date is for fiscal years beginning after June 15, 2000. FAS-133 addresses the accounting for freestanding foreign currency derivatives and certain foreign currency derivatives embedded in other instruments. In addition, in June 2000 FASB issued FAS-138 (Accounting for Certain Derivative Instruments and Certain Hedging Activities), which amended FAS-133 to address a limited number of issues. See Chapter 12, "Financial Instruments, Derivatives, and Hedging Activities," for the accounting for freestanding foreign currency derivatives and certain foreign currency derivatives embedded in other instruments.

Authoritative Literature

ARB-43	Chapter 12, Foreign Operations and Foreign Exchange
FAS-52	Foreign Currency Translation
FAS-95	Statement of Cash Flows
FAS-109	Accounting for Income Taxes
FAS-130	Reporting Comprehensive Income
FAS-131	Disclosures about Segments of an Enterprise and Related Information
FAS-133	Accounting for Derivative Instruments and Hedging Activities
FAS-138	Accounting for Certain Derivative Instruments and Certain Hedging Activities
FIN-37	Accounting for Translation Adjustments upon Sale of Part of an Investment in a Foreign Entity

DISCLOSURE REQUIREMENTS

Disclosure Requirements If FAS-133, as Amended by FAS-138, Has Not Been Adopted

The following disclosures should be made for foreign operations and currency translation:

1. Significant foreign operations, including foreign earnings reported in excess of amounts received in the United States (ARB-43, Ch. 12, pars. 5–6)
2. The aggregate exchange transaction gain or loss included in the determination of net income (FAS-52, par. 30)
3. An analysis of the change in the cumulative translation adjustments included as a component of accumulated other comprehensive income, including, at a minimum, the following (FAS-52, par. 31):
   a. Beginning and ending amounts of cumulative translation adjustments
   b. The aggregate adjustment for the period resulting from translation adjustments and gains and losses from hedges of a net investment in a foreign entity and long-term intercompany balances
   c. The amount of income taxes for the period allocated to translation adjustments

d. The amounts transferred from cumulative translation adjustments and included in determining net income for the period as a result of the sale or complete (or substantially complete) liquidation of an investment in a foreign entity

4. Exchange rate changes that occur after the balance sheet date, including the effects of rate changes on unsettled balances pertaining to foreign currency transactions. If the effects of rate changes cannot be determined, that fact should be disclosed (FAS-52, par. 143).

5. The following additional disclosures are optional and should be considered to supplement the required disclosures described above (FAS-52, par. 144):

   a. Mathematical effects of translating revenue and expenses at rates that are different from those used in previous financial statements

   b. Economic effects (such as selling prices, sales volume, and cost structures) of rate changes

Disclosure Requirements If FAS-133, as Amended by FAS-138, Has Been Adopted

The following disclosures should be made for foreign operations and currency translation:

1. Significant foreign operations, including foreign earnings reported in excess of amounts received in the United States (ARB-43, Ch. 12, pars. 5–6)

2. The aggregate exchange transaction gain or loss included in the determination of net income should be disclosed as follows (FAS-133, par. 45):

   a. For derivative instruments, as well as nonderivative instruments that may give rise to foreign currency transaction gains or losses, that have been designated and have qualified as *fair value hedging instruments* and for the related hedged items:

      — The net gain or loss recognized in earnings during the reporting period representing (i) the amount of the hedges' ineffectiveness and (ii) the component of the derivative instruments' gain or loss, if any, excluded from the assessment of hedge effectiveness and a description of where the net gain or loss is reported in the statement of income or other statement of financial performance

      — The amount of net gain or loss recognized in earnings when a hedged firm commitment no longer qualifies as a fair value hedge

b. For derivative instruments that have been designated and have qualified as *cash flow hedging instruments* and for the related hedged transactions:

   — The net gain or loss recognized in earnings during the reporting period representing (i) the amount of the hedges' ineffectiveness and (ii) the component of the derivative instruments' gain or loss, if any, excluded from the assessment of hedge effectiveness and a description of where the net gain or loss is reported in the statement of income or other statement of financial performance

   — A description of the transactions or other events that will result in the reclassification into earnings of gains and losses that are reported in accumulated other comprehensive income, and the estimated net amount of the existing gains or losses at the reporting date that is expected to be reclassified into earnings within the next 12 months

   — The maximum length of time over which the entity is hedging its exposure to the variability in future cash flows for forecasted transactions excluding those forecasted transactions related to the payment of variable interest on existing financial instruments

   — The amount of gains and losses reclassified into earnings as a result of the discontinuance of cash flow hedges because it is probable that the original forecasted transactions will not occur

c. For derivative instruments, as well as nonderivative instruments that may give rise to foreign currency transaction gains or losses, that have been designated and have qualified as hedges of the foreign currency exposure of a *net investment in a foreign operation*:

   — The net amount of gains or losses included in the cumulative translation adjustment during the reporting period

3. An analysis of the change in the cumulative translation adjustments included as a component of accumulated other comprehensive income, including, at a minimum, the following (FAS-52, par. 31):

   a. Beginning and ending amounts of cumulative translation adjustments

   b. The aggregate adjustment for the period resulting from translation adjustments and gains and losses from hedges of a net investment in a foreign entity and long-term intercompany balances

   c. The amount of income taxes for the period allocated to translation adjustments

   d. The amounts transferred from cumulative translation adjustments and included in determining net income for the period as a result of the sale or complete (or substantially complete) liquidation of an investment in a foreign entity

4. Exchange rate changes that occur after the balance sheet date, including the effects of rate changes on unsettled balances pertaining to foreign currency transactions. If the effects of rate changes cannot be determined, that fact should be disclosed (FAS-52, par. 143).

5. The following additional disclosures are optional and should be considered to supplement the required disclosures described above (FAS-52, par. 144):

   a. Mathematical effects of translating revenue and expenses at rates that are different from those used in previous financial statements

   b. Economic effects (such as selling prices, sales volume, and cost structures) of rate changes

EXAMPLES OF FINANCIAL STATEMENT DISCLOSURES

Except for freestanding foreign currency derivatives and certain foreign currency derivatives embedded in other instruments, the disclosure requirements for foreign operations and currency translation are substantially the same regardless of whether the provisions of FAS-133 have been adopted. Therefore, unless otherwise indicated, the illustrations in this section apply in situations involving foreign operations and foreign currency translation, regardless of whether the provisions of FAS-133 have been adopted. The following sample disclosures are available on the accompanying disc.

Example 14–1: Foreign Currency Adjustments—Functional Currency Is the Foreign Country's Local Currency

The financial position and results of operations of the Company's foreign subsidiaries are measured using the foreign subsidiary's local currency as the functional currency. Revenues and expenses of such subsidiaries have been translated into U.S. dollars at average exchange rates prevailing during the period. Assets and liabilities have been translated at the rates of exchange on the balance sheet date. The resulting translation gain and loss adjustments are recorded directly as a separate component of shareholders' equity, unless there is a sale or complete liquidation of the underlying foreign investments. Foreign currency translation adjustments resulted in gains of $425,000 and $366,000 in 2000 and 1999, respectively.

Transaction gains and losses that arise from exchange rate fluctuations on transactions denominated in a currency other than the functional currency are included in the results of operations as incurred. Foreign currency transaction losses included in operations totaled $57,000 in 2000 and $46,0000 in 1999.

Example 14–2: Foreign Currency Adjustments—Functional Currency Is the U.S. Dollar

The Company's functional currency for all operations worldwide is the U.S. dollar. Nonmonetary assets and liabilities are translated at historical rates and monetary assets and liabilities are translated at exchange rates in effect at the end of the year. Income statement accounts are translated at average rates for the year. Gains and losses from translation of foreign currency financial statements into U.S. dollars are included in current results of operations. Gains and losses resulting from foreign currency transactions are also included in current results of operations. Aggregate foreign currency translation and transaction losses included in operations totaled $138,000 in 2000 and $114,000 in 1999.

Example 14–3: Foreign Currency Adjustments—Certain Assets and Liabilities Are Remeasured at Current Exchange Rates While Others Are Remeasured at Historical Rates

The U.S. dollar is the functional currency of the Company's worldwide continuing operations. All foreign currency asset and liability amounts are remeasured into U.S. dollars at end-of-period exchange rates, except for inventories, prepaid expenses and property, plant, and equipment, which are remeasured at historical rates. Foreign currency income and expenses are remeasured at average exchange rates in effect during the year, except for expenses related to balance sheet amounts remeasured at historical exchange rates. Exchange gains and losses arising from remeasurement of foreign currency-denominated monetary assets and liabilities are included in income in the period in which they occur.

Example 14–4: Foreign Exchange Contracts—Prior to Adoption of FAS-133

The Company does not use derivative financial instruments for speculative or trading purposes. The Company enters into foreign exchange forward contracts and foreign exchange option contracts to hedge certain balance sheet exposures and intercompany balances against future movements in foreign exchange rates. Gains and losses on contracts designated as hedges of intercompany transactions that are permanent in nature are accrued as exchange rates change and are recognized in stockholders' equity as foreign currency translation adjustments. Gains and losses on contracts that are not permanent in nature or are not designated as hedges are accrued as exchange rates change and are recognized in operations. Gains and losses on contracts designated as hedges of identifiable foreign currency firm commitments are deferred and included in the measurement of the related foreign currency transaction.

Foreign exchange forward contracts are legal agreements between two parties to purchase and sell a foreign currency, for a price specified at the contract date. The foreign exchange forward contracts require the Company to exchange foreign currencies for U.S. dollars or vice versa, and generally mature in six months or less. As of December 31, 2000, and December 31, 1999, the Company had outstanding foreign exchange forward contracts with aggregate notional amounts of $5,400,000 and $7,200,000, respectively, that had remaining maturities of two months or less. Due to the short-term nature of these contracts, their fair values approximate their contract values as of December 31, 2000, and December 31, 1999. The fair value of foreign exchange forward contracts is based on prevailing financial market information.

The foreign exchange option contracts provide the Company with the right, but not the obligation, to exchange foreign currencies for U.S. dollars or vice versa and generally mature in one month. As of December 31, 2000, the Company had an outstanding foreign exchange option contract with a notional amount of $1,800,000 that had a remaining maturity of less than one month. Due to the short-term nature of this contract, its fair value approximates its contract value as of December 31, 2000. As of December 31, 1999, the Company did not have any foreign exchange option contracts. The fair value of foreign exchange option contracts is based on prevailing financial market information.

> **Note:** See Chapter 12, "Financial Instruments, Derivatives, and Hedging Activities," for additional examples.

Example 14–5: Foreign Exchange Contracts—After Adoption of FAS-133

The Company has adopted Financial Accounting Standards Board Statement No. 133 (Accounting for Derivative Instruments and Hedging Activities), as amended by FAS-138 (Accounting for Certain Derivative Instruments and Certain Hedging Activities), which requires that all derivative instruments be recorded on the balance sheet at fair value. On the date derivative contracts are entered into, the Company designates the derivative as either (i) a hedge of the fair value of a recognized asset or liability or of an unrecognized firm commitment (fair value hedge), (ii) a hedge of a forecasted transaction or of the variability of cash flows to be received or paid related to a recognized asset or liability (cash flow hedge), or (iii) a hedge of a net investment in a foreign operation (net investment hedge).

Changes in the fair value of derivatives are recorded each period in current earnings or other comprehensive income, depending on whether a derivative is designated as part of a hedge transaction and, if it is, depending on the type of hedge transaction. For fair value hedge transactions, changes in fair value of the derivative instrument are generally offset in the income statement by changes in the fair value of the item being hedged. For cash-flow hedge transactions, changes in the fair value of the derivative instrument are reported in other comprehensive income. For net investment hedge transactions, changes in the fair value are recorded as a component of the foreign currency translation account that is also included in other comprehensive income. The gains and losses on cash flow hedge transactions that are reported in other comprehensive income are reclassified to earnings in the periods in which earnings are effected by the variability of the cash flows of the hedged item. The ineffective portions of all hedges are recognized in current period earnings.

> **Note:** See Chapter 12, "Financial Instruments, Derivatives, and Hedging Activities," for additional examples.

Example 14–6: Analysis of the Change in Cumulative Foreign Currency Translation Adjustments

Accumulated other comprehensive income for 2000 and 1999 represents foreign currency translation items associated with the Company's European and South American operations. Following is an analysis of the changes in the cumulative foreign currency translation adjustment account for 2000 and 1999:

	Accumulated Other Comprehensive Income— Foreign Currency Translation	
	2000	*1999*
Balance at beginning of year	$2,250,000	$1,600,000
Foreign currency translation adjustments	1,317,000	1,100,000
Income tax effect relating to translation adjustments	(540,000)	(450,000)
Amount recognized in operations as a result of the sale of the Company's German subsidiary in 2000	(625,000)	-0-
Balance at end of year	$2,402,000	$2,250,000

Note: See Chapter 42, "Stockholders' Equity," for examples of the change in cumulative foreign currency translation adjustments as reflected in an entity's statement of stockholders' equity.

Example 14–7: Significant Exchange Rate Changes After the Balance Sheet Date of December 31, 2000

On January 13, 2001, the Brazilian government allowed the value of its currency, the Real, to float freely against other currencies. Between January 13, 2001, and March 17, 2001, the Real's exchange rate to the U.S. dollar has declined as much as 44% from the exchange rate on December 31, 2000. As nearly all the Company's transactions in Brazil are Real-denominated, translating the results of operations of the Company's Brazilian subsidiary into U.S. dollars at devalued exchange rates will result in a lower contribution to consolidated revenues and operating income. Based on the Real exchange rate to the U.S. dollar on March 17, 2001, the Company's currency translation of the foreign investment in its Brazilian subsidiary from the Real (functional currency) to the U.S. dollar would result in a devaluation of approximately $6 million. Currency devaluations resulting from translating assets and liabilities from the functional currency to the U.S. dollar are included as a component of other comprehensive income (loss) in stockholders' equity.

Example 14–8: Company Discloses Nature of Its Operations in Foreign Countries

Substantially all of the Company's products are manufactured in the Dominican Republic, Mexico (under the Maquiladora program), Switzerland, Ireland, and Slovakia. These foreign operations represent captive manufacturing facilities of the Company. The Company's operations are subject to various political, economic, and other risks and uncertainties inherent in the countries in which the Company operates. Among other risks, the Company's operations are subject to the risks of restrictions on transfer of funds; export duties, quotas, and embargoes; domestic and international customs and tariffs; changing taxation policies; foreign exchange restrictions; and political conditions and governmental regulations.

Example 14–9: Amount of Foreign Earnings Exceeds Amounts Actually Received in the United States

In 2000 and 1999, earnings from the Company's French subsidiary totaled $705,000 and $643,000, respectively; dividends received from this subsidiary totaled $500,000 and $400,000 in 2000 and 1999, respectively.

Example 14–10: Company Specifies Percentage of Net Sales Relating to Foreign Operations

Sales to customers outside the United States approximated 35% of net sales in 2000 and 25 % of net sales in 1999. An adverse change in either economic conditions abroad or the Company's relationship with significant foreign distributors could negatively affect the volume of the Company's international sales and the Company's results of operations.

Example 14–11: Concentration in Accounts Receivable from Foreign Customers

As of December 31, 2000, and December 31, 1999, approximately 38% and 35%, respectively, of the Company's total accounts receivable were due from four foreign customers.

Example 14–12: Revenues and Long-Lived Assets by Geographic Area

The following table indicates the Company's relative amounts of revenue and the long-lived assets for 2000 and 1999 by geographic area:

	2000		*1999*	
	Revenue	*Long-Lived Assets*	*Revenue*	*Long-Lived Assets*
United States	$50,719,000	$14,395,000	$47,611,000	$13,618,000
Europe:				
Germany	7,592,000	2,530,000	7,058,000	2,367,000
France	6,133,000	1,662,000	5,450,000	1,278,000
Italy	5,562,000	2,129,000	4,923,000	1,854,000
Other	4,397,000	1,012,000	3,820,000	1,299,000
Total Europe	23,684,000	7,333,000	21,251,000	6,798,000
Other foreign countries	3,789,000	1,126,000	3,214,000	1,011,000
Total	$78,192,000	$22,854,000	$72,076,000	$21,427,000

Example 14–13: Restrictions on Transfer of Assets of Foreign Operations

The governments and national banking systems of certain countries in which the Company has consolidated foreign affiliates impose various restrictions on the payment of dividends and transfer of funds out of those countries. Additionally, provisions of credit agreements entered into by certain foreign affiliates presently restrict the payment of dividends. The estimated U.S. dollar amount of the foreign net assets included in the Consolidated Balance Sheets that are restricted in some manner as to transfer to the Company was approximately $22 million and $19 million at December 31, 2000, and December 31, 1999, respectively.

Example 14–14: Company's Future Operations Are Dependent on Foreign Operations

The Company's future operations and earnings will depend on the results of the Company's operations in [*foreign country*]. There can be no assurance that the Company will be able to successfully conduct such operations, and a failure to do so would have a material adverse effect on the Company's financial position, results of operations, and cash flows. Also, the success of the Company's operations will be subject to numerous contingencies, some of which are beyond management's control. These contingencies include general and regional economic conditions, prices for the Company's products, competition, and changes in regulation. Since the Company is dependent on international operations, specifically those in [*foreign country*], the Company will be subject to various additional political, economic, and other uncertainties. Among other risks, the Company's operations will be subject to the risks of restrictions on transfer of funds; export duties, quotas, and embargoes; domestic and international customs and tariffs; changing taxation policies; foreign exchange restrictions; and political conditions and governmental regulations.

Example 14–15: Deferred Taxes Not Provided on Undistributed Earnings of Foreign Subsidiaries—Amount of Deferred Tax Liability Not Disclosed

A provision has not been made at December 31, 2000, for U.S. or additional foreign withholding taxes on approximately $12 million of undistributed earnings of foreign subsidiaries since it is the present intention of management to reinvest the undistributed earnings indefinitely in foreign operations. Generally, such earnings become subject to U.S. tax upon the remittance of dividends and under certain other circumstances. It is not practicable to estimate the amount of deferred tax liability on such undistributed earnings.

Example 14–16: Deferred Taxes Not Provided on Undistributed Earnings of Foreign Subsidiaries—Amount of Deferred Tax Liability Is Disclosed

The Company has not recorded deferred income taxes applicable to undistributed earnings of foreign subsidiaries that are indefinitely reinvested in foreign operations. Undistributed earnings amounted to approximately $6,000,000 and $5,200,000 at December 31, 2000, and December 31, 1999, respectively. If the earnings of such foreign subsidiaries were not definitely reinvested, a deferred tax liability of approximately $1,500,000 and $1,300,000 would have been required at December 31, 2000, and December 31, 1999, respectively.

Example 14–17: Deferred Taxes Recorded on Undistributed Earnings of Foreign Subsidiaries

At December 31, 2000, the accompanying consolidated balance sheet includes a deferred tax liability of $300,000 for the estimated income taxes that will be payable upon the anticipated future repatriation of approximately $1,000,000 of undistributed earnings of foreign subsidiaries in the form of dividends.

CHAPTER 15
GOING CONCERN

CONTENTS

EXECUTIVE SUMMARY

Information that raises uncertainty about an entity's ability to continue as a going concern generally relates to the entity's ability to meet its maturing obligations without selling operating assets, undergoing debt restructuring, or revising operations based on outside pressures or similar strategies. If there is substantial doubt about an entity's ability to continue as going concern for a period of time not to exceed one year beyond the balance sheet date, adequate disclosures should be made in the financial statements. If the substantial doubt about the entity's ability to continue as a going concern is alleviated, disclosures should be made of the conditions and events that initially caused the substantial doubt, their possible effects, and mitigating factors (e.g., management's plans).

Authoritative Literature

SAS-59	The Auditor's Consideration of an Entity's Ability to Continue as a Going Concern
FAS-5	Accounting for Contingencies

DISCLOSURE REQUIREMENTS

1. If, after considering management's plans, a conclusion is reached that there is substantial doubt about the entity's ability to continue as a going concern for a period of time not to exceed one year beyond the balance sheet date, the financial statements should include the following disclosures (AU 341.10):
   a. Pertinent conditions and events giving rise to the assessment of substantial doubt about the entity's ability to continue as a going concern for a period of time not to exceed one year beyond the balance sheet date
   b. The possible effects of such conditions and events
   c. Management's evaluation of the significance of those conditions and events and any mitigating factors
   d. Possible discontinuance of operations
   e. Management's plans (including relevant prospective financial information)
   f. Information about the recoverability or classification of recorded asset amounts or the amounts or classification of liabilities
2. When substantial doubt about the entity's ability to continue as a going concern for a period of time not to exceed one year from the balance sheet date is alleviated, the financial statements include the following disclosures (AU 341.11):
   a. The principal conditions and events that initially caused the auditor to believe there was substantial doubt
   b. The possible effects of such conditions and events, and any mitigating factors, including management's plans

EXAMPLES OF FINANCIAL STATEMENT DISCLOSURES

The following sample disclosures are available on the accompanying disc.

Example 15–1: Going-Concern Issues Arising from Recurring Losses and Cash Flow Problems

As shown in the accompanying Financial Statements, the Company has incurred recurring losses from operations, and as of December 31, 2000, the Company's current liabilities exceeded its current assets by $800,000 and its total liabilities exceeded its total assets by $1,900,000. These factors raise substantial doubt about the Company's ability to continue as a going concern. Management has instituted a cost reduction program that included a reduction in labor and fringe costs. In addition, the Company has redesigned certain product lines, increased sales prices on certain items, obtained more favorable material costs, and has instituted more efficient management techniques. Management believes these factors will contribute toward achieving profitability. The accompanying Financial Statements do not include any adjustments that might be necessary if the Company is unable to continue as a going concern.

Example 15–2: Going-Concern Issues Arising from Default of Certain Loan Agreements

The Company incurred a loss of approximately $3,200,000 in 2000 and continued to experience certain decreases in working capital. As a result, the Company is in technical default of certain covenants contained in its credit and loan agreement with its primary lender. In addition, this default has triggered events of default under certain other obligations of the Company, including a $2,000,000 interim capital financing notes and certain promissory notes secured by real estate and equipment. The holders of the interim capital financing notes and promissory notes may, at their option, give notice to the Company that amounts are immediately due and payable. As a result, $10,500,000 of the Company's total long-term debt has been classified as a current liability in the accompanying Balance Sheet at December 31, 2000.

The Company's default of the loan agreements described above raise substantial doubt about the Company's ability to continue as a going concern. The Company is currently working with all of its lenders to obtain necessary waivers under the terms of the various agreements and is negotiating with its primary lender to stabilize its lender relationships by establishing certain internal operating and management plans. The Company also retained the services of an outside consulting firm to institute and implement all required programs to accomplish management's objectives. The Company is also evaluating the disposal of certain assets, raising new capital for future operations, and selectively increasing certain product prices. However, there can be no assurance that the Company will be successful in achieving its objectives. The accompanying Financial Statements do not include any adjustments that might be necessary if the Company is unable to continue as a going concern.

Example 15–3: Company Has Sufficient Funds to Meet Its Needs over the Next Year But Is Uncertain about Whether It Can Accomplish Its Business Objectives over the Following Years

The Company has sustained recurring losses and negative cash flows from operations. Over the past year, the Company's growth has been funded through a combination of private equity, bank debt, and lease financing. As of December 31, 2000, the Company had approximately $200,000 of unrestricted cash. On January 12, 2001, the Company executed an agreement with a group of private investors whereby the Company issued $10,000,000 in convertible subordinated loan notes. The Company believes that, as a result of this, it currently has sufficient cash and financing commitments to meet its funding requirements over the next year. However, the Company has experienced and continues to experience negative operating margins and negative cash flows from operations, as well as an ongoing requirement for substantial additional capital investment. The Company expects that it will need to raise substantial additional capital to accomplish its business plan over the next several years. In addition, the Company may wish to selectively pursue possible acquisitions of businesses, technologies, content, or products complementary to those of the Company in the future in order to expand its presence in the marketplace and achieve operating efficiencies. The Company expects to seek to obtain additional funding through a bank credit facility or private equity. There can be no assurance as to the availability or terms upon which such financing and capital might be available.

Example 15–4: Company's Successful Operations Are Dependent on Those of Its Parent

The Company has historically relied on its parent to meet its cash flow requirements. The parent company has cash available in the amount of approximately $83,000 as of December 31, 2000, and a working capital deficit of $80 million. The Senior Secured Notes in the amount of $65 million have been reclassified because the Company's parent does not currently have sufficient funds to make the next interest payment (in the approximate amount of $6 million) due in May 2001. Failure by the parent to make such payment could allow the holders of the Notes to declare all amounts outstanding immediately due and payable. The Company and its parent will need additional funds to meet the development and exploratory obligations until sufficient cash flows are generated from anticipated production to sustain operations and to fund future development and exploration obligations.

The parent plans to generate the additional cash needed through the sale or financing of its domestic assets held for sale and the completion of additional equity, debt, or joint venture transactions. There is no assurance, however, that the parent will be able to sell or finance its assets held for sale or to complete other transactions in the future at commercially reasonable terms, if at all, or that the Company will be able to meet its future contractual obligations.

CHAPTER 16
INTEREST COST

CONTENTS

EXECUTIVE SUMMARY

Capitalization of Interest Cost

Interest cost should be capitalized as part of the cost of acquiring or constructing certain assets, such as a plant, a warehouse, or a real estate development. To qualify for interest capitalization, assets need a period of time to get them ready for their intended use, which may be either (1) for sale or (2) for use within the business. However, interest cannot be capitalized in the following circumstances:

1. For inventories that are routinely manufactured or otherwise produced in large quantities on a repetitive basis
2. For qualifying assets acquired using gifts or grants that are restricted by the grantor to acquisition of those assets to the extent that funds are available from such gifts or grants

If a specific borrowing is made to acquire the qualifying asset, the interest rate incurred on that borrowing may be used to determine the amount of interest costs to be capitalized. That interest rate is applied to the average accumulated expenditures for the period to calculate the amount of capitalized interest cost on the qualifying asset. Capitalized interest cost on average accumulated expenditures in excess of the amount of the specific borrowing is calculated by the use of the weighted-average interest rate incurred on other borrowings outstanding during the period.

If no specific borrowing is made to acquire the qualifying asset, the weighted-average interest rate incurred on other borrowings outstanding during the period is used to determine the amount of interest cost to be capitalized. The weighted-average interest rate is applied to the average accumulated expenditures for the period to calculate the amount of capitalized interest cost on the qualifying asset.

In situations involving qualifying assets financed with the proceeds of restricted tax-exempt borrowings, the amount of interest cost to be capitalized should be (1) all interest cost of those borrowings less (2) any interest earned on temporary investment of the proceeds of the borrowings from the date of the borrowing until the specified qualifying assets acquired with those borrowings are ready for their intended use.

Imputed Interest

When a note is exchanged for property, goods, or services in an arm's-length transaction, it is generally presumed that the interest stated on the note is fair and adequate. If no interest is stated or if the interest stated appears unreasonable, the transaction should be valued at the fair value of the note or property, goods, or services, whichever is more clearly determinable. If such fair value is not readily determinable, the transaction should be valued at the present value of the note, determined by discounting the future cash payments under the note by an appropriate interest rate. The difference between the face amount of the note and its present value represents a discount or premium, which should be amortized over the life of the note using the interest method, or a method that approximates the interest method. The discount or premium amount is not an asset or a liability separable from the note that gives rise to it; therefore, the discount or premium should be reported in the balance sheet as a direct deduction from or addition to the face amount of the note.

Disclosure of Amount of Interest Paid

Financial Accounting Standards Board Statement No. 95 (Statement of Cash Flows) requires that the amount of interest paid, net of amounts capitalized, be disclosed.

Authoritative Literature

APB-12	Omnibus Opinion—1967
APB-21	Interest on Receivables and Payables
FAS-34	Capitalization of Interest Cost
FAS-42	Determining Materiality for Capitalization of Interest Cost
FAS-58	Capitalization of Interest Cost in Financial Statements That Include Investments Accounted for by the Equity Method
FAS-62	Capitalization of Interest Cost in Situations Involving Certain Tax-Exempt Borrowings and Certain Gifts and Grants
FAS-95	Statement of Cash Flows
FIN-33	Applying FASB Statement No. 34 to Oil and Gas Producing Operations Accounted for by the Full Cost Method

DISCLOSURE REQUIREMENTS

The following disclosures should be made with respect to interest cost:

1. For an accounting period in which no interest cost is capitalized, the amount of interest cost incurred and charged to expense during the period (FAS-34, par. 21)
2. For an accounting period in which some interest cost is capitalized, the total amount of interest cost incurred during the period and the amount thereof that has been capitalized (FAS-34, par. 21)
3. The amount of interest cost incurred in connection with product financing arrangements (FAS-34, par. 21; FAS-49, par. 9)
4. For notes payable or receivable that require the imputation of interest, disclosures should include (APB-21, par. 16):
   a. A description of the note
   b. The effective interest rate
   c. The face amount of the note
   d. The amount of discount or premium resulting from present value determination
   e. The amortization of the discount or premium to interest

5. The amount of interest paid (net of amounts capitalized) for each period for which a statement of cash flows is presented (FAS-95, par. 29)

EXAMPLES OF FINANCIAL STATEMENT DISCLOSURES

The following sample disclosures are available on the accompanying disc.

Example 16–1: Interest Cost Capitalized

The Company capitalizes interest cost incurred on funds used to construct property, plant, and equipment. The capitalized interest is recorded as part of the asset to which it relates and is amortized over the asset's estimated useful life. Interest cost capitalized was $315,000 and $268,000 in 2000 and 1999, respectively.

> **Note:** The amount of interest cost capitalized may be disclosed as part of the note on property and equipment.

Example 16–2: Interest Cost Charged to Operations

The Company incurred interest cost of $472,000 in 2000 and $436,000 in 1999, all of which were charged to operations.

> **Note:** The amount of interest expense charged to operations may be disclosed on the face of the income statement, or as part of the debt footnote.

Example 16–3: Details of Interest Expense, Interest Capitalized, and Interest Paid Provided in a Separate Note

Details of interest cost incurred for the years ended December 31, 2000, and December 31, 1999 are as follows:

	2000	*1999*
Interest cost charged to operations	$523,000	$476,000
Interest cost capitalized	91,000	112,000
Total interest cost incurred	$614,000	$588,000

Interest paid during 2000 and 1999, net of capitalized interest, amounted to $511,000 and $458,000, respectively.

Example 16–4: Interest Cost Incurred in Connection with Product Financing Arrangement

In 2000, the Company entered into a product financing arrangement with a vendor for the purchase of $13 million of electronic connectors. Accordingly, this inventory and the related short-term debt have been included in the Balance Sheet at December 31, 2000. The vendor has also made commitments, on the Company's behalf, to purchase additional amounts of the electronic connectors for delivery in 2001. The average interest rate on the product financing arrangement was 7.3% at December 31, 2000. Interest expense incurred and paid under this product financing arrangement totaled $193,000 for 2000.

Example 16–5: Liability Requires Imputation of Interest

At December 31, 2000, the Company has included as a liability the present value, computed with an effective annual rate of 10%, of a death benefit related to the termination of an employment contract as a result of the death of the President in 2000. This termination death benefit will be paid in thirty-six equal monthly installments of $30,000 commencing in April 2001.

Example 16–6: Notes Receivable Require Imputation of Interest

In March 2000, the Company received $50,000 in cash and $2,200,000 in notes in full payment of outstanding trade receivables resulting from the reorganization by a major customer, pursuant to a bankruptcy decree. The notes vary in maturity from six months to five years. They include non-interest bearing notes and notes bearing interest at rates of 4% to 6%. The notes are recorded at the present value of the future cash flows, utilizing an imputed interest of 10%, which equals $2,017,000. Notes receivable are due as follows: $418,000 in 2001, $536,000 in 2002, $374,000 in 2003, $318,000 in 2004, and $196,000 in 2005.

CHAPTER 17
INTERIM FINANCIAL REPORTING

CONTENTS

EXECUTIVE SUMMARY

Interim financial reports may be issued quarterly, monthly, or at other intervals, and may include complete financial statements or summarized data. Each interim period should be viewed as an integral part of the annual period. The results for each interim period should be based on the accounting principles and reporting practices generally used by the entity to prepare its latest annual financial statements, with limited exceptions, such as a change in an accounting principle. Also, certain accounting principles may require modification at interim dates so that the interim period's results better relate to the annual results. For example, when interim physical inventory counts are not taken, inventories may be estimated at interim dates using the gross profit method. Similarly, income taxes may be estimated at interim periods to reflect the entity's best estimate of the effective tax rate expected to be applicable for the full year.

The following guidelines should be observed for recognizing revenues and expenses during interim periods:

1. Revenues should be recognized as earned on the same basis as followed for the full year.
2. Costs and expenses that are associated directly with revenue (e.g., material costs, wages and salaries, fringe benefits, manufacturing overhead, and warranties) should be reported in the same period that the related revenue is recognized.
3. All other costs and expenses should be charged against income in the interim period as incurred, or allocated among interim periods based on an estimate of time expired, benefit received, or other activity associated with the periods.
4. Certain costs and expenses are frequently subjected to year-end adjustments even though they can reasonably be approximated at interim dates. Examples of such items include allowances for uncollectible accounts, year-end bonuses, depreciation, and inventory shrinkage. Adjustments for such items should be estimated and assigned to the interim period so that the interim period bears a reasonable portion of the anticipated annual amount.
5. Material extraordinary items, unusual or infrequent transactions, and gains and losses on disposal of a business segment

should be recognized in the interim period in which they occur and should not be prorated over the full year.

6. Income taxes should be determined by applying an estimated annual effective tax rate, based on the current year's estimated annual results, to income or loss from continuing operations. The tax effects of extraordinary items, unusual or infrequent items, discontinued operations, and cumulative effects of accounting changes should be recorded in the interim period in which they occur.

Authoritative Literature

APB-28	Interim Financial Reporting
FAS-3	Reporting Accounting Changes in Interim Financial Statements
FAS-16	Prior Period Adjustments
FAS-109	Accounting for Income Taxes
FAS-128	Earnings Per Share
FAS-130	Reporting Comprehensive Income
FAS-131	Disclosures about Segments of an Enterprise and Related Information
FIN-18	Accounting for Income Taxes in Interim Periods

DISCLOSURE REQUIREMENTS

Disclosures Applicable to All Companies

The disclosure requirements for interim financial statements are basically the same as for annual financial statements, with the following exceptions:

1. If the company uses estimated gross profit rates to determine the cost of goods sold during interim periods or uses other methods different from those used at annual inventory dates, the company should make the following disclosures (APB-28, par. 14):
   a. The method used at the interim date
   b. Any significant adjustments that result from reconciliations with the annual physical inventory
2. When costs and expenses incurred in an interim period cannot be readily identified with the activities or benefits of other

interim periods, disclosures should be made about the nature and amount of such costs. (Disclosure is not required if items of a comparable nature are included in both the current interim period and the corresponding interim period of the preceding year.) (APB-28, par. 15)

3. If the entity's revenues are subject to material seasonal variations, the entity should make the following disclosures to avoid the possibility that interim results may be taken as fairly indicative of the estimated results for a full fiscal year (APB-28, par. 18):
   a. The seasonal nature of the business activities
   b. Information for 12-month periods ended at the interim date for the current and preceding years (Optional)
4. The reasons for significant variations in the customary relationship between income tax expense and pretax accounting income, if they are not otherwise apparent from the financial statements or from the nature of the entity's business, should be disclosed (APB-28, par. 19).
5. Extraordinary items, discontinued operations, unusual and infrequently occurring transactions, and events that are material to the operating results of the interim period should be reported separately and included in the determination of net income for the interim period in which they occur (APB-28, par. 21).
6. Contingencies and other uncertainties that could affect the fairness of presentation of the interim financial information should be disclosed. Such disclosures should be repeated in interim and annual reports until the contingencies have been removed or resolved or have become immaterial (APB-28, par. 22).
7. Disclosures should be made of any changes in accounting principles or practices from those applied in (APB-28, par. 23):
   a. The comparable interim period of the prior year
   b. The preceding interim periods in the current year
   c. The prior annual financial statements
8. If there were changes in accounting principles that required retroactive restatement of previously issued financial statements, the effect on all periods presented should be disclosed (APB-28, par. 25).
9. The effect of a change in accounting estimate, including a change in the estimated effective annual tax rate, should be disclosed if material in relation to any period presented (APB-28, par. 26).
10. The cumulative effects of an accounting change or of a correction of an error that are material to an interim period, but not

material to the estimated income for the full fiscal year or to the trend of earnings, should be disclosed separately in the interim period (APB-28, par. 29).

11. The gross and net of tax effects of prior-period adjustments of net income should be disclosed in the interim period in which the adjustments are made (APB-9, par. 26).
12. The following disclosures should be made in interim financial statements about an adjustment related to prior interim periods of the current fiscal year (FAS-16, par. 15):
    a. The effect on income from continuing operations and net income for each prior interim period of the current fiscal year
    b. Restated income from continuing operations and net income for each prior interim period
13. The following disclosures about a cumulative effect-type accounting change, other than changes to LIFO, should be made in interim financial reports (FAS-3, par. 11):
    a. In financial reports for the interim period in which the new accounting principle is adopted, the following disclosures should be made:
        — The nature of and justification for the change
        — The effect of the change on income from continuing operations and net income (and related per share amounts for public companies) for the interim period in which the change is made (If the change is made in a period other than the first interim period of a fiscal year, the effect of the change on income from continuing operations, net income, and related per share amounts for each prechange interim period of the fiscal year should be disclosed. Also, the restated income from continuing operations, net income, and related per share amounts for each prechange interim period of the fiscal year should be disclosed.)
        — Income from continuing operations and net income (and related per share amounts for public companies) computed on a pro forma basis for (i) the interim period in which the change is made and (ii) any interim periods of prior fiscal years for which financial information is being presented (If no financial information for interim periods of prior fiscal years is being presented, disclosure shall be made, in the period of change, of the actual and pro forma amounts of income from continuing operations, net income, and related per share amounts for the interim period of the immediately preceding fiscal year that corresponds to the interim period in which the changes are made.)

b. In year-to-date and last-12-months-to-date financial reports that include the interim period in which the new accounting principle is adopted, the following disclosures should be made:

 — The effect of the change on income from continuing operations and net income (and related per share amounts for public companies) for the interim period in which the change is made

 — Income from continuing operations and net income (and related per share amounts for public companies) computed on a pro forma basis for (i) the interim period in which the change is made and (ii) any interim periods of prior fiscal years for which financial information is being presented (If no financial information for interim periods of prior fiscal years is being presented, disclosure should be made, in the period of change, of the actual and pro forma amounts of income from continuing operations, net income, and related per share amounts for the interim period of the immediately preceding fiscal year that corresponds to the interim period in which the changes are made.)

c. In financial reports for subsequent (postchange) interim periods of the fiscal year in which the new accounting principle is adopted, disclosure should be made of the effect of the change on income from continuing operations and net income (and related per share amounts for public companies) for that postchange interim period

14. For changes in accounting principles when neither the cumulative effect of the change nor the pro forma amounts can be computed (principally a change to the LIFO method of inventory pricing), the following disclosures should be made (FAS-3, par. 12):

 a. An explanation of the reasons for omitting accounting for the cumulative effect of the change

 b. An explanation of the reasons for omitting disclosure of pro forma amounts for prior years

Additional Disclosures Applicable Only to Publicly Held Companies

1. Publicly traded companies that report summarized financial information to their security holders at interim dates (including reports on fourth quarters) should disclose the following as a minimum (APB-28, par. 30):

a. Sales or gross revenues
b. Provision for income taxes
c. Extraordinary items (including related income tax effects)
d. Cumulative effect of a change in accounting principles or practices
e. Net income
f. Comprehensive income
g. Basic and diluted earnings per share data for each period presented
h. Seasonal revenue, costs, or expenses
i. Significant changes in estimates or provisions for income taxes
j. Disposal of a segment of a business and extraordinary, unusual, or infrequently occurring items
k. Contingent items
l. Changes in accounting principles or estimates
m. Significant changes in financial position
n. The following information about reportable operating segments (including provisions related to restatement of segment information in previously issued financial statements):
   - Revenues from external customers
   - Intersegment revenues
   - A measure of segment profit or loss
   - Total assets for which there has been a material change from the amount disclosed in the last annual report
   - A description of differences from the last annual report in the basis of segmentation or in the measurement of segment profit or loss
   - A reconciliation of the total of the reportable segments' measures of profit or loss to the enterprise's consolidated income before income taxes, extraordinary items, discontinued operations, and the cumulative effect of changes in accounting principles. However, if, for example, an enterprise allocates items such as income taxes and extraordinary items to segments, the enterprise may choose to reconcile the total of the segments' measures of profit or loss to consolidated income after those items. Significant reconciling items shall be separately identified and described in that reconciliation

2. If financial information is not separately reported for the fourth quarter, or that information is not presented in the annual report, the following information about the fourth quarter should be disclosed in a note to the annual financial statements (FAS-3, par. 14):
   a. Disposal of a segment of a business
   b. Extraordinary, unusual, or infrequent transactions or events
   c. The aggregate effect of year-end adjustments that are material to the operating results of the fourth quarter
   d. Accounting changes presented in the manner required for interim accounting changes

EXAMPLES OF FINANCIAL STATEMENT DISCLOSURES

The following sample disclosures are available on the accompanying disc.

Example 17–1: Change in Depreciation Method for Property and Equipment Made in the First Interim Period of the Current Year

In the first quarter of 2000, the Company changed its method of computing depreciation of property and equipment from the double declining method used in prior years to the straight-line method, and the new method has been applied to equipment acquisitions of prior years. Management believes the new straight-line depreciation method will more accurately reflect its financial results by better matching costs of new property over the useful lives of these assets. In addition, the new depreciation method more closely conforms with that prevalent in the industry.

The cumulative effect of the change on prior years (after reduction for income taxes of $100,000) totaled $125,000 and is included in income of the first quarter of 2000. The effect of the change on the first quarter of 2000 was to increase income before cumulative effect of a change in accounting principle by $40,500 ($.04 per share) and net income $165,500 ($.17 per share). The pro forma amounts reflect the effect of retroactive application on depreciation, the change in provisions for incentive compensation that would have been made in 1999 had the new method been in effect, and related income taxes.

Note: The following table illustrates the manner of reporting the change in the first quarter of 2000, with comparative information for the first quarter of 1999.

Income Statement

	Three Months Ended March 31	
	2000	*1999*
Income before cumulative effect of a change in accounting principle	$1,100,000	$1,000,000
Cumulative effect on prior years (to December 31, 1999) of changing to a different depreciation method	125,000	-0-
Net income	$1,225,000	$1,000,000
Amounts per common share:		
Income before cumulative effect of a change in accounting principle	$1.10	$1.00
Cumulative effect on prior years (to December 31, 1999) of changing to a different depreciation method	.13	-0-
Net income	$1.23	$1.00
Pro forma amounts assuming the new depreciation method is applied retroactively:		
Net income	$1,100,000	$1,013,500
Net income per common share	$1.10	$1.01

Example 17–2: Change in Depreciation Method for Property and Equipment Made in an Interim Period Other Than the First Interim Period of the Current Year, with Year-to-Date Information and Comparative Information for Similar Periods of the Prior Year Presented

In the third quarter of 2000, the Company changed its method of computing depreciation of property and equipment from the double declining method used in prior years to the straight-line method, and the new method has been applied to equipment acquisitions of prior years. Management believes the new straight-line depreciation method will more accurately reflect its financial results by better matching costs of new property over the useful lives of these assets. In addition, the new depreciation method more closely conforms with that prevalent in the industry.

The cumulative effect of the change on prior years (after reduction for income taxes of $100,000) totaled $125,000 and is included in income of the nine months ended September 30, 2000. The effect of the change on the three months ended September 30, 2000, was to increase net income by $49,500 ($.05 per share); the effect of the change on the nine months ended September 30, 2000, was to increase income before cumulative effect of a change in accounting principle by

$135,000 ($.14 per share) and net income by $260,000 ($.26 per share). The pro forma amounts reflect the effect of retroactive application on depreciation, the change in provisions for incentive compensation that would have been made in 1999 had the new method been in effect, and related income taxes. The effect of the change on the first quarter of 2000 was to increase income before cumulative effect of a change in accounting principle by $40,500 ($.04 per share) to $1,100,000 ($1.10 per share) and net income by $165,500 ($.17 per share) to $1,225,000 ($1.23 per share). The effect of the change on the second quarter was to increase net income by $45,000 ($.04 per share) to $1,300,000 ($1.30 per share).

Note: The following table illustrates the manner of reporting the change in the third quarter of 2000, with year-to-date information and comparative information for similar periods of the prior year presented.

Income Statement

	Three Months Ended September 30		*Nine Months Ended September 30*	
	2000	*1999*	*2000*	*1999*
Income before cumulative effect of a change in accounting principle	$1,200,000	$1,100,000	$3,600,000	$3,300,000
Cumulative effect on prior years (to December 31, 1999) of changing to a different depreciation method	-0-	-0-	125,000	-0-
Net income	$1,200,000	$1,100,000	$3,725,000	$3,300,000
Amounts per common share:				
Income before cumulative effect of a change in accounting principle	$1.20	$1.10	$3.60	$3.30
Cumulative effect on prior years (to December 31, 1999) of changing to a different depreciation method	-0-	-0-	.13	-0-
Net income	$1.20	$1.10	$3.73	$3.30
Pro forma amounts assuming the new depreciation method is applied retroactively:				
Net income	$1,200,000	$1,122,500	$3,600,000	$3,367,500
Net income per common share	$1.20	$1.12	$3.60	$3.37

Example 17–3: Change to the LIFO Method of Inventory Pricing Made in the First Interim Period of the Current Year—Effect on Prior Years Is Not Determinable

In the first quarter of 2000, the Company changed its method of inventory pricing from the first-in, first-out (FIFO) method to the last-in, first-out (LIFO) method. Management believes the LIFO method results in a better matching of current costs with current revenues and minimizes the effect of price level changes on inventory valuations. Neither the cumulative effect of this accounting change for years prior to 2000 nor the pro forma effects of retroactive application of the LIFO method to prior years is reasonably determinable. The effect of the change on the first quarter of 2000 was to decrease net income by $40,500 ($.04 per share).

Note: The following table illustrates the manner of reporting the change in the first quarter of 2000, with comparative information for the first quarter of 1999.

Income Statement

	Three Months Ended March 31	
	2000	*1999*
Net income	$1,055,000	$1,000,000
Net income per common share	$1.06	$1.00

Example 17–4: Change to the LIFO Method of Inventory Pricing Made in an Interim Period Other Than the First Interim Period of the Current Year—Effect on Prior Years Is Not Determinable

In the third quarter of 2000, the Company changed its method of inventory pricing from the first-in, first-out (FIFO) method to the last-in, first-out (LIFO) method. Management believes the LIFO method results in a better matching of current costs with current revenues and minimizes the effect of price level changes on inventory valuations. Neither the cumulative effect of this accounting change for years prior to 2000 nor the pro forma effects of retroactive application of the LIFO method to prior years is reasonably determinable. The effect of the change on the three months and nine months ended September 30, 2000, was to decrease net income by $49,500 ($.05 per share) and $135,000 ($.14 per share), respectively. The effect of the change on the first and second quarters of 2000 was to decrease net income by $40,500 ($.04 per share) to $1,055,000 ($1.06 per share) and by $45,000 ($.05 per share) to $1,250,000 ($1.25 per share), respectively.

Note: The following table illustrates the manner of reporting the change in the third quarter of 2000, with year-to-date information and comparative information for similar periods of the prior year presented.

Income Statement

	Three Months Ended September 30		*Nine Months Ended September 30*	
	2000	*1999*	*2000*	*1999*
Net income	$1,145,000	$1,200,000	$3,450,000	$3,400,000
Net income per common share	$1.15	$1.20	$3.45	$3.40

Example 17–5: Quantities and Costs Used in Calculating Cost of Goods Sold on a Quarterly Basis Include Estimates of the Annual LIFO Effect

The quantities and costs used in calculating cost of goods sold for the three months and six months periods ended June 30, 2000, include estimates of the annual LIFO effect. The actual effect cannot be known until the year-end physical inventory is completed and quantity and price indices developed.

Example 17–6: Seasonal Nature of Operations due to Normal Maintenance

Although there is no pronounced seasonality in demand for the Company's products, typically the second quarter of the year is the Company's best in terms of profitability. Generally, in the third quarter of the year, plants are closed for the first week of July for scheduled normal maintenance.

Example 17–7: Nature of Operations Affected by Weather and Spending Patterns of Significant Customers

The Company has historically experienced variability in revenues, income before income taxes and net income on a quarterly basis. A significant amount of this variability is due to the fact that the Company's business is subject to seasonal fluctuations, with activity in its second and, occasionally, third fiscal quarters being adversely affected by weather. In addition, budgetary spending patterns of significant customers, which often run on a calendar year basis, have resulted in greater volatility of second fiscal quarter results. Therefore, the results of operations presented for the three months ended March 31, 2000, are not necessarily indicative of results of operations for the full year.

Example 17–8: Seasonal Nature of Operations Quantified

The Company's business is highly seasonal with between 65% and 80% of sales occurring in the second and third fiscal quarters combined.

Example 17–9: Unusual or Nonrecurring Item

The results of operations for the third quarter of 2000 include (1) a $798,000 ($483,000 after-tax) nonrecurring charge to address the impairment of existing manufacturing facilities in Carson City, Nevada, and to relocate certain contractual employees to the Company's new facility in Chandler, Arizona; (2) a gain of $1,500,000 ($908,000 after-tax) related to the termination of a license agreement, net of charges for related equipment write-offs and capacity adjustments; and (3) charges of $1,300,000 ($782,000 after-tax) for the settlement of certain environmental litigation.

Example 17–10: Extraordinary Item

In the second quarter of 2000, the Company prepaid the holders of its 11% privately placed senior notes. Accordingly, the Company recorded an extraordinary loss of $911,000 (net of income tax benefit of $625,000) related to the early retirement of debt.

Example 17–11: Significant Change in Income Tax Rate

The effective tax rate for the three-month period ended September 30, 2000, was 48%, which was higher than the tax rate for the preceding quarters. The higher tax rate is primarily the result of a proposed tax adjustment of approximately $1,200,000 by the Internal Revenue Service.

Example 17–12: Significant Items Affecting Fourth Quarter Results of Operations Disclosed—Financial Information Is Not Separately Reported for the Fourth Quarter

In the fourth quarter of 2000 the Company recorded net pretax charges for inventory and related reserves of approximately $3,500,000 and a goodwill write-down of $1,000,000 primarily as a result of changes in customer demand for certain Company products. In addition, the credit for income taxes in the fourth quarter of 2000 was favorably affected by approximately $1,000,000 as a result of the settlement of tax examinations for earlier years. These adjustments reduced fourth quarter net income per share by $0.10.

Example 17–13: Summarized Quarterly Data

The following sets forth certain unaudited quarterly statements of operations data for each of the Company's quarters for 2000 and 1999. In management's opinion, this quarterly information reflects all adjustments, consisting only of normal recurring adjustments, necessary for a fair presentation for the periods presented. Such quarterly results are not necessarily indicative of future results of operations and should be read in conjunction with the audited consolidated financial statements of the Company and the notes thereto.

	Dec. 31, 2000	*Sept. 30, 2000*	*June 30, 2000*	*March 31, 2000*
Net revenues	$7,014,000	$6,131,000	$5,227,000	$5,101,000
Cost of sales and expenses	3,176,000	3,192,000	3,027,000	2,749,000
Income before income taxes	3,838,000	2,939,000	2,200,000	2,352,000
Income tax expense	1,774,000	1,380,000	1,028,000	1,079,000
Net income	$2,064,000	$1,559,000	$1,172,000	$1,273,000
Basic earnings per share	$.62	$.46	$.35	$.39
Diluted earnings per share	$.59	$.44	$.33	$.36

	Dec. 31, 1999	*Sept. 30, 1999*	*June 30, 1999*	*March 31, 1999*
Net revenues	$5,914,000	$5,331,000	$5,460,000	$6,048,000
Cost of sales and expenses	3,116,000	2,804,000	2,343,000	2,307,000
Income before income taxes	2,798,000	2,527,000	3,117,000	3,741,000
Income tax expense	1,274,000	1,153,000	1,472,000	1,758,000
Net income	$1,524,000	$1,374,000	$1,645,000	$1,983,000
Basic earnings per share	$.53	$.48	$.50	$.61
Diluted earnings per share	$.49	$.44	$.46	$.55

CHAPTER 18
LEASES

CONTENTS

EXECUTIVE SUMMARY

A lease that transfers substantially all the benefits and risks inherent in the ownership of property should be capitalized. Such a lease is accounted for by the lessee as the acquisition of an asset and the incurrence of a liability. The lessor accounts for such a lease as a sale (sales-type lease) or financing (direct-financing lease). All other leases are referred to as operating leases and should be accounted for as the rental of property.

The following are the broad classifications of leases under generally accepted accounting principles (GAAP):

Lessees	*Lessors*
Capital lease	Sales-type lease
Operating lease	Direct-financing lease
	Operating lease

Sales-type and direct-financing leases are the lessor's equivalent for a capital lease by a lessee.

Accounting for Leases—Lessees

A lease should be classified as a capital lease by a lessee if the lease meets at least one of the following criteria:

1. By the end of the lease term, ownership of the leased property is transferred to the lessee.
2. The lease contains a bargain purchase option.
3. The lease term is at least 75% of the estimated remaining economic life of the leased property. This criterion is not applicable when the beginning of the lease term falls within the last 25% of the total estimated economic life of the leased property.
4. At the inception of the lease, the present value of the minimum lease payments is at least 90% of the fair value of the leased property. This criterion is not applicable when the beginning of the lease term falls within the last 25% of the total estimated economic life of the leased property.

If none of these criteria are met, the lessee should classify the lease as an operating lease.

In a capital lease, the lessee should record a capital asset and a lease obligation for the same amount. The amount recorded should be the lesser of (1) the fair value of the leased asset at the inception of the lease, or (2) the present value of the minimum lease payments as of the beginning of the lease term. Once capitalized, the leased asset should be depreciated like any owned asset.

Under an operating lease, the lessee generally should charge the lease payments to rent expense on a straight-line basis over the lease term, even if payments are not made on straight-line basis.

Accounting for Leases—Lessors

A *sales-type lease* is a type of capital lease that results in a profit or loss to the lessor and transfers substantially all the benefits and risks inherent in the ownership of the leased property to the lessee. In a sales-type lease, the fair value of the leased property at the inception of the lease differs from its cost or carrying amount, thereby resulting in a profit or loss to the lessor.

A *direct-financing lease* is a type of capital lease that does *not* result in a profit or loss to the lessor but does transfer substantially all the benefits and risks inherent in the ownership of the leased property to the lessee. In a direct-financing lease, the leased property's book value and fair value are the same; therefore, there is no resulting profit or loss.

A lessor should classify a lease as a sales-type or direct-financing lease, whichever is appropriate, if the lease at inception meets at least one of the four criteria discussed above and *both* of the following criteria:

1. Collection of the minimum lease payments is reasonably predictable.
2. No important uncertainties exist for unreimbursable costs yet to be incurred by the lessor. Important uncertainties include extensive warranties and material commitments beyond normal practice. *Executory costs*, such as insurance, maintenance, and taxes, are not considered important uncertainties.

If none of these criteria are met, the lease should be classified as an operating lease by a lessor.

A sales-type lease should be accounted for by a lessor as follows:

1. The lessor should determine the *gross investment in the lease,* which is (a) the minimum lease payments (net of amounts, if any, included therein for executory costs to be paid by the lessor, together with any profit thereon) plus (b) the unguaranteed residual value accruing to the benefit of the lessor.
2. The present value of the gross investment in the lease should be recorded as a receivable in the balance sheet.
3. The difference between the gross investment in the lease (as determined in item 1 above) and its present value (as determined in item 2 above) should be recorded as unearned income and amortized to income over the lease term by the interest method. (The unearned income is included in the balance sheet as a deduction from the related gross investment.)
4. The present value of the minimum lease payments should be recorded as the sales price. The carrying amount of the leased property, plus any initial direct costs and less the present value of the unguaranteed residual value, should be charged against income in the same period.

A direct-financing lease should be accounted for by a lessor as follows:

1. The lessor should determine the *gross investment in the lease,* which is (a) the minimum lease payments (net of amounts, if any, included therein for executory costs to be paid by the lessor, together with any profit thereon) plus (b) the unguaranteed residual value accruing to the benefit of the lessor.
2. The difference between the gross investment in the lease (as determined in item 1 above) and the carrying amount of the

leased property should be recorded as unearned income. The unearned income and any initial direct costs should be amortized to income over the lease term by the interest method.

3. The net investment in the lease (i.e., gross investment as determined in item 1 above plus any unamortized initial direct costs less the unearned income) should be recorded as a receivable in the balance sheet.

For operating leases, the lessor should include the cost of the property leased to the lessee in the lessor's balance sheet as property, plant, and equipment and should be depreciated. Material initial direct costs (those directly related to the negotiation and consummation of the lease) are deferred and allocated to income over the lease term. Rental income should be amortized over the lease term on a straight-line basis, unless some other systematic and rational basis is more representative of the time pattern in which income is earned.

Other Lease Matters

Leveraged leases shall be classified and accounted for in the same manner as nonleveraged leases. A *leveraged lease* is a type of direct financing lease that has certain additional characteristics, principally the involvement of a long-term creditor.

Additional requirements apply to sale-leaseback transactions, leases involving real estate, leases involving and between related parties, leases with governmental entities, money-over-money leases, wrap leases, leases in business combinations, and subleases.

Authoritative Literature

FAS-13	Accounting for Leases
FAS-22	Changes in the Provisions of Lease Agreements Resulting from Refundings of Tax-Exempt Debt
FAS-23	Inception of the Lease
FAS-27	Classification of Renewals or Extensions of Existing Sales-Type or Direct Financing Leases
FAS-28	Accounting for Sales with Leasebacks
FAS-29	Determining Contingent Rentals
FAS-91	Accounting for Nonrefundable Fees and Costs Associated with Originating or Acquiring Loans and Initial Direct Costs of Leases
FAS-94	Consolidation of All Majority-Owned Subsidiaries

FAS-98	Accounting for Leases: • Sale-Leaseback Transactions Involving Real Estate • Sales-Type Leases of Real Estate • Definition of the Lease Term • Initial Direct Costs of Direct Financing Leases
FAS-109	Accounting for Income Taxes
FAS-125	Accounting for Transfers and Servicing of Financial Assets and Extinguishments of Liabilities
FIN-19	Lessee Guarantee of the Residual Value of Leased Property
FIN-21	Accounting for Leases in a Business Combination
FIN-23	Leases of Certain Property Owned by a Governmental Unit or Authority
FIN-24	Leases Involving Only Part of a Building
FIN-26	Accounting for Purchase of a Leased Asset by the Lessee during the Term of the Lease
FIN-27	Accounting for a Loss on a Sublease
FTB 79-10	Fiscal Funding Clauses in Lease Agreements
FTB 79-12	Interest Rate Used in Calculating the Present Value of Minimum Lease Payments
FTB 79-13	Applicability of FASB Statement No. 13 to Current Value Financial Statements
FTB 79-14	Upward Adjustment of Guaranteed Residual Values
FTB 79-15	Accounting for Loss on a Sublease Not Involving the Disposal of a Segment
FTB 79-16(R)	Effect of a Change in Income Tax Rate on the Accounting for Leveraged Leases
FTB 79-17	Reporting Cumulative Effect Adjustment from Retroactive Application of FASB Statement No. 13
FTB 79-18	Transition Requirement of Certain FASB Amendments and Interpretations of FASB Statement No. 13
FTB 82-1	Disclosure of the Sale or Purchase of Tax Benefits through Tax Leases
FTB 85-3	Accounting for Operating Leases with Scheduled Rent Increases

FTB 86-2 Accounting for an Interest in the Residual Value of a Leased Asset:

- Acquired by a Third Party or
- Retained by a Lessor That Sells the Related Minimum Rental Payments

FTB 88-1 Issues Relating to Accounting for Leases:

- Time Pattern of the Physical Use of the Property in an Operating Lease
- Lease Incentives in an Operating Lease
- Applicability of Leveraged Lease Accounting to Existing Assets of the Lessor
- Money-Over-Money Lease Transactions
- Wrap Lease Transactions

DISCLOSURE REQUIREMENTS

Leases—Lessees

Lessees should make the following disclosures:

1. A general description of leasing arrangements, including, but not limited to, the following (FAS-13, par. 16):
   a. The basis on which contingent rental payments are determined
   b. The existence and terms of renewal or purchase options and escalation clauses
   c. Restrictions imposed by lease agreements such as those concerning dividends, additional debt, and further leasing
2. The nature and extent of leasing transactions with related parties (FAS-13, par. 29).
3. For capital leases, the following disclosures should be made (FAS-13, pars. 13 and 16):
   a. For each balance sheet presented, the gross amount of assets recorded under capital leases by major classes according to nature or function and the total amount of accumulated amortization thereon (this information may be combined with the comparable information for owned assets)
   b. Obligations related to assets recorded under capital leases should be separately identified in the balance sheet as obligations under capital leases, subject to the same considerations as other obligations in classifying them as current and noncurrent liabilities in classified balance sheets

c. Future minimum lease payments as of the date of the latest balance sheet presented, in the aggregate and for each of the five succeeding fiscal years, with separate deductions from the total for the amount representing executory costs (including any profit thereon), that are included in the minimum lease payments and for the amount of the imputed interest necessary to reduce the net minimum lease payments to present value

d. The total of minimum sublease rentals to be received in the future under noncancelable subleases as of the date of the latest balance sheet presented

e. Total contingent rentals actually incurred for each period for which an income statement is presented

f. Amortization of capitalized leases separately reported on the income statement or presented in a note to the financial statements (the amortization may be combined with depreciation expense, but that fact must be disclosed)

4. For operating leases, the following disclosures should be made (FAS-13, par. 16):

   a. For operating leases having initial or remaining noncancelable lease terms in excess of one year:

      — Future minimum rental payments required as of the date of the latest balance sheet presented, in the aggregate and for each of the five succeeding fiscal years

      — The total amount of minimum rentals to be received in the future under noncancelable subleases as of the date of the latest balance sheet presented

   b. For all operating leases (except for rental payments under leases with terms of a month or less that were not renewed):

      — Rental expense for each period for which an income statement is presented

      — Presentation of separate amounts for minimum rentals, contingent rentals, and sublease rental income

5. For seller-lessee transactions, a description of the terms of the sale-leaseback transaction, including future commitments, obligations, provisions, or circumstances that require or result in the seller-lessee's continuing involvement (FAS-98, par. 17).

6. If a sale-leaseback transaction is accounted for by the deposit method or as a real estate financing arrangement, the following disclosures should be made (FAS-98, par. 18):

   a. The obligation for future minimum lease payments as of the date of the latest balance sheet presented in the aggregate and for each of the five succeeding fiscal years

b. The total of minimum sublease rentals, if any, to be received in the future under noncancelable subleases in the aggregate and for each of the five succeeding fiscal years

Leases—Lessors

Lessors should make the following disclosures:

1. A general description of the lessor's leasing arrangements (FAS-13, par. 23).
2. The nature and extent of leasing transactions with related parties (FAS-13, par. 29).
3. For sales-type and direct-financing leases, the following disclosures should be made (FAS-13, par. 23; FAS-91, par. 25):
   a. The components of the net investment in sales-type and direct-financing leases as of the date of each balance sheet presented, as follows:
      — Future minimum lease payments to be received with separate deductions for (i) amounts representing executory costs, including any profit thereon, included in the minimum lease payments and (ii) the accumulated allowance for uncollectible minimum lease payments receivable
      — The unguaranteed residual values accruing to the benefit of the lessor
      — Initial direct costs for direct-financing leases only
      — Unearned income
   b. Future minimum lease payments to be received for each of the five succeeding fiscal years as of the date of the latest balance sheet presented
   c. Total contingent rentals included in income for each period for which an income statement is presented
4. For operating leases, the following disclosures should be made (FAS-13, par. 23):
   a. The cost and carrying amount, if different, of property on lease or held for leasing, by major classes of property according to nature or function, and the amount of accumulated depreciation in total as of the date of the latest balance sheet presented
   b. Minimum future rentals on noncancelable leases as of the date of the latest balance sheet presented, in the aggregate and for each of the five succeeding fiscal years
   c. Total contingent rentals included in income for each period for which an income statement is presented

5. For leveraged leases, the following disclosures should be made (FAS-13, par. 47):
   a. The amount of related deferred taxes presented separately from the remainder of the net income investment
   b. Separate presentation (in the income statement or in related notes) of pretax income from the leveraged lease, the tax effect of pretax income, and the amount of investment tax credit recognized as income during the period
   c. If leveraged leasing is a significant part of the lessor's business activities in terms of revenue, net income, or assets, the following components of the net investment in leveraged leases should be disclosed:
      — Rentals receivable, net of that portion of the rental applicable to principal and interest on the nonrecourse debt
      — A receivable for the amount of the investment tax credit to be realized on the transaction
      — The estimated residual value of the leased assets (the estimated residual value should not exceed the amount estimated at the inception of the lease, except as provided in FAS-23)
      — Unearned and deferred income consisting of (i) the estimated pretax lease income (or loss), after deducting initial direct costs, remaining to be allocated to income over the lease term and (ii) the investment tax credit remaining to be allocated to income over the lease term
6. Lessors that recognize contingent rental income should disclose (EITF 98-9):
   a. The accounting policy for recognizing contingent rental income
   b. If contingent rental income is recognized (accrued) prior to achieving the specified target that triggers the contingent rents, the effect on net income of accruing such rents prior to achieving the specified target should be disclosed

Leases—Tax Leases

1. If the entity is involved in the sale or purchase of tax benefits through tax leases, the entity should make the following disclosures (FTB 82-1, par. 4):
   a. The method of recognizing revenue
   b. The method of allocating the income tax benefits and asset costs to current and future periods

2. If unusual or infrequent, the nature and financial effects of sales or purchases of tax benefits through tax leases should be disclosed on the face of the income statement or in a note to the financial statements (FTB 82-1, par. 6).
3. Significant contingencies existing with respect to sales or purchases of tax benefits through tax leases should be disclosed (FTB 82-1, par. 7).
4. If comparative financial statements are presented, disclosures should be made of any changes in the method of accounting for sales or purchases of tax benefits through tax leases that significantly affect comparability (FTB 82-1, par. 7).
5. If a significant variation in the customary relationship between income tax expense and pretax accounting income occurs as a result of sales or purchases of tax benefits through tax leases, the estimated amount and nature of the variation should be disclosed (FAS-109, par. 288).

EXAMPLES OF FINANCIAL STATEMENT DISCLOSURES

The following sample disclosures are available on the accompanying disc.

Lessees

Example 18–1: Operating Leases Include Renewal Options, Increases in Future Minimum Payments, and Payment of Executory Costs

The Company leases many of its operating and office facilities for various terms under long-term, non-cancelable operating lease agreements. The leases expire at various dates through 2009 and provide for renewal options ranging from three months to six years. In the normal course of business, it is expected that these leases will be renewed or replaced by leases on other properties. The leases provide for increases in future minimum annual rental payments based on defined increases in the Consumer Price Index, subject to certain minimum increases. Also, the agreements generally require the Company to pay executory costs (real estate taxes, insurance, and repairs). Lease expense totaled $25,500,000 and $24,700,000 during 2000 and 1999, respectively.

The following is a schedule by year of future minimum rental payments required under the operating lease agreements:

Year Ending December 31	*Amount*
2001	$ 27,000,000
2002	29,500,000
2003	31,000,000
2004	33,500,000
2005	35,000,000
Thereafter	120,000,000
	$276,000,000

Total minimum lease payments do not include contingent rentals that may be paid under certain leases because of use in excess of specified amounts. Contingent rental payments were not significant in 2000 or 1999.

Example 18–2: Operating Leases Include Sublease Income

The Company leases corporate office and warehouse facilities, machinery and equipment, computers, and furniture under operating lease agreements expiring at various times through 2011. Substantially all of the leases require the Company to pay maintenance, insurance, property taxes, and percentage rent ranging from 3% to 12%, based on sales volume over certain minimum sales levels. Effective March 2000, the Company entered into a sublease agreement for its former warehouse facility, which expires in September 2004.

Minimum annual rental commitments under non-cancelable leases are as follows at December 31, 2000:

Year Ending December 31	*Minimum Lease Commitments*	*Sublease Income*	*Net Lease Commitments*
2001	$ 5,196,000	$247,000	$ 4,949,000
2002	4,962,000	247,000	4,715,000
2003	4,352,000	247,000	4,105,000
2004	3,511,000	185,000	3,326,000
2005	3,793,000	-0-	3,793,000
Thereafter	14,430,000	-0-	14,430,000
	$36,244,000	$926,000	$35,318,000

Rental expense, including common area maintenance, was $5,533,000 and $5,391,000, of which $77,000 and $45,000 was paid as percentage rent based on sales volume, for the years ended December 31, 2000, and December 31, 1999, respectively.

Example 18–3: Operating Leases Contain Purchase Option, Contingent Liability, and Restrictive Covenants

The Company has entered into lease agreements relating to certain corporate facilities that would allow the Company to purchase the facilities on or before the end of the lease term in March 2001 for a specified purchase price. If at the end of the lease term the Company does not purchase the property under lease or arrange a third-party purchase, then the Company would be obligated to the lessor for a guarantee payment equal to a specified percentage of the agreed purchase price for the property. The Company would also be obligated to the lessor for all or some portion of this amount if the price paid by the third party is below 15% of the specified purchase price.

As of December 31, 2000, the total amount related to the leased facilities for which the Company is contingently liable is $12,000,000. Under the terms of the agreements, the Company is required to maintain restricted investments, as collateral, of approximately $9,500,000 during the remainder of the lease term; this amount is shown as "Restricted long-term deposits" in the Company's Balance Sheet.

The lease agreements also require the Company to comply with certain covenants and to maintain certain financial ratios. As of December 31, 2000, the Company was in compliance with all ratios and covenants.

Example 18–4: Operating Leases Contain Rent Abatements and Provisions for Future Rent Increases That Are Amortized on the Straight-Line Method over the Lease Term

The Company has entered into several operating lease agreements, some of which contain provisions for future rent increases, rent free periods, or periods in which rent payments are reduced (abated). The total amount of rental payments due over the lease term is being charged to rent expense on the straight-line method over the term of the lease. The difference between rent expense recorded and the amount paid is credited or charged to "Deferred rent obligation," which is included in "Other current liabilities" in the accompanying Balance Sheet.

Example 18–5: Rent Expense Includes Contingent Rent and Sublease Rental Income

The following summary shows the composition of total rental expense for all operating leases:

	2000	*1999*
Minimum rents	$5,200,000	$4,750,000
Contingent rents	2,360,000	2,150,000
Less: Sublease rental income	(470,000)	(450,000)
Net rental expense	$7,090,000	$6,450,000

Contingent rents are based on factors other than the passage of time, primarily percentage of revenues in excess of specified amounts.

Example 18–6: Capital Leases—Future Minimum Lease Payments

The Company leases certain machinery and equipment under agreements that are classified as capital leases. The cost of equipment under capital leases is included in the Balance Sheets as property, plant, and equipment and was $6,943,000 and $6,822,000 at December 31, 2000, and December 31, 1999, respectively. Accumulated amortization of the leased equipment at December 31, 2000, and December 31, 1999, was approximately $4,720,000 and $4,245,000, respectively. Amortization of assets under capital leases is included in depreciation expense.

The future minimum lease payments required under the capital leases and the present value of the net minimum lease payments as of December 31, 2000, are as follows:

	Year Ending December 31	*Amount*
	2001	$1,250,000
	2002	975,000
	2003	820,000
	2004	745,000
	2005	620,000
	Thereafter	1,527,000
Total minimum lease payments		5,937,000
Less: Amount representing estimated taxes, maintenance, and insurance costs included in total amounts above		(125,000)
Net minimum lease payments		5,812,000
Less: Amount representing interest		(1,855,000)
Present value of net minimum lease payments		3,957,000
Less: Current maturities of capital lease obligations		(823,000)
Long-term capital lease obligations		$3,134,000

Example 18–7: Components of Property under Capital Leases

Assets recorded under capital leases and included in property and equipment in the Company's Balance Sheets consist of the following at December 31, 2000, and December 31, 1999:

	2000	*1999*
Distribution and manufacturing facility	$3,250,000	$3,250,000
Data processing equipment	1,975,000	1,050,000
Furniture and equipment	725,000	536,000
Transportation equipment	347,000	213,000
	6,297,000	5,049,000
Less: Accumulated amortization	(2,514,000)	(2,091,000)
	$3,783,000	$2,958,000

Example 18–8: Sale-Leaseback Transaction Accounted for as an Operating Lease Results in Deferred Gain That Is Being Amortized over the Term of the Lease

In March 2000, the Company sold certain machinery and equipment for $11,525,000. Under the agreement, the Company is leasing back the property from the purchaser over a period of 15 years. The Company is accounting for the leaseback as an operating lease. The gain of $1,630,000 realized in this transaction has been deferred and is being amortized to income in proportion to rent charged over the term of the lease. At December 31, 2000, the remaining deferred gain of $1,490,000 is shown as "Deferred gain on property sale" in the Company's Balance Sheet.

The lease requires the Company to pay customary operating and repair expenses and to observe certain operating restrictions and covenants, including restrictions on net worth and dividend payments. The lease contains renewal options at lease termination and purchase options at amounts approximating fair market value as of specified dates in the agreement. For the year ended December 31, 2000, the total rental expense incurred by the Company under this lease was $1,173,000. The minimum lease payments required by the lease are as follows:

Year Ending December 31	*Amount*
2001	$ 1,983,000
2002	1,621,000
2003	1,372,000
2004	1,011,000
2005	963,000
Thereafter	6,523,000
	$13,473,000

Example 18–9: Sale-Leaseback Transaction Accounted for as an Operating Lease Results in No Gain or Loss

In March 2000, the Company entered into an agreement with an independent third party to sell and leaseback certain machinery and equipment, which is accounted for as an operating lease. The net carrying value of the machinery and equipment sold was $8,250,000. Because the net carrying value of the machinery and equipment was equal to their sales price, there was no gain or loss recognized on the sale. The lease agreement entered into between the Company and the counterparty was for a minimum lease term of twelve months with three one-year renewal options. For the year ended December 31, 2000, the total rental expense incurred by the Company under this lease was $1,025,000.

Example 18–10: Sale-Leaseback Transaction Accounted for as a Financing Arrangement

In April 2000, the Company completed the refinancing of its headquarters facility under a sale-leaseback arrangement. The facility was sold for $8,230,000, of which $2,300,000 was received in the form of an interest bearing note receivable due in April 2005, and the remainder $5,930,000 in cash. The cash received was used to pay (1) existing mortgages on the property of $1,425,000, (2) expenses of the transaction of $350,000, and (3) bank debt of $4,155,000. The transaction has been accounted for as a financing arrangement, wherein the property remains on the Company's books and will continue to be depreciated. A financing obligation in the amount of $5,930,000, representing the proceeds, has been recorded under "Financing obligation, sale-leaseback" in the Company's Balance Sheet, and is being reduced based on payments under the lease.

The lease has a term of 12 years for the office and eight years for the warehouse and requires minimum annual rental payments as follows:

Year Ending December 31	*Amount*
2001	$1,100,000
2002	1,128,000
2003	1,156,000
2004	1,185,000
2005	1,215,000
Thereafter	3,216,000
	$9,000,000

The Company has the option to renew the lease at the end of the lease term and the option to purchase the property at the end of the warehouse lease.

Example 18–11: Contingency Resulting from Default under Lease Agreements

The Company leases certain plant machinery and equipment at its manufacturing facility in Boise, Idaho. As a result of the Company's default under its debt obligations, as more fully discussed in Note [*X*] to the financial statements, the Company is in default under these lease agreements. As a result, the lessors have the right to require the Company to prepay the remaining future lease payments required under the lease agreements. Because the Company has paid the lease payments and all lease payments are expected to be made in a timely manner, the Company does not expect that the lessors will assert this right under these lease agreements.

Example 18–12: Lease Termination Results in Contingent Liability

In September 2000, the Company notified the developer and landlord of its planned future headquarters in Paramount, California, that the Company intends to terminate the project. The Company had previously entered into a 15-year lease agreement for the new site. Although groundbreaking for the new site has not occurred, the Company anticipates that it will incur lease termination costs. The Company is not able to make a meaningful estimate of the amount or range of loss that could result from an unfavorable resolution of this matter. Consequently, the Company has not provided any accruals for lease termination costs in the financial statements.

Lessors

Example 18–13: Operating Leases

Operating leases arise from the leasing of the Company's machinery and equipment to retail customers, primarily in the construction industry in the United States. Initial lease terms generally range from 36 to 84 months. Depreciation expense for assets subject to operating leases is provided primarily on the straight-line method over the term of the lease in amounts necessary to reduce the carrying amount of the asset to its estimated residual value. Estimated and actual residual values are reviewed on a regular basis to determine that depreciation amounts are appropriate. Depreciation expense relating to machinery and equipment held as investments in operating leases was $373,000 for 2000 and $417,000 for 1999.

Investments in operating leases are as follows at December 31:

	2000	*1999*
Machinery and equipment, at cost	$4,373,000	$4,770,000
Lease origination costs	63,000	65,000
Accumulated depreciation	(813,000)	(765,000)
Allowance for credit losses	(50,000)	(90,000)
Net investments in operating leases	$3,573,000	$3,980,000

Future minimum rental payments to be received on non-cancelable operating leases are contractually due as follows as of December 31, 2000:

Year Ending December 31	*Amount*
2001	$ 883,000
2002	645,000
2003	422,000
2004	213,000
2005	105,000
Thereafter	75,000
	$2,343,000

Future minimum rental payments to be received do not include contingent rentals that may be received under certain leases because of use in excess of specified amounts. Contingent rentals were not significant in 2000 or 1999.

Example 18–14: Sales-Types Leases

The components of lease receivables for the net investment in sales-type leases are as follows at December 31:

	2000	*1999*
Total minimum lease receivables	$4,100,000	$3,600,000
Less: Allowance for uncollectible amounts	(125,000)	(100,000)
Net minimum lease payments receivable	3,975,000	3,500,000
Estimated residual values of leased property	230,000	145,000
Less: Unearned interest income	(710,000)	(625,000)
Net investment in sales-type leases	$3,495,000	$3,020,000
Current portion	$1,300,000	$1,050,000
Long-term portion	2,195,000	1,970,000
	$3,495,000	$3,020,000

Future minimum lease receivables due from customers under sales-type leases as of December 31, 2000, are as follows:

Year Ending December 31	*Amount*
2001	$ 852,000
2002	827,000
2003	793,000
2004	602,000
2005	464,000
Thereafter	562,000
	$4,100,000

Future minimum lease receivables do not include contingent rentals that may be received under certain leases because of use in excess of specified amounts. Contingent rentals were not significant in 2000 or 1999.

Example 18–15: Direct-Financing Leases

The components of lease receivables for the net investment in direct financing leases are as follows as of December 31:

	2000	*1999*
Total minimum lease receivables	$5,519,000	$5,837,000
Less: Allowance for credit losses	(80,000)	(143,000)
Net minimum lease payments receivable	5,439,000	5,694,000
Estimated residual values of leased property	3,720,000	2,923,000
Deferred initial direct costs	125,000	150,000
Less: Unearned income	(2,150,000)	(2,410,000)
Net investment in direct financing leases	$7,134,000	$6,357,000
Current portion	$2,760,000	$2,323,000
Long-term portion	4,374,000	4,034,000
	$7,134,000	$6,357,000

Future minimum lease receivables due from customers under direct-financing leases as of December 31, 2000, are as follows:

Year Ending December 31	*Amount*
2001	$1,906,000
2002	1,619,000
2003	949,000
2004	712,000
2005	233,000
Thereafter	100,000
	$5,519,000

Unearned income on direct financing leases is recognized in such a manner as to produce a constant periodic rate of return on the net investment in the direct-financing lease.

Future minimum lease receivables do not include contingent rentals that may be received under certain leases because of use in excess of specified amounts. Contingent rentals were not significant in 2000 or 1999.

Example 18–16: Leveraged Leases

Leveraged lease assets acquired by the Company are financed primarily through nonrecourse loans from third-party debt participants. These loans are secured by the lessee's rental obligations and the leased property. Net rents receivable represent gross rents less the principal and interest on the nonrecourse debt obligations. Unguaranteed residual values are principally based on independent appraisals of the values of leased assets remaining at the expiration of the lease. Leveraged lease investments are primarily related to heavy construction and drilling equipment, with original lease terms ranging from 5 to 15 years.

The Company's investment in leveraged leases consists of rentals receivable net of principal and interest on the related nonrecourse debt, estimated residual value of the leased property, and unearned income. The unearned income is recognized as leveraged lease revenue in income from investments over the lease term.

The Company's net investment in leveraged leases comprises the following at December 31, 2000, and December 31, 1999:

	2000	*1999*
Net lease receivables	$9,819,000	$8,761,000
Estimated unguaranteed residual values	10,863,000	9,910,000
Less: Unearned income	(10,150,000)	(9,613,000)
Investment in leveraged leases	$10,532,000	$9,058,000

Current portion	$ 2,031,000	$1,754,000
Long-term portion	8,501,000	7,304,000
	$10,532,000	$9,058,000

Deferred tax liability arising from leveraged leases totaled approximately $4,125,000 and $3,234,000 at December 31, 2000, and December 31, 1999, respectively.

The following is a summary of the components of income from leveraged leases for the years ended December 31, 2000, and December 31, 1999:

	2000	*1999*
Pretax leveraged lease income	$237,000	$151,000
Income tax effect	85,000	73,000
Income from leveraged leases	$322,000	$224,000

Leases with Related Parties

Example 18–17: Company Has a Long-Term Operating Lease with a Related Party

The Company leases its corporate headquarters and warehouse facility from a partnership owned by the two Company shareholders. The lease provides for monthly payments of $32,000, expires in 2011, and contains a renewal option for an additional seven years. Due to the current economic conditions of the Company, rent was reduced to $32,000 per month from $45,000 per month effective January 1, 2000. Rent expense incurred and paid to the partnership was $384,000 and $540,000 for 2000 and 1999, respectively.

The following is a schedule by year of future minimum rental payments due to the partnership under the operating lease agreement:

Year Ending December 31	*Amount*
2001	$ 384,000
2002	384,000
2003	416,000
2004	416,000
2005	450,000
Thereafter	2,700,000
	$4,750,000

Example 18–18: Company Has a Month-to-Month Operating Lease with a Related Party

The Company leases its administrative offices on a month-to-month basis from a partnership in which the Company's stockholder is a partner. Total rent paid to the partnership was $123,000 and $117,000 for the years ended December 31, 2000, and December 31, 1999, respectively.

Example 18–19: Company Discloses the Nature and Extent of Several Long-Term Operating Lease Agreements with Affiliated Entities

The Company leases various manufacturing facilities and equipment from companies owned by certain officers and directors of the Company, either directly or indirectly, through affiliates. The leases generally provide that the Company will bear the cost of property taxes and insurance.

Details of the principal operating leases with related parties as of December 31, 2000, including the effect of renewals and amendments executed subsequent to December 31, 2000, are as follows:

Name of Related Party/ Description of Lease	*Date of Lease*	*Term*	*Basic Annual Rental Amount*	*Future Minimum Rental Amounts*
Hope Realty Trust:				
Land & building—Chicago	12-13-90	15 years	$200,000	$1,000,000
Corporate offices	12-22-90	15 years	$100,000	$ 500,000
Machinery & equipment	11-30-95	10 years	$125,000	$ 625,000
John Jones Family Trust:				
Land & buildings—Atlanta	6-29-95	10 years	$150,000	$ 675,000
Furniture & computers	7-01-96	10 years	$100,000	$ 550,000
Mack Realty Trust:				
Land & building—Detroit	6-25-95	15 years	$200,000	$1,900,000
Corporate offices	12-28-95	10 years	$110,000	$ 550,000
Furniture & equipment	1-1-96	10 years	$ 80,000	$ 400,000

Rent incurred and paid to these related parties was $1,069,000 and $1,087,000 for the years ended December 31, 2000, and December 31, 1999, respectively.

Future minimum lease payments to these related parties as of December 31, 2000 are as follows:

Year Ending December 31	*Amount*
2001	$1,065,000
2002	1,110,000
2003	1,150,000
2004	1,205,000
2005	1,260,000
Thereafter	685,000
	$6,475,000

CHAPTER 19
LONG-TERM CONTRACTS

CONTENTS

EXECUTIVE SUMMARY

Under generally accepted accounting principles (GAAP), revenues from long-term contracts should be recognized under either the percentage-of-completion method or the completed-contract method. The percentage-of-completion method is appropriate in situations in which reliable estimates of the degree of completion are available, in which case a pro rata portion of the income from the contract is recognized in each accounting period covered by the contract. If reliable estimates are not available, the completed-contract method is used, in which income is deferred until the end of the contract period. The percentage-of-completion and the completed-contract methods are not alternatives; a contractor must use the appropriate method.

Regardless of the revenue recognition method used, an entity should accrue an anticipated loss on a contract whenever it becomes apparent that the total estimated contract costs (i.e., costs incurred to date, plus estimated costs to complete) will materially exceed the total estimated contract revenue.

Generally, four basic types of contracts are encountered in practice:

1. *Fixed-price or lump-sum contracts.* A fixed-price or lump-sum contract is a contract in which the price is not usually subject to adjustment because of costs incurred by the contractor.
2. *Time-and-material contracts.* Time-and-material contracts are contracts that generally provide for payments to the contractor on the basis of direct labor hours at fixed hourly rates and cost of materials or other specified costs.
3. *Cost-type contracts.* Cost-type contracts provide for reimbursement of allowable or otherwise defined costs incurred plus a fee that represents profit.
4. *Unit-price contracts.* Unit-price contracts are contracts under which the contractor is paid a specified amount for every unit of work performed.

Authoritative Literature

ARB-43	Chapter 11, Government Contracts
ARB-45	Long-Term Construction-Type Contracts

SOP 81-1 Accounting for Performance of Construction-Type and Certain Production-Type Contracts

DISCLOSURE REQUIREMENTS

The following disclosures are required for long-term contracts:

1. The method used to account for long-term contracts (i.e., the percentage-of-completion method or the completed-contract method) (ARB-45, par. 15)
2. Departure from the basic revenue recognition policy for a single contract or group of contracts (SOP 81-1, pars. 25 and 31)
3. The policies relating to combining and segmenting contracts, if applicable (SOP 81-1, par. 21)
4. When the percentage-of-completion method of accounting is used, the method of measuring the extent of progress toward completion should be disclosed (e.g., cost-to-cost, direct labor) (SOP 81-1, pars. 21 and 45)
5. If the completed-contract method is used, the criteria used to determine substantial completion (SOP 81-1, par. 52)
6. The amount of revenue from claims recognized in excess of the agreed contract price (SOP 81-1, pars. 65–67)
7. If the contractor recognizes revenues from claims only when the amounts have been received or awarded, the amounts of such revenues recorded during the period should be disclosed (SOP 81-1, par. 66)
8. The effect of significant revisions in contract estimates (SOP 81-1, par. 84)
9. The amount of advances, if any, offset against cost-type contract receivables (ARB-43, Ch. 11A, par. 22)
10. Provisions for losses on contracts should be disclosed separately as liabilities on the face of the balance sheet, if material (SOP 81-1, par. 89)
11. Provisions for losses on contracts that are material, unusual, or infrequent should be disclosed as a separate component of construction costs on the face of the income statement (SOP 81-1, par. 88)
12. The nature and amount of any large or unusual contract commitments (FAS-5, par. 18)
13. The unbilled costs and fees under cost-type contracts should be shown separately from billed accounts receivable (ARB-43, Ch. 11A, par. 21)

EXAMPLES OF FINANCIAL STATEMENT DISCLOSURES

The following sample disclosures are available on the accompanying disc.

Example 19–1: General Accounting Policy for Contracts under the Percentage-of-Completion Method

Sales and cost of sales related to long-term contracts are accounted for under the percentage-of-completion method. Sales under fixed-type contracts are generally recognized upon passage of title to the customer, which usually coincides with physical delivery or customer acceptance as specified in contractual terms. Such sales are recorded at the cost of items delivered or accepted plus a proportion of profit expected to be realized on a contract, based on the ratio of such costs to total estimated costs at completion. Sales, including estimated earned fees, under cost reimbursement-type contracts are recognized as costs are incurred.

Profits expected to be realized on contracts are based on the Company's estimates of total contract sales value and costs at completion. These estimates are reviewed and revised periodically throughout the lives of the contracts with adjustments to profits resulting from such revisions being recorded on a cumulative basis in the period in which the revisions are made. When management believes the cost of completing a contract, excluding general and administrative expenses, will exceed contract-related revenues, the full amount of the anticipated contract loss is recognized.

Revenues recognized in excess of amounts billed are classified as current assets under "Contract work-in-progress." Amounts billed to clients in excess of revenues recognized to date are classified as current liabilities under "Advance billings on contracts."

Example 19–2: General Accounting Policy for Contracts under the Completed-Contract Method

Revenues from fixed-price contracts are recognized on the completed-contract method. This method is used because the typical contract is completed in three months or less, and financial position and results of operations do not vary significantly from those that would result from use of the percentage-of-completion method. A contract is considered complete when all costs except significant items have been incurred and the installation is operating according to specifications or has been accepted by the customer. Revenues from time-and-material contracts are recognized currently as the work is performed.

Contract costs include all direct material and labor costs and those indirect costs related to contract performance, such as indirect labor, supplies, tools, repairs, and depreciation costs. General and administrative costs are charged to expense as incurred. Provisions for estimated losses on uncompleted contracts are made in the period in which such losses are determined.

Costs in excess of amounts billed are classified as current assets under "Costs in excess of billings on uncompleted contracts." Billings in excess of costs are classified as current liabilities under "Billings in excess of costs on uncompleted contracts."

Example 19–3: Revenue Recognized under Both the Completed-Contract and the Percentage-of-Completion Methods of Accounting

Revenue is recognized on both the completed-contract and the percentage-of-completion methods of accounting. The Company uses the percentage-of-completion method of accounting for all contracts that exceed $1 million in net operating revenues and recognizes such revenue upon incurring costs equal to the lesser of 25% of the contract costs or $500,000. Progress on percentage-of-completion contracts is measured generally by costs incurred to date compared with an estimate of total costs at the project's completion. Provision is made for anticipated losses, if any, on uncompleted contracts.

Example 19–4: Methods of Measuring Percentage of Completion Are Described

Revenues from long-term contracts are recognized on the percentage-of-completion method. Percentage-of-completion is measured principally by the percentage of costs incurred and accrued to date for each contract to the estimated total costs for each contract at completion. Certain of the Company's electrical contracting business units measure percentage-of-completion by the percentage of labor costs incurred to date for each contract to the estimated total labor costs for such contract.

The Company also enters into long-term contracts for the manufacture of products. Sales on production-type contracts are recorded as deliveries are made (units-of-delivery method of percentage-of-completion).

Example 19–5: Research and Development Contracts with Anticipated Losses

On a selective basis, the Company may enter into a contract to research and develop or manufacture a product with a loss anticipated at the date the contract is signed. These contracts are entered into in anticipation that profits will be obtained from future contracts for the same or similar products. These loss contracts often provide the Company with intellectual property rights that, in effect, establish it as the sole producer of certain products. Such losses are recognized at the date the Company becomes contractually obligated, with revisions made as changes occur in the related estimates to complete.

Example 19–6: Description of Segmented Contracts

Contracts are segmented between types of services, such as engineering and construction, and, accordingly, gross margin related to each activity is recognized as those separate services are rendered.

Example 19–7: Concentrations of Credit Risk

The majority of accounts receivable and all contract work-in-progress are from engineering and construction clients in various industries and locations throughout the United States. Most contracts require payments as the projects progress or in certain cases advance payments. The Company generally does not require collateral but in most cases can place liens against the property, plant, or equipment constructed or terminate the contract if a material default occurs. Accounts receivable from customers of the Company's Eastern operations are primarily concentrated in the steel and utility industries. The Company maintains adequate reserves for potential credit losses and such losses have been minimal and within management's estimates.

Example 19–8: Accounting for Cost Overruns under Fixed-Price Contracts

Under fixed-price contracts, the Company may encounter, and on certain programs from time to time has encountered, cost overruns caused by increased material, labor, or overhead costs; design or production difficulties; and various other factors such as technical and manufacturing complexity, which must be, and in such cases have been, borne by the Company. Adjustments to contract cost estimates are made in the periods in which the facts requiring such revisions become known. When the revised estimate indicates a loss, such loss is provided for currently in its entirety.

Example 19–9: Details of Contract Receivables Balance

Following are the details of contract receivables at December 31, 2000, and December 31, 1999:

	2000	*1999*
Amounts billed:		
Completed contracts	$1,217,000	$1,062,000
Contracts in progress	3,892,000	3,259,000
Retentions	813,000	768,000
	5,922,000	5,089,000
Unbilled	231,000	184,000
	6,153,000	5,273,000
Less: allowance for doubtful accounts	(197,000)	(239,000)
	$5,956,000	$5,034,000

Of the retentions balance and the unbilled amounts at December 31, 2000, approximately $613,000 is expected to be collected in the year 2001, with the balance to be collected in subsequent years as contract deliveries are made and warranty periods expire.

Example 19–10: Details of Costs and Estimated Earnings on Uncompleted Contracts Reconciled to the Balance Sheets

Costs and estimated earnings on uncompleted contracts and related amounts billed as of December 31, 2000, and December 31, 1999, are as follows:

	2000	*1999*
Costs incurred on uncompleted contracts	$2,737,507	$2,282,127
Estimated earnings	202,211	158,832
	2,939,718	2,440,959
Less: billings to date	(2,983,243)	(2,479,998)
	$(43,525)	$(39,039)

Such amounts are included in the accompanying Balance Sheets at December 31, 2000, and December 31, 1999, under the following captions:

	2000	*1999*
Costs and estimated earnings in excess of billings on uncompleted contracts	$91,569	$73,794
Billings in excess of costs and estimated earnings on uncompleted contracts	(135,094)	(112,833)
	$(43,525)	$(39,039)

Example 19–11: Allowances for Contract Losses Included in Current Liabilities

Other current liabilities at December 31, 2000, and December 31, 1999, include allowances for contract losses and other contract allowances aggregating $600,000 and $900,000, respectively.

Example 19–12: Contract Revenue from Claims Recognized When the Amounts Are Awarded or Resolved

The Company's policy is to recognize contract revenue from claims against customers and others on construction projects only when the amounts are awarded or resolved. Revenues from such claims amounted to $647,000 in 2000 and $483,000 in 1999.

Example 19–13: Contract Revenue from Claims Recognized When Realization Is Probable

The Company's policy is to recognize contract revenue from claims against customers and others on construction projects when realization is probable, the amount could be reasonably estimated, and the claim has reasonable legal basis. Claims involve the use of estimates and it is reasonably possible that revisions to the estimated recoverable amounts of recorded claims may be made in the near-term.

Example 19–14: Amounts Recognized from Claims and Pending Change Orders Disclosed and Identified in Balance Sheet Captions

Costs and estimated earnings in excess of billings on uncompleted contracts include unbilled revenues for pending change orders of approximately $590,000 and $417,000 at December 31, 2000, and December 31, 1999, respectively; and claims of approximately $370,000 and $223,000 at December 31, 2000, and December 31, 1999, respectively. In addition, accounts receivable as of December 31, 2000, and December 31, 1999, includes claims and contractually billed amounts related to such contracts of approximately $900,000 and $716,000, respectively. Generally, the customer will not pay contractually billed amounts to the Company until final resolution of related claims.

Example 19–15: Contingent Liability in Respect of Performance and Payment Bonds Issued by Sureties

The Company is contingently liable to sureties in respect of performance and payment bonds issued by the sureties in connection with certain contracts entered into by the Company in the normal course of business. The Company has agreed to indemnify the sureties for any payments made by them in respect of such bonds.

Example 19–16: Change from the Completed-Contract Method to the Percentage-of-Completion Method of Accounting

Effective January 1, 2000, the Company changed its method of accounting for long-term contracts from the completed-contract method to the percentage-of-completion method. The Company believes that the new method more accurately reflects periodic results of operations and conforms to revenue recognition practices predominant in the industry. The effect of this change was to increase 2000 net income by $600,000. The change has been applied to prior years by retroactively restating the financial statements presented for 1999. The effect of the restatement was to increase retained earnings as of January 1, 1999, by $1,000,000. The restatement decreased 1999 net income by $305,000.

> **Note:** The following table illustrates the retroactive application of the change as shown on the face of the Company's Statement of Retained Earnings or Statement of Stockholders' Equity (assume the Company's year-end is December 31 and the latest year presented is 2000).

Statement of Retained Earnings or Statement of Stockholders' Equity

	2000	*1999*
Retained earnings at beginning of year, as previously reported	$4,400,000	$2,900,000
Cumulative effect on prior years of retroactive restatement for accounting change	-0-	1,000,000
Retained earnings at beginning of year, as restated	4,400,000	3,900,000
Net income	650,000	500,000
Retained earnings at end of year	$5,050,000	$4,400,000

CHAPTER 20
NONMONETARY TRANSACTIONS

CONTENTS

EXECUTIVE SUMMARY

As a general rule, accounting for nonmonetary transactions (i.e., exchanges and nonreciprocal transfers that involve little or no monetary assets or liabilities) should be based on the fair value of the assets or services involved and any gain or loss should be recognized. However, certain exceptions exist for (a) exchanges involving similar assets, (b) nonreciprocal transfers to owners, and (c) exchanges in which fair value is not determinable.

An *exchange* is a reciprocal transfer in which each party to the transaction receives and/or gives up assets, liabilities, or services. Exchanges can be either monetary or nonmonetary, or a combination of both. Nonmonetary exchanges usually are for the mutual convenience of two businesses. An example would be an exchange of inventory for trucking services.

A *nonreciprocal transfer* is a transfer of assets or services in one direction, either from an enterprise to its owners or another entity, or from owners or another entity to the enterprise. Examples of nonreciprocal transfers are as follows:

1. Distribution of nonmonetary assets, such as marketable equity securities, to stockholders as dividends

2. Distribution of nonmonetary assets to stockholders to redeem or acquire outstanding capital stock of the entity
3. Distribution of nonmonetary assets, such as capital stock of subsidiaries, to stockholders in corporate liquidations or plans of reorganization that involve disposing of all or a significant segment of the business (such plans are variously referred to as *spin-offs, split-ups,* and *split-offs*)
4. Distribution of nonmonetary assets to groups of stockholders, pursuant to plans of rescission or other settlements relating to a prior business combination, to redeem or acquire shares of capital stock previously issued in a business combination
5. Charitable contributions by an entity
6. Contribution of land by a governmental unit for construction of productive facilities by an entity

When a nonmonetary asset is involuntarily converted to a monetary asset, a monetary transaction results, and a gain or loss should be recognized in the period of conversion. The gain or loss is the difference between the carrying amount of the nonmonetary asset and the proceeds from the conversion. Examples of involuntary conversion are the total or partial destruction of property through fire or other catastrophe, theft of property, or condemnation of property by a governmental authority (eminent domain proceedings).

Authoritative Literature

APB-29	Accounting for Nonmonetary Transactions
FAS-109	Accounting for Income Taxes
FIN-30	Accounting for Involuntary Conversions of Nonmonetary Assets to Monetary Assets

DISCLOSURE REQUIREMENTS

The following disclosures should be made regarding nonmonetary transactions (APB-29, par. 28):

1. The nature of the nonmonetary transaction
2. The basis of accounting for the assets transferred
3. Gains or losses recognized

In addition, gains and losses resulting from involuntary conversions of nonmonetary assets to monetary assets should be reported as either an extraordinary item or an unusual or infrequent item as appropriate (FIN-30, par. 4).

EXAMPLES OF FINANCIAL STATEMENT DISCLOSURES

The following sample disclosures are available on the accompanying disc.

Example 20–1: Barter Transactions

In 2000 and 1999, the Company entered into barter agreements whereby it delivered $1,165,000 and $1,059,000, respectively, of its inventory in exchange for future advertising credits and other items. The credits, which expire in November 2001, are valued at the lower of the Company's cost or market value of the inventory transferred. The Company has recorded barter credits of $115,000 and $236,000 in "Prepaid expenses and other current assets" at December 31, 2000, and December 31, 1999, respectively. At December 31, 2000, and December 31, 1999, "Other noncurrent assets" include $279,000 and $323,000, respectively, of such credits. Under the terms of the barter agreements, the Company is required to pay cash equal to a negotiated amount of the bartered advertising, or other items, and use the barter credits to pay the balance. These credits are charged to expense as they are used. During the years ended December 31, 2000, and December 31, 1999, approximately $1,080,000 and $751,000, respectively, were charged to expense for barter credits used.

The Company assesses the recoverability of barter credits periodically. Factors considered in evaluating the recoverability include management's plans with respect to advertising and other expenditures for which barter credits can be used. Any impairment losses are charged to operations as they are determinable. During the years ended December 31, 2000, and December 31, 1999, the Company charged $250,000 and $425,000, respectively, to operations for such impairment losses.

Example 20–2: Notes Receivable Balance Due from Related Parties Is Paid through Forfeiture of Bonuses

As of December 31, 1999, the Company had notes receivable due from certain executives and officers amounting to approximately $1,500,000. These notes bear interest at rates ranging from 7.25% to 7.85% and have maturities of six months to five years. In 2000, $625,000 of the notes receivable balance was paid through forfeiture of management bonuses.

Example 20–3: Common Stock Awarded as Compensation

During 2000 and 1999, common stock with an aggregate fair market value of $515,000 and $496,000, respectively, was awarded to key executives as compensation.

Example 20–4: Contribution of Subsidiary Stock

During 2000, the Company's contributions to the Advest Foundation consisted of 55,000 shares of the Company's majority-owned Plantex subsidiary. A pretax-gain of $120,000 was recorded on the donations. The shares contributed to the Advest Foundation had a market value of $425,000, which was recorded as a contribution expense in the accompanying 2000 Income Statement.

Example 20–5: Distribution of Nonmonetary Assets to Stockholders as Dividends

In 2000, the Company declared and paid a dividend to its stockholders in the form of shares of common stock of Santorest & Co., whose stock the Company held as an investment. The Company's stockholders received three shares of Santorest & Co. common stock for each share of the Company's stock held. As a result, retained earnings was charged a total of $317,000, which represents the aggregate market value of the shares of Santorest & Co. that were issued as a dividend. In connection with this transaction, the Company recognized a gain of $116,000 in 2000, which represents the excess of the aggregate market value of the shares of Santorest & Co. issued over the aggregate carrying value of these shares.

Example 20–6: Spin-Off of a Business Segment

In May 2000, the Company announced plans to spin off its electronic connectors business to shareholders in a tax-free distribution. In August 2000, the Company's Board of Directors approved the spin-off effective December 31, 2000, to shareholders of record as of December 17, 2000, through the issuance of shares in a new legal entity, Electors, Inc. Common shares were distributed on a basis of one share of Electors, Inc. for every five shares of the Company's common stock.

The consolidated financial results of the Company have been restated to reflect the divestiture of Electors, Inc. Accordingly, the revenues, costs, and expenses; assets and liabilities; and cash flows of Electors, Inc. have been excluded from their respective captions in the Consolidated Statements of Income, Consolidated Balance Sheets, and Consolidated Statements of Cash Flows. These items have been reported as "Income from discontinued operations, net of income taxes" in the Consolidated Statements of Income; "Net assets of discontinued operations" in the Consolidated Balance Sheets; and "Net cash flows from discontinued operations" and "Net investing and financing activities of discontinued operations" in the Consolidated Statements of Cash Flows.

As of December 31, 2000, the net assets of the discontinued segment of $4,289,000 have been charged against the Company's retained earnings to reflect the spin-off. During 2000, the Company recorded a pretax charge of $615,000 ($483,000 after taxes) for expenses related to the spin-off.

The following table summarizes financial information for the discontinued operations for all periods presented:

	2000	*1999*
Net sales	$8,300,000	$8,750,000
Income before income taxes	$ 211,000	$ 273,000
Net income	$ 107,000	$ 182,000
Current assets	$2,436,000	$2,543,000
Total assets	$8,161,000	$8,615,000
Current liabilities	$2,597,000	$1,796,000
Total liabilities	$3,872,000	$3,978,000
Net assets of discontinued operations	$4,289,000	$4,637,000

CHAPTER 21
PENSION PLANS

CONTENTS

EXECUTIVE SUMMARY

A *pension plan* may be broadly classified as either a defined benefit plan or a defined contribution plan. A *defined benefit pension plan* is one that contains a pension benefit formula, which generally describes the amount of pension benefit that each employee will receive for services performed during a specified period of employment. A *defined contribution pension plan* provides an individual account for each participant and specifies how contributions to each individual's account are determined.

Generally accepted accounting principles (GAAP) for employers' accounting for pension plans center on the determination of annual pension expense (identified as net periodic pension cost) and the presentation of an appropriate amount of pension liability in the statement of financial position. Net periodic pension cost has often been viewed as a single amount, but it is actually made up of several components that reflect different aspects of the employer's financial arrangements as well as the cost of benefits earned by employees.

A pension plan may be contributory or noncontributory; that is, the employees may be required to contribute to the plan (contributory), or the entire cost of the plan may be borne by the employer (noncontributory). A pension plan may be funded or unfunded; that is, the employees and/or the employer may make cash contributions to a pension plan trustee (funded), or the employer may make only credit entries on its books reflecting the pension liability under the plan (unfunded). Pension plans are accounted for on the accrual basis and any difference between net periodic pension cost charged against income and the amount actually funded is recorded as an accrued or prepaid pension cost.

Defined Benefit Pension Plans

An entity's *net periodic pension cost* represents the net amount of pension cost for a specified period that is charged against income. Under

GAAP, the components of net periodic pension cost are (a) service cost; (b) interest cost on the projected benefit obligation; (c) actual return on plan assets; (d) amortization of unrecognized prior service cost, if any; (e) recognition of net gain or loss, if any; and (f) amortization of any unrecognized net obligation or net asset.

Net periodic pension cost is estimated in advance at the beginning of a period based on actuarial assumptions relating to (a) the discount rate on the projected benefit obligation, (b) the expected long-term rate of return on pension plan assets, and (c) the average remaining service periods of active employees covered by the pension plan. At the end of the period, adjustments are made to account for the differences (actuarial gains or losses), if any, between the estimated and actual amounts.

If an employer's total contribution to its pension plan for the period is not equal to the amount of net periodic pension cost, the employer recognizes the difference either as a liability or as an asset (i.e., accrued/prepaid pension cost). A liability (unfunded accrued pension cost) is recognized if the amount of contribution is *less* than the amount of net periodic pension cost. If the amount of contribution is *more* than the amount of net periodic pension cost, the employer recognizes an asset (prepaid pension cost).

An employer's *unfunded accumulated benefit obligation* is the amount by which the accumulated benefit obligation exceeds the amount of the fair value of plan assets as of a specific date. GAAP requires an *additional minimum liability* to be recognized in the employer's statement of financial position if an unfunded accumulated benefit obligation exists and (a) an asset has been recognized as prepaid pension cost, (b) a liability has been recognized as unfunded accrued pension cost in an amount that is less than the amount of the existing unfunded accumulated benefit obligation, or (c) no accrued or prepaid pension cost has been recognized. If an asset has been recognized as prepaid pension cost, the additional minimum liability is the amount of the existing unfunded accumulated benefit obligation plus the amount of the prepaid pension cost. If a liability has been recognized as unfunded accrued pension cost in an amount that is less than the amount of the existing unfunded accumulated benefit obligation, the additional minimum liability is the amount of the existing unfunded accumulated benefit obligation reduced by the amount of the unfunded accrued pension cost. If no accrued or prepaid pension cost has been recognized, the additional minimum liability is the amount of the existing unfunded accumulated benefit obligation.

If an additional minimum liability is required to be recognized, generally an intangible asset in the same amount as the additional minimum liability is recognized. However, the amount of the intangible asset cannot exceed the total amount of any existing unrecognized prior service cost and any unrecognized net obligation. In the event that the intangible asset exceeds the total existing unrecognized prior service cost and unrecognized net obligation, the excess is reported as a separate negative component of stockholders' equity, net of related tax benefits.

If an employer sponsors more than one defined benefit pension plan, the assets of one plan should not be applied to reduce or eliminate the unfunded accrued pension cost and/or minimum additional liability of another plan, unless the employer clearly has the right to do so. An excess of plan assets over the accumulated benefit obligation or prepaid pension cost of one plan cannot be applied to reduce or eliminate a liability of another plan.

Defined Contribution Pension Plans

A defined contribution pension plan provides for individual accounts for each plan participant and contains the terms that specify how contributions are determined for each participant's individual account. Each periodic employer contribution is allocated to each participant's individual account in accordance with the terms of the plan, and pension benefits are based solely on the amount available in each participant's account at the time of his or her retirement. The amount available in each participant's account at the time of his or her retirement is the total of the amounts contributed by the employer, plus the returns earned on investments of those contributions, plus forfeitures of other participants' benefits that have been allocated to the participant's account, and less any allocated administrative expenses.

The net periodic pension cost of a defined contribution pension plan is the amount of contributions in a period that are made to the individual accounts of participants who performed services during that same period. Contributions for periods after an individual retires or terminates shall be estimated and accrued during periods in which the individual performs services.

Settlements, Curtailments, and Termination Benefits

A *settlement* of a pension plan is an irrevocable action that relieves the employer (or the plan) of primary responsibility for an obligation and eliminates significant risks related to the obligation and the assets used to effect the settlement. Examples of transactions that constitute a settlement include (a) making lump-sum cash payments to plan participants in exchange for their rights to receive specified pension benefits and (b) purchasing nonparticipating annuity contracts to cover vested benefits.

Gain or loss on a plan settlement is based on pension plan records that have been updated as of the day before the settlement. If the total pension plan obligation is settled by the employer, the maximum gain or loss is recognized. If part of the pension benefit obligation is settled, the employer must recognize a pro rata portion of the maximum gain or loss. For example, if a settlement results in a 40% reduction of the projected benefit obligation, an employer should recognize only 40% of the maximum gain or loss on the settlement. Gain or loss on a plan settlement is reported as an ordinary gain or loss, unless it meets the criteria of an extraordinary item.

A *curtailment* is a significant reduction in, or an elimination of, defined benefit accruals for present employees' future services. Examples of curtailments are (a) termination of employees' services earlier than expected, which may or may not involve closing a facility or discontinuing a segment of a business, and (b) termination or suspension of a plan so that employees do not earn additional defined benefits for future services.

If the total effects of a plan curtailment result in a loss, the loss is recognized when it is *probable* that the curtailment will occur and the effects of the curtailment can be *reasonably estimated*. If the total effects of a plan curtailment result in a gain, the gain is recognized only when the related employees terminate or the plan suspension or amendment is adopted. Gain or loss on the total effects of a pension plan curtailment is reported as an ordinary gain or loss, unless it meets the criteria of an extraordinary item.

Termination benefits are classified as either special or contractual. *Special termination benefits* are those that are offered to employees for a short period in connection with the termination of their employment. *Contractual termination benefits* are those that are required by the terms of an existing plan or agreement and that are provided only on the occurrence of a specified event, such as early retirement or the closing of a facility.

GAAP require employers to recognize the cost of termination benefits as a loss and corresponding liability. The recognition date depends on whether the benefits are special or contractual. The recognition date on which the employer records the loss and corresponding liability for special termination benefits occurs when (a) the employees accept the offer of the special termination benefits and (b) the amount of the cost of the benefits can be *reasonably estimated*. The recognition date on which the employer records the loss and corresponding liability for contractual termination benefits occurs when (a) it is *probable* that employees will be entitled to the benefits and (b) the amount of the cost of the benefits can be *reasonably estimated*. A loss on termination benefits is reported as an ordinary loss, unless it meets the criteria of an extraordinary item.

Authoritative Literature

APB-16	Business Combinations
FAS-87	Employers' Accounting for Pensions

FAS-88	Employers' Accounting for Settlements and Curtailments of Defined Benefit Pension Plans and for Termination Benefits
FAS-106	Employers' Accounting for Postretirement Benefits Other Than Pensions
FAS-109	Accounting for Income Taxes
FAS-130	Reporting Comprehensive Income
FAS-132	Employers' Disclosures about Pensions and Other Postretirement Benefits

DISCLOSURE REQUIREMENTS

The disclosure requirements for pension plans apply to both public and nonpublic entities. However, with respect to defined benefit pension plans, nonpublic entities are allowed to provide reduced disclosures, if they so elect, regardless of materiality.

Also, companies that have pension plans and other postretirement benefit plans may elect to present the required disclosures for their plans in a parallel format in a single note to the financial statements, since most of the disclosures about pension plans and postretirement benefit plans are similar.

Defined Benefit Pension Plans—Disclosure Requirements for All Public Entities and for Those Nonpublic Entities That Elect to Voluntarily Provide These Disclosures

The following disclosures should be made for defined benefit pension plans:

1. A description of the plan (FAS-132, par. 5)
2. For each income statement presented, the amount of net periodic pension cost recognized, showing separately the following (FAS-132, par. 5):
   a. Service cost component
   b. Interest cost component
   c. Expected return on plan assets for the period
   d. Amortization of the unrecognized transition obligation or asset
   e. Amount of recognized gains and losses
   f. Amount of prior service cost recognized
   g. Amount of gain or loss recognized due to a settlement or curtailment

3. For each balance sheet presented, the funded status of the plan, amounts not recognized in the entity's balance sheet, and amounts recognized in the entity's balance sheet, including the following (FAS-132, par. 5):
   a. The amount of any unamortized prior service cost
   b. The amount of unrecognized net gain or loss (including asset gains and losses not yet reflected in market-related value)
   c. The amount of any remaining unamortized, unrecognized net obligation, or net asset existing at the date of initial application of FAS-87
   d. The amount of net pension asset or liability
   e. Any intangible asset and the amount of accumulated other comprehensive income
4. For each balance sheet presented, a reconciliation of the beginning and ending balances of the benefit obligation, with separate disclosure of the following (FAS-132, par. 5):
   a. Service cost
   b. Interest cost
   c. Contributions by plan participants
   d. Actuarial gains and losses
   e. Foreign currency exchange rate changes
   f. Benefits paid
   g. Plan amendments
   h. Business combinations
   i. Divestitures
   j. Curtailments
   k. Settlements
   l. Special termination benefits
5. For each balance sheet presented, a reconciliation of the beginning and ending balances of the fair value of plan assets, including the effects of the following (FAS-132, par. 5):
   a. Actual return on plan assets
   b. Foreign currency exchange rate changes
   c. Contributions by employer
   d. Contributions by plan participants
   e. Benefits paid
   f. Business combinations
   g. Divestitures
   h. Settlements

6. For each income statement presented, the amount included within other comprehensive income arising from a change in the additional minimum pension liability recognized (FAS-132, par. 5)
7. For each balance sheet presented, the following assumptions used in the accounting for the plan (FAS-132, par. 5):
   a. The weighted-average assumed discount rate
   b. The weighted-average rate of compensation increase
   c. The weighted-average expected long-term rate of return on plan assets
8. The amounts and types of securities of the employer and related parties included in plan assets (FAS-132, par. 5)
9. The approximate amount of future annual benefits of plan participants covered by insurance contracts issued by the employer or related parties (FAS-132, par. 5)
10. Any significant transactions between the employer or related parties and the plan during the period (FAS-132, par. 5)
11. Any alternative amortization method used to amortize prior service costs or unrecognized net gains and losses (FAS-132, par. 5)
12. Any substantive commitment, such as past practice or a history of regular benefit increases, used as the basis for accounting for the benefit obligation (FAS-132, par. 5)
13. The cost of providing special or contractual termination benefits recognized during the period and a description of the nature of the event (FAS-132, par. 5)
14. An explanation of any significant change in the benefit obligation or plan assets not otherwise apparent in the above disclosures (FAS-132, par. 5)
15. For employers with two or more defined benefit pension plans, if disclosures for plans that have *projected* benefit obligations in excess of plan assets and for plans that have plan assets in excess of *projected* benefit obligations are presented on a combined basis, the following disclosures should be made separately (FAS-132, par. 6):
    a. The aggregate projected benefit obligations
    b. The aggregate fair value of plan assets
16. For employers with two or more defined benefit pension plans, if disclosures for plans that have *accumulated* benefit obligations in excess of plan assets and for plans that have plan assets in excess of *accumulated* benefit obligations are presented on a combined basis, the following disclosures should be made separately (FAS-132, par. 6):

   a. The aggregate accumulated benefit obligations
   b. The aggregate fair value of plan assets

17. If two or more defined benefit pension plans are combined, the amounts recognized as prepaid benefit costs and accrued benefit liabilities should be disclosed separately (FAS-132, par. 6)
18. Domestic and foreign defined benefit pension plans may be aggregated unless the benefit obligations of the foreign plans are significant relative to the total benefit obligation and the plans use significantly different assumptions (FAS-132, par. 7)

Defined Benefit Pension Plans—Reduced Disclosure Requirements for Nonpublic Entities

The following are the reduced disclosure requirements for defined benefit pension plans of nonpublic entities:

1. A brief description of the plan (FAS-132, par. 8)
2. For each balance sheet presented, the following information about the plan (FAS-132, par. 8):
   a. The benefit obligation
   b. The fair value of plan assets
   c. The funded status of the plan
   d. Employer contributions
   e. Participant contributions
   f. Benefits paid
3. For each balance sheet presented, the amounts recognized in the balance sheet, including (FAS-132, par. 8):
   a. The net pension prepaid assets or accrued liabilities
   b. The amount of any intangible asset recognized
   c. The amount of accumulated other comprehensive income recognized
4. For each income statement presented, the amount of net periodic benefit cost recognized and the amount included within other comprehensive income arising from a change in the minimum pension liability recognized pursuant to FAS-87, paragraph 37, as amended (FAS-132, par. 8)
5. For each balance sheet presented, the following assumptions used in the accounting for the plan (FAS-132, par. 8):
   a. The weighted-average assumed discount rate
   b. The weighted-average rate of compensation increase

   c. The weighted-average expected long-term rate of return on plan assets

6. The amounts and types of securities of the employer and related parties included in plan assets (FAS-132, par. 8)
7. The approximate amount of future annual benefits of plan participants covered by insurance contracts issued by the employer or related parties (FAS-132, par. 8)
8. Any significant transactions between the employer or related parties and the plan during the period (FAS-132, par. 8)
9. The nature and effect of significant nonroutine events, such as amendments, combinations, divestitures, curtailments, and settlements (FAS-132, par. 8)
10. For employers with two or more defined benefit pension plans, if disclosures for plans that have *projected* benefit obligations in excess of plan assets and for plans that have plan assets in excess of *projected* benefit obligations are presented on a combined basis, the following disclosures should be made separately (FAS-132, par. 6):
    a. The aggregate projected benefit obligations
    b. The aggregate fair value of plan assets
11. For employers with two or more defined benefit pension plans, if disclosures for plans that have *accumulated* benefit obligations in excess of plan assets and for plans that have plan assets in excess of *accumulated* benefit obligations are presented on a combined basis, the following disclosures should be made separately (FAS-132, par. 6):
    a. The aggregate accumulated benefit obligations
    b. The aggregate fair value of plan assets
12. If two or more defined benefit pension plans are combined, the amounts recognized as prepaid benefit costs and accrued benefit liabilities should be disclosed separately (FAS-132, par. 6)
13. Domestic and foreign defined benefit pension plans may be aggregated unless the benefit obligations of the foreign plans are significant relative to the total benefit obligation and the plans use significantly different assumptions (FAS-132, par. 7)

Defined Contribution Pension Plans

The following disclosures should be made for defined contribution pension plans:

1. A brief description of the plan (FAS-132, par. 9)
2. The amount of cost recognized as expense during the period (FAS-132, par. 9)

3. The nature and effect of significant matters affecting comparability of information for all periods presented, such as a change in the rate of employer contributions, business combinations, or divestitures (FAS-132, par. 9)

Multiemployer Pension Plans

The following disclosures should be made for multiemployer pension plans:

1. The amount of employer contributions during the period (amounts attributable to pensions and other postretirement benefit plans may be combined) (FAS-132, par. 10)
2. A description of the nature and effect of any changes affecting comparability, such as a change in the rate of employer contributions, business combinations, or divestitures (FAS-132, par. 10)
3. If it is either probable or reasonably possible that an employer would withdraw from a multiemployer plan under circumstances that would give rise to a withdrawal obligation, disclosure of the information required by FAS-5 should be made (FAS-132, par. 11)

EXAMPLES OF FINANCIAL STATEMENT DISCLOSURES

The following sample disclosures are available on the accompanying disc.

Example 21–1: Defined Benefit Pension Plans with No Minimum Liability

The Company sponsors two funded defined benefit pension plans for eligible employees who are 21 years of age with one or more years of service and who are not covered by collective bargaining agreements. Benefits paid to retirees are based on age at retirement, years of credited service, and average compensation. The Company's funding policy is to contribute the larger of the amount required to fully fund the Plan's current liability or the amount necessary to meet the funding requirements as defined by the Internal Revenue Code.

The Company also sponsors an unfunded Executive Pension Plan. This plan is nonqualified and provides certain key employees defined pension benefits that supplement those provided by the Company's other retirement plans.

The following table sets forth the benefit obligation, fair value of plan assets, and the funded status of the Company's Plans; amounts recognized in the Company's financial statements; and the principal weighted average assumptions used:

	2000	*1999*
Change in projected benefit obligation:		
Benefit obligation at beginning of year	$27,800,000	$23,200,000
Service cost	1,700,000	1,500,000
Interest cost	1,900,000	2,000,000
Actuarial loss	4,700,000	1,900,000
Divestitures	(100,000)	-0-
Curtailments	(6,800,000)	-0-
Benefits paid	(300,000)	(800,000)
Benefit obligation at end of year	$28,900,000	$27,800,000
Change in plan assets:		
Fair value of plan assets at beginning of year	$22,700,000	$18,300,000
Actual return on plan assets	1,200,000	4,500,000
Employer contributions	1,300,000	700,000
Divestitures	(300,000)	-0-
Benefits paid	(900,000)	(800,000)
Fair value of plan assets at end of year	$24,000,000	$22,700,000
Funded status	$(4,900,000)	$(5,100,000)
Unrecognized net actuarial gain	(1,700,000)	(1,800,000)
Unrecognized prior service cost	700,000	1,900,000
Unrecognized net transition obligation	(200,000)	(300,000)
Accrued pension cost	$(6,100,000)	$(5,300,000)
Amounts recognized in the balance sheets consist of:		
Prepaid pension cost included with other assets	$300,000	$300,000
Accrued pension cost included with accrued liabilities	(6,400,000)	(5,600,000)
Net amount recognized at end of year	$(6,100,000)	$(5,300,000)
Weighted-average assumptions as of December 31:		
Discount rate	6.50%	7.25%
Expected return on plan assets	9.75%	9.75%
Rate of compensation increase	5.00%	5.25%

Components of net periodic benefit cost are as follows:

	2000	*1999*
Service cost—Benefits earned during the period	$1,700,000	$1,500,000
Interest cost on projected benefit obligations	1,900,000	2,000,000
Expected return on plan assets	(1,800,000)	(1,300,000)
Amortization of prior service cost	100,000	200,000
Amortization of actuarial loss	200,000	-0-
Net periodic benefit cost	$2,100,000	$2,400,000

The following table summarizes the Company-sponsored pension plans that have projected benefit obligations in excess of plan assets and the accumulated benefit obligation of the unfunded Executive Pension Plan in which the accumulated benefit obligation exceeds plan assets:

	2000	*1999*
Projected benefit obligation in excess of plan assets:		
Projected benefit obligation	$3,900,000	$4,200,000
Fair value of plan assets	$2,800,000	$2,600,000
Accumulated benefit obligation in excess of plan assets:		
Accumulated benefit obligation	$1,300,000	$1,100,000
Fair value of plan assets	$ -0-	$ -0-

The plan's assets are invested in directed trusts. Assets in the directed trusts are invested in common stocks, U.S. government obligations, corporate bonds, international equity mutual funds, real estate, and money market funds.

Example 21–2: Defined Benefit Pension Plans with No Minimum Liability—Alternative Reduced Disclosures for a Nonpublic Entity

Note: Example 21–2 illustrates the alternative reduced disclosures for a nonpublic entity using the same facts in Example 21–1.

The Company sponsors two funded defined benefit pension plans for eligible employees who are 21 years of age with one or more years of service and who are not covered by collective bargaining agreements. Benefits paid to retirees are based on age at retirement,years of credited service, and average compensation. The Company's funding policy is to contribute the larger of the amount required to fully fund the Plan's current liability or the amount necessary to meet the funding requirements as defined by the Internal Revenue Code.

The Company also sponsors an unfunded Executive Pension Plan. This plan is nonqualified and provides certain key employees defined pension benefits that supplement those provided by the Company's other retirement plans.

	2000	*1999*
Benefit obligation at December 31	$28,900,000	$27,800,000
Fair value of plan assets at December 31	24,000,000	22,700,000
Funded status	$(4,900,000)	$ (5,100,000)
Accrued pension cost	$(6,100,000)	$ (5,300,000)
Amounts recognized in the balance sheets consist of:		
Prepaid pension cost included with other assets	$300,000	$300,000
Accrued pension cost included with accrued liabilities	(6,400,000)	(5,600,000)
Net amount recognized at end of year	$(6,100,000)	$ (5,300,000)
Weighted-average assumptions as of December 31:		
Discount rate	6.50%	7.25%
Expected return on plan assets	9.75%	9.75%
Rate of compensation increase	5.00%	5.25%
Benefit cost	$ 2,100,000	$ 2,400,000
Employer contributions	$ 1,300,000	$ 700,000
Benefits paid	$ 300,000	$ 800,000

The following table summarizes the Company-sponsored pension plans that have projected benefit obligations in excess of plan assets and the accumulated benefit obligation of the unfunded Executive Pension Plan in which the accumulated benefit obligation exceeds plan assets:

	2000	*1999*
Projected benefit obligation in excess of plan assets:		
Projected benefit obligation	$3,900,000	$4,200,000
Fair value of plan assets	$2,800,000	$2,600,000
Accumulated benefit obligation in excess of plan assets:		
Accumulated benefit obligation	$1,300,000	$1,100,000
Fair value of plan assets	$ -0-	$ -0-

The plan's assets are invested in directed trusts. Assets in the directed trusts are invested in common stocks, U.S. government obligations, corporate bonds, international equity mutual funds, real estate, and money market funds.

Example 21–3: Disclosures for a Defined Benefit Pension Plan That Recognizes a Minimum Liability

The Company and its subsidiaries sponsor numerous defined benefit pension plans. The following table sets forth the benefit obligation, fair value of plan assets, and the funded status of the Company's Plans; amounts recognized in the Company's financial statements; and the principal weighted average assumptions used:

	2000	*1999*
Change in benefit obligation:		
Benefit obligation at beginning of year	$1,266,000	$1,200,000
Service cost	76,000	72,000
Interest cost	114,000	108,000
Amendments	(20,000)	-0-
Actuarial gain	(25,000)	-0-
Benefits paid	(125,000)	(114,000)
Benefit obligation at end of year	$1,286,000	$1,266,000
Change in plan assets:		
Fair value of plan assets at beginning of year	$1,156,000	$ 968,000
Actual return on plan assets	29,000	188,000
Employer contribution	139,000	114,000
Benefits paid	(125,000)	(114,000)
Fair value of plan assets at end of year	$1,199,000	$1,156,000

	2000	*1999*
Funded status	$ (87,000)	$(110,000)
Unrecognized actuarial loss	83,000	38,000
Unrecognized prior service cost	170,000	225,000
Net amount recognized	$166,000	$153,000
Amounts recognized in the statement of financial position consist of:		
Prepaid benefit cost	$255,000	$227,000
Accrued benefit liability	(153,000)	(127,000)
Intangible asset	50,000	53,000
Accumulated other comprehensive income	14,000	-0-
Net amount recognized	$166,000	$153,000
Weighted-average assumptions as of December 31:		
Discount rate	9.25%	9.00%
Expected return on plan assets	10.00%	10.00%
Rate of compensation increase	5.00%	5.00%

Components of net periodic benefit cost are as follows:

	2000	*1999*
Service cost	$ 76,000	$ 72,000
Interest cost	114,000	108,000
Expected return on plan assets	(116,000)	(97,000)
Amortization of prior service cost	35,000	35,000
Recognized actuarial loss	17,000	11,000
Net periodic benefit cost	$126,000	$129,000

The projected benefit obligation, accumulated benefit obligation, and fair value of plan assets for the pension plans with accumulated benefit obligations in excess of plan assets were $263,000, $237,000, and $84,000, respectively, as of December 31, 2000, and $247,000, $222,000, and $95,000, respectively, as of December 31, 1999.

The provisions of Financial Accounting Standards Board Statement No. 87 (Employers' Accounting for Pensions) require the Company to record an additional minimum liability of $64,000 and $53,000 at December 31, 2000, and December 31, 1999, respectively. This liability represents the amount by which the accumulated benefit obligation exceeds the sum of the fair market value of plan assets and accrued amounts previously recorded. The additional liability may be offset by an intangible asset to the extent of previously unrecognized prior service cost. The intangible assets of $50,000 and $53,000 at December 31, 2000, and December 31, 1999, respectively, are included on the line item entitled "Other assets" in the Balance Sheets. The remaining amounts of $14,000 and $0 are recorded as a component of stockholders' equity, net of related tax benefits of $8,000 and $0, on the line item titled "Accumulated other comprehensive income (loss)" in the Balance Sheets at December 31, 2000, and December 31, 1999, respectively.

Example 21–4: Disclosures about Defined Benefit Pension Plans and Other Postretirement Benefit Plans Are Presented in a Parallel Format in a Single Note to the Financial Statements

The Company and its subsidiaries sponsor numerous defined benefit pension plans and other postretirement benefit plans. The following tables set forth the benefit obligation, fair value of plan assets, and the funded status of the Company's Plans; amounts recognized in the Company's financial statements; and the principal weighted average assumptions used:

	Pension Benefits		*Postretirement Benefits*	
	2000	*1999*	*2000*	*1999*
Change in benefit obligation:				
Benefit obligation at beginning of year	$1,266,000	$1,200,000	$738,000	$700,000
Service cost	76,000	72,000	36,000	32,000
Interest cost	114,000	108,000	65,000	63,000
Plan participants' contributions	-0-	-0-	20,000	13,000
Amendments	120,000	-0-	75,000	-0-
Actuarial gain	(25,000)	-0-	(24,000)	-0-
Acquisition	900,000	-0-	600,000	-0-
Benefits paid	(125,000)	(114,000)	(90,000)	(70,000)
Benefit obligation at end of year	$2,326,000	$1,266,000	$1,420,000	$738,000

	Pension Benefits		*Postretirement Benefits*	
	2000	*1999*	*2000*	*1999*
Change in plan assets:				
Fair value of plan assets at beginning of year	$1,068,000	$ 880,000	$ 206,000	$ 87,000
Actual return on plan assets	29,000	188,000	(3,000)	24,000
Acquisition	1,000,000	-0-	25,000	-0-
Employer contribution	75,000	114,000	171,000	152,000
Plan participants' contributions	-0-	-0-	20,000	13,000
Benefits paid	(125,000)	(114,000)	(90,000)	(70,000)
Fair value of plan assets at end of year	$2,047,000	$1,068,000	$ 329,000	$ 206,000
Funded status	$ (279,000)	$ (198,000)	$(1,091,000)	$(532,000)
Unrecognized net actuarial loss	83,000	38,000	59,000	60,000
Unrecognized prior service cost	260,000	160,000	585,000	540,000
Prepaid (accrued) benefit cost	$ 64,000	$ 0	$ (447,000)	$ 68,000

Weighted-average assumptions as of December 31:				
Discount rate	9.25%	9.00%	9.00%	9.00%
Expected return on plan assets	10.00%	10.00%	10.00%	10.00%
Rate of compensation increase	5.00%	5.00%	N/A	N/A

For measurement purposes, a 10% annual rate of increase in the per capita cost of covered healthcare benefits was assumed for 2001. The rate was assumed to decrease gradually to 4% for 2007 and remain at that level thereafter.

Components of net periodic benefit cost are as follows:

	Pension Benefits		*Postretirement Benefits*	
	2000	*1999*	*2000*	*1999*
Service cost	$76,000	$72,000	$36,000	$32,000
Interest cost	114,000	108,000	65,000	63,000
Expected return on plan assets	(107,000)	(88,000)	(21,000)	(9,000)
Amortization of prior service cost	20,000	20,000	30,000	30,000
Recognized net actuarial loss	8,000	2,000	1,000	1,000
Net periodic benefit cost	$111,000	$114,000	$111,000	$117,000

The Company acquired Massari, Ltd. on December 31, 2000, including its pension plans. As a result, the Company's plans were amended to establish parity with the benefits provided by Massari, Ltd.

The Company has multiple nonpension postretirement benefit plans. The healthcare plans are contributory, with participants' contributions adjusted annually; the life insurance plans are noncontributory. The accounting for the healthcare plans anticipates future cost sharing changes to the written plan that are consistent with the Company's expressed intent to increase retiree contributions each year by 50% of the excess of the expected general inflation rate over 6%. On December 31, 2000, the Company amended its postretirement healthcare plans to provide long-term care coverage.

Assumed healthcare cost trend rates have a significant effect on the amounts reported for the healthcare plans. A 1% point change in assumed healthcare cost trend rates would have the following effects:

	1% Point Increase	*1% Point Decrease*
Effect on total of service and interest cost components	$ 22,000	$ (20,000)
Effect on postretirement benefit obligation	$173,000	$(156,000)

Example 21–5: Profit Sharing Plan

The Company has a qualified profit sharing plan that covers substantially all full-time employees meeting certain eligibility requirements. The annual contribution is discretionary as determined by the Board of Directors; however, the contributions cannot exceed 15% of compensation for the eligible employees in any one tax year. The Company's contributions to the plan were $325,000 for 2000 and $215,000 for 1999.

Example 21–6: 401(k) Savings Plan

The Company has a 401(k) Plan (Plan) to provide retirement and incidental benefits for its employees. Employees may contribute from 1% to 15% of their annual compensation to the Plan, limited to a maximum annual amount as set periodically by the Internal Revenue Service. The Company matches employee contributions dollar for dollar up to a maximum of $1,500 per year per person. All matching contributions vest immediately. In addition, the Plan provides for discretionary contributions as determined by the board of directors. Such contributions to the Plan are allocated among eligible participants in the proportion of their salaries to the total salaries of all participants.

Company matching contributions to the Plan totaled $632,000 in 2000 and $595,000 in 1999. No discretionary contributions were made in 2000 or 1999.

Example 21–7: Money Purchase Pension Plan

The Company sponsors a trusted defined contribution money purchase pension plan covering substantially all employees meeting minimum age and service requirements and not covered by collective bargaining agreements. Contributions are based on a percentage of each eligible employee's compensation and are at about 10% of each covered employee's salary. The Company's contributions to the plan totaled $346,000 for 2000 and $271,000 for 1999.

Example 21–8: Incentive Bonus Plan

The Company has an Incentive Bonus Plan (Bonus Plan) for the benefit of its employees, including executive officers. The total amount of cash bonus awards to be made under the Bonus Plan for any plan year depends primarily on the Company's sales and net income for such year.

For any plan year, the Company's sales and net income must meet or exceed, or in combination with other factors satisfy, levels targeted by the Company in its business plan, as established at the beginning of each fiscal year, for any bonus awards to be made. Aggregate bonus awards to all participants under the Bonus Plan may not exceed 7% of the Company's net income. The board of directors has the authority to determine the total amount of bonus awards, if any, to be made to the eligible employees for any plan year based on its evaluation of the Company's financial condition and results of operations, the Company's business and prospects, and such other criteria as the Board may determine to be relevant or appropriate. The Company expensed $822,000 in 2000 and $320,000 in 1999 in conjunction with the Bonus Plan.

Example 21–9: Combined Disclosures of Defined Contribution Pension Plans and Defined Contribution Postretirement Plans

The Company sponsors several defined contribution pension plans covering substantially all employees. Employees may contribute to these plans and these contributions are matched in varying amounts by the Company. Defined contribution pension expense for the Company was $543,000 for 2000 and $429,000 for 1999.

Also, the Company sponsors defined contribution postretirement healthcare and life insurance benefit plans. Contributions to these plans were $311,000 in 2000 and $304,000 in 1999.

Example 21–10: Union-Sponsored Multiemployer Pension Plans

The Company participates in various multi-employer union-administered defined benefit pension plans that principally cover production workers. Total contributions to these plans were $472,000 for 2000 and $461,000 for 1999.

Example 21–11: Liability Resulting from Withdrawal from Multiemployer Pension Plan Is Recognized in the Financial Statements

Effective October 13, 2000, the Company decided to withdraw its participation in the Glass Workers Industry Pension Plan. As a result, the Company will be required to contribute its share of the Plan's unfunded benefit obligation. The Company's actuaries have advised that the Company's required contribution at the withdrawal date will be approximately $734,000. As a result, a provision for that amount has been charged against earnings in the 2000 Statement of Operations.

Example 21–12: Company Would Not Have a Material Liability If It Withdrew from Multiemployer Pension Plan

The Company's contributions to union-sponsored, defined benefit, multiemployer pension plans were $511,000 in 2000 and $473,000 in

1999. These plans are not administered by the Company and contributions are determined in accordance with provisions of negotiated labor contracts. As of December 31, 2000, the actuarially computed values of vested benefits for these plans were primarily equal to or less than the net assets of the plans. Therefore, the Company would have no material withdrawal liability. However, the Company has no present intention of withdrawing from any of these plans, nor has the Company been informed that there is any intention to terminate such plans.

Example 21–13: Curtailment and Special Termination Benefits

In January 2000, the Company offered a limited program of Retirement Enhancements. The Retirement Enhancements program provided for unreduced retirement benefits to the first 150 employees who retired before December 31, 2001. In addition, each retiring participant could elect a lump-sum payment of $25,000 or a $400 monthly supplement payable until age 62. As of December 31, 2000, a total of 125 employees applied for retirement under this program. The Retirement Enhancements program represented a curtailment and special termination benefits under Financial Accounting Standards Board Statement No. 88 (Employers' Accounting for Settlements and Curtailments of Defined Benefit Pension Plans and for Termination Benefits). The Company recorded a charge of $2,936,000 in 2000 to cover the Retirement Enhancements program.

CHAPTER 22
POSTEMPLOYMENT BENEFITS

CONTENTS

EXECUTIVE SUMMARY

Postemployment benefits are benefits provided to former or inactive employees, their beneficiaries, and covered dependents after employment but before retirement. Postemployment benefits may be provided in cash or in kind and may be paid as a result of a disability, layoff, death, or other event. They include, but are not limited to, salary continuation, supplemental unemployment benefits, severance benefits, disability-related benefits (including workers' compensation), job training and counseling, and continuation of benefits such as healthcare benefits and life insurance coverage.

Postemployment benefits should be accrued if they meet all of the following conditions:

1. They relate to services already rendered.
2. The employee's right to be paid postemployment benefits vests or accumulates.

3. It is probable the benefits will be paid.
4. The amount that will be paid can be reasonably estimated.

Postemployment benefits that do not meet all of the above criteria should be accounted for as contingencies; accordingly, they should be:

1. Accrued if (a) information available prior to issuance of the financial statements indicates that it is probable that a liability has been incurred at the balance sheet date and (b) the amount of the liability can be reasonably estimated
2. Disclosed (but not accrued) if (a) it is probable a liability exists but the amount of the liability cannot be reasonably estimated or (b) it is reasonably possible, but not probable, that a liability exists

Authoritative literature does not specifically address how to measure the postemployment benefit obligation. However, the literature does state that companies may refer to the guidance on measuring pension obligations (Chapter 21, "Pension Plans") and obligations for postretirement benefits other than pensions (Chapter 23, "Post-retirement Benefits Other Than Pensions"), to the extent similar issues apply to the postemployment benefits.

In addition, authoritative literature does not provide explicit guidance on discounting; therefore, the use of discounting in measuring postemployment benefit obligations is permitted but not required.

Authoritative Literature

FAS-112	Employers' Accounting for Postemployment Benefits
FAS-123	Accounting for Stock-Based Compensation

DISCLOSURE REQUIREMENTS

Authoritative literature does not require an entity to disclose the amount of postemployment benefits. However, if the entity has not accrued an obligation for postemployment benefits only because the amount cannot be reasonably estimated, the entity should disclose that fact in the financial statements (FAS-112, par. 7).

EXAMPLES OF FINANCIAL STATEMENT DISCLOSURES

The following sample disclosures are available on the accompanying disc.

Example 22–1: Company Discloses Amount of Postemployment Benefits Charged to Operations

> **Note:** Although authoritative literature does not require that the amount of postemployment benefits be disclosed, such disclosure is considered informative.

The Company provides certain postemployment benefits to eligible former or inactive employees and their dependents during the period subsequent to employment but prior to retirement and accrues for the related cost over the service lives of the employees. These benefits include certain disability and healthcare coverage and severance benefits. Postemployment benefit costs charged to operations in 2000 and 1999 totaled $97,000 and $73,000, respectively.

Example 22–2: Company Does Not Disclose Amount of Postemployment Benefits Charged to Operations

> **Note:** Although authoritative literature does not require that the amount of postemployment benefits be disclosed, such disclosure is considered informative.

The Company provides certain postemployment benefits to eligible former or inactive employees and their dependents during the period subsequent to employment but prior to retirement and accrues for the related cost over the service lives of the employees. These benefits include certain disability and healthcare coverage and severance benefits.

Example 22–3: Company Uses Discounting to Measure the Postemployment Benefit Obligation

> **Note:** The use of discounting in measuring postemployment benefit obligations is permitted but not required.

The Company provides certain benefits to former or inactive employees after employment but before retirement and accrues for the related cost over the service lives of the employees. Those benefits include, among others, disability, severance, and workers' compensation. The assumed discount rate used to measure the postemployment benefit liability was 7% at December 31, 2000, and 6.5% at December 31, 1999.

Example 22–4: Company Is Self-Insured under Its Postemployment Benefit Plans

The Company is self-insured under its employees' short-term and long-term disability plans, which are the primary benefits paid to inactive employees prior to retirement. Following is a summary of the obligation for postemployment benefits included in the Company's balance sheets at December 31, 2000, and December 31, 1999:

	2000	*1999*
Included with "Salaries and related liabilities"	$105,000	$102,000
Included with "Other long-term liabilities"	693,000	607,000
	$798,000	$709,000

Example 22–5: Company Has Not Accrued a Liability for Postemployment Benefits Because the Amount Cannot Be Reasonably Estimated

Financial Accounting Standards Board Statement No. 112 (Employers' Accounting for Postemployment Benefits) requires employers to recognize an obligation for benefits provided to former or inactive employees after employment but before retirement. The Company provides the following postemployment benefits to former and inactive employees: supplemental unemployment benefits, disability-related benefits, and job training and counseling. It is not practicable for the Company to reasonably estimate the amount of its obligation for postemployment benefits; accordingly, no liability for postemployment benefits has been recorded in the accompanying financial statements. The Company's policy is to recognize the costs of such postemployment benefits when actually paid.

CHAPTER 23
POSTRETIREMENT BENEFITS OTHER THAN PENSIONS

CONTENTS

EXECUTIVE SUMMARY

A *postretirement benefit plan* is one in which an employer agrees to provide certain postretirement benefits to current and former employees after they retire, upon the occurrence of a covered event, such as retirement, death, disability, or termination of employment. Generally accepted accounting principles (GAAP) require the accrual of postretirement benefits in a manner similar to the recognition of net periodic pension cost for pension plans.

A postretirement plan may be broadly classified as either a defined benefit plan or a defined contribution plan. In a *defined benefit postretirement plan,* the benefit may be defined in terms of a specified monetary amount (such as a life insurance benefit) or a specified type of benefit (such as all or a percentage of the cost of specified surgical procedures). A *defined contribution postretirement plan* provides an individual account for each participant and specifies how contributions to each individual's account are determined.

A postretirement benefit plan may be *contributory* (employees may be required to contribute to the plan) or *noncontributory* (the entire cost of the plan is borne by the employer).

Also, a postretirement benefit plan may be *funded* or *unfunded*—that is, the employees and/or the employer may make cash contributions to a postretirement benefit plan trustee (i.e., funded), or the employer may make only credit entries on its books reflecting the postretirement benefit liability under the plan and pay all benefits from its general assets (i.e., unfunded).

Defined Benefit Postretirement Plans

The entity's primary objectives when accounting for a defined benefit postretirement plan are to (1) charge postretirement benefit costs to operations over the period employee services are rendered and (2) charge liabilities and credit assets when retirement benefits are paid. The annual cost of a defined benefit postretirement plan consists of the following components: (1) service cost; (2) interest cost on the plan's obligation to provide benefits; (3) actual return on plan assets; (4) amortization of unrecognized prior service cost, if any; (5) recognition of net gain or loss, if any; and (6) amortization of any unrecognized net obligation or net asset.

Net periodic postretirement cost is estimated in advance at the beginning of a period based on actuarial assumptions such as the discount rate on accumulated benefit obligation, the expected long-term rate of return on postretirement plan assets, and future compensation levels. At the end of the period, adjustments are made to account for the differences (actuarial gains or losses), if any, between the estimated and actual amounts.

Most postretirement benefit plans include healthcare benefits, which require the use of additional unique assumptions such as per capita claims cost (the current cost of providing postretirement healthcare benefit at each age at which a participant is expected to receive benefits), and healthcare cost trend rates.

If an employer's total contribution to its postretirement plan for the period is not equal to the amount of net periodic postretirement cost, the employer recognizes the difference either as a liability or as an asset (i.e., accrued/prepaid postretirement cost). A liability (unfunded accrued postretirement cost) is recognized if the amount of contribution is *less* than the amount of net periodic postretirement cost. If the amount of contribution is *more* than the amount of net periodic postretirement cost, an asset (prepaid postretirement cost) is recognized.

Defined Contribution Postretirement Plans

A *defined contribution postretirement plan* provides for individual accounts for each plan participant and contains the terms that specify how contributions are determined for each participant's individual account. Each periodic employer contribution is allocated to each participant's individual account in accordance with the terms of the plan, and postretirement benefits are based solely on the amount available in each participant's account at the time of his or her retirement. The amount available in each participant's account at the time of his or her retirement is the total of the amounts contributed by the employer, plus the returns earned on investments of those contributions, plus forfeitures of other participants' benefits that have been allocated to the participant's account, and less any allocated administrative expenses.

A defined contribution postretirement plan may require the employer to contribute to the plan only for periods in which an employee renders services, or the employer may be required to continue making payments for periods after the employee retires or terminates employment. To the extent an employer's contribution is made in the same period as the employee renders services, the employer's net periodic postretirement benefit cost equals the amount of contributions required for that period. If the plan requires the employer to continue contributions after the employee retires or terminates, the employer should make accruals during the employee's service period of the estimated amount of contributions to be made after the employee's retirement or termination.

Settlements, Curtailments, and Termination Benefits

A *settlement* of a postretirement plan is an irrevocable action that relieves the employer (or the plan) of primary responsibility for an obligation and eliminates significant risks related to the obligation and the assets used to effect the settlement. Examples of transactions that constitute a settlement include (1) making lump-sum cash payments to plan participants in exchange for their rights to receive specified postretirement benefits and (2) purchasing nonparticipating insurance contracts to cover the accumulated postretirement benefit obligation for some or all of the participants in the plan.

When a postretirement benefit obligation is settled, the maximum gain or loss to be recognized in income is the unrecognized gain or loss plus any unrecognized transition asset. This maximum gain or loss includes any gain or loss resulting from the remeasurement of plan assets and of the accumulated postretirement benefit obligation at the time of settlement.

A *curtailment* is an event that either (1) significantly reduces the expected years of future service of active plan participants or (2) eliminates the accrual of defined benefits for some or all of the future services of a significant number of active plan participants. Examples of curtailments are (1) termination of employees' services earlier than expected, which may or may not involve closing a facility or discontinuing a segment of a business, and (2) termination or suspension of a plan so that employees do not earn additional benefits for future services.

The unrecognized prior service cost associated with the portion of the future years of service that had been expected to be rendered, but as a result of a curtailment are no longer expected to be rendered, is a loss. If a curtailment occurs as the result of the termination of a significant number of employees who were plan participants, the curtailment loss consists of (1) the portion of the remaining unrecognized prior-service cost attributable to the previously estimated number of remaining future years of service of all terminated employees plus (2) the portion of the remaining unrecognized transition obligation attributable to the previously estimated number of remaining future years of service.

If a curtailment results from terminating the accrual of additional benefits for the future services of a significant number of employees, the curtailment loss consists of (1) the pro rata amount of the remaining unrecognized prior service cost plus (2) the pro rata amount of the remaining unrecognized transition obligation.

A curtailment may cause a gain by decreasing the accumulated postretirement benefit obligation, or a loss by increasing that obligation. If a curtailment decreases the accumulated obligation, the gain from this decrease is first used to offset any unrecognized net loss, and the excess is a curtailment gain. If a curtailment increases the accumulated obligation, the loss from this increase is first used to offset any unrecognized net gain, and the excess is a curtailment loss.

Termination benefits are classified as either special or contractual. *Special termination benefits* are those that are offered to employees for a short period in connection with the termination of their employment. *Contractual termination benefits* are those that are required by the terms of an existing plan or agreement and that are provided only on the occurrence of a specified event, such as early retirement or the closing of a facility.

GAAP require the recognition of the cost of termination benefits as a loss and corresponding liability. The recognition date depends on whether the benefits are special or contractual. Special termination benefits should be accrued when (1) the employees accept the offer of the special termination benefits and (2) the amount of the cost of the benefits can be *reasonably estimated*. The recognition date on which the employer records the loss and corresponding liability for contractual termination benefits occurs when (1) it is *probable* that employees will be entitled to the benefits and (2) the amount of the benefits to be provided can be *reasonably estimated*.

Authoritative Literature

FAS-88	Employers' Accounting for Settlements and Curtailments of Defined Benefit Pension Plans and for Termination Benefits
FAS-106	Employers' Accounting for Postretirement Benefits Other Than Pensions
FAS-112	Employers' Accounting for Postemployment Benefits
FAS-132	Employers' Disclosures about Pensions and Other Postretirement Benefits

DISCLOSURE REQUIREMENTS

The disclosure requirements for postretirement benefit plans apply to both public and nonpublic entities. However, with respect to defined benefit postretirement plans, nonpublic entities are allowed to provide reduced disclosures, if they so elect, regardless of materiality.

Also, companies that have pension plans and other postretirement benefit plans may elect to present the required disclosures for their plans in a parallel format in a single note to the financial statements, because most of the disclosures about pension plans and postretirement benefit plans are similar.

Defined Benefit Postretirement Plans—Disclosure Requirements for All Public Entities and for Those Nonpublic Entities That Elect to Voluntarily Provide These Disclosures

The following disclosures should be made for defined benefit postretirement plans:

1. A brief description of the plan (FAS-132, par. 5)
2. For each income statement presented, the amount of net periodic benefit cost for the period, showing separately the following (FAS-132, par. 5):
   a. Service cost component
   b. Interest cost component
   c. Expected return on plan assets for the period
   d. Amortization of the unrecognized transition obligation or asset
   e. Amount of recognized gains and losses
   f. Amount of prior service cost recognized
   g. Amount of gain or loss recognized due to a settlement or curtailment
3. For each balance sheet presented, the funded status of the plan, amounts not recognized in the entity's balance sheet, and amounts recognized in the entity's balance sheet, including the following (FAS-132, par. 5):
   a. The amount of any unamortized prior service cost
   b. The amount of unrecognized net gain or loss (including asset gains and losses not yet reflected in market-related value)
   c. The amount of any remaining unamortized, unrecognized net obligation or net asset existing at the date of initial application of FAS-106
   d. The net postretirement benefit prepaid assets or accrued liabilities
4. For each balance sheet presented, a reconciliation of the beginning and ending balances of the benefit obligation, with separate disclosure of the following (FAS-132, par. 5):
   a. Service cost
   b. Interest cost
   c. Contributions by plan participants
   d. Actuarial gains and losses
   e. Foreign currency exchange rate changes
   f. Benefits paid
   g. Plan amendments
   h. Business combinations
   i. Divestitures
   j. Curtailments

k. Settlements

l. Special termination benefits

5. For each balance sheet presented, a reconciliation of the beginning and ending balances of the fair value of plan assets, including the effects of the following (FAS-132, par. 5):

   a. Actual return on plan assets

   b. Foreign currency exchange rate changes

   c. Contributions by employer

   d. Contributions by plan participants

   e. Benefits paid

   f. Business combinations

   g. Divestitures

   h. Settlements

6. For each balance sheet presented, the following assumptions used in the accounting for the plan (FAS-132, par. 5):

   a. The weighted-average assumed discount rate

   b. The weighted-average rate of compensation increase (for pay-related plans)

   c. The weighted-average expected long-term rate of return on plan assets

7. The assumed healthcare cost trend rate(s) for the next year used to measure the expected cost of benefits covered by the plan (gross eligible charges), a general description of the direction and pattern of change in the assumed trend rates thereafter, together with the ultimate trend rate(s) and when that rate is expected to be achieved (FAS-132, par. 5)

8. The effect of a 1% point increase and the effect of a 1% point decrease in the assumed healthcare cost trend rates on (1) the aggregate of the service and interest cost components of net periodic postretirement healthcare benefit cost of the current period and (2) the accumulated postretirement benefit obligation for healthcare benefits as of the current balance sheet (FAS-132, par. 5)

9. The amounts and types of securities of the employer and related parties included in plan assets (FAS-132, par. 5)

10. The approximate amount of future annual benefits of plan participants covered by insurance contracts issued by the employer or related parties (FAS-132, par. 5)

11. Any significant transactions between the employer or related parties and the plan during the period (FAS-132, par. 5)

12. Any alternative amortization method used to amortize prior service costs or unrecognized net gains and losses (FAS-132, par. 5)
13. Any substantive commitment, such as past practice or a history of regular benefit increases, used as the basis for accounting for the benefit obligation (FAS-132, par. 5)
14. The cost of providing special or contractual termination benefits recognized during the period and a description of the nature of the event (FAS-132, par. 5)
15. An explanation of any significant change in the benefit obligation or plan assets not otherwise apparent in the above disclosures (FAS-132, par. 5)
16. For employers with two or more defined benefit postretirement plans, if disclosures for *underfunded plans* (those that have accumulated postretirement benefit obligations in excess of plan assets) and *overfunded plans* (those that have plan assets in excess of accumulated postretirement benefit obligations) are presented on a combined basis, the following disclosures should be made separately with respect to plans that are *underfunded* (FAS-132, par. 6):
    a. The aggregate accumulated postretirement benefit obligation
    b. The aggregate fair value of plan assets
17. If two or more defined benefit postretirement plans are combined, the amounts recognized as prepaid benefit costs and accrued benefit liabilities should be disclosed separately (FAS-132, par. 6)
18. Domestic and foreign defined benefit postretirement plans may be aggregated unless the benefit obligations of the foreign plans are significant relative to the total benefit obligation and the plans use significantly different assumptions (FAS-132, par. 6)

Defined Benefit Postretirement Plans—Reduced Disclosure Requirements for Nonpublic Entities

The following are the reduced disclosure requirements for defined benefit postretirement plans of nonpublic entities:

1. A brief description of the plan (FAS-132, par. 8)
2. For each balance sheet presented, the following information about the plan (FAS-132, par. 8):
    a. The benefit obligation
    b. The fair value of plan assets

c. The funded status of the plan

d. Employer contributions

e. Participant contributions

f. Benefits paid

3. For each balance sheet presented, amounts recognized in the balance sheet, including the net postretirement benefit prepaid assets or accrued liabilities (FAS-132, par. 8)

4. The amount of net periodic benefit cost recognized as expense for all income statements presented (FAS-132, par. 8)

5. For each balance sheet presented, the following assumptions used in the accounting for the plan (FAS-132, par. 8):

   a. The weighted-average assumed discount rate

   b. The weighted-average rate of compensation increase (for pay-related plans)

   c. The weighted-average expected long-term rate of return on plan assets

6. The assumed healthcare cost trend rate(s) for the next year used to measure the expected cost of benefits covered by the plan (gross eligible charges) and a general description of the direction and pattern of change in the assumed trend rates thereafter, together with the ultimate trend rate(s) and when that rate is expected to be achieved (FAS-132, par. 8)

7. The amounts and types of securities of the employer and related parties included in plan assets (FAS-132, par. 8)

8. The approximate amount of future annual benefits of plan participants covered by insurance contracts issued by the employer or related parties (FAS-132, par. 8)

9. Any significant transactions between the employer or related parties and the plan during the period (FAS-132, par. 8)

10. The nature and effect of significant nonroutine events, such as amendments, combinations, divestitures, curtailments, and settlements (FAS-132, par. 8)

11. For employers with two or more defined benefit postretirement plans, if disclosures for *underfunded plans* (those that have accumulated postretirement benefit obligations in excess of plan assets) and *overfunded plans* (those that have plan assets in excess of accumulated postretirement benefit obligations) are presented on a combined basis, the following disclosures should be made separately with respect to plans that are *underfunded* (FAS-132, par. 6):

    a. The aggregate accumulated postretirement benefit obligation

    b. The aggregate fair value of plan assets

12. If two or more defined benefit postretirement plans are combined, the amounts recognized as prepaid benefit costs and accrued benefit liabilities should be disclosed separately (FAS-132, par. 6)
13. Domestic and foreign defined benefit postretirement plans may be aggregated unless the benefit obligations of the foreign plans are significant relative to the total benefit obligation and the plans use significantly different assumptions (FAS-132, par. 7)

Defined Contribution Postretirement Plans

The following disclosures should be made for defined contribution postretirement plans:

1. A brief description of the plan (FAS-132, par. 9)
2. The amount of cost recognized as expense during the period (FAS-132, par. 9)
3. The nature and effect of significant matters affecting comparability of information for all periods presented, such as a change in the rate of employer contributions, business combinations, or divestitures (FAS-132, par. 9)

Multiemployer Postretirement Benefit Plans

The following disclosures should be made for multiemployer postretirement benefit plans:

1. The amount of employer contributions during the period (amounts attributable to pensions and other postretirement benefit plans may be combined) (FAS-132, par. 10)
2. A description of the nature and effect of any changes affecting comparability, such as a change in the rate of employer contributions, business combinations, or divestitures (FAS-132, par. 10)
3. If it is either probable or reasonably possible that (a) an employer would withdraw from a multiemployer postretirement benefit plan under circumstances that would give rise to a withdrawal obligation or (b) an employer's contribution to a multiemployer postretirement benefit plan would be increased during the remainder of a contract period in order to maintain a negotiated level of benefit coverage (a maintenance of benefits clause), disclosure of the information required by FAS-5 should be made (FAS-132, par. 11)

EXAMPLES OF FINANCIAL STATEMENT DISCLOSURES

The following sample disclosures are available on the accompanying disc.

Example 23–1: Defined Benefit Postretirement Plans

The Company has multiple nonpension postretirement benefit plans. The healthcare plans are contributory, with participants' contributions adjusted annually; the life insurance plans are noncontributory. The accounting for the healthcare plans anticipates future cost sharing changes to the written plan that are consistent with the Company's expressed intent to increase retiree contributions each year by 50% of the excess of the expected general inflation rate over 6%. On December 31, 2000, the Company amended its postretirement healthcare plans to provide long-term care coverage.

The following tables set forth the benefit obligation, fair value of plan assets, and the funded status of the Company's Plans; amounts recognized in the Company's financial statements; and the principal weighted-average assumptions used:

	2000	*1999*
Change in benefit obligation:		
Benefit obligation at beginning of year	$738,000	$700,000
Service cost	36,000	32,000
Interest cost	65,000	63,000
Plan participants' contributions	20,000	13,000
Amendments	75,000	-0-
Actuarial gain	(24,000)	-0-
Acquisition	600,000	-0-
Benefits paid	(90,000)	(70,000)
Benefit obligation at end of year	$1,420,000	$738,000
Change in plan assets:		
Fair value of plan assets at beginning of year	$206,000	$87,000
Actual return on plan assets	(3,000)	24,000
Acquisition	25,000	-0-
Employer contribution	171,000	152,000
Plan participants' contributions	20,000	13,000
Benefits paid	(90,000)	(70,000)
Fair value of plan assets at end of year	$329,000	$206,000

	2000	*1999*
Funded status	$(1,091,000)	$(532,000)
Unrecognized net actuarial loss	59,000	60,000
Unrecognized prior service cost	585,000	540,000
Prepaid (accrued) benefit cost	$(447,000)	$68,000

Weighted-average assumptions as of December 31:		
Discount rate	9.00%	9.00%
Expected return on plan assets	10.00%	10.00%

For measurement purposes, a 10% annual rate of increase in the per capita cost of covered healthcare benefits was assumed for 2001. The rate was assumed to decrease gradually to 4% for 2007 and remain at that level thereafter.

Components of net periodic benefit cost are as follows:

	2000	*1999*
Service cost	$36,000	$32,000
Interest cost	65,000	63,000
Expected return on plan assets	(21,000)	(9,000)
Amortization of prior service cost	30,000	30,000
Recognized net actuarial loss	1,000	1,000
Net periodic benefit cost	$111,000	$117,000

The Company acquired Massari, Ltd. on December 31, 2000, including its postretirement benefit plans. As a result, the Company's plans were amended to establish parity with the benefits provided by Massari, Ltd.

Assumed healthcare cost trend rates have a significant effect on the amounts reported for the healthcare plans. A 1% point change in assumed healthcare cost trend rates would have the following effects:

	1% Point Increase	*1% Point Decrease*
Effect on total of service and interest cost components	$ 22,000	$ (20,000)
Effect on postretirement benefit obligation	$173,000	$(156,000)

Example 23–2: Defined Benefit Postretirement Plans—Alternative Reduced Disclosures for a Nonpublic Entity

Note: Example 23–2 illustrates the alternative reduced disclosures for a nonpublic entity, using the same facts in Example 23–1.

The Company has multiple nonpension postretirement benefit plans. The healthcare plans are contributory, with participants' contributions adjusted annually; the life insurance plans are noncontributory.

	Postretirement Benefits	
	2000	*1999*
Benefit obligation at December 31	$1,420,000	$738,000
Fair value of plan assets at December 31	329,000	206,000
Funded status	$(1,091,000)	$(532,000)
Prepaid (accrued) benefit cost recognized	$(447,000)	$68,000
Weighted-average assumptions as of December 31:		
Discount rate	9.00%	9.00%
Expected return on plan assets	10.00%	10.00%

For measurement purposes, a 10% annual rate of increase in the per capita cost of covered healthcare benefits was assumed for 2001. The rate was assumed to decrease gradually to 4% for 2007 and remain at that level thereafter.

Benefit cost	$111,000	$117,000
Employer contribution	$171,000	$152,000
Plan participants' contributions	$20,000	$13,000
Benefits paid	$90,000	$70,000

The Company acquired Massari, Ltd. on December 31, 2000, increasing the postretirement benefit obligation by $600,000 and related plan assets by $25,000. Amendments during the year to the Company's plans increased the postretirement benefit obligation by $75,000.

Example 23–3: Disclosures about Defined Benefit Postretirement Plans and Pension Plans Are Presented in a Parallel Format in a Single Note to the Financial Statements

The Company and its subsidiaries sponsor numerous defined benefit pension plans and other postretirement benefit plans. The following tables set forth the benefit obligation, fair value of plan assets, and the funded status of the Company's Plans; amounts recognized in the Company's financial statements; and the principal weighted-average assumptions used:

	Pension Benefits		*Postretirement Benefits*	
	2000	*1999*	*2000*	*1999*
Change in benefit obligation:				
Benefit obligation at beginning of year	$1,266,000	$1,200,000	$738,000	$700,000
Service cost	76,000	72,000	36,000	32,000
Interest cost	114,000	108,000	65,000	63,000
Plan participants' contributions	-0-	-0-	20,000	13,000
Amendments	120,000	-0-	75,000	-0-
Actuarial gain	(25,000)	-0-	(24,000)	-0-
Acquisition	900,000	-0-	600,000	-0-
Benefits paid	(125,000)	(114,000)	(90,000)	(70,000)
Benefit obligation at end of year	$2,326,000	$1,266,000	$1,420,000	$738,000
Change in plan assets:				
Fair value of plan assets at beginning of year	$1,068,000	$880,000	$206,000	$87,000
Actual return on plan assets	29,000	188,000	(3,000)	24,000
Acquisition	1,000,000	-0-	25,000	-0-
Employer contribution	75,000	114,000	171,000	152,000
Plan participants' contributions	-0-	-0-	20,000	13,000
Benefits paid	(125,000)	(114,000)	(90,000)	(70,000)
Fair value of plan assets at end of year	$2,047,000	$1,068,000	$329,000	$206,000
Funded status	$(279,000)	$(198,000)	$(1,091,000)	$(532,000)
Unrecognized net actuarial loss	83,000	38,000	59,000	60,000
Unrecognized prior service cost	260,000	160,000	585,000	540,000
Prepaid (accrued) benefit cost	$64,000	$0	$(447,000)	$68,000

Weighted-average assumptions as of December 31:				
Discount rate	9.25%	9.00%	9.00%	9.00%
Expected return on plan assets	10.00%	10.00%	10.00%	10.00%
Rate of compensation increase	5.00%	5.00%	N/A	N/A

Components of net periodic benefit cost are as follows:

	Pension Benefits		*Postretirement Benefits*	
	2000	*1999*	*2000*	*1999*
Service cost	$76,000	$72,000	$36,000	$32,000
Interest cost	114,000	108,000	65,000	63,000
Expected return on plan assets	(107,000)	(88,000)	(21,000)	(9,000)
Amortization of prior service cost	20,000	20,000	30,000	30,000
Recognized net actuarial loss	8,000	2,000	1,000	1,000
Net periodic benefit cost	$111,000	$114,000	$111,000	$117,000

The Company acquired Massari, Ltd. on December 31, 2000, including its pension plans. As a result, the Company's plans were amended to establish parity with the benefits provided by Massari, Ltd.

The Company has multiple nonpension postretirement benefit plans. The healthcare plans are contributory, with participants' contributions adjusted annually; the life insurance plans are noncontributory. The accounting for the healthcare plans anticipates future cost sharing changes to the written plan that are consistent with the Company's expressed intent to increase retiree contributions each year by 50% of the excess of the expected general inflation rate over 6%. On December 31, 2000, the Company amended its postretirement healthcare plans to provide long-term care coverage.

Assumed healthcare cost trend rates have a significant effect on the amounts reported for the healthcare plans. A 1% point change in assumed healthcare cost trend rates would have the following effects:

	1% Point Increase	*1% Point Decrease*
Effect on total of service and interest cost components	$ 22,000	$ (20,000)
Effect on postretirement benefit obligation	$173,000	$(156,000)

Example 23–4: Defined Contribution Postretirement Plans

The Company sponsors defined contribution postretirement healthcare and life insurance benefit plans. Contributions to these plans were $236,000 in 2000 and $222,000 in 1999.

Example 23–5: Combined Disclosures of Defined Contribution Postretirement Plans and Defined Contribution Pension Plans

The Company sponsors several defined contribution pension plans covering substantially all employees. Employees may contribute to these plans and their contributions are matched in varying amounts by the Company. Defined contribution pension expense for the Company was $543,000 for 2000 and $429,000 for 1999.

Also, the Company sponsors defined contribution postretirement healthcare and life insurance benefit plans. Contributions to these plans were $311,000 in 2000 and $304,000 in 1999.

Example 23–6: Union-Sponsored Multiemployer Postretirement Benefit Plans

The Company participates in various multi-employer, union-administered postretirement benefit plans, which provide for healthcare and life insurance benefits to both active employees and retirees. Total contributions to these plans were $423,000 for 2000 and $410,000 for 1999.

CHAPTER 24 QUASI-REORGANIZATIONS AND REORGANIZATIONS UNDER THE BANKRUPTCY CODE

CONTENTS

EXECUTIVE SUMMARY

Quasi-Reorganizations

Under carefully defined circumstances, contributed or paid-in capital generally may be used to restructure a corporation, including the elimination of a deficit in retained earnings. This procedure is called a *quasi-reorganization* or *corporate readjustment*. In a quasi-reorganization, a company reduces the carrying amounts of its balance sheet accounts to fair value; the offsetting adjustment should be charged to retained earnings. If the adjustment exceeds the balance in the retained earnings account, any difference should be charged to additional paid-in capital. A new retained earnings account should be established at the effective date of such readjustment, and the effective date generally should be disclosed for a period of ten years.

Reorganizations under the Bankruptcy Code

The accounting followed by entities reorganizing as going concerns under Chapter 11 of the Bankruptcy Code is similar in many ways to the fresh-start accounting of a quasi-reorganization. However, there are some differences and, therefore, formal reorganizations under the Bankruptcy Code should not be confused with quasi-reorganizations. For example, in a quasi-reorganization, a formal plan to restructure liabilities and debt to creditors is not adopted.

An entity should adopt fresh-start accounting upon its emergence from Chapter 11 if (1) the reorganization value of the assets of the emerging entity immediately before the date of confirmation by the Court is less than the total of all postpetition liabilities and allowed claims and (2) holders of existing voting shares immediately before confirmation receive less than 50% of the voting shares of the emerging entity.

Authoritative Literature

ARB-43	Chapter 7, Capital Accounts
	Chapter 7A, Quasi-Reorganization or Corporate Readjustment
ARB-46	Discontinuance of Dating Earned Surplus
FAS-109	Accounting for Income Taxes
SOP 90-7	Financial Reporting by Entities in Reorganization Under the Bankruptcy Code
PB-11	Accounting for Preconfirmation Contingencies in Fresh-Start Reporting

DISCLOSURE REQUIREMENTS

Quasi-Reorganizations

1. The nature and a description of the quasi-reorganization should be adequately disclosed in the financial statements. After a quasi-reorganization or corporate readjustment, a new retained earnings account should be established and dated to show that it runs from the effective date of the readjustment. This dating should be disclosed in the financial statements un-

til such time as the effective date is no longer deemed to possess any special significance, which is generally not more than ten years (ARB-46, par. 2).

2. Companies that recognize the tax benefits of prior deductible temporary differences and carryforwards in income rather than contributed capital (i.e., companies that have previously adopted FAS-96 and effected a quasi-reorganization that involved only the elimination of a deficit in retained earnings) should disclose the following (FAS-109, par. 39):
   a. The date of the quasi-reorganization
   b. The manner of reporting the tax benefits and that it differs from present accounting requirements for other entities
   c. The effect of those tax benefits on income from continuing operations, income before extraordinary items, and net income (and on related per share amounts, if applicable)

Reorganizations under the Bankruptcy Code

1. Companies that have filed petitions with the Bankruptcy Court and expect to reorganize as going concerns under Chapter 11 should disclose the following (SOP 90-7, pars. 23–31 and 34):
   a. Prepetition liabilities, including claims that become known after a petition is filed, which are not subject to reasonable estimation
   b. Principal categories of claims subject to compromise
   c. The extent to which reported interest expense differs from stated contractual interest
   d. Details of operating cash receipts and payments resulting from the reorganization if the indirect method is used in the statement of cash flows
   e. In the earnings per share calculation, whether it is probable that the plan will require the issuance of common stock or common stock equivalents, thereby diluting current equity interests
2. In the consolidated financial statements of one or more entities in reorganization under Chapter 11 and of one or more entities not in reorganization proceedings, the following disclosures should be made (SOP 90-7, pars. 32–33):
   a. Condensed combined financial statements of the entities in reorganization proceedings
   b. Intercompany receivables and payables of entities in reorganization

3. For companies that have emerged from Chapter 11 under confirmed plans that adopt fresh start reporting, the following disclosures should be made (SOP 90-7, par. 39):
   a. Adjustments to the historical amounts of individual assets and liabilities
   b. The amount of debt forgiveness
   c. The amount of prior retained earnings or deficit eliminated
   d. Significant matters relating to the determination of reorganization value such as:
      - The method(s) used to determine reorganization value and factors such as discount rates, tax rates, the number of years for which cash flows are projected, and the method of determining terminal value
      - Sensitive assumptions about which there is a reasonable possibility of the occurrence of a variation that would significantly affect the measurement of reorganization value
      - Assumptions about anticipated conditions that are expected to be different from current conditions, unless otherwise apparent
4. For companies that have emerged from Chapter 11 under confirmed plans that adopt fresh start reporting and have recorded an adjustment that resulted from a preconfirmation contingency, the following disclosures should be made (PB-11, pars. 8–9):
   a. The adjustment in income or loss from continuing operations of the emerged entity

EXAMPLES OF FINANCIAL STATEMENT DISCLOSURES

The following sample disclosures are available on the accompanying disc.

Quasi-Reorganizations

Example 24–1: Quasi-Reorganization Adopted in Connection with Ownership Change and Restructuring of Operations

In recognition of the change in ownership of the Company and the restructuring of operations, the Company believes that future operations are not burdened with the problems of the past. As a result, the Company believed it to be appropriate to adjust the carrying value of assets and liabilities to their fair value as of January 1, 2000.

Following extensive research and consultations with legal counsel and independent accountants, management recommended, and the Company's Board of Directors approved, a quasi-reorganization to be effective as of January 1, 2000. Accordingly, all assets and liabilities of the Company have been retroactively restated as of January 1, 2000, to their fair value, determined as follows:

- Inventories—market value reduced by selling costs and a reasonable profit allowance
- Property, plant, and equipment—recent appraisal values
- Debt due beyond one year—principal and interest payments due beyond one year have been discounted at 10%
- Convertible subordinated debentures—appraisal from an investment banker
- Liability for pension plans—amounts have been discounted at 10%

> **Note:** The following table illustrates the caption used in the Company's stockholders' equity section to show the dating of retained earnings from the effective date of the quasi-reorganization of January 1, 2000.

	2000	*1999*
Common stock	$20,000	$700,000
Additional paid-in-capital	80,000	900,000
Retained earnings since January 1, 2000, in connection with quasi-reorganization	373,000	-0-
Accumulated deficit (prior to quasi-reorganization)	-0-	(1,325,000)
Total stockholder's equity	$473,000	$275,000

Reorganizations under the Bankruptcy Code

Example 24–2: Petition for Relief under Chapter 11

On February 13, 2000, ABC Company (the Debtor) filed petitions for relief under Chapter 11 of the federal bankruptcy laws in the United States Bankruptcy Court for the Western District of Tennessee. Under Chapter 11, certain claims against the Debtor in existence prior to the filing of the petitions for relief under the federal bankruptcy laws are stayed while the Debtor continues business operations as Debtor-in-possession. These claims are reflected in the December 31, 2000, Balance Sheet as "Liabilities subject to compromise." Additional claims (liabilities subject to compromise) may arise subsequent to the filing date resulting from rejection of executory contracts, including leases, and from the determination by the court (or agreed to by parties in interest) of allowed claims for contingencies and other disputed amounts. Claims secured against the Debtor's assets (secured claims) also are stayed, although the holders of such claims have the right to move the court for relief from the stay. Secured claims are secured primarily by liens on the Debtor's property, plant, and equipment.

The Debtor received approval from the Bankruptcy Court to pay or otherwise honor certain of its prepetition obligations, including employee wages and product warranties. The Debtor has determined that there is insufficient collateral to cover the interest portion of scheduled payments on its prepetition debt obligations. Contractual interest on those obligations amounts to $[*amount*], which is $[*amount*] in excess of reported interest expense; therefore, the Debtor has discontinued accruing interest on these obligations.

Example 24–3: Emergence from Bankruptcy

Upon emergence from its Chapter 11 proceedings in April 2000, the Company adopted "fresh-start" reporting in accordance with AICPA Statement of Position No. 90-7 (Financial Reporting by Entities in Reorganization Under the Bankruptcy Code) as of March 31, 2000. The Company's emergence from these proceedings resulted in a new reporting entity with no retained earnings or accumulated deficit as of March 31, 2000. Accordingly, the Company's financial information shown for periods prior to March 31, 2000, is not comparable to consolidated financial statements presented on or subsequent to March 31, 2000.

The Bankruptcy Court confirmed the Company's plan of reorganization. The confirmed plan provided for the following:

Secured Debt—The Company's $[*amount*] of secured debt (secured by a first mortgage lien on a building located in Nashville, Tennessee) was exchanged for $[*amount*] in cash and a $[*amount*] secured note, payable in annual installments of $[*amount*] commencing on July 1, 2001, through June 30, 2004, with interest at 13% per annum, with the balance due on July 1, 2005.

Priority Tax Claims—Payroll and withholding taxes of $[*amount*] are payable in equal annual installments commencing on July 1, 2001, through July 1, 2006, with interest at 11% per annum.

Senior Debt—The holders of approximately $[*amount*] of senior subordinated secured notes received the following instruments in exchange for their notes: (a) $[*amount*] in new senior secured debt, payable in annual installments of $[*amount*] commencing March 1,

2001, through March 1, 2004, with interest at 12% per annum, secured by first liens on certain property, plant, and equipment, with the balance due on March 1, 2005; (b) $[*amount*] of subordinated debt with interest at 14% per annum due in equal annual installments commencing on October 1, 2001, through October 1, 2007, secured by second liens on certain property, plant, and equipment; and (c) [*percent*]% of the new issue of outstanding voting common stock of the Company.

Trade and Other Miscellaneous Claims—The holders of approximately $[*amount*] of trade and other miscellaneous claims received the following for their claims: (a) $[*amount*] in senior secured debt, payable in annual installments of $[*amount*] commencing March 1, 2001, through March 1, 2004, with interest at 12% per annum, secured by first liens on certain property, plant, and equipment, with the balance due on March 1, 2005; (b) $[*amount*] of subordinated debt, payable in equal annual installments commencing October 1, 2001, through October 1, 2006, with interest at 14% per annum; and (c) [*percent*]% of the new issue of outstanding voting common stock of the Company.

Subordinated Debentures—The holders of approximately $[*amount*] of subordinated unsecured debt received, in exchange for the debentures, [*percent*]% of the new issue outstanding voting common stock of the Company.

Preferred Stock—The holders of [*number*] shares of preferred stock received [*percent*]% of the outstanding voting common stock of the new issue of the Company in exchange for their preferred stock.

Common Stock—The holders of approximately [*number*] outstanding shares of the Company's existing common stock received, in exchange for their shares, [*percent*]% of the new outstanding voting common stock of the Company.

CHAPTER 25
RELATED-PARTY DISCLOSURES

CONTENTS

EXECUTIVE SUMMARY

In general terms, *related parties* exist when there is a relationship that offers the potential for transactions at less than arm's-length, favorable treatment, or the ability to influence the outcome of events differently from that which might result in the absence of that relationship. A related party may be any of the following:

- *Affiliate*—An affiliate is a party that directly or indirectly controls, is controlled by, or is under common control with another party.

- *Principal owner*—This is generally the owner of record or known beneficial owner of more than 10% of the voting interests of an entity.
- *Management*—Persons having responsibility for achieving objectives of the entity and requisite authority to make decisions that pursue those objectives. This normally includes members of the board of directors, chief executive officer, chief operating officer, president, treasurer, any vice president in charge of a principal business function (e.g., sales, administration, finance), and any other individual who performs similar policymaking functions.
- *Immediate family of management or principal owners*—Generally, this includes spouses, brothers, sisters, parents, children, and spouses of these persons.
- *A parent company and its subsidiaries*—This is typically an entity that "directly or indirectly has a controlling financial interest" in a subsidiary company.
- *Trusts for the benefit of employees*—Trusts for the benefit of employees include pension and profit-sharing trusts that are managed by, or under the trusteeship of, the entity's management.
- *Other parties*—Other parties include any other party that has the ability to significantly influence the management or operating policies of the entity, to the extent that it may be prevented from fully pursuing its own separate interests. The ability to exercise significant influence may be indicated in several ways, such as representation on the board of directors, participation in policy-making processes, material intercompany transactions, interchange of managerial personnel, or technological dependency.

Common related-party transactions include the following:

- Contracts that carry no interest rate or an unrealistic interest rate
- Nonmonetary transactions that involve the exchange of similar assets
- Loan agreements that contain no repayment schedule
- Loans to parties that do not possess the ability to repay
- Services or goods purchased from a party at little or no cost to the entity
- Maintenance of bank balances as compensating balances for the benefit of another
- Intercompany billings based on allocation of common costs
- Leases to an entity from its principal shareholder

Financial statement disclosure of related party transactions is required by GAAP in order for those statements to fairly present financial position, results of operations, and cash flows.

Authoritative Literature

ARB-43	Chapter 1A, Rules Adopted by Membership
FAS-57	Related Party Disclosures
FAS-109	Accounting for Income Taxes

DISCLOSURE REQUIREMENTS

The following disclosures should be made for material related-party transactions:

1. The nature of the relationship of the parties involved (FAS-57, par. 2)
2. A description of the transactions, including transactions to which no amounts or nominal amounts were ascribed, for each of the periods for which income statements are presented, and any other information deemed necessary to an understanding of the effects of the transactions on the financial statements (FAS-57, par. 2)
3. The dollar amounts of transactions for each of the periods for which income statements are presented and the effects of any change in the method of establishing the terms from those used in the preceding period (FAS-57, par. 2)
4. Amounts due from or to related parties as of the date of each balance sheet presented and, if not otherwise apparent, the terms and manner of settlement (FAS-57, par. 2)
5. When the company and one or more other entities are under common ownership or management control and the existence of that control could result in operating results or financial position of the company significantly different from those that would have resulted if the company were autonomous, then the nature of the control relationship should be disclosed even though there are no related-party transactions (FAS-57, par. 4)

Disclosures concerning related-party transactions should *not* be worded in a manner that implies that the transactions were consummated on terms equivalent to those that prevail in arm's-length transactions, unless such representations can be substantiated (FAS-57, par. 3).

EXAMPLES OF FINANCIAL STATEMENT DISCLOSURES

The following sample disclosures are available on the accompanying disc.

Example 25–1: Advances Made to Related Parties for Expansion and Financing Needs

The Company has made advances to PRC Development, an entity owned by the president and certain officers of the Company, primarily to accommodate expansion and other financing needs of this related entity. Such advances bear interest at rates equal to the Company's weighted average cost of borrowing, which for the years ended December 31, 2000, and December 31, 1999, was 7.25% and 7.75%, respectively. Interest charged to PRC Development for the years ended December 31, 2000, and December 31, 1999, was $379,000 and $493,000, respectively.

Example 25–2: Company's Corporate Services Agreement with a Related Entity Provides for Payment of a Fee Based on Company's Net Sales

The Company has a corporate services agreement with Odeyssa, Inc., an entity that is controlled by the Company's chairman of the board of directors and president. Under the terms of the agreement, the Company pays a fee to Odeyssa, Inc. for various corporate support staff, administrative services, and research and development services. Such fee equals 2.2% of the Company's net sales, subject to certain adjustments, and totaled $1,975,000 and $1,836,000 in 2000 and 1999, respectively.

Example 25–3: Demand Note Receivable from Stockholder Is Classified as Noncurrent Because Repayment Is Not Anticipated During the Next Year

At December 31, 2000, and December 31, 1999, the Company has a note receivable of $295,200 and $268,400, respectively, due from its stockholder that is due upon demand. This note is unsecured and bears interest at 10%. Accrued interest on this note totaled $51,200 and $24,400 as of December 31, 2000, and December 31, 1999, respectively, and is included in the note receivable balance. The note receivable has been classified as noncurrent in the accompanying Balance Sheets because repayment is not anticipated during the next year.

Example 25–4: Notes Receivable Balance Due from Related Parties Is Paid through Forfeiture of Bonuses

As of December 31, 1999, the Company had notes receivable due from certain executives and officers amounting to approximately $1,500,000. These notes bear interest at rates ranging from 7.25% to 7.85% and have maturities of six months to five years. In 2000, $625,000 of the notes receivable balance was paid through forfeiture of management bonuses.

Example 25–5: Company Is Forgiving Loan Balance Due from an Officer

On May 19, 1997, the Company loaned $500,000 to Dave Jones, a senior vice president of the Company. Mr. Jones executed an unsecured promissory note in favor of the Company that matures on May 18, 2002. In 1999, the Company forgave a total of $200,000 of outstanding principal amount and $47,000 in accrued interest. In 2000, the Company forgave a total of $100,000 of outstanding principal amount and $31,000 in accrued interest. The remaining outstanding balance of the loan as of December 31, 2000, was $205,000, representing $200,000 in principal and $5,000 in accrued interest, and bears interest at a rate of 7.95%.

Example 25–6: Loan Payable to Related Company Is Secured and Subordinated to Bank Debt

In November 1999, Cubes, Ltd., an entity that is partially owned by a minority shareholder of the Company, loaned $1,000,000 to the Company for working capital and equipment financing. The loan is payable in five annual installments of $200,000, plus applicable interest, beginning November 2000. Interest accrues at the prevailing prime rate plus 1.75% (9% at December 31, 2000). The loan is secured by inventory, accounts receivable, and machinery and equipment, and is subordinated to the Company's line of credit with the bank. At December 31, 2000, and December 31, 1999, the outstanding balance due was $800,000 and $1,000,000, respectively.

Example 25–7: Loan Covenants Restrict Payment on Shareholder Loan Made to Company

At December 31, 2000, and December 31, 1999, the Company's shareholder has advanced $200,000 and $182,000, respectively, to the Company. These loans are represented by three separate demand notes, are unsecured, and carry interest at 10%. Loan covenants and restrictions prohibit the shareholder from receiving any payment on these loans until such time that other loan commitments are satisfied. Accordingly, these shareholder loans are recorded as long-term debt in the accompanying financial statements.

Example 25–8: Financial Services Agreement with a Related Entity Provides for a Fee at Less Than Prevailing Market Rate

GBG Capital Management (GBG), an entity in which an officer of the Company holds a beneficial interest, performs services for the Company as its agent in connection with negotiations regarding various financial arrangements of the Company. In January 1999, the Company entered into a Financial Services Agreement for five years with GBG pursuant to which GBG has agreed to render financial advisory and related services to the Company for a fee equal to 90% of the fees that would be charged to the Company by unaffiliated third parties for the same or comparable services. Each year, the Company pays GBG an annual $1,000,000 retainer as an advance against payments due pursuant to this agreement and reimburses GBG for its reasonable out-of-pocket expenses. The Company paid fees to GBG totaling $1,500,000 in 2000 and $1,300,000 in 1999 relating to several business acquisitions and dispositions made by the Company.

Example 25–9: Company's Consulting Agreement with a Shareholder Provides for Future Payment for a Covenant Not to Compete

For the years ended December 31, 2000, and December 31, 1999, consulting service fees in the amount of $326,000 and $302,000, respectively, were paid to Dr. Mark Makhoul, a shareholder. Dr. Makhoul provides consulting services to the Company pursuant to a consulting agreement that terminates on December 31, 2003 (subject to extension for an additional five-year term) and for which he receives annual payments of $300,000. The Company also reimburses Dr. Makhoul for his out-of-pocket expenses in performing such consulting services. In addition, the Company has agreed to pay to Dr. Makhoul $250,000 for a period of 24 months following the termination of his consulting relationship with the Company in exchange for his agreement not to compete with the Company during this period.

Example 25–10: Company Pays Royalties in Connection with Patents and Licensing Rights Acquired from Related Party

The Company has patents and licensing rights that were acquired from John Teen, the Company's president and major stockholder. As consideration, the Company pays royalties equal to 2.5% of gross sales on all manufactured products covered by the patents and licensing rights. In 2000 and 1999, the Company paid royalties of $1,379,000 and $1,243,000, respectively, to Mr. Teen.

Example 25–11: A Director of the Company Is a Partner in the Law Firm That Acts as Counsel to the Company

A director of the Company is a partner in the law firm that acts as counsel to the Company. The Company paid legal fees and expenses to the law firm in the amount of approximately $375,000 in 2000 and $210,000 in 1999.

Example 25–12: A Director of the Company Is an Owner in an Insurance Agency That Has Written Policies for the Company

A director of the Company has an ownership interest in an insurance agency that has written general liability policies for the Company with premiums totaling $136,000 in 2000 and $122,000 in 1999.

Example 25–13: Company Purchased Land and Buildings from Directors

During 2000, the Company purchased land and buildings adjoining one of its plants from two Company directors for $1,250,000. The board of directors unanimously approved the purchase, with the two directors involved in the transaction abstaining.

Example 25–14: Company Sold Building to Chief Executive Officer at a Price That is within the Range of Appraised Values

In 2000, the Company sold a building to its chief executive officer for $3,750,000 in cash, which was approved by the Company's board of directors. The sales price was in excess of book value, resulting in a gain of $490,000, and was within the range of appraised values. The building had previously been offered for sale to the public for six months.

Example 25–15: Salary Advance Made to Officer as Part of New Employment Contract

During 2000, the Company made a $100,000 salary advance to Jane Apostol, an officer, as part of a new employment contract that required her to relocate to Los Angeles, California. According to the terms of the contract, Ms. Apostol is required to repay the loan at $20,000 per year for the next five years, beginning in 2001.

Example 25–16: Related Party Supplies Inventory Materials to the Company

The Company has an agreement with Just, Inc., an entity in which a major stockholder of the Company owns a significant interest, which provides for purchases by the Company of electrical equipment, subassemblies, and spare parts. Purchases from Just, Inc. for 2000 and 1999 totaled $2,900,000 and $3,750,000, respectively. Accounts payable to Just, Inc. amounted to $1,010,000 and $1,236,000 at December 31, 2000, and December 31, 1999, respectively. In addition, in 2000 the Company made advance payments to Just, Inc. for future inventory purchases in return for lower prices on certain components.

Advance payments of $420,000 were included in prepaid expenses at December 31, 2000.

Example 25–17: Company Sells a Substantial Portion of Its Products to a Related Entity

The Company sells a substantial portion of its medical instruments products to Horizons, Ltd., an entity in which the Company's vice-president of operations is a majority stockholder. During 2000 and 1999, the Company sold approximately $10,400,000 and $8,732,000 of products to Horizons, Ltd. Trade receivables from Horizons, Inc. were $1,923,000 and $1,544,000 at December 31, 2000, and December 31, 1999, respectively.

Example 25–18: Related Parties Reimburse the Company for Allocated Overhead and Administrative Expenses

The Company's managed limited partnerships reimburse the Company for certain allocated overhead and administrative expenses. These expenses generally consist of salaries and related benefits paid to corporate personnel, rent, data processing services, and other corporate facilities costs. The Company provides engineering, marketing, administrative, accounting, information management, legal, and other services to the partnerships. Allocations of personnel costs have been based primarily on actual time spent by Company employees with respect to each partnership managed. Remaining overhead costs are allocated based on the pro rata relationship of the partnership's revenues to the total revenues of all businesses owned or managed by the Company. The Company believes that such allocation methods are reasonable. Amounts charged to managed partnerships and other affiliated companies have directly offset the Company's general and administrative expenses by approximately $5,100,000 and $5,400,000 for the years ended December 31, 2000, and December 31, 1999, respectively.

Example 25–19: Company Has Several Long-Term Operating Lease Agreements with Affiliated Entities

The Company leases various manufacturing facilities and equipment from companies owned by certain officers and directors of the Company, either directly or indirectly, through affiliates. The leases generally provide that the Company will bear the cost of property taxes and insurance.

Details of the principal operating leases with related parties as of December 31, 2000, including the effect of renewals and amendments executed subsequent to December 31, 2000, are as follows:

Name of Related Party/ Description of Lease	*Date of Lease*	*Term*	*Basic Annual Rental Amount*	*Future Minimum Rental Amounts*
Hope Realty Trust:				
Land & building—Chicago	12-13-90	15 years	$200,000	$1,000,000
Corporate offices	12-22-90	15 years	$100,000	$ 500,000
Machinery & equipment	11-30-95	10 years	$125,000	$ 625,000
John Jones Family Trust:				
Land & buildings—Atlanta	6-29-95	10 years	$150,000	$ 675,000
Furniture & computers	7-1-96	10 years	$100,000	$ 550,000
Kilmer Realty Trust:				
Land & building—Detroit	6-25-95	15 years	$200,000	$1,900,000
Corporate offices	12-28-95	10 years	$110,000	$ 550,000
Furniture & equipment	1-1-96	10 years	$ 80,000	$ 400,000

Rent incurred and paid to these related parties was $1,069,000 and $1,087,000 for the years ended December 31, 2000, and December 31, 1999, respectively.

Future minimum lease payments to these related parties as of December 31, 2000, are as follows:

Year Ending December 31	*Amounts*
2001	$1,065,000
2002	1,110,000
2003	1,150,000
2004	1,205,000
2005	1,260,000
Thereafter	685,000
	$6,475,000

Example 25–20: Company Has a Month-to-Month Lease with a Related Party

The Company leases its administrative offices on a month-to-month basis from a partnership in which the Company's stockholder is a partner. Total rent paid to the partnership was $123,000 and $117,000 for the years ended December 31, 2000, and December 31, 1999, respectively.

Example 25–21: Companies under Common Control May Experience Change in Operations

The Company's 80% shareholder also controls other entities whose operations are similar to those of the Company. Although there were no transactions between the Company and these entities in 2000 or 1999, the 80% shareholder is, nevertheless, in a position to influence the sales volume of the Company for the benefit of the other entities that are under his control.

Example 25–22: Guarantee of Indebtedness of Related Entity

As of December 31, 2000, the Company is contingently liable as guarantor with respect to $5,400,000 of indebtedness of Escaped, Inc., an entity that is owned by the Company's stockholders. No material loss is anticipated by reason of such guarantee.

Example 25–23: Loss Recorded as a Result of Guarantee of Indebtedness of an Affiliate

In 2000, the Company accrued a loss of $400,000 for a loan to an insolvent affiliate that was guaranteed by the Company.

Example 25–24: Guarantee of Indebtedness of Joint Venture Obligates Company to Advance Funds to the Joint Venture if Certain Loan Covenants Are Not Met

The Company holds a 25% ownership interest in Stellark, Inc., which has a $7,000,000 line of credit agreement (Agreement) with First Nations Bank. Under terms of the Agreement, the Company is obligated to advance to Stellark, Inc. a maximum of $2,500,000 if its working capital falls below $500,000 or its current ratio is less than one. Any funds advanced under this agreement are available to First Nations Bank. In addition, First Nations Bank may have claims against the Company in an amount not to exceed $2,000,000 of any unsatisfied required advances. At December 31, 2000, Stellark, Inc. was in compliance with the terms of the Agreement with First Nations Bank.

Example 25–25: Shareholders' Stock Purchase Agreement

The Company and the shareholders have established a Stock Purchase Agreement whereby the Company is obligated to purchase, in the event of the death of any shareholder, all of the decedent's outstanding shares. The repurchase price is determined pursuant to a formula provided in the agreement. The Company has purchased insurance on the lives of the shareholders to help meet its obligation under the Stock Purchase Agreement.

Example 25–26: Purchase of Deceased Shareholder's Stock at Fair Value

In March 2000, the death of a shareholder triggered the Buy/Sell provisions of the Stock Purchase Agreement dated January 1, 1988. The provisions of the Agreement required the Company to purchase the shareholder's stock at fair market value, with a minimum cash payment of 10%.

The fair market value of the stock, as determined by an independent valuation, was $2,675,000. The Company paid $1,000,000 in life insurance policy proceeds against the purchase price. The remaining balance of $1,675,000 was financed at 10%, representing the current corporate borrowing rate, and is payable in 36 equal monthly installments to the shareholder's estate.

Example 25–27: Sales Commissions Payable to Related Entities

Sales commissions are payable to a company owned by one of the Company's principal stockholders for sales obtained by this related entity. These commissions amounted to approximately $540,000 and $473,000 for the years ended December 31, 2000, and December 31, 1999, respectively, of which $145,000 and $132,000 are included in accrued expenses at December 31, 2000, and December 31, 1999, respectively.

CHAPTER 26
RESEARCH AND DEVELOPMENT COSTS

CONTENTS

EXECUTIVE SUMMARY

Generally, research and development costs should be charged to expense when incurred rather than recorded as inventory, component of overhead, or otherwise capitalized. However, intangibles purchased from others and the costs of materials, equipment, and facilities acquired or constructed for research and development activities, and that have alternative future uses, should be capitalized and depreciated over their useful lives. Depreciation expense related to such capitalized costs should be considered research and development costs.

Research and development costs acquired in a business combination accounted for under the purchase method should be assigned a portion of the purchase price based on their fair values, if any. The subsequent accounting by the acquiring entity of these research and development assets is that costs assigned to assets with alternative future uses are capitalized and all others are expensed at the date of consummation of the business combination.

If an entity enters into an arrangement with other parties that fund its research and development, the accounting and reporting for research and development costs depend on the nature of the obligation that the entity incurs in the arrangement. The nature of the obligation in such arrangements can be classified in one of the following categories:

1. *The obligation is solely to perform contractual research and development services for others.* In such situations, the research and development costs incurred should be capitalized as inventory and charged to cost of sales when revenue is recognized.
2. *The obligation represents a liability to repay all of the funds provided by the other parties.* In such situations, the entity should estimate and accrue the liability to repay the other parties and charge research and development costs to expense as incurred.
3. *The obligation is partly to perform contractual services and partly a liability to repay some, but not all, of the funds provided by the other parties.* In such situations, research and development costs are charged partly to expense and partly to cost of sales. The portion charged to cost of sales is related to the funds provided by the other parties that do not have to be repaid by the entity. The portion charged to expense is related to the funds provided by the other parties that are likely to be repaid by the entity.

Costs incurred to establish the technological feasibility of computer software to be sold, leased, or otherwise marketed are research and development costs and should be charged to expense when incurred. After technological feasibility has been established, costs incurred for computer software to be sold, leased, or otherwise marketed should be capitalized and amortized on a product-by-product basis.

Authoritative Literature

FAS-2	Accounting for Research and Development Costs
FAS-68	Research and Development Arrangements
FAS-86	Accounting for the Costs of Computer Software to Be Sold, Leased, or Otherwise Marketed
FIN-4	Applicability of FASB Statement No. 2 to Business Combinations Accounted for by the Purchase Method
FIN-6	Applicability of FASB Statement No. 2 to Computer Software
FTB 84-1	Accounting for Stock Issued to Acquire the Results of a Research and Development Arrangement

DISCLOSURE REQUIREMENTS

The financial statements should include the following disclosures:

1. For an entity that accounts for its obligations under a research and development arrangement as a contract to perform research and development for others (FAS-68, par. 14):
   a. The terms of significant agreements under the research and development arrangement (including royalty arrangements, purchase provisions, license agreement, and commitments to provide additional funding) as of the date of each balance sheet presented
   b. The amount of compensation earned and costs incurred under such contracts for each period for which an income statement is presented
2. Total research and development costs charged to expense in each period for which an income statement is presented (FAS-2, par. 13)
3. For research and development assets acquired in a business combination accounted for as a purchase and that have no alternative future use, the portion of the purchase price that has been allocated to research and development and charged to expense at the date of consummation of the business combination (FIN-4, par. 5)
4. Research and development costs incurred for computer software to be sold, leased, or otherwise marketed should be disclosed either separately or as part of total research and development costs for each period presented (FAS-86, par. 12)
5. If an entity has capitalized costs incurred for computer software costs to be sold, leased, or otherwise marketed, the following disclosures should be made (FAS-86, par. 11):
   a. Unamortized computer software costs included in each balance sheet presented
   b. The total amount charged to expense in each income statement presented for amortization of capitalized computer software costs and for amounts written down to net realizable value

EXAMPLES OF FINANCIAL STATEMENT DISCLOSURES

The following sample disclosures are available on the accompanying disc.

Example 26–1: Research and Development Costs Charged to Expense as Incurred

Expenditures for research activities relating to product development and improvement are charged to expense as incurred. Such expenditures amounted to $546,000 in 2000 and $612,000 in 1999.

Example 26–2: Product Development Costs Deferred

The Company defers certain costs related to the preliminary activities associated with the manufacture of its products, which the Company has determined have future economic benefit. These costs are then expensed in the period in which the initial shipment of the related product is made. Management periodically reviews and revises, when necessary, its estimate of the future benefit of these costs and expenses them if it deems there no longer is a future benefit. At December 31, 2000, and December 31, 1999, product development costs capitalized totaled $817,000 and $734,000, respectively.

Example 26–3: Contract to Perform Research and Development Services for Others

The Company has two contracts with Panax, Inc. under which it is obligated to perform certain specific research and development activities. The Company receives royalties under the terms of one of the contracts and licensing fees under the terms of the other contract. Under both contracts, Panax, Inc. can require the Company to purchase their interest in the research and development. Also, under certain circumstances, the Company is obligated to use its own funds if the amount of funds provided by Panax, Inc. is not sufficient to complete the research and development effort.

Compensation earned and costs incurred by the Company under these contracts for the years ended December 31, 2000, and December 31, 1999, are as follows:

	2000	*1999*
Royalties and other fees earned	$1,385,000	$1,266,000
Costs incurred charged to operations	$1,102,000	$1,014,000

At December 31, 2000, and December 31, 1999, the Company's commitments to provide additional funding under these contracts amounted to $517,000 and $433,000, respectively.

Example 26–4: Research and Development Costs Acquired in a Purchase Business Combination Are Capitalized

In October 2000, the Company purchased the Chickadee brand from Seliga & Co. for $9,500,000 in cash. Under the terms of the agreement, the Company purchased the Chickadee name, accounts and notes receivable, and tooling and assumed certain liabilities. The company also incurred $500,000 of direct, acquisition-related costs, which were capitalized as part of the purchase price. The acquisition was recorded using the purchase method of accounting. Accordingly, the purchase price has been allocated to the assets acquired and liabilities assumed based on the estimated fair values at the date of acquisition.

The purchase price exceeded the estimated fair values of the net assets acquired by $3,200,000. Of this amount, $1,325,000 was assigned to "Purchased in-process research and development," which is being amortized on the straight-line method over the estimated remaining lives of individual projects, ranging from two to five years. The amounts charged to these projects include only costs of materials, equipment, and facilities that the Company deems to have future benefit. The remainder of the excess purchase price, amounting to $1,875,000, has been recorded as goodwill and is being amortized on the straight-line method over ten years. Amortization expense charged to operations for 2000 totaled $157,000, of which $111,000 related to the acquired research and development.

The operating results of this acquisition are included in the Company's consolidated results of operations from the date of acquisition. The following table presents the allocation of the purchase price, including related acquisition costs, to the assets and liabilities acquired:

Accounts and notes receivable	$2,000,000
Tooling equipment	4,900,000
Goodwill	1,875,000
Purchased in-process research and development	1,325,000
Accounts payable	(600,000)
Total purchase price	$9,500,000

Example 26–5: Research and Development Costs Acquired in a Purchase Business Combination Are Expensed

"Purchased in-process research and development" expense in the 2000 Statement of Operations represents the value assigned to research and development projects in a purchase business combination of the Chickadee brand from Seliga & Co. These projects were commenced but not yet completed at the date of acquisition, for which technological feasibility has not been established and which have no alternative future use in research and development activities or otherwise. In accordance with Financial Accounting Standards Board Statement No. 2 (Accounting for Research and Development Costs), as interpreted by FASB Interpretation No. 4 (Applicability of FASB Statement No. 2 to Business Combinations Accounted for by the Purchase Method), amounts assigned to purchased in-process research and development meeting the above criteria must be charged to expense at the date of consummation of the purchase business combination. In 2000, a charge of $1,325,000 was recorded for purchased in-process research and development costs in conjunction with this business combination, based on preliminary allocations of purchase price.

In 1999, a charge of $762,000 was recorded for purchased in-process research and development costs in conjunction with the purchase of Novatex, Inc. (see Note [X]), based on an independent appraisal.

Example 26–6: Capitalized Costs of Computer Software to Be Sold, Leased, or Otherwise Marketed

Research and development costs are charged to expense as incurred. However, the costs incurred for the development of computer software that will be sold, leased, or otherwise marketed are capitalized when technological feasibility has been established. These capitalized costs are subject to an ongoing assessment of recoverability based on anticipated future revenues and changes in hardware and software technologies. Costs that are capitalized include direct labor and related overhead.

Amortization of capitalized software development costs begins when the product is available for general release. Amortization is provided on a product-by-product basis on either the straight-line method over periods not exceeding two years or the sales ratio method. Unamortized capitalized software development costs determined to be in excess of net realizable value of the product are expensed immediately.

During the years ended December 31, 2000, and December 31, 1999, amortization of costs related to computer software products held for sale totaled $57,000 and $46,000, respectively. In addition, in September 2000, the Company charged $173,000 to operations as a write-down of capitalized computer software costs to their estimated net realizable value.

CHAPTER 27
SEGMENT INFORMATION

CONTENTS

EXECUTIVE SUMMARY

Generally accepted accounting principles (GAAP) require that public entities report certain information (1) about operating segments in complete sets of financial statements and in condensed financial statements of interim periods and (2) about the segments' principal products and services, the geographic areas in which they operate, and their major customers. Although the disclosures about segments of an entity are not required for *nonpublic* business entities or for not-for-profit organizations, such entities are encouraged to provide the same information as public business entities.

Operating segments are components of an entity that meet all of the following criteria:

1. Engage in business activities from which revenues may be earned and in which expenses may be incurred
2. Operating results are regularly reviewed by the entity's chief operating decision maker (e.g., chief executive officer, chief operating officer, or a group of individuals) for purposes of making decisions about resource allocation and performance evaluation
3. Discrete financial information is available

An entity should report separately information about each operating segment that meets any of the following quantitative criteria:

1. The operating segment's total revenues (both external, such as sales to other entities, and intersegment, such as sales between operating segments) make up 10% or more of the combined revenue of all reported operating segments
2. The absolute amount of the reported profit or loss of the operating segment is 10% or more of the greater (in absolute amount) of (a) the combined reported profit of all operating segments that did not report a loss or (b) the combined reported loss of all operating segments that did report a loss
3. The operating segment's assets are 10% or more of the combined assets of all operating segments

For purposes of the above criteria, two or more operating segments may be aggregated into a single operating segment if the segments have similar economic characteristics and if the segments are similar in each of the following areas:

1. The nature of their products and services
2. The nature of their production processes
3. Their type or class of customers
4. Their distribution methods
5. The nature of their regulatory environment , if applicable, (e.g., banking, insurance)

The following are other situations in which separate information about an operating segment should be reported:

- If total external revenue reported by operating segments constitutes less than 75% of total consolidated revenue, then additional operating segments should be identified as reportable segments (even if they do not meet the quantitative criteria above) until at least 75% of the total consolidated revenue is included in reportable segments.

- Information about other business activities and operating segments that are not reportable should be combined and disclosed in an "all other" category.
- If a prior-year reportable segment fails to meet one of the quantitative criteria in the current reporting period, but management believes the segment to be of continuing significance, then information about that segment shall continue to be presented.
- If an operating segment meets the criteria as a reportable segment for the first time in the current period, prior-year segment information that is presented for comparative purposes should be restated to reflect the new reportable segment as a separate segment, unless it is impracticable.

There may be a practical limit to the number of reportable segments that an entity separately discloses so that segment information does not become extremely detailed. As a practical matter, authoritative literature indicates that as the number of reportable segments exceeds ten, an entity should consider whether a practical limit has been reached.

Authoritative Literature

FAS-131	Disclosures about Segments of an Enterprise and Related Information
FTB 79-4	Segment Reporting of Puerto Rican Operations
FTB 79-5	Meaning of the Term "Customer" as It Applies to Health Care Facilities under FASB Statement No. 14

DISCLOSURE REQUIREMENTS

The following information should be disclosed for each period for which a complete set of financial statements is presented:

1. Factors used to identify the entity's reportable segments, including the basis of organization such as (FAS-131, par. 26):
   a. Differences in products and services
   b. Geographic areas
   c. Regulatory environments
   d. A combination of factors
2. Types of products and services from which each reportable segment derives its revenues (FAS-131, par. 26)

3. The amount of profit or loss and total assets for each reportable segment (FAS-131, par. 27)
4. The following financial information about each reportable segment, if the specified amounts are included in the determination of segment profit or loss reviewed by the chief operating decision maker (FAS-131, par. 27):
   a. Revenues from external customers
   b. Revenues from transactions with other operating segments
   c. Interest revenue (this may be reported net of interest expense if a majority of the segment's revenues are from interest and the chief operating decision maker relies primarily on net interest revenue to assess performance)
   d. Interest expense
   e. Depreciation, depletion, and amortization
   f. Unusual items, as described in APB Opinion No. 30
   g. Equity in the net income of investees accounted for by the equity method
   h. Income tax expense or benefit
   i. Extraordinary items
   j. Significant noncash items other than depreciation, depletion, and amortization
5. The following financial information about each reportable segment, if the specified amounts are included in the determination of segment assets reviewed by the chief operating decision maker (FAS-131, par. 28):
   a. The amount of investment in equity-method investees
   b. Total expenditures for additions to long-lived assets (other than financial instruments, long-term customer relationships of a financial institution, mortgage and other servicing rights, deferred policy acquisition costs, and deferred tax assets)
6. An explanation of the measurements used for segment profit or loss and segment assets for each reportable segment, including, at a minimum, the following information (FAS-131, par. 31):
   a. The basis of accounting for any transactions between reportable segments
   b. The nature of any differences between the measurements of the reportable segments' profit or loss and the entity's consolidated income before income taxes, extraordinary items,

discontinued operations, and cumulative effect of changes in accounting principles

c. The nature of any differences between the measurements of the reportable segments' assets and the entity's consolidated assets

d. The nature of any changes from prior periods in the measurement methods used to determine reported segment profit or loss and the effect, if any, of those changes on the amount of segment profit or loss

e. The nature and effect of any asymmetrical allocations to segments (e.g., an entity might allocate depreciation expense to a segment without allocating the related depreciable assets to that segment)

7. Reconciliations of all of the following items (FAS-131, par. 32):

   a. The total of the reportable segments' revenues to the entity's consolidated revenues

   b. The total of the reportable segments' profit or loss to the entity's consolidated income before income taxes, extraordinary items, discontinued operations, and cumulative effect of changes in accounting principles (However, if an entity allocates items such as income taxes and extraordinary items to segments, the entity may choose to reconcile the total of the segments' profit or loss to consolidated income after those items.)

   c. The total of the reportable segments' assets to the entity's consolidated assets

   d. The total of the reportable segments' amounts for every other significant item of information disclosed to the corresponding consolidated amount (e.g., an entity may choose to disclose liabilities for its reportable segments, in which case the entity would reconcile the total of reportable segments' liabilities for each segment to the entity's consolidated liabilities if the segment liabilities are significant)

8. The following items are required to be disclosed on an entity-wide basis, unless they are disclosed as part of the information about reportable segments (Entities that have a single reportable segment must also disclose this information.) (FAS-131, pars. 36–39):

   a. Revenues from external customers for each product and service or each group of similar products and services, based on information used to produce the entity's general-purpose financial statements (unless it is impracticable to do so, in which case the entity should disclose that fact)

b. The following information about geographic areas, based on information used to produce the entity's general-purpose financial statements (unless it is impracticable to do so, in which case the entity should disclose that fact):

— Revenues from external sources (i) attributed to the entity's country of domicile and (ii) attributed to all foreign countries in total from which the entity derives revenues. If revenues from external customers attributed to an individual foreign country are material, the entity should disclose those revenues separately; the entity should disclose the basis for attributing revenues from external customers to individual countries.

— Long-lived assets (other than financial instruments, long-term customer relationships of a financial institution, mortgage and other servicing rights, deferred policy acquisition costs, and deferred tax assets) located in (i) the entity's country of domicile and (ii) all foreign countries in total in which the entity holds assets. If assets in an individual foreign country are material, the entity should disclose those assets separately.

c. The extent of the entity's reliance on a single external customer from which 10% or more of revenues are derived, the amount of revenues earned from each such single customer, and the operating segment reporting the revenue

9. The following information should be disclosed about each reportable segment in condensed financial statements of interim periods (FAS-131, par. 33):

a. Revenues from external customers

b. Intersegment revenues

c. Segment profit or loss

d. Total assets for which there has been a material change from the amount disclosed in the last annual report

e. A description of differences from the last annual report in the basis of segmentation or in the basis of measurement of segment profit or loss

f. A reconciliation of the total reportable segments' profit or loss to the entity's consolidated income before income taxes, extraordinary items, discontinued operations, and cumulative effect of changes in accounting principles (However, if an entity allocates items such as income taxes and extraordinary items to segments, the entity may reconcile the total of the segments' profit or loss to consolidated income after those items.)

10. If an entity changes the structure of its internal organization in a manner that causes the composition of its reportable segments to change, the corresponding information for earlier periods, including interim periods, should be restated, unless it is impracticable to do so. The entity should also disclose that it has restated the segment information for earlier periods. (If the segment information for earlier periods, including interim periods, is not restated to reflect the change, the entity should disclose in the year in which the change occurs segment information for the current period under both the old basis and the new basis of segmentation, unless it is impracticable to do so.) (FAS-131, pars. 34–35)

EXAMPLES OF FINANCIAL STATEMENT DISCLOSURES

The following sample disclosures are available on the accompanying disc.

Example 27–1: Company Operates in a Single Business Segment and Discloses Entity-Wide Geographic Data and Sales to Major Customers

The Company operates in a single business segment that includes the design, development, and manufacture of electronic surveillance equipment and products for the commercial electronics industry. The following table summarizes the Company's revenues and long-lived assets in different geographic locations:

	2000	*1999*
Revenues:		
United States	$59,820,000	$54,338,000
Singapore	11,341,000	9,102,000
Other foreign countries	20,145,000	17,010,000
Total	$91,306,000	$80,450,000
Long-lived assets:		
United States	$16,764,000	$15,430,000
Singapore	6,450,000	6,020,000
Other foreign countries	1,230,000	1,113,000
Total	$24,444,000	$22,563,000

Geographic area data is based on product shipment destination. Export sales as a percentage of revenues were 40% for 2000 and 35% for 1999.

In 2000 and 1999, sales to a single customer were 13% and 11% of total sales, respectively.

The geographic summary of long-lived assets is based on physical location.

Example 27–2: Company's Operations Are Classified Into Two Principal Reportable Segments: Domestic and International Operations

The Company manages its operations through two business segments: domestic and international. Each unit sells railroad electronics and related products as well as services to railroads and transit authorities. The international business segment sells the Company's products and services outside the U.S.

The Company evaluates performance based on net operating profit. Administrative functions such as finance, treasury, and information systems are centralized. However, where applicable, portions of the administrative function expenses are allocated between the operating segments. The operating segments do not share manufacturing or distribution facilities. In the event any materials and/or services are provided to one operating segment by the other, the transaction is valued according to the company's transfer policy, which approximates market price. The costs of operating the manufacturing plants are captured discretely within each segment. The Company's property, plant and equipment, inventory, and accounts receivable are captured and reported discretely within each operating segment.

Summary financial information for the two reportable segments is as follows:

	2000	*1999*
United States Operations:		
Net sales	$25,200,000	$22,400,000
Operating income	2,150,000	2,410,000
Assets	15,600,000	14,400,000
Accounts receivable	5,070,000	4,510,000
Inventory	4,250,000	4,325,000
International Operations:		
Net sales	$1,360,000	$1,310,000
Operating income	69,000	31,000
Assets	65,000	59,000
Accounts receivable	171,000	143,000
Inventory	56,000	42,000

	2000	1999
Consolidated Operations:		
Net sales	$26,560,000	$23,710,000
Operating income	2,219,000	2,441,000
Assets	15,665,000	14,459,000
Accounts receivable	5,241,000	4,653,000
Inventory	4,306,000	4,367,000

Example 27–3: Company Has Five Operating Segments That Are Aggregated into Three Reportable Segments and Are Reconciled to the Company's Consolidated Amounts

The Company has five principal operating segments, which are the design, manufacturing and marketing of (1) semiconductor test systems, (2) backplane connection systems, (3) circuit-board test systems, (4) telecommunication test systems, and (5) software test systems. These operating segments were determined based on the nature of the products and services offered. *Operating segments* are defined as components of an enterprise about which separate financial information is available that is evaluated regularly by the chief operating decision-maker in deciding how to allocate resources and in assessing performance. The Company's chief executive officer and chief operating officer have been identified as the chief operating decision makers. The Company's chief operating decision makers direct the allocation of resources to operating segments based on the profitability and cash flows of each respective segment.

The Company has determined that there are three reportable segments: (1) semiconductor test systems segment, (2) backplane connection systems segment, and (3) other test systems segment. The other test systems segment comprises circuit-board test systems, telecommunication test systems, and software test systems; these operating segments were not separately reported as they do not meet any of the quantitative thresholds under Financial Accounting Standards Board Statement No. 131 (Disclosures about Segments of an Enterprise and Related Information).

The Company evaluates performance based on several factors, of which the primary financial measure is business segment income before taxes. The accounting policies of the business segments are the same as those described in "Note 1: Summary of Significant Accounting Policies." Intersegment sales are accounted for at fair value as if sales were to third parties. The following tables show the operations of the Company's reportable segments:

	Semiconductor Test Systems Segment	*Backplane Connection Systems Segment*	*Other Test Systems Segment*	*Corporate and Eliminations*	*Consolidated*
2000					
Sales to unaffiliated customers	$19,670,000	$5,458,000	$4,975,000	$-0-	$30,103,000
Intersegment sales	-0-	275,000	-0-	(275,000)	-0-
Net sales	19,670,000	5,733,000	4,975,000	(275,000)	30,103,000
Income before taxes (1)	2,125,000	692,000	531,000	(450,000)	2,898,000
Total assets (2)	10,391,000	3,850,000	2,700,000	6,200,000	23,141,000
Property additions (3)	1,400,000	640,000	150,000	700,000	2,890,000
Interest expense	120,000	74,000	53,000	-0-	247,000
Depreciation and amortization (3)	545,000	280,000	200,000	320,000	1,345,000
1999					
Sales to unaffiliated customers	$17,840,000	$4,940,000	$4,310,000	-0-	$27,090,000
Intersegment sales	-0-	210,000	-0-	(210,000)	-0-
Net sales	17,840,000	5,150,000	4,310,000	(210,000)	27,090,000
Income before taxes (1)	1,930,000	584,000	487,000	(400,000)	2,601,000
Total assets (2)	10,110,000	3,725,000	2,574,000	5,900,000	22,309,000
Property additions (3)	1,050,000	420,000	170,000	400,000	2,040,000
Interest expense	113,000	67,000	48,000	-0-	228,000
Depreciation and amortization (3)	510,000	240,000	180,000	290,000	1,220,000

(1) Income before taxes of the principal businesses exclude the effects of employee profit sharing, management incentive compensation, other unallocated expenses, and net interest income.

(2) *Total business assets* are the owned or allocated assets used by each business. *Corporate assets* consist of cash and cash equivalents, marketable securities, unallocated fixed assets of support divisions and common facilities, and certain other assets.

(3) Corporate property additions and depreciation and amortization expense include items attributable to the unallocated fixed assets of support divisions and common facilities.

Information as to the Company's sales in different geographical areas is as follows:

	2000	*1999*
Sales to unaffiliated customers:		
United States	$16,112,000	$13,143,000
Asia Pacific region	5,477,000	6,374,000
Europe	4,993,000	4,065,000
Japan	2,300,000	2,439,000
Other	1,221,000	1,069,000
	$30,103,000	$27,090,000

Sales are attributable to geographic areas based on location of customer. Neither the Company nor any of its segments depends on any single customer, small group of customers, or government for more than 10% of its sales.

Also, because a substantial portion of the Company's sales are derived from the sales of product manufactured in the United States, long-lived assets located outside the United States are less than 10%.

Example 27–4: Company Discloses Sales to Major Customers and the Identity of the Segments Reporting the Sales

> **Note:** Example 27–4 assumes the same facts as in Example 27–3, except that the Company has sales to major customers, for which disclosure is required of (1) the total amount of sales to the major customer and (2) the identity of the segment reporting the sales.

In 2000 and 1999, sales to a customer of the Company's Semiconductor Test Systems segment totaled approximately $4,214,000 (14%), and $3,522,000 (13%), respectively, of the Company's consolidated sales. In 2000 and 1999, sales to a different customer of the Company's Backplane Connection Systems segment totaled $3,913,000 (13%), and $3,251,000 (12%), respectively, of the Company's consolidated sales.

Example 27–5: Company Discloses Its Exposure to Economic Conditions in Foreign Countries

The Company has operations in Hong Kong, China, and Brazil. These countries have experienced illiquidity, volatile currency exchange rates and interest rates, and reduced economic activity. The Company will be affected for the foreseeable future by economic conditions in these regions, although it is not possible to determine the extent of the effects.

CHAPTER 28
STOCK-BASED COMPENSATION, STOCK OPTION PLANS, AND STOCK PURCHASE PLANS

CONTENTS

EXECUTIVE SUMMARY

Stock issued to employees may include compensation (compensatory plan) or may not include compensation (noncompensatory plan). A *compensatory plan* is one in which services rendered by employees are compensated for by the issuance of stock. The measurement of compensation expense included in compensatory plans is the primary problem in accounting for stock issued to employees.

Generally accepted accounting principles (GAAP) for stock-based compensation plans are established primarily in Accounting Principles Board Opinion No. 25 (Accounting for Stock Issued to Employees) and Financial Accounting Standards Board Statement No. 123 (Accounting for Stock-Based Compensation). APB-25 is based on the intrinsic value method of accounting. FAS-123 established a method of accounting for stock-based compensation that is based on the fair value of stock options and similar instruments. Adoption of the fair value based method of accounting under FAS-123 is encouraged but not required for all stock-based compensation arrangements with *employees*. However, the fair value based method of accounting under FAS-123 must be adopted as the measurement basis for transactions in which an entity acquires goods or services from *nonemployees* in exchange for equity instruments.

APB-25

The essential characteristics of noncompensatory stock options or stock purchase plans are as follows:

1. Substantially all full-time employees meeting limited employment qualifications may participate.
2. Stock is offered equally to eligible employees, but the plan may limit the total amount of shares that can be purchased.
3. The time permitted to exercise the rights is limited to a reasonable period.
4. Any discount from the market price is no greater than would be a reasonable offer of stock to shareholders or others.

Plans that do not have these characteristics are classified as compensatory plans.

Under traditional stock option and stock purchase plans, an employer corporation grants options to purchase shares of its stock, sometimes at a price lower than the prevailing market, making it possible for the individual exercising the option to have at least a potential profit at the time of acquisition. Compensatory plans result in compensation expense on the books of the Company and in compensation income to the recipient. Under APB-25, the cost of compensation is measured by the excess of the quoted market price of the stock over the option price on the measurement date. This is referred to as the *intrinsic value method.* The measurement date is the first date on which the employer knows (1) the number of shares the employee is to receive and (2) the option or purchase price. Usually, the measurement date is the grant date.

Compensation expense related to compensatory plans should be recognized as an expense over the period of employment attributable to the option. If this period is not stated, a reasonable estimate must be made, taking into account the circumstances implied by the terms of the agreement. Stock issued in accordance with a plan for past and future services of an employee is allocated between expired costs and future costs. Future costs are charged to the periods in which the employee performs services. In the event stock options are exercised before the related compensation cost is actually incurred, a deferred or prepaid compensation account is set up. Unearned compensation cost should be written off to the period(s) in which they were actually earned, and any balances at a reporting date should be deducted from stockholders' equity.

FAS-123

Under FAS-123, a plan is noncompensatory if it meets the following criteria:

1. Substantially all full-time employees meeting limited employment qualifications may participate.
2. The plan has no option features other than the following:
   a. Employees are permitted a short period of time, not exceeding 31 days, after the purchase price has been fixed to enroll in the plan
   b. The purchase price is based solely on the stock's market price at the date of purchase, and employees are permitted to cancel participation before the purchase date and receive a refund of amounts previously paid
3. The discount from the market price does not exceed the greater of (a) a per-share discount that would be reasonable in a recurring offer of stock to stockholders or others, or (b) the per-share amount of stock issuance costs avoided by not having to raise a significant amount of capital by a public offering. A discount of 5% or less would meet this criterion.

Plans that do not have these characteristics are classified as compensatory plans.

FAS-123 establishes a method of accounting for stock compensation plans that is based on the fair value of employee stock options and similar equity instruments. The method is in contrast to that described in APB-25, which is based on the intrinsic value of equity instruments. Companies are permitted to continue using the method of accounting described in APB-25 but are required to disclose pro forma net income (and earnings per share if presented), determined as if the fair value method of FAS-123 had been used to measure compensation cost.

The general principle underlying FAS-123 is that equity instruments are recognized at the fair value of the consideration received for them. In a transaction with third parties for goods and services, fair value may be the value of the consideration received or the value of the equity instruments issued, whichever is more reliably measurable. Applying this general principle to stock compensation results in the equity instruments being measured and recognized at their fair value and the compensation cost being the excess of that amount over any amount paid by the employee. For example, if an employee pays $10 for a stock option valued at $30, $20 is the amount of compensation attributed to employee services.

The objective of the measurement process described in FAS-123 is to estimate the fair value, based on the stock price at the grant date, of equity instruments to be issued to employees when they have satisfied all conditions required to earn the right to benefit from the instruments. The fair value of an option estimated at the grant date is not subsequently adjusted for changes in the price of the underlying stock or other variables (e.g., changes in volatility, the life of the option, dividends on the stock, or the risk-free interest rate).

Authoritative Literature

ARB-43	Chapter 13B, Compensation Involved in Stock Option and Stock Purchase Plans
APB-25	Accounting for Stock Issued to Employees
FAS-123	Accounting for Stock-Based Compensation
FAS-128	Earnings per Share
FIN-28	Accounting for Stock Appreciation Rights and Other Variable Stock Option or Award Plans
FIN-38	Determining the Measurement Date for Stock Option, Purchase, and Award Plans Involving Junior Stock
FIN-44	Accounting for Certain Transactions Involving Stock Compensation—an Interpretation of APB Opinion No. 25

FTB 97-1	Accounting under Statement 123 for Certain Employee Stock Purchase Plans with a Look-Back Option
SOP 93-6	Employers' Accounting for Stock Ownership Plans

DISCLOSURE REQUIREMENTS

Stock-Based Compensation Plans

All entities must disclose the following information, regardless of the method used (APB-25 or FAS-123) to account for employee stock-based compensation arrangements (FAS-123, pars. 46–48):

1. A description of the stock-based compensation plan, including the general terms of awards, such as vesting requirements, maximum term of options granted, and number of shares authorized for grants of options or other equity instruments
2. For each year for which an income statement is presented, the number and weighted-average exercise prices of options that were:
   a. Outstanding at the beginning of the year
   b. Outstanding at the end of the year
   c. Granted during the year
   d. Exercised during the year
   e. Exercisable at the end of the year
   f. Forfeited during the year
   g. Expired during the year
3. The weighted-average fair value (as of grant date) of options granted during the year (If the exercise price of some options differs from the market price of the stock on the grant date, weighted-average exercise prices and weighted-average fair values of options should be disclosed separately for options whose exercise price (a) equals, (b) exceeds, or (c) is less than the market price of the stock on the date of grant.)
4. The number and weighted-average fair value (as of grant date) of equity instruments other than options (e.g., shares of nonvested stock) granted during the year
5. A description of the method and significant assumptions used during the year to estimate the fair values of options, including (a) risk-free interest rate, (b) expected life, (c) expected volatility, and (d) expected dividends
6. Total compensation cost recognized in the financial statements
7. The terms of significant modifications of outstanding awards

8. The range of exercise prices, the weighted-average exercise price, and the weighted-average remaining contractual life for options outstanding as of the date of the latest balance sheet presented, and for each range:
   a. The number, weighted-average exercise price, and weighted-average remaining contractual life of options outstanding
   b. The number and weighted-average exercise price of options currently exercisable

An entity that grants options under multiple stock-based employee compensation plans should provide the foregoing information separately for different types of awards to the extent that the differences in the characteristics of the awards make separate disclosure important to an understanding of the entity's use of stock-based compensation (FAS-123, pars. 46–48).

In addition to the above, if the entity is accounting for stock-based compensation under APB-25, rather than FAS-123, pro forma net income (and pro forma earnings per share, if earnings per share is presented) should be disclosed as if the fair value based method prescribed by FAS-123 had been applied (FAS-123, par. 45).

Employee Stock Ownership Plans

The financial statements of a company sponsoring an ESOP should disclose the following information:

1. A description of the plan (SOP 93-6, par. 53a)
2. The basis for determining contributions (SOP 93-6, par. 53a)
3. The employee groups covered (SOP 93-6, par. 53a)
4. The nature and effects of significant matters affecting comparability of information for all periods presented (SOP 93-6, par. 53a)
5. For leveraged ESOPs and pension reversion ESOPs, the basis for releasing shares and how dividends on allocated and unallocated shares are used (SOP 93-6, par. 53a)
6. The following accounting policies for blocks of both "old ESOP shares" and "new ESOP shares" (The following disclosures are required if the employer has both old ESOP shares for which it does not adopt the guidance in SOP 93-6 and new ESOP shares for which the guidance in SOP 93-6 is required; *old ESOP shares* are those acquired or held by the plan on or before December 31, 1992.) (SOP 93-6, par. 53b):
   a. The method of measuring compensation
   b. The classification of dividends on ESOP shares

   c. The treatment of ESOP shares for earnings per share computations

7. The amount of plan compensation cost recognized for each period for which an income statement is presented (SOP 93-6, par. 53c)

8. If the employer does not adopt SOP 93-6 for the old ESOP shares, the following disclosures should be made at the balance sheet date for both old ESOP shares and new ESOP shares (SOP 93-6, par. 53d):

   a. The number of allocated shares

   b. The number of committed-to-be-released shares

   c. The number of suspense shares held by the ESOP

9. The fair value of unearned ESOP shares at the balance sheet date for shares accounted for under SOP 93-6 (This disclosure need not be made for old ESOP shares for which the employer does not apply the guidance in SOP 93-6 for those shares.) (SOP 93-6, par. 53e)

10. The existence and nature of any repurchase obligation, including disclosure of the fair value of the shares allocated as of the balance sheet date that are subject to a repurchase obligation (SOP 93-6, par. 53f)

11. If an employer has, in substance, guaranteed the debt of an ESOP, the employer's financial statements should disclose the following (SOP 76-3, par. 10):

    a. The compensation element and the interest element of annual contributions to the ESOP

    b. The interest rate and debt terms

EXAMPLES OF FINANCIAL STATEMENT DISCLOSURES

The following sample disclosures are available on the accompanying disc.

Example 28–1: Single Stock Compensation Plan—Company Applies APB-25; Pro Forma Effect under FAS-123 Is Disclosed

The Company has a Stock Option Plan (Plan) under which officers, key employees, and non-employee directors may be granted options to purchase shares of the Company's authorized but unissued common stock. The maximum number of shares of the Company's common stock available for issuance under the Plan is 10 million shares. As of December 31, 2000, the maximum number of shares available for future grants under the Plan is 4,200,000 shares. Under the Plan, the option exercise price is equal to the fair market value of the Company's common stock at the date of grant. Options currently expire no later than 10 years from the grant date and generally vest within five years. Proceeds received by the Company from exercises of stock options are credited to common stock and additional paid-in capital. Additional information with respect to the Plan's stock option activity is as follows:

	Number of Shares	*Weighted Average Exercise Price*
Outstanding at December 31, 1998	3,378,000	$ 7.49
Granted	630,000	$36.23
Exercised	(472,000)	$ 3.06
Cancelled	(88,000)	$16.38
Outstanding at December 31, 1999	3,448,000	$13.12
Granted	480,000	$38.35
Exercised	(600,000)	$ 4.59
Cancelled	(203,000)	$23.64
Outstanding at December 31, 2000	3,125,000	$18.13
Options exercisable at December 31, 1999	1,152,000	$3.66
Options exercisable at December 31, 2000	1,038,000	$6.11

The following tables summarize information about stock options outstanding and exercisable at December 31, 2000:

	Stock Options Outstanding		
Range of Exercise Prices	*Number of Shares Outstanding*	*Weighted Average Remaining Contractual Life in Years*	*Weighted Average Exercise Price*
$1.46–$5.55	558,000	2.2	$ 2.83
$5.62–$11.10	702,000	4.9	$ 7.18
$11.42–$34.75	892,000	6.9	$15.16
$34.85–$60.80	973,000	8.8	$37.51
	3,125,000	6.2	$18.13

	Stock Options Exercisable	
Range of Exercise Prices	*Number of Shares Exercisable*	*Weighted Average Exercise Price*
$1.46–$5.55	558,000	$ 2.83
$5.62–$11.10	376,000	$ 6.16
$11.42–$34.75	70,000	$16.82
$34.85–$60.80	34,000	$37.53
	1,038,000	$ 6.11

The Company has elected to follow APB Opinion No. 25 (Accounting for Stock Issued to Employees) in accounting for its employee stock options. Accordingly, no compensation expense is recognized in the Company's financial statements because the exercise price of the Company's employee stock options equals the market price of the Company's common stock on the date of grant. If under Financial Accounting Standards Board Statement No. 123 (Accounting for Stock-Based Compensation) the Company determined compensation costs based on the fair value at the grant date for its stock options, net earnings and earnings per share would have been reduced to the following pro forma amounts:

	2000	*1999*
Net earnings:		
As reported	$3,750,000	$3,195,000
Pro forma	$3,600,000	$3,050,000
Basic earnings per share:		
As reported	$1.10	$.80
Pro forma	$1.06	$.76
Diluted earnings per share:		
As reported	$1.06	$.78
Pro forma	$1.02	$.74

The weighted average estimated fair value of stock options granted during 2000 and 1999 was $17.71 and $16.95 per share, respectively. These amounts were determined using the Black-Scholes option-pricing model, which values options based on the stock price at the grant date, the expected life of the option, the estimated volatility of the stock, the expected dividend payments, and the risk-free interest rate over the expected life of the option. The assumptions used in the Black-Scholes model were as follows for stock options granted in 2000 and 1999:

	2000	*1999*
Risk-free interest rate	5.3%	6.6%
Expected volatility of common stock	45.5%	30.5%
Dividend yield	1.4%	1.5%
Expected life of options	6 years	6 years

The Black-Scholes option valuation model was developed for estimating the fair value of traded options that have no vesting restrictions and are fully transferable. Because option valuation models require the use of subjective assumptions, changes in these assumptions can materially affect the fair value of the options, and the Company's options do not have the characteristics of traded options, the option valuation models do not necessarily provide a reliable measure of the fair value of its options.

Example 28–2: Multiple Stock Compensation Plans—Company Applies APB-25; Pro Forma Effect under FAS-123 Is Disclosed

The Company's Omnibus Stock Plan provides for the granting of 15 million shares of common stock for awards of options under the Company's 1993 Stock Option Plan, the 1993 Employee Stock Purchase Plan, and the 1995 Stock Incentive Plan.

Under the 1993 Stock Option Plan, options to purchase up to 10,500,000 shares of common stock may be granted to officers, employees, and consultants to the Company. The Company may grant options that are either qualified (incentive stock options) or nonqualified under the Internal Revenue Code of 1986, as amended. Options under the Plan will generally vest over a three-year period and the option term may not exceed ten years. Total options granted under this plan amounted to 128,100 in 2000 and 148,313 in 1999.

The Company's 1993 Employee Stock Purchase Plan provides that eligible employees may contribute up to 10% of their base earnings toward the semiannual purchase of the Company's common stock, at a price equal to 85% of the lower of the market value of the common stock on the first and last day of the applicable period. There are limitations on the number of shares that can be purchased in any period. Total shares issued under this plan were 127,082 in 2000 and 160,906 in 1999. Because the plan is noncompensatory, no charges to operations have been recorded.

The 1995 Stock Incentive Plan permits the issuance of options of common stock in the form of incentive stock options, nonstatutory stock options, stock appreciation rights, performance shares, restricted stock, or unrestricted stock to selected employees of the Company. Options under the plan vest over a three-year period. Stock appreciation rights entitle recipients to receive an amount determined in whole or in part by appreciation in the fair market value of the stock between the date of the award and the date of exercise. Performance share awards entitle recipients to acquire shares of stock upon attainment of specified performance goals. Restricted stock awards entitle recipients to acquire shares of stock, subject to the right of the Company to repurchase under certain circumstances all or part of the shares at their purchase price (or to require forfeiture of such shares if purchased at no cost) from the recipient. Restricted shares vest over a five-year period. Unearned compensation, representing the fair market value of the shares at the date of issuance, is charged to earnings over the vesting period. Total options granted under this plan amounted to 760,763 in 2000 and 1,209,471 in 1999. No stock appreciation rights or performance shares were granted in 2000 or 1999.

In addition to the above plans, the Company's 1993 Director Stock Option Plan provides for the grant of nonqualified stock options to the Company's nonemployee directors. The total number of shares to be issued under this plan may not exceed 100,000 shares. Options granted under the 1993 Director Stock Option Plan have an exercise price equal to the fair market value of the common stock on the date of the grant and a term equal to ten years. Total options granted under this plan amounted to 8,055 in 2000 and 5,310 in 1999.

Pursuant to Financial Accounting Standards Board Statement No. 123 (Accounting for Stock-Based Compensation), the Company has elected to account for its stock option plans under the provisions of APB Opinion No. 25 (Accounting for Stock Issued to Employees). Accordingly, no compensation cost has been recognized for the stock option plans. The Company has evaluated the pro forma effects of FAS-123 and as such, net earnings, basic earnings per common share, and diluted earnings per common share would have been as follows:

	2000	*1999*
Net earnings (loss):		
As reported	$(3,686,000)	$1,480,000
Pro forma	$(3,753,000)	$1,420,000
Basic earnings per share:		
As reported	$(1.03)	$.47
Pro forma	$(1.05)	$.45
Diluted earnings per share:		
As reported	$(1.03)	$.44
Pro forma	$(1.05)	$.42

The fair value of each option was estimated on the date of grant using the Black-Scholes option pricing model and the following assumptions:

	2000	*1999*
Risk-free interest rate	5.43%	6.17%
Expected volatility of common stock	35.5%	52.1%
Dividend yield	-0-	1.31%
Expected life of options	10 years	10 years

The following is a summary of the status of all of the Company's stock option plans as of December 31, 2000, and December 31, 1999 and changes during the years ended on those dates:

	Number of Shares	*Weighted Average Exercise Price*
Outstanding at December 31, 1998	4,056,000	$25.29
Granted	1,524,000	$45.48
Exercised	(507,000)	$14.09
Cancelled	(55,000)	$23.12
Outstanding at December 31, 1999	5,018,000	$32.58
Granted	1,024,000	$45.94
Exercised	(370,000)	$16.52
Cancelled	(128,000)	$32.44
Outstanding at December 31, 2000	5,544,000	$33.96
Options exercisable at December 31, 1999	340,000	$21.19
Options exercisable at December 31, 2000	451,000	$23.73

The following tables summarize information about stock options outstanding and exercisable at December 31, 2000:

	Stock Options Outstanding		
Range of Exercise Prices	*Number of Shares Outstanding*	*Weighted Average Remaining Contractual Life in Years*	*Weighted Average Exercise Price*
$8.69–$13.56	84,000	0.9	$13.28
$16.56–$24.31	702,000	3.0	$19.09
$25.13–$35.00	2,247,000	6.6	$31.54
$39.75–$45.94	2,511,000	8.1	$45.61
	5,544,000	6.5	$33.96

Range of Exercise Prices	*Stock Options Exercisable* — *Number of Shares Exercisable*	*Weighted Average Exercise Price*
$8.69–$13.56	52,000	$13.54
$16.56–$24.31	233,000	$18.40
$25.13–$35.00	99,000	$27.96
$39.75–$45.94	67,000	$43.91
	451,000	$23.73

Example 28–3: Multiple Stock Compensation Plans—Company Applies FAS-123

At December 31, 2000, the Company has three stock-based compensation plans, which are described below. The Company accounts for the fair value of its grants under those plans in accordance with Financial Accounting Standards Board Statement No. 123 (Accounting for Stock-Based Compensation). The compensation cost that has been charged against income for those plans was $7,900,000 and $6,400,000 for 2000 and 1999, respectively.

The Company has a fixed stock option plan, ABC Company Employee Stock Option Plan, under which the Company may grant options to its employees for up to 10 million shares of common stock. The exercise price of each option equals the market price of the Company's stock on the date of grant and an option's maximum term is ten years. Options are granted on January 1 and vest at the end of the third year. The weighted average estimated fair value of stock options granted during 2000 and 1999 was $17.71 and $16.95 per share, respectively. A summary of the status of the Company's fixed stock option plan as of December 31, 2000, and December 31, 1999, and changes during the years ending on those dates is presented below:

Fixed Stock Option Plan	*Number of Shares*	*Weighted Average Exercise Price*
Outstanding at December 31, 1998	4,500,000	$34.29
Granted	900,000	$50.48
Exercised	(700,000)	$27.09
Cancelled	(100,000)	$46.12
Outstanding at December 31, 1999	4,600,000	$38.58
Granted	1,000,000	$55.94
Exercised	(850,000)	$34.52
Cancelled	(90,000)	$51.44
Outstanding at December 31, 2000	4,660,000	$42.96

Options exercisable at December 31, 1999	2,924,000	$35.19
Options exercisable at December 31, 2000	2,873,000	$41.73

The following tables summarize information about fixed stock options outstanding and exercisable at December 31, 2000:

	Stock Options Outstanding		
Range of Exercise Prices	*Number of Shares Outstanding*	*Weighted Average Remaining Contractual Life in Years*	*Weighted Average Exercise Price*
$25.69–$33.56	1,107,000	3.6	$29.28
$39.56–$41.31	467,000	5.0	$40.09
$46.13–$50.19	1,326,000	6.6	$48.54
$55.75–$60.94	1,760,000	8.5	$57.61
	4,660,000	6.5	$42.96

	Stock Options Exercisable	
Range of Exercise Prices	*Number of Shares Exercisable*	*Weighted Average Exercise Price*
$25.69–$33.56	952,000	$29.54
$39.56–$41.31	325,000	$40.40
$46.13–$50.19	1,199,000	$48.96
$55.75–$60.94	397,000	$55.91
	2,873,000	$41.73

Also, the Company has a performance-based stock option plan, Enterprise 2001 Stock Option Plan, under which the Company grants selected executives and other key employees stock option awards, whose vesting is contingent upon increases in the Company's market share for its principal product. If at the end of three years market share has increased by at least 5% from the date of grant, one-third of the options under the award vest to active employees. However, if at that date market share has increased by at least 10%, two-thirds of the options under the award vest, and if market share has increased by 20% or more, all of the options under the award vest. The number of shares subject to options under this plan cannot exceed 5 million. The exercise price of each option, which has a ten-year life, is equal to the market price of the Company's common stock on the date of grant. The weighted average estimated fair value of stock options granted during 2000 and 1999 was $19.97 and $24.32 per share, respectively. A summary of the status of the Company's performance-based stock option plan as of December 31, 2000, and December 31, 1999, and changes during the years ending on those dates is presented below:

Performance-Based Stock Option Plan	*Number of Shares*	*Weighted Average Exercise Price*
Outstanding at December 31, 1998	1,635,000	$48.29
Granted	980,000	$55.48
Exercised	(40,000)	$47.09
Cancelled	(42,000)	$50.12
Outstanding at December 31, 1999	2,533,000	$51.58
Granted	995,000	$60.94
Exercised	(100,000)	$46.52
Cancelled	(604,000)	$51.44
Outstanding at December 31, 2000	2,824,000	$55.96
Options exercisable at December 31, 1999	780,000	$46.19
Options exercisable at December 31, 2000	936,000	$47.73

As of December 31, 2000, the performance-based stock options of 2,824,000 outstanding under the Plan have exercise prices between $46.52 and $60.94, and a weighted-average remaining contractual life of 7.7 years. The Company expects that approximately one-third of the nonvested awards at December 31, 2000, will eventually vest based on projected market share.

The Company's third stock-based compensation plan is an employee stock purchase plan, ABC Company Employee Stock Purchase Plan, under which the Company is authorized to issue up to 10 million shares of common stock to its full-time employees, nearly all of whom are eligible to participate. Under the terms of the Plan, employees can choose each year to have up to 6% of their annual base earnings withheld to purchase the Company's common stock. The purchase price of the stock is 85% of the lower of its beginning-of-year or end-of-year market price. Approximately 75% to 80% of eligible employees have participated in the Plan in the last 3 years. Under the Plan, the Company sold 723,000 shares and 629,000 shares to employees in 2000 and 1999, respectively.

For all three plans, the fair value of each option was estimated on the date of grant using the Black-Scholes option pricing model with the following assumptions:

	Risk-Free Interest Rate	*Expected Volatility of Stock*	*Expected Dividend Yield*	*Life of Options*
2000				
Fixed stock option plan	6.7%	26%	1.5%	5 years
Performance-based stock option plan	6.9%	26%	1.5%	6 years
Employee stock purchase plan	6.2%	24%	1.5%	1 year
1999				
Fixed stock option plan	5.7%	24%	1.5%	6 years
Performance-based stock option plan	5.8%	24%	1.5%	6 years
Employee stock purchase plan	5.2%	22%	1.5%	1 year

Example 28–4: Stock Option Plan—Option Repricing

> **Note:** Example 28–4 illustrates only the option repricing portion of the note. All other disclosures about the plan and the related assumptions, as illustrated in Examples 28–1 to 28–3, would be required.

Sharp declines in the market price of the Company's common stock during 2000 resulted in many outstanding employee stock options being exercisable at prices that exceeded the current market price, thereby substantially impairing the effectiveness of such options as performance incentives. Consistent with the Company's philosophy of using such equity incentives to motivate and retain management and employees, the Company's board of directors (the Board) determined it to be in the best interests of the Company and its shareholders to restore the performance incentives intended to be provided by employee stock options by repricing such options at a price equal to the average price since the decline, or $9.475 per share. Consequently, on August 19, 2000, the Company's Board decided to cancel options to purchase 450,000 shares, which were granted during 1999 at $29.50 per share; new options to purchase 450,000 shares at $9.475 were then granted. All vesting under the canceled options was lost and new vesting periods were started. The effect of this option repricing on the pro forma disclosures is considered a modification of the terms of the outstanding options. Accordingly, the 2000 pro forma disclosure includes compensation cost for the incremental fair value, under FAS-123, resulting from such modification.

Example 28–5: Stock Option Plan—Exercise Price of Some Options Differs from the Market Price of the Stock on the Grant Date

> **Note:** Example 28–5 illustrates only the disclosure requirements when the exercise price of stock options differs from the market price of the Company's common stock on the grant date. All other disclosures about the plan and the related assumptions, as illustrated in Examples 28–1 to 28–3, would be required.

The following table presents information about stock options granted during the year where the exercise price of some options differed from the market price of the Company's stock on the grant date:

	Number of Shares Granted	*Weighted Average Exercise Price*
Year ended December 31, 2000:		
Exercise price equals market value	3,878,000	$25.88
Exercise price greater than market value	5,000	$28.56
Exercise price less than market value	137,000	$ 1.28
	4,020,000	$25.04
Year ended December 31, 1999:		
Exercise price equals market value	2,953,000	$21.15
Exercise price greater than market value	6,000	$32.75
Exercise price less than market value	194,000	$ 3.59
	3,153,000	$20.09

Example 28–6: Employee Stock Purchase Plan—Company Applies APB-25; Pro Forma Effect under FAS-123 Is Disclosed

The Company's 1991 Employee Stock Purchase Plan (Plan) is a plan under which employee participants may purchase shares of the Common Stock at 85% of market value on the first or last business day of the twelve-month plan period beginning each January, whichever value is lower. Such purchases are limited to 10% of the employee's regular pay. A maximum aggregate of 1,000,000 shares has been reserved under the Plan, 423,643 of which were available for future purchases at December 31, 2000. In January 2001, 82,450 shares were purchased at $20.11 per share and in January 2000, 64,312 shares were purchased at $18.36 per share. The Company applies APB Opinion No. 25 (Accounting for Stock Issued to Employees) and related Interpretations in accounting for the Plan. Accordingly, no compensation cost has been recognized in the accompanying financial statements. Had compensation cost for the Company's employee stock purchase plan been determined consistent with the provisions of Financial Accounting Standards Board Statement No. 123 (Accounting for Stock-Based Compensation), net earnings, basic earnings per common share, and diluted earnings per common share would have been as follows:

	2000	*1999*
Net earnings		
As reported	$2,343,000	$1,375,000
Pro forma	$2,037,000	$1,211,000
Basic earnings per share:		
As reported	$1.21	$.79
Pro forma	$1.05	$.70
Diluted earnings per share:		
As reported	$1.16	$.72
Pro forma	$1.01	$.63

The pro forma value of the employees' purchase rights was estimated using the Black-Scholes model and the following assumptions: no dividend yield, an expected life of one year, expected volatility of 36.2%, and a risk-free interest rate of 5.7%. The weighted-average fair value of these purchase rights granted in 2000 and 1999 was $11.64 and $8.42, respectively.

Example 28–7: Restricted Stock Plan—Company Applies APB-25; Pro Forma Effect under FAS-123 Is Not Disclosed Due to Immateriality

The Company has a Restricted Stock Plan covering 1,500,000 shares of common stock, the purpose of which is to permit grants of shares, subject to restrictions, to key employees of the Company as a means of retaining and rewarding them for long-term performance and to increase their ownership in the Company. Shares awarded under the plan entitle the shareholder to all rights of common stock ownership except that the shares may not be sold, transferred, pledged, exchanged or otherwise disposed of during the restriction period. The restriction period is determined by a committee, appointed by the board of directors, and may not exceed ten years.

The Company accounts for its Restricted Stock Plan under APB Opinion No. 25 (Accounting for Stock Issued to Employees). During 2000 and 1999, 95,000 shares and 83,000 shares, respectively, were granted with restriction periods of four to six years at market prices ranging from $13.125 to $18.475 in 2000 and $11.375 to $16.875 in 1999.

The shares were recorded at the market value on the date of issuance as deferred compensation and the related amount is being amortized to operations over the respective vesting period. During the years ended December 31, 2000, and December 31, 1999, unearned compensation charged to operations related to these shares of restricted stock was $375,000 and $290,000, respectively. At December 31, 2000, the weighted-average grant date fair value and weighted-average contractual life for outstanding shares of restricted stock was $15.03 and 5.2 years, respectively.

The pro forma net income impact under Financial Accounting Standards Board Statement No. 123 (Accounting for Stock-Based Compensation) is not material.

A summary of restricted stock award share activity follows:

	2000	*1999*
Awards available for grant—Beginning of year	728,000	186,000
New awards authorized	400,000	725,000
Available awards terminated	(200,000)	(100,000)
Restricted shares awarded	(95,000)	(83,000)
Awards available for grant—End of year	833,000	728,000

Example 28–8: Non-Plan Independent Consultant Stock Options

During the year ended December 31, 2000, the Company's board of directors approved the grant of stock options to an independent consultant to purchase an aggregate of 50,000 shares of its common stock. These options have an exercise price of $11.49 and as of December 31, 2000, none of these option shares were vested. As a result, the Company has recorded $215,000 in deferred compensation, which will be amortized to expense over the three-year vesting period of the options. For the year ended December 31, 2000, an amount of $36,000 has been amortized to expense. These options were not issued as part of any of the Company's registered Stock Option Plans.

Example 28–9: FASB Interpretation No. 44 of APB-25 Relating to Transactions Involving Stock Compensation

In March 2000, FASB issued Interpretation No. 44 (FIN-44) (Accounting for Certain Transactions Involving Stock Compensation—an Interpretation of APB Opinion No. 25). This Interpretation clarifies the definition of employee for purposes of applying APB Opinion No. 25 (Accounting for Stock Issued to Employees), the criteria for determining whether a plan qualifies as a noncompensatory plan, the accounting consequence of various modifications to the terms of a previously fixed stock option or award, and the accounting for an exchange of stock compensation awards in a business combination. This Interpretation is effective July 1, 2000, but certain conclusions in this Interpretation cover specific events that occur after either December 15, 1998, or January 12, 2000. The Company believes that FIN-44 will not have a material effect on the consolidated financial position or results of operations.

Example 28–10: Leveraged ESOP

The Company sponsors a leveraged employee stock ownership plan (ESOP) that covers all U.S. employees who work twenty or more hours per week. The Company makes annual contributions to the ESOP equal to the ESOP's debt service less dividends received by the ESOP. All dividends received by the ESOP are used to pay debt service. The ESOP shares initially were pledged as collateral for its debt. As the debt is repaid, shares are released from collateral and allocated to active employees, based on the proportion of debt service paid in the year. The Company accounts for its ESOP in accordance with SOP 93-6 (Employers' Accounting for Employee Stock Ownership Plans). Accordingly, the debt of the ESOP is recorded as debt and the shares pledged as collateral are reported as unearned ESOP shares in the Balance Sheet. As shares are released from collateral, the Company reports compensation expense equal to the current market price of the shares, and the shares become outstanding for earnings-per-share computations. Dividends on allocated ESOP shares are recorded as a reduction of retained earnings; dividends on unallocated ESOP shares are recorded as a reduction of debt and accrued interest. ESOP compensation expense was $275,000 and $250,000 for 2000 and 1999, respectively. The ESOP shares as of December 31, 2000, and December 31, 1999, were as follows:

	2000	*1999*
Allocated shares	80,000	40,000
Shares released for allocation	40,000	40,000
Unreleased shares	80,000	120,000
Total ESOP shares	200,000	200,000
Fair value of unreleased shares at December 31	$1,200,000	$1,500,000

Example 28–11: Leveraged ESOP Used to Fund Employer's Portion of 401(k) Plan

The Company sponsors a 401(k) savings plan under which eligible employees may choose to save up to 6% of salary income on a pre-tax basis, subject to certain IRS limits. The Company matches 50% of employee contributions with Company common stock. The shares for this purpose are provided principally by the Company's employee stock ownership plan (ESOP), supplemented as needed by newly issued shares. The Company makes annual contributions to the ESOP equal to the ESOP's debt service less dividends received by the ESOP. All dividends received by the ESOP are used to pay debt service. The ESOP shares initially were pledged as collateral for its debt. As the debt is repaid, shares are released from collateral and allocated to employees who made 401(k) contributions that year, based on the proportion of debt service paid in the year. The Company accounts for its ESOP in accordance with SOP 93-6 (Employers' Accounting for Employee Stock Ownership Plans). Accordingly, the shares pledged as collateral are reported as unearned ESOP shares in the balance sheet. As shares are released from collateral, the Company reports compensation expense equal to the current market price of the shares, and the shares become outstanding for earnings-per-share computations. Dividends on allocated ESOP shares are recorded as a reduction of retained earnings; dividends on unallocated ESOP shares are recorded as a reduction of debt and accrued interest.

Compensation expense for the 401(k) match and the ESOP was $325,000 and $305,000 for 2000 and 1999, respectively. The ESOP shares as of December 31, 2000, and December 31, 1999 were as follows:

	2000	*1999*
Allocated shares	85,000	40,000
Shares released for allocation	50,000	45,000
Unreleased shares	75,000	115,000
Total ESOP shares	210,000	200,000
Fair value of unreleased shares at December 31	$850,000	$1,150,000

CHAPTER 29
SUBSEQUENT EVENTS

CONTENTS

EXECUTIVE SUMMARY

There are two types of subsequent events that require consideration:

1. Events that provide additional evidence with respect to conditions that existed at the balance sheet date and affect the estimates inherent in the process of preparing financial statements (Type 1). These events have a direct effect on the financial statements and require adjustment.
2. Events that provide evidence with respect to conditions that did not exist at the date of the balance sheet but arose subsequent to that date (Type 2). These events have no direct effect on the financial statements and should not result in an adjustment; however, disclosure may be required in notes to the financial statements.

Examples of subsequent events that have a direct effect on the financial statements and require an adjustment of account balances in the current year's financial statements, if material, include:

- A customer with an outstanding accounts receivable balance as of the balance sheet date and that declares bankruptcy in the subsequent period
- The subsequent settlement of a litigation at an amount that is different from the amount recorded in the financial statements
- The subsequent sale of property not being used in operations at a price less than the carrying value in the financial statements
- The subsequent sale of investments at a price less than the carrying value in the financial statements
- Payment of contingent liabilities

The following are examples of subsequent events that do not result in an adjustment of financial statement accounts but may be so significant that they require disclosure for fair presentation of the financial statements:

- Issuance of bonds or equity securities
- Acquisition of a business
- Litigation that arises subsequent to the balance sheet date
- Uninsured loss of inventories as a result of fire or flood
- Loss of receivables resulting from conditions that arose subsequent to the balance sheet date
- Interruption of production by natural disaster, governmental action, or labor stoppage
- Decline in market value of inventory as a consequence of government action barring further sale of the client's products
- Significant realized and unrealized gains and losses that result from changes in quoted market prices of securities arising after the balance sheet date
- Material commitments to purchase property, plant, and equipment
- Material commitments under a long-term lease agreement
- Sale of assets

Authoritative Literature

SAS-1	Section 560, Subsequent Events

DISCLOSURE REQUIREMENTS

In order for the financial statements not to be misleading, appropriate disclosures should be made of subsequent events based on information that becomes available prior to the issuance of the financial statements. An entity should consider supplementing the historical financial statements by providing pro forma data disclosure in the footnotes, giving effect to the subsequent event as if it had occurred as of the date of the financial statements (FAS-5, par. 11; AU 560.05–.07 and 560.09).

EXAMPLES OF FINANCIAL STATEMENT DISCLOSURES

The following sample disclosures are available on the accompanying disc.

Business Combinations and Joint Ventures

Example 29–1: Business Acquisition for Cash Accounted for under the Purchase Method

On February 15, 2001, the Company completed the acquisition of Itec for $5 million in cash, subject to adjustment upon finalizing the closing balance sheet. Itec is a Boston-based company and leading supplier of high-density and general-purpose AC/DC converters and ring generators distributed primarily throughout North America. The acquisition will be accounted for under the purchase method, whereby the purchase price will be allocated to the underlying assets and liabilities based on their estimated fair values. The resulting goodwill from this transaction, which is currently estimated at $1,500,000, will be amortized over twenty years. The goodwill estimate is preliminary, pending the results of appraisals, an audit, and further financial analysis. For the year ended December 31, 2000, Itec had sales of approximately $6.3 million and net income of approximately $593,000.

In addition, the Company may pay up to $1,500,000 earnout consideration to Itec's stockholders based on Itec's attaining certain defined operational performance objectives through June 30, 2002. The source of funds for the acquisition was a combination of the Company's available cash, as well as advances totaling $3 million under its existing credit facility. In connection with the Itec acquisition, the Company amended its credit facility with its primary bank to waive certain requirements and amend certain provisions.

Example 29–2: Business Acquisition for Cash, Debt, and Stock Accounted for under the Purchase Method

On January 18, 2001, the Company entered into a definitive agreement to acquire all of the outstanding capital stock of Communix, a leading supplier of automotive coatings. The agreed purchase price consists of (i) a cash component of $500,000 payable at closing, (ii) a promissory note in the amount of $1 million due one year after closing (and payable in cash or in the Company's common stock at the option of the sellers), (iii) a promissory note in the amount of $2 million due two years after closing (and payable in cash or in the Company's common stock at the option of the Company), and (iv) the issuance of 500,000 shares of the Company's common stock.

The acquisition will be accounted for under the purchase method, whereby the purchase price will be allocated to the underlying assets and liabilities based on their estimated fair values. No goodwill is expected to result from this transaction. For the year ended December 31, 2000, Communix had sales of approximately $10 million and net income of approximately $1,200,000.

Example 29–3: Business Acquisition Accounted for under the Pooling-of-Interests Method

On February 19, 2001, the Company signed a definitive agreement to merge with Evitec, a leading manufacturer of commercial air distribution products. The Company will exchange approximately 2.4 million shares of its common stock for all the outstanding stock of Evitec and will reserve approximately 100,000 shares of its common stock for issuance under Evitec's stock option plan, which the Company will assume in the transaction. The business combination will be accounted for as a pooling-of-interests. Retained earnings will be restated as of January 1, 2001, to reflect the pooling-of-interests combination.

Example 29–4: Joint Venture

On February 1, 2001, the Company and Medwax commenced operations of SOSP, Inc., a 50/50 joint venture to manufacture and distribute electronic connectors. Concurrent with the formation of the joint venture, the Company contributed assets to the venture with a net book value at December 31, 2000, of about $500,000 and will provide funds, as needed by the venture, up to $3 million per year through 2005.

Casualty Loss

Example 29–5: Inventory Destroyed in Fire

In February 2001, the Company suffered a fire in its main warehouse located in Hillsborough, Virginia. The Company estimates that inventory with a recorded value of approximately $1,200,000 was destroyed. Although the exact amount of the loss is not currently determinable, the Company expects to recover 50% to 75% of the value through insurance proceeds.

Debt/Financing

Example 29–6: New Financing Arrangement

On January 29, 2001, the Company entered into a Revolving Loan Agreement (the Loan Agreement) with Ace State Bank. The Loan Agreement provides for borrowings through January 31, 2006 (the Maturity Date). Borrowings will bear interest at the bank's prime rate. The maximum amount that may be outstanding under the Loan Agreement is $20,000,000 through December 31, 2002. Thereafter, the maximum amount of borrowings that may be outstanding under the Loan Agreement is reduced by $1,000,000 in calendar 2003 and by $1,000,000 in each of the following calendar years up to the Maturity Date. Under the terms of the Loan Agreement, the Company will pay Ace State Bank $200,000 plus an unused commitment fee during the term of the Loan Agreement. The Company will also pay legal, accounting, and other fees and expenses in connection with the Loan Agreement.

Example 29–7: Issuance of Convertible Subordinated Notes

On January 12, 2001, the Company executed an agreement with a group of institutional investors whereby the Company issued $12 million in convertible subordinated loan notes. These notes bear an interest rate of 11% per year and mature in 2003.

Example 29–8: Maximum Borrowing under Line of Credit

In February and March 2001, the Company borrowed $800,000 under its line of credit for working capital purposes. As a result, the Company has borrowed the maximum amount available under the credit line. The Company is negotiating with the bank to increase its credit line limit by $2,000,000. However, there can be no assurance that the Company will be successful in increasing its credit line.

Discontinued Operations

Example 29–9: Discontinued Operations Presented as Net Amounts in the Financial Statements

On January 31, 2001, the Company concluded the sale of its diagnostic chemical kits business for approximately $14,000,000 in cash and is expected to report a net after-tax gain of approximately $900,000 from disposal of these operations in 2001. As a result of the sale, activities of the diagnostic chemical kits business have been accounted for as discontinued operations. These results are presented as net amounts in the Consolidated Statements of Income, with prior periods restated to conform to the current presentation. Selected operating results for these discontinued operations are presented in the following table:

	2000	*1999*
Revenues	$8,100,000	$6,700,000
Costs and expenses	$8,500,000	$7,940,000
Net loss	$(230,000)	$(640,000)

Net assets of the diagnostic chemical kits operations, which are presented as a net amount in the Consolidated Balance Sheets at December 31, 2000, and December 31, 1999, were as follows:

	2000	*1999*
Current assets	$390,000	$475,000
Property and equipment, net	12,180,000	11,973,000
Other noncurrent assets	310,000	296,000
Liabilities	(400,000)	(611,000)
Net assets	$12,480,000	$12,133,000

Inventory

Example 29–10: Commitment to Sell Inventory at Fixed Price

On January 15, 2001, the Company entered into an agreement with a customer to sell a specified minimum number of units of its Eglaze adhesive products over the next thirty months at a fixed price of $10,200,000. The fixed price is equal to approximately 5% above the aggregate selling price at current market prices.

Leases

Example 29–11: New Operating Lease Agreement

In February 2001, the Company entered into an operating lease agreement for a manufacturing plant to be constructed in Carson, New Jersey. The total cost of assets to be covered by the lease is limited to $15,000,000. The manufacturing facility is scheduled for completion in June 2002. Payments under the lease will be determined and will commence upon completion of construction and will continue through the initial lease term of five years. The Company has options to renew the lease for two five-year periods and to purchase the facility at its estimated fair market value at any time during the lease term.

Example 29–12: Contingent Liability Relating to Lease Termination

In March 2001, the Company notified the developer and landlord of its planned future headquarters in Paramount, California, that the Company intends to terminate the project. The Company had previously entered into a 15-year lease agreement for the new site. Although groundbreaking for the new site has not occurred, the Company anticipates that it will incur lease termination costs. However, the Company is not able to make a meaningful estimate of the amount or range of loss that could result from an unfavorable resolution of this matter.

License Agreement

Example 29–13: License Fee Commitments under License Agreement

In February 2001, the Company entered into an agreement to license software to be incorporated into its data conferencing products. Under the agreement, the Company is obligated to pay annual minimum license fees, ranging from $150,000 to $350,000 through the year 2004 and the Company may cancel the agreement at any time, provided the Company has paid a minimum of $1,000,000 in connection with the agreement.

Litigation

Example 29–14: Patent Infringement Lawsuit

On February 13, 2001, the Company was named as a defendant in a patent infringement suit brought by Pasterine, Ltd., alleging that certain of the Company's products infringe seven patents that Pasterine Ltd. allegedly owns and is seeking a judgment of infringement for each of these asserted patents and other costs. The Company is reviewing the suit and, based on advice from legal counsel, believes that the complaints are without merit. However, no assurance can be given that this matter will be resolved in the Company's favor.

Example 29–15: Sexual Discrimination Lawsuit

In March 2001, the Company and two principal officers were named as defendants in a lawsuit brought by a former employee alleging sexual discrimination. Management believes that the lawsuit is without merit and the outcome will not have a material adverse effect on the financial position or results of operations of the Company.

Example 29–16: Settlement of Threatened Litigation in Connection with Event Occurring after Year End

In January 2001, the Company breached its contract with a supplier by failing to buy a minimum amount of certain specified products for the month of January, which the Company was committed to buy under terms of the agreement. The supplier threatened litigation to enforce the terms of the contract. As a result, on March 29, 2001, the Company agreed to pay $400,000 to the supplier in an out-of-court settlement. The amount will be charged to operations in 2001.

Property and Equipment

Example 29–17: Purchase of Assets

On March 4, 2001, the Company entered into an agreement to purchase a new warehouse and distribution center at a total cost of $4,700,000. The Company opened escrow and made a deposit of $500,000. The purchase price is expected to be financed by the Company's primary bank over five years at an interest rate of 1% above the bank's prime rate.

Example 29–18: Sale of Assets

On January 23, 2001, the Company sold one of its warehouse and distribution facility for $4,400,000, with an after tax gain of $890,000. The proceeds were used to repay long-term borrowings.

Example 29–19: Sale and Leaseback of Facility

Subsequent to December 31, 2000, the Company entered into a sale and leaseback agreement with regard to its manufacturing facility in Grand Rapids, Michigan. The transaction has been recorded as a sale with the cash proceeds of $11 million used to repay borrowings of $7.5 million and the remainder used for working capital purposes. The Company recorded a gain of $2.5 million on the sale.

Under the terms of the agreement, the Company has committed to lease a portion of the facility for 12 years. The present value of minimum lease payments at inception of the obligation approximates $4 million.

Related Parties

Example 29–20: Advances Made to Related Parties

In February and March 2001, the Company made advances totaling $1,200,000 to PRC Development, an entity owned by the president and certain officers of the Company, primarily to accommodate expansion and other financing needs of this related entity. Such advances are unsecured, bear interest at 10%, and are payable in semiannual installments starting April 1, 2002.

Stockholders' Equity

Example 29–21: Conversion of Debentures into Common Stock

On March 1, 2001, the holders of the Company's 10% convertible debentures have elected to convert an aggregate of $4,000,000 principal amount of the debentures into 696,520 shares of the Company's common stock on May 25, 2001.

Example 29–22: Sale of Common Stock

On February 11, 2001, the Company sold 300,000 shares of its common stock at $10 per share. The proceeds will be used for working capital purposes and to pay off long-term debt of approximately $1,300,000.

Example 29–23: Stock Option Plan

In February 2001, the Company adopted a Stock Option Plan (Plan) that provides for the granting of stock options to certain key employees. The Plan reserves 450,000 shares of common stock, including 200,000 shares granted to the president under his employment arrangement. Options under the Plan are to be granted at no less than fair market value of the shares at the date of grant.

Example 29–24: Stock Split

On March 1, 2001, the Company's board of directors declared a two-for-one stock split of the common stock effected in the form of a 25% stock dividend, to be distributed on or about April 10, 2001, to holders of record on March 23, 2001. Accordingly, all references to number of shares, except shares authorized, and to per share information in the consolidated financial statements have been adjusted to reflect the stock split on a retroactive basis.

Example 29–25: Amendment to Certificate of Incorporation to Decrease Number of Authorized Shares

Subsequent to December 31, 2000, the board of directors approved a proposal to amend the Certificate of Incorporation to decrease the number of authorized shares of common stock from 50,000,000 shares to 5,000,000 shares and to effect a one-for-ten reverse split of common stock whereby each ten shares of common stock will be exchanged for one share of common stock. The Amendment will have no effect on the par value of the common stock.

Example 29–26: Cash Dividend

On January 27, 2001, the Company declared a cash dividend of $0.07 per share payable on March 3, 2001, to shareholders of record on February 10, 2001.

Part II—
Balance Sheet

CHAPTER 30
ASSETS AND LIABILITIES: GENERAL

CONTENTS

EXECUTIVE SUMMARY

The distinction between current and noncurrent assets and liabilities in a classified balance sheet is an important feature of financial reporting because considerable interest in the liquidity of the reporting enterprise exists. One way to measure a company's liquidity is to have separate classification of current assets and liabilities. Therefore, classified balance sheets should present current assets and current liabilities separately from other assets and liabilities. Resources that are expected to be realized in cash, sold, or consumed during the next year (or operating cycle, if longer) are classified as *current assets.* Assets not expected to be realized within one year (or operating cycle, if longer) should be included as *noncurrent.* Asset valuation allowances (e.g., uncollectible accounts) should be deducted from the assets to which they relate. Also, a description of assets pledged, subject to liens, or otherwise encumbered should be disclosed.

The major assets are generally presented in the following order:

- Cash
- Short-term investments (including marketable securities)
- Trade accounts receivable
- Inventories
- Long-term investments (including marketable securities)
- Property, plant, and equipment
- Intangible assets
- Other noncurrent assets (e.g., deferred charges, deposits)

Current liabilities are obligations that are reasonably expected to be settled by either liquidating current assets or creating other current liabilities. Current liabilities include obligations that, by their terms, are due and payable on demand. This includes long-term obligations that are callable because a violation of an objective acceleration clause in a long-term debt agreement may exist at the date of the debtor's balance sheet. Such callable obligations must be classified as a current liability at the debtor's balance sheet date unless one of the following conditions is met:

1. The creditor has waived or subsequently lost the right to demand repayment for more than one year (or operating cycle, if longer) from the balance sheet date.
2. For long-term obligations containing a grace period within which the debtor may cure the violation, it is probable that the violation will be cured within that period, which would prevent the obligation from being callable.

A short-term obligation can be excluded from current liabilities only if the company intends to refinance it on a long-term basis and the intent is supported by the ability to refinance that is demonstrated in one of the following ways:

1. A long-term obligation or equity security whose proceeds are used to retire the short-term obligation is issued after the date of the balance sheet but before the issuance of the financial statements.
2. Before the issuance of the financial statements, the company has entered into an agreement that enables it to refinance a short-term obligation on a long-term basis.

The major liabilities are generally presented in the order of maturity as follows:

- Demand notes and other short-term debt
- Trade accounts payable
- Accrued expenses
- Long-term debt (including capital lease obligations)
- Other long-term liabilities

Offsetting assets and liabilities (i.e., the display of a recognized asset and a recognized liability as one net amount in a financial statement) is improper except where a right of setoff exists. The following four criteria must be met for the right to offset assets and liabilities to exist:

1. Each party owes the other party specific amounts.
2. The reporting party has the right to set off the amount payable, by contract or other agreement, with the amount receivable from the other party.

3. The reporting party intends to set off.
4. The right of setoff is enforceable by law.

Authoritative Literature

ARB-43	Chapter 3A, Current Assets and Current Liabilities
APB-10	Omnibus Opinion—1966
APB-12	Omnibus Opinion—1967
FAS-6	Classification of Short-Term Obligations Expected to Be Refinanced
FAS-78	Classification of Obligations That Are Callable by the Creditor
FIN-8	Classification of a Short-Term Obligation Repaid prior to Being Replaced by a Long-Term Security
FIN-39	Offsetting of Amounts Related to Certain Contracts
FTB 79-3	Subjective Acceleration Clauses in Long-Term Debt Agreements

DISCLOSURE REQUIREMENTS

Assets and liabilities must be identified clearly in the financial statements, and the basis for determining the stated amounts must be disclosed fully.

For specific disclosure requirements, see individual chapters relating to specific balance sheet accounts.

EXAMPLES OF FINANCIAL STATEMENT DISCLOSURES

See individual chapters relating to specific balance sheet accounts for examples of financial statement disclosures.

CHAPTER 31
CASH AND CASH EQUIVALENTS

CONTENTS

EXECUTIVE SUMMARY

Cash generally consists of cash on hand, available funds on deposit at a financial institution, and negotiable instruments (e.g., money orders, personal checks). Cash equivalents generally consist of highly liquid investments (e.g., certificates of deposit, money market accounts) with initial maturity of three months or less.

The following are common balance sheet captions used to describe cash and cash equivalents on the face of a balance sheet:

- Cash (this is used if there are no cash equivalents)
- Cash and cash equivalents
- Cash and equivalents
- Cash, including certificates of deposit
- Cash and short-term investments

Cash overdrafts not having free cash balances against which they may be offset should be classified as a current liability. The following are common balance sheet captions used to describe the overdraft as a current liability on the face of a balance sheet:

- Overdraft
- Cash overdraft
- Bank overdraft
- Checks drawn in excess of available bank balances

To be classified as a current asset, cash and cash equivalents must be readily available to pay current obligations and free from any contractual restrictions. Cash that is restricted or in escrow should be segregated from the general cash category; the restricted cash is either classified in the current asset or in the noncurrent asset section, depending on the date of availability or disbursement. If the cash is to be used for payment of existing or maturing obligations (within a year or within the operating cycle, whichever is longer), classification as a current asset is appropriate; otherwise, it should be shown as a noncurrent asset.

Authoritative Literature

ARB-43	Chapter 3A, Current Assets and Current Liabilities
FAS-5	Accounting for Contingencies
FAS-95	Statement of Cash Flows

FAS-105 Disclosure of Information About Financial Instruments with Off-Balance-Sheet Risk and Financial Instruments with Concentrations of Credit Risk

DISCLOSURE REQUIREMENTS

Restrictions on cash should be properly disclosed and the amount of restricted cash and cash equivalents should be segregated from cash available for current operations (ARB-43, Ch. 3A, par. 6).

Significant concentrations of credit risk arising from cash on deposit with banks in excess of federally insured limits should be appropriately disclosed (FAS-105, par. 20).

There is no generally accepted accounting principles (GAAP) requirement to disclose compensating balance agreements unless the agreement legally restricts the use of the funds. For legally restrictive compensating balance agreements, the following disclosures should be made:

- The terms of the compensating balance agreement
- The amount of the compensating balance requirement
- The amount required to be maintained to assure future credit availability and the terms of that agreement
- The maintenance of compensating balances for the benefit of a related party

EXAMPLES OF FINANCIAL STATEMENT DISCLOSURES

The following sample disclosures are available on the accompanying disc.

Example 31–1: Note Discloses the Components of Cash and Cash Equivalents

Cash and cash equivalents consist of the following:

	2000	*1999*
Cash	$102,000	$116,000
Certificates of deposit	200,000	250,000
Money market funds	300,000	125,000
Commercial paper	500,000	500,000
Total	$1,102,000	$991,000

Example 31–2: Restricted Cash from Industrial Revenue Bonds Is Shown as a Noncurrent Asset

	2000	*1999*
Noncurrent assets:		
Restricted cash from industrial revenue bonds	$1,200,000	$ -0-
Intangible assets	200,000	220,000
Deposits	125,000	100,000
Total noncurrent assets	$1,525,000	$320,000

At December 31, 2000, the Company had borrowings under Industrial Revenue and Job Development Authority Bonds available for and restricted for the construction of a new facility and the purchase of certain equipment. The unexpended portion of such funds totaling $1,200,000 have been classified as "Restricted cash from industrial revenue bonds" in the accompanying Balance Sheet.

Example 31–3: Cash Not Available for Use in Operations and Restricted for Capital Expenditures Is Shown as a Noncurrent Asset

	2000	*1999*
Noncurrent assets:		
Cash restricted for capital expenditures	$3,200,000	$ -0-
Intangible assets	200,000	220,000
Deposits	125,000	100,000
Total noncurrent assets	$3,525,000	$320,000

The Company has classified as restricted certain cash and cash equivalents that are not available for use in its operations. At December 31, 2000, the Company had commitments to construct additional warehouse 2000, the Company expended $5,400,000 on this capital program and had $3,200,000 in cash and cash equivalents on hand restricted for use in completing this project.

Example 31–4: Restricted Cash Has Both a Current and Noncurrent Portion

	2000	*1999*
Current assets:		
Cash	$723,000	$1,325,000
Restricted cash for litigation settlement	600,000	-0-
Accounts receivable	4,736,000	4,244,000
Inventory	4,317,000	3,978,000
Total current assets	$10,376,000	$9,547,000
Property and equipment, net	$6,759,000	$6,316,000

Noncurrent assets:		
Restricted cash for litigation settlement	900,000	-0-
Deposits	125,000	100,000
Total assets	$18,160,000	$15,963,000

At December 31, 2000, the Company has $1,500,000 of restricted cash of which $900,000 is classified as a noncurrent asset. The restricted cash serves as collateral for an irrevocable standby letter of credit that provides financial assurance that the Company will fulfill its obligations with respect to certain litigation settlement discussed in Note [X]. The cash is held in custody by the issuing bank, is restricted as to withdrawal or use, and is currently invested in money market funds. Income from these investments is paid to the Company. The current portion of restricted cash of $600,000 represents the amount of current liability for amounts billed to the Company for certain repairs agreed to be made under the settlement agreement.

Example 31–5: Note Discloses Cash Equivalents That Include Securities Purchased under Agreement to Resell

The Company considers all investments purchased with initial maturity of three months or less to be cash equivalents. On December 31, 2000, and December 31, 1999, the Company purchased $2,500,000 and $2,000,000, respectively, of U.S. government securities under agreements to resell on January 4, 2001, and January 4, 2000, respectively, which are included in cash and cash equivalents in the accompanying Balance Sheets. Due to the short-term nature of the agreements, the Company did not take possession of the securities, which were instead held in the Company's safekeeping account at the bank.

Example 31–6: General Accounting Policy Describes the Components of Cash Equivalents and Indicates There Is No Exposure to Credit Risk

Cash equivalents include money market accounts, certificates of deposit, and commercial paper, all of which have maturities of three months or less. Cash equivalents are stated at cost plus accrued interest, which approximates market value. The maximum amount placed in any one financial institution is limited in order to reduce risk. The Company does not believe it is exposed to any significant credit risk on cash and cash equivalents.

Example 31–7: General Accounting Policy Describes Cash Equivalents and Indicates at Times They May Exceed the FDIC Insurance Limit

Cash and cash equivalents include all cash balances and highly liquid investments with an initial maturity of three months or less. The

Company places its temporary cash investments with high credit quality financial institutions. At times such investments may be in excess of the Federal Deposit Insurance Corporation (FDIC) insurance limit.

Example 31–8: Concentration of Credit Risk for Cash Deposits at Banks

Financial instruments that potentially subject the Company to concentrations of credit risk consist principally of cash deposits. Accounts at each institution are insured by the Federal Deposit Insurance Corporation (FDIC) up to $100,000. At December 31, 2000, and December 31, 1999, the Company had approximately $2,317,000 and $1,945,000 in excess of FDIC insured limits, respectively.

Example 31–9: Concentration of Credit Risk for Cash Deposits at Brokerage Firms

Financial instruments that potentially subject the Company to concentrations of credit risk consist principally of cash deposits at a brokerage firm. The accounts at the brokerage firm contain cash and securities. Balances are insured up to $500,000, with a limit of $100,000 for cash, by the Securities Investor Protection Corporation (SIPC). At December 31, 2000, and December 31, 1999, the Company had approximately $434,000 and $369,000 in excess of SIPC insured limits, respectively.

Example 31–10: Compensating Balance Requirement Is Based on a Percentage of the Available Line of Credit

As part of its line of credit agreement with a bank, the Company is expected to maintain average compensating cash balances that are based on a percentage of the available credit line. The amount of compensating balances required at December 31, 2000, was $300,000. The compensating balances are held under agreements that do not legally restrict the use of such funds and, therefore, the funds are not segregated on the face of the balance sheet. The compensating cash balances are determined daily by the bank based on cash balances shown by the bank, adjusted for average uncollected funds and Federal Reserve requirements. During the year ended December 31, 2000, the Company was in substantial compliance with the compensating balance requirements. Funds on deposit with the bank and considered in the compensating balances are subject to withdrawal; however, the availability of the line of credit is dependent on the maintenance of sufficient average compensating balances.

> **Note:** Alternatively, the disclosure of compensating balances may be included in the note disclosure of the related debt agreement.

Example 31–11: Compensating Balance Requirement Is a Fixed Amount

As part of its line of credit agreement with a bank, the Company has agreed to maintain average compensating balances of $150,000. The balances are not legally restricted as to withdrawal and serve as part of the Company's normal operating cash.

> **Note:** Alternatively, the disclosure of compensating balances may be included in the note disclosure of the related debt agreement.

Example 31–12: Change in Method of Classifying Cash Equivalents and Restatement of Prior-Year Balances

During the year ended December 31, 2000, the Company changed the method of classifying cash equivalents and has restated prior-year balances to reflect the change. All highly liquid investments with original maturities of three months or less at date of purchase are carried at cost and considered to be cash equivalents. These investments were previously classified as marketable securities. All other investments not considered to be a cash equivalent now are categorized separately as investments.

CHAPTER 32
ACCOUNTS AND NOTES RECEIVABLE

CONTENTS

EXECUTIVE SUMMARY

For financial statement purposes, accounts and notes receivable are generally classified into two categories: (1) trade receivables and (2) nontrade receivables. *Trade receivables* are amounts owed by customers for goods and services sold as part of the normal operations of the business and include open accounts, notes, and installment contracts. *Nontrade receivables,* or other receivables, include items such as advances to officers and employees, interest and dividend receivables, tax refund claims, and receivables from sales of assets. Technically, a great distinction does not exist between accounts and notes receivable, except that typically a note receivable (1) involves a formal promissory note, (2) carries interest, and (3) is of a longer duration.

Valuation allowances for losses on trade receivables should be recorded if a loss is probable and the amount of the loss can be reasonably estimated, and should be deducted from the related receivables. Similarly, a note receivable generally is considered impaired, and a valuation allowance should be recorded, when it is probable that a creditor will be unable to collect all amounts due, including principal and interest, according to the contractual terms and schedules of the loan agreement. If a loan is considered to be impaired, its value generally should be measured based on the present value of expected future cash flows discounted at the note's effective interest rate.

When a note is exchanged for property, goods, or services in an arm's-length transaction, it is generally presumed that the interest stated on the note is fair and adequate. If no interest is stated or if the interest stated appears unreasonable, the transaction should be valued at the fair value of the note or property, goods, or services, whichever is more clearly determinable. If such fair value is not readily determinable, the transaction should be valued at the present value of the note, determined by discounting the future cash payments under the note by an appropriate interest rate.

Unearned finance charges, interest, or discount on installment receivables should be amortized using the interest method, or a method that approximates the interest method, and should be shown as a reduction of the applicable receivables. Installment receivables should be allocated between current and noncurrent assets in the balance sheet, where applicable.

When an entity transfers any of its receivables to another entity, the entity should determine whether the transferred receivables should be recorded as sales under Financial Accounting Standards Board Statement No. 140 (Accounting for Transfers and Servicing of Financial Assets and Extinguishments of Liabilities). According to FAS-140, transfers of receivables should be recorded as sales (to the extent that the consideration received for the transferred receivables does not include rights to receive all or portions of specified cash inflows of such receivables) if all of the following conditions are met:

1. The transferred receivables have been isolated from the transferor (i.e., they are beyond the reach of the transferor and its creditors).
2. The transferee obtains the unconditional right to pledge or exchange the transferred receivables.
3. The transferor does not maintain effective control over the transferred receivables either through (a) an agreement that entitles and obligates the transferor to repurchase or redeem the receivables before their maturity or (b) the ability to unilaterally cause the holder to return specific receivables, other than through a cleanup-call.

Upon completion of a transfer of receivables to be accounted for as a sale, an entity should remove all receivables sold from the balance sheet, recognize the consideration received at fair value, and recognize a gain or loss on the sale.

Transactions that do not meet the above criteria for a sale of receivables should be accounted for as a secured borrowing.

Authoritative Literature

ARB-43	Chapter 1A, Rules Adopted by Membership
APB-10	Omnibus Opinion—1966
APB-21	Interest on Receivables and Payables
FAS-114	Accounting by Creditors for Impairment of a Loan
FAS-118	Accounting by Creditors for Impairment of a Loan—Income Recognition and Disclosures
FAS-140	Accounting for Transfers and Servicing of Financial Assets and Extinguishments of Liabilities

DISCLOSURE REQUIREMENTS

1. For transfers of receivables, the disclosures should include the following (FAS-140, par. 17):
   a. If the entity has entered into repurchase agreements or securities lending transactions, its policy for requiring collateral or other security
   b. If the entity has pledged any of its assets as collateral that are not reclassified and separately reported in the balance sheet, the carrying amount and classification of those assets as of the date of the latest balance sheet presented

c. If the entity has accepted collateral that it is permitted by contract or custom to sell or repledge, the following disclosures should be made as of the date of each balance sheet presented:

   (1) The fair value of the collateral

   (2) The portion of that collateral that it has sold or repledged

   (3) Information about the sources and uses of that collateral

d. If it is not practicable to estimate the fair value of certain assets obtained or liabilities incurred in connection with the transfers of receivables during the period, a description of those items and the reasons why it is not practicable to estimate their fair value

e. If the entity has securitized receivables during any period presented and accounts for that transfer as a sale, the following disclosures should be made for each major asset type (e.g., credit card receivables, automobile loans, mortgage loans):

   (1) The accounting policies for initially measuring the retained interests, if any, including the methodology (whether quoted market price, prices based on sales of similar assets and liabilities, or prices based on valuation techniques) used in determining their fair value

   (2) The characteristics of securitizations (a description of the transferor's continuing involvement with the transferred receivables, including, but not limited to: servicing; recourse; and restrictions on retained interests) and the gain or loss from sale of receivables in securitizations

   (3) The key assumptions used in measuring the fair value of retained interests at the time of securitization, including at a minimum: quantitative information about discount rates; expected prepayments including the expected weighted-average life of prepayable receivables; and anticipated credit losses, if applicable

   (4) Cash flows between the securitization SPE (special purpose entity) and the transferor, unless reported separately elsewhere in the financial statements or notes, including: proceeds from new securitizations; proceeds from collections reinvested in revolving-period securitizations; purchases of delinquent or foreclosed loans; servicing fees; and cash flows received on interests retained

f. If the entity has retained interests in securitized receivables at the date of the latest balance sheet presented, the following disclosures should be made for each major asset type (e.g., credit card receivables, automobile loans, mortgage loans):

(1) The accounting policies for subsequently measuring those retained interests, including the methodology (whether quoted market price, prices based on sales of similar assets and liabilities, or prices based on valuation techniques) used in determining their fair value

(2) The key assumptions used in subsequently measuring the fair value of those interests, including at a minimum: quantitative information about discount rates; expected prepayments including the expected weighted-average life of prepayable financial assets; and anticipated credit losses, including expected static pool losses if applicable

(3) A sensitivity analysis or stress test showing the hypothetical effect on the fair value of those interests of two or more unfavorable variations from the expected levels for each key assumption that is reported under (2) above independently from any change in another key assumption, and a description of the objectives, methodology, and limitations of the sensitivity analysis or stress test

(4) For the securitized receivables and any other financial assets that it manages together with them:

   (i) The total principal amount outstanding, the portion that has been derecognized, and the portion that continues to be recognized in each category reported in the balance sheet, at the end of the period

   (ii) Delinquencies at the end of the period

   (iii) Credit losses, net of recoveries, during the period

   (iv) Average balances during the period (this disclosure item is encouraged but not required)

2. For impaired loans, the disclosures should include the following (FAS-118, pars. 6 and 24):

   a. As of the date of each statement of financial position presented, the total recorded investment in the impaired loans at the end of each period and (i) the amount of that recorded investment for which there is a related allowance for credit losses and the amount of that allowance and (ii) the amount of that recorded investment for which there is no related allowance for credit losses

   b. The creditor's policy for recognizing interest income on impaired loans, including how cash receipts are recorded

   c. For each period for which results of operations are presented:

- The average recorded investment in the impaired loans during each period
- The related amount of interest income recognized during the time within that period that the loans were impaired
- The amount of interest income recognized using a cash-basis method of accounting during the time within that period that the loans were impaired, unless not practicable

d. For each period for which results of operations are presented, disclosures should be made of the activity in the total allowance for credit losses related to loans, including the following:

- The balance in the allowance at the beginning and end of each period
- Additions charged to operations
- Direct write-downs charged against the allowance
- Recoveries of amounts previously charged off

3. For notes receivable that require the imputation of interest, or that bear interest at an inappropriate rate, the disclosures should include the following (APB-21, par. 16):

   a. A description of the note

   b. The effective interest rate

   c. The face amount of the note

   d. The amount of discount or premium resulting from present value determination

   e. The amortization of the discount or premium, as interest expense

4. For troubled debt restructurings, the creditor should include the disclosures in items 2a through 2d and the following (FAS-15, par. 40):

   a. The amount of commitments, if any, to lend additional funds to debtors who are party to the restructuring

For amounts due from related parties, see the disclosure requirements in Chapter 25, "Related Party Disclosures."

EXAMPLES OF FINANCIAL STATEMENT DISCLOSURES

The following sample disclosures are available on the accompanying disc. For additional information see:

- Chapter 2, "Accounting Policies," for examples of general accounting policy disclosures relating to accounts receivable
- Chapter 12, "Financial Instruments," for sample disclosures of fair value of financial instruments, including accounts and notes receivable
- Chapter 18, "Leases, " for sample disclosures of lease receivables
- Chapter 19, "Long-Term Contracts," for sample disclosures of contract receivables and related concentrations in connection with long-term contracts
- Chapter 25, "Related Party Disclosures," for sample disclosures of accounts receivable due from related parties

Example 32–1: Company Requires No Collateral and Concentrations of Credit Risk Virtually Limited

Concentrations of credit risk with respect to accounts receivable are limited because a large number of geographically diverse customers make up the Company's customer base, thus spreading the trade credit risk. At December 31, 2000, and December 31, 1999, no single group or customer represents greater than 10% of total accounts receivable. The Company controls credit risk through credit approvals, credit limits, and monitoring procedures. The Company performs ongoing credit evaluations of its customers but generally does not require collateral to support accounts receivable.

Example 32–2: Company Requires Collateral and Has Concentrations in Accounts Receivable

The Company sells its products to distributors and original equipment manufacturers throughout the United States. The Company performs ongoing credit evaluations of its customers' financial condition and, generally, requires collateral, such as letters of credit, whenever deemed necessary. At December 31, 2000, three customers, each of which accounted for more than 10% of the Company's accounts receivable, accounted for 58% of total accounts receivable in aggregate. At December 31, 1999, four customers, each of which accounted for more than 10% of the Company's accounts receivable, accounted for 52% of total accounts receivable in aggregate.

Example 32–3: Details of Current Accounts Receivable

Accounts receivable consist of the following at December 31, 2000, and December 31, 1999:

	2000	*1999*
Trade receivables	$8,659,000	$9,054,000
Income taxes receivable	216,000	192,000
Due from officers and employees	200,000	100,000
Interest and dividend receivable	81,000	73,000
Receivable from affiliate	354,000	297,000
Insurance claim receivable	162,000	175,000
Litigation settlement (received in January 2001)	314,000	-0-
	9,986,00	9,891,000
Allowance for doubtful accounts	(418,000)	(504,000)
Allowance for returns and discounts	(376,000)	(452,000)
	$9,192,000	$8,935,000

Example 32–4: Allowances for Commitments Regarding Price Concessions and Sales Returns Are Based on Historical Experience

The Company has agreements with distributor customers that, under certain conditions, allow for returns of overstocked inventory and provide protection against price reductions initiated by the Company. Allowances for these commitments are included in the Balance Sheets as reductions in trade accounts receivable. The Company adjusts sales to distributors through the use of allowance accounts based on historical experience. During 2000 and 1999, provisions for these commitments were recorded in the amounts of $2,679,000 and $3,182,000, respectively.

Example 32–5: Write-Off of a Significant Account Receivable Balance

The "Special charge" of $513,000 in the 2000 Statement of Operations relates to the write-off of receivables due from a customer who filed for protection under Chapter 11 of the U.S. Bankruptcy Code during the year. The write-off was necessary because the Company's receivable was unsecured and the amount that the Company may ultimately recover, if any, is not presently determinable.

Example 32–6: Receivable from Sale of Assets

In December 2000, the Company sold substantially all of the assets of its electrical tools division for a gain of $716,000. The sales price of $4,825,000 consisted of $1,500,000 in cash and a term note of $3,325,000. The term note bears interest at 2% above the prime rate

(11% at December 31, 2000). Interest and principal payments on the note are due monthly until maturity at December 31, 2004. Certain mandatory prepayments are required upon the occurrence of certain events. The note receivable is collateralized by the assets of the purchaser.

Principal contractual maturities on the note receivable are as follows:

Year	*Maturities*
2001	$ 1,200,000
2002	850,000
2003	800,000
2004	475,000
	$ 3,325,000

Example 32–7: Notes Receivable Requiring Imputation of Interest Are Received in Payment of Outstanding Trade Receivables from Major Customer Pursuant to a Bankruptcy Decree

In March 2000, the Company received $50,000 in cash and $2,200,000 in notes in full payment of outstanding trade receivables resulting from the reorganization by a major customer, pursuant to a bankruptcy decree. The notes vary in maturity from six months to five years. They include non-interest bearing notes and notes bearing interest at rates of 4% to 6%. The notes are recorded at the present value of the future cash flows, utilizing an imputed interest of 10%, which equals $2,017,000. During 2000, the Company received all scheduled payments on a timely basis. In management's opinion, the remaining balance is collectible. Notes receivable are due as follows: $418,000 in 2001, $536,000 in 2002, $374,000 in 2003, $318,000 in 2004, and $196,000 in 2005.

The trade receivables balance due from the customer of $3,136,000 exceeded the fair value of the settlement amounts received by $1,069,000 and, accordingly, a loss in that amount has been charged to operations in 2000.

Example 32–8: Installment Receivables

Installment receivables bear interest at rates ranging from 8% to 13% and have initial terms of three to seven years. Installment receivables were reduced for unearned finance charges of $1,284,000 and $918,000 at December 31, 2000, and December 31, 1999, respectively. Unearned finance charges are amortized to interest income using a method that approximates the interest method. The installment receivables are collateralized by security interests in the related machinery and equipment sold to customers.

Details of installment receivables at December 31, 2000, and December 31, 1999 are as follows:

	2000	*1999*
Due in:		
2000	$ -0-	$1,637,000
2001	1,961,000	1,176,000
2002	1,381,000	833,000
2003	1,006,000	522,000
2004	675,000	420,000
2005	385,000	382,000
Thereafter	719,000	200,000
Gross installment receivables	6,127,000	5,170,000
Less: unearned finance charges	(1,284,000)	(918,000)
Less: allowance for doubtful receivables	(566,000)	(419,000)
Installment receivables, net	$4,277,000	$3,833,000
Current balance	$1,711,000	$1,039,000
Long-term balance	2,566,000	2,794,000
	$4,277,000	$3,833,000

An analysis of the allowance for doubtful installment receivables for 2000 and 1999 follows:

	2000	*1999*
Balance, beginning of the year	$419,000	$390,000
Provision charged to operations	322,000	317,000
Amounts written off	(225,000)	(363,000)
Recoveries	50,000	75,000
Balance, end of the year	$566,000	$419,000

Example 32–9: Impaired Loans

The Company's impaired notes receivable, including current portion, are as follows at December 31, 2000, and December 31, 1999:

	2000	*1999*
Impaired notes with related allowances	$3,589,000	$1,743,000
Credit loss allowance on impaired notes	(1,176,000)	(718,000)
	2,413,000	1,025,000
Impaired notes with no related allowances	211,000	763,000
Net impaired notes receivable	$2,624,000	$1,788,000

Average investments in impaired notes were $3,140,000 in 2000 and $1,413,000 in 1999.

Activity in the allowance for credit losses is as follows:

	2000	*1999*
Balance, beginning of the year	$718,000	$597,000
Provision charged to operations	617,000	269,000
Amounts written off	(224,000)	(241,000)
Recoveries	65,000	93,000
Balance, end of the year	$1,176,000	$718,000

Interest income on impaired loans is recognized only when payments are received and totaled $289,000 in 2000 and $173,000 in 1999.

Example 32–10: Noncurrent Receivables from Related Parties

At December 31, 2000, and December 31, 1999, "Other noncurrent receivables" in the Balance Sheets consist of accounts and notes receivable from employees and officers that are due on demand and are uncollateralized. The notes receivable carry interest at rates ranging from 6% to 10% per annum. Accrued interest receivable included in these balances totaled $43,000 and $31,000 at December 31, 2000, and December 31, 1999, respectively. The aggregate receivable balances have been classified as noncurrent assets because they are not expected to be collected within one year from the Balance Sheet dates.

Example 32–11: Transfer of Accounts Receivable Qualifies as a Sale

The Company has agreements to sell interests in pools of the Company's trade receivables, in an amount not to exceed $6,000,000 at any one time. Participation interests in new receivables may be sold, as collections reduce previously sold accounts. The receivables are sold at a discount that is included in selling, administrative, and general expenses in the Statements of Operations, and amounted to $210,000 and $162,000 in 2000 and 1999, respectively. Sales of trade accounts receivable are reflected as a reduction of accounts receivable in the accompanying Balance Sheets and the proceeds received are included in cash flows from operating activities in the accompanying Statements of Cash Flows. Gross proceeds from the sales of receivables were $4,900,000 and $3,618,000 in 2000 and 1999, respectively.

Example 32–12: Transfer of Accounts Receivable Does Not Qualify as a Sale

The Company has an asset securitization program with a large financial institution to sell, with recourse, certain eligible trade receivables up to a maximum of $12 million. As receivables transferred to the financial institution are collected, the Company may transfer additional receivables up to the predetermined facility limit. Gross receivables transferred to the financial institution amounted to $9,760,000 and $10,397,000 in 2000 and 1999, respectively. The Company retains the right to repurchase transferred receivables under the program and, therefore, the transaction does not qualify as a sale under the terms of Financial Accounting Standards Board Statement No. 140 (Accounting for Transfers and Servicing of Financial Assets and Extinguishments of Liabilities). Included in the Balance Sheets as receivables at December 31, 2000, and December 31, 1999, are account balances totaling $2,412,000 and $2,867,000, respectively, of uncollected receivables transferred to the financial institution.

Example 32–13: Factored Accounts Receivable and Factoring Agreement

Accounts receivable comprise the following at December 31, 2000, and December 31, 1999:

	2000	*1999*
Receivables assigned to factor	$6,125,000	$3,655,000
Advances to (from) factor	(2,264,000)	616,000
Amounts due from factor	3,861,000	4,271,000
Unfactored accounts receivable	758,000	869,000
Allowances for returns and allowances	(415,000)	(463,000)
	$4,204,000	$4,677,000

Pursuant to a factoring agreement, the Company's principal bank acts as its factor for the majority of its receivables, which are assigned on a pre-approved basis. At December 31, 2000, and December 31, 1999, the factoring charge amounted to 0.25% of the receivables assigned. The Company's obligations to the bank are collateralized by all of the Company's accounts receivable, inventories, and equipment. The advances for factored receivables are made pursuant to a revolving credit and security agreement, which expires on March 31, 2002. Pursuant to the terms of the agreement, the Company is required to maintain specified levels of working capital and tangible net worth, among other covenants.

Example 32–14: Finance Receivables Income Recognition Policy

Interest income on finance receivables is recorded as earned and is based on the average outstanding daily balance for wholesale and retail receivables. Accrued interest is classified with finance receivables. Loan origination payments made to dealers for certain retail installment sales contracts are deferred and amortized over the estimated life of the contract. Fees earned on revolving charge transactions are recognized upon assessment.

Example 32–15: Finance Receivables Credit Losses Policy

The provision for credit losses on finance receivables is charged to income in amounts sufficient to maintain the allowance for uncollectible accounts at a level management believes is adequate to cover the losses of principal and accrued interest in the existing portfolio. The Company's wholesale and other large loan charge-off policy is based on a loan-by-loan review. Retail revolving charge receivables are charged off at the earlier of 180 days contractually past due or when otherwise deemed to be uncollectible. Retail installment receivables are generally charged off at 120 days contractually past due. Repossessed inventory is recorded at net realizable value at time of repossession and any deficiency is charged off at that time.

CHAPTER 33
INVENTORY

CONTENTS

EXECUTIVE SUMMARY

Inventory usually is classified as (1) finished goods, (2) work in process, or (3) raw materials. Inventories exclude long-term assets that are subject to depreciation. Inventories are classified as current assets, except when there are excessive quantities that may not reasonably be expected to be used or sold within the normal operating cycle of a business. In this event, the excess inventory is classified as noncurrent.

Generally, inventory should be stated at the *lower of cost or market. Cost* is the sum of the expenditures and charges, direct and indirect, incurred in bringing inventories to their existing condition or location. Cost may be determined by specific identification or by the association of the flow of cost factors, such as first-in, first-out (FIFO); last-in, first-out (LIFO); and average cost.

In the phrase *lower of cost or market,* the term *market* means current replacement cost, whether by purchase or by reproduction, and is limited to the following maximum and minimum amounts:

- *Maximum*—The estimated selling price less any costs of completion and disposal, referred to as net realizable value
- *Minimum*—The net realizable value, less an allowance for normal profit

The write-down of inventory to market usually is reflected in cost of goods sold, unless the amount is unusually material, in which case the loss should be identified separately in the income statement.

Losses on firm purchase commitments for inventory goods are measured in the same manner as inventory losses and, if material, recognized in the accounts and disclosed separately in the income statement.

Inventories used in discontinued segments of a business should be written down to their net realizable value and the amount of write-down included as part of the gain or loss recognized on the disposal of the discontinued segment.

Interim Financial Reporting

Generally, the same principles and methods are used to value inventories for interim financial statements as are used for annual reports. For practical purposes, however, the following exceptions apply:

1. An estimated gross profit frequently is used to determine the cost of goods sold during an interim period. This is acceptable for generally accepted accounting principles (GAAP), as long as periodic physical inventories are taken to adjust the gross profit percentage used.

2. When the LIFO method is used for interim financial statements and a LIFO layer is depleted, in part or in whole, that is expected to be replaced before the end of the fiscal period, the expected cost of replacement for the depleted LIFO inventory can be used in determining cost of goods sold for the interim period.
3. Inventory losses from market declines, other than those expected to be recovered before the end of the fiscal year, are included in the results of operations of the interim period in which the loss occurs. Subsequent gains from market price recovery in later interim periods are included in the results of operation in which the gain occurs, but only to the extent of the previously recognized losses.
4. Standard costs are acceptable in determining inventory valuations for interim financial reporting. Unplanned or unanticipated purchase price, volume, or capacity variances should be included in the results of operations of the interim period in which they occur. Anticipated and planned purchase price, volume, or capacity variances that are expected to be recovered by the end of the fiscal year are deferred at interim dates. In general, the same procedures for standard costs used at the end of the fiscal year should be used for interim financial reporting.

Business Combinations

Inventory acquired in a business combination accounted for by the purchase method is valued as follows:

- *Raw materials*—Current replacement cost
- *Work-in-process*—Net realizable value for finished goods, less costs to complete and dispose, and a reasonable profit for the completion and selling effort
- *Finished goods*—Net realizable value less costs of disposal and a reasonable profit for the selling effort

Inventories acquired in a business combination accounted for as a pooling of interests are valued at the same cost as that to the acquired entity.

Authoritative Literature

ARB-43	Chapter 4, Inventory Pricing
APB-16	Business Combinations
APB-28	Interim Financial Reporting
FAS-133	Accounting for Derivative Instruments and Hedging Activities

DISCLOSURE REQUIREMENTS

The following disclosures about inventories are required to be disclosed in a company's financial statements:

1. The basis for carrying inventories (e.g., cost) (ARB-43, Ch. 3A, par. 9; ARB-43, Ch. 4)
2. The method of determining cost (e.g., FIFO) (ARB-43, Ch. 3A, par. 9; ARB-43, Ch. 4)
3. Any inventories stated above cost (ARB-43, Ch. 4, par. 16)
4. Major categories of inventories (raw materials, work in process, finished goods, and supplies), if practicable (ARB-43, Ch. 3A, par. 4)
5. Material losses resulting from the write-down from cost to market (ARB-43, Ch. 4, par. 14)
6. Material net losses on inventory firm purchase commitments (ARB-43, Ch. 4, par. 17)

The following disclosures, although not required by GAAP, are commonly found in practice as they are considered informative:

1. If the LIFO inventory method is used, the difference between the LIFO amount and replacement cost (LIFO reserve)
2. The effect on income due to liquidation of a portion of LIFO inventory

EXAMPLES OF FINANCIAL STATEMENT DISCLOSURES

The following sample disclosures are available on the accompanying disc.

Example 33–1: Basis of Valuation and Method of Determining Cost Are Included in Summary of Accounting Policies Note

Inventories are stated at the lower of cost (first-in, first-out) or market (net realizable value).

> **Note:** See Chapter 2, "Accounting Policies," for additional examples of inventory disclosures that are typically included as part of the general note describing the company's accounting policies.

Example 33–2: Disclosure of Major Components of Inventory under FIFO

Inventories, consisting of material, material overhead, labor, and manufacturing overhead, are stated at the lower of cost (first-in, first-out) or market and consist of the following at December 31:

	2000	*1999*
Raw materials	$ 9,826,000	$ 6,286,000
Work-in-process	3,061,000	1,167,000
Finished goods	6,188,000	8,501,000
	$19,075,000	$15,954,000

Example 33–3: Disclosure of Major Components of Inventory under LIFO

Inventories consist of the following at December 31:

	2000	*1999*
Finished Goods	$ 9,803,000	$ 8,014,000
Work-in-progress	5,047,000	5,386,000
Raw materials	2,003,000	2,042,000
FIFO inventories	16,853,000	15,442,000
Less provision for LIFO method of valuation	(1,230,000)	(1,402,000)
LIFO inventories	$15,623,000	$14,040,000

Example 33–4: Inventories Valued on Both Average Cost and LIFO Methods

At December 31, 2000, and December 31, 1999, approximately 59% and 53% of total inventories, respectively, were valued on a LIFO basis; the cost of other inventories is principally determined under the average cost method. If all inventories were valued on an average cost basis, total inventories would have been $951,000 and $873,000 higher at December 31, 2000, and December 31, 1999, respectively.

Example 33–5: Reserves for Obsolete Inventories Disclosed

At December 31, 2000 and December 31, 1999, the reserve for obsolescence was $1,051,000 and $805,000, respectively. Reserves for obsolescence were increased by $1,782,000 and $1,209,000 for 2000 and 1999, respectively. Reserves for obsolescence were reduced, due to inventory written off, by $1,132,000 and $759,000 for 2000 and 1999, respectively.

Example 33–6: Material Losses Resulting from the Write-Down of Inventory to Its Net Realizable Value

Due to changing market conditions in the electronics industry, in 2000 management conducted a thorough review of the inventory in all of its product lines. As a result, a provision for inventory losses of $4,421,000 was charged against operations in 2000 to write down inventory to its net realizable value. This was based on the Company's best estimates of product sales prices and customer demand patterns, and its plans to transition its products. It is at least reasonably possible that the estimates used by the Company to determine its provision for inventory losses will be materially different from the actual amounts or results. These differences could result in materially higher than expected inventory provisions, which could have a materially adverse effect on the Company's results of operations and financial condition in the near term.

Example 33–7: Inventory Held as a Noncurrent Asset

In 2000, the Company purchased inventory quantities in excess of amounts expected to be utilized in the Company's operating cycle at very favorable terms. At December 31, 2000, inventory of $780,000 shown on the balance sheet as a noncurrent asset represents that portion of the inventory acquired in excess of amounts expected to be sold in the next twelve months.

Example 33–8: Inventories Produced in a "Maquiladora" Operation

The Company operates its Mexican manufacturing facilities under the "Maquiladora" program. Pursuant to this program, materials and components owned by the Company are transferred to the Mexican subsidiaries where they are used to produce finished goods. The finished goods are returned to the United States and the Company reimburses the Mexican subsidiaries for their manufacturing costs without any intended significant profit or loss of consequence.

Example 33–9: Liquidation of LIFO Inventory Quantities

In 2000 and 1999, certain inventory quantities were reduced, resulting in liquidations of LIFO inventory quantities carried at lower costs prevailing in prior years. The effect was to increase net income by $676,000 in 2000 and $493,000 in 1999.

Example 33–10: Purchase Contracts

In connection with the EFTX transaction in January 1999, EFTX and the Company entered into a manufacturing agreement whereby the Company committed to purchase minimum amounts of goods and services used in its normal operations during the first 48 months after the transaction. Future annual minimum purchases remaining under the agreement are $19 million and $22 million for 2001 and 2002, respectively. During 2000 and 1999, the Company's total purchases under the agreement were $17 million and $13 million, respectively.

Example 33–11: Firm Price Commitment Manufacturing and Supply Agreement

The Company entered into a firm price commitment manufacturing and supply agreement in connection with the acquisition of the F&D trademarks purchased in 2000. The agreement was entered into with the seller of the trademarks upon request by the Company to obtain from the seller tools and other manufacturing resources of the seller for the manufacture of products. The manufacturing and supply agreement has created a firm commitment by the Company for a minimum of $4,500,000. A minimum payment of $500,000 on the agreement was due on December 31, 2000, with three additional payments of $400,000 and five additional payments of $560,000 to follow thereafter, through December 31, 2004, which is also the date on which the agreement terminates.

Example 33–12: Commitment to Sell Inventory at a Fixed Price

At December 31, 2000, the Company has an agreement with a customer to sell a specified minimum number of units of its Eglaze adhesive products over the next thirty months at a fixed price of $10,200,000. The fixed price is equal to approximately 5% above the aggregate selling price at current market prices.

Example 33–13: Materials Prices Are Linked to the Commodity Markets and Are Subject to Change

The principal raw materials purchased by the Company (fabricated aluminum, plastics, metals, and copper) are subject to changes in market price as these materials are linked to the commodity markets. To the extent that the Company is unable to pass on cost increases to customers, the cost increases could have a significant impact on the results of operations of the Company.

CHAPTER 34
INVESTMENTS: DEBT AND EQUITY SECURITIES

CONTENTS

EXECUTIVE SUMMARY

The topic of this chapter applies to both current and noncurrent investments in debt and equity securities. The primary issue in accounting and reporting for debt and equity investments is the appropriate use of market value. Generally accepted accounting principles (GAAP) require that investments in equity securities that have readily determinable fair values and all investments in debt securities be classified in three categories (held-to-maturity, trading securities, and available-for-sale) and be given specific accounting treatments, as follows:

Classification	*Accounting Treatment*
1. *Held-to-maturity*—Debt securities that the entity has the positive intent and ability to hold to maturity.	Amortized cost, reduced for nontemporary losses that are charged to earnings. Other unrealized gains or losses should not be recognized.
2. *Trading securities*—Debt and equity securities bought and held primarily for sale in the near term (e.g., the entity's normal operating cycle).	Fair value, with unrealized holding gains and losses included in earnings.
3. *Available-for-sale*—Debt and equity securities that do not meet the criteria to be classified as held-to-maturity or trading.	Fair value, with unrealized holding gains and losses reported in other comprehensive income. Nontemporary losses should be charged to earnings.

The following are examples of debt and equity securities:

Debt Securities	*Equity Securities*
U.S. treasury securities	Common stock
U.S. government agency securities	Preferred stock
Municipal securities	Warrants
Corporate bonds	Rights
Convertible debt	Call options
Commercial paper	Put options
Collateralized mortgage obligations	
Preferred stock that must be redeemed	
Real estate mortgage investment conduits	
Interest-only and principal-only strips	

Held-to-maturity securities should be classified as noncurrent assets until they are within one year of maturity; at that time, they should be classified as current. Trading securities should always be classified as current assets. Available-for-sale securities are classified as current or noncurrent, as appropriate.

Financial Accounting Standards Board Statement No. 115 (Accounting for Certain Investments in Debt and Equity Securities) is the primary source of GAAP for investments in debt and equity securities. However, FAS-115 is amended by FAS-133 (Accounting for Derivative Instruments and Hedging Activities), which was initially effective for fiscal years beginning after June 15, 1999. FAS-137 (Accounting for Derivative Instruments and Hedging Activities—Deferral of the Effective Date of FASB Statement No. 133) amends FAS-133 by delaying its effective date by one year, making the provisions of FAS-133 effective for fiscal years beginning after June 15, 2000.

FAS-115 does not apply to investments in derivative instruments that are subject to the requirements of FAS-133. See Chapter 11, "Financial Instruments," for the accounting and disclosure requirements applicable to investments in derivative instruments. FAS-115 also does not apply to not-for-profit entities.

Authoritative Literature

FAS-115	Accounting for Certain Investments in Debt and Equity Securities
FAS-124	Accounting for Certain Investments Held by Not-for-Profit Organizations

FAS-130	Reporting Comprehensive Income
FAS-133	Accounting for Derivative Instruments and Hedging Activities
FAS-140	Accounting for Transfers and Servicing of Financial Assets and Extinguishments of Liabilities
FTB 79-19	Investor's Accounting for Unrealized Losses on Marketable Securities Owned by an Equity Method Investee
FTB 94-1	Application of Statement 115 to Debt Securities Restructured in a Troubled Debt Restructuring

DISCLOSURE REQUIREMENTS

In June 1998, the FASB issued FAS-133, which amends FAS-115. FAS-133 was originally effective for all fiscal quarters of fiscal years beginning after June 15, 1999. Due to the complexity of FAS-133, the FASB issued, in June 1999, FAS-137 (Accounting for Derivative Instruments and Hedging Activities—Deferral of the Effective Date of FASB Statement No.133), which delays the effective date of FAS-133 by one year. Therefore, FAS-133 is effective for all fiscal quarters of fiscal years beginning after June 15, 2000.

This section discusses the disclosure requirements in effect prior to and subsequent to the adoption of FAS-133.

Disclosure Requirements if FAS-133 Has *Not* Been Adopted

Note: FAS-133 is effective for all fiscal quarters of fiscal years beginning after June 15, 2000.

1. For securities classified as available-for-sale and separately for securities classified as held-to-maturity, the following disclosures should be made, by major security type, as of each date for which a balance sheet is presented (FAS-115, par. 19):
   a. The aggregate fair value
   b. Gross unrealized holding gains
   c. Gross unrealized holding losses
   d. Amortized cost basis

   Note: Financial institutions should disclose the above information for the following types of securities: (i) equity securities, (ii) debt securities issued by the U.S. Treasury and other U.S. government corporations and agencies, (iii) debt securities issued by states of the United States and political subdivisions of the states, (iv) debt securities issued by foreign governments, (v) corporate debt securities, (vi) mortgage-backed securities, and (vii) other debt securities.

2. For investments in debt securities classified as available-for-sale and separately for securities classified as held-to-maturity, the following disclosures should be made (FAS-115, par. 20):
   a. Information about the contractual maturities of the securities as of the date of the most recent balance sheet presented (Maturity information may be combined in appropriate groupings for companies other than financial institutions.)
   b. The basis for allocation of securities not due at a single maturity date, if such securities are allocated over several maturity groupings

   Note: Financial institutions should disclose the fair value and the amortized cost of debt securities based on at least the following four maturity groupings: (i) within one year, (ii) after one year and up to the fifth year, (iii) after five years and up to the tenth year, and (iv) after ten years.

3. The following disclosures should be made for each period for which an income statement is presented (FAS-115, par. 21):
   a. The proceeds from sales of available-for-sale securities and the gross realized gains and the gross realized losses on those sales
   b. The basis on which cost was determined in computing realized gain or loss (i.e., specific identification, average cost, or other method used)
   c. The gross gains and gross losses included in earnings from transfers of securities from the available-for-sale category into the trading category (Such transfers should be rare.)
   d. The change in net unrealized holding gain or loss on available-for-sale securities that has been included in other comprehensive income during the period
   e. The change in net unrealized holding gain or loss on trading securities that has been included in earnings during the period
4. For any sales of or transfers from securities classified as held-to-maturity, the following disclosures should be made for each period for which an income statement is presented (FAS-115, par. 22):
   a. The amortized cost amount of the sold or transferred security

b. The related realized or unrealized gain or loss at the date of sale or transfer

c. The circumstances leading to the decision to sell or transfer the security

Disclosure Requirements if FAS-133 Has Been Adopted

Note: FAS-133 is effective for all fiscal quarters of fiscal years beginning after June 15, 2000.

1. For securities classified as available-for-sale, the following disclosures should be made, by major security type, as of each date for which a balance sheet is presented (FAS-133, par. 534):

   a. The aggregate fair value

   b. Total gains for securities with net gains in accumulated other comprehensive income

   c. Total losses for securities with net losses in accumulated other comprehensive income

   Note: Financial institutions should disclose the above information for the following types of securities: (i) equity securities, (ii) debt securities issued by the U.S. Treasury and other U.S. government corporations and agencies, (iii) debt securities issued by states of the United States and political subdivisions of the states, (iv) debt securities issued by foreign governments, (v) corporate debt securities, (vi) mortgage-backed securities, and (vii) other debt securities.

2. For securities classified as held-to-maturity, the following disclosures should be made, by major security type, as of each date for which a balance sheet is presented (FAS-133, par. 534):

   a. The aggregate fair value

   b. Gross unrecognized holding gains

   c. Gross unrecognized holding losses

   d. Net carrying amount

   e. Gross gains and losses in accumulated other comprehensive income for any derivatives that hedged the forecasted acquisition of the held-to-maturity securities

3. For investments in debt securities classified as available-for-sale and separately for securities classified as held-to-maturity, the following disclosures should be made (FAS-115, par. 20):

a. Information about the contractual maturities of the securities as of the date of the most recent balance sheet presented (Maturity information may be combined in appropriate groupings for companies other than financial institutions.)

b. The basis for allocation of securities not due at a single maturity date, if such securities are allocated over several maturity groupings

Note: Financial institutions should disclose the fair value and the net carrying amount (if different from fair value) of debt securities based on at least the following four maturity groupings: (i) within one year, (i) after one year and up to the fifth year, (iii) after five years and up to the tenth year, and (iv) after ten years.

4. The following disclosures should be made for each period for which an income statement is presented (FAS-115, par. 21; FAS-133, par. 534):

   a. The proceeds from sales of available-for-sale securities and the gross realized gains and the gross realized losses on those sales

   b. The method used to determine the cost of a security sold or the amount reclassified out of accumulated other comprehensive income into earnings (i.e., specific identification, average cost, or other method used)

   c. The gross gains and gross losses included in earnings from transfers of securities from the available-for-sale category into the trading category (Such transfers should be rare.)

   d. The amount of the net unrealized holding gain or loss on available-for-sale securities that has been included in accumulated other comprehensive income for the period

   e. The amount of gains and losses reclassified out of accumulated other comprehensive income into earnings for the period

   f. The portion of trading gains and losses for the period that relates to trading securities still held at the balance sheet date

5. For any sales of or transfers from securities classified as held-to-maturity, the following disclosures should be made for each period for which an income statement is presented (FAS-115, par. 22; FAS-133, par. 534):

   a. The net carrying amount of the sold or transferred security

   b. The net gain or loss in accumulated other comprehensive income for any derivative that hedged the forecasted acquisition of the held-to-maturity security

c. The related realized or unrealized gain or loss at the date of sale or transfer

d. The circumstances leading to the decision to sell or transfer the security

EXAMPLES OF FINANCIAL STATEMENT DISCLOSURES

Except for debt and equity securities that are embedded in derivative instruments, the disclosure requirements for investments in debt and equity securities are similar regardless of whether the provisions of FAS-133 have been adopted. The following sample disclosures are available on the accompanying disc.

Illustrative Disclosures Prior to Adoption of FAS-133 (Examples 34–1 to 34–8)

Example 34–1: Accounting Policy Note Explains Classification of Marketable Securities as Held-to-Maturity, Trading, and Available-for-Sale

The Company determines the appropriate classification of its investments in debt and equity securities at the time of purchase and reevaluates such determinations at each balance sheet date. Debt securities are classified as held-to-maturity when the Company has the positive intent and ability to hold the securities to maturity. Debt securities for which the Company does not have the intent or ability to hold to maturity are classified as available-for-sale. Held-to-maturity securities are recorded as either short-term or long-term on the Balance Sheet based on contractual maturity date and are stated at amortized cost. Marketable securities that are bought and held principally for the purpose of selling them in the near term are classified as trading securities and are reported at fair value, with unrealized gains and losses recognized in earnings. Debt and marketable equity securities not classified as held-to-maturity or as trading, are classified as available-for-sale and are carried at fair market value, with the unrealized gains and losses, net of tax, included in the determination of comprehensive income and reported in shareholders' equity.

The fair value of substantially all securities is determined by quoted market prices. The estimated fair value of securities for which there are no quoted market prices is based on similar types of securities that are traded in the market.

Example 34–2: Available-for-Sale Securities Are Classified between Debt and Equity Securities

Available-for-sale securities consist of the following:

	December 31, 2000			
	Gross Amortized Cost	Gross Unrealized Gains	Estimated Unrealized Losses	Fair Value
U.S. government securities	$1,412,000	$-0-	$(6,000)	$1,406,000
Commercial paper	1,347,000	5,000	(2,000)	1,350,000
Corporate bonds	1,153,000	51,000	(17,000)	1,187,000
Fixed rate notes	100,000	-0-	-0-	100,000
Total debt securities	4,012,000	56,000	(25,000)	4,043,000
Common stock	822,000	100,000	(56,000)	866,000
Preferred stock	140,000	5,000	-0-	145,000
Total equity securities	962,000	105,000	(56,000)	1,011,000
Total available-for-sale securities	$4,974,000	$161,000	$(81,000)	$5,054,000

	December 31, 1999			
	Gross Amortized Cost	Gross Unrealized Gains	Estimated Unrealized Losses	Fair Value
U.S. government securities	$1,161,000	$-0-	$(4,000)	$1,157,000
Commercial paper	1,632,000	9,000	(6,000)	1,635,000
Corporate bonds	1,788,000	12,000	(73,000)	1,727,000
Fixed rate notes	150,000	-0-	-0-	150,000
Total debt securities	4,731,000	21,000	(83,000)	4,669,000
Common stock	615,000	37,000	(26,000)	626,000
Preferred stock	110,000	4,000	-0-	114,000
Total equity securities	725,000	41,000	(26,000)	740,000
Total available-for-sale securities	$5,456,000	$62,000	$(109,000)	$5,409,000

During the years ended December 31, 2000, and December 31, 1999, available-for-sale securities were sold for total proceeds of $823,000 and $617,000, respectively. The gross realized gains on these sales totaled $127,000 and $104,000 in 2000 and 1999, respectively. For purpose of determining gross realized gains, the cost of securities sold is based on specific identification. The change in net unrealized holding gains on available-for-sale securities in the amount of $127,000 and $53,000 has been charged to other comprehensive income for the years ended December 31, 2000, and December 31, 1999, respectively.

The amortized cost and estimated fair value of investments in debt securities at December 31, 2000, by contractual maturity, were as follows:

	Amortized Cost	*Estimated Fair Value*
Due in 1 year or less	$2,381,000	$2,388,000
Due in 1–2 years	1,137,000	1,161,000
Due in 2–5 years	273,000	273,000
Due after 5 years	221,000	221,000
Total investments in debt securities	$4,012,000	$4,043,000

Actual maturities may differ from contractual maturities because some borrowers have the right to call or prepay obligations with or without call or prepayment penalties.

Example 34–3: Available-for-Sale Securities Are Classified between Current and Noncurrent Assets

Available-for-sale securities consist of the following:

	December 31, 2000			
	Gross Amortized Cost	*Gross Unrealized Gains*	*Estimated Unrealized Losses*	*Fair Value*
Current:				
Municipal bonds and notes	$748,000	$-0-	$(4,000)	$744,000
Asset-backed securities	302,000	6,000	(2,000)	306,000
U.S. government obligations	675,000	12,000	(7,000)	680,000
Total current securities	1,725,000	18,000	(13,000)	1,730,000

	December 31, 2000			
	Gross Amortized Cost	*Gross Unrealized Gains*	*Estimated Unrealized Losses*	*Fair Value*
Noncurrent:				
Municipal bonds	679,000	8,000	(6,000)	681,000
Corporate bonds	274,000	-0-	(9,000)	265,000
Common stock	413,000	47,000	(26,000)	434,000
Preferred stock	279,000	24,000	(13,000)	290,000
Total noncurrent securities	1,645,000	79,000	(54,000)	1,670,000
Total available-for-sale securities	$3,370,000	$97,000	$(67,000)	$3,400,000

	December 31, 1999			
	Gross Amortized Cost	*Gross Unrealized Gains*	*Estimated Unrealized Losses*	*Fair Value*
Current:				
Municipal bonds and notes	$623,000	$-0-	$(3,000)	$620,000
Asset-backed securities	291,000	4,000	(1,000)	294,000
U.S. government obligations	600,000	10,000	(6,000)	604,000
Total current securities	1,514,000	14,000	(10,000)	1,518,000
Noncurrent:				
Municipal bonds	610,000	7,000	(5,000)	612,000
Corporate bonds	296,000	-0-	(11,000)	285,000
Common stock	471,000	43,000	(29,000)	485,000
Preferred stock	342,000	28,000	(17,000)	353,000
Total noncurrent securities	1,719,000	78,000	(62,000)	1,735,000
Total available-for-sale securities	$3,233,000	$92,000	$(72,000)	$3,253,000

Proceeds from the sales of available-for-sale securities were $511,000 and $307,000 during 2000 and 1999, respectively. Gross realized gains on those sales during 2000 and 1999 were $107,000 and

$95,000, respectively. Gross realized losses on those sales during 2000 and 1999 were $53,000 and $46,000, respectively. For purpose of determining gross realized gains and losses, the cost of securities sold is based on average cost. The change in net unrealized holding gains on available-for-sale securities in the amount of $10,000 and $36,000 has been charged to other comprehensive income for the years ended December 31, 2000, and December 31, 1999, respectively.

The amortized cost and estimated fair value of investments in debt securities at December 31, 2000, by contractual maturity, were as follows:

	Amortized Cost	*Estimated Fair Value*
Within one year	$1,514,000	$1,518,000
After 1–5 years	756,000	750,000
After 5–10 years	150,000	147,000
	$2,420,000	$2,415,000

Actual maturities may differ from contractual maturities because some borrowers have the right to call or prepay obligations with or without call or prepayment penalties.

Example 34–4: Trading Securities

The Company's short-term investments comprise equity and debt securities, all of which are classified as trading securities, and are carried at their fair value based on the quoted market prices of the securities at December 31, 2000, and December 31, 1999. Net realized and unrealized gains and losses on trading securities are included in net earnings. For purpose of determining realized gains and losses, the cost of securities sold is based on specific identification.

The composition of trading securities, classified as current assets, is as follows at December 31, 2000 and December 31, 1999:

	December 31, 2000		*December 31, 1999*	
	Cost	*Fair Value*	*Cost*	*Fair Value*
Treasury bills	$2,796,000	$2,796,000	$2,515,000	$2,515,000
Mutual funds	883,000	765,000	691,000	653,000
Common stock	617,000	501,000	574,000	452,000
Preferred stock	311,000	294,000	282,000	258,000
Total trading securities	$4,607,000	$4,356,000	$4,062,000	$3,878,000

Investment income for the years ended December 31, 2000, and December 31, 1999, consists of the following:

	2000	*1999*
Gross realized gains from sale of trading securities	$162,000	$129,000
Gross realized losses from sale of trading securities	(71,000)	(46,000)
Dividend and interest income	194,000	123,000
Net unrealized holding losses	(67,000)	(134,000)
Net investment income	$218,000	$ 72,000

Example 34–5: Held-to-Maturity Securities

At December 31, 2000, and December 31, 1999, the Company held investments in marketable securities that were classified as held-to-maturity and consisted of the following:

	December 31, 2000			
	Gross Amortized Cost	*Gross Unrealized Gains*	*Estimated Unrealized Losses*	*Fair Value*
U.S. government securities	$4,997,000	$8,000	$(3,000)	$5,002,000
States and municipalities	1,170,000	75,000	(10,000)	1,235,000
Corporate bonds	1,219,000	67,000	(11,000)	1,275,000
Total held-to-maturity securities	$7,386,000	$150,000	$(24,000)	$7,512,000

	December 31, 1999			
	Gross Amortized Cost	*Gross Unrealized Gains*	*Estimated Unrealized Losses*	*Fair Value*
U.S. government securities	$3,624,000	$9,000	$(2,000)	$3,631,000
States and municipalities	1,641,000	95,000	(16,000)	1,720,000
Corporate bonds	1,023,000	61,000	(13,000)	1,071,000
Total held-to-maturity securities	$6,288,000	$165,000	$(31,000)	$6,422,000

During the years ended December 31, 2000, and December 31, 1999, held-to-maturity securities were sold for total proceeds of $917,000 and $733,000, respectively. The gross realized gains on these sales totaled $58,000 and $64,000 in 2000 and 1999, respectively. For purpose of determining gross realized gains, the cost of securities sold is based on specific identification.

The amortized cost and estimated fair value of held-to-maturity securities at December 31, 2000, by contractual maturity, were as follows:

	Amortized Cost	*Estimated Fair Value*
Due in one year or less	$1,380,000	$1,380,000
Due in 2–5 years	5,481,000	5,592,000
Due in 6–10 years	525,000	540,000
Total investments in held-to-maturity securities	$7,386,000	$7,512,000

Actual maturities may differ from contractual maturities because some borrowers have the right to call or prepay obligations with or without call or prepayment penalties.

Example 34–6: Estimated Fair Value of Held-to-Maturity Securities Approximates Cost

At December 31, 2000, and December 31, 1999, the Company had marketable debt securities that were classified as held-to-maturity and carried at amortized cost. Held-to-maturity securities consisted of the following:

	2000	*1999*
Current:		
U.S. government securities	$ 1,714,000	$-0-
Commercial paper	1,975,000	1,810,000
Certificates of deposits	1,315,000	600,000
Corporate notes	2,417,000	1,976,000
Total current held-to-maturity securities	7,421,000	4,386,000
Noncurrent:		
U.S. government securities	3,411,000	3,100,000
Commercial paper	-0-	-0-
Certificates of deposits	-0-	-0-
Corporate notes	3,719,000	2,418,000
Total noncurrent held-to-maturity securities	7,130,000	5,518,000
Total held-to-maturity securities	$14,551,000	$9,904,000

At December 31, 2000, maturities for noncurrent held-to-maturity securities were between one and two years. At December 31, 2000, and December 31, 1999, the estimated fair value of each investment approximated its amortized cost and, therefore, there were no significant unrealized gains or losses.

Example 34–7: Decline in Market Value Is Considered Other Than Temporary

At December 31, 2000, the Company wrote down to fair market value certain equity security investments. The write-down amounted to $157,000 and was due to a decline in the fair value of the equity security which, in the opinion of management, was considered to be other than temporary. The write-down is included in general and administrative expenses in the accompanying statement of operations for 2000.

Example 34–8: Transfer of Held-to-Maturity Debt Securities to Available-for-Sale Category

During 2000, the Company transferred all its held-to-maturity debt securities to the available-for-sale category. The amortized cost of these securities at the time of transfer was $3,540,000 and the unrealized gain was $236,000 ($150,000 after income taxes). Although the Company's intention to hold a majority of its debt securities to maturity has not changed, the transfer was made to increase flexibility in responding to future changes.

Illustrative Disclosures Subsequent to Adoption of FAS-133 (Examples 34–9 to 34–16)

Example 34–9: Accounting Policy Note Explains Classification of Marketable Securities as Held-to-Maturity, Trading, and Available-for-Sale

The Company determines the appropriate classification of its investments in debt and equity securities at the time of purchase and reevaluates such determinations at each balance sheet date. Debt securities are classified as held-to-maturity when the Company has the positive intent and ability to hold the securities to maturity. Debt securities for which the Company does not have the intent or ability to hold to maturity are classified as available-for-sale. Held-to-maturity securities are recorded as either short-term or long-term on the Balance Sheet based on contractual maturity date and are stated at amortized cost. Marketable securities that are bought and held principally for the purpose of selling them in the near term are classified as trading securities and are reported at fair value, with unrealized gains and losses recognized in earnings. Debt and marketable equity securities not classified as held-to-maturity or as trading, are classified as available-for-sale, and are carried at fair market value, with the unrealized gains and losses, net of tax, included in the determination of comprehensive income and reported in shareholders' equity.

The fair value of substantially all securities is determined by quoted market prices. The estimated fair value of securities for which there are no quoted market prices is based on similar types of securities that are traded in the market.

Example 34–10: Available-for-Sale Securities Are Classified between Debt and Equity Securities

Available-for-sale securities consist of the following:

	December 31, 2000		
	Gains in Accumulated Other Comprehensive Income	*Losses in Accumulated Other Comprehensive Income*	*Estimated Fair Value*
U.S. government securities	$-0-	$(6,000)	$1,406,000
Commercial paper	5,000	(2,000)	1,350,000
Corporate bonds	51,000	(17,000)	1,187,000
Fixed rate notes	-0-	-0-	100,000
Total debt securities	56,000	(25,000)	4,043,000
Common stock	100,000	(56,000)	866,000
Preferred stock	5,000	-0-	145,000
Total equity securities	105,000	(56,000)	1,011,000
Total available-for-sale securities	$161,000	$(81,000)	$5,054,000

	December 31, 1999		
	Gains in Accumulated Other Comprehensive Income	*Losses in Accumulated Other Comprehensive Income*	*Estimated Fair Value*
U.S. government securities	$-0-	$(4,000)	$1,157,000
Commercial paper	9,000	(6,000)	1,635,000
Corporate bonds	12,000	(73,000)	1,727,000
Fixed rate notes	-0-	-0-	150,000
Total debt securities	21,000	(83,000)	4,669,000

Common stock	37,000	(26,000)	626,000
Preferred stock	4,000	-0-	114,000
Total equity securities	41,000	(26,000)	740,000
Total available-for-sale securities	$62,000	$(109,000)	$5,409,000

During the years ended December 31, 2000, and December 31, 1999, available-for-sale securities were sold for total proceeds of $823,000 and $617,000, respectively. The gross realized gains on these sales totaled $127,000 and $104,000 in 2000 and 1999, respectively. For purpose of determining gross realized gains, the cost of securities sold is based on specific identification. Net unrealized holding gains on available-for-sale securities in the amount of $127,000 and $53,000 for the years ended December 31, 2000, and December 31, 1999, respectively, have been included in accumulated other comprehensive income.

Contractual maturities of available-for-sale debt securities at December 31, 2000, are as follows:

	Estimated Fair Value
Due in one year or less	$2,388,000
Due in 1–2 years	1,161,000
Due in 2–5 years	273,000
Due after 5 years	221,000
Total investments in debt securities	$4,043,000

Actual maturities may differ from contractual maturities because some borrowers have the right to call or prepay obligations with or without call or prepayment penalties.

Example 34–11: Available-for-Sale Securities Are Classified between Current and Noncurrent Assets

Available-for-sale securities consist of the following:

	December 31, 2000		
	Gains in Accumulated Other Comprehensive Income	*Losses in Accumulated Other Comprehensive Income*	*Estimated Fair Value*
Current:			
Municipal bonds and notes	$-0-	$(4,000)	$744,000
Asset-backed securities	6,000	(2,000)	306,000
U.S. government obligations	12,000	(7,000)	680,000
Total current securities	18,000	(13,000)	1,730,000

	December 31, 2000		
	Gains in Accumulated Other Comprehensive Income	*Losses in Accumulated Other Comprehensive Income*	*Estimated Fair Value*
Noncurrent:			
Municipal bonds	8,000	(6,000)	681,000
Corporate bonds	-0-	(9,000)	265,000
Common stock	47,000	(26,000)	434,000
Preferred stock	24,000	(13,000)	290,000
Total noncurrent securities	79,000	(54,000)	1,670,000
Total available-for-sale securities	$97,000	$(67,000)	$3,400,000

	December 31, 1999		
	Gains in Accumulated Other Comprehensive Income	*Losses in Accumulated Other Comprehensive Income*	*Estimated Fair Value*
Current:			
Municipal bonds and notes	$-0-	$(3,000)	$620,000
Asset-backed securities	4,000	(1,000)	294,000
U.S. government obligations	10,000	(6,000)	604,000
Total current securities	14,000	(10,000)	1,518,000
Noncurrent:			
Municipal bonds	7,000	(5,000)	612,000
Corporate bonds	-0-	(11,000)	285,000
Common stock	43,000	(29,000)	485,000
Preferred stock	28,000	(17,000)	353,000
Total noncurrent securities	78,000	(62,000)	1,735,000
Total available-for-sale securities	$92,000	$(72,000)	$3,253,000

Proceeds from the sales of available-for-sale securities were $511,000 and $307,000 during 2000 and 1999, respectively. Gross realized gains on those sales during 2000 and 1999 were $107,000 and $95,000, respectively. Gross realized losses on those sales during 2000 and 1999 were $53,000 and $46,000, respectively. For purpose of determining gross realized gains and losses, the cost of securities sold is based on average cost. Net unrealized holding gains on available-for-sale securities in the amount of $10,000 and $36,000 for the years ended December 31, 2000, and December 31, 1999, respectively, have been included in accumulated other comprehensive income.

Contractual maturities of available-for-sale debt securities at December 31, 2000, are as follows:

	Estimated Fair Value
Within one year	$1,518,000
After 1–5 years	750,000
After 5–10 years	147,000
	$2,415,000

Actual maturities may differ from contractual maturities because some borrowers have the right to call or prepay obligations with or without call or prepayment penalties.

Example 34–12: Trading Securities

The Company's short-term investments comprise equity and debt securities, all of which are classified as trading securities and are carried at their fair value based on the quoted market prices of the securities at December 31, 2000, and December 31, 1999. Net realized and unrealized gains and losses on trading securities are included in net earnings. For purpose of determining realized gains and losses, the cost of securities sold is based on specific identification.

The composition of trading securities, classified as current assets, is as follows at December 31, 2000, and December 31, 1999:

	December 31, 2000		*December 31, 1999*	
	Cost	*Fair Value*	*Cost*	*Fair Value*
Treasury bills	$2,796,000	$2,796,000	$2,515,000	$2,515,000
Mutual funds	883,000	765,000	691,000	653,000
Common stock	617,000	501,000	574,000	452,000
Preferred stock	311,000	294,000	282,000	258,000
Total trading securities	$4,607,000	$4,356,000	$4,062,000	$3,878,000

Investment income for the years ended December 31, 2000, and December 31, 1999, consists of the following:

	2000	*1999*
Gross realized gains from sale of trading securities	$162,000	$129,000
Gross realized losses from sale of trading securities	(71,000)	(46,000)
Dividend and interest income	194,000	123,000
Net unrealized holding losses	(67,000)	(134,000)
Net investment income	$218,000	$72,000

Example 34–13: Held-to-Maturity Securities

At December 31, 2000, and December 31, 1999, the Company held investments in marketable securities that were classified as held-to-maturity and consisted of the following:

	December 31, 2000			
	Gross Net Carrying Amount	*Gross Unrecognized Holding Gains*	*Unrecognized Holding Losses*	*Estimated Fair Value*
U.S. government securities	$4,997,000	$8,000	$(3,000)	$5,002,000
States and municipalities	1,170,000	75,000	(10,000)	1,235,000
Corporate bonds	1,219,000	67,000	(11,000)	1,275,000
Total held-to-maturity securities	$7,386,000	$150,000	$(24,000)	$7,512,000

	December 31, 1999			
	Gross Net Carrying Amount	*Gross Unrecognized Holding Gains*	*Unrecognized Holding Losses*	*Estimated Fair Value*
U.S. government securities	$3,624,000	$9,000	$(2,000)	$3,631,000
States and municipalities	1,641,000	95,000	(16,000)	1,720,000
Corporate bonds	1,023,000	61,000	(13,000)	1,071,000
Total held-to-maturity securities	$6,288,000	$165,000	$(31,000)	$6,422,000

During the years ended December 31, 2000, and December 31, 1999, held-to-maturity securities were sold for total proceeds of $917,000 and $733,000, respectively. The gross realized gains on these sales totaled $58,000 and $64,000 in 2000 and 1999, respectively. For purpose of determining gross realized gains, the cost of securities sold is based on specific identification.

Contractual maturities of held-to-maturity securities at December 31, 2000, are as follows:

	Net Carrying Amount
Due in one year or less	$1,380,000
Due in 2–5 years	5,481,000
Due in 6–10 years	525,000
Total investments in held-to-maturity securities	$7,386,000

Actual maturities may differ from contractual maturities because some borrowers have the right to call or prepay obligations with or without call or prepayment penalties.

Example 34–14: Estimated Fair Value of Held-to-Maturity Securities Approximates Cost

At December 31, 2000, and December 31, 1999, the Company had marketable debt securities that were classified as held-to-maturity and carried at amortized cost. Held-to-maturity securities consisted of the following:

	2000	*1999*
Current:		
U.S. government securities	$ 1,714,000	$-0-
Commercial paper	1,975,000	1,810,000
Certificates of deposits	1,315,000	600,000
Corporate notes	2,417,000	1,976,000
Total current held-to-maturity securities	7,421,000	4,386,000
Noncurrent:		
U.S. government securities	3,411,000	3,100,000
Commercial paper	-0-	-0-
Certificates of deposits	-0-	-0-
Corporate notes	3,719,000	2,418,000
Total noncurrent held-to-maturity securities	7,130,000	5,518,000
Total held-to-maturity securities	$14,551,000	$9,904,000

At December 31, 2000, maturities for noncurrent held-to-maturity securities were between one and two years. At December 31, 2000, and December 31, 1999, the estimated fair value of each investment approximated its amortized cost and, therefore, there were no significant unrecognized holding gains or losses.

Example 34–15: Decline in Market Value Is Considered Other Than Temporary

At December 31, 2000, the Company wrote down to fair market value certain equity security investments. The write-down amounted to $157,000 and was due to a decline in the fair value of the equity security which, in the opinion of management, was considered to be other than temporary. The write-down is included in general and administrative expenses in the accompanying statement of operations for 2000.

Exhibit 34–16: Transfer of Held-to-Maturity Debt Securities to Available-for-Sale Category

During 2000, the Company transferred all its held-to-maturity debt securities to the available-for-sale category. The net carrying amount of these securities at the time of transfer was $3,540,000 and the unrealized gain was $236,000 ($150,000 after income taxes). Although the Company's intention to hold a majority of its debt securities to maturity has not changed, the transfer was made to increase flexibility in responding to future changes.

CHAPTER 35
INVESTMENTS: EQUITY AND COST METHODS

CONTENTS

EXECUTIVE SUMMARY

The equity method of accounting for investments in common stock is appropriate if an investment enables the investor to significantly influence the operating or financial decisions of the investee. Absent evidence to the contrary, an investor is presumed to have the ability to significantly influence an investee if it owns (directly or indirectly) 20% or more of the investee's voting stock. The authoritative literature presumes that significant influence does not exist in an investment of less than 20%. However, this presumption may be overcome by evidence to the contrary. Therefore, significant influence over the operating and financial policies of an investment of less than 20% can occur. The 20% cutoff is intended to be a guideline, subject to individual judgment rather than a rigid rule.

The equity method is not intended as a substitute for consolidated financial statements when the conditions for consolidation are present. Under the equity method, an investment is initially recorded at cost. Thereafter, the carrying amount of the investment is (1) increased for the investor's proportionate share of the investee's earnings or (2) decreased for the investor's proportionate share of the investee's losses or for dividends received from the investee. The effect of this treatment is that net income for the period and stockholders' equity at the end of the period are the same as if the companies had been consolidated.

An investor's share of earnings or losses from its investment usually is shown as a single amount (called a *one-line consolidation*) in the income statement. The following procedures are appropriate in applying the equity method:

1. Intercompany profits and losses are eliminated by reducing the investment balance and the income from investee for the investor's share of the unrealized intercompany profits and losses.
2. Any difference between the underlying equity in net assets of the investee and the cost of the investment is amortized over the period of the remaining lives of the investee assets that give rise to the difference.
3. The investment is shown in the investor's balance sheet as a single amount and earnings or losses are shown as a single amount (one-line consolidation) in the income statement, except for the investor's share of (a) extraordinary items and (b) prior-period adjustments, which are shown separately.
4. Capital transactions of the investee that affect the investor's share of stockholders' equity are accounted for as if the investee were consolidated.
5. Gain or loss is recognized when an investor sells the common stock investment, equal to the difference between the selling price and the carrying amount of the investment at the time of sale.
6. If the investee's financial reports are not timely enough for an investor to apply the equity method currently, the investor may use the most recent available financial statements, and the lag in time created should be consistent from period to period.
7. Other than temporary declines, a loss in value of an investment should be recognized in the books of the investor.
8. When the investee has losses, applying the equity method decreases the basis of the investment. The investment account generally is not reduced below zero, at which point the use of the equity method is discontinued, unless the investor has guaranteed obligations of the investee or is committed to provide financial support. The investor resumes the equity method when the investee subsequently reports net income and the net income exceeds the investor's share of any net losses not recognized during the period of discontinuance.

9. Dividends for cumulative preferred stock of the investee are deducted before the investor's share of earnings or losses is computed, whether the dividend was declared or not.

10. The investor's shares of earnings or losses from an investment accounted for by the equity method are based on the outstanding shares of the investee without regard to common stock equivalents.

Authoritative Literature

APB-18	The Equity Method of Accounting for Investments in Common Stock
FAS-94	Consolidation of All Majority-Owned Subsidiaries
FIN-35	Criteria for Applying the Equity Method of Accounting for Investments in Common Stock
FTB 79-19	Investor's Accounting for Unrealized Losses on Marketable Securities Owned by an Equity Method Investee

DISCLOSURE REQUIREMENTS

1. An entity's financial statements should include the following disclosures about an investment accounted for under the equity method (when determining the extent of the disclosures, the investment's significance to the investor's financial position and results of operations should be considered) (APB-18, par. 20):

   a. The name of the investee

   b. The percentage ownership of the investee's common stock

   c. The accounting policies of the investor with respect to the investment in common stock

   d. The difference, if any, between the amount of the carrying value of the investment and the amount of underlying equity in net assets and the accounting treatment of the difference

   e. The aggregate market value of investments for which quoted market prices are available (not required for investments in common stock of subsidiaries)

   f. When investments in common stock of corporate joint ventures or other investments accounted for under the equity method are, in the aggregate, material, summarized information of assets, liabilities, and results of operations of the investees should be presented in notes or separate statements, either individually or in groups

g. Material effects of possible conversions of outstanding convertible securities, exercise of outstanding options and warrants, and other contingent issuances that could have a significant effect on the investor's share of reported earnings or losses

2. If the equity method is not used for an investment of 20% or more of the voting stock of the investee company, disclosure of the reason is required. Conversely, if the equity method is used for an investment of less than 20%, disclosure of the reason is required (APB-18, par. 20, footnote 13).
3. Investments accounted for on the equity method should be shown in the balance sheet of the investor as a single amount, and the investor's share of earnings or losses of investees should be shown in the income statement as a single amount, with separate identification of the investor's share of the investee's extraordinary items, the cumulative effect of changes in accounting principles, and gains or losses from the disposition of a business segment (APB-18, par. 19).
4. The investor's proportional share of prior-period adjustments made by the investee company should be presented as part of the retained earnings of the investor company (APB-18, par. 19).

EXAMPLES OF FINANCIAL STATEMENT DISCLOSURES

The following sample disclosures are available on the accompanying disc.

Example 35–1: General Accounting Policy Describes the Equity Method of Accounting

The equity method of accounting is used when the Company has a 20% to 50% interest in other entities. Under the equity method, original investments are recorded at cost and adjusted by the Company's share of undistributed earnings or losses of these entities. Nonmarketable investments in which the Company has less than 20 % interest and in which it does not have the ability to exercise significant influence over the investee are initially recorded at cost and periodically reviewed for impairment.

Example 35–2: Disclosure of Summarized Information of Assets, Liabilities, and Results of Operations of Investees Accounted for on the Equity Method

The Company's investments in companies that are accounted for on the equity method of accounting consist of the following: (1) 25% interest in Kalass, Inc., which is engaged in the manufacture and sale of automotive replacement radiators; (2) 30% interest in Safir Industries, a manufacturer of water pumps; and (3) 50% interest in Tetera Co., a manufacturer of rubber bearings. The investments in these companies amounted to $5,542,000 and $4,668,000 at December 31, 2000, and December 31, 1999, respectively.

The combined results of operations and financial position of the Company's equity basis investments are summarized below:

	2000	*1999*
Condensed income statement information:		
Net sales	$51,173,000	$49,742,000
Gross margin	$17,321,000	$16,235,000
Net income	$2,174,000	$1,839,000
Company's equity in net income of affiliates	$874,000	$716,000
Condensed balance sheet information:		
Current assets	$29,316,000	$31,067,000
Noncurrent assets	20,011,000	17,374,000
Total assets	$49,327,000	$48,441,000
Current liabilities	$26,851,000	$28,992,000
Noncurrent liabilities	12,787,000	11,603,000
Equity	9,689,000	7,846,000
Total liabilities and equity	$49,327,000	$48,441,000

Note: The following tables illustrate the captions used in the Company's Balance Sheets and Income Statements for its equity basis investments described above.

Balance Sheet Presentation

	2000	*1999*
Total current assets	$36,823,000	$37,015,000
Equity in net assets of and advances to affiliates	5,542,000	4,668,000
Property and equipment	11,610,000	10,539,000
Other assets	411,000	402,000
	$54,386,000	$52,624,000

Income Statement Presentation

	2000	*1999*
Income before income taxes	$8,941,000	$7,916,000
Provision for income taxes	(3,576,000)	(3,287,000)
Income before equity in net income of affiliates	5,365,000	4,629,000
Equity in net income of affiliates	874,000	716,000
Net income	$6,239,000	$5,345,000

Example 35–3: Investment Accounted for on the Equity Method Is Reduced to Zero—Investor Is Not Obligated to Provide Additional Financial Support to Investee

The Company has a 40% interest in Shana, Ltd., a manufacturer of medical diagnostic products, which has been accounted for on the equity method since 1995. The Company's 2000 operations include a loss of $1,975,000, which represents the Company's share of loss on its investment in Shana, Ltd. The loss resulted largely from Shana, Ltd.'s decision to write-down certain assets, predominantly property and intangibles, in light of current market conditions affecting the medical supplies industry. The loss reduced the Company's investment in Shana, Ltd. to zero and, as a consequence, the Company's future financial results will not be negatively affected by Shana, Ltd.'s ongoing operations. The Company has no obligation to fund future operating losses of Shana, Ltd.

Example 35–4: Investment Accounted for on the Equity Method Is Reduced to Zero—Investor Is Obligated to Provide Additional Financial Support to Investee

The Company has a 40% interest in Shana, Ltd., a manufacturer of medical diagnostic products, which has been accounted for on the equity method since 1995. The Company's 2000 operations include a loss of $1,975,000, which represents the Company's share of loss on its investment in Shana, Ltd. The loss resulted largely from Shana, Ltd.'s decision to write-down certain assets, predominantly property and intangibles, in light of current market conditions affecting the medical supplies industry. The loss reduced the Company's investment in Shana, Ltd. to zero.

Under the terms of an agreement with Shana, Ltd., the Company is obligated to advance additional funds to Shana, Ltd. through July 2003. As a result, the Company recorded an additional loss of $2,360,000 in 2000, which represents the estimated amount of such required future advances under the terms of the agreement.

Example 35–5: Equity Method Used for Less Than 20% Owned Investee because Investor Exercises Significant Influence Over Investee's Operating and Financial Activities

The Company has a 15% interest in Fadar, a producer of chemical-based materials, which is accounted for on the equity method because the Company exercises significant influence over Fadar's operating and financial activities. Therefore, the Company's investment in Fadar, which was initially carried at cost, is adjusted annually for the Company's proportionate share of Fadar's earnings or losses.

Example 35–6: Cost Method Applied to 20% or More Owned Subsidiary Due to Lack of Significant Influence Over Investee's Operating and Financial Activities

At December 31, 2000, and December 31, 1999, "Investment in associated company" as shown on the Company's Balance Sheet consists of the cost of an investment in Acker, Inc., in which the Company has a 45% interest. Prior to 1999, the Company's 45% ownership in this Canadian affiliate was recorded on the equity basis. In 1999, the Company concluded that it could no longer exert a significant influence over Acker, Inc.'s operating and financial activities; therefore, the Company began accounting for this investment using the cost method effective January 1, 1999. The carrying value of this investment at December 31, 2000, and December 31, 1999, was $725,000, which approximates the Company's pro rata share of Acker, Inc.'s underlying value.

Example 35–7: Company Resumes Applying the Equity Method, Which Was Previously Suspended in Prior Years Due to Losses by Investee

The Company has a 30% interest in Fadar, a producer of chemical-based materials. In 1998, when the Company's share of losses equaled the carrying value of its investment, the Company suspended the use of the equity method, and no additional losses were recognized since the Company was not obligated to provide further financial support for Fadar. The Company's unrecorded share of Fadar's losses for 1998 and 1999 totaled $210,000. In 2000, Fadar reported earnings of $1,200,000, of which the Company's share was $360,000. Accordingly, the Company has included $150,000 in income in 2000, which represents the excess of the Company's share of Fadar's earnings for 2000 over the Company's share of prior unrecorded losses.

Example 35–8: Financial Statements Currently Include on the Equity Basis of Accounting the Accounts of a Previously Consolidated Business

On January 1, 2000, the Company transferred its medical equipment business segment and contributed certain assets and liabilities, totalling $15 million and $4 million, respectively, to a joint venture named Hope Enterprises (a partnership). The Company's equity interest in the joint venture is 35%. As a result, the 1999 income statement, which included the accounts of the medical equipment business segment on a consolidated basis, has been restated to reflect adjustments of line items for revenue and costs applicable to the medical equipment business segment transferred to the joint venture and to reflect the losses of this business on the equity basis of accounting.

Example 35–9: Change to Equity Method From Cost Method Due to Increasing Stake in Investee

During 2000, the Company bought an additional 25% interest in Bodair Co., thereby increasing its holdings to 40%. As a result, the Company changed its method of accounting for this investment from the cost method to the equity method. Under the cost method, the investment is recorded at cost and dividends are treated as income when received. Under the equity method, the Company records its proportionate share of the earnings or losses of Bodair Co. The effect of the change was to increase 2000 net income by $437,000 ($.23 per share). The financial statements for 1999 have been restated for the change, which resulted in an increase of net income for 1999 of $211,000 ($.12 per share). Retained earnings as of the beginning of 1999 has been increased by $589,000 for the effect of retroactive application of the new method.

Example 35–10: Nonmarketable Investments Are Impaired and Written Down to Net Realizable Value

At December 31, 2000, and December 31, 1999, "Other long term investments" of $2,057,000 and $2,819,000, respectively, consist of nonmarketable investments in private companies and venture capital partnerships, which are carried at the lower of cost or net realizable value. The estimated aggregate fair value of these investments approximated their carrying amount. The fair values of these investments were estimated based on the most recent rounds of financing and securities transactions and on other pertinent information, including financial condition and operating results of the investees. The Company wrote-down certain investments by $762,000 in 2000 and $604,000 in 1999 to their estimated net realizable value due to deterioration in the investees' financial condition and the decision by the Company to liquidate its position in investments no longer meeting its overall strategic objectives.

Example 35–11: Company Discloses That It Is Not Practicable to Estimate the Fair Value of Its Nonmarketable Investment

It is not practicable to estimate the fair value of the Company's 11% investment in the common stock of Linkets, Inc., a producer of precision fasteners, because of the lack of quoted market prices and the inability to estimate fair value without incurring excessive costs. However, management believes that the carrying amount (on the cost method) of $1,571,000 at December 31, 2000, and December 31, 1999, was not impaired.

Example 35–12: Disclosure of Nature of Transactions between Company and Investee

The Company uses the equity method to account for its 39% investment in Coreson, Inc., a manufacturer of electrical and electronic products and systems. Included in accounts receivable of the Company at December 31, 2000, and December 31, 1999, are amounts due from Coreson, Inc. of $298,000 and $357,000, respectively. Included in accounts payable of the Company at December 31, 2000, and December 31, 1999, are amounts due to Coreson, Inc. of $481,000 and $517,000, respectively. Transactions with Coreson, Inc. consist of the following:

	2000	*1999*
Sales to Coreson, Inc.	$2,415,000	$2,074,000
Purchases from Coreson, Inc.	$6,712,000	$5,649,000

Example 35–13: Disclosure of Cumulative Unremitted Earnings and Dividends Received

The Company's investment in and advances to joint venture at December 31, 2000, and December 31, 1999, consists of its 25% investment in Keset, Inc., a manufacturer of electronic components. The amount of cumulative unremitted earnings of this joint venture included in the Company's consolidated retained earnings at December 31, 2000, was $3,892,000. During the years ended December 31, 2000, and December 31, 1999, distributions in the amounts of $600,000 and $550,000, respectively, were received from Keset, Inc.

Example 35–14: Company Has an Obligation to Guarantee Debt of Investee

The Company has an obligation to guarantee a pro rata share of debt incurred by Keeler, a joint venture in which the Company has a 45% interest, up to a maximum of $5,000,000. At December 31, 2000, the Company has guaranteed the payment of $1,710,000 of the affiliate's indebtedness.

Example 35–15: Underlying Net Assets Exceed Investment Accounted for on the Equity Method—Excess Relates to Depreciable Assets

The Company's investment in and advances to joint venture at December 31, 2000, and December 31, 1999, consists of its 32% investment in Bisara, Co. a manufacturer of medical instruments, which is accounted for on the equity method. At December 31, 2000, and December 31, 1999, the Company's share of the underlying net assets of Bisara, Co. exceeded its investment by $1,543,000 and $1,807,000, respectively. The excess, which relates to certain property, plant, and equipment, is being amortized into income over the estimated remaining lives of the assets.

Example 35–16: Carrying Value of Investment Accounted for on the Equity Method Exceeds Underlying Net Assets—Excess Relates to Depreciable Assets

The Company accounts for its 29% investment in Kamas, Inc., an engineering and construction enterprise, under the equity method. At December 31, 2000, and December 31, 1999, the carrying value of the investment in Kamas, Inc. exceeded the Company's share of the underlying net assets of Kamas, Inc. by $1,123,000 and $1,207,000, respectively. The excess, which relates to certain property, plant, and equipment, is being amortized against the Company's share of Kamas, Inc.'s net income over the useful lives of the assets that gave rise to the difference.

Example 35–17: Carrying Value of Investment Accounted for on the Equity Method Exceeds Underlying Net Assets—Excess Does Not Relate to Any Specific Accounts and Is Considered to Be Goodwill

The Company accounts for its 43.5% investment in Madaris, Inc., a manufacturer of electronic components, under the equity method. At December 31, 2000, and December 31, 1999, the carrying value of the investment in Madaris, Inc. exceeded the Company's share of the underlying net assets of Madaris, Inc. by $716,000 and $814,000, respectively. The excess, which the Company is unable to relate to any specific accounts of Madaris, Inc., is considered to be goodwill and is being amortized on the straight line method over ten years.

Example 35–18: Excess of the Fair Value of the Assets Sold or Transferred to Investee over the Investor's Book Value Is Deferred and Amortized

The Company conducts some of its operations through various joint venture and other partnership forms that are accounted for using the equity method. When the Company sells or transfers assets to an affiliated company that is accounted for using the equity method and the affiliated company records the assets at fair value, the excess of the fair value of the assets over the Company's net book value is deferred and amortized over the expected lives of the assets. Deferred gains included in the Company's other liabilities were $135,000 and $102,000 at December 31, 2000, and December 31, 1999, respectively.

Example 35–19: Potential Conversion of Outstanding Convertible Securities and Exercise of Options and Warrants of Investee May Have a Significant Effect on Investor's Share of Reported Earnings

The Company has a 35% interest in Fadar, Inc. a producer of chemical-based materials, which is accounted for on the equity method. At December 31, 2000, and December 31, 1999, Fadar, Inc. had outstanding convertible securities, options, and warrants that, if in the aggregate were converted and exercised, would have reduced the Company's interest to 26% and, accordingly, would have reduced the Company's share of earnings in Fadar, Inc. for 2000 and 1999 by $195,000 and $167,000, respectively.

Example 35–20: Investor's Proportionate Share of Extraordinary Item Reported by Investee

The extraordinary item of $320,000 represents the Company's proportionate share of a gain realized on the extinguishment of debt by Kametz, Ltd., a manufacturer of electronic parts in which the Company has a 40% interest that is accounted for on the equity method. The Company has not provided any income tax related to its share of the extraordinary gain because it is the Company's intention to reinvest all undistributed earnings of Kametz, Ltd. indefinitely.

Note: The following table illustrates the portion of the Income Statement reflecting the Company's proportionate share of extraordinary item reported by Kametz, Ltd.

Income Statement Presentation

	2000	1999
Income before income taxes	$8,941,000	$7,916,000
Provision for income taxes	(3,576,000)	(3,287,000)
Income before equity in net income of affiliate and extraordinary item	5,365,000	4,629,000
Equity in net income of affiliate, excluding extraordinary gain of $320,000 in 2000	554,000	716,000
Income before extraordinary item	5,919,000	5,345,000
Extraordinary item—equity in undistributed extraordinary gain of affiliate	320,000	-0-
Net income	$6,239,000	$5,345,000

CHAPTER 36
PROPERTY, PLANT, AND EQUIPMENT

CONTENTS

EXECUTIVE SUMMARY

Fixed assets (also referred to as *property, plant, and equipment; plant assets; capital assets;* or *tangible long-lived assets*) are used in production, distribution, and services by all enterprises. Examples include land, buildings, furniture, fixtures, machinery, equipment, and vehicles. The nature of the assets employed by a particular enterprise is determined by the nature of its activities.

Fixed assets have two primary characteristics:

1. They are acquired for use in operations and enter into the revenue-generating stream indirectly. They are held primarily for use, not for sale.
2. They have relatively long lives.

Generally accepted accounting principles (GAAP) generally require a fixed asset to be recorded at its cost, which includes all normal expenditures of readying an asset for its intended use. However, unnecessary expenditures that do not add to the utility of the asset are charged to expense.

The asset's cost, less any salvage value, is charged to expense (i.e., depreciated) over the asset's estimated useful life in a systematic and rational manner. Commonly used depreciation methods include straight-line, units of production, sum-of-the-years'-digits, and declining balance, although other methods may meet the criteria of *systematic* and *rational.*

If an entity constructs an asset for the entity's own use, the entity should capitalize the related interest cost incurred as part of the cost of the asset until the asset is substantially complete and ready for its intended use. Once the interest cost is capitalized, it should be depreciated in the same manner as other costs of the underlying asset.

Long-lived assets to be held and used by an entity should be reviewed for impairment whenever events or changes in circumstances indicate that the carrying amount of an asset may not be recoverable. In performing the review for recoverability, the entity should estimate the future cash flows expected to result from the use of the asset and its eventual disposition. If the sum of the expected future cash flows (undiscounted and without interest charges) is less than the carrying amount of the asset, an impairment loss should be recognized. Measurement of an impairment loss for long-lived assets that an entity expects to hold and use should be based on the fair value of the asset.

Long-lived assets to de disposed of (other than as part of a disposal of a business segment) should be reported at the lower of carrying amount or fair value less costs to sell.

For capitalized leased assets, see Chapter 18 "Leases."

Authoritative Literature

ARB-43	Chapter 9A, Depreciation and High Costs
	Chapter 9C, Emergency Facilities—Depreciation, Amortization, and Income Taxes
APB-6	Status of Accounting Research Bulletins
APB-12	Omnibus Opinion—1967
FAS-34	Capitalization of Interest Cost
FAS-92	Regulated Enterprises—Accounting for Phase-in Plans
FAS-93	Recognition of Depreciation by Not-for-Profit Organizations
FAS-109	Accounting for Income Taxes
FAS-121	Accounting for the Impairment of Long-Lived Assets and for Long-Lived Assets to Be Disposed Of

DISCLOSURE REQUIREMENTS

Depreciable Assets

1. The following disclosures of depreciable assets and depreciation are required in the financial statements or notes thereto (APB-12, par. 5):
   a. The basis of determining the amounts shown in the balance sheet, such as cost
   b. Balances of major classes of depreciable property presented by nature or function at the balance sheet date
   c. Accumulated depreciation presented by major classes of assets or in total at the balance sheet date
   d. A description of the method(s) used to compute depreciation for major classes of depreciable assets
   e. The amount of depreciation expense for each year for which an income statement is presented
2. Property, plant, and equipment that is idle or held for sale should be identified and presented separately from property,

plant, and equipment currently used in the business (generally accepted disclosure)

3. The amount of interest capitalized as part of the cost of property, plant, and equipment should be disclosed (FAS-34, par. 21)
4. Assets pledged as security for loans should be disclosed (FAS-5, par. 18)
5. The following disclosures, although not required by GAAP, are in some cases made by companies when they are considered useful:
   a. The accounting treatment for maintenance and repairs, betterments, and renewals
   b. The policy for adjusting accumulated depreciation when property and equipment is disposed of, and the treatment of any gain or loss on disposition
   c. The rates or lives used in computing depreciation

Impairment of Long-Lived Assets and Long-Lived Assets to Be Disposed Of

1. The following disclosures should be made for impaired assets to be held and used (FAS-121, par. 14):
   a. A description of the impaired assets and the facts and circumstances leading to the impairment
   b. The amount of the impairment loss and how the fair value of the impaired assets was determined
   c. The caption in the income statement in which the impairment loss is aggregated if that loss has not been presented as a separate caption or reported parenthetically on the face of the statement
   d. If applicable, the business segment(s) affected
2. The following disclosures should be made for all assets to be disposed of for each period presented during which those assets are held (FAS-121, par. 19):
   a. A description of the assets to be disposed of, the facts and circumstances leading to the expected disposal, the expected disposal date, and the carrying amount of those assets
   b. If applicable, the business segment(s) in which assets to be disposed of are held
   c. The loss, if any, resulting from writing down the assets to fair value less cost to sell
   d. The caption in the income statement in which the impairment gains or losses are aggregated if those gains or losses

have not been presented as a separate caption or reported parenthetically on the face of the statement

e. The gain or loss, if any, resulting from changes in the carrying amounts of assets to be disposed of that arise from subsequent revisions in estimates of fair value less cost to sell

f. The results of operations for assets to be disposed of to the extent that those results are included in the entity's results of operations for the period and can be identified

EXAMPLES OF FINANCIAL STATEMENT DISCLOSURES

All of the following sample disclosures are available on the accompanying disc. For additional information, see:

- Chapter 1, "Accounting Changes," for disclosures required in connection with a change in depreciation methods or useful lives
- Chapter 2, "Accounting Policies," for additional examples of disclosures of property, plant, and equipment that are typically included as part of the company's general note on significant accounting policies
- Chapter 18, "Leases," for disclosures required by lessees and lessors of assets held under capitalized leases

Example 36-1: Basis for Recording Assets and Depreciation Methods

Property and equipment are recorded at cost. Depreciation is provided over the estimated useful lives of the related assets using the straight-line method for financial statement purposes. The Company uses other depreciation methods (generally accelerated) for tax purposes where appropriate. Amortization of leasehold improvements is computed using the straight-line method over the shorter of the remaining lease term or the estimated useful lives of the improvements.

Example 36-2: Different Methods of Depreciation Used for Depreciable Assets

Property, equipment, and special tools are stated at cost, less accumulated depreciation and amortization. Property and equipment placed in service before January 1, 1993, are depreciated using an accelerated method that results in accumulated depreciation of approximately two-thirds of the asset cost during the first half of the estimated useful life of the asset. Property and equipment placed in service after December 31, 1992, are depreciated using the straight-line method of depreciation over the estimated useful life of the asset. Special tools are amortized using an accelerated method over periods of time representing the estimated productive life of those tools.

Example 36–3: Estimated Service Lives of Property and Equipment Disclosed

The estimated service lives of property and equipment are principally as follows:

Buildings and improvements	3–40 years
Machinery and equipment	2–15 years
Computer software	2–7 years
Transportation vehicles	2–6 years

> **Note:** Disclosure of estimated service lives of property and equipment is not required by GAAP. However, in some cases companies disclose the information because it is considered useful.

Example 36–4: Policy for Repairs and Maintenance, Capitalization, and Disposal of Assets Disclosed

Repairs and maintenance are expensed as incurred. Expenditures that increase the value or productive capacity of assets are capitalized. When property and equipment are retired, sold, or otherwise disposed of, the asset's carrying amount and related accumulated depreciation are removed from the accounts and any gain or loss is included in operations.

> **Note:** Disclosure of policy for repairs and maintenance, capitalization, and disposal of assets is not required by GAAP. However, in some cases companies disclose the information because it is considered useful.

Example 36–5: Review of Carrying Value of Property and Equipment for Impairment

The Company reviews the carrying value of property, plant, and equipment for impairment whenever events and circumstances indicate that the carrying value of an asset may not be recoverable from the estimated future cash flows expected to result from its use and eventual disposition. In cases where undiscounted expected future cash flows are less than the carrying value, an impairment loss is recognized equal to an amount by which the carrying value exceeds the fair value of assets. The factors considered by management in performing this assessment include current operating results, trends, and prospects, as well as the effects of obsolescence, demand, competition, and other economic factors.

Example 36–6: Components of Property and Equipment Disclosed in a Note

The following is a summary of property and equipment, at cost less accumulated depreciation, at December 31:

	2000	*1999*
Land	$1,500,000	$1,500,000
Buildings and improvements	6,250,000	6,250,000
Data processing equipment	1,975,000	1,050,000
Furniture and fixtures	725,000	536,000
Transportation equipment	347,000	213,000
Leasehold improvements	290,000	230,000
Construction in progress	200,000	100,000
	11,287,000	9,879,000
Less: accumulated depreciation	(2,804,000)	(2,091,000)
	$8,483,000	$7,788,000

Depreciation of property, plant, and equipment amounted to $713,000 for 2000 and $671,000 for 1999.

Note: Alternatively, the components of property and equipment may be disclosed on the face of the balance sheet.

Example 36–7: Property and Equipment Include Assets Acquired under Capital Leases

Property, plant, and equipment include gross assets acquired under capital leases of $493,000 and $414,0000 at December 31, 2000, and December 31, 1999, respectively. Related amortization included in accumulated depreciation was $251,000 and $176,000 at December 31, 2000, and December 31, 1999, respectively. Capital leases are included as a component of vehicles and equipment and machinery. Amortization of assets under capital leases is included in depreciation expense.

Example 36–8: Interest Cost Capitalized

The Company capitalizes interest cost incurred on funds used to construct property, plant, and equipment. The capitalized interest is recorded as part of the asset to which it relates and is amortized over the asset's estimated useful life. Interest cost capitalized was $315,000 and $268,000 in 2000 and 1999, respectively.

Example 36–9: Property Held for Sale

In July 2000, the Company signed a letter of intent to sell substantially all its plant assets at its manufacturing facility in Cleveland, Ohio. These assets have been classified as "Property held for sale" in the Company's Balance Sheet.

Example 36–10: Commitment Required under Construction in Progress

The Company is constructing a new facility, which is scheduled to be completed in 2002. As of December 31, 2000, the Company incurred and capitalized in "Construction in progress" $1,600,000. The estimated cost to be incurred in 2001 and 2002 to complete construction of the facility is approximately $12 million.

Example 36–11: Impairment Write-Down Recognized as a Result of Change in Policy for Replacing Property and Equipment

Effective October 1, 2000, management approved a revision to the Company's policy of replacing certain transportation equipment and heavy duty machinery and equipment. Under the revised policy, the Company replaces transportation equipment after eight years, and heavy duty machinery and equipment after ten years. The previous policy was to not replace transportation equipment before it was a minimum of ten years old, and heavy duty machinery and equipment before they were a minimum of 12 years old. As a result of this decision, the Company recognized an impairment write-down of $4,736,000 in 2000 for those transportation equipment and heavy duty machinery and equipment scheduled for replacement in the next two years under the new policy. Depreciable lives were also adjusted effective October 1, 2000, to reflect the new policy.

Example 36–12: Impairment of Assets Held and Used Recognized as a Result of Strategic Review of Certain Operations

In 2000, during the course of the Company's strategic review of its diagnostic chemicals kits operations, the Company assessed the recoverability of the carrying value of certain fixed assets, which resulted in impairment losses of $1,400,000. These losses reflect the amounts by which the carrying values of these assets exceed their estimated fair values determined by their estimated future discounted cash flows. The impairment loss is recorded as a component of operating expenses in the income statement for 2000.

Example 36–13: Impairment of Assets to Be Disposed Of

In 2000, the Company adopted a plan to dispose of most of its plant assets, machinery and equipment, and furniture and fixtures relating to its manufacturing facility in Boise, Idaho. The Company expects that the final sale and disposal of the assets will be completed in the year 2001. In connection with the plan of disposal, the Company determined that the carrying values of some of the underlying assets exceeded their fair values. Consequently, the Company recorded an impairment loss of $1,715,000, which represents the excess of the carrying values of the assets over their fair values. The impairment loss is recorded as a component of "Other expenses" in the Income Statement for 2000.

Example 36–14: Gain from Sale of Assets

In October 2000, the Company sold its manufacturing plant building in Boise, Idaho, for $2,374,000. The net pretax gain from the sale was $1,693,000 and is included in "Gain from sale of assets" in the 2000 Statement of Operations.

Example 36–15: Deferred Revenue on Sale of Plant and Equipment

In March 2000, the Company sold its Toledo, Ohio, facility for approximately $16 million. The provisions of the contract state that the Company will continue to own and occupy the warehouse portion of the facility for a period of up to ten years (the "Reservation Period"). The contract also contains a buyout clause, at the buyer's option and under certain circumstances, of the remaining Reservation Period. Under the provisions of Statement of Financial Accounting Standards (FAS) No. 66, *Accounting for Sales of Real Estate,* the Company is required to account for this as a financing transaction as the Company continues to have substantial involvement with the facility during the Reservation Period or until the buyout option is exercised. Under this method, the cash received is reflected as non-current deferred revenue, and the assets and the accumulated depreciation remain on the Company's books. Depreciation expense continues to be recorded each period, and imputed interest expense is also recorded and added to deferred revenue. Offsetting this is the imputed fair value lease income on the non-Company occupied portion of the building. A pretax gain, which will be recognized at the earlier of the exercise of the buyout option or the expiration of the Reservation Period, is estimated to be $10 million to $12 million. The annual cost of operating the warehouse portion of the facility is not material.

CHAPTER 37
INTANGIBLE ASSETS

CONTENTS

EXECUTIVE SUMMARY

Intangible assets are long-lived assets used in the production of goods and services. They are similar to property, plant, and equipment except that they lack physical properties. Examples of intangible assets include copyrights, patents, trademarks, and goodwill. They generally are subject to amortization over their estimated useful lives, subject to certain limitations for intangibles acquired on or before October 31, 1970.

The cost of intangible assets acquired from other enterprises or individuals should be recorded as an asset and should be amortized over the period of its estimated useful life, not exceeding 40 years. Costs of developing, maintaining, or restoring intangible assets that are not specifically identifiable should be recorded as expenses when incurred. The excess of the cost of an acquired enterprise over the sum of identifiable net assets (usually called *goodwill*) is the most common unidentifiable intangible asset.

Ordinarily, goodwill and similar intangible assets cannot be disposed of apart from the enterprise as a whole. However, if a large segment or separable group of assets of an acquired company or the entire acquired company is sold or otherwise liquidated, all or part of the unamortized goodwill recognized in the acquisition should be included in the cost of the assets sold.

In certain situations, the sum of the market or appraised values of identifiable assets less liabilities assumed may exceed the cost of the assets or business enterprise being acquired. Under these circumstances, the values assigned to the noncurrent assets being acquired are reduced proportionately (except long-term investments in marketable securities) to absorb the excess value. A deferred credit for an excess of assigned values of identifiable assets over cost (*negative goodwill*) is not recorded unless the noncurrent assets have been reduced to zero. If, after reducing the noncurrent assets (except long-term investments in marketable securities) to zero, a deferred credit still remains, it is recorded as an excess of acquired net assets over cost (negative goodwill) and amortized systematically to income over the period expected to benefit but not in excess of 40 years. The method and period of amortization should be disclosed adequately in the financial statements. No part of the negative goodwill should be credited directly to stockholders' equity at the date of acquisition.

In some cases, the carrying amount of long-lived assets may exceed what a company will eventually recover from continuing to use the assets. Therefore, a company should regularly assess whether an intangible asset, or a group of intangible assets, is impaired and should be written off or adjusted. In assessing whether the carrying amount of an intangible asset is recoverable, the entity should estimate the future cash flows expected to result from the use of the asset and its eventual disposition. If the sum of the expected future cash flows (undiscounted and without interest charges) is less than the carrying amount of the asset, an impairment loss should be recognized to adjust the asset to its fair value.

Once the carrying amount of an impaired intangible asset has been written down to fair value, that value becomes the asset's new cost. Consequently, subsequent increases in fair value should not be recorded.

FASB Outstanding Exposure Draft

As this book goes to press, FASB has an outstanding exposure draft of a Statement of Financial Accounting Standards (Business Combinations and Intangible Assets) that may have an important effect on accounting for intangible assets. The primary effects of the exposure draft would be that the pooling-of-interests method of accounting for business combinations would no longer be allowed and intangible assets (including goodwill) would be subject to a maximum life of 20 years rather than 40 years, as is current practice. The requirement that intangible assets older than the 20-year maximum be amortized could be overcome if the asset clearly is expected to generate identifiable cash flows beyond that time, and either the asset is exchangeable or control over the future economic benefits is obtained through contractual or other legal rights. In these circumstances, the intangible asset would not be amortized until its life is determined to be finite.

Following are some of the more important conclusions that have been reached or confirmed in recent FASB deliberations:

- Goodwill should be recognized initially as an asset because it meets the definition of an asset in CON-6 (Recognition and Measurement in Financial Statements of Business Enterprises).
- Goodwill should be measured initially as the excess of the cost of the acquired enterprise over the sum of the amounts assigned to identifiable assets acquired less liabilities assumed.
- An identifiable intangible asset should be recognized separately if it is separable or if control over the future economic benefits of the asset is obtained through contractual or other legal rights.
- The scope of the project will include purchased intangibles but not internally developed intangibles.

The practitioner should be alert to the issuance of a final pronouncement that would affect the guidance provided in this chapter.

Authoritative Literature

ARB-43	Chapter 5, Intangible Assets
APB-16	Business Combinations
APB-17	Intangible Assets
FAS-44	Accounting for Intangible Assets of Motor Carriers
FAS-72	Accounting for Certain Acquisitions of Banking or Thrift Institutions
FAS-109	Accounting for Income Taxes
FAS-121	Accounting for the Impairment of Long-Lived Assets and for Long-Lived Assets to Be Disposed Of
FAS-135	Rescission of FASB Statement No. 75 and Technical Corrections
FIN-9	Applying APB Opinions No. 16 and 17 When a Savings and Loan Association or a Similar Institution Is Acquired in a Business Combination Accounted for by the Purchase Method

DISCLOSURE REQUIREMENTS

Intangible Assets

1. The following disclosures of intangible assets are required in the financial statements or notes thereto (APB-17, pars. 30–31):
   a. The amortization method and amortization period for specific intangible assets
   b. If an intangible asset is *not* amortized, the reason for the lack of amortization
   c. If the period over which an intangible asset is amortized has been significantly reduced, the reason for the reduction

Impairment of Long-Lived Assets and Long-Lived Assets to Be Disposed Of

1. The following disclosures should be made for impaired assets to be held and used (FAS-121, par. 14):
   a. A description of the impaired assets and the facts and circumstances leading to the impairment
   b. The amount of the impairment loss and how the fair value of the impaired assets was determined
   c. The caption in the income statement in which the impairment loss is aggregated if that loss has not been presented as

a separate caption or reported parenthetically on the face of the statement

d. If applicable, the business segment(s) affected

2. The following disclosures should be made for all assets to be disposed of for each period presented during which those assets are held (FAS-121, par. 19):

   a. A description of the assets to be disposed of, the facts and circumstances leading to the expected disposal, the expected disposal date, and the carrying amount of those assets

   b. If applicable, the business segment(s) in which assets to be disposed of are held

   c. The loss, if any, resulting from writing down the assets to fair value less cost to sell

   d. The caption in the income statement in which the impairment gains or losses are aggregated if those gains or losses have not been presented as a separate caption or reported parenthetically on the face of the statement

   e. The gain or loss, if any, resulting from changes in the carrying amounts of assets to be disposed of that arise from subsequent revisions in estimates of fair value less cost to sell

   f. The results of operations for assets to be disposed of to the extent that those results are included in the entity's results of operations for the period and can be identified

EXAMPLES OF FINANCIAL STATEMENT DISCLOSURES

The following sample disclosures are available on the accompanying disc. For additional examples of disclosures of intangible assets that are typically included as part of a company's general note on significant accounting policies see Chapter 2, "Accounting Policies."

Example 37–1: Accounting Policy for Goodwill

Cost in excess of net assets of businesses acquired (goodwill) represents the unamortized excess of the cost of acquiring a business over the fair values of the net assets received at the date of acquisition. It is being amortized on a straight-line basis over periods ranging from five to 40 years and is stated net of accumulated amortization of $470,000 and $420,000 at December 31, 2000, and December 31, 1999, respectively. Amortization expense charged to operations was $50,000 for 2000 and $45,000 for 1999.

Example 37–2: Accounting Policy for Patents

The Company capitalizes the costs of acquiring patents on its products and the costs of patents obtained through acquisition. Patents are being amortized on a straight-line basis over a period of ten to 25 years and are stated net of accumulated amortization of $195,000 and $173,000 at December 31, 2000, and December 31, 1999, respectively. Amortization expense charged to operations was $22,000 for 2000 and $19,000 for 1999.

Example 37–3: Accounting Policy for Trademarks

Costs incident to the creation and registration of trademarks, including legal fees, are capitalized. Trademarks are being amortized on a straight-line basis over a period of five to 15 years and are stated at cost net of accumulated amortization of $213,000 and $184,000 at December 31, 2000, and December 31, 1999, respectively. Amortization expense charged to operations was $29,000 for 2000 and $24,000 for 1999.

Example 37–4: Accounting Policy for Organization Costs

Organization costs, including legal fees, are expensed as incurred. Organization costs charged to operations totaled $23,000 and $12,000 for 2000 and 1999, respectively.

Example 37–5: Accounting Policy for Deferred Financing Costs

Costs relating to obtaining the mortgage debt and the Industrial Revenue Bond financing are capitalized and amortized over the term of the related debt using the straight-line method. Accumulated amortization at December 31, 2000, and December 31, 1999, was $38,000 and $29,000, respectively. Amortization of deferred financing costs charged to operations was $9,000 for 2000 and $7,000 for 1999. When a loan is paid in full, any unamortized financing costs are removed from the related accounts and charged to operations.

Example 37–6: Accounting Policy for Assessing Carrying Value of Intangible Assets for Impairment

Management periodically reviews the carrying value of acquired intangible assets to determine whether an impairment may exist. The Company considers relevant cash flow and profitability information, including estimated future operating results, trends, and other available information, in assessing whether the carrying value of intangible assets can be recovered. If the Company determines that the carrying value of intangible assets will not be recovered from the undiscounted future cash flows of the acquired business, the Company considers the carrying value of such intangible assets as impaired and reduces them by a charge to operations in the amount of the impairment. An impairment charge is measured as any deficiency in the amount of estimated undiscounted future cash flows of the acquired business available to recover the carrying value related to the intangible assets.

Example 37–7: Components of Intangible Assets Disclosed in a Note

Intangible assets consist of the following at December 31:

	2000	*1999*
Cost in excess of net assets of businesses acquired (goodwill)	$1,700,000	$1,700,000
Patents	450,000	370,000
Trademarks	300,000	210,000
Trade names	415,000	300,000
Copyrights	175,000	175,000
Intellectual property	420,000	225,000
Customer lists	790,000	620,000
Covenant not to compete	600,000	300,000
	4,850,000	3,900,000
Less: accumulated amortization	(1,440,000)	(1,090,000)
Net intangible assets	$3,410,000	$2,810,000

Amortization of intangible assets amounted to $350,000 for 2000 and $270,000 for 1999.

Note: Alternatively, the components of intangible assets may be disclosed on the face of the balance sheet.

Example 37–8: Excess of Purchase Price in Business Combination Assigned to Specifically Identifiable Intangible Assets and Goodwill

In July 2000, the Company acquired Xtec, Inc. in a business combination accounted for as a purchase. The purchase price of $4,000,000, which was all paid in cash, exceeded the net assets acquired by

$2,300,000. Of that excess amount, approximately $1,500,000 was assigned to patents, trademarks, and copyrights, which are being amortized on the straight-line method over their remaining lives, ranging from five to 15 years. The remaining amount of $800,000 was considered goodwill and is being amortized on the straight-line method over 30 years. Amortization expense charged to operations was $140,000 in 2000 and $82,000 in 1999.

Example 37–9: Additional Goodwill Resulting from Future Contingent Payments

The initial purchase price in excess of the fair value of identifiable net assets acquired (goodwill) of XYZ Corp. is being amortized on a straight-line basis over 15 years. Additional goodwill resulting from future contingent purchase price payments earned will be amortized on a straight-line basis over the remaining life of the original 15-year period. The earn-out agreement provides for contingent payments, not to exceed $1,500,000, payable in cash, based on the profitability of XYZ Corp. over a four-year period from the acquisition date.

Example 37–10: Negative Goodwill

The Company purchased its subsidiary, DEF Corp., at a cost, which was below the fair value of the subsidiary's net assets at the date of acquisition. The difference, negative goodwill, represents the unallocated portion of the excess of net assets acquired over cost of the subsidiary and is being amortized on the straight-line basis over 25 years.

Example 37–11: Goodwill Impairment Results in Reduction of Amortization Period

In 2000, the Company recognized $2,600,000 in impairment losses on certain identified assets. The largest portion of the loss, $2,100,000, represents impaired goodwill of the Company's electronic components operation. Despite the Company's efforts to improve the operations at this division, several internal and external factors have impacted, and are expected to continue to impact, results of operations. As a result, projected future cash flows from this division were determined to be less than the carrying value of the division's long-lived assets, including goodwill. The revised carrying value of the goodwill was calculated using discounted estimated future cash flows. Management also determined that the useful life of the goodwill should be reduced from 20 years to ten years. The residual goodwill, $1,300,000, will be amortized over the remaining ten years on a straight-line basis.

Goodwill of the electronic components division will continue to be monitored for impairment in accordance with the Company's policy.

Example 37–12: Goodwill Completely Eliminated due to Financial Condition and Operating Results of the Company

In December 2000, the Company recorded a goodwill write-down of $3,450,000, which eliminated all remaining goodwill of the Company. Goodwill was determined to have been impaired because of the current financial condition of the Company and the Company's inability to generate future operating income without substantial sales volume increases, which are highly uncertain. Furthermore, the Company's anticipated future cash flows indicate that the recoverability of goodwill is not reasonably assured. Prior to December 2000, goodwill was being amortized using the straight-line method over 25 years. The goodwill write-down is included as a component of operating expenses in 2000.

Example 37–13: Impairment Write-Down Recognized as a Result of Strategic Review of Certain Operations

In 2000, during the course of the Company's strategic review of its diagnostic chemicals kits operations, the Company recorded a pretax charge of $3,200,000 ($1,970,000 after tax) relating to the impairment of certain intangible assets held for use when it was determined that future undiscounted cash flows associated with these assets were insufficient to recover their carrying value. The impaired assets principally represent the company's historical ownership interest in product rights and license agreements. The assets were written down to fair value, which was determined on the basis of future discounted cash flows and confirmed by independent appraisal.

Example 37–14: Amount Initially Assigned to Goodwill in Business Combination Subsequently Revised

In October 1999, the Company acquired XDEG, Inc., a leading provider of healthcare information products. The Company issued 3,000,000 shares of common stock and 700,000 common stock options with a total fair value of $35,000,000 in exchange for all outstanding shares of XDEG, Inc. The Company accounted for the acquisition using the purchase method of accounting for business combinations. The purchase price and costs associated with the acquisition exceeded the preliminary estimated fair value of net assets acquired by $10,200,000, which was preliminarily assigned to goodwill.

During 2000, the Company completed the valuation of the intangible assets acquired in the XDEG, Inc. transaction. Pursuant to the valuation, the Company expensed $4,400,000 of the excess purchase price representing purchased in-process technology that previously had been assigned to goodwill. In management's judgment, this amount reflects the amount the Company would reasonably expect to pay an unrelated party for each project included in the technology. The value of in-process research and development of $4,400,000 represented approximately 37% of the purchase price and was determined by estimating the costs to develop the purchased technology into commercially viable products, then estimating the resulting net cash flows from each project that was incomplete at the acquisition date, and discounting the resulting net cash flows to their present value. The $4,400,000 charge is included as a component of "Other charges" in the accompanying Consolidated Statements of Operations for the year ended December 31, 2000. Based on the final valuation, the remaining excess purchase price of $5,800,000 was assigned to existing technologies, trade names, and goodwill. The pro forma effects of the XDEG, Inc. acquisition on the consolidated financial statements were not material.

Example 37–15: Covenant Not to Compete Agreements

Covenant not to compete agreements (net) of $623,000 and $823,000 at December 31, 2000, and December 31, 1999, respectively, represents the portion of the purchase price associated with the 1999 acquisition of Baysol Co. allocated to noncompetition agreements. Under these agreements, the former stockholders of Baysol Co. agreed not to compete with the Company for a period of five years. The related cost is being amortized on the straight-line method over the terms of the agreements. Accumulated amortization related to the covenant not to compete agreements totaled $377,000 and $177,000 at December 31, 2000, and December 31, 1999, respectively. Amortization expense charged to operations was $200,000 for 2000 and $177,000 for 1999.

Example 37–16: Patent Acquisition

In 1998, the Company acquired certain patents pertaining to technology incorporated into certain of the Company's products. The Company paid approximately $1,975,000 for these patents and related expenses upon entering into the agreement. In April 2000, this agreement was amended such that the Company paid approximately $1,215,000 for additional patent rights and related expenses. The cost of these patents is being amortized over the patents' expected life of ten years.

Example 37–17: License Agreement

In 2000, the Company entered into an agreement to license the rights to certain laboratory equipment developed and manufactured by another company. The purchase price paid for the license was $400,000 in cash. The cost of the licensing agreement acquired was recorded as an intangible asset and is being amortized over the period of its estimated benefit period of ten years. At December 31, 2000, accumulated amortization was $30,000. Under the terms of the agreement, the Company is also required to pay royalties, as defined, to the licensors semiannually.

CHAPTER 38
OTHER ASSETS: CURRENT AND NONCURRENT

CONTENTS

EXECUTIVE SUMMARY

Rarely is the nature of other assets appearing in the current or noncurrent asset sections of an entity's balance sheet disclosed in the financial statements. This is generally because such assets are not material to the financial statements taken as a whole. Typically, other assets include items such as prepaid expenses, deferred charges, and deposits. However, if several other assets are included as a single line item in the balance sheet, it is generally informative to include the details of such items in a note to the financial statements.

Other assets generally have one main characteristic: They represent costs and expenditures that are expected to benefit future periods. They include payments in advance for services to be rendered to the entity by others in the future. Therefore, if a current expenditure has an economic benefit obtainable in a future period and is quantifiable, the expenditure most likely qualifies to be reported as an other asset in the financial statements.

Some items in the other assets category are sufficiently important in specific financial statement contexts and have already been covered in other chapters. Chapter 38 includes only examples of the most common types of other assets, current and noncurrent, found in practice that have not already been addressed in other chapters.

Authoritative Literature

ARB-43	Chapter 3A, Current Assets and Current Liabilities
APB-10	Omnibus Opinion—1966
APB-12	Omnibus Opinion—1967

DISCLOSURE REQUIREMENTS

If other assets are material to the financial statements, the following generally accepted disclosures should be made:

1. A description of the asset and the basis of its valuation
2. If applicable, the method of amortization, the amortization period, the amount of amortization expense, and the accumulated amortization

EXAMPLES OF FINANCIAL STATEMENT DISCLOSURES

The following sample disclosures are available on the accompanying disc.

Example 38–1: Prepaid Expenses

Prepaid expenses comprise the following at December 31, 2000, and December 31, 1999:

	2000	*1999*
Royalty advances	$132,000	$116,000
Prepaid insurance	92,000	85,000
Prepaid advertising costs	74,000	48,000
Prepaid rent	29,000	27,000
Prepaid taxes	20,000	25,000
Other prepaid expenses	14,000	12,000
	$361,000	$313,000

Example 38–2: Deposits

At December 31, 2000, the Company has deposits with vendors totaling $100,000 for the purchase of machinery and equipment.

Example 38–3: Deferred Advertising Costs

Direct response advertising costs, consisting primarily of catalog book production, printing, and postage costs, are capitalized and amortized over the expected life of the catalog, not to exceed six months. Prepaid expenses at December 31, 2000, and December 31, 1999, include deferred advertising costs of $275,000 and $350,000, respectively. Total advertising expenses were $1,900,000 and $1,600,000 in 2000 and 1999, respectively.

> **Note:** For additional examples of disclosures relating to advertising costs, see Chapter 3, "Advertising Costs."

Example 38–4: Deferred Financing Costs

Costs relating to obtaining the mortgage debt and the Industrial Revenue Bond financing are capitalized and amortized over the term of the related debt using the straight-line method. Accumulated amortization at December 31, 2000, and December 31, 1999, was $38,000 and $29,000, respectively. Amortization of deferred financing costs charged to operations was $9,000 for 2000 and $7,000 for 1999. When a loan is paid in full, any unamortized financing costs are removed from the related accounts and charged to operations.

Example 38–5: Organization Costs

Organization costs, including legal fees, are expensed as incurred. Organization costs charged to operations totaled $23,000 and $12,000 for 2000 and 1999, respectively.

Example 38–6: Covenant Not to Compete Agreements

Covenant not to compete agreements (net) of $623,000 and $823,000 at December 31, 2000, and December 31, 1999, respectively, represents the portion of the purchase price associated with the 1999 acquisition of Baysol Co. allocated to noncompetition agreements. Under these agreements, the former stockholders of Baysol Co. agreed not to compete with the Company for a period of five years. The related cost is being amortized on the straight-line method over the terms of the agreements. Accumulated amortization related to the covenant not to compete agreements totaled $377,000 and $177,000 at December 31, 2000, and December 31, 1999, respectively. Amortization expense charged to operations was $200,000 for 2000 and $177,000 for 1999.

Example 38–7: Assets Held for Sale

In September 2000, the Company formalized its plan to sell its medical instruments operations. Accordingly, operating results for this business have been presented as discontinued operations in the Statement of Operations for 2000. Amounts in the Statement of Operations for 1999 have been restated to conform to the 2000 discontinued operations presentation.

The Company is in the process of negotiating the sale of these operations and expects that the sale will be completed within one year. The net assets of the discontinued business held for sale, totaling $2,630,000, have been included as a current asset in the accompanying Balance Sheet at December 31, 2000, under the caption "Net assets held for sale—discontinued operations." The net assets have been recorded at their estimated net realizable value and consist of the following:

Accounts receivable	$ 506,000
Inventories	543,000
Property, plant, and equipment, net	2,163,000
Other assets	176,000
Total assets	3,388,000
Accounts payable	612,000
Other accrued liabilities	146,000
Total liabilities	758,000
Net assets held for sale	$2,630,000

Example 38–8: Cash Surrender Value of Life Insurance, Net of Policy Loans

The Company has purchased insurance on the lives of certain key executive officers. As beneficiary, the Company receives the cash surrender value if the policy is terminated and, upon death of the insured, receives all benefits payable. Cash value of life insurance is reported in the financial statements net of policy loans. The loans carry interest at a rate of 6.5%, require interest only payments annually, and are collateralized by the cash value of the policies. A summary of "Net cash value of life insurance" as reported in the accompanying Balance Sheets at December 31, 2000, and December 31, 1999, is as follows:

	2000	*1999*
Cash surrender value of life insurance	$1,156,000	$1,005,000
Policy loans balances outstanding	(418,000)	(329,000)
Net cash value of life insurance	$738,000	$676,000

Example 38–9: Life Insurance Contracts Used to Fund Deferred Compensation Plan

The Company has a deferred compensation plan that permits management and highly compensated employees to defer portions of their compensation and earn a guaranteed interest rate on the deferred amounts. The salaries that have been deferred since the plan's inception have been accrued and the only expense, other than salaries, related to this plan is the interest on the deferred amounts. Interest expense during 2000 and 1999 includes $103,000 and $68,000, respectively, related to this plan. The Company has included in "Deferred employee benefits" $1,150,000 and $935,000 at December 31, 2000, and December 31, 1999, respectively, to reflect its liability under this plan. To fund this plan, the Company purchases corporate-owned whole-life insurance contracts on the related employees. The Company has included in "Other assets" $1,200,000 and $967,000 at December 31, 2000, and December 31, 1999, respectively, which represents cash surrender value of these policies.

CHAPTER 39
INCOME TAXES

CONTENTS

EXECUTIVE SUMMARY

The tax consequences of many transactions recognized in the financial statements are included when determining income taxes currently payable in the same accounting period. Sometimes, tax laws differ from the recognition and measurement requirements of financial reporting standards. Differences arise between the tax bases of assets or liabilities and their reported amounts in the financial statements. These differences are called *temporary differences* and they give rise to deferred tax assets and liabilities.

Temporary differences ordinarily reverse when the related asset is recovered or the related liability is settled. A *deferred tax liability* or *deferred tax asset* represents the increase or decrease in taxes payable or refundable in future years as a result of temporary differences and carryforwards at the end of the current year.

The objectives of accounting for income taxes are to recognize:

- The amount of taxes payable or refundable for the current year
- The deferred tax liabilities and assets that result from future tax consequences of events that have been recognized in the enterprise's financial statements or tax returns

To implement these objectives, the following basic principles should be observed at the date of the financial statements:

1. Recognize a *tax liability or asset* for the amount of taxes currently payable or refundable.
2. Recognize a *deferred tax liability or asset* for the estimated future tax effects of temporary differences or carryforwards.
3. Measure *current* and *deferred tax assets* and *liabilities* based on provisions of enacted tax laws.
4. Reduce the amount of any deferred *tax assets* by a valuation allowance, if necessary, based on available evidence.

The following are exceptions to these basic principles:

1. Certain exceptions to the requirements for recognition of deferred tax assets and liabilities for the areas addressed by Accounting Principles Board Opinion No. 23 (Accounting for Income Taxes—Special Areas), as amended by Financial Accounting Standards Board Statement No. 109 (Accounting for Income Taxes), paragraphs 31–34, notably the investments in foreign subsidiaries and joint ventures
2. Special transitional procedures for temporary differences related to deposits in statutory reserve funds by U.S. steamship enterprises
3. Accounting for leveraged leases as required by FAS-13 (Accounting for Leases) and FASB Interpretation No. 21 (Accounting for Leases in a Business Combination)
4. Prohibition of the recognition of a deferred tax liability or asset related to goodwill for which amortization is not deductible for tax purposes
5. Accounting for income taxes under Accounting Research Bulletin No. 51 (Consolidated Financial Statements)
6. Prohibition of the recognition of a deferred tax liability or asset for differences related to assets and liabilities accounted for under FAS-52 (Foreign Currency Translation)

The emphasis placed on the balance sheet by the asset/liability method of accounting for income taxes is evident from the focus on the recognition of deferred tax liabilities and assets. The change in these liabilities and assets is combined with the income taxes currently payable or refundable to determine income tax expense.

The following five steps are required to complete the annual computation of deferred tax liabilities and assets:

1. Identify the types and amounts of existing temporary differences and the nature and amount of each type of operating loss and tax credit carryforward and the remaining length of the carryforward period.
2. Measure the total deferred tax liability for taxable temporary differences using the applicable tax rate.
3. Measure the total deferred tax asset for deductible temporary differences and operating loss carryforwards using the applicable tax rate.
4. Measure deferred tax assets for each type of tax credit carryforward.
5. Reduce deferred tax assets by a valuation allowance if it is more likely than not that some or all of the deferred tax assets will not be realized.

Determining the need for and calculating the amount of the valuation allowance requires the following steps at the end of each accounting period:

1. Determine the amount of the deferred tax asset recognized on each deductible temporary difference, operating loss, and tax credit carryforward. These are not offset by the deferred tax liability on taxable temporary differences.
2. Assess the sources of future taxable income that may be available to recognize the deductible differences and carryforwards by considering the following:
   a. Future reversals of existing taxable temporary differences
   b. Taxable income in prior carryback year(s) if carryback is permitted under tax law
   c. Future taxable income exclusive of reversing differences and carryforwards
   d. Tax planning strategies that would make income available at appropriate times in the future that would otherwise not be available
3. Based on all available evidence, make a judgment concerning the realizability of the deferred tax asset.
4. Record the amount of the valuation allowance, or change in the valuation allowance.

Authoritative Literature

APB-2	Accounting for the "Investment Credit"
APB-4	Accounting for the "Investment Credit" (Amending No. 2)

APB-10	Omnibus Opinion—1966
APB-23	Accounting for Income Taxes—Special Areas
FAS-37	Balance Sheet Classification of Deferred Income Taxes
FAS-95	Statement of Cash Flows
FAS-109	Accounting for Income Taxes
FAS-115	Accounting for Certain Investments in Debt and Equity Securities
FAS-123	Accounting for Stock-Based Compensation
FAS-130	Reporting Comprehensive Income
FIN-18	Accounting for Income Taxes in Interim Periods
FTB 79-9	Accounting in Interim Periods for Changes in Income Tax Rates
FTB 82-1	Disclosure of the Sale or Purchase of Tax Benefits though Tax Leases

DISCLOSURE REQUIREMENTS

1. If a classified balance sheet is presented, the following items should be disclosed (ARB-43, Ch. 3A; FAS-109, par. 41):
   a. Income taxes currently payable or refundable
   b. Current and noncurrent deferred tax assets, including the valuation allowance, if any
   c. Current and noncurrent deferred tax liabilities
2. The following components of the net deferred tax liability or asset recognized in the balance sheet should be disclosed (FAS-109, par. 43):
   a. The total of all deferred tax liabilities for taxable temporary differences
   b. The total of all deferred tax assets for deductible temporary differences, operating loss carryforwards, and tax credit carryforwards
   c. The total valuation allowance recognized for deferred tax assets
3. The net change during the year in the total valuation allowance account should be disclosed (FAS-109, par. 43).
4. The following components (where applicable) of income tax expense related to continuing operations for each year presented should be disclosed (FAS-109, par. 45):

a. Current tax expense or benefit

b. Deferred tax expense or benefit (exclusive of items listed below)

c. Investment tax credits

d. Government grants (to the extent they have been used to reduce income tax expense)

e. Benefits arising from operating loss carryforwards

f. Tax expense arising from allocating tax benefits either directly to contributed capital or to reduce goodwill or other noncurrent intangible assets of an acquired company

g. Adjustments to a deferred tax liability or asset arising from changes in tax laws, tax rates, or the entity's tax status

h. Adjustments to the beginning balance in the valuation allowance account related to deferred tax assets that arise due to changes in the amount of assets expected to be realized

5. The amount of income tax expense or benefit should be disclosed for each of the following items for each year for which the items are presented (FAS-109, par. 46; APB-9, par. 26; APB-9, par. 20):

   a. Continuing operations

   b. Discontinued operations

   c. Extraordinary items

   d. The cumulative effect of accounting changes

   e. Prior-period adjustments

   f. Items charged or credited directly to shareholders' equity

   g. Other comprehensive income

6. For a particular tax paying component of an enterprise and within a particular tax jurisdiction (e.g., federal, state, or local), the following items should be disclosed (FAS-109, par. 42):

   a. The amount of current deferred tax liabilities and assets offset and presented as a single amount

   b. The amount of noncurrent deferred tax liabilities and assets offset and presented as a single amount

   c. The net current deferred tax asset or liability and the net noncurrent deferred tax asset or liability within each tax jurisdiction shown separately for each tax paying component

7. If the entity is a member of a group that files a consolidated tax return, the following disclosures should be made in the entity's separately issued financial statements (FAS-109, par. 49):

   a. The amount of current and deferred tax expense for each statement of income presented

b. The amount of any tax-related balances due to or from affiliates as of the date of each balance sheet presented

c. The principal provisions of the method by which the consolidated amount of current and deferred tax expense is allocated to members of the group, and the nature and effect of any changes in that method (and in determining related balance to or from affiliates) during the years for which the disclosures in items 7a and 7b are presented

8. In addition to the above, the notes to the financial statements should also disclose:

   a. The types of significant temporary differences and carryforwards (FAS-109, par. 43)

   b. The nature of significant reconciling items between (i) the reported amount of income tax expense attributable to continuing operations for the year and (ii) the amount of income tax expense that would result from applying domestic federal statutory tax rates to pretax income from continuing operations (FAS-109, par. 47)

   c. The amounts and expiration dates for operating loss and tax credit carryforwards for tax purposes (FAS-109, par. 48)

   d. The portion of the valuation allowance for deferred tax assets for which subsequently recognized tax benefits will be allocated to reduce goodwill or other noncurrent intangible assets of an acquired entity or directly to contributed capital (FAS-109, par. 48)

   e. The method of accounting for the investment tax credit (deferral method or flow-through method) and related amounts (APB-4, par. 11)

   f. The change in an entity's tax status that becomes effective after year end but before the financial statements are issued (FAS-109, QA-11)

   g. The nature and effect of any other significant matters affecting comparability of information for all periods presented, if not otherwise evident (FAS-109, par. 47)

9. The following items should be disclosed when a deferred tax liability is not recognized because of the exceptions allowed by APB-23 (i.e., undistributed earnings of subsidiaries or corporate joint ventures, bad debt reserves of savings and loan associations, or policy holders' surplus of life insurance companies) or for deposits in statutory reserve funds by U.S. steamship companies (FAS-109, par. 44):

   a. Description of temporary differences that did *not* create a deferred tax liability and the event(s) that would cause the temporary differences to become taxable

b. Cumulative amount of each type of temporary difference

c. Amount of unrecognized deferred tax liability arising from temporary differences related to investments in foreign subsidiaries and foreign corporate joint ventures that are considered permanent (If it is not practical to compute the amount, then that fact should be stated.)

d. Amount of unrecognized deferred tax liability for temporary differences related to (i) undistributed domestic earnings, (ii) bad-debt reserve for tax purposes of U.S. savings and loan associations or other qualified thrift lenders, (iii) the policyholders' surplus of a life insurance enterprise, and (iv) statutory reserve funds of a U.S. steamship enterprise

10. If the amount of income tax benefit realized from the exercise of employee stock options is credited to equity but is not presented as a separate line item in the statement of changes in stockholders' equity or in the statement of cash flows, the amount of that income tax benefit should be disclosed (EITF 00-15).

It should be noted that several distinctions are made in the disclosures required by public entities and those required by nonpublic entities. The two most significant ones are summarized as follows:

	Public/Nonpublic Company Disclosures	
	Public	*Nonpublic*
Temporary differences and carryforwards	Approximation of tax effect of each type	Description of types
Statutory reconciliation	Reconciliation in percentages or dollars	Description of major reconciling items

EXAMPLES OF FINANCIAL STATEMENT DISCLOSURES

The following sample disclosures are available on the accompanying disc. For examples of income tax disclosures that are typically described in a note summarizing a company's significant accounting policies, see Chapter 2, "Accounting Policies."

Example 39–1: Company's Disclosure of the Provision for Income Taxes, Reconciliation of Statutory Rate to Effective Rate, and Significant Components of Deferred Tax Assets and Liabilities

Note: A non-public company may, alternatively, describe in a narrative format the major reconciling items between the statutory tax rate and effective tax rate and the significant components of deferred tax assets and liabilities as shown in Example 39–2.

The federal and state income tax provision (benefit) is summarized as follows:

	Year Ended December 31	
	2000	*1999*
Current:		
Federal	$250,000	$(45,000)
State	50,000	5,000
	300,000	(40,000)
Deferred:		
Federal	(80,000)	(125,000)
State	(20,000)	30,000
	(100,000)	(95,000)
Total provision (benefit) for income taxes	$200,000	$(135,000)

A reconciliation of the provision (benefit) for income taxes with amounts determined by applying the statutory U.S. federal income tax rate to income before income taxes is as follows:

	Year Ended December 31	
	2000	*1999*
Computed tax at the federal statutory rate of 34%	$700,000	$(150,000)
State taxes, net of federal benefit	30,000	20,000
Write-down of asset not deductible	80,000	450,000
Foreign sales corporation benefits	(15,000)	(10,000)
Corporate-owned life insurance	10,000	-0-
Tax exempt interest	(75,000)	(15,000)
Research and development tax credits	(290,000)	-0-
Operating loss carryforwards	(300,000)	(400,000)
Reduction in valuation allowance	-0-	(20,000)
Settlement of prior years' audit issues	50,000	-0-
Adjustment of prior years' accruals	15,000	-0-
Other	(5,000)	(10,000)
Provision (benefit) for income taxes	$200,000	$(135,000)
Effective income tax rate	10%	(31%)

Deferred income taxes reflect the net tax effects of temporary differences between the carrying amounts of assets and liabilities for financial reporting purposes and the amounts used for income tax purposes. Significant components of the Company's deferred tax assets and liabilities are as follows:

	Year Ended December 31	
	2000	*1999*
Deferred tax assets:		
Inventory capitalization	$450,000	$675,000
Inventory obsolescence	300,000	125,000
LIFO inventory valuation	200,000	150,000
Intercompany profit in inventory	75,000	50,000
Allowance for doubtful accounts	50,000	100,000
Allowance for sales returns	100,000	150,000
Warranty expense	300,000	400,000
Postretirement benefit obligation	250,000	125,000
Deferred compensation	100,000	50,000
Accrued vacation	125,000	75,000
Deferred revenue	275,000	200,000
Unrealized foreign exchange losses	15,000	10,000
Net operating losses carryforwards	300,000	400,000
Tax credits carryforwards	200,000	100,000
AMT credit	50,000	25,000
Other	5,000	10,000
Total deferred tax assets	2,795,000	2,645,000
Deferred tax liabilities:		
Difference between book and tax depreciation	1,755,000	1,515,000
Unrealized gains on marketable securities	75,000	60,000
Unrealized foreign exchange gains	25,000	40,000
Unremitted earnings of subsidiaries	75,000	50,000
Other	15,000	5,000
Total deferred tax liabilities	1,945,000	1,670,000
Net deferred tax asset before valuation allowance	850,000	975,000
Valuation allowance	(200,000)	(500,000)
Net deferred tax asset	$650,000	$475,000

Example 39–2: Company's Disclosure of the Provision for Income Taxes, Major Reconciling Items between the Statutory Tax Rate and Effective Tax Rate, and the Significant Components of Deferred Tax Assets and Liabilities

> **Note:** Example 39–2 is applicable only to non-public entities. For a sample disclosure that is applicable to a public entity, see Example 39–1.

The federal and state income tax provision (benefit) is summarized as follows:

	Year Ended December 31	
	2000	*1999*
Current:		
Federal	$250,000	$(45,000)
State	50,000	5,000
	300,000	(40,000)
Deferred:		
Federal	(80,000)	(125,000)
State	(20,000)	30,000
	(100,000)	(95,000)
Total provision (benefit) for income taxes	$200,000	$(135,000)

The Company's effective income tax rate is lower than what would be expected if the federal statutory rate were applied to income before income taxes primarily because of certain expenses deductible for financial reporting purposes that are not deductible for tax purposes, tax-exempt interest income, research and development tax credits, and operating loss carryforwards.

Deferred income taxes reflect the net tax effects of temporary differences between the carrying amounts of assets and liabilities for financial reporting purposes and the amounts used for income tax purposes. The major temporary differences that give rise to the deferred tax assets and liabilities are as follows: inventory capitalization, LIFO inventory valuation, provision for doubtful accounts, warranty expense, postretirement benefit obligation, deferred compensation, depreciation, net operating losses carryforwards, and tax credits carryforwards.

Example 39–3: Disclosure of Net Operating Losses and Tax Credits Carryforwards

At December 31, 2000, the Company has available unused net operating losses and investment tax credits carryforwards that may be applied against future taxable income and that expire as follows:

Year of Expiration	*Net Operating Losses Carryforwards*	*Investment Tax Credits Carryforwards*
2001	$3,000,000	$1,000,000
2002	1,000,000	2,000,000
2003	6,000,000	4,000,000
2004	4,000,000	3,000,000
2005	3,000,000	1,000,000
Thereafter up to 2013	8,000,000	2,000,000
	$25,000,000	$13,000,000

In addition, the Company has available Alternative Minimum Tax credit carryforwards for tax purposes of approximately $1,800,000, which may be used indefinitely to reduce regular federal income taxes.

Example 39–4: Company Has Substantial Net Operating Loss Carryforwards and a Valuation Allowance Is Recorded

The Company recognizes the amount of taxes payable or refundable for the current year and recognizes deferred tax liabilities and assets for the expected future tax consequences of events and transactions that have been recognized in the Company's financial statements or tax returns. The Company currently has substantial net operating loss carryforwards. The Company has recorded a 100% valuation allowance against net deferred tax assets due to uncertainty of their ultimate realization.

Example 39–5: Company Discloses Its Consideration of Sufficient Positive Evidence to Support Its Conclusion Not to Record a Valuation Allowance

A significant portion of the deferred tax assets recognized relate to net operating loss and credit carryforwards. Because the Company operates in multiple overseas jurisdictions, it considered the need for a valuation allowance on a country-by-country basis, taking into account the effects of local tax law. Where a valuation allowance was not recorded, the Company believes that there was sufficient positive evidence to support its conclusion not to record a valuation allowance. Management believes that the Company will utilize the loss carryforwards in the future because: (1) prior to the restructuring charges, the Company had a history of pre-tax income; (2) a significant portion of the loss carryforwards resulted from restructuring costs; (3) management believes that the restructuring of the Company's businesses will reduce their cost structures and that the Company will be profitable and will generate taxable income in the near term; (4) management is aware of viable tax strategies that could be implemented to accelerate taxable income in order to realize a substantial portion of the recorded deferred tax assets; and (5) a significant portion of the net operating losses have an indefinite life or do not expire in the near term. However, there can be no assurance that the Company will generate taxable income or that all of its loss carryforwards will be utilized.

Example 39–6: Change in Valuation Allowance During the Year Is Described

In 2000, the valuation allowance increased approximately $1,950,000, composed of increases to allowances due to the uncertainty of realizing research and development tax credits, tax benefits from certain asset impairment write-downs, and net operating loss carryforwards.

Example 39–7: Valuation Allowances Related to Preacquisition NOL Carryforwards of Acquired Business Are Being Applied to Reduce Goodwill Arising from the Acquisition

Valuation allowances related to the preacquisition net operating loss carryforwards of Instarr, Inc., which was acquired by the Company in 1997, are being applied to reduce goodwill arising from the acquisition as the related tax benefits are realized. During 2000 and 1999, reversals of valuation allowances applied to reduce goodwill totaled $4,200,000 and $3,100,000, respectively. Any subsequent decreases in the deferred tax valuation allowance will also be recorded as a reduction to goodwill.

Example 39–8: Reduction in Valuation Allowance Recorded as an Increase in Additional Paid-In Capital in Connection with "Fresh-Start" Accounting

As of December 31, 1998, the Company had various net deferred tax assets made up primarily of the expected future tax benefit of net operating loss carryforwards, various credit carryforwards, and reserves not yet deductible for tax purposes. A valuation allowance was provided in full against these net deferred tax assets upon the Company's emergence from bankruptcy when "fresh-start" reporting was adopted.

During 2000 and 1999, the Company reduced the valuation allowance related to the remaining net tax assets by $2,800,000 and

$1,900,000, respectively. The reduction reflects the Company's expectation that it is more likely than not that it will generate future taxable income to utilize this amount of net deferred tax assets. The benefit from this reduction was recorded as an increase in additional paid-in capital in accordance with Statement of Position No. 90-7.

Example 39–9: Tax Benefits Associated with Stock Options Recorded as an Increase to Additional Paid-In Capital

During 2000 and 1999, the Company recognized certain tax benefits related to stock option plans in the amount of $1,200,000 and $800,000, respectively. Such benefits were recorded as a reduction of income taxes payable and an increase in additional paid-in capital.

Example 39–10: Deferred Taxes Not Provided on Undistributed Earnings of Foreign Subsidiaries—Amount of Deferred Tax Liability Not Disclosed

A provision has not been made at December 31, 2000, for U.S. or additional foreign withholding taxes on approximately $10 million of undistributed earnings of foreign subsidiaries because it is the present intention of management to reinvest the undistributed earnings indefinitely in foreign operations. Generally, such earnings become subject to U.S. tax upon the remittance of dividends and under certain other circumstances. It is not practicable to estimate the amount of deferred tax liability on such undistributed earnings.

Example 39–11: Deferred Taxes Not Provided on Undistributed Earnings of Foreign Subsidiaries—Amount of Deferred Tax Liability Is Disclosed

The Company has not recorded deferred income taxes applicable to undistributed earnings of foreign subsidiaries that are indefinitely reinvested in foreign operations. Undistributed earnings amounted to approximately $6,000,000 and $5,200,000 at December 31, 2000, and December 31, 1999, respectively. If the earnings of such foreign subsidiaries were not definitely reinvested, a deferred tax liability of approximately $1,500,000 and $1,300,000 would have been required at December 31, 2000, and December 31, 1999, respectively.

Example 39–12: Deferred Taxes Recorded on Undistributed Earnings of Foreign Subsidiaries

At December 31, 2000, the accompanying consolidated Balance Sheet includes a deferred tax liability of $300,000 for the estimated income taxes that will be payable upon the anticipated future repatriation of approximately $1,000,000 of undistributed earnings of foreign subsidiaries in the form of dividends.

Example 39–13: Subchapter S Status Terminated

Prior to January 1, 2000, the Company had operated as a C corporation. Effective January 1, 2000, the stockholders of the Company elected to be taxed under Subchapter S of the Internal Revenue Code. During such period, federal income taxes were the responsibility of the Company's stockholders, as were certain state income taxes. As of the effective date of the election, the Company was responsible for Federal built-in-gain taxes to the extent applicable. Accordingly, the consolidated statement of operations for the year ended December 31, 2000, provides for such taxes. The S corporation election terminated in connection with the consummation of the initial public offering of the Company's common stock on October 10, 2000.

Example 39–14: Conversion from Cash Basis to Accrual Basis for Tax Purposes Results in a Deferred Tax Liability

In the current year, the Company converted from a cash basis to accrual basis for tax purposes in conjunction with its conversion to a C corporation. Due to temporary differences in recognition of revenue and expenses, income for financial reporting purposes exceeded income for income tax purposes. The conversion to the accrual basis along with these temporary differences resulted in the recognition of a net deferred tax liability and a corresponding one-time charge to expense of $3.5 million as of December 31, 2000.

Example 39–15: Company Is in Dispute with Taxing Authority over Tax Assessment

The Company is in dispute over a 1999 tax assessment, including penalties and interest, by the Ohio Department of Revenue and Taxation for the years 1994 through 1998 in the approximate amount of approximately $9.5 million. The Company has filed written protests as to these assessments and will vigorously contest the asserted deficiencies through the administrative appeals process and, if necessary, litigation. The Company believes that adequate provision has been made in the financial statements for any liability.

Example 39–16: Company's Tax Returns Are under Examination by the IRS

The Internal Revenue Service is currently examining the Company's tax returns for years 1997 through 1999. Management believes the ultimate resolution of this examination will not result in a material adverse effect to the Company's financial position or results of operations.

Example 39–17: IRS Has Completed Examination and Issued a Deficiency Notice—No Accrual Made

The Internal Revenue Service (IRS) has completed an examination of the federal income tax returns filed by the Company for the years ended December 31, 1997, and December 31, 1998. The IRS has proposed to disallow certain deductions taken by the Company in connection with an acquisition and has sent the Company a statutory notice of deficiency. The Company disagrees with the position of the IRS, intends to pursue its judicial remedies, and is confident that, upon final resolution of the issue, the proposed tax deficiencies will be substantially reduced. No provision has been made in the financial statements for the proposed additional taxes and interest because the ultimate liability cannot be reasonably estimated. Full loss of the contested deductions, plus interest costs through December 31, 2000, would result in a charge to net earnings of approximately $750,000.

Example 39–18: Settlement Reached with IRS about Proposed Adjustments—Accrual Made

The Internal Revenue Service (IRS) has proposed certain adjustments to the Company's federal tax returns for 1997 and 1998. The Company has entered into an agreement with the IRS concerning some of the proposed adjustments and has reached an informal understanding with the IRS regarding the others. The provision for current income taxes for 2000 include an additional $450,000 resulting from the settlement with the IRS. As of December 31, 2000, the Company has accrued the additional tax liability of $450,000, plus $92,000 for estimated interest due.

CHAPTER 40
DEBT OBLIGATIONS AND CREDIT ARRANGEMENTS

CONTENTS

EXECUTIVE SUMMARY

Debt Obligations and Credit Arrangements

Debt obligations that, by their terms, are due and payable on demand should be presented as a current liability in the balance sheet. Current liabilities include long-term obligations that are callable because a violation of an objective acceleration clause in a long-term debt agreement may exist at the date of the debtor's balance sheet. Such callable obligations must be classified as a current liability at the debtor's balance sheet date unless one of the following conditions is met:

1. The creditor has waived or subsequently lost the right to demand repayment for more than one year (or operating cycle, if longer) from the balance sheet date.
2. For long-term obligations containing a grace period within which the debtor may cure the violation, it is probable that the violation will be cured within that period, therefore preventing the obligation from being callable.

A short-term obligation can be excluded from current liabilities only if the company intends to refinance the obligation on a long-term basis and the intent is supported by the ability to refinance in one of the following ways:

1. A long-term obligation or equity security whose proceeds are used to retire the short-term obligation is issued after the date of the balance sheet but before the issuance of the financial statements.
2. Before the issuance of the financial statements, the company has entered into an agreement that enables it to refinance a short-term obligation on a long-term basis.

When a note is exchanged for property, goods, or services in an arm's length transaction, it is generally presumed that the interest stated on the note is fair and adequate. If no interest is stated or if the interest stated appears unreasonable, the transaction should be valued at the fair value of the note or property, goods, or services, whichever is more clearly determinable. If such fair value is not readily determinable, the transaction should be valued at the present value of the note, determined by discounting the future cash payments under the note by an appropriate interest rate. The difference between the face amount of the note and its present value represents a discount or premium, which should be amortized over the life of the note using the interest method, or a method that approximates the interest method. The discount or premium amount is not an asset or a liability separable from the note that gives rise to it; therefore, the discount or premium should be reported in the balance sheet as a direct deduction from or addition to the face amount of the note.

When convertible debt is issued without an embedded beneficial conversion feature (i.e., a conversion feature that is *not* in-the-money at the commitment date), no value should be assigned to the conversion feature because it generally is inseparable from the debt. Consequently, the transaction should be recorded entirely as the issuance of debt. When debt is converted into stock, the debt obligation and unamortized premium or discount should be eliminated; the issuance of the shares should be recorded as outstanding stock and additional paid-in capital.

When debt is issued with detachable stock purchase warrants, a portion of the proceeds should be allocated to the warrants and recorded as additional paid-in capital because the warrants and debt are viewed as separate securities.

Debt Extinguishment

An *extinguishment of debt* is the reacquisition of debt, or removal of debt from the balance sheet, prior to or at the maturity date of that debt. Debt is extinguished and should be de-recognized in the debtor's financial statements only in the following circumstances:

1. The debtor pays the creditor and is relieved of its obligations for the liability. This includes (a) the transfer of cash, other financial assets, goods, or services, or (b) the debtor's reacquisition of its outstanding debt securities, whether the securities are canceled or held as treasury bonds.
2. The debtor is legally released from being the primary obligor under the liability, either judicially or by the creditor. If a third party assumes nonrecourse debt in conjunction with the sale of an asset that serves as sole collateral for that debt, the sale and related assumption effectively accomplish a legal release of the seller-debtor.

Gain or loss on the extinguishment is the difference between the total reacquisition cost of the debt to the debtor and the net carrying amount of the debt on the debtor's books at the date of extinguishment. The gain or loss on the extinguishment of debt is recognized immediately in the year of extinguishment and, if material, is reported as an extraordinary item net of related tax effects. However, gains or losses from the extinguishment of debt made within one year to meet sinking fund requirements are not classified as extraordinary items but are included in income from continuing operations. This also applies to any debt that has the same characteristics as sinking fund requirements, such as a required annual extinguishment of a specific percentage of outstanding debt prior to its maturity. Gains or losses from the maturity of serialized debt are classified as extraordinary items, however, because serial debt does not have the same characteristics as debt pursuant to sinking fund requirements.

Debt Restructuring

The types of debt restructuring include (a) transfer of assets or transfer of an equity interest in full settlement, (b) modification of the terms of the debt, or (c) a combination of the two.

If a debtor satisfies a debt in full by transferring assets, or by granting an equity interest, to a creditor, and the fair market value of the assets transferred or equity interest granted is less than the carrying value of the debt, the debtor generally should recognize the difference as an extraordinary gain. In addition, the debtor should recognize a gain or loss for any difference between the carrying value of the assets transferred and their fair value, which should be reported as ordinary gain or loss on transfer of assets.

A troubled debt restructuring involving only modification of terms of a payable (i.e., not involving a transfer of assets or grant of an equity interest) should be accounted for prospectively. However, if the carrying amount of the debt exceeds the total future cash payments specified by the new terms, the debtor should reduce the debt's carrying amount to the total future cash payments specified by the new terms and recognize an extraordinary gain on debt restructuring.

Unconditional Purchase Obligations

An unconditional purchase obligation is an obligation to transfer funds in the future for fixed or minimum amounts or quantities of goods or services at fixed or minimum prices. Such obligations often are in the form of "take-or-pay contracts" or "throughput agreements," which generally require the buyer to pay specified amounts periodically, even if delivery of goods is not taken or the service is not used. Liabilities created by purchase obligations may or may not be recorded under current accounting standards. However, all unconditional purchase obligations should be disclosed in the financial statements regardless of whether they have been recorded as liabilities.

Product Financing Arrangements

A product financing arrangement is a transaction in which an entity sells products to another entity and, in a related transaction, agrees to repurchase the products at a specified price over a specified period. A product financing arrangement should be accounted for as a borrowing rather than as a sale. It should be noted that the accounting for product financing arrangements differs from the accounting for long-term unconditional purchase obligations. In a product financing arrangement, the entity is in substance the owner of the product and, therefore, should report the product as an asset and the related obligation as a liability. In contrast, at the time a contract is entered into under an unconditional purchase obligation arrangement, either the product does not yet exist or the product exists in a form unsuitable to the buyer; in other words, the buyer has a right to receive a future product but is *not* the substantive owner of an existing product.

Authoritative Literature

ARB-43	Chapter 3A, Current Assets and Current Liabilities
APB-10	Omnibus Opinion—1966
APB-12	Omnibus Opinion—1967
APB-14	Accounting for Convertible Debt and Debt Issued with Stock Purchase Warrants
APB-21	Interest on Receivables and Payables
APB-26	Early Extinguishment of Debt

FAS-4	Reporting Gains and Losses from Extinguishment of Debt
FAS-6	Classification of Short-Term Obligations Expected to Be Refinanced
FAS-15	Accounting by Debtors and Creditors for Troubled Debt Restructurings
FAS-22	Changes in the Provisions of Lease Agreements Resulting from Refundings of Tax-Exempt Debt
FAS-47	Disclosure of Long-Term Obligations
FAS-49	Accounting for Product Financing Arrangements
FAS-64	Extinguishments of Debt Made to Satisfy Sinking-Fund Requirements
FAS-78	Classification of Obligations That Are Callable by the Creditor
FAS-84	Induced Conversions of Convertible Debt
FAS-91	Accounting for Nonrefundable Fees and Costs Associated with Originating or Acquiring Loans and Initial Direct Costs of Leases
FAS-111	Rescission of FASB Statement No. 32 and Technical Corrections
FAS-114	Accounting by Creditors for Impairment of a Loan
FAS-129	Disclosure of Information about Capital Structure
FAS-140	Accounting for Transfers and Servicing of Financial Assets and Extinguishments of Liabilities
FIN-8	Classification of a Short-Term Obligation Repaid prior to Being Replaced by a Long-Term Security
FIN-39	Offsetting of Amounts Related to Certain Contracts
FTB 79-3	Subjective Acceleration Clauses in Long-Term Debt Agreements
FTB 80-1	Early Extinguishment of Debt through Exchange for Common or Preferred Stock
FTB 80-2	Classification of Debt Restructurings by Debtors and Creditors
FTB 81-6	Applicability of Statement 15 to Debtors in Bankruptcy Situations

DISCLOSURE REQUIREMENTS

Debt Obligations and Credit Arrangements

The following disclosures should be made about debt obligations and credit arrangements:

1. The terms, interest rates, maturity dates, and subordinate features of significant categories of debt (e.g., notes payable to banks, line of credit agreements, related-party notes) (generally accepted disclosure)
2. Any restrictive covenants (e.g., restrictions on additional borrowings, obligations to maintain minimum working capital or restrict dividends) and assets mortgaged, pledged, or otherwise subject to lien (FAS-5, pars. 18–19)
3. If a short-term obligation expected to be refinanced on a long-term basis is excluded from current liabilities (FAS-6, par. 15):
   a. A general description of the financing agreement
   b. The terms of any new obligation incurred or expected to be incurred or equity securities issued or expected to be issued as a result of the refinancing
4. For each of the five years following the date of the latest balance sheet presented (FAS-47, par. 10):
   a. The combined aggregate amount of maturities and sinking fund requirements for all long-term borrowings
   b. The amount of redemption requirements for all issues of capital stock that are redeemable at fixed or determinable prices on fixed or determinable dates, separately by issue or combined
5. The conversion features and descriptions of convertible debt, including the pertinent rights and privileges of the convertible debt (APB-14, pars. 16–18)
6. For debt securities that carry an unreasonable interest rate or are non-interest-bearing (APB-21, par. 16):
   a. The unamortized discount or premium that is reported in the balance sheet as a direct deduction from or as an addition to the face amount of the note
   b. The face amount of the note
   c. The effective interest rate
   d. Amortization of discount or premium reported as interest in the income statement
   e. Related debt issue costs that are reported as deferred charges in the balance sheet
7. If the debtor has violated a provision of a long-term debt agreement at the balance sheet date but classifies the obligation as noncurrent because it is probable (likely) that the violation will be cured within the grace period, the circumstances should be described (FAS-78, par. 5)
8. When events of default under a credit agreement have occurred at any time prior to the date of the accountant's report and have

not been cured or waived or a valid waiver has been obtained for only a stated period of time (SAS-1, AU 560) (EITF 86-30):

   a. The nature and amount of the default

   b. The period for which the violation has been waived

9. Significant changes in long-term obligations subsequent to the date of the financial statements disclosed (FAS-5, par. 11)

Debt Extinguishment

The following disclosures should be made about debt extinguishment:

1. If debt was considered to be extinguished by in-substance defeasance under the provisions of FAS-76, prior to January 1, 1997 (FAS-140, par. 17b):
   a. A general description of the transaction
   b. The amount of debt that is considered extinguished at the end of the period so long as that debt remains outstanding
2. If assets are set aside after January 1, 1997 solely for satisfying scheduled payments of a specific obligation, a description of the nature of restrictions placed on those assets (FAS-140, par. 17c)
3. Gains or losses from extinguishment of debt that are classified as extraordinary items (FAS-4, par. 9)
4. The following information, to the extent not shown separately on the face of the income statement (FAS-4, par. 9):
   a. A description of the extinguishment transactions, including the sources of any funds used to extinguish debt if it is practicable to identify the sources
   b. The income tax effect in the period of extinguishment
   c. If applicable, the per share amount of the aggregate gain or loss, net of related income tax effect

Debt Restructuring

The following disclosures should be made about debt restructuring:

1. For the period in which the debt is restructured (FAS-15, par. 25):
   a. For each restructuring, a description of the principal changes in terms, the major features of settlement, or both
   b. Aggregate gain on restructuring of payables and the related income tax effect

   c. Aggregate net gain or loss on transfers of assets recognized during the period

   d. If applicable, the per share amount of the aggregate gain on restructuring, net of related income tax effect

2. For periods subsequent to the period in which the debt was restructured (FAS-15, par. 26):

   a. The extent to which amounts contingently payable are included in the carrying amount of restructured payables

   b. Total amounts that are contingently payable on restructured payables and the conditions under which those amounts would become payable or would be forgiven when there is at least a reasonable possibility that a liability for contingent payments will be incurred

Unconditional Purchase Obligations

The following disclosures should be made about unconditional purchase obligations:

1. For unconditional purchase obligations that have *not* been recorded (FAS-47, pars. 6–8):

   a. The nature and term of the obligation

   b. The amount of the fixed and determinable portion of the obligation as of the date of the latest balance sheet presented in the aggregate and, if determinable, for each of the five succeeding fiscal years

   c. The nature of any variable components of the obligation

   d. The amounts purchased under the obligation for each period for which an income statement is presented

   e. The amount of imputed interest necessary to reduce the unconditional purchase obligation to its present value (optional)

2. For unconditional purchase obligations that have been recorded, the following disclosures should be made for each of the five years following the date of the latest balance sheet presented (FAS-47, par. 10):

   a. The aggregate amounts of payments for unconditional purchase obligations

   b. The combined aggregate amount of maturities and sinking fund requirements

   c. The amount of redemption requirements for all issues of capital stock that are redeemable at fixed or determinable prices on fixed or determinable dates, separately by issue or combined

Product Financing Arrangements

The disclosure requirements for product financing arrangements are the same as for debt obligations discussed above; there are no additional disclosure requirements that are unique to product financing arrangements.

EXAMPLES OF FINANCIAL STATEMENT DISCLOSURES

The following sample disclosures are available on the accompanying disc. For examples of disclosures of capital lease obligations, see Chapter 18, "Leases."

Short-Term and Long-Term Debt Obligations

Example 40–1: Borrowings under Revolving Line of Credit and Restrictive Covenants

The Company has available a revolving line of credit with a bank for the lesser of (a) $5,000,000, or (b) the sum of 80% of eligible domestic trade accounts receivable and 55% of eligible inventory, as defined. The line of credit expires in November 2001, unless extended. Borrowings under the line of credit bear interest (10.25% at December 31, 2000) at one of the following rates as selected by the Company: LIBOR plus 1% to 2.25%, or the bank's prime rate plus .5%. All borrowings are collateralized by substantially all assets of the Company. The outstanding balance on the line of credit was $4,436,000 and $3,879,00 at December 31, 2000, and December 31, 1999, respectively. Borrowings under the line are subject to certain financial covenants and restrictions on indebtedness, dividend payments, financial guarantees, business combinations, and other related items. As of December 31, 2000, the Company is in compliance with all covenants. Retained earnings available for the payment of cash dividends was $ 657,000 at December 31, 2000.

Example 40–2: Details of Short-Term Debt

Short-term debt consists of the following at December 31, 2000, and December 31, 1999:

	2000	*1999*
Demand note payable to bank, secured by machinery and equipment, interest at 10%	$2,137,000	$1,785,000
Demand notes payable to an entity owned by a majority stockholder, unsecured, interest rates ranging from 8% to 11%	971,000	813,000
Demand note payable to a former stockholder, unsecured, interest at 12%	624,000	674,000
Notes payable to officers with initial maturities of 6 to 12 months, unsecured, interest at 9%	237,000	218,000
	$3,969,000	$3,490,000

Example 40–3: Details of Long-Term Debt

Long-term debt consists of the following at December 31, 2000, and December 31, 1999:

	2000	*1999*
Mortgage note payable to bank in monthly installments of $86,000, including interest at 9.25%, due in December 2011, secured by office building	$7,155,000	$7,514,000
Industrial Revenue Bonds with varying quarterly principal payments due through December 2009, including interest at 85% of the current prime rate (8.72% at December 31, 2000), collateralized by property, plant, and equipment	5,767,000	6,158,000
8% convertible subordinated debentures, due in May 2014 with annual sinking fund requirements of $280,000, convertible into 833,126 shares of common stock at any time prior to maturity	5,160,000	5,440,000
Note payable to bank in quarterly installments of $47,000, including interest at prime plus 1% (10.25% at December 31, 2000), due in August 2007, secured by machinery and equipment	922,000	1,013,000
Note payable to an entity owned by a majority stockholder in semi-annual installments of $75,000, plus interest at 10%, due in April 2005, unsecured	611,000	701,000

	2000	*1999*
Note payable to supplier in monthly installments of $19,000, non-interest bearing (imputed interest of 12%), due in December 2002, secured by equipment, less unamortized discount of $51,000 at December 31, 2000, and $112,000 at December 31, 1999	398,000	565,000
Other	317,000	492,000
Total debt	20,330,000	21,883,000
Less: current portion	(1,636,000)	(1,519,000)
Long-term debt, less current portion	$18,694,000	$20,364,000

Future maturities of long-term debt are as follows as of December 31, 2000:

2001	$ 1,636,000
2002	1,758,000
2003	1,520,000
2004	1,619,000
2005	1,748,000
Thereafter	12,049,000
	$20,330,000

Example 40–4: Debt Issued with Stock Purchase Warrants

In May 2000, the Company sold in a private placement to qualified buyers and accredited investors 10,000 Note Units (the Note Offering). Each Note Unit consisted of $1,000 principal amount of 13.5% unsecured Notes (collectively, the Notes) due May 1, 2007, and one Common Stock Purchase Warrant (collectively the Note Warrants) to purchase 85 shares of the Company's common stock, par value $0.01 per share (the Common Stock), at an exercise price of $3.09 per share, first exercisable after May 20, 2001. Total funds received of $10,000,000 were allocated $2,000,000 to the Note Warrants and $8,000,000 to the Notes. The value allocated to the Note Warrants is being amortized to interest expense over the term of the Notes. At December 31, 2000, the unamortized discount on the Notes is approximately $1,825,000.

Interest on the Notes is payable semi-annually on May 1 and November 1. The Notes will mature on May 1, 2007. The Notes are not redeemable at the option of the Company prior to May 1, 2005.

On or after May 1, 2005, the Notes are redeemable at the option of the Company, in whole or in part, at an initial redemption price of 106.75% of the aggregate principal amount of the Notes until May 1,

2006, and at par thereafter, plus accrued and unpaid interest, if any, to the date of redemption.

Example 40–5: Issuance of Convertible Subordinated Debt

In February 2000, the Company issued $10,000,000 of 9% convertible subordinated notes, due on February 1, 2005. Interest is payable semi-annually in February and August. The notes are convertible by the holders into shares of the Company's common stock at any time at a conversion price of $8.50 per share. The notes are subordinated in right of payment to all existing and future senior indebtedness, as defined in the indenture. The notes are redeemable after February 1, 2003, at the option of the Company at 101.6% of the principal amount, declining to 100.8% of the principal amount on February 1, 2004, and thereafter until maturity, at which time the notes will be redeemed at par, plus accrued interest. The proceeds were primarily used to repay debt under the Company's bank borrowings and for general corporate purposes.

Example 40–6: Long-Term Debt Classified as a Current Liability Due to Covenant Violations

As a result of operating losses, the Company was unable to remain in compliance with the financial covenants arising under substantially all of its long-term note agreements. The creditors have not waived the financial covenant requirements. The Company has been working with the different creditors to restructure the existing debt; however, an agreement satisfactory to the Company has not been reached. A total of $7,856,000 of long-term debt is subject to accelerated maturity and, as such, the creditors may, at their option, give notice to the Company that amounts owed are immediately due and payable. As a result, the full amount of the related long-term debt has been classified as a current liability in the accompanying Balance Sheet at December 31, 2000. Regardless of the non-compliance with financial covenants, the Company has made every scheduled payment of principal and interest.

Example 40–7: Long-Term Debt Classified as a Current Liability Due to Company's Likelihood of Missing Its Next Interest Payment

At December 31, 2000, the long-term portion of the Senior Secured Notes was reclassified to a current liability due to the uncertainty surrounding the Company's ability to make its next interest payment in the approximate amount of $273,000 due in May 2001.

Example 40–8: Long-Term Debt Classified as a Current Liability Because Company Anticipates to Pay Debt within a Year from the Balance Sheet Date

The entire outstanding balance of the industrial revenue bond issue, totaling $2,876,000 at December 31, 2000, has been classified as a current liability as the Company anticipates repaying the entire balance during 2001 upon the sale of the Company's manufacturing facility in Gary, Indiana.

Example 40–9: Short-Term Debt Classified as Long-Term Because Company Has Both Ability and Intent to Refinance the Debt

Commercial paper debt is due within one year, but has been classified as long-term because the Company has the ability through a $25,000,000 credit agreement to convert this obligation into longer term debt. The credit agreement expires in 2003 and provides for interest on borrowings at prevailing rates. The Company intends to refinance the commercial paper debt by replacing them with long-term debt.

Example 40–10: Short-Term Debt Classified as Long-Term Because Proceeds of Long-Term Financing Issued Subsequent to Balance Sheet Date Were Used to Retire the Short-Term Debt

On February 13, 2001, the Company borrowed $1,000,000 from a financial institution at 1% above the prime rate. The loan is secured by inventory and accounts receivable, is payable in quarterly installments of principal and interest, and matures in December 2004. The Company has used a portion of the proceeds to pay off the outstanding balance of the 10% short-term notes payable to a finance company, totaling $473,000 at December 31, 2000. Accordingly, that balance of $473,000 has been classified as long-term debt at December 31, 2000.

Example 40–11: Short-Term Debt Classified as Long-Term Because Proceeds from Sale of Stock Subsequent to Balance Sheet Date Are Expected to Be Used to Retire the Short-Term Debt

On January 28, 2001, the Company sold 300,000 shares of its $.01 par value common stock for $5 per share. Of the total proceeds of $1,500,000, the Company expects to use $695,000 to refinance on a long-term basis the outstanding principal balance of its 11% short-term notes payable to a vendor. Accordingly, the amount of $695,000 has been classified as long-term debt at December 31, 2000.

Example 40–12: Shareholder Demand Loan Classified as Long-Term Debt Due to Loan Covenants That Restrict Payment

At December 31, 2000, and December 31, 1999, the Company's shareholder has advanced $200,000 and $182,000, respectively, to the Company. These loans are represented by three separate demand notes, are unsecured, and carry interest at 10%. Loan covenants and restrictions prohibit the shareholder from receiving any payment on these loans until such time that other loan commitments are satisfied. Accordingly, these shareholder loans are recorded as long-term debt in the accompanying financial statements.

Example 40–13: Bank Waives Noncompliance with Financial Covenants

The Company's credit agreement with the bank contains certain financial covenants that require, among other things, maintenance of minimum amounts and ratios of working capital; minimum amounts of tangible net worth; maximum ratio of indebtedness to tangible net worth; and limits purchases of property, plant and equipment. Certain financial covenants have not been met, and the bank has waived such noncompliance.

Credit Arrangements and Compensating Balances

Example 40–14: Unused Available Line of Credit

The Company has a demand bank line of credit totalling $6,000,000, including letters of credit, under which the Company may borrow on an unsecured basis at the bank's prime rate. There were no amounts outstanding under this line of credit at December 31, 2000, and December 31, 1999. The credit agreement requires compliance with certain financial covenants and expires on April 30, 2002.

Example 40–15: Borrowings under Line of Credit May Be Converted Into a Term Loan

The line of credit agreement allows the Company to convert the borrowing to a term loan for any outstanding amount upon request prior to the expiration of the agreement.

Example 40–16: Factoring Agreement

Pursuant to a factoring agreement, the Company's principal bank acts as its factor for the majority of its receivables, which are assigned on a pre-approved basis. At December 31, 2000, and December 31, 1999, the factoring charge amounted to 0.25% of the receivables assigned. The Company's obligations to the bank are collateralized by all of the Company's accounts receivable, inventories, and equipment. The advances for factored receivables are made pursuant to a revolving credit and security agreement, which expires on March 31, 2002. Pursuant to the terms of the agreement, the Company is required to maintain specified levels of working capital and tangible net worth, among other covenants.

The Company draws down working capital advances and opens letters of credit (up to an aggregate maximum of $10 million) against the facility in amounts determined on a formula that is based on factored receivables, inventory, and cost of imported goods under outstanding letters of credit. Interest is charged at the bank's prime lending rate plus 1% per annum (10.5% at December 31, 2000) on such advances. As of December 31, 2000, the Company was in compliance with the covenants under its revolving credit facility.

Example 40–17: Letters of Credit—Inventory

At December 31, 2000, and December 31, 1999, the Company has outstanding irrevocable letters of credit in the amount of $1,800,000 and $700,000, respectively. These letters of credit, which have terms from two months to one year, collateralize the Company's obligations to third parties for the purchase of inventory. The fair value of these letters of credit approximates contract values based on the nature of the fee arrangements with the issuing banks.

Example 40–18: Letters of Credit—Contracts and Debt Obligations

At December 31, 2000, standby letters of credit of approximately $2,400,000 have been issued under an agreement, expiring September 30, 2001, which is being maintained as security for performance and advances received on long-term contracts and as security for debt service payments under industrial revenue bond loan agreements. The agreement provides a maximum commitment for letters of credit of $3,500,000 and requires an annual commitment fee of $25,000.

Example 40–19: Compensating Balance Requirement Is Based on a Percentage of the Available Line of Credit

As part of its line of credit agreement with a bank, the Company is expected to maintain average compensating cash balances, which are based on a percentage of the available credit line. The amount of compensating balances required at December 31, 2000, was $300,000.

The compensating balances are held under agreements that do not legally restrict the use of such funds and, therefore, the funds are not segregated on the face of the Balance Sheet. The compensating cash balances are determined daily by the bank based upon cash balances shown by the bank, adjusted for average uncollected funds and Federal Reserve requirements. During the year ended December 31, 2000, the Company was in substantial compliance with the compensating balance requirements. Funds on deposit with the bank and considered in the compensating balances are subject to withdrawal; however, the availability of the line of credit is dependent upon the maintenance of sufficient average compensating balances.

Example 40–20: Compensating Balance Requirement Is a Fixed Amount

As part of its line of credit agreement with a bank, the Company has agreed to maintain average compensating balances of $150,000. The balances are not legally restricted as to withdrawal and serve as part of the Company's normal operating cash.

Debt Extinguishment

Example 40–21: Extraordinary Charge from Early Extinguishment of Debt Represents Unamortized Discount and Call Premium

In September 2000, the Company redeemed various outstanding notes and debentures with an aggregate principal value of $2,769,000. The Company paid a premium to the debenture holders, and the transaction resulted in an extraordinary charge. The extraordinary loss of $452,000, net of a tax benefit of $165,000, principally represents the premium paid in connection with the early extinguishment of the debt and unamortized discount. The payments were made out of available cash.

Example 40–22: Extraordinary Charge from Early Extinguishment of Debt Represents Prepayment Penalties and Write-Off of Unamortized Deferred Financing Costs

During August 2000, the Company prepaid the holders of certain privately placed senior notes an aggregate amount of $8,250,000 with proceeds from its Credit Facility. Interest on these privately placed senior notes ranged from 9.50% to 12.50%. In connection with this transaction, the Company was required to pay prepayment penalties of $375,000 and wrote off the remaining unamortized deferred financing costs of approximately $96,000; the total of $471,000 before applicable income tax benefit of $188,000 has been recorded as a net extraordinary loss of $283,000 in the 2000 Statement of Operations.

Debt Restructuring

Example 40–23: Terms of Troubled Debt Modified—Carrying Amount of Troubled Debt Exceeds Future Cash Payments

At December 31, 1999, the Company had a 12% note payable to its primary bank with an outstanding principal balance of $1,756,000, due in December 2005. In September 2000, the Company reached an agreement with the bank to modify the terms of the note, due to cash flow problems experienced by the Company. The bank has agreed to accept a cash payment of $250,000 and installment payments on a note for a total of $900,000 at no interest, due in December 2005. As a result, the amount of the note to the bank was reduced by $606,000 to reflect the revised terms, and an extraordinary gain of $352,000, net of income tax of $254,000, has been included in the Statement of Operations for 2000.

Example 40–24: Terms of Troubled Debt Modified—Future Cash Payments Exceed Carrying Value of Troubled Debt

At December 31, 1999, the Company had an 11% note payable to its primary bank with an outstanding principal balance of $1,500,000, due in December 2001. In September 2000, the Company reached an agreement with the bank to modify the terms of the note, due to cash flow problems experienced by the Company. The bank has agreed to extend the due date of the note until December 2004 and to reduce the interest rate to 9%. The modifications have resulted in an effective interest rate of 8.2% to be applied to the carrying amount of the debt prospectively. Interest expense through the revised maturity date of December 2004 will be reduced accordingly.

Example 40–25: Transfer of Assets and Grant of Equity Interest in Full Settlement of Troubled Debt Restructuring

In March 2000, the Company reached an agreement with its principal vendor to transfer fixed assets and to grant 50,000 shares of the Company's $.01 par value common stock to the vendor in full settlement of a 12% note payable to the vendor due in February 2002. At the date of transfer, the fair market value of the fixed assets and common stock transferred exceeded their carrying value by $179,000; accordingly, an ordinary gain of $179,000 has been included in the Statement of Operations in 2000. At the date of transfer, the carrying value of the debt payable to the vendor exceeded the fair market value of the fixed assets and common stock transferred by $611,000; accordingly, an extraordinary gain of $397,000, net of income tax of $214,000, has been included in the Statement of Operations in 2000.

Example 40–26: Modified Terms of Troubled Debt Restructuring Include Future Contingent Payments

Due to significant cash flow problems, in April 2000 the Company modified the terms of its 10% note payable to a principal vendor with an outstanding balance of $1,618,000, due in quarterly installments through May 2005. The vendor has agreed to (1) accept 2,000,000 shares of the Company's $.01 par value common stock, (2) reduce the required quarterly payments by $35,000 through May 2005, and (3) receive an additional $50,000 annual payment for each year in which the Company's cash flow from operations exceeds $250,0000. As a result of these modifications, the Company recorded an extraordinary gain of $315,000, net of income tax of $170,000, in the Statement of Operations in 2000.

Unconditional Purchase Obligations

Example 40–27: Unconditional Obligation under a Throughput Agreement—Includes Optional Disclosure of Present Value of Required Payments

To secure access to facilities to process high damping rubber compound, the Company has signed a processing agreement with BJ Rubber allowing the Company to submit 150,000 tons for processing annually for 15 years. Under the terms of the agreement, the Company may be required to advance funds against future processing charges if BJ Rubber is unable to meet its financial obligations. The aggregate amount of required payments at December 31, 2000, is as follows:

2001	$215,000
2002	200,000
2003	185,000
2004	175,000
2005	150,000
Thereafter	1,260,000
Total	2,185,000
Less: amount representing interest	(1,487,000)
Present value of required payments	$698,000

In addition, the Company is required to pay a proportional share of the variable operating expenses of the plant. The Company's total processing charges under the agreement for 2000 and 1999 was $289,000 and $266,000, respectively.

Example 40–28: Unconditional Obligation under Take-or-Pay Agreement—Includes Optional Disclosure of Present Value of Required Payments

To assure a long-term supply, the Company has contracted to purchase 20% of the production of microprocessors of Microteks, Inc. through the year 2005 and to make minimum annual payments as follows, whether or not it is able to take delivery:

2001	$5,000,000
2002	5,000,000
2003	4,500,000
2004	4,500,000
2005	4,000,000
Total	23,000,000
Less: amount representing interest	(10,125,000)
Present value of required payments	$12,875,000

In addition, the Company must reimburse Microteks, Inc. for a proportional share of its plant operating expenses. The Company's total purchases under the agreement were $5,769,000 and $5,432,000 in 2000 and 1999, respectively.

Example 40–29: Unconditional Purchase Obligation in Connection with Acquisition—Disclosure of Present Value of Minimum Payments Not Made (Present Value Disclosure Is Optional)

In connection with the EFTX acquisition in January 1999, EFTX and the Company entered into a manufacturing agreement whereby the Company committed to purchase minimum amounts of goods and services used in its normal operations during the first 48 months after the transaction. Future annual minimum purchases remaining under the agreement are $19 million and $22 million for 2001 and 2002, respectively. During 2000 and 1999, the Company's total purchases under the agreement were $17 million and $13 million, respectively.

Product Financing Arrangements

Example 40–30: Obligations and Commitments under Product Financing Arrangement

In 2000, the Company entered into a product financing arrangement with a vendor for the purchase of $13 million of electronic connectors. Accordingly, this inventory and the related short-term debt have been included in the Balance Sheet at December 31, 2000. The vendor has also made commitments, on the Company's behalf, to purchase additional amounts of the electronic connectors for delivery in 2001. The average interest rate on the product financing arrangement was 7.3% at December 31, 2000. Interest expense incurred and paid under this product financing arrangement totaled $186,000 for 2000. The Company is obligated to pay the vendor under this product financing arrangement upon its receipt of the products.

Subsequent Events Involving Debt Obligations and Credit Arrangements

Example 40–31: Subsequent Event—New Financing Arrangement

On January 29, 2001, the Company entered into a Revolving Loan Agreement (the Loan Agreement) with Ace State Bank. The Loan Agreement provides for borrowings through January 31, 2006 (the Maturity Date). Borrowings will bear interest at the bank's prime rate. The maximum amount that may be outstanding under the Loan Agreement is $20,000,000 through December 31, 2002. Thereafter, the maximum amount of borrowings that may be outstanding under the Loan Agreement is reduced by $1,000,000 in calendar 2003 and by $1,000,000 in each of the following calendar years up to the Maturity Date. Under the terms of the Loan Agreement, the Company will pay Ace State Bank $200,000 plus an unused commitment fee during the term of the Loan Agreement. The Company will also pay legal, accounting, and other fees and expenses in connection with the Loan Agreement.

Example 40–32: Subsequent Event—Issuance of Convertible Subordinated Notes

On January 12, 2001, the Company executed an agreement with a group of institutional investors whereby the Company issued $12 million in convertible subordinated loan notes. These notes bear an interest rate of 11% per year and mature in 2003. The Company intends to use the proceeds for general corporate purposes, including working capital and machinery and equipment purchases, and to finance the construction of the Company' s new facility in Dayton, Ohio.

Example 40–33: Subsequent Event—Maximum Borrowing under Line of Credit

In February and March 2001, the Company borrowed $800,000 under its line of credit for working capital purposes. As a result, the Company has borrowed the maximum amount available under the credit line. The Company is negotiating with the bank to increase its credit line limit by $2,000,000. However, there can be no assurance that the Company will be successful in increasing its credit line.

CHAPTER 41
OTHER LIABILITIES: CURRENT AND NONCURRENT

CONTENTS

EXECUTIVE SUMMARY

The most common types of current and noncurrent liabilities are discussed in numerous chapters throughout this book. For example:

- Capital lease obligations are discussed in Chapter 18.
- Obligations relating to pension plans, postemployment benefits, and postretirement benefits are discussed in Chapters 21–23.
- Current and deferred income tax liabilities are discussed in Chapter 39.
- Debt obligations (short-term and long-term debt) are discussed in Chapter 40.

The discussion and examples in this chapter address both current and noncurrent liabilities that have not been covered in other chapters of this book.

Current liabilities may be listed in the balance sheet in order of maturity, according to amount (largest to smallest), or in order of liquidation preference. However, generally, trade accounts payable or short-term debt is listed first and a catchall caption such as "Other liabilities" or "Accrued expenses" is typically listed last. Current liabilities typically include the following:

- Trade accounts payable
- Short-term debt (e.g., notes and loans, including borrowings under line of credit arrangements)
- Current maturities of long-term debt
- Current maturities of capital lease obligations
- Employee related liabilities (e.g., salaries, wages, bonuses, commissions, and related benefits)
- Taxes (e.g., income taxes payable, deferred income taxes, and sales taxes)
- Dividends payable
- Accrued interest
- Customer deposits and advances
- Deferred income
- Accrued expenses (e.g., product warranties, royalties)

Long-term liabilities primarily consist of debt obligations (e.g., bonds, mortgages, notes, and capital leases), deferred income taxes, and a catchall caption such as "Other long-term liabilities."

If several "Other liabilities" type items (current or noncurrent) are included as a single line item in the balance sheet, and the amount is material, it is generally informative to include the details of such items in a note to the financial statements.

Authoritative Literature

ARB-43	Chapter 3A, Current Assets and Current Liabilities
APB-10	Omnibus Opinion—1966
APB-12	Omnibus Opinion—1967

DISCLOSURE REQUIREMENTS

Detail and supplemental information concerning current and noncurrent liabilities should be sufficiently included in the financial statements, or notes thereto, to meet the requirement of adequate informative disclosure. If other liabilities, current or noncurrent, are material to the financial statements, disclosures should include a description of the liability, its carrying value, and the basis of its valuation.

EXAMPLES OF FINANCIAL STATEMENT DISCLOSURES

The following sample disclosures are available on the accompanying disc.

Example 41–1: Details of Other Current Liabilities

> **Note:** Example 41–1 is a comprehensive example of the details of current liabilities provided in a note to the financial statements. It assumes that the items are material and, therefore, have not been grouped. The order in which the items are presented in the note will depend on the individual circumstances, but, generally, the items are presented according to amount (largest to smallest).

Other current liabilities consist of the following at December 31, 2000, and December 31, 1999:

	2000	*1999*
Accrued income taxes	$300,000	$250,000
Gift certificate and credit memo liability	153,000	157,000
Sales tax payable	140,000	132,000
Accrued salaries, wages, and related payroll taxes	120,000	115,000
Deferred revenue	102,000	111,000
Customer deposits	93,000	91,000
Accrued warranties	88,000	83,000

	2000	*1999*
Accrued sales returns and discounts	70,000	78,000
Accrued royalties payable	61,000	68,000
Accrued commissions	59,000	53,000
Accrued profit sharing contribution	46,000	42,000
Accrued insurance	37,000	31,000
Accrued rent	26,000	24,000
Accrued interest	19,000	15,000
Dividends payable	16,000	10,000
	$1,330,000	$1,260,000

Example 41–2: Accrued Product Liability and Warranty Claims

The Company's financial statements include accruals for potential product liability and warranty claims based on the Company's claims experience. Such costs are accrued at the time revenue is recognized. At December 31, 2000, and December 31, 1999, accrued product warranties totaled $373,000 and $419,000, respectively, and are included in "Other current liabilities" in the accompanying Balance Sheets.

Example 41–3: Deferred Revenue

Revenue under maintenance agreements is deferred and recognized over the term of the agreements (typically two years) on a straight-line basis. At December 31, 2000, and December 31, 1999, deferred revenue totaled $556,000 and $471,000, respectively, of which the amount recognizable within one year is included under "Accrued liabilities" in the accompanying Balance Sheets.

Example 41–4: Deferred Rent

The Company has entered into operating lease agreements for its corporate office and warehouse, some of which contain provisions for future rent increases, or periods in which rent payments are reduced (abated). In accordance with generally accepted accounting principles, the Company records monthly rent expense equal to the total of the payments due over the lease term, divided by the number of months of the lease term. The difference between rent expense recorded and the amount paid is credited or charged to "Deferred rent" which is reflected as a separate line item in the accompanying Balance Sheets.

Example 41–5: Accrued Rebates

The Company enters into contractual agreements for rebates on certain products with its customers. These amounts are recorded as a reduction of gross sales to arrive at net sales, and a corresponding accrual is made in the balance sheet. At December 31, 2000, and December 31, 1999, "Accrued expenses" include accrued rebates of $298,000 and $347,000, respectively.

Example 41–6: Accrual for Litigation Based on Company's Best Estimate

The Company is a defendant in a lawsuit, filed by a former supplier of electronic components alleging breach of contract, which seeks damages totaling $750,000. The Company proposed a settlement in the amount of $500,000, based on the advice of the Company's legal counsel, and this amount represents the Company's best estimate for which the litigation will settle. Consequently, $500,000 was charged to operations in 2000 and a corresponding liability has been recorded under "Litigation accrual" as of December 31, 2000, in the accompanying financial statements. However, if the settlement offer is not accepted by the plaintiff and the case goes to trial, the amount of the ultimate loss to the Company, if any, may equal the entire amount of damages of $750,000 sought by the plaintiff.

Example 41–7: Accrual for Lawsuit Settlement Recorded at Present Value of Amount to Be Paid

In October 2000, the Company settled a legal action brought by a group of employees alleging certain discriminatory employment practices by the Company. Under the settlement, the Company has agreed to provide monetary relief in the amount of approximately $2,500,000, to be paid in installments over a five-year period. The present value of the cost of the settlement and estimated additional legal fees, totalling $1,900,000, have been included in results of operations for 2000. At December 31, 2000, the current portion of the liability recorded is approximately $500,000 and is included in "Other current liabilities"; the remaining amount of $1,400,000 is classified as a noncurrent liability under "Lawsuit settlement liability" in the accompanying Balance Sheets.

Example 41–8: Liability under Self-Insured Group Medical Insurance Plan

The Company sponsors a self-insured group medical insurance plan. The plan is designed to provide a specified level of coverage, with stop-loss coverage provided by a commercial insurer. The Company's maximum claim exposure is limited to $35,000 per person per policy year. At December 31, 2000, the Company had 244 employees enrolled in the plan. The plan provides non-contributory coverage for employees and contributory coverage for dependents. The Company's contributions totaled $617,000 in 2000 and $564,000 in 1999.

The Company provides accruals based on the aggregate amount of the liability for reported claims and an estimated liability for claims incurred but not reported. At December 31, 2000, and December 31, 1999, "Other liabilities" include accrued liability related to this plan of $116,000 and $149,000, respectively.

Example 41–9: Accrued Liability Relating to Lease Termination

In September 2000, the Company notified the developer and landlord of its planned future headquarters in Paramount, California, that the Company intends to terminate the project. The Company had previously entered into a 15-year lease agreement for the new site. Although groundbreaking for the new site has not occurred, the Company anticipates that it will incur lease termination costs and related penalties in the amount of $450,000. Consequently, the Company has included under "Other liabilities" an accrual for $450,000 as of December 31, 2000, for estimated lease termination costs.

Example 41–10: Accrued Liability for Estimated Environmental Remediation Costs

The Company is involved in environmental remediation and ongoing compliance at several sites. At December 31, 2000, the Company estimated, based on engineering studies, total remediation and ongoing monitoring costs to be made in the future to be approximately $6,500,000, including the effects of inflation. Accordingly, the Company recorded a liability of approximately $4,000,000, which represents the net present value of the estimated future costs discounted at 6%. This is management's best estimate of these liabilities, although possible actual costs could range up to 50% higher. The Company has not anticipated any third-party payments in arriving at these estimates.

> **Note:** See Chapter 9, "Contingencies, Risks, Uncertainties, and Concentrations," for additional examples regarding accruals for estimated environmental remediation costs.

Example 41–11: Allowances for Contract Losses

Other current liabilities at December 31, 2000, and December 31, 1999, include allowances for contract losses aggregating $512,000 and $390,000, respectively.

Example 41–12: Accrued Loss for Guarantee of Indebtedness of an Affiliate

As of December 31, 2000, the Company accrued a loss of $300,000 for a loan to an insolvent affiliate, which was guaranteed by the Company. The accrued loss amount is included in "Other current liabilities" in the accompanying Balance Sheet.

Example 41–13: Minority Interest in Consolidated Subsidiary

"Minority interest in consolidated subsidiary" represents the minority stockholders' proportionate share of the equity of Nostars, Inc. At December 31, 2000, and December 31, 1999, the Company owned 22% of Nostars, Inc.'s capital stock, representing 75% voting control. The Company's 75% controlling interest requires that Nostars, Inc.'s operations be included in the consolidated financial statements. The 78% equity interest of Nostars, Inc. that is not owned by the Company is shown as "Minority interest in consolidated subsidiary" in the 2000 and 1999 Consolidated Statement of Earnings and Consolidated Balance Sheet.

> **Note:** The following table illustrates the presentation of minority interest in the consolidated balance sheets between the liabilities section and the stockholder's equity section. Whereas minority interests are insignificant and do not warrant a separate classification in the consolidated balance sheets, some entities have disclosed minority interests among other liabilities.

	2000	*1999*
Total current liabilities	$15,000,000	$13,000,000
Long-term debt	6,000,000	5,000,000
Deferred income taxes	1,500,000	2,300,000
Minority interest in consolidated subsidiary	1,100,000	1,400,000
Stockholders' equity	7,600,000	6,900,000
Total liabilities and stockholders' equity	$31,200,000	$28,600,000

Example 41–14: Termination Benefit Payable

At December 31, 2000, the Company has included as a liability the present value, computed with an effective annual rate of 10%, of a death benefit related to the termination of an employment contract as a result of the death of the president in 2000. This termination death benefit will be paid in 36 equal monthly installments of $30,000 commencing in April 2001.

CHAPTER 42
STOCKHOLDERS' EQUITY

CONTENTS

EXECUTIVE SUMMARY

Stockholders' equity includes the following three broad categories:

1. *Contributed capital*—This represents (a) the amounts paid by common and preferred stockholders when they purchased the company's stock and (b) the amounts arising from subsequent transactions such as treasury stock transactions.

2. *Retained earnings*—This represents the amount of previous income of the company that has not been distributed to owners as dividends or transferred to contributed capital.
3. *Accumulated other comprehensive income*—Under current accounting literature, other comprehensive income includes (a) unrealized gains and losses on available-for-sale marketable securities, (b) minimum pension liability adjustments, (c) foreign currency translation adjustments and gains and losses from certain foreign currency transactions, and (d) changes in the market value of certain futures contracts that qualify as a hedge. Components of other comprehensive income are covered in more detail in Chapter 48, "Comprehensive Income," because comprehensive income may be reported in an income statement, in a separate statement of comprehensive income that begins with net income, or in a statement of changes in stockholder's equity.

Generally, the components of stockholders' equity are presented in the following order in the balance sheet:

- Preferred stock
- Common stock
- Additional paid-in capital
- Retained earnings (accumulated deficit)
- Accumulated other comprehensive income (loss)
- Treasury stock

Capital transactions should generally be excluded from the determination of income but should be adequately disclosed in the financial statements.

Capital Stock

Capital stock represents the legal or stated capital provided by stockholders. Capital stock may consist of common or preferred shares. Common stock usually has (a) the right to vote, (b) the right to share in earnings, (c) a preemptive right to a proportionate share of any additional common stock issued, and (d) the right to share in assets on liquidation. Preferred stock carries certain specified preferences or privileges over common stock. For example, preferred shares may be (a) voting or nonvoting, (b) participating or nonparticipating as to the earnings of the corporation, (c) cumulative or noncumulative as to the payment of dividends, (d) callable for redemption at a specified price, or (e) convertible to common stock.

A corporation's charter contains the types and amounts of stock that it can legally issue, which is called the *authorized capital stock*.

When part or all of the authorized capital stock is issued, it is called *issued capital stock.* Because a corporation may own issued capital stock in the form of treasury stock, the amount of issued capital stock in the hands of stockholders is called *outstanding capital stock.*

If capital stock is issued for the acquisition of property and it appears that, at about the same time and pursuant to a previous agreement or understanding, some portion of the stock so issued is donated to the corporation, the par value of the stock is not an appropriate basis for valuing the property. Rather, the property should be recorded at its fair value.

Additional Paid-in Capital

Generally, stock is issued with a par value. No-par value stock may or may not have a stated value. *Par* or *stated value* is the amount that is established in the stock account at the time the stock is issued. When stock is issued above or below par value, a premium or discount on the stock is recorded, respectively. A discount reduces paid-in or contributed capital; a premium increases paid-in or contributed capital. A premium on stock is often referred to as "Additional paid-in capital" or "Paid-in capital in excess of par value." Because the issuance of stock at a discount is not legal in many jurisdictions, discounts on stock are not frequently encountered.

Stock Subscriptions Receivable

A corporation may sell its capital stock by subscriptions. An individual subscriber becomes a stockholder upon subscribing to the capital stock, and, upon full payment of the subscription, a stock certificate evidencing ownership in the corporation is issued. When the subscription method is used to sell capital stock, a subscription receivable account is debited and a capital stock subscribed account is credited. On payment of the subscription, the subscription receivable account is credited and cash or other assets are debited. On the actual issuance of the stock certificates, the capital stock subscribed account is debited and the regular capital stock account is credited.

Stock subscriptions receivable generally should be reported as a deduction from stockholders' equity. They should be shown as an asset only in rare circumstances when the receivables mature in a relatively short period of time and there is substantial evidence of ability and intent to pay.

Treasury Stock

Treasury stock is a company's own capital stock that has been issued and subsequently reacquired. It is ordinarily presented as a reduction in the amount of stockholders' equity. Treasury stock is not considered an asset, because it is widely held that a corporation cannot own part of itself. The status of treasury stock is similar to that of authorized but unissued capital stock. Dividends on a company's own stock are not considered a part of income. Gains and losses on sales of treasury stock should be accounted for as adjustments to capital and not as part of income.

Stock Dividends

A *dividend* is a pro rata distribution by a corporation, based on shares of a particular class, and usually represents a distribution based on earnings. Cash dividends are the most common type of dividend distribution and are recorded on the books of the corporation as a liability (dividends payable) on the date of declaration. Stock dividends are distributions of a company's own capital stock to its existing stockholders in lieu of cash. Stock dividends are accounted for by transferring an amount equal to the fair market value of the stock from retained earnings to paid-in capital.

Stock Splits

When a stock distribution is generally more than 20% to 25% of the outstanding shares immediately before the distribution, it is considered a stock split. A stock split increases the number of shares of capital stock outstanding, and a reverse stock split decreases the number of shares of capital stock outstanding. In both straight and reverse stock splits, the total dollar amount of stockholders' equity does not change. The par or stated value per share of capital stock, however, decreases or increases in proportion with the increase or decrease in the number of shares outstanding.

Dividends-in-Kind

Dividends payable in assets of the corporation other than cash (e.g., marketable securities) are commonly referred to as *dividends-in-kind.* Such dividend distributions of nonmonetary assets to stockholders should be recorded at the fair value of the assets transferred, and a gain or loss should be recognized on the disposition of the asset.

Retained Earnings

If a portion of retained earnings is appropriated for loss contingencies, the appropriation of retained earnings should be shown within the stockholder's equity section of the balance sheet and be clearly identified as an appropriation of retained earnings.

Costs or losses should not be charged to an appropriation of retained earnings, and no part of the appropriation should be transferred to income.

Authoritative Literature

ARB-43	Chapter 1A, Rules Adopted by Membership
	Chapter 1B, Opinion Issued by Predecessor Committee
	Chapter 7B, Stock Dividends and Stock Split-ups
ARB-51	Consolidated Financial Statements
APB-6	Status of Accounting Research Bulletins
APB-10	Omnibus Opinion—1966
APB-12	Omnibus Opinion—1967
APB-14	Accounting for Convertible Debt and Debt Issued with Stock Purchase Warrants
APB-29	Accounting for Nonmonetary Transactions
FAS-5	Accounting for Contingencies
FAS-129	Disclosure of Information about Capital Structure
FTB 85-6	Accounting for a Purchase of Treasury Shares at a Price Significantly in Excess of the Current Market Price of the Shares and the Income Statement Classification of Costs Incurred in Defending against a Takeover Attempt

DISCLOSURE REQUIREMENTS

The following disclosures should be made.

1. For each class of capital stock (generally accepted practice):
   a. Shares authorized, issued, and outstanding
   b. Par value or stated value
   c. The number of shares reserved for future issuance and the purpose for such reservation
2. For preferred stock or other senior stock that has a preference in involuntary liquidation considerably in excess of the par or stated values of the shares (FAS-129, pars. 6–7):
   a. The liquidation preference of the stock (the relationship between the preference in liquidation and the par or stated

value of the shares) (This disclosure should be made in the equity section on the face of the balance sheet, in the aggregate, rather than the notes.)

   b. The aggregate or per-share amounts at which preferred stock may be called or is subject to redemption through sinking-fund operations or otherwise

   c. The aggregate and per-share amounts of arrearages in cumulative preferred dividends

3. The rights and privileges of the various securities outstanding, including (FAS-129, par. 4):
   a. Dividend, liquidation, or call preferences
   b. Participation rights
   c. Call prices and dates
   d. Conversion or exercise prices or rates and pertinent dates
   e. Sinking fund requirements
   f. Unusual voting rights
   g. Significant terms of contracts to issue additional shares

4. The number of shares issued on conversion, exercise, or otherwise during at least the most recent annual fiscal period and any subsequent interim period presented (FAS-129, par. 5)

5. For each of the five years following the date of the latest balance sheet presented, the amount of redemption requirements for all issues of capital stock redeemable at fixed or determinable prices on fixed or determinable dates (FAS-47, par. 10 and FAS-129, par. 8)

6. Dividends declared but not yet paid at the balance sheet (ARB-43, Ch. 3A, par. 7)

7. Restrictions on dividend payments (FAS-5, pars. 18–19)

8. For retained earnings:
   a. Appropriations of retained earnings for loss contingencies separately shown in the stockholders' equity section and clearly identified as such (FAS-5, par. 15)
   b. The nature and extent to which retained earnings is restricted (APB-6, par. 13)

9. For each period in which both a balance sheet and statement of income are presented, the changes in stockholders' equity, including (APB-12, par. 10):
   a. Changes in the separate accounts comprising stockholders' equity
   b. Changes in the number of shares of equity securities during at least the most recent annual fiscal period

10. Stock subscriptions receivable presented as a contra-equity account, or if shown as an asset, the receivable should be clearly labeled and segregated from any other type of asset (generally accepted practice)

11. For treasury stock (APB-6, par. 13):

    a. The method used to account for the treasury stock

    b. The number of shares of treasury stock held

    c. Accounting treatment in accordance with state law if it is at variance with generally accepted accounting principles (GAAP)

12. If treasury stock is acquired for purposes other than retirement (formal or constructive), or if the ultimate disposition has not yet been decided (APB-6, par. 12b):

    a. The cost should be shown separately as a deduction from the total of capital stock, additional paid-in capital, and retained earnings; or

    b. The par value of the shares should be charged to the specific stock issue and the excess of purchase price over the par value should be allocated between additional paid-in capital and retained earnings (alternatively, the excess may be charged entirely to retained earnings).

13. If treasury stock of the entity is shown as an asset, the circumstances for such classification should be adequately disclosed (ARB-43, Ch. 1A, par. 4)

14. If treasury shares are purchased at a stated price significantly in excess of the current market price of the shares, disclosure should include the amounts allocated to other elements of the transaction and the related accounting treatment (FTB 85-6)

15. Capital shares reserved for future issuance in connection with a business combination (APB-16, pars. 78 and 95)

16. If a stock dividend, split, or reverse split occurs after the date of the latest balance sheet presented but before the issuance of the financial statements (generally accepted practice):

    a. An explanation of the stock dividend, split, or reverse split and the date

    b. The retroactive effect provided in the balance sheet

17. For warrants or rights outstanding as of the most recent balance sheet date (generally accepted practice):

    a. The title and aggregate amount of securities called for by warrants or rights outstanding

    b. The period during which warrants or rights are exercisable

    c. The exercise price

EXAMPLES OF FINANCIAL STATEMENT DISCLOSURES

The following sample disclosures are available on the accompanying disc.

Presentation of Components of Stockholders' Equity

Example 42–1: Details of Stockholders' Equity on the Face of the Balance Sheet

	2000	*1999*
Stockholders' Equity:		
3% cumulative preferred stock; par value $.10; authorized 1,000,000 shares; issued and outstanding 200,000 shares in 2000 and 100,000 shares in 1999; aggregate liquidation preference of $2,400,000 in 2000 and $1,200,000 in 1999	$20,000	$10,000
6% convertible preferred stock; par value $.50; authorized 1,000,000 shares; issued and outstanding 400,000 shares in 2000 and 300,000 shares in 1999	200,000	150,000
Class A common stock; par value $.01; authorized 100,000,000 shares; issued and outstanding 15,000,000 shares in 2000 and 13,000,000 shares in 1999	150,000	130,000
Class B common stock; par value $.01; authorized 50,000,000 shares; issued and outstanding 10,000,000 shares in 2000 and 1999	100,000	100,000
Additional paid-in capital	5,475,000	4,692,000
Retained earnings	1,413,000	1,017,000
Accumulated other comprehensive income	80,000	65,000
Less: stock subscriptions receivable	(180,000)	-0-
Less: treasury stock, at cost—150,000 shares in 2000 and 1999	(675,000)	(675,000)
Total stockholders' equity	$6,583,000	$5,489,000

Example 42–2: Statement of Changes in Stockholders' Equity

Note: The following is a comprehensive presentation of changes in components of stockholders' equity shown as a separate statement in the financial statements.

	Preferred Stock		*Common Stock*		*Additional Paid-in Capital*	*Retained Earnings*	*Accumulated Other Compre-hensive Income*	*Stock Subscrip-tions Receivable*	*Treasury Stock*		*Total Stock-holders' Equity*
	Shares	*Amount*	*Shares*	*Amount*					*Shares*	*Amount*	
Balance at December 31, 1998	100,000	$10,000	250,000	$2,500	$418,000	$111,000	$56,000	$(8,000)	(4,000)	$(40,000)	$549,500
Net income	-0-	-0-	-0-	-0-	-0-	316,000	-0-	-0-	-0-	-0-	316,000
Foreign currency adjustment	-0-	-0-	-0-	-0-	-0-	-0-	(27,000)	-0-	-0-	-0-	(27,000)
Unrealized gain on marketable securities	-0-	-0-	-0-	-0-	-0-	-0-	34,000	-0-	-0-	-0-	34,000
Cash dividends ($.16 per share)	-0-	-0-	-0-	-0-	-0-	(58,000)	-0-	-0-	-0-	-0-	(58,000)
Exercise of stock options	-0-	-0-	150,000	1,500	198,500	-0-	-0-	-0-	-0-	-0-	200,000
Repurchase of preferred stock	(20,000)	(2,000)	-0-	-0-	(48,000)	-0-	-0-	-0-	-0-	-0-	(50,000)
Payment received on stock sale	-0-	-0-	-0-	-0-	-0-	-0-	-0-	6,000	-0-	-0-	6,000
Purchase of 10,000 shares	-0-	-0-	-0-	-0-	-0-	-0-	-0-	-0-	(10,000)	(50,000)	(50,000)
Balance at December 31, 1999	80,000	8,000	400,000	4,000	568,500	369,000	63,000	(2,000)	(14,000)	(90,000)	920,500
Net income	-0-	-0-	-0-	-0-	-0-	243,000	-0-	-0-	-0-	-0-	243,000
2 for 1 stock split	-0-	-0-	400,000	4,000	(4,000)	-0-	-0-	-0-	-0-	-0-	-0-
Conversion of 8% debentures	-0-	-0-	100,000	1,000	149,000	-0-	-0-	-0-	-0-	-0-	150,000
Stock issued for acquisition	-0-	-0-	50,000	500	199,500	-0-	-0-	-0-	-0-	-0-	200,000
Stock exchanged for services	-0-	-0-	20,000	200	59,800	-0-	-0-	-0-	-0-	-0-	60,000
Foreign currency adjustment	-0-	-0-	-0-	-0-	-0-	-0-	(11,000)	-0-	-0-	-0-	(11,000)
Unrealized gain on marketable securities	-0-	-0-	-0-	-0-	-0-	-0-	17,000	-0-	-0-	-0-	17,000
Dividends	-0-	-0-	-0-	-0-	-0-	(225,000)	-0-	-0-	-0-	-0-	(225,000)
Balance at December 31, 2000	80,000	$8,000	970,000	$9,700	$972,800	$387,000	$69,000	$(2,000)	(14,000)	$(90,000)	$1,354,500

Capital Stock

Example 42–3: Description of Rights and Privileges of Capital Stock—Capital Structure Consists of Common Stock

At December 31, 2000, the authorized capital of the Company consists of 40,000,000 shares of capital stock comprising 30,000,000 shares of no par common stock and 10,000,000 shares of no par Class A common stock. Both classes of stock have a stated value of $.001 per share. The Class A Common Stock has certain preferential rights with respect to cash dividends and upon liquidation of the Company. In the case of cash dividends, the holders of the Class A Common Stock will be paid one-half cent per share per quarter in addition to any amount payable per share for each share of Common Stock. In the event of liquidation, holders of the Class A Common Stock are entitled to a preference of $1 per share. After such amount is paid, holders of the Common Stock are entitled to receive $1 per share for each share of Common Stock outstanding. Any remaining amount would be distributed to the holders of the Class A Common Stock and the Common Stock on a pro rata basis.

In general, with respect to the election of directors, the holders of Class A Common Stock, voting as a separate class, are entitled to elect that number of directors, which constitutes 25% of the total membership of the board of directors. Holders of common stock, voting as a separate class, are entitled to elect the remaining directors. In all other matters not requiring a class vote, the holders of the Common Stock and the holders of Class A Common Stock vote as a single class provided that holders of Class A Common Stock have one-tenth of a vote for each share held and the holders of the Common Stock have one vote for each share held.

Example 42–4: Description of Rights and Privileges of Capital Stock—Capital Structure Consists of Common and Preferred Stock

The Company has three classes of capital stock: Preferred Stock, Common Stock, and Class B Common Stock. Holders of Common Stock are entitled to one vote for each share held. Holders of Class B Common Stock generally vote as a single class with holders of Common Stock but are entitled to ten votes for each share held. The Common Stock and Class B Common Stock have equal liquidation and dividend rights except that any regular quarterly dividend declared shall be $.05 per share less for holders of Class B Common Stock. Class B Common Stock is nontransferable, except under certain conditions, but may be converted into Common Stock on a share-for-share basis at any time.

The preferred stock has an annual dividend rate of 6% and is cumulative. Preferred stockholders are not entitled to voting privileges except on matters involving liquidation, dissolution, or merger of the Company, in which case they are entitled to one vote for each ten shares held.

Example 42–5: Redemption of Convertible Preferred Stock during the Reporting Period

In December 2000, the Company redeemed all 200,000 outstanding shares of 5.75% Series A Convertible Preferred Stock (the Preferred Stock). The Preferred Stock was issued to certain former shareholders of Mederatus, Inc. as a portion of the total consideration of the Company's 1998 acquisition of Mederatus, Inc. The redemption price per share of stock was $10.40 per share, or $2,080,000 in the aggregate, which included a redemption premium of $.40 per share, or $80,000 in the aggregate. The redemption premium of $80,000 is deducted from net earnings to arrive at net earnings applicable to common shareholders in the accompanying Statements of Operations.

Example 42–6: Conversion of Subordinated Debentures into Common Stock during the Reporting Period

During 2000, $4,500,000 of the Company's $5,000,000 of 6% Convertible Subordinated Debentures due in 2005 were converted into 680,000 shares of the Company's common stock at the conversion price of $10.50 per share. As a result of the conversion, $67,000 of costs associated with the issuance of the debentures was charged against additional paid-in capital.

Example 42–7: Common Stock Reserved for Future Issuance

At December 31, 2000, and December 31, 1999, the Company has reserved 1,389,000 and 1,016,000 shares of its authorized but unissued common stock for possible future issuance in connection with the following:

	2000	*1999*
Exercise and future grants of stock options	660,000	404,000
Exercise of stock warrants	394,000	311,000
Conversion of preferred stock	217,000	183,000
Contingently issuable shares in connection with the XYZ business combination	118,000	118,000
	1,389,000	1,016,000

Example 42–8: Change from Stated to Par Value

On May 1, 2000, the Company was reincorporated in Delaware. As a result, each of the Company's classes of stock was changed from a stated value of $.05 per share to a par value of $.01 per share, resulting in a decrease in common stock and an increase in additional paid-in capital of $235,000. At the same time, the authorized number of shares of common stock was increased from 10 million to 25 million.

Example 42–9: Amendment to Certificate of Incorporation

On October 26, 2000, the Company's stockholders approved an amendment to the Certificate of Incorporation reducing the par value of the Common Stock from $1 to $.01 per share and increasing the number of authorized shares of Common Stock from 1 million to 10 million. As a result of the reduction in par value, the "Common stock" account was reduced by $250,000 and the "Additional paid-in capital" account was increased by the same amount in the accompanying Statement of Stockholders' Equity for 2000.

Example 42–10: Mandatorily Redeemable Preferred Stock

In connection with its acquisition of ABC Company in 1999, the Company sold 30,000 shares of Series B 8.5% Cumulative Redeemable Preferred Stock ("Series B") and warrants to purchase up to 1,800,000 shares of Non-Voting Common Stock at $.01 per share for total consideration of $3,000,000. The number of warrants to be issued was subject to adjustment in the event the Company redeemed all or a portion of the Series B prior to its mandatory redemption date. The Series B was non-voting and was entitled to a liquidation preference of $100 per share plus any unpaid dividends. Dividends are cumulative and accrue at an annual rate of 8.5%. The Series B was redeemable by the Company at its redemption price at any time on or before the mandatory redemption date of December 31, 2003. The redemption price, as defined, equaled the liquidation preference amount plus all accrued and unpaid dividends.

The Company accounted for the Series B as mandatorily redeemable preferred stock. Accordingly, the Company accrued dividends and amortized any discount over the redemption period with a charge to additional paid-in capital (APIC). The Company recorded a discount on the Series B at the time of its issuance for the estimated fair value of the warrants ($1,050,000). The Company valued the maximum amount of warrants that would be issued up to the mandatory redemption date of the Series B as of the acquisition date, January 23, 1999, and the mandatory redemption date, December 31, 2003.

Dividends and accretion on the Series B were $410,000 and $1,070,000 for the years ended December 31, 1999 and 2000, respectively. The Series B were redeemed in August 2000 for $2,600,000. In connection with this early redemption, the Company recorded a one-time charge to APIC of $1,070,000, which represented the difference between the carrying value of the Series B and the redemption value. This amount is included in dividends and accretion in the accompanying financial statements.

Balance Sheet Presentation

	2000	*1999*
Total current liabilities	$15,000,000	$13,000,000
Long-term debt	6,000,000	5,000,000
Deferred income taxes	1,500,000	2,300,000
Mandatorily redeemable preferred stock	-0-	2,360,000
Stockholders' equity	7,600,000	6,900,000
Total liabilities and stockholders' equity	$30,100,000	$29,560,000

Statement of Changes in Stockholders' Equity Presentation

	Preferred Stock		*Common Stock*		*Additional Paid-in*	*Retained*	*Total Stock-holders'*
	Shares	*Amount*	*Shares*	*Amount*	*Capital*	*Earnings*	*Equity*
Balance at December 31, 1998	100,000	$10,000	200,000	$2,000	$2,418,000	$111,000	$2,541,000
Net income	-0-	-0-	-0-	-0-	-0-	316,000	316,000
Cash dividends	-0-	-0-	-0-	-0-	-0-	(58,000)	(58,000)
Exercise of stock options	-0-	-0-	150,000	1,500	198,500	-0-	200,000
Issuance of common stock warrants	-0-	-0-	-0-	-0-	1,050,000	-0-	1,050,000
Dividends and accretion on mandatorily redeemable preferred stock	-0-	-0-	-0-	-0-	(410,000)	-0-	(410,000)
Balance at December 31, 1999	100,000	10,000	350,000	3,500	3,256,500	369,000	3,639,000
Net income	-0-	-0-	-0-	-0-	-0-	243,000	243,000
Dividends and accretion on mandatorily redeemable preferred stock	-0-	-0-	-0-	-0-	(1,070,000)	-0-	(1,070,000)
Stock exchanged for services	-0-	-0-	20,000	200	59,800	-0-	60,000
Balance at December 31, 2000	100,000	$10,000	370,000	$3,700	$2,246,300	$612,000	$2,872,000

Treasury Stock

Example 42–11: Treasury Stock Purchase

In fiscal 1999, the board of directors authorized the purchase of up to 1,200,000 shares of the Company's common stock, which may be used to meet the Company's common stock requirements for its stock benefit plans. In fiscal 2000, the board of directors increased the number of shares of common stock that the Company is authorized to repurchase under this plan by 200,000 shares. During fiscal 2000 and 1999, the Company repurchased 473,000 and 518,000 shares, respectively, at an aggregate cost of $4,565,000 and $3,238,000, respectively.

Example 42–12: Treasury Stock Sale

In October 2000, the Company sold 125,000 shares of common stock previously held in the treasury for $625,000. The aggregate purchase price of the treasury shares sold exceeded the aggregate sales price by $156,000 and has been charged to "Additional paid-in capital."

Receivables from Sale of Stock

Example 42–13: Outstanding Receivables from Sale of Stock Reported as a Reduction of Stockholders' Equity

Notes receivable from stock sales resulting from the exercise of stock options for notes totaled $218,000 and $203,000 at December 31, 2000, and December 31, 1999, respectively, and are reported as a reduction of stockholders' equity. The notes are full recourse promissory notes bearing interest at variable rates ranging from 6.25% to 8.50% and are collateralized by the stock issued upon exercise of the stock options. Interest is payable semi-annually and principal is due from 2001 through 2004.

Options and Warrants

Example 42–14: Repricing of Stock Options

In order to continue to attract and retain employees, the board of directors authorized the repricing of options to purchase shares of common stock effective as of the close of business on September 30, 2000, to the then fair market value of $8.50 per share. Under the terms of the repricing, optionees were required to extend their existing vesting schedules in exchange for the repriced options. All repriced options maintained the same expiration terms. Approximately 700,000 options were repriced under this program, which accounted for approximately 8% of options outstanding as of the effective date. The board of directors and executive officers were excluded from the repricing.

Example 42–15: Warrants Activity for the Period and Summary of Outstanding Warrants

During the years ended December 31, 2000, and December 31, 1999, the board of directors approved the issuance of warrants to purchase an aggregate of 565,000 shares of the Company's common stock. Such warrants are exercisable at prices ranging from $9.50 to $20.625 per share, vest over periods up to 48 months, and expire at various times through April 2009.

During the years ended December 31, 2000, and December 31, 1999, certain warrant holders exercised warrants to purchase 278,000 and 11,000 shares, respectively, of the Company's common stock for an aggregate of $673,000 and $22,000, respectively.

Included in the issuance of warrants to purchase 565,000 aggregate shares of the Company's common stock is a warrant to purchase 50,000 shares that was issued to a director under the terms of a consulting agreement during fiscal 1999. Such issuance was accounted for under Financial Accounting Standards Board Statement No. 123 using the Black-Scholes option pricing model (with the same assumptions as those used for the option), which resulted in the recording of $233,000 and $50,000 in compensation cost during the years ended December 31, 2000, and December 31, 1999, respectively.

A summary of warrant activity for 2000 and 1999 is as follows:

	Number of Warrants	*Weighted Average Exercise Price*	*Warrants Exercisable*	*Weighted Average Exercise Price*
Outstanding, December 31, 1998	427,000	4.44	409,916	$4.13
Granted	350,000	11.95		
Exercised	(11,000)	2.00		
Outstanding, December 31, 1999	766,000	7.42	493,082	4.91
Granted	215,000	17.31		
Exercised	(278,000)	2.42		
Outstanding, December 31, 2000	703,000	12.42	482,166	12.20

At December 31, 2000, the range of warrant prices for shares under warrants and the weighted average remaining contractual life is as follows:

	Warrants Outstanding			Warrants Exercisable	
Range of Warrant Exercise Price	*Number of Warrants*	*Weighted Average Exercise Price*	*Weighted Average Remaining Contractual Life*	*Number Exercisable*	*Weighted Average Exercise Price*
$6.00–9.50	200,000	$ 7.81	5.83	200,000	$ 7.81
11.78–12.81	288,000	11.96	6.01	92,166	12.11
16.88–20.63	215,000	17.31	9.22	190,000	16.88
	703,000			482,166	

Cash and Stock Dividends

Example 42–16: Cash Dividends

On February 16, 2000, the board of directors approved an annual cash dividend for 2000 of $0.03 per share payable on April 15, 2000, to holders of common stock as of close of business on April 1, 2000. Cash dividends paid in 2000 totaled $213,000 and have been charged to retained earnings.

Example 42–17: Stock Dividends

On December 1, 2000, the Company paid a 2% stock dividend to shareholders of record on November 10, 2000. Based on the number of common shares outstanding on the record date, the Company issued 200,000 new shares. The fair market value of the additional shares issued, aggregating $613,000, was charged to retained earnings, and common stock and additional paid-in capital were increased by $2,000 and $611,000, respectively. All references in the accompanying financial statements to the number of common shares and per share amounts are based on the increased number of shares giving retroactive effect to the stock dividend.

Example 42–18: Dividends in Arrears Deferred

Payments of annual dividends for 2000 and 1999 were deferred by the Company's board of directors on the outstanding preferred stocks because of losses sustained by the Company. As of December 31, 2000, preferred dividends in arrears amounted to $400,000, or $2 per share, on the 5% Cumulative Preferred Stock.

Example 42–19: Dividends in Arrears Paid in Amended New Shares of Preferred Stock

Prior to November 1998, dividends with respect to the Series A Preferred Stock were in arrearage. Effective November 10, 1998, the Series A Preferred Stock was amended, reclassified, and converted to Amended Series A Preferred Stock. As a consequence of such consent, all dividend arrearages, and accrued and unpaid dividends were paid in additional shares of Amended Series A Preferred Stock.

Dividends-in-Kind

Example 42–20: Dividend-in-Kind Consists of a Spin-Off of a Business Segment

In May 2000, the Company announced plans to spin off its electronic connectors business to shareholders in a tax-free distribution. In August 2000, the Company's board of directors approved the spin-off effective December 31, 2000, to shareholders of record as of December 17, 2000, through the issuance of shares in a new legal entity, Electors, Inc. Common shares were distributed on a basis of one share of Electors, Inc. for every five shares of the Company's common stock.

The consolidated financial results of the Company have been restated to reflect the divestiture of Electors, Inc. Accordingly, the revenues, costs, and expenses; assets and liabilities; and cash flows of Electors, Inc. have been excluded from their respective captions in the Consolidated Statements of Income, Consolidated Balance Sheets, and Consolidated Statements of Cash Flows. These items have been reported as "Income from discontinued operations, net of income taxes" in the Consolidated Statements of Income; "Net assets of discontinued operations" in the Consolidated Balance Sheets; and "Net cash flows from discontinued operations" and "Net investing and financing activities of discontinued operations" in the Consolidated Statements of Cash Flows.

As of December 31, 2000, the net assets of the discontinued segment of $4,289,000 have been charged against the Company's retained earnings to reflect the spin-off. During 2000, the Company recorded a pretax charge of $615,000 ($483,000 after taxes) for expenses related to the spin-off.

The following table summarizes financial information for the discontinued operations for all periods presented:

	2000	*1999*
Net sales	$8,300,000	$8,750,000
Income before income taxes	$211,000	$273,000
Net income	$107,000	$182,000
Current assets	$2,436,000	$2,543,000
Total assets	$8,161,000	$8,615,000
Current liabilities	$2,597,000	$1,796,000
Total liabilities	$3,872,000	$3,978,000
Net assets of discontinued operations	$4,289,000	$4,637,000

Stock Splits

Example 42–21: Stock Split During the Reporting Period

On January 30, 2000, the Company's board of directors declared a two-for-one stock split, effected in the form of a stock dividend, on the shares of the Company's common stock. Each shareholder of record on February 20, 2000, received an additional share of common stock for each share of common stock then held. The stock was issued March 19, 2000. The Company retained the current par value of $.01 per share for all shares of common stock. All references in the financial statements to the number of shares outstanding, per share amounts, and stock option data of the Company's common stock have been restated to reflect the effect of the stock split for all periods presented.

Stockholders' equity reflects the stock split by reclassifying from "Additional paid-in capital" to "Common stock" an amount equal to the par value of the additional shares arising from the split.

Example 42–22: Stock Split Subsequent to the Balance Sheet Date

On February 18, 2001, subsequent to the date of the report of independent auditors, the Company's board of directors authorized a two-for-one split of the common stock effected in the form of a 100% stock dividend to be distributed on or about March 31, 2001, to holders of record on March 5, 2001. Accordingly, all references to numbers of common shares and per share data in the accompanying financial statements have been adjusted to reflect the stock split on a retroactive basis. The par value of the additional shares of common stock issued in connection with the stock split will be credited to "Common stock" and a like amount charged to "Additional paid-in-capital" in 2001.

Other Comprehensive Income

Example 42–23: Components of Other Comprehensive Income and Accumulated Other Comprehensive Income

> **Note:** See Chapter 48, "Comprehensive Income," for additional examples of disclosures regarding comprehensive income.

The pretax, tax, and after-tax effects of the components of other comprehensive income (loss) for 2000 and 1999 are as follows:

	Pretax	*Tax*	*After-tax*
2000			
Unrealized gains on available-for-sale securities	$102,000	$(43,000)	$59,000
Foreign currency translation adjustment	(23,000)	-0-	(23,000)
Minimum pension liability adjustment	(193,000)	81,000	(112,000)
Other comprehensive income (loss)	$(114,000)	$38,000	$(76,000)
1999			
Unrealized gains on available-for-sale securities	$357,000	$(140,000)	$217,000
Foreign currency translation adjustment	(130,000)	-0-	(130,000)
Minimum pension liability adjustment	(46,000)	18,000	(28,000)
Other comprehensive income (loss)	$181,000	$(122,000)	$59,000

Balances of related after-tax components comprising accumulated other comprehensive income (loss), included in stockholders' equity, at December 31, 2000, and December 31, 1999, are as follows:

	December 31	
	2000	*1999*
Unrealized gains on available-for-sale securities	$311,000	$252,000
Foreign currency translation adjustment	(176,000)	(153,000)
Minimum pension liability adjustment	(256,000)	(144,000)
Accumulated other comprehensive income (loss)	$(121,000)	$(45,000)

Stock Purchase Buy/Sell Agreement

Example 42–24: Stock Purchase Agreement between Company and Stockholders

The Company has entered into an agreement with its stockholders whereby, upon the death of a stockholder, the Company is obligated to purchase all of the decedent's outstanding shares. The purchase price is determined based on a formula provided in the agreement. Under the current formula, the obligation ranges between $450,000 and $2,675,000 at December 31, 2000. The obligation is required to be paid with at least 25% cash and a promissory note for the balance payable over three years.

Part III—
Income Statement

CHAPTER 43
REVENUES AND GAINS

CONTENTS

EXECUTIVE SUMMARY

Generally accepted accounting principles (GAAP), as well as recognized industry practices, generally call for revenue recognition at the point of sale. Revenue usually is recognized when the earning process is complete and an exchange has taken place. The earning process is not complete until collection of the sales price is reasonably assured. The installment method of recognizing revenue is not acceptable unless collection of the sale price is *not* reasonably estimated or assured.

Revenue from sales transactions in which the buyer has a right to return the product should be recognized at time of sale only if *all* of the following conditions are met:

1. The price between the seller and the buyer is substantially fixed or determinable.
2. The seller has received full payment, or the buyer is indebted to the seller and the indebtedness is not contingent on the resale of the merchandise.

3. Physical destruction, damage, or theft of the merchandise would not change the buyer's obligation to the seller.
4. The buyer has economic substance and is not a front or conduit existing for the benefit of the seller.
5. No significant obligations exist for the seller to help the buyer resell the merchandise.
6. A reasonable estimate can be made of the amount of future returns.

If all of the above conditions are met, revenue is recognized on sales for which a right of return exists, provided that an appropriate provision is made for costs or losses that may occur in connection with the return of merchandise from the buyer. If those conditions are not met, revenue recognition should be postponed.

Revenue from the sale of separately priced extended warranty and product maintenance contracts should be deferred and generally recognized in income on a straight-line basis. Costs that are directly related to the acquisition of those contracts are deferred and charged to expense in proportion to the revenue recognized. All other costs are charged to expense as incurred.

Gains are increases in equity (net assets) from peripheral or incidental transactions of an entity and from all other transactions and other events and circumstances affecting the entity during a period, except those that result from revenues or investments by owners. The most common types of gains are discussed in numerous chapters throughout this book. For example:

- Gain contingencies are covered in Chapter 9.
- Foreign exchange gains are covered in Chapter 14.
- Gains resulting from marketable securities and other investments are covered in Chapters 34 and 35.

Authoritative Literature

ARB-43	Chapter 1A, Rules Adopted by Membership
APB-10	Omnibus Opinion—1966
FAS-48	Revenue Recognition When Right of Return Exists
FTB 90-1	Accounting for Separately Priced Extended Warranty and Product Maintenance Contracts

DISCLOSURE REQUIREMENTS

There are no specific disclosures about revenues that are prescribed by authoritative literature, except as follows:

1. Significant amounts of discounts, returns, and allowances are generally disclosed (generally accepted practice).
2. Sales with significant rights of return should be excluded from the income statement and disclosed, if significant (FAS-48, pars. 3–7).

Pronouncements covered in other chapters of this book may require specific disclosures about revenues or gains related to specific types of transactions (e.g., revenues related to long-term contracts, as discussed in Chapter 19; gains on sale of marketable securities and other investments, as discussed in Chapters 34 and 35).

EXAMPLES OF FINANCIAL STATEMENT DISCLOSURES

Most of the disclosures that are typically associated with revenues and gains are covered throughout this book. Individual chapters should be consulted for specific disclosure requirements and examples of financial statement disclosures. This chapter provides only examples of disclosures relating to revenues and gains that are not covered elsewhere in this book. For additional information, see the following chapters:

- Chapter 1, "Accounting Changes," for changes in revenue recognition methods
- Chapter 2, "Accounting Policies," for revenue recognition policies and concentrations in sources of revenues
- Chapter 9 "Contingencies, Risks, Uncertainties, and Concentrations," for concentrations in accounts receivable, concentrations in sources of revenue, and gains from litigation
- Chapter 14, "Foreign Operations and Currency Translation," for revenues and gains resulting from foreign operations
- Chapter 18, "Leases," for revenues from leasing transactions
- Chapter 19, "Long-Term Contracts," for revenues under long-term contracts
- Chapter 25, "Related Party Disclosures," for revenues and gains resulting from transactions with related parties
- Chapter 27, "Segment Information," for revenues by major business segments
- Chapter 32, "Accounts and Notes Receivable," for balance sheet accounts arising from various revenue sources
- Chapter 34, "Investments: Debt and Equity Securities," for gains on sale of marketable securities
- Chapter 35, "Investments: Equity and Cost Methods," for earnings from investees accounted for under the equity method

- Chapter 45, "Discontinued Operations," for revenues and gains applicable to discontinued operations
- Chapter 46, "Extraordinary Items," for extraordinary gains

The following sample disclosures are available on the accompanying disc.

Example 43–1: Revenue Recognition Policy for a Manufacturing Company

Revenues are recorded when products are shipped to customers or, in instances where products are configured to customer requirements, upon the successful completion of the Company's final test procedures. The Company is generally not contractually obligated to accept returns, except for defective product. However, the Company may permit its customers to return or exchange products and may provide pricing allowances on products unsold by a customer. Revenue is recorded net of an allowance for estimated returns, price concessions, and other discounts. Such allowance is reflected as a reduction to accounts receivable when the Company expects to grant credits for such items; otherwise, it is reflected as a liability.

Example 43–2: Revenue Recognition Policy for Royalties

Royalty revenue is recognized by the Company upon fulfillment of its contractual obligations and determination of a fixed royalty amount or, in the case of ongoing royalties, upon sale by the licensee of royalty-bearing products, as estimated by the Company.

Example 43–3: Components of Other Income Disclosed in a Note to the Financial Statements

The components of other income for the years ended December 31, 2000, and December 31, 1999, are as follows:

	2000	*1999*
Interest income	$161,000	$143,000
Gain on sale of fixed assets	78,000	37,000
Royalties	45,000	41,000
Rental income	63,000	58,000
Miscellaneous other income	18,000	22,000
Total other income	$365,000	$301,000

Example 43–4: Other Income Resulting from Termination of License Agreement

Other revenues for the year ended December 31, 2000, includes a gain of $473,000 related to the termination of a license agreement, net of charges for related equipment write-offs and capacity adjustments, under which the Company had produced plastic multipack carriers for beverage cans.

Example 43–5: Income from Life Insurance Proceeds

Due to the death of the Company's president and chief executive officer in February 2000, the Company realized non-taxable income from life insurance proceeds in the amount of $1,243,000, which is separately stated in the Statement of Operations for the year ended December 31, 2000.

Example 43–6: Gain from Sale of Assets

In October 2000, the Company sold its manufacturing plant building in Boise, Idaho, for $2,374,000. The net pretax gain from the sale was $1,693,000 and is included in "Gain from sale of assets" in the 2000 Statement of Operations.

Example 43–7: Reclassifications of Revenue Items

Previously, the Company classified as sales revenue amounts charged on sales invoices for delivery of its products, and related delivery expense was included in cost of sales. Commencing in 2000, the Company is classifying delivery revenue as a reduction of delivery expense. Prior net sales and cost of sales have been reclassified accordingly for comparative periods presented in the accompanying financial statements. This change in classification has no effect on previously reported net income.

CHAPTER 44
EXPENSES AND LOSSES

CONTENTS

EXECUTIVE SUMMARY

Accounting literature recognizes two basic types of expenses: direct and indirect. *Direct expenses* are those that are clearly associated with the production of revenue during a period or with the production of assets held for future sale (e.g., inventories). *Indirect expenses* are all other costs, such as selling and administrative expenses.

Losses are decreases in equity (net assets) from peripheral or incidental transactions of an entity and from all other transactions and other events and circumstances affecting the entity during a period, except those that result from expenses or distributions to owners.

Disclosures that are typically associated with expenses and losses are covered throughout this book. Individual chapters, such as the following, should be consulted for specific disclosure requirements and examples of financial statement disclosures:

- Chapter 1, "Accounting Changes," for changes in recognition methods for costs and expenses
- Chapter 2, "Accounting Policies," for general accounting policies for expenses
- Chapter 3, "Advertising Costs," for capitalized and expensed advertising costs
- Chapter 7, "Compensated Absences," for vacation pay and sick pay expense
- Chapter 9, "Contingencies, Risks, Uncertainties, and Concentrations," for concentrations in accounts payable, purchases from vendors, and loss contingencies
- Chapter 14, "Foreign Operations and Currency Translation," for expenses and losses resulting from foreign operations
- Chapter 16, "Interest Cost," for interest capitalized, expensed, and paid
- Chapter 18, "Leases," for rental expense

- Chapter 19, "Long-Term Contracts," for cost recognition methods under long-term contracts
- Chapter 21, "Pension Plans,"; Chapter 22, "Postemployment Benefits,"; and Chapter 23, "Postretirement Benefits Other Than Pensions," for pension and other retirement related costs
- Chapter 25, "Related Party Disclosures," for expenses and losses resulting from transactions with related parties
- Chapter 26, "Research and Development Costs," for expense and capitalization of research and development costs
- Chapter 27, "Segment Information," for revenues by major business segments
- Chapter 28, "Stock-Based Compensation, Stock Option Plans, and Stock Purchase Plans," for compensation expense in connection with such plans
- Chapter 34, "Investments: Debt and Equity Securities," for losses on sale of marketable securities
- Chapter 35, "Investments: Equity and Cost Methods," for losses from investees accounted for under the equity method
- Chapter 36, "Property, Plant, and Equipment," for depreciation expense and impairment losses related to fixed assets
- Chapter 37, "Intangible Assets," for amortization expense and impairment losses related to intangible assets, including goodwill
- Chapter 39, "Income Taxes," for current and deferred income tax expense
- Chapter 45, "Discontinued Operations," for expenses and losses applicable to discontinued operations
- Chapter 46, "Extraordinary Items," for extraordinary losses

CHAPTER 45
DISCONTINUED OPERATIONS

CONTENTS

EXECUTIVE SUMMARY

Discontinued operations result from the disposal of identifiable segments of a business. *Identifiable segments* of a business are components that represent a major class of a firm's business, usually taking the form of a subsidiary, division, department, or other identifiable entity. Segments of a business have separate assets and results of operations and activities that can be distinguished clearly for financial reporting purposes. Facts that indicate there is no separate identity suggest that the disposal of that part of the business should not be classified as a segment of a business for purposes of discontinued operations accounting.

An estimate of the gain or loss that ultimately will result from the disposal of a segment of a business is made at the measurement date, based on estimates of the net realizable value. If a loss is expected from the discontinuance of a business segment, the estimated loss should be provided for as of the measurement date. If a gain is expected, it should be recognized when realized.

Operations of a segment that have been or will be discontinued should be reported separately as a component of income before extraordinary items and the cumulative effect of accounting changes, if applicable. Discontinued operations are presented in two parts: (1) income or loss from operations of the discontinued segment and (2) gain or loss on disposal. Each component should be presented net of tax.

Authoritative Literature

APB-9	Reporting the Results of Operations
APB-30	Reporting the Results of Operations—Reporting the Effects of Disposal of a Segment of a Business, and Extraordinary, Unusual, and Infrequently Occurring Events and Transactions
FAS-16	Prior Period Adjustments

DISCLOSURE REQUIREMENTS

The following disclosures are required for discontinued operations:

1. Results of discontinued operations reported separately from continuing operations, net of income taxes (APB-30, par. 8)
2. Gains or losses from disposal of a segment of a business reported separately from continuing operations, net of income taxes (APB-30, par. 8)
3. The results of operations of a segment that has been or will be discontinued reported separately as a component of income before extraordinary items and the cumulative effect of accounting changes using the following captions (APB-30, par. 8):
    a. Income from continuing operations before income taxes
    b. Provision for income taxes
    c. Income from continuing operations
    d. Income (loss) from operations of discontinued segment (less applicable income taxes)

   e. Loss on disposal of discontinued segment, including provisions for operating losses during phase-out period (less applicable income taxes)

4. Revenues applicable to the discontinued operations (APB-30, par. 8)
5. The following disclosures should be made for the period encompassing the measurement date (APB-30, par. 18):
   a. The identity of the segment of business that has been or will be discontinued
   b. The expected disposal date, if known
   c. The expected manner of disposal
   d. A description of the remaining assets and liabilities of the segment at the balance sheet date
   e. The income or loss from discontinued operations and any proceeds from disposal of the segment during the period from the measurement date to the date of the balance sheet
6. The following disclosures should be made for years subsequent to the measurement date that include the period of disposal (APB-30, par. 18):
   a. Identification of the segment of business that has been discontinued
   b. The disposal date
   c. The manner of disposition
   d. A description of the remaining assets and liabilities, if any, of the segment at the balance sheet date
   e. The income or loss from discontinued operations and any proceeds from disposal of the segment during the period from the measurement date to the date of the balance sheet compared with prior estimates
7. The following disclosures should be made for each adjustment in the current period of a loss on disposal of a business segment that was reported in a prior period (APB-30, par. 25; FAS-16, par. 6):
   a. The year of origin, nature, and amount
   b. The adjustment classified separately in the current period as a gain or loss on disposal of a segment

EXAMPLES OF FINANCIAL STATEMENT DISCLOSURES

The following sample disclosures are available on the accompanying disc.

Example 45-1: Presentation of Discontinued Operations in an Income Statement That Does Not Include Extraordinary Items or Cumulative Effect of Accounting Change

	2000	1999
Income from continuing operations before income taxes	$2,078,000	$2,774,000
Provision for income taxes	(874,000)	(1,138,000)
Income from continuing operations	1,204,000	1,636,000
Discontinued operations:		
Income (loss) from operations of discontinued segment, net of income tax benefit of $134,000 in 2000 and expense of $241,000 in 1999	(318,000)	473,000
Estimated loss on disposal of business segment, including provision of $217,000 for operating losses during phase-out period, less applicable income taxes of $181,000	(412,000)	-0-
Net income	$474,000	$2,109,000

Example 45–2: Presentation of Discontinued Operations in an Income Statement That Includes Extraordinary Item or Cumulative Effect of Accounting Change

	2000	1999
Income from continuing operations before income taxes	$2,078,000	$2,774,000
Provision for income taxes	(874,000)	(1,138,000)
Income from continuing operations	1,204,000	1,636,000
Discontinued operations:		
Income (loss) from operations of discontinued segment, net of income tax benefit of $134,000 in 2000 and expense of $241,000 in 1999	(318,000)	473,000
Estimated loss on disposal of business segment, including provision of $217,000 for operating losses during phase-out period, less applicable income taxes of $181,000	(412,000)	-0-
Income before extraordinary item and cumulative effect of accounting change	474,000	2,109,000
Extraordinary item—Gain on early extinguishment of debt, net of income tax expense of $1,487,000	2,231,000	-0-
Income before cumulative effect of accounting change	2,705,000	2,109,000

Cumulative effect on prior years of change in accounting for product maintenance contracts, net of tax effect of $878,000	(1,356,000)	-0-
Net income	$1,349,000	$2,109,000

Example 45–3: Description of Discontinued Operations for the Period Encompassing the Measurement Date

> **Note:** For Example 45–3, assume the following: the measurement date is September 1,2000; the expected disposal date is June 1, 2001; the Company's year end is December 31; and comparative financial statements are presented for 2000 and 1999. See Example 45–1 for the presentation of the discontinued operations on the face of the income statement.

On September 1, 2000, the Company determined to discontinue operations at its Paramount division, a manufacturer of electronic power systems, and put the assets and business up for sale. The expected disposal date is June 1, 2001. Paramount's sales for the years ended December 31, 2000, and December 31, 1999, were $7,359,000 and $6,986,000, respectively. In conjunction with the discontinuance of operations, the Company recorded a provision for disposition of $412,000 (net of income tax benefit of $181,000) for costs estimated to be incurred prior to Paramount's disposition, including $217,000 for expected operating losses during the phase-out period from September 1, 2000, through June 1, 2001. Approximately $83,000 of the expected operating loss was incurred in 2000. The results of Paramount's operations have been reported separately as discontinued operations in the Statements of Operations. Prior year financial statements for 1999 have been restated to present the operations of the Paramount division as a discontinued operation.

The net assets of the discontinued operations have been recorded at their estimated net realizable value under the caption "Net assets of discontinued operations" in the accompanying Balance Sheets at December 31, 2000, and December 31, 1999, and consist of the following:

	2000	*1999*
Accounts receivable	$ 403,000	$ 488,000
Inventories	622,000	723,000
Property and equipment, net	1,954,000	1,995,000
Other assets	123,000	100,000
Total assets	3,102,000	3,306,000
Accounts payable	862,000	1,156,000
Accrued liabilities	134,000	221,000
Total liabilities	996,000	1,377,000
Net assets of discontinued operations	$2,106,000	$ 1,929,000

Example 45–4: Description of Discontinued Operations for the Period Encompassing the Disposal Date

> **Note:** For Example 45–4, assume the same facts as in Example 45–3, but the financial statements presented are for the years ended December 31, 2001 (the year of disposal), and December 31, 2000.

On September 1, 2000, the Company determined to discontinue operations at its Paramount division, a manufacturer of electronic power systems, and put the assets and business up for sale. On June 1, 2001, the Company completed the sale of this division for a total cash proceeds of $1,730,000. The assets sold consisted primarily of accounts receivable, inventories, property and equipment, and other assets. The buyer also assumed certain accounts payable and accrued liabilities.

In 2000, the Company estimated a loss on the disposal of Paramount of $412,000 (net of income tax benefit of $181,000), which included $217,000 for expected operating losses during the phase-out period from September 1, 2000, through June 1, 2001. Approximately $83,000 of the expected operating loss was incurred in 2000. Actual operating losses of Paramount during the period from January 1, 2001, through May 31, 2001, exceeded the estimate by $50,000 (net of income tax benefit of $30,000), and the actual loss on the sale of net assets exceeded the estimate by $60,000 (net of income tax benefit of $36,000). Accordingly, the accompanying Statement of Operations for 2000 includes an additional loss of $110,000.

Paramount's sales for the five months ended May 31, 2001, and for the year ended December 31, 2000, were $2,863,000 and $7,359,000, respectively.

The following is a summary of the net assets sold as initially estimated at December 31, 2000, and as finally reported on the closing date of June 1, 2001:

	June 1, 2001	*December 31, 2000*
Accounts receivable	$387,000	$403,000
Inventories	602,000	622,000
Property and equipment, net	1,904,000	1,954,000
Other assets	100,000	123,000
Total assets	2,993,000	3,102,000
Accounts payable	858,000	862,000
Accrued liabilities	125,000	134,000
Total liabilities	983,000	996,000
Net assets of discontinued operations	$2,010,000	$2,106,000

Note: The following table illustrates the reporting of the discontinued operations on the face of the Statements of Operations for years subsequent to the measurement date (i.e., 2000), including the period of disposal (i.e., 2001).

	2001	*2000*
Income from continuing operations before income taxes	$1,814,000	$2,078,000
Provision for income taxes	(6711,000)	(874,000)
Income from continuing operations	1,143,000	1,204,000
Discontinued operations:		
Loss from operations of discontinued segment, net of income tax benefit of $134,000	-0-	(318,000)
Loss on disposal of business segment, including provision of $217,000 in 2000 for operating losses during phase-out period, net of income tax benefits of $66,000 in 2001 and $181,000 in 2000	(110,000)	(412,000)
Net income	$1,033,000	$474,000

Example 45–5: Spin-Off of a Business Segment during the Reporting Period

In May 2000, the Company announced plans to spin off its electronic connectors business to shareholders in a tax-free distribution. In August 2000, the Company's board of directors approved the spin-off effective December 31, 2000, to shareholders of record as of December 17, 2000, through the issuance of shares in a new legal entity, Electors, Inc. Common shares were distributed on a basis of one share of Electors, Inc. for every five shares of the Company's common stock.

The consolidated financial results of the Company have been restated to reflect the divestiture of Electors, Inc. Accordingly, the revenues, costs, and expenses; assets and liabilities; and cash flows of Electors, Inc. have been excluded from their respective captions in the Consolidated Statements of Income, Consolidated Balance Sheets, and Consolidated Statements of Cash Flows. These items have been reported as "Income from discontinued operations, net of income taxes" in the Consolidated Statements of Income; "Net assets of discontinued operations" in the Consolidated Balance Sheets; and "Net cash flows from discontinued operations" and "Net investing and financing activities of discontinued operations" in the Consolidated Statements of Cash Flows.

As of December 31, 2000, the net assets of the discontinued segment of $4,289,000 have been charged against the Company's retained earnings to reflect the spin-off. During 2000, the Company recorded a pre-tax charge of $615,000 ($483,000 after taxes) for expenses related to the spin-off.

The following table summarizes financial information for the discontinued operations for all periods presented:

	2000	*1999*
Net sales	$8,300,000	$8,750,000
Income before income taxes	$211,000	$273,000
Net income	$107,000	$182,000
Current assets	$2,436,000	$2,543,000
Total assets	$8,161,000	$8,615,000
Current liabilities	$2,597,000	$1,796,000
Total liabilities	$3,872,000	$3,978,000
Net assets of discontinued operations	$4,289,000	$4,637,000

Example 45–6: Adjustment of Loss Reported in Prior Period on Discontinued Operations

In 1999, the Company sold all of the assets, net of certain liabilities, associated with its Stretchflex product line. The estimated loss on disposal of this segment recorded in 1999 was $940,000 (net of income tax benefit of $576,000). In 2000, the Company revised its estimated loss on disposal of the segment by $200,000 for the estimated loss on a note received in connection with the sale. A tax benefit was not recorded on this loss in 2000 due to limitations on current tax recognition.

Note: The following table illustrates the reporting of the adjustment of loss on the face of the Statements of Operations.

	2000	*1999*
Income from continuing operations before income taxes	$1,563,000	$1,832,000
Provision for income taxes	(601,000)	(658,000)
Income from continuing operations	962,000	1,174,000
Discontinued operations:		
Income from operations of discontinued segment, net of income tax expense of $382,000	-0-	609,000
Estimated loss on disposal of business segment, net of income tax benefit of $576,000 in 1999	(200,000)	(940,000)
Net income	$762,000	$843,000

Example 45–7: Subsequent Event—Discontinued Operations

On January 24, 2001, the Company signed a definitive agreement to sell its Aquatech retail and wholesale distribution business unit. The Company anticipates the sale to be completed by June 30, 2001. The results of operations of Aquatech have been reported separately as discontinued operations. Prior year financial statements have been restated to present the operations of Aquatech as a discontinued operation. The loss on disposal, net of income tax benefits of $450,000, is estimated to be $871,000 and is recorded in the accompanying Statement of Operations for 2000. Aquatech's revenues were $6,750,000 and $5,936,000 for 2000 and 1999, respectively.

For financial reporting purposes, the assets and liabilities of Aquatech to be sold have been classified in the accompanying Balance Sheets as of December 31, 2000, and December 31, 1999, under "Assets of discontinued operations held for sale" and comprise the following:

	2000	*1999*
Assets:		
Accounts receivable	$637,000	$418,000
Inventories	3,570,000	2,913,000
Other current assets	37,000	22,000
Property, plant and equipment, net	1,322,000	1,174,000
Other assets	62,000	65,000
Total assets	5,628,000	4,592,000
Liabilities:		
Accounts payable	1,698,000	1,996,000
Accrued liabilities	211,000	678,000
Other noncurrent liabilities	35,000	47,000
Total liabilities	1,944,000	2,721,000
Assets of discontinued operations held for sale	$3,684,000	$1,871,000

Note: The following table illustrates the reporting of the discontinued operations on the face of the Statements of Operations for 2000 and 1999.

	2000	*1999*
Income from continuing operations before income taxes	$3,124,000	$1,976,000
Provision for income taxes	(1,218,000)	(738,000)
Income from continuing operations	1,906,000	1,238,000

	2000	*1999*
Discontinued operations:		
Income (loss) from operations of discontinued segment, net of income tax benefit of $393,000 in 2000 and expense of $224,000 in 1999	(612,000)	383,000
Estimated loss on disposal of business segment, net of income tax benefit of $450,000	(871,000)	-0-
Net income	$423,000	$1,621,000

CHAPTER 46
EXTRAORDINARY ITEMS

CONTENTS

EXECUTIVE SUMMARY

Extraordinary items are events and transactions that are distinguished by their unusual nature *and* by the infrequency of their occurrence. Therefore, *both* of the following criteria should be met to classify an event or transaction as an extraordinary item:

1. *Unusual nature*—The underlying event or transaction possesses a high degree of abnormality and is of a type clearly unrelated to, or only incidentally related to, the ordinary and typical activities of the enterprise, taking into account the environment in which the enterprise operates.

2. *Infrequency of occurrence*—The underlying event or transaction is of a type that would not reasonably be expected to recur in the foreseeable future, taking into account the environment in which the enterprise operates.

Extraordinary items should be presented separately in the income statement, net of any related income tax effect. If the income statement includes discontinued operations or the cumulative effect of accounting changes, extraordinary items should be presented following discontinued operations and preceding the cumulative effect of accounting changes.

Events or transactions that are *either* unusual or infrequent, but not both (and therefore do not meet the criteria for extraordinary items), should be classified and reported as separate components of income from continuing operations. See Chapter 47, "Unusual or Infrequent Items," for a discussion of unusual or infrequent items.

Authoritative Literature

APB-9	Reporting the Results of Operations
APB-30	Reporting the Results of Operations—Reporting the Effects of Disposal of a Segment of a Business, and Extraordinary, Unusual, and Infrequently Occurring Events and Transactions
FAS-4	Reporting Gains and Losses from Extinguishment of Debt
FAS-16	Prior Period Adjustments

DISCLOSURE REQUIREMENTS

The following disclosures are required for extraordinary items:

1. A description of the nature of an extraordinary event or transaction and the principal items entering into the computation of the gain or loss (APB-30, par. 11)
2. The following captions used on the face of the income statement when there is an extraordinary item (and there are no discontinued operations or changes in accounting principles) (APB-30, pars. 10–12):
   a. Income before extraordinary items
   b. Extraordinary item (less applicable income taxes)
   c. Net income

d. Earnings per share amounts before extraordinary items and net income, where applicable

3. The following disclosures should be made for each adjustment in the current period of an element of an extraordinary item that was reported in a prior period (APB-30, par. 25):

   a. The year of origin, nature, and amount

   b. The adjustment classified separately in the current period as an extraordinary item

EXAMPLES OF FINANCIAL STATEMENT DISCLOSURES

The following sample disclosures are available on the accompanying disc.

Example 46–1: Presentation of Extraordinary Items in an Income Statement That Does Not Include Discontinued Operations and Cumulative Effect of Accounting Change

	2000	*1999*
Income before income taxes and extraordinary items	$2,078,000	$2,774,000
Provision for income taxes	(874,000)	(1,138,000)
Income before extraordinary items	1,204,000	1,636,000
Extraordinary items:		
Gain on early extinguishment of debt, less income tax of $233,000	-0-	417,000
Insurance settlement for earthquake damage, less income tax expense of $310,000	624,000	-0-
Net income	$1,828,000	$2,053,000

Example 46–2: Presentation of Extraordinary Items in an Income Statement That Includes Discontinued Operations and Cumulative Effect of Accounting Change

	2000	*1999*
Income (loss) from continuing operations before income taxes	$4,914,000	$(1,811,000)
Income taxes	(2,113,000)	652,000
Income (loss) from continuing operations	2,801,000	(1,159,000)

	2000	*1999*
Discontinued operations:		
Loss from operations of discontinued segment, net of income tax benefit of $617,000 in 2000 and $1,515,000 in 1999	(1,568,000)	(3,726,000)
Gain on disposal of business segment, net of income tax expense of $ 986,000	1,347,000	-0-
Income (loss) before extraordinary item and cumulative effect of accounting change	2,580,000	(4,885,000)
Extraordinary item—Loss on early extinguishment of debt, net of income tax benefit of $165,000	(452,000)	-0-
Income (loss) before cumulative effect of accounting change	2,128,000	(4,885,000)
Cumulative effect on prior years of change in accounting for product maintenance contracts, net of tax effect of $878,000	(1,356,000)	-0-
Net income (loss)	$772,000	$(4,885,000)

Example 46–3: Extraordinary Loss Related to Early Extinguishment of Debt

In September 2000, the Company redeemed various outstanding notes and debentures with an aggregate principal value of $2,769,000. The Company paid a premium to the debenture holders, and the transaction resulted in an extraordinary charge. The extraordinary loss of $452,000, net of a tax benefit of $165,000, principally represents the premium paid in connection with the early extinguishment of the debt and unamortized discount. The payments were made out of available cash.

Example 46–4: Extraordinary Gain Related to Troubled Debt Restructuring

At December 31, 1999, the Company had a 12% note payable to its primary bank with an outstanding principal balance of $1,756,000, due in December 2005. In September 2000, the Company reached an agreement with the bank to modify the terms of the note, due to cash flow problems experienced by the Company. The bank has agreed to accept a cash payment of $250,000 and installment payments on a note for a total of $900,000 at no interest, due in December 2005. As a result, the amount of the note to the bank was reduced by $606,000 to reflect the revised terms, and an extraordinary gain of $352,000, net of income tax of $254,000, has been included in the Statement of Operations for 2000.

Example 46–5: Extraordinary Loss Related to Write-Off of Debt Issuance Costs

In April 2000, the Company had an extraordinary loss of $213,000 net of an income tax benefit of $86,000 for the write-off of debt issuance costs relating to the former revolving credit facility, which was replaced by the new long-term credit agreement.

Example 46–6: Extraordinary Gain Related to Insurance Settlement for Earthquake Damage

In September 2000, the Company's headquarters building in Apple Valley, California, was severely damaged by an earthquake. After the settlement with the insurer in December 2000, the Company retired the building and recognized an extraordinary gain of $624,000, net of income taxes of $310,000, during 2000.

Example 46–7: Adjustment of Prior Period Extraordinary Item

In September 1999, the Company's warehouse in Los Angeles, California, was substantially damaged by fire. As a result, the Company recorded in 1999 an extraordinary loss of $918,000 (net of income tax benefit of $491,000 and net of insurance proceeds of $1,836,000). Included in the 1999 extraordinary loss was a provision for estimated inventory damage. During 2000, the Company determined that actual inventory damage exceeded its original estimate. Therefore, an extraordinary loss of $386,000, net of income tax benefit of $211,000, has been included in the Statement of Operations for 2000.

> **Note:** The following table illustrates the reporting of the adjustment of loss on the face of the Statements of Operations.

	2000	*1999*
Income before income taxes and extraordinary items	$1,563,000	$1,832,000
Provision for income taxes	(601,000)	(658,000)
Income before extraordinary items	962,000	1,174,000
Extraordinary item:		
Fire loss, net of income tax benefit of $211,000 in 2000 and $491,000 in 1999	(386,000)	(918,000)
Net income	$ 576,000	$256,000

Example 46–8: Investor's Proportionate Share of Investee's Extraordinary Gain

The extraordinary item of $320,000 represents the Company's proportionate share of a gain realized on the extinguishment of debt by Kametz, Ltd., a manufacturer of electronic parts in which the Company has a 40% interest that is accounted for on the equity method. The Company has not provided any income tax related to its share of the extraordinary gain because it is the Company's intention to reinvest all undistributed earnings of Kametz, Ltd. indefinitely.

Note: The following table illustrates the portion of the income statement reflecting the Company's proportionate share of extraordinary item reported by Kametz, Ltd.

	2000	*1999*
Income before income taxes	$8,941,000	$7,916,000
Provision for income taxes	(3,576,000)	(3,287,000)
Income before equity in net income of affiliate and extraordinary item	5,365,000	4,629,000
Equity in net income of affiliate, excluding extraordinary gain of $320,000 in 2000	554,000	716,000
Income before extraordinary item	5,919,000	5,345,000
Extraordinary item—Equity in undistributed extraordinary gain of affiliate	320,000	-0-
Net income	$6,239,000	$5,345,000

CHAPTER 47
UNUSUAL OR INFREQUENT ITEMS

CONTENTS

EXECUTIVE SUMMARY

Events or transactions that are *either* unusual or infrequent, but not both (and therefore do not meet the criteria for extraordinary items), should be classified and reported as separate components of income from continuing operations. However, the income statement presentation should *not* imply that the event is an extraordinary item. Therefore, the separately identified item should *not* be reported net of its related tax effect as a separate line item following income from continuing operations. Instead, it should be classified separately as a component of ordinary income or loss.

Employee termination benefits and costs incurred to exit an activity, including certain restructuring costs, are typical examples of transactions that are "unusual or infrequent." A liability should be recorded for employee termination benefits in the period that management approves a plan of termination if *all* of the following conditions are met:

1. Prior to the financial statement date, management commits to the plan of termination and determines the actual benefits that terminated employees will receive
2. The benefit arrangement is communicated to employees in sufficient detail, prior to issuance of the financial statements, to allow them to determine the benefits they will receive if they are terminated

3. The termination plan specifically indicates the number of employees to be terminated, their job classifications, and their locations
4. The time to complete the termination plan is short enough so that significant changes to the plan are *not* likely

An entity may incur additional costs (other than for employee termination benefits) to exit an activity. A liability for such costs should be recorded at the date management commits to an exit plan (i.e., the commitment date) and should include all exit costs that can be reasonably estimated. An exit cost is one that meets the following two criteria:

1. The cost was not incurred prior to the commitment date and will be incurred as a direct result of the exit plan
2. The cost was incurred under a contractual obligation prior to the commitment date and will either continue after the activity is stopped with no economic benefit or will result in a cancellation penalty when cancelled

Examples of exit costs include a cancellation penalty for a lease related to a facility that will no longer be used and relocation costs incurred from moving the operations of a facility that will be closed to another facility.

Authoritative Literature

APB-9	Reporting the Results of Operations
APB-30	Reporting the Results of Operations—Reporting the Effects of Disposal of a Segment of a Business, and Extraordinary, Unusual, and Infrequently Occurring Events and Transactions
EITF 94-3	Liability Recognition for Certain Employee Termination Benefits and Other Costs to Exit an Activity (Including Certain Costs Incurred in a Restructuring)

DISCLOSURE REQUIREMENTS

The nature and financial effects of material transactions that are either unusual or infrequent (but not both) should be disclosed and presented as a separate component of income from continuing operations (APB-30, par. 26).

Employee Termination Benefits and Other Costs to Exit an Activity (Including Certain Restructuring Costs)

1. The following disclosures should be made about accrued employee termination benefits (EITF 94-3):
   a. The amount of the termination benefits accrued and charged to expense and the classification of these costs in the income statement
   b. The number of employees to be terminated
   c. A description of the employee group(s) to be terminated
   d. The amount of actual termination benefits paid and charged against the liability accrued for employee termination benefits
   e. The number of employees actually terminated as a result of the termination plan
   f. The amount of any adjustments to the liability accrued for employee termination benefits
2. The following disclosures should be made about an entity's plan to exit an activity for all periods until the exit plan is fully executed, if the activities that will not be continued are significant to an entity's revenue or operating results, or the exit costs recognized at the commitment date are material (EITF 94-3):
   a. A description of the major actions included in the exit plan and the particular activities that will not be continued, including the method of disposition and anticipated date of completion
   b. A description of the type and amount of exit costs recognized as liabilities and the classification of the exit costs in the income statement
   c. A description of the type and amount of exit costs paid and charged against the liability
   d. The amount of any adjustments to the liability
   e. The revenues and net operating income or losses from activities that will not be continued if those activities have separately identifiable operations, for all periods presented

EXAMPLES OF FINANCIAL STATEMENT DISCLOSURES

The following sample disclosures are available on the accompanying disc.

Example 47–1: Unusual Expenses

In September 2000, the Company recorded unusual expenses of $1,044,000 before taxes. This is presented separately as a component of income from operations in the Statement of Operations. The unusual expenses relate to (1) $712,000 incurred in pre-opening costs for two new company-owned stores opened in Los Angeles, California, and Chicago, Illinois; (2) $217,000 incurred in the hiring of the new chief executive officer; and (3) $115,000 of cost of litigation associated with such hiring.

Note: The following table illustrates the portion of the income statement reflecting an unusual or infrequent item.

	2000	*1999*
Net sales	$82,174,000	$74,311,000
Costs and expenses:		
Cost of sales	50,947,000	46,816,000
Selling expenses	4,142,000	3,268,000
General and administrative expenses	23,743,000	19,492,000
Unusual expenses	1,044,000	-0-
	79,876,000	69,576,000
Income before income taxes	$2,298,000	$4,735,000

Example 47–2: Restructuring Charges

In 2000, the Company recorded $4,300,000 of restructuring charges primarily associated with the Company's restructuring plan adopted in the second quarter of 2000. The Company's restructuring plans and associated costs consisted of (a) $2,950,000 to terminate approximately 100 employees, (b) $1,075,000 to downsize and close excess facilities, and (c) $275,000 of other restructuring expenses. The Company's restructuring plan was primarily aimed at reducing the cost of excess personnel and capacity in its services business.

The employee severance costs of $2,950,000 include severance benefits, notice pay, and outplacement services. All terminations and termination benefits were communicated to the affected employees prior to year-end and severance benefits are expected to be paid in full in 2001.

The charges of $1,075,000 to downsize and close excess facilities were incurred in connection with the closure of four sales and engineering facilities and included $456,000 in abandonment costs for the related leasehold improvements. These closure and exit costs include payments required under lease contracts (less any applicable sublease income) after the properties were abandoned, lease buyout costs, and restoration costs associated with certain lease arrangements. Asset related costs written off consist of leasehold improvements to facilities that were abandoned and whose estimated fair market value is zero.

The other restructuring charges of $275,000 consist primarily of cancellation fees associated with certain vendor arrangements and abandoned software.

At December 31, 2000, outstanding liabilities related to severance and employee benefits totaled $2,136,000 and are included in "Payroll and related benefits," and the remaining liabilities for other restructuring charges, totaling $782,000, are included in "Other current liabilities" in the accompanying Balance Sheets.

CHAPTER 48
COMPREHENSIVE INCOME

CONTENTS

EXECUTIVE SUMMARY

Generally accepted accounting principles (GAAP) require comprehensive income and its components to be reported when a company presents a full set of financial statements that report financial position, results of operations, and cash flows. The term *comprehensive income* refers to net income plus other comprehensive income, i.e., certain revenues, expenses, gains, and losses that are reported as separate components of stockholders' equity instead of net income. Under current accounting standards, other comprehensive income includes the following:

1. Unrealized holding gains and losses on available-for-sale securities

2. Unrealized holding gains and losses that result from a debt security being transferred into the available-for-sale category from the held-to-maturity category
3. Subsequent decreases (if not an other-than-temporary impairment) or increases in the fair value of available-for-sale securities previously written down as impaired
4. Foreign currency translation adjustments
5. Gains and losses on foreign currency transactions that are designated as, and are effective as, economic hedges of a net investment in a foreign entity, commencing as of the designation date
6. Gains and losses on intercompany foreign currency transactions that are of a long-term investment nature, when the entities to the transaction are consolidated, combined, or accounted for by the equity method
7. Minimum pension liability adjustments
8. A change in the fair value of a derivative instrument that qualifies as the hedging instrument in a cash flow hedge

An entity is required to (1) present items of other comprehensive income by their nature in a financial statement *and* (2) display the accumulated balance of other comprehensive income separately from retained earnings and additional paid-in capital in the equity section of a balance sheet.

Authoritative Literature

FAS-130	Reporting Comprehensive Income
FAS-133	Accounting for Derivative Instruments and Hedging Activities

DISCLOSURE REQUIREMENTS

The following are the presentation and disclosure requirements for comprehensive income:

1. Comprehensive income should be displayed in one of the following three alternative presentation formats (FAS-130, pars. 14 and 22):

   a. In a single statement of income and comprehensive income that extends a traditional income statement to include (following net income) the elements of other comprehensive income and the total of comprehensive income

   b. In a separate statement of comprehensive income that begins with net income and includes the elements of other comprehensive income and then a total of comprehensive income

   c. In the statement of changes in equity

2. The components of other comprehensive income should be displayed either (i) net of related income tax effects *or* (ii) before related tax effects with one amount shown for the aggregate income tax expense or benefit related to the total of other comprehensive income items (FAS-130, par. 24)

3. The amount of income tax expense or benefit allocated to each component of other comprehensive income, including reclassification adjustments, should be disclosed either (i) on the face of the financial statement in which the components are displayed *or* (ii) in the notes to the financial statements (FAS-130, par. 25)

4. Reclassification adjustments for each classification of other comprehensive income (other than minimum pension liability adjustments) should be disclosed either (i) on the face of the financial statement in which comprehensive income is reported *or* (ii) in the notes to the financial statements (FAS-130, par. 20)

5. The accumulated balance of other comprehensive income should be reported separately from retained earnings and additional paid-in capital in the equity section of the balance sheet (FAS-130, par. 26)

6. The ending accumulated balances for each item in accumulated other comprehensive income should be disclosed either (i) on the face of the balance sheet, (ii) in a statement of changes in equity, *or* (iii) in the notes to the financial statements (FAS-130, par. 26)

7. If FAS-133 has been adopted, the following disclosures should be made (FAS-133 is effective for all fiscal quarters of fiscal years beginning after June 15, 2000):

   a. The net gain or loss on derivative instruments designated as cash flow hedging instruments (including qualifying foreign currency cash flow hedges) should be reported as a separate classification within other comprehensive income (FAS-133, par. 46)

   b. The following disclosures should be made as part of the disclosures of accumulated other comprehensive income (FAS-133, par. 47):

- — The beginning and ending accumulated derivative gain or loss
- — The related net change associated with current period hedging transactions
- — The net amount of any reclassification into earnings

EXAMPLES OF FINANCIAL STATEMENT DISCLOSURES

The following sample disclosures are available on the accompanying disc.

Example 48–1: Comprehensive Income Reported in a Single Statement of Income and Comprehensive Income

ABC Company
Statement of Income and Comprehensive Income
Years Ended December 31, 2000, and December 31, 1999

	2000	*1999*
Revenues	$12,760,000	$11,312,000
Costs and expenses	(12,663,000)	(11,226,000)
Other income and expenses, net	10,000	5,000
Income from operations before tax	107,000	91,000
Income tax expense	(44,000)	(37,000)
Net income	63,000	54,000
Other comprehensive income, net of tax:		
Unrealized gains on securities:		
Unrealized holding gains arising during the period	13,000	18,000
Less: reclassification adjustment for gains included in net income	(2,000)	(4,000)
	11,000	14,000
Minimum pension liability adjustment	(2,000)	(5,000)
Foreign currency translation adjustment	8,000	3,000
Other comprehensive income, net of tax	17,000	12,000
Comprehensive income	$ 80,000	$ 66,000

Note: Components of other comprehensive income also could be displayed on a before tax basis, with one amount shown for the aggregate income tax effect as follows:

	2000	*1999*
Net income	$63,000	$54,000
Other comprehensive income, before tax:		
Unrealized gains on securities:		
Unrealized holding gains arising during the period	18,000	26,000
Less: reclassification adjustment for gains included in net income	(3,000)	(6,000)
	15,000	20,000
Minimum pension liability adjustment	(4,000)	(9,000)
Foreign currency translation adjustment	11,000	4,000
Other comprehensive income, before tax	22,000	15,000
Income tax expense related to items of other comprehensive income	(5,000)	(3,000)
Other comprehensive income, net of tax	17,000	12,000
Comprehensive income	$80,000	$66,000

Example 48–2: Comprehensive Income Reported in a Separate Statement of Comprehensive Income

ABC Company
Statement of Comprehensive Income
Years Ended December 31, 2000, and December 31, 1999

	2000	*1999*
Net income	$63,000	$54,000
Other comprehensive income, net of tax:		
Unrealized gains on securities:		
Unrealized holding gains arising during the period	13,000	18,000
Less: reclassification adjustment for gains included in net income	(2,000)	(4,000)
	11,000	14,000
Minimum pension liability adjustment	(2,000)	(5,000)
Foreign currency translation adjustment	8,000	3,000
Other comprehensive income, net of tax	17,000	12,000
Comprehensive income	$80,000	$66,000

Example 48–3: Comprehensive Income Reported in a Statement of Changes in Equity

ABC Company
Statement of Changes in Stockholders' Equity
Years Ended December 31, 2000, and December 31, 1999

	Common Stock Shares	*Common Stock Amount*	*Additional Paid-in Capital*	*Retained Earnings*	*Accumulated Other Comprehensive Income*	*Total*
Balance at December 31, 1998	1,250,000	$125,000	$250,000	$49,000	$13,000	$437,000
Comprehensive income:						
Net income				54,000		54,000
Unrealized gains on securities, net of reclassification adjustment					14,000	14,000
Minimum pension liability adjustment					(5,000)	(5,000)
Foreign currency translation adjustment					3,000	3,000
Total comprehensive income						66,000
Common stock issued	250,000	25,000	50,000			75,000
Dividends				(15,000)		(15,000)
Balance at December 31, 1999	1,500,000	150,000	300,000	88,000	25,000	563,000
Comprehensive income:						
Net income				63,000		63,000
Unrealized gains on securities, net of reclassification adjustment					11,000	11,000
Minimum pension liability adjustment					(2,000)	(2,000)
Foreign currency translation adjustment					8,000	8,000
Total comprehensive income						80,000
Common stock issued	500,000	50,000	100,000			150,000
Dividends				(10,000)		(10,000)
Balance at December 31, 2000	2,000,000	$200,000	$400,000	$141,000	$42,000	$783,000

Example 48–4: Income Tax Expense or Benefit Allocated to Each Component of Other Comprehensive Income, Including Reclassification Adjustments

The pretax, tax, and after-tax effects of the components of other comprehensive income (loss) for 2000 and 1999 are as follows:

	Pre-tax Amount	*Tax (Expense) Benefit*	*After-tax Amount*
2000			
Unrealized gains on securities:			
Unrealized holding gains arising during the period	$18,000	$(5,000)	$13,000
Less: reclassification adjustment for gains included in net income	(3,000)	1,000	(2,000)
Net unrealized gains	15,000	(4,000)	11,000
Minimum pension liability adjustment	(4,000)	2,000	(2,000)
Foreign currency translation adjustment	11,000	(3,000)	8,000
Other comprehensive income	$22,000	$(5,000)	$17,000
1999			
Unrealized gains on securities:			
Unrealized holding gains arising during the period	$26,000	$(8,000)	$18,000
Less: reclassification adjustment for gains included in net income	(6,000)	2,000	(4,000)
Net unrealized gains	20,000	(6,000)	14,000
Minimum pension liability adjustment	(9,000)	4,000	(5,000)
Foreign currency translation adjustment	4,000	(1,000)	3,000
Other comprehensive income	$15,000	$(3,000)	$12,000

Note: Alternatively, the tax amounts for each component of other comprehensive income can be displayed parenthetically on the face of the financial statement in which comprehensive income is reported.

Example 48–5: Display of Accumulated Other Comprehensive Income Separately as a Component of Equity in a Balance Sheet

	2000	*1999*
Stockholders' Equity:		
Common stock; par value $.10; authorized 10,000,000 shares; issued and outstanding 2,000,000 shares in 2000 and 1,500,000 shares in 1999	$200,000	$150,000
Additional paid-in capital	400,000	300,000
Retained earnings	141,000	88,000
Accumulated other comprehensive income	42,000	25,000
Total stockholders' equity	$783,000	$563,000

Example 48–6: Details of the Accumulated Balances for Each Component Comprising Accumulated Other Comprehensive Income

Balances of related after-tax components comprising accumulated other comprehensive income (loss), included in stockholders' equity, at December 31, 2000, and December 31, 1999, are as follows:

	Unrealized Gains on Securities	*Minimum Pension Liability Adjustment*	*Foreign Currency Translation Adjustment*	*Accumulated Other Comprehensive Income*
Balance at December 31, 1998	$12,000	$5,000	$(4,000)	$13,000
Change for 1999	14,000	(5,000)	3,000	12,000
Balance at December 31, 1999	26,000	-0-	(1,000)	25,000
Change for 2000	11,000	(2,000)	8,000	17,000
Balance at December 31, 2000	$37,000	$(2,000)	$7,000	$42,000

Note: Alternatively, the balances of each classification within accumulated other comprehensive income can be displayed in a statement of changes in equity or in a balance sheet.

CHAPTER 49
EARNINGS PER SHARE

CONTENTS

EXECUTIVE SUMMARY

Earnings per share (EPS) is an important measure of corporate performance for investors and other users of financial statements. EPS figures must be presented in the income statement of a publicly held company and must be presented in a manner consistent with the captions included in the company's income statement. Certain securities, such as convertible bonds, preferred stock, and stock options, permit their holders to become common stockholders or add to the number of shares of common stock already held. When potential reduction, called *dilution,* of EPS figures is inherent in a company's capital structure, a dual presentation of EPS is required—basic EPS and diluted EPS.

For purposes of presenting earnings per share, a distinction is made between enterprises with a simple capital structure and those with a complex capital structure. A *simple capital structure* is one that consists of capital stock and includes no potential for dilution via conversions, exercise of options, or other arrangements that would increase the number of shares outstanding. For organizations with complex capital structures, two EPS figures are presented with equal prominence on the face of the income statement: basic EPS and diluted EPS. The difference between basic EPS and diluted EPS is that *basic EPS* considers only outstanding common stock, whereas *diluted EPS* incorporates the potential dilution from all potentially dilutive securities that would have reduced EPS.

Basic EPS excludes dilution and is computed by dividing income available to common stockholders by the weighted-average number of common shares outstanding for the period. Diluted EPS reflects the potential dilution that could occur if securities or other contracts to issue common stock were exercised or converted into common stock or resulted in the issuance of common stock that then shared in the earnings of the entity. The computation of diluted EPS should not assume conversion, exercise, or contingent issuance of securities that would have an anti-dilutive effect on earnings per share.

Authoritative Literature

FAS-128 Earnings per Share

DISCLOSURE REQUIREMENTS

The following are the required disclosures relating to earnings per share (Nonpublic companies are *not* required to present earnings per share.):

1. For each period for which an income statement is presented:
   a. A reconciliation of the numerators and denominators of the basic EPS and the diluted EPS computations for income from continuing operations, including the individual income and share amount effects of all securities that affect EPS; insignificant reconciling items need not be itemized as part of the reconciliation and can be aggregated (FAS-128, pars. 40 and 138)
   b. The effect that has been given to preferred dividends in determining the income available to common stockholders in computing basic EPS (FAS-128, par. 40)

c. Securities (including those issuable pursuant to contingent stock agreements) that could potentially dilute EPS in the future, but which were not included in the calculation of diluted EPS because to do so would have been antidilutive for the periods presented (FAS-128, par. 40)

2. For the latest period for which an income statement is presented, a description of any transaction that occurs after the end of the most recent period but before the issuance of the financial statements that would have changed materially the number of common shares or potential common shares outstanding at the end of the period if the transaction had occurred before the end of the period (FAS-128, par. 41)

3. When prior EPS amounts have been restated in compliance with an accounting standard requiring restatement, the per share effect of the restatement should be disclosed (FAS-128, pars. 57–58)

4. When the number of common shares outstanding increases as a result of a stock dividend or stock split, or decreases as a result of a reverse stock split, the computations of basic EPS and diluted EPS should be adjusted retroactively for all periods presented to reflect such changes in the number of shares, and that fact should be disclosed (FAS-128, par. 54)

5. If changes in common stock resulting from stock dividends, stock splits, or reverse stock splits occur after the close of the period but before the issuance of the financial statements, the per-share computations for all periods presented should be based on the new number of shares, and that fact should be disclosed (FAS-128, par. 54)

EXAMPLES OF FINANCIAL STATEMENT DISCLOSURES

The following sample disclosures are available on the accompanying disc.

Example 49–1: Earnings per Share Calculation Shows Reconciliation of Denominator

Basic net earnings per share is computed using the weighted average number of common shares outstanding. The dilutive effect of potential common shares outstanding is included in diluted net earnings per share. The computations of basic net earnings per share and diluted net earnings per share for 2000 and 1999 are as follows:

	2000	*1999*
Net earnings from continuing operations	$10,174,000	$9,143,000
Basic weighted average shares	6,119,000	6,625,000
Effect of dilutive securities:		
Common and convertible preferred stock options	90,200	55,400
Convertible preferred stock	70,800	42,600
Dilutive potential common shares	6,280,000	6,723,000
Net earnings per share from continuing operations:		
Basic	$ 1.66	$ 1.38
Diluted	$ 1.62	$ 1.36

Example 49–2: Dilutive Potential Common Shares Are Calculated in Accordance with the Treasury Stock Method That Is Described

Basic earnings per common share for the years ended December 31, 2000, and December 31, 1999, are calculated by dividing net income by weighted average common shares outstanding during the period. Diluted earnings per common share for the years ended December 31, 2000, and December 31, 1999, are calculated by dividing net income by weighted average common shares outstanding during the period plus dilutive potential common shares, which are determined as follows:

	2000	*1999*
Weighted average common shares	20,745,000	21,881,000
Effect of dilutive securities:		
Warrants	5,550,000	4,734,000
Options to purchase common stock	219,000	241,000
Dilutive potential common shares	26,514,000	26,856,000

Dilutive potential common shares are calculated in accordance with the treasury stock method, which assumes that proceeds from the exercise of all warrants and options are used to repurchase common stock at market value. The amount of shares remaining after the proceeds are exhausted represents the potentially dilutive effect of the securities. The increasing number of warrants used in the calculation is a result of the increasing market value of the Company's common stock.

Example 49–3: Diluted Net Earnings per Share Excludes Potential Common Stock with Antidilutive Effect

Basic earnings per share is computed by dividing net income by the weighted average number of common shares outstanding during the period. Diluted earnings per share is computed by dividing net income by the weighted average number of common shares and dilutive potential common shares outstanding during the period.

The following is a reconciliation of the number of shares used in the calculation of basic earnings per share and diluted earnings per share for the years ended December 31, 2000, and December 31, 1999:

	2000	*1999*
Net income	$5,323,000	$10,471,000
Weighted average number of common shares outstanding	7,419,000	7,699,000
Incremental shares from the assumed exercise of dilutive stock options	198,000	174,000
Dilutive potential common shares	7,617,000	7,873,000
Net earnings per share:		
Basic	$ 0.72	$ 1.36
Diluted	$ 0.70	$ 1.33

Options to purchase 37,950 and 68,925 shares were outstanding at December 31, 2000, and December 31, 1999, respectively, but were not included in the computation of diluted net income per share because the exercise price of the options was greater than the average market price of the common shares and, therefore, the effect would be antidilutive.

Example 49–4: EPS Calculations Are Adjusted for Tax-Effected Interest Expense to Calculate Diluted Earnings per Share and for Stock Split

In December 2000, the Company issued a two-for-one stock split effected in the form of a 100% stock dividend. Previously reported share and earnings per share amounts have been restated. Basic earnings per share is computed by dividing net earnings by the weighted average number of common shares outstanding. Diluted earnings per share is computed by dividing net earnings by the sum of the weighted average number of common shares outstanding and the weighted average number of potential common shares outstanding. The calculations of basic and diluted earnings per share for 2000 and 1999 are as follows:

	2000	*1999*
Calculation of basic earnings per share:		
Net earnings	$1,614,000	$1,160,000
Weighted average number of common shares outstanding	1,471,000	1,459,000
Basic earnings per share	$ 1.10	$ 0.80
Calculation of diluted earnings per share:		
Net earnings	$1,614,000	$1,160,000
Tax-effected interest expense attributable to 3% Notes	23,000	23,000
Net earnings assuming dilution	$1,637,000	$1,183,000
Weighted average number of common shares outstanding	1,471,000	1,459,000
Effect of potentially dilutive securities:		
3% Notes	48,000	48,000
Employee stock plans	28,000	17,000
Weighted average number of common shares outstanding assuming dilution	1,547,000	1,524,000
Diluted earnings per share	$ 1.06	$ 0.78

Employee stock plans represent shares granted under the Company's employee stock purchase plan and stock option plans. For 2000 and 1999, shares issuable upon conversion of the Company's 3% Notes were included in weighted average shares assuming dilution for purposes of calculating diluted earnings per share. To calculate diluted earnings per share, net earnings are adjusted for tax-effected net interest and issue costs on the 3% Notes and divided by weighted average shares assuming dilution.

Example 49–5: EPS Calculations Include Cumulative Effect of Change in Accounting Principle

Basic net income per share is computed by dividing net income available to common stockholders by the weighted average number of common shares outstanding during the period and excludes the dilutive effect of stock options. Diluted net income per share gives effect to all dilutive potential common shares outstanding during a period. A reconciliation of the numerators and denominators of the basic and diluted income per share for 2000 and 1999 is presented below:

	2000	*1999*
Basic earnings per share:		
Income before cumulative effect of change in accounting principle	$4,200,000	$3,700,000
Cumulative effect of change in accounting principle	-0-	(400,000)
Net income	$4,200,000	$3,300,000
Weighted shares outstanding—Basic	2,545,000	2,185,000
Per share:		
Income before cumulative effect of change in accounting principle	$ 1.65	$ 1.69
Cumulative effect of change in accounting principle	-0-	(0.18)
Basic earnings per share	$ 1.65	$ 1.51
Diluted earnings per share:		
Income before cumulative effect of change in accounting principle	$4,200,000	$3,700,000
Effect of 5.75% convertible subordinated notes	110,000	170,000
Income before cumulative effect of change in accounting principle including the effect of dilutive securities	4,310,000	3,870,000
Cumulative effect of change in accounting principle	-0-	(400,000)
Net income	$4,310,000	$3,470,000
Weighted shares outstanding—Basic	2,545,000	2,185,000
Effect of dilutive securities:		
Stock options	112,000	125,000
5.75% convertible subordinated notes	115,000	220,000
Weighted shares outstanding—Diluted	2,772,000	2,530,000
Per share:		
Income before cumulative effect of change in accounting principle	$ 1.55	$ 1.53
Cumulative effect of change in accounting principle	-0-	(0.16)
Diluted earnings per share	$ 1.55	$ 1.37

Example 49–6: EPS Calculations Include Discontinued Operations and Extraordinary Items

> **Note:** Example 49–6 illustrates (1) the presentation of earnings per share on the face of the income statement and (2) the computation of basic earnings per share and diluted earnings per share for income from continuing operations in a note to the financial statements.

Income Statement

	2000	*1999*
Income from continuing operations	$8,750,000	$7,450,000
Discontinued operations:		
Income from discontinued operations, net of taxes	500,000	-0-
Gain on disposition of business, net of taxes	600,000	-0-
Extraordinary items, net of taxes	-0-	(700,000)
Net income	$9,850,000	$6,750,000
Earnings per share—Basic:		
Income from continuing operations	$ 0.51	$ 0.45
Discontinued operations	0.06	-0-
Extraordinary items	-0-	(0.04)
Net income	$ 0.57	$ 0.41
Earnings per share—Diluted:		
Income from continuing operations	$ 0.50	$ 0.44
Discontinued operations	0.06	-0-
Extraordinary items	-0-	(0.04)
Net income	$ 0.56	$ 0.40
Weighted average number of shares—Basic	17,160,000	16,600,000
Weighted average number of shares assuming dilution	17,530,000	16,825,000

Note to the Financial Statements

Basic earnings per share is computed by dividing net income by the weighted average number of common shares outstanding during the period. Diluted earnings per share is computed by dividing net income by the weighted average number of common shares and dilutive potential common shares outstanding during the period. The computation of basic earnings per share and diluted earnings per share for "Income from continuing operations" is as follows:

	2000	*1999*
Income from continuing operations	$8,750,000	$7,450,000
Weighted average number of common shares outstanding—Basic	17,160,000	16,600,000
Effect of dilutive securities—Stock options	370,000	225,000
Weighted average number of common shares outstanding—Diluted	17,530,000	16,825,000
Net earnings per share from continuing operations:		
Basic	$ 0.51	$ 0.45
Diluted	$ 0.50	$ 0.44

Example 49–7: Earnings per Share Amounts for Prior Period Have Been Restated to Give Effect to the Adoption of a New Accounting Standard

In 2000, the Company adopted Financial Accounting Standards Board Statement (FAS) No. [*number*] [*title*], which requires [*describe briefly the requirements of the new standard*]. The effect of this change was to [*increase/decrease*] 2000 net income by $[*amount*], basic earnings per share by $[*amount*], and diluted earnings per share by $[*amount*]. The financial statements for 1999 have been retroactively restated for the change, which resulted in an [*increase/decrease*] in net income for 1999 of $[*amount*]. Earnings per share amounts for 1999 have been restated to give effect to the application of the new accounting standard. The effect of the restatement was to [*increase/decrease*] 1999 basic earnings per share by $[*amount*] and diluted earnings per share by $[*amount*]. Retained earnings as of January 1, 1999, has been adjusted for the effect of retroactive application of the new Statement.

Part IV—
Statement of Cash Flows

CHAPTER 50
STATEMENT OF CASH FLOWS

CONTENTS

EXECUTIVE SUMMARY

A statement of cash flows is required as part of a complete set of financial statements prepared in conformity with generally accepted accounting principles (GAAP) for all business enterprises. A statement of cash flows specifies the amount of net cash provided by or used by an enterprise during a period from (1) operating activities, (2) investing activities, and (3) financing activities. The statement of cash flows indicates the net effect of these cash flows on the enterprise's cash and cash equivalents. A reconciliation of beginning and ending cash and cash equivalents is included in the statement of cash flows. Also, a statement of cash flows should contain separate related disclosures about all investing and financing activities of an enterprise that affect its financial position but do not directly affect its cash flows during the period. Descriptive terms such as "Cash" or "Cash and cash equivalents" are required in the statement of cash flows, whereas ambiguous terms such as "Funds" are inappropriate.

Cash equivalents are short-term, highly liquid investments that are (1) readily convertible to known amounts of cash and (2) so near their maturities that they present insignificant risk of changes in value because of changes in interest rates. As a general rule, only investments with original maturities of three months or less qualify as cash equivalents. Examples of items commonly considered to be cash equivalents include Treasury bills, commercial paper, money market funds, and federal funds sold.

GAAP specifically prohibit reporting cash flow per share.

Authoritative Literature

FAS-95	Statement of Cash Flows
FAS-102	Statement of Cash Flows—Exemption of Certain Enterprises and Classification of Cash Flows from Certain Securities Acquired for Resale
FAS-104	Statement of Cash Flows—Net Reporting of Certain Cash Receipts and Cash Payments and Classification of Cash Flows from Hedging Transactions
FAS-115	Accounting for Certain Investments in Debt and Equity Securities
FAS-117	Financial Statements of Not-for-Profit Organizations
FAS-133	Accounting for Derivative Instruments and Hedging Activities

DISCLOSURE REQUIREMENTS

The following are required disclosures related to statements of cash flows:

1. The accounting policy for determining which items are treated as cash and cash equivalents (FAS-95, par. 10)
2. If the indirect method of reporting cash flows is used, a reconciliation of net income to net cash provided or used by operating activities (presented in notes to the financial statements or on the face of the statement of cash flows) (FAS-95, par. 6)
3. Information about noncash investing and financing activities that affect assets or liabilities (FAS-95, par. 32)
4. If the indirect method of reporting cash flows from operating activities is used, disclosures should include the amounts of interest paid (net of amounts capitalized) and income taxes paid during the period (FAS-95, par. 29)

EXAMPLES OF FINANCIAL STATEMENT DISCLOSURES

The following sample disclosures are available on the accompanying disc.

Example 50–1: Statement of Cash Flows—Indirect Method

	Year Ended December 31	
	2000	*1999*
Operating activities:		
Net income (loss)	$36,000,000	$19,000,000
Adjustments to reconcile net income (loss) to net cash provided by (used in) operating activities:		
Depreciation and amortization	7,500,000	3,700,000
Amortization of deferred compensation	1,300,000	800,000
Deferred taxes	(1,500,000)	(500,000)
Changes in operating assets and liabilities, net of effects from acquired companies:		
Accounts receivable	(20,000,000)	(8,000,000)
Inventory	(4,500,000)	(1,200,000)
Income taxes receivable	(3,500,000)	(2,400,000)

Prepaid expenses and other assets	(2,000,000)	(500,000)
Accounts payable	14,000,000	7,000,000
Other accrued liabilities	5,500,000	3,500,000
Net cash provided by (used in) operating activities	32,800,000	21,400,000
Investing activities:		
Net assets of acquired companies, net of cash acquired	(16,000,000)	(10,000,000)
Purchases of property and equipment	(11,000,000)	(12,000,000)
Purchases of investments	(2,000,000)	(1,000,000)
Net cash provided by (used in) investing activities	(29,000,000)	(23,000,000)
Financing activities:		
Proceeds from bank term loan	1,000,000	5,700,000
Payments on bank term loan	(500,000)	(7,000,000)
Payments on capital lease obligations	(700,000)	(800,000)
Proceeds from issuance of common stock	2,000,000	3,000,000
Payments on repurchase of preferred stock	(200,000)	(300,000)
Net cash provided by (used in) financing activities	1,600,000	600,000
Effect of exchange rate changes on cash and cash equivalents	(100,000)	200,000
Increase (decrease) in cash and cash equivalents	5,300,000	(800,000)
Cash and cash equivalents at beginning of year	2,300,000	3,100,000
Cash and cash equivalents at end of year	$7,600,000	$2,300,000

Example 50–2: Statement of Cash Flows—Direct Method, Including Reconciliation of Net Income to Net Cash from Operating Activities

	Year Ended December 31	
	2000	*1999*
Cash flows from operating activities:		
Cash received from customers	28,000,000	22,000,000
Cash paid to suppliers and employees	(25,500,000)	(21,700,000)
Interest received	200,000	100,000

	Year Ended December 31	
	2000	*1999*
Interest paid	(1,000,000)	(1,500,000)
Income tax refunds received	400,000	100,000
Income taxes paid	(1,500,000)	(2,000,000)
Other cash received (paid)	(200,000)	100,000
Net cash provided by (used in) operating activities	400,000	(2,900,000)
Cash flows from investing activities:		
Payments for business acquisitions, net of cash acquired	(1,500,000)	(1,000,000)
Purchases of property and equipment	(500,000)	(500,000)
Proceeds from disposition of capital equipment	400,000	1,700,000
Purchases of short-term investments	(300,000)	(100,000)
Proceeds from short-term investments	200,000	400,000
Net cash provided by (used in) investing activities	(1,700,000)	500,000
Cash flows from financing activities:		
Proceeds from short-term borrowings	3,000,000	100,000
Repayment of long-term debt	(700,000)	(200,000)
Proceeds from issuance of long-term debt	800,000	1,500,000
Proceeds from issuance of common stock	200,000	400,000
Net cash provided by (used in) financing activities	3,300,000	1,800,000
Effect of exchange rate changes on cash and cash equivalents	(400,000)	(100,000)
Increase (decrease) in cash and cash equivalents	1,600,000	(700,000)
Cash and cash equivalents at beginning of year	1,200,000	1,900,000
Cash and cash equivalents at end of year	$2,800,000	$1,200,000

Reconciliation of Net Income (Loss) to Net Cash Provided by (Used in) Operating Activities

	Year Ended December 31	
	2000	*1999*
Net income (loss)	$(3,500,000)	$4,700,000
Adjustments to reconcile net income (loss) to net cash provided by (used in) operating activities:		
Depreciation and amortization	1,700,000	1,500,000
Deferred income taxes	(500,000)	200,000
Foreign exchange (gains) losses	(150,000)	100,000
Loss (gain) on sale of equipment	(100,000)	250,000
Inventory write-off	400,000	300,000
Changes in operating assets and liabilities, net of effects of business acquisitions:		
Accounts receivable	2,000,000	(3,850,000)
Inventory	(4,000,000)	(2,000,000)
Income taxes receivable	300,000	100,000
Prepaid expenses and other assets	700,000	(600,000)
Accounts payable	1,650,000	(2,500,000)
Other accrued liabilities	1,900,000	(1,100,000)
Net cash provided by (used in) operating activities	$400,000	$(2,900,000)

Example 50–3: Cash Flow Statement—Discontinued Operations

Note: Financial Accounting Standards Board Statement No. 95 (Statement of Cash Flows) does not require discontinued operations to be separately disclosed in cash flow statements. Example 50–3 is provided for entities that nevertheless choose to report such category.

	Year Ended December 31	
	2000	*1999*
Cash flows from operating activities:		
Net income	$6,000,000	$9,000,000
Adjustments to reconcile net income to net cash provided by operating activities:		
Depreciation and amortization	2,500,000	1,700,000
Estimated loss on disposal of discontinued operations	2,400,000	-0-
Increase in accounts receivable	(2,000,000)	(6,000,000)
Increase in accounts payable	3,000,000	4,000,000
Net cash provided by operating activities	11,900,000	8,700,000
Cash flows from investing activities:		
Purchases of property and equipment	(7,000,000)	(2,000,000)
Net investing activities of discontinued operations	(3,000,000)	(1,200,000)
Net cash used in investing activities	(10,000,000)	(3,200,000)
Cash flows from financing activities:		
Payments on capital lease obligations	(700,000)	(800,000)
Net financing activities of discontinued operations	(500,000)	(400,000)
Net cash used in financing activities	(1,200,000)	(1,200,000)
Increase (decrease) in cash and cash equivalents	700,000	4,300,000
Cash and cash equivalents at beginning of year	6,500,000	2,200,000
Cash and cash equivalents at end of year	$7,200,000	$6,500,000

Example 50–4: Cash Flow Statement—Extraordinary Items

> **Note:** FAS-95 does not require extraordinary items to be separately disclosed in cash flow statements. Example 50–4 is provided for entities that nevertheless choose to report such category.

	Year Ended December 31	
	2000	*1999*
Cash flows from operating activities:		
Net income	$36,000,000	$19,000,000
Adjustments to reconcile net income to net cash provided by operating activities:		
Depreciation and amortization	7,500,000	3,700,000
Extraordinary loss on early extinguishment of debt	2,300,000	-0-
Net cash provided by operating activities	45,800,000	22,700,000

(Remaining details omitted.)

Example 50–5: Cash Flow Statement—Cumulative Effect of Accounting Changes

> **Note:** FAS-95 does not require the cumulative effect of accounting changes to be separately disclosed in cash flow statements. Example 50–5 is provided for entities that nevertheless choose to report such category.

	Year Ended December 31	
	2000	*1999*
Cash flows from operating activities:		
Net income	$6,000,000	$9,000,000
Adjustments to reconcile net income to net cash provided by operating activities:		
Depreciation and amortization	1,500,000	1,700,000
Cumulative effect of changing overhead recorded in inventory	(400,000)	-0-
Net cash provided by operating activities	7,100,000	10,700,000

(Remaining details omitted.)

Example 50–6: Foreign Currency Cash Flows

Financial Accounting Standards Board Statement No. 95 (Statement of Cash Flows) specifies that the effect of exchange rate changes on cash balances held in foreign currencies be reported as a separate part of the reconciliation of the change in cash and cash equivalents in the Statement of Cash Flows.

Note: For examples of reporting foreign currency cash flows, see Examples 50–1 and 50–2.

Example 50–7: Cash Overdraft Reported as a Financing Activity

	Year Ended December 31	
	2000	*1999*
Cash flows from financing activities:		
Proceeds of long-term borrowings	1,000,000	500,000
Payments on capital lease obligations	(700,000)	(800,000)
Net increase (decrease) in bank overdrafts	500,000	(400,000)
Net cash provided by (used in) financing activities	800,000	(700,000)

(Remaining details omitted.)

Example 50–8: Other Adjustments to Arrive at Net Cash Flows from Operating Activities

Note: Example 50–8 is a comprehensive illustration of adjustments to arrive at net cash flows from operating activities, other than changes in operating assets and liabilities. The objective of these adjustments is to account for noncash operating activities, by adding noncash expenses to net income and subtracting noncash revenues from net income. For complete examples of statements of cash flows under the direct and indirect methods, see Examples 50–1 and 50–2.

	Year Ended December 31	
	2000	*1999*
Cash flows from operating activities:		
Net income	$4,000,000	$5,000,000
Adjustments to reconcile net income to net cash provided by operating activities:		
Cash value of life insurance	(100,000)	(200,000)
Common stock issued to employees	500,000	100,000
Depreciation and amortization	1,500,000	1,700,000
Foreign currency translation loss (gain)	100,000	(300,000)
Gain on litigation settlement	(600,000)	(100,000)
Imputed interest on debt	300,000	100,000
Inventory write-down	200,000	300,000
LIFO effect	200,000	(250,000)
Loss (gain) on sale of property and equipment	100,000	(200,000)
Minority interest in net income (loss) of consolidated subsidiary	(400,000)	300,000
Provision for environmental remediation	200,000	700,000
Provision for losses on accounts receivable	700,000	500,000
Provision related to early retirement program	1,100,000	900,000
Restructuring charges	900,000	600,000
Undistributed (earnings) losses of affiliate	300,000	(400,000)
Write-down of certain long-lived assets	150,000	200,000
Write-off of advances to affiliates	500,000	200,000
Changes in operating assets and liabilities:		
Accounts receivable	600,000	(400,000)
(Remaining details omitted.)		
Net cash provided by operating activities	10,250,000	8,750,000

(Remaining details omitted.)

Example 50–9: Cash Flows from Investing Activities

> **Note:** Example 50–9 is a comprehensive illustration of cash flows provided by and used in investing activities. For complete examples of statements of cash flows under the direct and indirect methods, see Examples 50–1 and 50–2.

	Year Ended December 31	
	2000	*1999*
Cash flows from investing activities:		
Additions to long-term notes receivable	(600,000)	(900,000)
Collections of loans to officers	250,000	150,000
Deconsolidation of joint ventures	(200,000)	(500,000)
Increase in intangibles	(400,000)	(200,000)
Investment in and advances to affiliates	(500,000)	(700,000)
Payment for business acquisitions, net of cash acquired	(1,000,000)	(2,000,000)
Payments on long-term notes receivable	200,000	300,000
Proceeds from property insurance settlement	200,000	400,000
Proceeds from sale of assets held for resale	600,000	150,000
Proceeds from sale of marketable securities and investments	6,000,000	2,000,000
Proceeds from sale of property and equipment	1,000,000	3,000,000
Purchase of marketable securities and investments	(3,000,000)	(6,000,000)
Purchase of minority interests	(150,000)	(100,000)
Purchases of property and equipment	(1,000,000)	(2,000,000)
Repayments from (loans to) employees	100,000	(50,000)
Restricted funds held in escrow	(1,200,000)	(1,500,000)
Sale (purchase) of available-for-sale securities	1,800,000	(400,000)
Sale (purchase) of investments held-to-maturity	(600,000)	500,000
Net cash provided by (used in) investing activities	1,500,000	(7,850,000)

(Remaining details omitted.)

Example 50–10: Cash Flows from Financing Activities

Note: Example 50–10 is a comprehensive illustration of cash flows provided by and used in financing activities. For complete examples of statements of cash flows under the direct and indirect methods, see Examples 50–1 and 50–2.

	Year Ended December 31	
	2000	*1999*
Cash flows from financing activities:		
Capital contributions from (distributions to) minority interests	(200,000)	150,000
Debt issue costs	(300,000)	(100,000)
Decrease (increase) in funds restricted for payment of long-term debt	600,000	(400,000)
Loans to ESOP	(400,000)	(300,000)
Net borrowings under line-of-credit agreement	1,000,000	2,000,000
Net increase (decrease) in bank overdrafts	400,000	(600,000)
Payment of debt and capital lease obligations	(3,500,000)	(800,000)
Payment of dividends	(100,000)	(200,000)
Premiums paid on early retirement of debt	(500,000)	(300,000)
Proceeds from issuance of common stock	700,000	600,000
Proceeds from issuance of long-term debt	2,000,000	3,000,000
Proceeds from notes receivable—Stock	100,000	200,000
Proceeds from stock options exercised	200,000	300,000
Proceeds of preferred stock issued to ESOP	250,000	150,000
Reduction of loan to ESOP	150,000	100,000
Repurchase of common stock	(1,500,000)	(1,300,000)
Treasury stock issued	400,000	500,000
Treasury stock purchased	(600,000)	(700,000)
Net cash provided by (used in) financing activities	(1,300,000)	2,300,000

(Remaining details omitted.)

Noncash Investing and Financing Activities

Example 50–11: Note Receivable Received in Connection with Sale of Business

In 2000, the Company sold certain assets of its frozen food distribution business. The selling price was $2,800,000, which included a cash payment of $1,000,000 and a note receivable of $1,800,000 payable in three equal annual installments.

Example 50–12: Casualty Results in an Insurance Claim Receivable

On August 13, 2000, the Company experienced a major fire, which destroyed a significant part of the manufacturing facility. The total amount of the insurance claim was for $8,500,000. The Company has received $7,000,000 in cash and the balance of $1,500,000 is recorded as an insurance claim receivable due from the insurance company.

Example 50–13: Forgiveness of Note Receivable

During the year ended December 31, 2000, the Company forgave a note receivable, including interest, totaling $210,000, in connection with its sales quota agreement with Sarak, Inc.

Example 50–14: Conversion of Accounts Receivable to Notes Receivable

During the year ended December 31, 2000, the Company converted $350,000 of accounts receivable to notes receivable.

Example 50–15: Note Receivable Balance Reduced for Expenses Incurred

During the year ended December 31, 2000, the Company reduced its note receivable balance from its affiliate, Sisak Corp., by $125,000 for a management fee charged by the affiliate.

Example 50–16: Property Acquired under Capital Lease Obligations

The Company acquired equipment of $430,000 and $310,000 in 2000 and 1999, respectively, under capital lease obligations.

Example 50–17: Note Payable Issued in Connection with Property Acquisition

During the years ended December 31, 2000, and December 31, 1999, the Company issued notes payable for $450,000 and $375,000, respectively, in connection with the acquisition of certain property and equipment.

Example 50–18: Property Distributed to Shareholder as Salary

In 2000, the Company distributed an automobile with a book value of $17,900 to a 5% shareholder as salary.

Example 50–19: Property Acquired in Exchange for Services Rendered

In 2000, the Company acquired furniture and equipment with a value of $38,500 in exchange for consulting services rendered.

Example 50–20: Issuance of Common Stock as Payment for Consulting Services

In 2000, the Company issued 65,000 shares of Common Stock, valued at $260,000, to a consultant in payment for consulting services performed under a consulting agreement dated July 1, 2000.

Example 50–21: Issuance of Preferred Stock and Warrants as Payment of Accrued Interest

In 2000, the Company issued 30,000 shares of Amended Series A Preferred Stock and 150,000 warrants to acquire shares of Common Stock, in respect of approximately $750,000 of accrued interest payable to certain institutional holders of secured subordinated debt.

Example 50–22: Issuance of Warrants Recorded as Stock Dividends

In 2000, the Company issued warrants to holders of its Series B Preferred Stock at $0.15 per share, which was recorded as a preferred stock dividend of approximately $400,000.

Example 50–23: Issuance of Warrants as Finder's Fee

During May 2000, the Company issued to a finder 20,000 warrants to purchase 20,000 shares of common stock, as compensation for the placement with its clients of 200,000 units, comprising shares of common stock and warrants to purchase common stock.

Example 50–24: Conversion of Preferred Stock into Common Stock

In April 2000, the 4,000 shares of 5% redeemable convertible preferred stock with a total stockholders' equity value of $4,800,000 were converted into an aggregate of 100,000 shares of the Company's common stock.

Example 50–25: Common Stock Issued Pursuant to Conversion of Bridge Financing Notes

500,000 shares of common stock were issued in 2000 pursuant to the conversion of bridge financing promissory notes, which provided net proceeds of $2,000,000.

Example 50–26: Issuance of Stock Dividends

In 2000, the Company declared and issued a stock dividend of 2,545,000 common shares resulting in a transfer from retained earnings to additional paid-in capital of $725,000.

Example 50–27: Purchase Method Business Combinations

Supplemental cash flow information regarding the Company's acquisitions in 2000 and 1999 are as follows:

	2000	*1999*
Fair value of assets acquired	$3,100,000	$2,900,000
Less liabilities assumed	(900,000)	(200,000)
Net assets acquired	2,200,000	2,700,000
Less shares issued	(300,000)	(400,000)
Less cash acquired	(100,000)	(200,000)
Business acquisitions, net of cash acquired	$1,800,000	$2,100,000

Example 50–28: Assets and Liabilities Contributed to Newly Formed Joint Venture

In April 2000, the Company contributed its medical diagnostics business to a newly formed, equally owned joint venture with Sabak, Inc. This transaction had the following non-cash effect on the Company's 2000 balance sheet:

Current assets	$(300,000)
Property and equipment	(900,000)
Long-term receivables	500,000
Current liabilities	600,000

Example 50–29: Increase in Goodwill and Payables under Contingent Purchase Price Obligations

During 2000, the Company recorded a payable to the former owners of Lisba, Inc. and increased goodwill by $325,000 under its contingent purchase price obligations.

Example 50–30: Transfer of Inventory to Property and Equipment

During the years ended December 31, 2000, and December 31, 1999, the Company transferred $80,000 and $95,000 of inventory to property and equipment, respectively.

Example 50–31: Refinance of Term Loan

During the year ended December 31, 2000, the Company refinanced a term loan of $3,500,000 for the same amount.

Example 50–32: Insurance Premiums Financed

During 2000 and 1999, the Company financed $75,000 and $63,000, respectively, of insurance premiums relating to general liability and workers' compensation. The liability is recorded as a note payable.

Accounting Policy for Cash Equivalents

Example 50–33: Cash Equivalents Include Money Market Accounts and Short-Term Investments

Cash and cash equivalents include cash on hand, money market accounts, and short-term investments with original maturities of three months or less.

Example 50–34: Cash Equivalents Include Marketable Securities

For purposes of the Statements of Cash Flows, marketable securities purchased with an original maturity of three months or less are considered cash equivalents.

Example 50–35: Cash Equivalents Exclude Securities Held in Trust

The Company considers all short-term debt securities purchased with an initial maturity of three months or less and not held in trust to be cash equivalents.

Example 50–36: Cash Equivalents Include Repurchase Agreements

At December 31, 2000, cash equivalents include overnight repurchase agreements.

Example 50–37: Negative Book Cash Balances Are Included in Accounts Payable

Cash equivalents consist of all highly liquid investments with an original maturity of three months or less. As a result of the Company's cash management system, checks issued but not presented to the banks for payment may create negative book cash balances. Such negative balances are included in trade accounts payable and totaled $3,700,000 and $2,900,000 as of December 31, 2000, and December 31, 1999, respectively.

Disclosure of Interest and Income Taxes Paid (When the Indirect Method Is Used)

Example 50–38: Interest and Income Taxes Paid

Cash paid for interest and income taxes for 2000 and 1999 were as follows:

	2000	*1999*
Interest, net of amount capitalized of $113,000 in 2000	$166,000	$244,000
Income taxes	$100,000	$125,000

FINANCIAL STATEMENT DISCLOSURES CHECKLIST

CLIENT NAME: ______________________________

DATE OF FINANCIAL STATEMENTS: ______________________________

Prepared by ______________________________

Date ______________________________

Reviewed by ______________________________

Date ______________________________

INSTRUCTIONS

This checklist is intended to be used as a guide for determining whether the financial statements of nonpublic for-profit type entities include the necessary disclosures as required by generally accepted accounting principles. It should be noted that this checklist does not address the specialized disclosure requirements of specialized industries, not-for-profit organizations, the SEC, or the Governmental Accounting Standards Board.

Most of the questions addressed in this checklist refer to specific authoritative literature and use the following acronyms:

- FAS—Statement of Financial Accounting Standards
- FIN—Financial Accounting Standards Board Interpretation
- CON—Financial Accounting Standards Board Statement of Financial Accounting Concepts
- FTB—Financial Accounting Standards Board Technical Bulletin
- EITF—Consensus Position of the FASB Emerging Issues Task Force
- ARB—Accounting Research Bulletin
- APB—Accounting Principles Board Opinion
- QA—FASB Question-and-Answer documents
- AU—Statement on Auditing Standards, Professional Standards, published by the AICPA

- SOP—AICPA Statement of Position of the Accounting Standards Division
- PB—Practice Bulletin of the AICPA Accounting Standards Executive Committee

Some of the questions included in the checklist do not refer to any specific authoritative literature. Nevertheless, the disclosure items they address are considered informative disclosures for users of the financial statements and usually are disclosed. These disclosures are generally accepted by auditors and, accordingly, are referenced as "Generally accepted practice" in this checklist.

This checklist is divided into the following four major financial statement parts:

- Part I—Balance Sheet
- Part II—Income Statement
- Part III—Statement of Cash Flows
- Part IV—Other Financial Statement Topics and Disclosures

Review the topics within each of the four major parts for possible disclosures. The page number for each topic is provided this checklist's Table of Contents for quick reference. For each topic that is applicable, check the "Item Present" column; otherwise, check the "Item Not Present" column. For each topic checked "Item Present," complete the individual checklist items by placing a checkmark in the appropriate "Yes," "No," or "N/A" (not applicable) column. Any item marked "No" should be explained in the checklist or in a separate memorandum. It is not necessary to complete the individual checklist items for topics checked "Item Not Present."

This Financial Statement Disclosures Checklist has been updated through the following authoritative pronouncements:

- FAS-140 (September 2000)
- FTB 97-1 (December 1997)
- FIN-44 (March 2000)
- FASB Question-and-Answer documents through FAS-140 (February 2001)
- EITF 00-27 (November 2000)
- SOP 00-3 (December 2000)
- PB-15 (January 1997)

TABLE OF CONTENTS

PART I—BALANCE SHEET

PART II—INCOME STATEMENT

PART III—STATEMENT OF CASH FLOWS

PART IV—OTHER FINANCIAL STATEMENT TOPICS AND DISCLOSURES

	Page No.	*Item Present*	*Item Not Present*
Foreign Operations and Currency Translation	51.76	______	______
Going-Concern Disclosures	51.80	______	______
Impairment of Certain Loans	51.81	______	______
Impairment of Long-Lived Assets and Long-Lived Assets to Be Disposed Of	51.82	______	______
Interest Cost	51.83	______	______
Interim Financial Reporting	51.84	______	______
Leases—Lessees	51.90	______	______
Leases—Lessors	51.92	______	______
Leases—Tax Leases	51.94	______	______
Lending Activities	51.95	______	______
Limited Liability Companies or Partnerships (LLCs or LLPs)	51.95	______	______
Long-Term Contracts	51.96	______	______
Nonmonetary Transactions	51.97	______	______
Pension and Postretirement Benefit Plans:	51.97	______	______
• Pension and Postretirement Defined Benefit Plans—Reduced Disclosure Requirements for Nonpublic Companies	51.97	______	______
• Pension and Postretirement Defined Benefit Plans—Public Companies (and Nonpublic Companies That Elect to Voluntarily Provide Additional Disclosures)	51.100	______	______
• Pension and Postretirement Defined Contribution Plans—All Companies	51.104	______	______
• Pension and Postretirement Multiemployer Plans—All Companies	51.104	______	______
Postemployment Benefits	51.105	______	______
Prior-Period Adjustments (Correction of Errors)	51.105	______	______
Quasi-Reorganizations and Reorganizations under the Bankruptcy Code:	51.106	______	______

	Page No.	*Item Present*	*Item Not Present*
• Quasi-Reorganizations	51.106	______	______
• Reorganizations under the Bankruptcy Code	51.107	______	______
Related-Party Transactions	51.109	______	______
Research and Development	51.110	______	______
Segment Information	51.111	______	______
Stock-Based Compensation	51.115	______	______
Subsequent Events	51.117	______	______
Termination Claims	51.117	______	______
Transfers and Servicing of Financial Assets	51.117	______	______
• Transfers of Financial Assets	51.118	______	______
• Servicing of Financial Assets and Liabilities	51.120	______	______
Troubled Debt Restructuring—Creditors	51.121	______	______
Troubled Debt Restructuring—Debtors	51.122	______	______

PART I—BALANCE SHEET

	Yes	*No*	*N/A*
GENERAL DISCLOSURES			
1. If a classified balance sheet is used, does the balance sheet contain classifications for:	___	___	___
a. Total current assets? (Generally accepted practice)	___	___	___
b. Total current liabilities? (FAS-6, par. 15)	___	___	___
2. Are items classified as current assets expected to be realized within one year (or within the entity's operating cycle)? (ARB-43, Ch. 3A)	___	___	___
3. If a company's normal operating cycle is longer than one year and the balance sheet is classified, has disclosure been made of the practice followed for the classification of current assets and liabilities, including the following: (ARB-43, Ch. 3A)	___	___	___
a. An estimate of the amounts not realizable or payable within one year, if practicable?	___	___	___
b. The amount of liabilities maturing in each year, if practicable, and applicable interest rates or range of rates?	___	___	___
4. Are contra-valuation accounts properly disclosed? (CON-6, par. 34)	___	___	___
CASH AND CASH EQUIVALENTS			
1. Are cash overdrafts not subject to offset by other cash accounts in the same financial institution classified as current liabilities? (Generally accepted practice)	___	___	___
2. Are checks from customers held as of the end of the period accounted for as cash? (Generally accepted practice)	___	___	___
3. Are checks payable to vendors held as of the end of the period accounted for as accounts payable? (Generally accepted practice)	___	___	___
4. Are the following items excluded from the cash classification: (ARB-43, Ch. 3A, par. 6)	___	___	___

	Yes	*No*	*N/A*
a. Cash amounts restricted as to withdrawal or use for other than current operations?	___	___	___
b. Cash amounts designated for expenditure in the acquisition or construction of noncurrent assets?	___	___	___
c. Cash amounts segregated for the liquidation of long-term debt?	___	___	___
5. Are significant concentrations of credit risk arising from cash deposits in excess of federally insured amounts disclosed? (FAS-105, par. 20)	___	___	___
6. Have the following disclosures been made for legally restrictive compensating balance agreements: (Generally accepted practice)	___	___	___
a. The terms of the compensating balance agreement?	___	___	___
b. The amount of the compensating balance requirement?	___	___	___
c. The amount required to be maintained to assure future credit availability and the terms of that agreement?	___	___	___
d. The maintenance of compensating balances for the benefit of a related party?	___	___	___

ACCOUNTS AND NOTES RECEIVABLE

1. Are trade notes and accounts receivable reported under a heading separate from other receivables? (ARB-43, Ch. 1A, par. 5)	___	___	___
2. Are notes and accounts receivable from officers, employees, or affiliated companies reported under separate headings? (ARB-43, Ch. 1A, par. 5)	___	___	___
3. Are valuation allowances (such as uncollectible accounts and returned goods) deducted from the related accounts and notes receivable? (APB-12, par. 3)	___	___	___
4. Are unearned discounts (other than cash or quantity discounts and the like), interest, and finance charges included in receivables deducted from the face of the related receivables? (APB-6, par. 14; APB-21, par. 16)	___	___	___

	Yes	No	N/A
5. Is the unamortized balance of loan origination, commitment, other fees and costs, and purchase premiums and discounts recognized as adjustments of yield pursuant to FAS-91 reported on the company's balance sheet as part of the related loan balance? (FAS-91, par. 8)	___	___	___
6. Do notes receivable that require the imputation of interest as required by APB-21 include the following presentation or disclosures: (APB-21, par. 16)	___	___	___
a. Is the related discount (premium) reported in the balance sheet as a direct deduction from (addition to) the face amount of the notes?	___	___	___
b. Does the description include the effective interest rate?	___	___	___
c. Is the face amount of the notes disclosed in the financial statements or in the notes?	___	___	___
d. Is the amortization of discount or premium classified as part of interest expense?	___	___	___
e. Are the related issuance costs presented on the balance sheet as deferred costs?	___	___	___
7. Have disclosures been made for transfers of receivables? (See "Transfers and Servicing of Financial Assets")	___	___	___
8. Are disclosures made with respect to guarantees to repurchase receivables or related property that has been sold or otherwise assigned? (FAS-5, par. 12)	___	___	___
9. Are significant concentrations of credit risk arising from receivables disclosed? (See "Financial Instruments—Other Disclosures," Items 3 and 6)	___	___	___
10. Have the disclosures required by FAS-118 been made for impaired loans? (See "Impairment of Certain Loans")	___	___	___
11. Have the applicable fair value disclosures been made? (See "Financial Instruments—Other Disclosures," Items 4 and 7)	___	___	___

Yes No N/A

INVENTORY

1. Are major categories of inventories (raw materials, work in process, finished goods, and supplies) presented? (ARB-43, Ch. 3A, par. 4) ___ ___ ___
2. Have the basis for carrying inventories and the method of determining cost been disclosed? (ARB-43, Ch. 3A, par. 9; ARB-43, Ch. 4) ___ ___ ___
3. Are valuation allowances for inventory losses deducted from related inventory balances? (CON-6, par. 34) ___ ___ ___
4. If material, are losses resulting from the write-down from cost to market disclosed? (ARB-43, Ch. 4, par. 14) ___ ___ ___
5. If the LIFO inventory method is used, is the difference between the LIFO amount and replacement cost (LIFO reserve) disclosed? (Generally accepted practice) ___ ___ ___
6. Are amounts from the liquidation of a LIFO layer disclosed? (Generally accepted practice) ___ ___ ___
7. Has overhead been allocated to inventory in accordance with GAAP? (ARB-43, Ch. 4, par. 8) ___ ___ ___
8. Have material losses on inventory purchase commitments been recorded and properly disclosed? (ARB-43, Ch. 4, par. 17) ___ ___ ___

INVESTMENTS—DEBT AND EQUITY SECURITIES

Questions 1 through 7 apply if FAS-133 (Accounting for Derivative Instruments and Hedging Activities) Has ***not*** *Been Adopted (***Note:*** FAS-133 is effective for all fiscal quarters of fiscal years beginning after June 15, 2000.)*

1. For securities classified as available-for-sale and separately for securities classified as held-to-maturity, have the following disclosures been made, by major security type, as of each date for which a balance sheet is presented: (FAS-115, par. 19) ___ ___ ___

	Yes	*No*	*N/A*
a. The aggregate fair value?	___	___	___
b. Gross unrealized holding gains?	___	___	___
c. Gross unrealized holding losses?	___	___	___
d. Amortized cost basis?	___	___	___
Note: Financial institutions should disclose the above information for the following types of securities: (1) equity securities, (2) debt securities issued by the U.S. Treasury and other U.S. government corporations and agencies, (3) debt securities issued by states of the United States and political subdivisions of the states, (4) debt securities issued by foreign governments, (5) corporate debt securities, (6) mortgage-backed securities, and (7) other debt securities.	___	___	___
2. For investments in debt securities classified as available-for-sale and separately for securities classified as held-to-maturity, have the following disclosures been made: (FAS-115, par. 20)	___	___	___
a. Information about the contractual maturities of the securities as of the date of the most recent balance sheet presented? (*Note:* Maturity information may be combined in appropriate groupings for companies other than financial institutions.)	___	___	___
b. The basis for allocation of securities not due at a single maturity date, if such securities are allocated over several maturity groupings?	___	___	___
Note: Financial institutions should disclose the fair value and the amortized cost of debt securities based on at least the following four maturity groupings: (1) within one year, (2) after 1 year through 5 years, (3) after 5 years through 10 years, and (4) after 10 years.			
3. Have the following disclosures been made for each period for which an income statement is presented: (FAS-115, par. 21)	___	___	___
a. The proceeds from sales of available-for-sale securities and the gross realized gains and the gross realized losses on those sales?	___	___	___

Yes No N/A

b. The basis on which cost was determined in computing realized gain or loss (i.e., specific identification, average cost, or other method used)? ___ ___ ___

c. The gross gains and gross losses included in earnings from transfers of securities from the available-for-sale category into the trading category? (*Note:* Such transfers should be rare.) ___ ___ ___

d. The change in net unrealized holding gain or loss on available-for-sale securities that has been included in other comprehensive income during the period? ___ ___ ___

e. The change in net unrealized holding gain or loss on trading securities that has been included in earnings during the period? ___ ___ ___

4. For any sales of or transfers from securities classified as held-to-maturity, have the following disclosures been made for each period for which an income statement is presented: (FAS-115, par. 22) ___ ___ ___

   a. The amortized cost amount of the sold or transferred security? ___ ___ ___

   b. The related realized or unrealized gain or loss at the date of sale or transfer? ___ ___ ___

   c. The circumstances leading to the decision to sell or transfer the security? ___ ___ ___

5. Have the following been disclosed about futures contracts accounted for as hedges: (FAS-80, par. 12) ___ ___ ___

   a. Nature of the assets, liabilities, firm commitments, or anticipated transactions that are hedged with futures contracts? ___ ___ ___

   b. Method of accounting for futures contracts including a description of the events or transactions that cause changes in the contracts' values to be recognized in income? ___ ___ ___

6. Have the required disclosures been made for transfers of financial assets? (See "Transfers and Servicing of Financial Assets") ___ ___ ___

Yes No N/A

7. Has the policy for accounting for the premium paid to acquire an option classified as held-to-maturity or available-for-sale been disclosed? (EITF 96-11) ___ ___ ___

*Questions 8 through 14 apply if FAS-133 (Accounting for Derivative Instruments and Hedging Activities) Has Been Adopted (**Note:** FAS-133 is effective for all fiscal quarters of fiscal years beginning after June 15, 2000.)*

8. For securities classified as available-for-sale, have the following disclosures been made, by major security type, as of each date for which a balance sheet is presented: (FAS-133, par. 534) ___ ___ ___
   a. The aggregate fair value? ___ ___ ___
   b. Total gains for securities with net gains in accumulated other comprehensive income? ___ ___ ___
   c. Total losses for securities with net losses in accumulated other comprehensive income? ___ ___ ___

Note: Financial institutions should disclose the above information for the following types of securities: (1) equity securities, (2) debt securities issued by the U.S. Treasury and other U.S. government corporations and agencies, (3) debt securities issued by states of the United States and political subdivisions of the states, (4) debt securities issued by foreign governments, (5) corporate debt securities, (6) mortgage-backed securities, and (7) other debt securities.

9. For securities classified as held-to-maturity, have the following disclosures been made, by major security type, as of each date for which a balance sheet is presented: (FAS-133, par. 534) ___ ___ ___
   a. The aggregate fair value? ___ ___ ___
   b. Gross unrecognized holding gains? ___ ___ ___
   c. Gross unrecognized holding losses? ___ ___ ___
   d. Net carrying amount? ___ ___ ___
   e. Gross gains and losses in accumulated other comprehensive income for any derivatives

Yes *No* *N/A*

that hedged the forecasted acquisition of the held-to-maturity securities? ___ ___ ___

10. For investments in debt securities classified as available-for-sale and separately for securities classified as held-to-maturity, have the following disclosures been made: (FAS-115, par. 20) ___ ___ ___

    a. Information about the contractual maturities of the securities as of the date of the most recent balance sheet presented? (*Note:* Maturity information may be combined in appropriate groupings for companies other than financial institutions.) ___ ___ ___

    b. The basis for allocation of securities not due at a single maturity date, if such securities are allocated over several maturity groupings? ___ ___ ___

Note: Financial institutions should disclose the fair value and the net carrying amount (if different from fair value) of debt securities based on at least the following four maturity groupings: (1) within one year, (2) after 1 year through 5 years, (3) after 5 years through 10 years, and (4) after 10 years. ___ ___ ___

11. Have the following disclosures been made for each period for which an income statement is presented: (FAS-115, par. 21; FAS-133, par. 534) ___ ___ ___

    a. The proceeds from sales of available-for-sale securities and the gross realized gains and the gross realized losses on those sales? ___ ___ ___

    b. The method used to determine the cost of a security sold or the amount reclassified out of accumulated other comprehensive income into earnings (i.e., specific identification, average cost, or other method used)? ___ ___ ___

    c. The gross gains and gross losses included in earnings from transfers of securities from the available-for-sale category into the trading category? (*Note:* Such transfers should be rare.) ___ ___ ___

    d. The amount of the net unrealized holding gain or loss on available-for-sale securities that has been included in accumulated other comprehensive income for the period? ___ ___ ___

	Yes	No	N/A
e. The amount of gains and losses reclassified out of accumulated other comprehensive income into earnings for the period?	___	___	___
f. The portion of trading gains and losses for the period that relates to trading securities still held at the balance sheet date?	___	___	___
12. For any sales of or transfers from securities classified as held-to-maturity, have the following disclosures been made for each period for which an income statement is presented: (FAS-115, par. 22; FAS-133, par. 534)	___	___	___
a. The net carrying amount of the sold or transferred security?	___	___	___
b. The net gain or loss in accumulated other comprehensive income for any derivative that hedged the forecasted acquisition of the held-to-maturity security?	___	___	___
c. The related realized or unrealized gain or loss at the date of sale or transfer?	___	___	___
d. The circumstances leading to the decision to sell or transfer the security?	___	___	___
13. Has the policy for accounting for the premium paid to acquire an option classified as held-to-maturity or available-for-sale been disclosed? (EITF 96-11)	___	___	___
14. Have the required disclosures been made for transfers of financial assets? (See "Transfers and Servicing of Financial Assets")	___	___	___

INVESTMENTS—EQUITY AND COST METHODS

	Yes	No	N/A
1. Have the following disclosures been made with respect to investments in common stock of 20% or more when the equity method is used: (APB-18, par. 20)	___	___	___
a. The name of each investee and percentage of ownership of common stock?	___	___	___
b. The accounting policies of the investor with respect to the investment in common stock?	___	___	___

	Yes	*No*	*N/A*
c. The difference, if any, between the amount of the carrying value of the investment and the amount of underlying equity in net assets and the accounting treatment of the difference?	___	___	___
d. The aggregate market value of investments for which quoted market prices are available (not required for investments in common stock of subsidiaries)?	___	___	___
e. When investments in common stock of corporate joint ventures or other investments accounted for under the equity method are, in the aggregate, material, has summarized information of assets, liabilities, and results of operations of the investees been presented in notes or separate statements, either individually or in groups?	___	___	___
f. Material effects of possible conversions of outstanding convertible securities, exercise of outstanding options and warrants, and other contingent issuances that could have a significant effect on the investor's share of reported earnings or losses?	___	___	___
2. Is the reason for not using the equity method when the investor company owns 20% or more of the voting stock of the investee company, and the name of the significant investee, disclosed? (APB-18, par. 20, footnote 13)	___	___	___
3. Is the reason for using the equity method when the investor company owns less than 20% of the voting stock of the investee company, and the name of the significant investee, disclosed? (APB-18, par. 20, footnote 13)	___	___	___
4. Is the investment presented in the balance sheet as a single amount rather than as proportional amounts of specific assets and liabilities of the investee company? (APB-18, par. 19)	___	___	___
5. Is the equity in the earnings of the investee company presented in the investor company's income statement as a single amount, except for the proportional amount of gains/losses from the disposition of a business segment, extraordinary gains/losses, and the cumulative effects of changes in accounting principles? (APB-18, par. 19)	___	___	___

Yes No N/A

6. Is the proportional share of prior-period adjustments made by the investee company, if any, presented as part of the retained earnings of the investor company? (APB-18, par. 19) ___ ___ ___
7. Is the policy disclosed for determining the amount of equity method losses after the common stock investment has been reduced to zero as a result of previous losses? (EITF 99-10) ___ ___ ___

PROPERTY, PLANT, AND EQUIPMENT

1. Have the following disclosures been made with respect to depreciable assets: (APB-12, par. 5) ___ ___ ___
   a. The basis of determining the amounts shown in the balance sheet, such as cost? ___ ___ ___
   b. Balances of major classes of depreciable property presented by nature or function at the balance sheet date? ___ ___ ___
   c. Accumulated depreciation presented by major classes of assets or in total at the balance sheet date? ___ ___ ___
   d. A general description of the method(s) used to compute depreciation for major classes of depreciable assets? ___ ___ ___
   e. The amount of depreciation expense for each year for which an income statement is presented? ___ ___ ___
2. Is property, plant, and equipment that is idle or held for sale identified and presented separately from property, plant, and equipment currently used in the business? (Generally accepted practice) ___ ___ ___
3. Is the amount of interest capitalized as part of the cost of plant and equipment disclosed? (FAS-34, par. 21) ___ ___ ___
4. Are property and equipment pledged as security for loans disclosed? (FAS-5, par. 18) ___ ___ ___
5. Have the following **optional** disclosures been made, if they are considered useful: (*Note:* Although not required by GAAP, these disclosures are in some cases made by companies when they are considered useful to a better understanding of the company's accounting policies.): ___ ___ ___

	Yes	No	N/A
a. The accounting treatment for maintenance and repairs, betterments, and renewals?	___	___	___
b. The policy for adjusting accumulated depreciation when property and equipment is disposed of, and the treatment of any gain or loss on disposition?	___	___	___
c. The rates or lives used in computing depreciation?	___	___	___
6. If property, plant, and equipment are impaired or are to be disposed of, have the disclosures required by FAS-121 been made? (See "Impairment of Long-Lived Assets and Long-Lived Assets to Be Disposed Of")	___	___	___

INTANGIBLE ASSETS

	Yes	No	N/A
1. Is the amortization method and amortization period for specific intangible assets disclosed? (APB-17, par. 30)	___	___	___
2. If an intangible is not amortized, is the reason for the lack of amortization disclosed? (Generally accepted practice)	___	___	___
3. If the period over which an intangible is amortized has been significantly reduced, has the reason for the reduction been disclosed? (APB-17, par. 31)	___	___	___
4. If intangible assets are impaired or are to be disposed of, have the disclosures required by FAS-121 been made? (See "Impairment of Long-Lived Assets and Long-Lived Assets to Be Disposed Of")	___	___	___

INCOME TAXES

	Yes	No	N/A
1. If a classified balance sheet is presented, have the following been disclosed: (ARB-43, Ch. 3A; FAS-109, par. 41)	___	___	___
a. Income taxes currently payable or refundable?	___	___	___
b. Current and noncurrent deferred tax assets, including the valuation allowance, if any?	___	___	___
c. Current and noncurrent deferred tax liabilities?	___	___	___

	Yes	*No*	*N/A*
2. Have the following components of the net deferred tax liability or asset recognized in the balance sheet been disclosed: (FAS-109, par. 43)	___	___	___
a. The total of all deferred tax liabilities for taxable temporary differences?	___	___	___
b. The total of all deferred tax assets for deductible temporary differences, operating loss carryforwards, and tax credit carryforwards?	___	___	___
c. The total valuation allowance recognized for deferred tax assets?	___	___	___
3. Has the net change during the year in the total valuation allowance account been disclosed? (FAS-109, par. 43)	___	___	___
4. Are the following components (where applicable) of income tax expense related to continuing operations for each year presented: (FAS-109, par. 45)	___	___	___
a. Current tax expense or benefit?	___	___	___
b. Deferred tax expense or benefit (exclusive of items listed below)?	___	___	___
c. Investment tax credits?	___	___	___
d. Government grants (to the extent they have been used to reduce income tax expense)?	___	___	___
e. Benefits arising from operating loss carryforwards?	___	___	___
f. Tax expense arising from allocating tax benefits either directly to contributed capital or to reduce goodwill or other noncurrent intangible assets of an acquired company?	___	___	___
g. Adjustments to a deferred tax liability or asset arising from changes in tax laws, tax rates, or the entity's tax status?	___	___	___
h. Adjustments to the beginning balance in the valuation allowance account related to deferred tax assets that arise due to changes in the amount of assets expected to be realized?	___	___	___
5. Is income tax expense or benefit (intra-period income tax allocation) for each of the following disclosed for each year for which the items are presented: (FAS-109, par. 46; APB-9, par. 26; APB-20, par. 20)	___	___	___

	Yes	*No*	*N/A*
a. Continuing operations?	___	___	___
b. Discontinued operations?	___	___	___
c. Extraordinary items?	___	___	___
d. The cumulative effect of accounting changes?	___	___	___
e. Prior-period adjustments?	___	___	___
f. Items charged or credited directly to shareholders' equity?	___	___	___
g. Other comprehensive income	___	___	___
6. For a particular tax-paying component of an enterprise and within a particular tax jurisdiction (e.g., federal, state, or local): (FAS-109, par. 42)	___	___	___
a. Have all current deferred tax liabilities and assets been offset and presented as a single amount?	___	___	___
b. Have all noncurrent deferred tax liabilities and assets been offset and presented as a single amount?	___	___	___
c. Have the net current deferred tax asset or liability and the net noncurrent deferred tax asset or liability within each tax jurisdiction been shown separately for each tax-paying component?	___	___	___
7. If the entity is a member of a group that files a consolidated tax return, are the following disclosures made in its separately issued financial statements: (FAS-109, par. 49)	___	___	___
a. The amount of current and deferred tax expense for each statement of income presented?	___	___	___
b. The amount of any tax-related balances due to or from affiliates as of the date of each balance sheet presented?	___	___	___
c. The principal provisions of the method by which the consolidated amount of current and deferred tax expense is allocated to members of the group, and the nature and effect of any changes in that method (and in determining related balance to or from affiliates) during the years for which the disclosures in a. and b. above are presented?	___	___	___

Yes No N/A

8. Have types of significant temporary differences and carryforwards been disclosed? (FAS-109, par. 43) ___ ___ ___

9. Has the nature of significant reconciling items been disclosed between (a) the reported amount of income tax expense attributable to continuing operations for the year and (b) the amount of income tax expense that would result from applying domestic federal statutory tax rates to pretax income from continuing operations? (*Note:* A numerical reconciliation, such as the one described in 15 b. below, is not required for nonpublic companies.) (FAS-109, par. 47) ___ ___ ___

10. Have the amounts and expiration dates for operating loss and tax credit carryforwards for tax purposes been disclosed? (FAS-109, par. 48) ___ ___ ___

11. Has the portion of the valuation allowance for deferred tax assets for which subsequently recognized tax benefits will be allocated to reduce goodwill or other noncurrent intangible assets of an acquired entity or directly to contributed capital been disclosed? (FAS-109, par. 48) ___ ___ ___

12. Have the nature and effect of any other significant matters affecting comparability of information for all periods presented been disclosed if not otherwise evident from the disclosures discussed in this section? (FAS-109, par. 47) ___ ___ ___

13. Is the method of accounting for the investment tax credit (deferral method or flow-through method) and related amount used in the determination of income tax expense disclosed? (APB-4, par. 11) ___ ___ ___

14. Are proper disclosures made when a change in an entity's tax status becomes effective after year end but before the financial statements are issued? (QA-11, FAS-109) ___ ___ ___

15. Have the following required disclosures been made for *public* companies (optional for nonpublic companies): (FAS-109, par. 43) ___ ___ ___

    a. The approximate tax effect of each type of temporary difference and carryforward that gives rise to a significant portion of deferred tax liabilities and assets (before allocation of valuation allowance)? (FAS-109, par. 43) ___ ___ ___

Yes No N/A

b. A reconciliation (using percentages or dollar amounts) of the reported amount of income tax expense attributable to continuing operations for the year to the amount of income tax expense that would result from applying domestic federal statutory tax rates to pretax income from continuing operations? (*Note:* If alternative tax systems exist, such as the U.S. alternative minimum tax, the regular tax rate should be used.) (FAS-109, par. 47) ___ ___ ___

16. Are the following items disclosed when a deferred tax liability is not recognized because of the exceptions allowed by APB-23 (i.e., undistributed earnings of subsidiaries or corporate joint ventures, bad debt reserves of savings and loan associations, or policy holders' surplus of life insurance companies) or for deposits in statutory reserve funds by U.S. steamship companies: (FAS-109, par. 44) ___ ___ ___

    a. Description of temporary differences that did not create a deferred tax liability and the event(s) that would cause the temporary differences to become taxable? ___ ___ ___

    b. Cumulative amount of each type of temporary difference? ___ ___ ___

    c. Amount of unrecognized deferred tax liability arising from temporary differences related to investments in foreign subsidiaries and foreign corporate joint ventures that are considered permanent? (If it is not practical to compute the amount, then that fact should be stated.) ___ ___ ___

    d. Amount of unrecognized deferred tax liability for temporary differences related to (1) undistributed domestic earnings, (2) bad-debt reserve for tax purposes of U.S. savings and loan associations or other qualified thrift lenders, (3) the policyholders' surplus of a life insurance enterprise, and (4) statutory reserve funds of a U.S. steamship enterprise? ___ ___ ___

17. For companies that recognize the tax benefits of prior deductible temporary differences and carryforwards in income rather than contributed capital (i.e., companies that have previously adopted FAS-96 and effected a quasi-reorgani-

Yes No N/A

zation that involved only the elimination of a deficit in retained earnings), have the following disclosures been made: (FAS-109, par. 39) ___ ___ ___

a. The date of the quasi-reorganization? ___ ___ ___

b. The manner of reporting the tax benefits and that it differs from present accounting requirements for other entities? ___ ___ ___

c. The effect of those tax benefits on income from continuing operations, income before extraordinary items, and net income (and on related per share amounts, if applicable)? ___ ___ ___

18. Has disclosure been made of the amount of income tax benefit realized from the exercise of employee stock options, if the amount of that benefit is credited to equity but is not presented as a separate line item in the statement of changes in stockholders' equity or in the statement of cash flows? (EITF 00-15) ___ ___ ___

CURRENT LIABILITIES

1. Are liabilities due on demand, or within a year from the balance sheet date (or operating cycle, if longer), presented as current liabilities and segregated by type? (ARB-43, Ch. 3A, par. 7) ___ ___ ___

2. With respect to accounting for compensated absences: (FAS-43, pars. 6, 7, 15) ___ ___ ___

   a. Are liabilities appropriately accrued and reported for employees' compensation for future absences? ___ ___ ___

   b. If the entity has not accrued a liability for compensated absences because the amount cannot be reasonably estimated, has that fact been disclosed? ___ ___ ___

3. With respect to real and personal property taxes: (ARB-43, Ch. 10A, par. 16) ___ ___ ___

   a. Is an accrued liability, whether estimated or definitely known, included in current liabilities? ___ ___ ___

   b. If estimates are used for accrual and are subject to a substantial measure of uncertainty, has the liability been disclosed as estimated? ___ ___ ___

Yes No N/A

DEBT OBLIGATIONS AND CREDIT ARRANGEMENTS

1. Are significant categories of debt (e.g., notes payable to banks, related-party notes, capital lease obligations) and the terms, interest rates, maturity rates, and subordinate features disclosed? (Generally accepted practice) ___ ___ ___
2. Are restrictive covenants (e.g., restrictions on additional borrowings, obligations to maintain minimum working capital or restrict dividends) and pledged assets disclosed? (FAS-5, pars. 18–19) ___ ___ ___
3. Are the following disclosures made for debt securities that carry an unreasonable interest rate or are non-interest-bearing: (APB-21, par. 16) ___ ___ ___
   a. The unamortized discount or premium that is reported in the balance sheet as a direct deduction from or as an addition to the face amount of the note? ___ ___ ___
   b. The face amount of the note? ___ ___ ___
   c. The effective interest rate? ___ ___ ___
   d. Amortization of discount or premium reported as interest in the income statement? ___ ___ ___
   e. Related debt issue costs that are reported as deferred charges in the balance sheet? ___ ___ ___
4. Are the following disclosures made for each of the five years following the date of the latest balance sheet presented: (FAS-47, par. 10) ___ ___ ___
   a. The combined aggregate amount of maturities and sinking fund requirements for all long-term borrowings? ___ ___ ___
   b. The amount of redemption requirements for all issues of capital stock that are redeemable at fixed or determinable prices on fixed or determinable dates, separately by issue or combined? ___ ___ ___
5. If a short-term obligation expected to be refinanced on a long-term basis is excluded from current liabilities, are the following disclosures made: (FAS-6, par. 15) ___ ___ ___
   a. A general description of the financing agreement? ___ ___ ___

	Yes	No	N/A
b. The terms of any new obligation incurred or expected to be incurred or equity securities issued or expected to be issued as a result of the refinancing?	___	___	___
6. Are current maturities of long-term debt presented as current liabilities? (ARB-43, Ch. 3A, par. 7)	___	___	___
7. Are debt obligations that, by their terms, are due on demand or will be due on demand within one year (or operating cycle, if longer) from the balance sheet date, even though liquidation may not be expected within that period, included in current liabilities? (FAS-78, par. 5)	___	___	___
8. Do current liabilities include long-term obligations that are or will be callable by the creditor either because the debtor's violation of a provision of the debt agreement at the balance sheet date makes the obligation callable or because the violation, if not cured within a specified grace period, will make the obligation callable unless one of the following conditions is met: (FAS-78, par. 5)	___	___	___
a. The creditor has waived or subsequently lost the right to demand repayment for more than one year (or operating cycle, if longer) from the balance sheet date?	___	___	___
b. For long-term obligations containing a grace period within which the debtor may cure the violation, it is probable that the violation will be cured within that period, thus preventing the obligation from becoming callable?	___	___	___
c. If an obligation under (b) above is classified as a long-term liability, are the circumstances disclosed?	___	___	___
9. Are the conversion features and descriptions of convertible debt adequately disclosed and do they explain the pertinent rights and privileges of the convertible debt? (APB-14, pars. 16–18)	___	___	___
10. Have the following disclosures been made when events of default under a credit agreement have occurred at any time prior to the date of the accountant's report and have not been cured or waived or a valid waiver has been obtained for			

	Yes	*No*	*N/A*
only a stated period of time (SAS-1, AU 560) (EITF 86–30):	___	___	___
a. The nature and amount of the default?	___	___	___
b. The period for which the violation has been waived?	___	___	___
11. Are significant changes in long-term obligations subsequent to the date of the financial statements disclosed? (FAS-5, par. 11)	___	___	___
12. For unrecorded, unconditional purchase obligations, have the following disclosures been made: (FAS-47, pars. 6–8)	___	___	___
a. The nature and term of the obligation?	___	___	___
b. The amount of the fixed and determinable portion of the obligation as of the date of the latest balance sheet presented in the aggregate and, if determinable, for each of the five succeeding fiscal years?	___	___	___
c. The nature of any variable components of the obligation?	___	___	___
d. The amounts purchased under the obligation for each period for which an income statement is presented?	___	___	___
e. The amount of imputed interest necessary to reduce the unconditional purchase obligation to its present value (optional disclosure)?	___	___	___
13. For recorded, unconditional purchase obligations, have the following disclosures been made for each of the five years following the date of the latest balance sheet presented: (FAS-47, par. 10)	___	___	___
a. The aggregate amounts of payments for unconditional purchase obligations?	___	___	___
b. The combined aggregate amount of maturities and sinking fund requirements?	___	___	___
c. The amount of redemption requirements for all issues of capital stock that are redeemable at fixed or determinable prices on fixed or determinable dates, separately by issue or combined?	___	___	___
14. Have the applicable fair value disclosures been made? (See "Financial Instruments—Other Disclosures," Items 4 and 7)	___	___	___

Yes No N/A

STOCKHOLDERS' EQUITY

1. Are the following disclosures made for each class of capital stock: (Generally accepted practice) ___ ___ ___
   a. Shares authorized, issued, and outstanding? ___ ___ ___
   b. Par value or stated value? ___ ___ ___
   c. The number of shares reserved for future issuance and the purpose for such reservation? ___ ___ ___
2. Are the following disclosures made for preferred stock or other senior stock that has a preference in involuntary liquidation considerably in excess of the par or stated values of the shares: (FAS-129, pars. 6–7) ___ ___ ___
   a. The liquidation preference of the stock (the relationship between the preference in liquidation and the par or stated value of the shares)? (*Note:* That disclosure should be made in the equity section of the balance sheet in the aggregate, rather than the notes.) ___ ___ ___
   b. The aggregate or per-share amounts at which preferred stock may be called or is subject to redemption through sinking-fund operations or otherwise? ___ ___ ___
   c. The aggregate and per-share amounts of arrearages in cumulative preferred dividends? ___ ___ ___
3. Have the following disclosures been made of the rights and privileges of the various securities outstanding: (FAS-129, par. 4) ___ ___ ___
   a. Dividend, liquidation, or call preferences? ___ ___ ___
   b. Participation rights? ___ ___ ___
   c. Call prices and dates? ___ ___ ___
   d. Conversion or exercise prices or rates and pertinent dates? ___ ___ ___
   e. Sinking fund requirements? ___ ___ ___
   f. Unusual voting rights? ___ ___ ___
   g. Significant terms of contracts to issue additional shares? ___ ___ ___
4. Have the number of shares issued on conversion, exercise, or otherwise during at least the most recent annual fiscal period and any subse-

	Yes	*No*	*N/A*
quent interim period presented been disclosed? (FAS-129, par. 5)	___	___	___
5. Is there a disclosure for each of the five years following the date of the latest balance sheet presented for the amount of redemption requirements for all issues of capital stock redeemable at fixed or determinable prices on fixed or determinable dates? (FAS-47, par. 10 and FAS-129, par. 8)	___	___	___
6. Are dividends declared but not yet paid at the balance sheet date classified as a current liability? (ARB-43, Ch. 3A, par. 7)	___	___	___
7. Are restrictions on dividend payments disclosed? (FAS-5, pars. 18–19)	___	___	___
8. Are appropriations for loss contingencies shown in the stockholders' equity section and clearly identified as such? (FAS-5, par. 15)	___	___	___
9. Are disclosures made of the nature and extent to which retained earnings is restricted? (APB-6, par. 13)	___	___	___
10. Are the following disclosures relative to changes in stockholders' equity made for each period in which both a balance sheet and statement of income are presented (the disclosures may be in the form of a separate statement, in a note to the financial statements, or in the body of the balance sheet): (APB-12, par. 10)	___	___	___
a. Changes in the separate accounts comprising stockholders' equity?	___	___	___
b. Changes in the number of shares of equity securities during at least the most recent annual fiscal period?	___	___	___
11. Are stock subscriptions receivable presented as a contra-equity account (or if shown as an asset, is the receivable clearly labeled and segregated from any other type of asset)? (Generally accepted practice)	___	___	___
12. Are the following disclosures made with respect to treasury stock: (APB-6, par. 13)	___	___	___
a. The method used to account for the treasury stock?	___	___	___
b. The number of shares of treasury stock held?	___	___	___

	Yes	*No*	*N/A*
c. Accounting treatment in accordance with state law if it is at variance with GAAP?	___	___	___
13. If treasury stock is acquired for purposes other than retirement (formal or constructive), or if the ultimate disposition has not yet been decided, has it been accounted for in one of the following ways: (APB-6, par. 12b)	___	___	___
a. Has the cost been shown separately as a deduction from the total of capital stock, additional paid-in capital, and retained earnings? or	___	___	___
b. Has the par value of the shares been charged to the specific stock issue and the excess of purchase price over the par value allocated between additional paid-in capital and retained earnings? (Alternatively, the excess may be charged entirely to retained earnings.)	___	___	___
14. If treasury stock of the entity is shown as an asset, have the circumstances for such classification been disclosed? (ARB-43, Ch. 1A, par. 4)	___	___	___
15. If an agreement to purchase treasury shares also involves the receipt or payment of consideration in exchange for stated or unstated rights or privileges, has the purchase price been allocated properly and the accounting treatment disclosed? (FTB 85-6)	___	___	___
16. Is disclosure made of capital shares reserved for future issuance in connection with a business combination (APB-16, pars. 78 and 95)?	___	___	___
17. If a stock dividend, split, or reverse split occurs after the date of the latest balance sheet presented, but before the issuance of the financial statements have the following disclosures been made: (Generally accepted practice)	___	___	___
a. An explanation of the stock dividend, split, or reverse split and the date?	___	___	___
b. The retroactive effect provided in the balance sheet?	___	___	___
18. Have the following disclosures been made for warrants or rights outstanding as of the most recent balance sheet date: (Generally accepted practice)	___	___	___

	Yes	No	N/A
a. The title and aggregate amount of securities called for by warrants or rights outstanding?			
b. The period during which warrants or rights are exercisable?			
c. The exercise price?			
19. Is the accumulated balance of other comprehensive income displayed separately from retained earnings and additional paid-in capital in the equity section of the balance sheet? (FAS-130, par. 26)			
20. Is each classification of accumulated other comprehensive income presented in one of the following manners: (FAS-130, par. 26)			
a. On the face of the balance sheet as a separate component of equity?			
b. On the statement of changes in stockholders' equity?			
c. In the notes to the financial statements?			
21. If FAS-133 (Accounting for Derivative Instruments and Hedging Activities) has been adopted, have the following been separately disclosed as part of the disclosures of accumulated other comprehensive income: (FAS-133, par. 47) (*Note:* FAS-133 is effective for all fiscal quarters of fiscal years beginning after June 15, 2000.)			
a. The beginning and ending accumulated derivative gain or loss?			
b. The related net change associated with current period hedging transactions?			
c. The net amount of any reclassification into earnings?			

PART II—INCOME STATEMENT

COMPREHENSIVE INCOME

	Yes	No	N/A
1. Are elements of comprehensive income displayed in one of the following three alternative presentation formats: (FAS-130, pars. 14, 22)			

	Yes	No	N/A
a. In a single statement of income and comprehensive income that extends a traditional income statement to include (following net income) the elements of other comprehensive income and the total of comprehensive income?	___	___	___
b. In a separate statement of comprehensive income which begins with net income and includes the elements of other comprehensive income and then a total of comprehensive income?	___	___	___
c. In the statement of changes in stockholders' equity?	___	___	___
2. Are components of other comprehensive income shown either (a) net of related tax effects, or (b) before related tax effects with one amount shown for the aggregate income tax expense or benefit related to the total of other comprehensive income items? (FAS-130, par. 24)	___	___	___
3. Has the amount of income tax expense or benefit allocated to each component of other comprehensive income, including reclassification adjustments, been disclosed either (a) on the face of the financial statement in which the components are displayed, or (b) in the notes to the financial statements? (FAS-130, par. 25)	___	___	___
4. Have reclassification adjustments for each classification of other comprehensive income (other than minimum pension liability adjustments) been disclosed either (a) on the face of the financial statement in which comprehensive income is reported, or (b) in the notes to the financial statements? (FAS-130, par. 20)	___	___	___
5. Has the accumulated balance of other comprehensive income been reported separately from retained earnings and additional paid-in capital in the equity section of the balance sheet? (FAS-130, par. 26)	___	___	___
6. Has the ending accumulated balances for each item in accumulated other comprehensive income been disclosed either (a) on the face of the balance sheet, (b) in a statement of changes in equity, or (c) in the notes to the financial statements? (FAS-130, par. 26)	___	___	___

Yes No N/A

7. If FAS-133 (Accounting for Derivative Instruments and Hedging Activities) has been adopted, have the following disclosures been made: (*Note:* FAS-133 is effective for all fiscal quarters of fiscal years beginning after June 15, 2000.) ___ ___ ___
   a. The net gain or loss on derivative instruments designated as cash flow hedging instruments (including qualifying foreign currency cash flow hedges) reported as a separate classification within other comprehensive income? (FAS-133, par. 46) ___ ___ ___
   b. As part of the disclosures of accumulated other comprehensive income: (FAS-133, par. 47) ___ ___ ___
      (1) The beginning and ending accumulated derivative gain or loss? ___ ___ ___
      (2) The related net change associated with current period hedging transactions? ___ ___ ___
      (3) The net amount of any reclassification into earnings? ___ ___ ___

EARNINGS PER SHARE

Note: Nonpublic companies are NOT required to present earnings per share.

1. Have the following disclosures been made for each period for which an income statement is presented: ___ ___ ___
   a. A reconciliation of the numerators and denominators of the basic and diluted EPS computations for income from continuing operations, including the individual income and share amount effects of all securities that affect EPS. Insignificant reconciling items need not be itemized as part of the reconciliation and can be aggregated? (FAS-128, pars. 40, 138) ___ ___ ___
   b. The effect that has been given to preferred dividends in determining the income available to common stockholders in computing basic EPS? (FAS-128, par. 40) ___ ___ ___

	Yes	*No*	*N/A*
c. Securities (including those issuable pursuant to contingent stock agreements) that could potentially dilute EPS in the future, but which were not included in the calculation of diluted EPS because to do so would have been antidilutive for the periods presented? (FAS-128, par. 40)	___	___	___
2. For the latest period for which an income statement is presented, have disclosures been made of any transaction that occurs after the end of the most recent period but before the issuance of the financial statements that would have changed materially the number of common shares or potential common shares outstanding at the end of the period if the transaction had occurred before the end of the period? (FAS-128, par. 41)	___	___	___
3. When prior EPS amounts have been restated in compliance with an accounting standard requiring restatement, has disclosure been made of the per share effect of the restatement? (FAS-128, pars. 57–58)	___	___	___
4. When the number of common shares outstanding increases as a result of a stock dividend or stock split, or decreases as a result of a reverse stock split, have the computations of basic and diluted EPS been adjusted retroactively for all periods presented to reflect such changes in the number of shares, and has that fact been disclosed? (FAS-128, par. 54)	___	___	___
5. If changes in common stock resulting from stock dividends, stock splits, or reverse stock splits occur after the close of the period but before the issuance of the financial statements, have the per-share computations for all periods presented been based on the new number of shares, and has that fact been disclosed? (FAS-128, par. 54)	___	___	___

INCOME STATEMENT PRESENTATION—DISCONTINUED OPERATIONS

1. Are the results of continuing operations reported separately from discontinued operations? (APB-30, par. 8)	___	___	___

Yes *No* *N/A*

2. Are gains or losses from disposal of a segment of a business reported in conjunction with the related results of discontinued operations? (APB-30, par. 8) ___ ___ ___
3. Are the results of operations of a segment that has been or will be discontinued reported separately as a component of income before extraordinary items and the cumulative effect of accounting changes using the following captions: (APB-30, par. 8) ___ ___ ___
   a. Income from continuing operations before income taxes? ___ ___ ___
   b. Provision for income taxes? ___ ___ ___
   c. Income from continuing operations? ___ ___ ___
   d. Income (loss) from operations of discontinued segment, less applicable income taxes? ___ ___ ___
   e. Loss on disposal of discontinued segment, including provisions for operating losses during phase-out period, less applicable income taxes? ___ ___ ___
4. Are revenues applicable to the discontinued operations disclosed in a related note? (APB-30, par. 8) ___ ___ ___
5. Are the results of operations of a disposed segment, less applicable income taxes, presented as a separate component of income before extraordinary items on income statements of current and prior years that include results of operations prior to the measurement date? (APB-30, par. 13) ___ ___ ___
6. Are the following disclosures made for the period encompassing the measurement date: (APB-30, par. 18) ___ ___ ___
   a. The identity of the segment of business that has been or will be discontinued? ___ ___ ___
   b. The expected disposal date, if known? ___ ___ ___
   c. The expected manner of disposal? ___ ___ ___
   d. A description of the remaining assets and liabilities of the segment at the balance sheet date? ___ ___ ___
   e. The income or loss from discontinued operations and any proceeds from disposal of the

Yes No N/A

segment during the period from the measurement date to the date of the balance sheet? ___ ___ ___

7. Are the following disclosures made for years subsequent to the measurement date that include the period of disposal: (APB-30, par. 18) ___ ___ ___
   a. Identification of the segment of business that has been discontinued? ___ ___ ___
   b. The disposal date? ___ ___ ___
   c. The manner of disposition? ___ ___ ___
   d. A description of the remaining assets and liabilities, if any, of the segment at the balance sheet date? ___ ___ ___
   e. The income or loss from discontinued operations and any proceeds from disposal of the segment during the period from the measurement date to the date of the balance sheet compared with prior estimates? ___ ___ ___
8. For each adjustment in the current period of a loss on disposal of a business segment that was reported in the prior period, have the following been disclosed in the current period: (APB-30, par. 25; FAS-16, par. 6) ___ ___ ___
   a. Year of origin, nature, and amount? ___ ___ ___
   b. Classified separately in the current period as a gain or loss on disposal of a segment? ___ ___ ___

INCOME STATEMENT PRESENTATION—EXTRAORDINARY ITEMS

1. Are items unusual in nature *and* infrequent in occurrence classified as extraordinary items? (APB-30, par. 20) ___ ___ ___
2. Are the proportional amounts of an investee company's extraordinary items presented on the face of the investor company's income statement as extraordinary if they are material? (APB-18, par. 19) ___ ___ ___
3. Are descriptive captions and the amounts for individual extraordinary events or transactions presented (preferably) on the face of the income statement or disclosed in related notes? (APB-30, par. 11) ___ ___ ___

	Yes	No	N/A
4. Are the nature of an extraordinary event or transaction and the principal items entering into the computation of the gain or loss described? (APB-30, par. 11)	___	___	___
5. Are the following captions used when there is an extraordinary item (and there are no discontinued operations or changes in accounting principles): (APB-30, pars. 10–12)	___	___	___
a. Income before extraordinary items?	___	___	___
b. Extraordinary item (less applicable income taxes)?	___	___	___
c. Net income?	___	___	___
d. Earnings per share amounts before extraordinary items and net income, where applicable?	___	___	___
6. Are extraordinary gains and losses arising from extinguishments of debt described sufficiently to enable users of financial statements to evaluate their significance? (FAS-4, par. 9)	___	___	___
7. Are the following disclosures made on the face of the income statement or in a single note to the financial statements (or adequately cross-referenced if more than one note is used), for extraordinary gains and losses arising from extinguishments of debt: (FAS-4, par. 9)	___	___	___
a. Description of the transaction, including the sources of any funds used to extinguish debt if it is practicable to identify the sources?	___	___	___
b. Income tax effect in the period of extinguishment?	___	___	___
c. Per-share amount of the aggregate gain or loss, net of related income tax effect?	___	___	___
8. Are the following transactions or events *not* reported as extraordinary items: (APB-30, par. 23)	___	___	___
a. Writedown or writeoff of receivables, inventories, equipment leased to others, or intangible assets?	___	___	___
b. Gains or losses from exchange or translation of foreign currencies, including those relating to major devaluations and revaluations?	___	___	___
c. Gains or losses on disposal of a segment of a business?	___	___	___

	Yes	No	N/A
d. Other gains or losses from sale or abandonment of property, plant, or equipment used in the business?	___	___	___
e. Effects of a strike, including those against competitors and major suppliers?	___	___	___
f. Adjustments of accruals on long-term contracts?	___	___	___
9. Are gains or losses arising from the disposal of a significant part of the assets or a separable segment of a previously separate enterprise originally accounted for as a pooling-of-interests classified as an extraordinary item if (a) the profit or loss is material in relation to the net income of the combined enterprise and (b) the disposition is within two years after the combination is consummated? (APB-16, par. 60)	___	___	___
10. Are additional gains or losses arising in the current period but related to transactions or events that were previously reported as extraordinary items presented in the following manner: (APB-30, par. 25)	___	___	___
a. Separately disclosed as to year of origin, nature, and amount?	___	___	___
b. Classified separately in the current period as an extraordinary item?	___	___	___

INCOME STATEMENT PRESENTATION—UNUSUAL OR INFREQUENT ITEMS

	Yes	No	N/A
1. Are material transactions that are either unusual in nature *or* infrequent in occurrence (but not both and, therefore, not meeting the criteria for extraordinary items) not classified as extraordinary items? (APB-30, par. 26)	___	___	___
2. Are material transactions that are either unusual in nature or infrequent in occurrence (but not both) presented in the following manner: (APB-30, par. 26)	___	___	___
a. Reported as a separate component of income from continuing operations?	___	___	___
b. Nature and financial effects disclosed on the income statement (preferably) or in a note to the financial statements?	___	___	___

	Yes	*No*	*N/A*
c. Not reported in a manner that would imply that the item is extraordinary?	___	___	___
d. Not reported on an earnings-per-share basis?	___	___	___

REVENUES, GAINS, EXPENSES, AND LOSSES

1. Is the statement of operations classified into appropriate functional areas such as sales, costs of goods sold, operating expenses, and other items? (Generally accepted practice)	___	___	___
2. Are income before income taxes and net income identified on the income statement? (Generally accepted practice)	___	___	___
3. Have significant amounts of discounts, returns, and allowances been disclosed? (Generally accepted practice)	___	___	___
4. Are cost of goods sold and expenses shown net of purchase discounts? (Generally accepted practice)	___	___	___
5. Have sales with significant rights of return been excluded from the income statement, and disclosed if significant? (FAS-48, pars. 3–7)	___	___	___

PART III—STATEMENT OF CASH FLOWS

1. Is a statement of cash flows presented as a basic financial statement for each period for which an income statement is presented? (FAS-95, par. 3)	___	___	___
2. Is the statement presented in a manner to reconcile beginning and ending balances of cash (or cash and cash equivalents)? (FAS-95, par. 26)	___	___	___
3. Are the beginning and ending balances of cash (or cash and cash equivalents) as shown in the statement of cash flows the same amounts as similarly titled line items or subtotals in the balance sheet? (FAS-95, par. 7)	___	___	___
4. Is the accounting policy for determining which items are treated as cash equivalents disclosed? (FAS-95, par. 10)	___	___	___

Yes *No* *N/A*

5. Are gross amounts of cash receipts and cash payments presented in the statement of cash flows, except for certain items that have a quick turnover, large amounts, or short maturities, which may be presented on a net basis? (FAS-95, pars. 11–13) ___ ___ ___

6. Are cash flows classified as resulting from operating, investing, and financing activities? (FAS-95, pars. 6, 14) ___ ___ ___

7. Are the following items classified as cash inflows from investing activities: (FAS-95, par. 16) ___ ___ ___

   a. Receipts from collections or sales of (1) loans made by the enterprise and (2) other entities' debt instruments (other than cash equivalents and certain debt instruments that are acquired specifically for resale) that were purchased by the enterprise? ___ ___ ___

   b. Receipts from sales of equity instruments of other enterprises (other than certain equity instruments carried in a trading account) and from returns on investment in those instruments? ___ ___ ___

   c. Receipts from sales of property, plant, and equipment, and other productive assets? ___ ___ ___

8. Are the following items classified as cash outflows from investing activities: (FAS-95, par. 17) ___ ___ ___

   a. Disbursements for loans made by the enterprise and payments to acquire debt instruments of other entities (other than cash equivalents and certain debt instruments that are acquired specifically for resale)? ___ ___ ___

   b. Payments to acquire equity instruments of other enterprises (other than certain equity instruments carried in a trading account)? ___ ___ ___

   c. Payments at the time of purchase or soon before or after purchase to acquire property, plant, and equipment and other productive assets? ___ ___ ___

9. Are the following items classified as cash inflows from financing activities: (FAS-95, par. 19) ___ ___ ___

   a. Proceeds from issuing equity instruments? ___ ___ ___

	Yes	No	N/A
b. Proceeds from issuing bonds, mortgages, notes, and from other short-term or long-term borrowings?			
10. Are the following items classified as cash outflows from financing activities: (FAS-95, par. 20)			
a. Payments of dividends or other distributions to owners, including outlays to reacquire the enterprise's instruments?			
b. Repayments of amounts borrowed?			
c. Other principal payments to creditors who have extended long-term credit?			
11. At a minimum, are the following classes of operating cash receipts and payments separately reported when the direct method is used to compute cash flows provided or used by operating activities: (FAS-95, par. 27)			
a. Cash collected from customers, including lessees, licensees, and other customers?			
b. Interest and dividends received?			
c. Other operating cash receipts, if any?			
d. Cash paid to employees and other suppliers of goods or services, including suppliers of insurance, advertising, and the like?			
e. Interest paid?			
f. Income taxes paid?			
g. Other operating cash payments, if any?			
12. If the indirect method is used to compute cash flows provided or used by operating activities, is a reconciliation of net income to operating cash flows presented on the face of the statement of cash flows or in a separate schedule? (FAS-95, par. 6)			
13. If the direct method is used to compute cash flows provided or used by operating activities, is a reconciliation of net cash flows from operating activities provided in a separate schedule? (FAS-95, par. 29)			
14. Is information about noncash investing and financing activities presented in a narrative or summarized in a schedule? (FAS-95, par. 32)			

Yes No N/A

15. If the indirect method of reporting cash flows from operating activities is used, are amounts of interest paid (net of amounts capitalized) and income taxes paid during the period disclosed? (FAS-95, par. 29) ___ ___ ___
16. If cash flows from derivative instruments that are accounted for as fair value hedges or cash flow hedges are classified in the same category as the cash flows from the items being hedged, is that accounting policy disclosed? (FAS-104, par. 7) ___ ___ ___

PART IV—OTHER FINANCIAL STATEMENT TOPICS AND DISCLOSURES

ACCOUNTING CHANGES—CHANGES IN ACCOUNTING ESTIMATE

1. For a change in accounting estimate that affects several future periods (e.g., change in service lives of depreciable assets, actuarial assumptions affecting pension costs), has the effect on income before extraordinary items and net income (and on related per share amounts when presented) of the current period been disclosed? (APB-20, par. 33) ___ ___ ___
2. For a change in accounting estimate made each period in the ordinary course of accounting for items such as uncollectible accounts or inventory obsolescence, has disclosure been made of the effect, if material, on income before extraordinary items and net income (and on related per share amounts when presented)? (APB-20, par. 33) ___ ___ ___

ACCOUNTING CHANGES—CHANGES IN ACCOUNTING PRINCIPLE

1. Are the following disclosures made for a change in accounting principle in the year in which the change occurs: (APB-20, par. 17)
   a. The nature of the change in accounting principle? ___ ___ ___

	Yes	*No*	*N/A*
b. The justification for the change in accounting, including a clear explanation of why the newly adopted accounting principle is preferable?	___	___	___
c. The effect of the change in accounting principle on income before extraordinary items and net income (and related per share amounts when presented)?	___	___	___
2. Are the effects of the following changes presented by restating prior years' financial statements: (APB-20, par. 28)	___	___	___
a. A change from the LIFO method of inventory pricing to another method?	___	___	___
b. A change in the method of accounting for long-term construction-type contracts?	___	___	___
c. A change to or from the full-cost method of accounting that is used in extractive industries?	___	___	___
d. A change from retirement-replacement-betterment accounting to depreciation accounting?	___	___	___
3. For those changes in accounting principles reported by restating prior years' financial statements, are the following disclosures made: (APB-20, par. 28)	___	___	___
a. The nature of and justification for a change in accounting principle?	___	___	___
b. The effect of the change on income before extraordinary items and net income (and on related per share amounts when presented) for all periods presented?	___	___	___
4. For a change in accounting principle that is accounted for as a cumulative effect adjustment: (APB-20, pars. 19–26)	___	___	___
a. Have the financial statements for prior periods included for comparative purposes been presented as previously reported?	___	___	___
b. Has the cumulative effect of change to the new accounting principle on the amount of retained earnings at the beginning of the period in which the change is made been included in net income of the period of the change?	___	___	___

Yes No N/A

c. Has the amount of the cumulative effect been shown as a separate item in the income statement between the captions "extraordinary items" and "net income" and the related tax effects (and related per share amounts when presented) been disclosed? ___ ___ ___

d. Has the effect of adopting the new accounting principle on income before extraordinary items and on net income (and on related per share amounts when presented) of the period of the change been disclosed? ___ ___ ___

e. Have pro forma amounts of income before extraordinary items and net income been shown on the face of the income statements for all periods presented as if the newly adopted accounting principle had been applied during all periods affected? ___ ___ ___

f. If the pro forma amounts cannot be computed or reasonably estimated for individual prior periods, although the cumulative effect on retained earnings at the beginning of the period of change can be determined, has the reason for not showing the pro forma amounts by periods been disclosed? ___ ___ ___

g. If the amount of the cumulative effects of a change in accounting principle on retained earnings at the beginning of the period of change cannot be computed (generally limited to a change from the FIFO inventory method to LIFO), are the following disclosures made: ___ ___ ___

(1) The effect of the change on the results of operations (and on related per share amounts when presented) for the period of change? ___ ___ ___

(2) The reason for omitting (a) accounting for the cumulative effect and (b) disclosures of pro forma amounts for prior years? ___ ___ ___

5. Are the following disclosures made for a change in the method of depreciation, depletion, or amortization for newly acquired assets while a different method continues to be used for assets

	Yes	No	N/A
of that class acquired in previous years: (APB-20, par. 24)	___	___	___
a. Description of the nature of the change in method?	___	___	___
b. The effect of the change in method on income before extraordinary items and net income (and on related per share amounts when presented) for the year in which the change in method occurred?	___	___	___
6. If an accounting change is not considered material for the period in which the change occurs, but it is reasonably certain that the change will have a material effect on financial statements of subsequent years, are appropriate disclosures made whenever the financial statements of the year of change are presented? (APB-20, par. 38)	___	___	___

ACCOUNTING CHANGES—CHANGES IN REPORTING ENTITY

	Yes	No	N/A
1. Are prior years' financial statements restated for a change in the reporting entity, including the following: (APB-20, pars. 12 and 34)	___	___	___
a. A business combination accounted for by the pooling-of-interests method?	___	___	___
b. Presenting consolidated or combined statements in place of statements of individual enterprises?	___	___	___
c. Changing specific subsidiaries comprising the group of enterprises for which consolidated financial statements are presented?	___	___	___
d. Changing the enterprises included in combined financial statements?	___	___	___
2. Are the following disclosures made for a change in reporting entity for the period in which the change has occurred: (APB-20, par. 35)	___	___	___
a. A description of the nature of the change?	___	___	___
b. A description of the reason for the change?	___	___	___
c. The effect of the change on income before extraordinary items and net income (and on related per share amounts when presented) for all periods presented?	___	___	___

Yes No N/A

ACCOUNTING POLICIES AND RECLASSIFICATIONS

1. Is a summary of significant accounting policies presented and does it include important judgments about the appropriateness of principles relating to revenue recognition and asset cost allocation to current and future periods, and in particular include the following: (APB-22, pars. 8–15) ___ ___ ___
   a. Selection from existing acceptable alternative accounting principles and methods? ___ ___ ___
   b. Principles and methods peculiar to the industry (even if the principle or method is predominant in the industry)? ___ ___ ___
   c. Unusual or innovative applications of GAAP (including principles and methods peculiar to the industry)? ___ ___ ___
2. Are material changes in classifications made to previously issued financial statements disclosed? (ARB-43, Ch. 2A, par. 3; AU 420.16) ___ ___ ___

ADVERTISING COSTS

1. Are the following disclosures made for direct-response advertising: (SOP 93-7, par. 49) ___ ___ ___
   a. A description of the direct-response advertising reported as assets, if any? ___ ___ ___
   b. The accounting policy for it? ___ ___ ___
   c. The amortization period? ___ ___ ___
2. For non-direct response advertising costs, are disclosures made about whether such costs are expensed as incurred for the first time the advertising takes place? (SOP 93-7, par. 49) ___ ___ ___
3. Is the disclosure made of the total amount charged to advertising expense for each income statement presented, with separate disclosure of amounts, if any, representing a writedown to net realizable value? (SOP 93-7, par. 49) ___ ___ ___
4. Is disclosure made of the total amount of advertising costs reported as assets in each balance sheet presented? (SOP 93-7, par. 49) ___ ___ ___

Yes No N/A

5. Is the amount of revenue and expense recognized from advertising barter transactions disclosed for each income statement period presented? (EITF 99-17) (*Note:* Entities providing advertising in barter transactions that do not qualify for recognition at fair value under EITF 99-17 should disclose for each income statement presented the volume and type of advertising provided and received, such as the number of equivalent pages, number of minutes, or the overall percentage of advertising volume.) ___ ___ ___

BUSINESS COMBINATIONS—POOLING OF INTERESTS

1. Are the following disclosures made when a business combination is accounted for as a pooling-of-interests: (APB-16, pars. 56 and 64) ___ ___ ___
   a. Name and brief description of the enterprises combined, except for an enterprise whose name is carried forward to the combined enterprise? ___ ___ ___
   b. Statement that the business combination was accounted for using the pooling-of-interests method? ___ ___ ___
   c. Description and number of shares of stock issued in the business combination? ___ ___ ___
   d. Details (including revenues, extraordinary items, net income, other changes in stockholders' equity, and amount of and manner of accounting for intercompany transactions) of the results of operations of the previously separate enterprises for the period before the business combination is consummated that are included in the current combined net income? ___ ___ ___
   e. Descriptions of the nature of adjustments of net assets of the combining enterprises to adopt the same accounting practices and of the effects of the changes on net income reported previously by the separate enterprises and now are presented in comparative financial statements? ___ ___ ___

Yes *No* *N/A*

f. Details (including, at minimum, revenues, expenses, extraordinary items, net income, and other changes in stockholders' equity for the period excluded from the reported results of operations) of an increase or decrease in retained earnings from changing the fiscal year of a combining enterprise? ___ ___ ___

g. Reconciliations of amounts of revenues and earnings previously reported by the enterprise that issues the stock to effect the combination with the combined amounts currently presented in financial statements and historical summaries? (Alternatively, a new enterprise formed to effect a combination may instead disclose the earnings of separate enterprises that comprise combined earnings for prior periods.) ___ ___ ___

h. The nature of and effects on earnings per share of nonrecurring intercompany transactions involving long-term assets and liabilities that were not eliminated from current period income? ___ ___ ___

2. If a transaction expected to be treated as a pooling has been initiated, and a portion of the stock has been acquired, but the pooling is not consummated at the date of the financial statements, have combined results of operations of all prior periods and the entire current period been disclosed as they will be reported if the combination is later accounted for as a pooling? (APB-16, par. 62) ___ ___ ___

3. Is information disclosed in notes to financial statements furnished on a pro forma basis for a proposed business combination (to be accounted for as a pooling-of-interests) that is given to stockholders of combining enterprises? (APB-16, par. 64) ___ ___ ___

4. For a business combination (to be accounted for as a pooling-of-interests) consummated before the financial statements are issued but that is either incomplete as of the date of the financial statements or initiated after that date, are details (including revenues, net income, earnings per share, and the effects of anticipated changes in

	Yes	*No*	*N/A*
accounting methods as if the combination had been consummated at the date of the financial statements) of the effects of the business combination disclosed in notes to the financial statements? (APB-16, par. 65)	___	___	___

BUSINESS COMBINATIONS—PURCHASE

1. Are the following disclosures made when a business combination is accounted for as a purchase (several relatively minor acquisitions may be combined for disclosure purposes): (APB-16, par. 95)	___	___	___
a. Name and brief description of the acquired enterprise?	___	___	___
b. Statement that the business combination was accounted for using the purchase method?	___	___	___
c. Period for which results of operations of the acquired enterprise are included in the income statement of the acquiring enterprise?	___	___	___
d. Cost of the acquired enterprise and, if applicable, the number of shares of stock issued or issuable and the amount assigned to the issued and issuable shares?	___	___	___
e. Description of the plan for amortization of acquired goodwill, the amortization method, and periods?	___	___	___
f. Contingent payments, options, or commitments specified in the acquisition agreement and their proposed accounting treatment?	___	___	___
2. For research and development assets acquired in a business combination accounted for as a purchase that have no alternative future use, has disclosure been made of the portion of the purchase price that has been allocated to research and development and charged to expense at the date of consummation of the business combination? (FIN-4, par. 5)	___	___	___
3. Has consideration that is issued or issuable at the end of a contingency period or that is held in escrow been disclosed? (APB-16, par. 78)	___	___	___
4. Are the following disclosures (optional for nonpublic clients) made on a pro forma basis for			

Yes No N/A

business combinations accounted for as a purchase: (APB-16, par. 96; FAS-79, par. 6) ___ ___ ___

a. Results of operations for the current period as though the enterprises had combined at the beginning of the period, unless the acquisition was at or near the beginning of the period? ___ ___ ___

b. Results of operations for the immediately preceding period as though the enterprises had combined at the beginning of that period if comparative financial statements are presented? ___ ___ ___

c. At a minimum, *pro forma* disclosures including revenues, income before extraordinary items, net income, and earnings per share? ___ ___ ___

5. If preacquisition contingencies (for business combinations accounted for as a purchase) are not allocated as required by FAS-38, are the amount and nature of adjustments determined after December 15, 1980, disclosed? (FAS-38, pars. 6 and 10) ___ ___ ___

6. Are the following disclosures made if a combined entity plans to incur costs from exiting an activity of an acquired entity, involuntarily terminating employees of an acquired entity, or relocating employees of an acquired entity and the activities of the acquired entity that will not be continued are significant to the combined entity's revenues or operating results or the cost recognized from those activities as of the consummation date are material to the combined entity: (EITF 95-3, par. 13a-b) ___ ___ ___

   a. For the period in which a purchase business combination occurs: ___ ___ ___

      (1) When the plans to exit an activity or involuntarily terminate or relocate employees of the acquired entity are not final as of the balance sheet date, a description of any unresolved issues, the types of additional liabilities that may result in an adjustment to the purchase price allocation, and how any adjustment will be reported? ___ ___ ___

      (2) A description of the type and amount of liabilities assumed in the purchase

Yes No N/A

price allocation for costs to exit an activity or involuntarily terminate or relocate employees? ___ ___ ___

(3) A description of the major actions that make up the plan to exit an activity or involuntarily terminate or relocate employees of an acquired entity? ___ ___ ___

(4) A description of activities of the acquired entity that will not be continued, including the method of disposition, and the anticipated date of completion and description of employee groups to be terminated or relocated? ___ ___ ___

b. For all periods presented subsequent to the acquisition date in which a purchase business combination occurred, until a plan to exit an activity or involuntarily terminate or relocate employees of an acquired entity is fully executed: ___ ___ ___

(1) A description of the type and amount of exit costs, involuntary employee termination costs, and relocation costs paid and charged against the liability? ___ ___ ___

(2) The amount of any adjustments to the liability account and whether the corresponding entry was an adjustment of the costs of the acquired entity or included in the determination of net income for the period? ___ ___ ___

CHANGING PRICES

1. Have the following disclosures been made, for each of the five most recent years: (FAS-89, par. 7) ___ ___ ___

a. Net sales and other operating revenues? ___ ___ ___

b. Income from continuing operations on a current cost basis? ___ ___ ___

c. Purchasing power gain or loss on net monetary items? ___ ___ ___

d. Increase or decrease in the current cost or lower recoverable amount of inventory and property, plant, and equipment, net of inflation? ___ ___ ___

	Yes	*No*	*N/A*
e. The aggregate foreign currency translation adjustment on a current cost basis, if applicable?	___	___	___
f. Net assets at year-end on a current cost basis?	___	___	___
g. Income per common share from continuing operations on a current cost basis?	___	___	___
h. Cash dividends declared per common share?	___	___	___
i. Market price per common share at year-end?	___	___	___
j. The Consumer Price Index—All Urban Consumers (CPI-U) used for each year's current cost/constant purchasing power calculations?	___	___	___
k. If the Company has a significant foreign operation measured in a functional currency other than the U.S. dollar, has disclosure been made of whether adjustments to the current cost information to reflect the effects of general inflation are based on the U.S. general price level index or on a functional currency general price level index?	___	___	___
2. In addition to the disclosures in item 1 above, if income from continuing operations on a current cost/constant purchasing power basis differs significantly from the income from continuing operations reported in the primary financial statements, has the following additional information been disclosed: (FAS-89, pars. 11–13)	___	___	___
a. Components of income from continuing operations for the current year on a current cost/constant purchasing power basis?	___	___	___
b. Separate amounts for the current cost or lower recoverable amount at the end of the current year of inventory and property, plant, and equipment?	___	___	___
c. The increase or decrease in current cost or lower recoverable amount before and after adjusting for the effects of inflation of inventory and property, plant, and equipment for the current year?	___	___	___
d. The principal types of information used to calculate the current cost of (1) inventory, (2) property, plant, and equipment, (3) cost of goods sold, and (4) depreciation, depletion, and amortization expense?	___	___	___

	Yes	*No*	*N/A*
e. Any differences between (1) the depreciation methods, estimates of useful lives, and salvage values of assets used for calculations of current cost/constant purchasing power depreciation and (2) the methods and estimates used for calculations of depreciation in the primary financial statements?	___	___	___
3. For companies with mineral resource assets (other than oil and gas), such as metal ores, coal, etc., have the following additional disclosures been made: (FAS-89, par. 14)	___	___	___
a. Estimates of significant quantities of proved mineral reserves or proved and probable mineral reserves (whichever is used for cost amortization purposes) at the end of the year or at the most recent date during the year for which estimates can be made?	___	___	___
b. If the mineral reserves include deposits containing one or more significant mineral products, the estimated quantity, expressed in physical units or in percentages of reserves, of each mineral product that is recoverable in significant commercial quantities?	___	___	___
c. Quantities of each significant mineral produced during the year?	___	___	___
d. Quantity of significant proved, or proved and probable, mineral reserves purchased or sold in place during the year?	___	___	___
e. The average market price of each significant mineral product or, for mineral products transferred within the enterprise, the equivalent market price prior to use in a manufacturing process?	___	___	___
4. When determining the quantities of mineral reserves to be reported in item 3 above, have the following been applied: (FAS-89, par. 15)	___	___	___
a. If consolidated financial statements are issued, 100 percent of the quantities attributable to the parent company and 100 percent of the quantities attributable to its consolidated subsidiaries (whether or not wholly owned) should be included?	___	___	___

Yes No N/A

b. If the company's financial statements include investments that are proportionately consolidated, the company's quantities should include its proportionate share of the investee's quantities? ___ ___ ___

c. If the company's financial statements include investments that are accounted for by the equity method, the investee's quantities should not be included in the disclosures of the company's quantities. However, the company's share of the investee's quantities of reserves should be reported separately, if significant? ___ ___ ___

COMMITMENTS

1. Have disclosures included a description of the commitment, the terms of the commitment, and the amount of the commitment, for large or unusual commitments such as the following: ___ ___ ___
   a. Unused letters of credit? (FAS-5, par. 18) ___ ___ ___
   b. Obligation to reduce debt? (FAS-5, par. 18) ___ ___ ___
   c. Obligation to maintain working capital? (FAS-5, par. 18) ___ ___ ___
   d. Obligation to restrict dividends? (FAS-5, par. 18) ___ ___ ___
   e. Commitments for major capital expenditures? (FAS-5, par. 18) ___ ___ ___
   f. Assets pledged as security for loans? (FAS-5, par. 18) ___ ___ ___
   g. Net losses on inventory purchase commitments? (ARB-43, Ch. 4, par. 17) ___ ___ ___
   h. Other commitments? (FAS-5, par. 18) ___ ___ ___

COMPUTER SOFTWARE TO BE SOLD, LEASED, OR OTHERWISE MARKETED

1. Have research and development costs incurred for computer software to be sold, leased, or otherwise marketed been disclosed either separately or as part of total research and development costs for each period presented? (FAS-86, par. 12) ___ ___ ___

Yes No N/A

2. If an entity has capitalized costs incurred for computer software costs to be sold, leased, or otherwise marketed, have the following disclosures been made: (FAS-86, par. 11) ___ ___ ___
   a. Unamortized computer software costs included in each balance sheet presented? ___ ___ ___
   b. The total amount charged to expense in each income statement presented for amortization of capitalized computer software costs and for amounts written down to net realizable value? ___ ___ ___

CONSOLIDATED AND COMBINED FINANCIAL STATEMENTS

1. Is the consolidation policy followed by the client apparent by the headings on the financial statements, other information in the statements, or disclosed in notes? (ARB-51, par. 5; ARB-22, par. 13) ___ ___ ___
2. Are intercompany accounts and intercompany profits or losses on assets eliminated as part of the preparation of consolidated financial statements? (ARB-51, par. 6) ___ ___ ___
3. If the consolidated financial statements are prepared using the financial statements of a subsidiary that has a different year end than the parent, are disclosures made for intervening events that materially affect financial position or results of operations? (ARB-51, par. 4; FAS-12, pars. 18–20; FASB INT-13) ___ ___ ___
4. If the entity is a member of a group that files a consolidated tax return, are the following disclosures made in its separately issued financial statements: (FAS-109, par. 49) ___ ___ ___
   a. The amount of current and deferred tax expense for each statement of income presented? ___ ___ ___
   b. The amount of any tax-related balances due to or from affiliates as of the date of each balance sheet presented? ___ ___ ___
   c. The principal provisions of the method by which the consolidated amount of current

Yes No N/A

and deferred tax expense is allocated to members of the group, and the nature and effect of any changes in that method (and in determining related balance to or from affiliates) during the years for which the disclosures in items a and b above are presented? ___ ___ ___

5. Is summarized information about assets, liabilities, and results of operations relating to majority-owned subsidiaries that were unconsolidated in financial statements for fiscal years 1986 or 1987, but which are now consolidated based on FAS-94, disclosed? (FAS-94, par. 14) ___ ___ ___

CONTINGENCIES, RISKS, UNCERTAINTIES, AND CONCENTRATIONS

Loss and Gain Contingencies

1. If loss contingencies have been accrued, has consideration been given to describing the nature and amount of the accrual for the financial statements not to be misleading? (FAS-5, par. 9) ___ ___ ___
2. If no accrual is made for a loss contingency, or if an exposure to loss exists in excess of the amount accrued, have the following disclosures been made when there is at least a reasonable possibility that a loss or an additional loss may have been incurred: (FAS-5, par. 10) ___ ___ ___
   a. The nature of the contingency? ___ ___ ___
   b. An estimate of the possible loss or range of loss, or a statement that such an estimate cannot be made? ___ ___ ___
3. Are the following disclosures made (when it is necessary to keep the financial statements from being misleading) for losses and loss contingencies that arise subsequent to the date of the financial statements: (FAS-5, par. 11) ___ ___ ___
   a. The nature of the loss or loss contingency? ___ ___ ___
   b. An estimate of the amount or range of loss, or possible loss, or a statement that an estimate cannot be made? ___ ___ ___

Yes No N/A

4. Are the following disclosures made for certain *remote* loss contingencies relating to guarantees made for outside parties (such as guarantees of indebtedness of others, obligations of commercial banks under stand-by letters of credit, and guarantees to repurchase receivables or other properties that have been sold or assigned): (FAS-5, par. 12) ___ ___ ___
   a. The nature of the loss contingency? ___ ___ ___
   b. The nature and amount of the guarantee? ___ ___ ___
   c. If subject to estimation, the value of any recovery from other outside parties that could be expected to result? ___ ___ ___
5. Are loss contingencies relating to guarantees (direct, indirect, written, or oral) made for outside parties disclosed, including the nature and amounts thereof, and the value of any recovery that could be expected to result, if estimable? (FAS-5, par. 12) ___ ___ ___
6. Are there adequate disclosures for unasserted claims or assessments if it is considered probable that a claim will be asserted and there is a reasonable possibility that a loss will arise from the matter? (FAS-5, par. 10) ___ ___ ___
7. Have contingencies that might result in gains been adequately disclosed but not reflected in the financial statements since to do so might be to recognize revenue before to its realization? (Care should be exercised to avoid misleading implications about the likelihood of realization.) (FAS-5, par. 17) ___ ___ ___

Environmental Remediation Contingencies

1. Has the following information been disclosed about recorded accruals for environmental remediation loss contingencies and related assets for third-party recoveries: (SOP 96-1, pars. 7.11, 7.20) ___ ___ ___
   a. Whether the accrual for environmental remediation liabilities is measured on a discounted basis? ___ ___ ___

Yes No N/A

b. The nature and amount of the accrual if necessary for the financial statements not to be misleading? ___ ___ ___

c. If any portion of the accrued obligation is discounted, the undiscounted amount of the obligation and the discount rate used? ___ ___ ___

d. If it is at least reasonably possible that the accrued obligation or any recognized asset for third-party recoveries will change within one year of the date of the financial statements and the effect is material, an indication that it is at least reasonably possible that a change in the estimate will occur in the near term? ___ ___ ___

2. Have the following disclosures been made about unaccrued environmental remediation contingencies, including exposures in excess of amounts accrued: (SOP 96-1, par. 7.21) ___ ___ ___

   a. A description of the reasonably possible loss contingency and an estimate of the possible loss, or the fact that such an estimate cannot be made? ___ ___ ___

   b. If it is at least reasonably possible that the estimated loss (or gain) contingency will change within one year of the date of the financial statements and the effect is material, an indication that it is at least reasonably possible that a change in the estimate will occur in the near term? ___ ___ ___

3. Have the following **optional** disclosures been made by entities that elect to disclose such items: (*Note:* Entities are *encouraged*, but not required, to disclose this information.) (SOP 96-1, par. 7.22) ___ ___ ___

   a. The estimated time frame of disbursements for recorded amounts if expenditures are expected to continue over the long term? ___ ___ ___

   b. The estimated time frame for realization of recognized probable recoveries, if realization is not expected in the near term? ___ ___ ___

   c. The factors that cause the estimates to be sensitive to change with respect to (1) the accrued obligation, (2) any recognized asset for

Yes No N/A

third-party recoveries, or (3) reasonably possible loss exposures, or disclosed gain contingencies? ___ ___ ___

d. If an estimate of the probable or reasonable possible loss or range of loss cannot be made, the reasons why it cannot be made? ___ ___ ___

e. If information about the reasonably possible loss or the recognized and additional reasonably possible loss for an environmental remediation obligation related to an individual site is relevant to an understanding of the financial position, cash flows, or results of operations of the entity, are the following disclosures made with respect to the site: ___ ___ ___

(1) The total amount accrued for the site? ___ ___ ___

(2) The nature of any reasonably possible loss contingency or additional loss, and an estimate of the possible loss or the fact that an estimate cannot be made and the reasons why it cannot be made? ___ ___ ___

(3) Whether other potentially responsible parties are involved and the entity's estimated share of the obligation? ___ ___ ___

(4) The status of regulatory proceedings? ___ ___ ___

(5) The estimated time frame for resolution of the contingency? ___ ___ ___

4. If an environmental liability for a specific cleanup site is discounted because it meets the criteria for discounting in EITF 93-5 and the effect of discounting is material, do the financial statements disclose the undiscounted amounts of the liability and any related recovery and the discount rate used? (EITF 93-5) ___ ___ ___

Risks, Uncertainties, and Concentrations

1. Are the following disclosures made about the entity's nature of operations, including: (SOP 94-6, par. 10) ___ ___ ___

   a. A description of the entity's major products or services? ___ ___ ___

	Yes	No	N/A
b. The principal markets (e.g., industries and types of customers) for the entity's products or services?	___	___	___
c. If the entity operates in more than one business, the relative importance of the entity's operations in each business and the basis for that determination (e.g., based on assets, revenues, or earnings)? (*Note:* Relative importance need not be quantified and could be conveyed by use of terms such as *predominately, about equally*, or *major.*)	___	___	___
2. Is disclosure made that the preparation of financial statements in conformity with GAAP requires the use of management's estimates? (SOP 94-6, par. 11)	___	___	___
3. Are the following disclosures made regarding significant estimates used in the determination of the carrying amounts of assets or liabilities or in disclosure of gain or loss contingencies, if (1) it is at least reasonably possible that the effect on the financial statements of the estimates will change within one year of the date of the financial statements due to one or more future confirming events, and (2) the effect of the change would be material to the financial statements: (SOP 94-6, par. 13–15)	___	___	___
a. The nature of the estimate?	___	___	___
b. An indication that it is at least reasonably possible that a change in the estimate will occur in the near term?	___	___	___
c. The factors that cause the estimate to be sensitive to change? (This disclosure is encouraged, but not required.)	___	___	___
d. If the entity uses risk-reduction techniques to mitigate losses or the uncertainty that may result from future events and, as a result, determines that the criteria described above are not met, the disclosures in a, b, and c are encouraged, but not required?	___	___	___
4. Are the following concentrations disclosed if (1) the concentration exists at the date of the financial statements, (2) the concentration makes			

Yes No N/A

the entity vulnerable to the risk of a near-term severe impact, and (3) it is at least reasonably possible that the events that could cause the severe impact will occur in the near term: (SOP 94-6, pars. 21, 22, and 24) ___ ___ ___

a. Concentrations in the volume of business transacted with a particular customer, supplier, lender, grantor, or contributor? (For purposes of this disclosure, it is always considered at least reasonably possible that any customer, grantor, or contributor will be lost in the near term.) ___ ___ ___

b. Concentrations in revenue from particular products, services, or fund-raising events? ___ ___ ___

c. Concentrations in the available sources of supply of materials, labor, or services, or of licenses or other rights used in the entity's operations? ___ ___ ___

d. Concentrations in the market or geographic area in which the entity conducts its operations? (For purposes of this disclosure, it is always considered at least reasonably possible that operations located outside an entity's home country will be disrupted in the near term.) ___ ___ ___

e. For concentrations of labor subject to collective bargaining agreements, the percentage of the labor force covered by a collective bargaining agreement and the percentage of the labor force covered by a collective agreement that will expire within one year? ___ ___ ___

f. For concentrations of operations located outside the entity's home country, the carrying amounts of net assets and the geographic areas in which they are located? ___ ___ ___

DEVELOPMENT STAGE ENTERPRISES

1. Are the following included in the financial statements issued by a development stage enterprise: (FAS-7, par. 11) ___ ___ ___

   a. A balance sheet, including any cumulative net losses reported with a descriptive cap-

Yes No N/A

tion, such as "deficit accumulated during the development stage," in the stockholders' equity section? ___ ___ ___

b. An income statement showing amounts of revenues and expenses for each period covered by the income statement and, in addition, cumulative amounts from the enterprise's inception? ___ ___ ___

c. A statement of cash flows showing the cash inflows and cash outflows for each period for which an income statement is presented and, in addition, cumulative amounts from the enterprise's inception? ___ ___ ___

d. A statement of stockholders' equity showing from the enterprise's inception: ___ ___ ___

(1) For each issuance, the date and number of shares of stock, warrants, rights, or other equity securities issued for cash and for other consideration? ___ ___ ___

(2) For each issuance, the dollar amounts (per share or other equity unit and in total) assigned to the consideration received for shares of stock, warrants, rights, or other equity securities? (Dollar amounts should be assigned to any noncash consideration received.) ___ ___ ___

(3) For each issuance involving noncash consideration, the nature of the noncash consideration and the basis for assigning amounts? ___ ___ ___

2. Are the financial statements identified as those of a development-stage enterprise? (FAS-7, par. 12) ___ ___ ___

3. Is there a description of the nature of the development-stage activities in which the enterprise is engaged? (FAS-7, par. 12) ___ ___ ___

4. If this is the first year which the client is not considered to be a development-stage enterprise, is there a disclosure that in prior years the client had been in the development stage? (FAS-7, par. 12) ___ ___ ___

5. If the client is no longer a development-stage enterprise and financial statements from the years

Yes No N/A

of the development stage are presented on a comparative basis, are the cumulative amounts and other additional disclosures related to a development-stage enterprise as described in items 1 through 4 above omitted from presentation? (FAS-7, par. 13) ___ ___ ___

EMPLOYEE STOCK OWNERSHIP PLANS (ESOPs)

1. Do the financial statements of an employer sponsoring an ESOP disclose the following information about the plan: (SOP 93-6, par. 53a) ___ ___ ___
   a. A description of the plan? ___ ___ ___
   b. The basis for determining contributions? ___ ___ ___
   c. The employee groups covered? ___ ___ ___
   d. The nature and effects of significant matters affecting comparability of information for all periods presented? ___ ___ ___
   e. For leveraged ESOPs and pension reversion ESOPs, the basis for releasing shares and how dividends on allocated and unallocated shares are used? ___ ___ ___
2. Are the following accounting policies for blocks of both "old ESOP shares" and "new ESOP shares" disclosed (the following disclosures are required if the employer has both old ESOP shares for which it does not adopt the guidance in SOP 93-6 and new ESOP shares for which the guidance in SOP 93-6 is required; old ESOP shares are those acquired or held by the plan on or before December 31, 1992): (SOP 93-6, par. 53b) ___ ___ ___
   a. The method of measuring compensation? ___ ___ ___
   b. The classification of dividends on ESOP shares? ___ ___ ___
   c. The treatment of ESOP shares for earnings per share computations? ___ ___ ___
3. Is disclosure made of the amount of plan compensation cost recognized during the period? (SOP 93-6, par. 53c) ___ ___ ___

Yes *No* *N/A*

4. Are the following disclosures made at the balance sheet date for both old ESOP shares and new ESOP shares, if the employer does not adopt SOP 93-6 for the old shares: (SOP 93-6, par. 53d) ___ ___ ___
   a. The number of allocated shares? ___ ___ ___
   b. The number of committed-to-be-released shares? ___ ___ ___
   c. The number of suspense shares held by the ESOP? ___ ___ ___
5. Is disclosure made of the fair value of unearned ESOP shares at the balance sheet date for shares accounted for under SOP 93-6? (This disclosure need not be made for old ESOP shares for which the employer does not apply the guidance in SOP 93-6 for those shares.) (SOP 93-6, par. 53e) ___ ___ ___
6. Is disclosure made of the existence and nature of any repurchase obligation, including disclosure of the fair value of the shares allocated as of the balance sheet date, which are subject to a repurchase obligation? (SOP 93-6, par. 53f) ___ ___ ___
7. If an employer has, in substance, guaranteed the debt of an ESOP, have the employer's financial statements disclosed the following: (SOP 76-3, par. 10) ___ ___ ___
   a. The compensation element and the interest element of annual contributions to the ESOP? ___ ___ ___
   b. The interest rate and debt terms? ___ ___ ___

EMPLOYEE TERMINATION BENEFITS AND OTHER COSTS TO EXIT AN ACTIVITY (INCLUDING CERTAIN RESTRUCTURING COSTS)

1. Are the following disclosures made about accrued employee termination benefits: (EITF 94-3) ___ ___ ___
   a. The amount of the termination benefits accrued and charged to expense and the classification of these costs in the income statement?

	Yes	*No*	*N/A*
b. The number of employees to be terminated?	___	___	___
c. A description of the employee group(s) to be terminated?	___	___	___
d. The amount of actual termination benefits paid and charged against the liability accrued for employee termination benefits?	___	___	___
e. The number of employees actually terminated as a result of the termination plan?	___	___	___
f. The amount of any adjustments to the liability accrued for employee termination benefits?	___	___	___
2. Are the following disclosures about an entity's plan to exit an activity made in the financial statements for all periods until the exit plan is fully executed if the activities that will not be continued are significant to an entity's revenue or operating results or the exit costs recognized at the commitment date are material: (EITF 94-3)	___	___	___
a. A description of the major actions included in the exit plan and the particular activities that will not be continued, including the method of disposition and anticipated date of completion?	___	___	___
b. A description of the type and amount of exit costs recognized as liabilities and the classification of the exit costs in the income statement?	___	___	___
c. A description of the type and amount of exit costs paid and charged against the liability?	___	___	___
d. The amount of any adjustments to the liability?	___	___	___
e. The revenues and net operating income or losses from activities that will not be continued if those activities have separately identifiable operations, for all periods presented?	___	___	___

EXTINGUISHMENTS OF LIABILITIES

1. If debt was considered to be extinguished by in-substance defeasance under the provisions of FAS-76, prior to January 1, 1997, have the following disclosures been made: (FAS-140, par. 17b)	___	___	___

	Yes	No	N/A
a. A general description of the transaction?	___	___	___
b. The amount of debt that is considered extinguished at the end of the period so long as that debt remains outstanding?	___	___	___
2. If assets are set aside after January 1, 1997 solely for satisfying scheduled payments of a specific obligation, has a description of the nature of restrictions placed on those assets been disclosed? (FAS-140, par. 17c)	___	___	___
3. Have gains or losses from extinguishment of debt that are classified as extraordinary items been described in sufficient detail to enable users of financial statements to evaluate their significance? (FAS-4, par. 9)	___	___	___
4. Has the following information, to the extent not shown separately on the face of the income statement, been disclosed in a single note to the financial statements to evaluate its significance: (FAS-4, par. 9)	___	___	___
a. A description of the extinguishment transactions, including the sources of any funds used to extinguish debt if it is practicable to identify the sources?	___	___	___
b. The income tax effect in the period of extinguishment?	___	___	___
c. If applicable, the per share amount of the aggregate gain or loss, net of related income tax effect?	___	___	___

FINANCIAL INSTRUMENTS— DERIVATIVES AND HEDGING ACTIVITIES

Questions 1 through 4 apply if FAS-133 (Accounting for Derivative Instruments and Hedging Activities), as amended by FAS-138, has **not** *been adopted. (***Note:** *FAS-133 and FAS-138 are effective for all fiscal quarters of fiscal years beginning after June 15, 2000.)*

1. Have the following disclosures been made, either in the body of the financial statements or in the accompanying notes, about derivative fi-

Yes No N/A

nancial instruments held or issued for trading purposes: (FAS-119, par. 10) ___ ___ ___

a. The average fair value of those derivative financial instruments during the reporting period, presented together with the related fair value at the balance sheet date, distinguishing between those that are assets and those that are liabilities? ___ ___ ___

b. The net gains or losses arising from trading activities (often referred to as net trading revenues) during the reporting period disaggregated by class, business activity, risk, or other category that is consistent with the management of those activities and where those net trading gains or losses are reported in the income statement? (If the disaggregation is other than by class, the entity also should describe for each category the classes of derivative financial instruments, other financial instruments, and nonfinancial assets and liabilities from which the net trading gains or losses arose.) ___ ___ ___

2. Have the following disclosures been made about derivative financial instruments held or issued for purposes other than trading: (FAS-119, par. 11) ___ ___ ___

   a. The entity's objectives for holding or issuing the instruments? ___ ___ ___

   b. The context needed to understand the entity's objectives? ___ ___ ___

   c. The entity's strategies for achieving those objectives, including the classes of derivative financial instruments used? ___ ___ ___

   d. A description of how each class of derivative financial instrument is reported in the financial statements, including the policies for recognizing (or reasons for not recognizing) and measuring the derivative financial instruments held or issued, and when recognized, where those instruments and related gains and losses are reported in the balance sheet and income statement? ___ ___ ___

   e. For derivative financial instruments that are held or issued and accounted for as hedges of

Yes No N/A

anticipated transactions (both firm commitments and forecasted transactions for which there is no firm commitment), have the following disclosures been made: ___ ___ ___

(1) A description of the anticipated transactions whose risks are hedged, including the period of time until the anticipated transactions are expected to occur? ___ ___ ___

(2) A description of the classes of derivative financial instruments used to hedge the anticipated transactions? ___ ___ ___

(3) The amount of hedging gains and losses explicitly deferred? ___ ___ ___

(4) A description of the transactions or other events that result in the recognition in earnings of gains or losses deferred by hedge accounting? ___ ___ ___

3. In disclosing the fair value of a derivative financial instrument, did the entity **not** (1) combine, aggregate, or net that fair value with the fair value of nonderivative financial instruments or (2) net that fair value with the fair value of other derivative financial instruments, except to the extent that the offsetting of carrying amounts in the balance sheet is permitted? (FAS-119, par. 15) ___ ___ ___

4. Have the following disclosures been made for futures contracts that have been accounted for as hedges: (FAS-80, par. 12) ___ ___ ___

   a. The nature of the assets, liabilities, firm commitments, or anticipated transactions that are hedged with futures contracts? ___ ___ ___

   b. The method of accounting for the futures contracts? ___ ___ ___

   c. The description of the events or transactions that result in recognition in income of changes in value of the futures contracts? ___ ___ ___

*Questions 5 through 9 apply if FAS-133 (Accounting for Derivative Instruments and Hedging Activities), as amended by FAS-138, has been adopted. (**Note:** FAS-133 and FAS-138 are effective for all fiscal quarters of fiscal years beginning after June 15, 2000.)*

Yes *No* *N/A*

5. Have the following disclosures been made for all derivative instruments (and for nonderivative instruments designated and qualifying as hedging instruments): (FAS-133, par. 44) ___ ___ ___

   a. The entity's objectives for holding or issuing the instruments? ___ ___ ___

   b. The context needed to understand the entity's objectives? ___ ___ ___

   c. The entity's strategies for achieving these objectives? ___ ___ ___

   d. The entity's risk management policy for each type of hedge, including a description of the items or transactions for which risks are hedged? ___ ___ ___

   e. For derivative instruments not designated as hedging instruments, the purpose of the derivative activity? ___ ___ ___

   f. Do the disclosures for items 5a. through 5e. above distinguish between: ___ ___ ___

      (1) Derivative instruments (and nonderivative instruments) designated as fair value hedging instruments? ___ ___ ___

      (2) Derivative instruments designated as cash flow hedging instruments? ___ ___ ___

      (3) Derivative instruments (and nonderivative instruments) designated as hedging instruments for hedges of the foreign currency exposure of a net investment in a foreign operation? ___ ___ ___

      (4) All other derivatives? ___ ___ ___

6. Have the following disclosures been made for derivative instruments designated and qualifying as fair value hedging instruments (as well as nonderivative instruments that may give rise to foreign currency transaction gains or losses) and for the related hedged items, for each reporting period for which a complete set of financial statements is presented: (FAS-133, par. 45) ___ ___ ___

   a. The net gain or loss recognized in earnings during the reporting period representing (a) the amount of the hedges' ineffectiveness and (b) the component of the derivative in-

	Yes	*No*	*N/A*
struments' gain or loss, if any, excluded from the assessment of hedge effectiveness, and (c) a description of where the net gain or loss is reported in the statement of income or other statement of financial performance?	___	___	___
b. The amount of net gain or loss recognized in earnings when a hedged firm commitment no longer qualifies as a fair value hedge?	___	___	___
7. Have the following disclosures been made for derivative instruments that have been designated and qualifying as cash flow hedging instruments and for the related hedged transactions: (FAS-133, par. 45)	___	___	___
a. The net gain or loss recognized in earnings during the reporting period representing (a) the amount of the hedges' ineffectiveness, (b) the component of the derivative instruments' gain or loss, if any, excluded from the assessment of hedge effectiveness, and (c) a description of where the net gain or loss is reported in the statement of income or other statement of financial performance?	___	___	___
b. A description of the transactions or other events that will result in the reclassification into earnings of gains and losses that are reported in accumulated other comprehensive income, and the estimated net amount of the existing gains or losses at the reporting date that is expected to be reclassified into earnings within the next 12 months?	___	___	___
c. The maximum length of time over which the entity is hedging its exposure to the variability in future cash flows for forecasted transactions excluding those forecasted transactions related to the payment of variable interest on existing financial instruments?	___	___	___
d. The amount of gains and losses reclassified into earnings as a result of the discontinuance of cash flow hedges because it is probable that the original forecasted transactions will not occur?	___	___	___
8. Has the following disclosure been made for derivative instruments designated and qualifying as hedging instruments for hedges of the foreign			

	Yes	*No*	*N/A*
currency exposure of a net investment in a foreign operation (as well as for nonderivative instruments that may give rise to foreign currency transaction gains or losses): (FAS-133, par. 45)	___	___	___
a. The net amount of gains or losses included in the cumulative translation adjustment during the reporting period?	___	___	___
9. Have the following disclosures been made as part of reporting changes in the components of other comprehensive income: (FAS-133, pars. 46 and 47)	___	___	___
a. The net gain or loss on derivative instruments designated and qualifying as cash flow hedging instruments that are reported in comprehensive income are displayed as a separate classification within other comprehensive income?	___	___	___
b. As part of the disclosures of accumulated other comprehensive income, are the following disclosed separately:	___	___	___
(1) The beginning and ending accumulated derivative gain or loss?	___	___	___
(2) The related net change associated with current-period hedging transactions?	___	___	___
(3) The net amount of any reclassification into earnings?	___	___	___

FINANCIAL INSTRUMENTS—OTHER DISCLOSURES

Questions 1 through 5 apply if FAS-133 (Accounting for Derivative Instruments and Hedging Activities), as amended by FAS-138, has ***not*** *been adopted. (****Note:*** *FAS-133 and FAS-138 are effective for all fiscal quarters of fiscal years beginning after June 15, 2000.)*

1. For financial instruments with off-balance-sheet risk, have the following disclosures been made by category of financial instrument:	___	___	___
a. The face or contract amount (or notional principal amount if there is no face or contract amount)? (FAS-105, par. 17)	___	___	___

Yes No N/A

b. The nature and terms of the financial instruments, including at a minimum a discussion of (1) the credit and market risk of those instruments, (2) the cash requirements of those instruments, and (3) the related accounting policy? (FAS-105, par. 17) ___ ___ ___

c. Have the disclosures required in 1a. and 1b. above: (FAS-119, pars. 8 and 14) ___ ___ ___

(1) Distinguished between financial instruments held or issued for trading purposes (including dealing and other trading activities measured at fair value with gains and losses recognized in earnings) and financial instruments held or issued for purposes other than trading? ___ ___ ___

(2) Included a description of the leverage features and their general effect on the credit and market risk, cash requirements, and related accounting policy? ___ ___ ___

(3) Been made for options and other derivatives that do not have off-balance-sheet risk? ___ ___ ___

(4) Been made by category of financial instrument (for example, class of financial instrument, business activity, or risk), distinguishing between those held for trading purposes and those held for purposes other than trading? ___ ___ ___

2. For financial instruments with off-balance-sheet credit risk, have the following disclosures been made: (FAS-105, par. 18) ___ ___ ___

a. The amount of accounting loss the entity would incur if any party to the financial instrument failed completely to perform according to the terms of the contract and the collateral or other security, if any, for the amount due proved to be of no value to the entity? ___ ___ ___

b. The entity's policy of requiring collateral or other security to support financial instruments subject to credit risk? ___ ___ ___

c. Information about the entity's access to that collateral or other security? ___ ___ ___

	Yes	*No*	*N/A*
d. The nature and a brief description of the collateral or other security supporting those financial instruments?	___	___	___
3. Have significant concentrations of credit risk arising from all financial instruments been disclosed, including the following about each significant concentration: (FAS-105, par. 20)	___	___	___
a. Information about the activity, region, or economic characteristic that identifies the concentration?	___	___	___
b. The amount of accounting loss caused by credit risk the entity would incur if parties to the financial instruments that make up the concentration failed completely to perform according to the terms of the contract and the collateral or other security, if any, for the amount due proved to be of no value to the entity?	___	___	___
c. The entity's policy of requiring collateral or other security to support financial instruments subject to credit risk?	___	___	___
d. Information about the entity's access to the collateral or other security?	___	___	___
e. The nature and a brief description of the collateral or other security supporting those financial instruments?	___	___	___
4. Have the following information about fair value of financial instruments been disclosed either in the body of the financial statements or in the accompanying notes: (*Note:* These disclosures about the fair value of financial instruments are optional, not required, for an entity that meets **all** of the following criteria: (1) the entity is a nonpublic entity, (2) the entity's total assets are less than $100 million on the date of the financial statements, and (3) the entity has not held or issued any derivative financial instruments during the reporting period.) (FAS-107, pars. 10 and 14; FAS-119, par. 15)	___	___	___
a. Fair value of financial instruments for which it is practicable to estimate fair value? (For trade receivables and payables, no disclosure is required when the carrying amount ap-			

Yes No N/A

proximates fair value). In connection with this item: ___ ___ ___

(1) When disclosure is made in the accompanying notes, is the fair value presented together with the related carrying amount in a form that makes it clear whether the fair value and carrying amount represent assets or liabilities and how the carrying amounts relate to what is reported in the balance sheet? ___ ___ ___

(2) Has disclosure been made in a single note or, if disclosed in more than a single note, does one of the notes include a summary table that contains the fair value and related carrying amounts and cross-references to the locations of the remaining disclosures? ___ ___ ___

b. The methods and significant assumptions used to estimate the fair value of financial instruments? (The disclosures should distinguish between financial instruments held or issued for trading purposes, including dealing and other trading activities measured at fair value with gains and losses recognized in earnings, and financial instruments held or issued for purposes other than trading.) ___ ___ ___

c. In disclosing the fair value of a derivative financial instrument, did the entity **not** (1) combine, aggregate, or net that fair value with the fair value of nonderivative financial instruments or (2) net that fair value with the fair value of other derivative financial instruments, except to the extent that the offsetting of carrying amounts in the balance sheet is permitted? ___ ___ ___

d. For financial instruments for which it is concluded that estimating fair value is not practicable, have disclosures been made of (1) information related to estimating the fair value of the financial instrument (such as the carrying amount, effective interest rate, and maturity), and (2) the reasons why it is not practicable to estimate fair value? ___ ___ ___

Yes No N/A

5. Have the required disclosures been made for transfers of financial instruments? (See "Transfers and Servicing of Financial Assets") ___ ___ ___

*Questions 6 through 8 apply if FAS-133 (Accounting for Derivative Instruments and Hedging Activities), as amended by FAS-138, has been adopted. (**Note:** FAS-133 and FAS-138 are effective for all fiscal quarters of fiscal years beginning after June 15, 2000.)*

6. Have significant concentrations of credit risk arising from all financial instruments been disclosed, including the following about each significant concentration: (FAS-133, par. 531) ___ ___ ___
   a. Information about the activity, region, or economic characteristic that identifies the concentration? ___ ___ ___
   b. The maximum amount of loss due to credit risk that, based on the gross fair value of the financial instrument, the entity would incur if parties to the financial instruments that make up the concentration failed completely to perform according to the terms of the contracts and the collateral or other security, if any, for the amount due proved to be of no value to the entity? ___ ___ ___
   c. The entity's policy of requiring collateral or other security to support financial instruments subject to credit risk? ___ ___ ___
   d. Information about the entity's access to the collateral or other security? ___ ___ ___
   e. The nature and a brief description of the collateral or other security supporting those financial instruments? ___ ___ ___
   f. The entity's policy of entering into master netting arrangements to mitigate the credit risk of financial instruments, information about the arrangements for which the entity is a party, and a brief description of the terms of those arrangements, including the extent to which they would reduce the entity's maximum amount of loss due to credit risk? ___ ___ ___

Yes *No* *N/A*

7. Have the following information about fair value of financial instruments been disclosed either in the body of the financial statements or in the accompanying notes: (*Note:* These disclosures about the fair value of financial instruments are optional, not required, for an entity that meets **all** of the following criteria: (1) the entity is a nonpublic entity, (2) the entity's total assets are less than $100 million on the date of the financial statements, and (3) the entity has not held or issued any derivative financial instruments during the reporting period.) (FAS-107, pars. 10 and 14; FAS-133, pars. 531 and 532) ___ ___ ___
   a. Fair value of financial instruments for which it is practicable to estimate fair value? (For trade receivables and payables, no disclosure is required when the carrying amount approximates fair value). In connection with this item: ___ ___ ___
      (1) When disclosure is made in the accompanying notes, is the fair value presented together with the related carrying amount in a form that makes it clear whether the fair value and carrying amount represent assets or liabilities and how the carrying amounts relate to what is reported in the balance sheet? ___ ___ ___
      (2) Has disclosure been made in a single note or, if disclosed in more than a single note, does one of the notes include a summary table that contains the fair value and related carrying amounts and cross-references to the locations of the remaining disclosures? ___ ___ ___
   b. The methods and significant assumptions used to estimate the fair value of financial instruments? ___ ___ ___
   c. In disclosing the fair value of a financial instrument, did the entity **not** net that fair value with the fair value of other financial instruments, except to the extent that the offsetting of carrying amounts in the balance sheet is permitted? ___ ___ ___

Yes No N/A

d. For financial instruments for which it is concluded that estimating fair value is not practicable, have disclosures been made of (1) information related to estimating the fair value of the financial instrument (such as the carrying amount, effective interest rate, and maturity), and (2) the reasons why it is not practicable to estimate fair value? ___ ___ ___

8. Have the required disclosures been made for transfers of financial instruments? (See "Transfers and Servicing of Financial Assets") ___ ___ ___

FOREIGN OPERATIONS AND CURRENCY TRANSLATION

Questions 1 through 5 apply if FAS-133 (Accounting for Derivative Instruments and Hedging Activities), as amended by FAS-138, has **not** *been adopted (***Note:*** FAS-133 and FAS-138 are effective for all fiscal quarters of fiscal years beginning after June 15, 2000.)*

1. Are significant foreign operations disclosed, including foreign earnings reported in excess of amounts received in the United States? (ARB-43, Ch. 12, pars. 5–6) ___ ___ ___
2. Is the aggregate exchange transaction gain or loss (included in the determination of net income) disclosed on the income statement or in a related note? (FAS-52, par. 30) ___ ___ ___
3. Is there an analysis of the change in the cumulative translation adjustments (included as a component of accumulated other comprehensive income), and does the analysis include the following: (FAS-52, par. 31) ___ ___ ___
   a. Beginning and ending amounts of cumulative translation adjustments? ___ ___ ___
   b. The aggregate adjustment for the period resulting from translation adjustments and gains and losses from hedges of a net investment in a foreign entity and long-term intercompany balances? ___ ___ ___
   c. The amount of income taxes for the period allocated to translation adjustments? ___ ___ ___

Yes No N/A

d. The amounts transferred from cumulative translation adjustments and included in determining net income for the period as a result of the sale or complete (or substantially complete) liquidation of an investment in a foreign entity? ___ ___ ___

4. Are the following disclosures made for rate changes that occur after the date of the client's financial statements: (FAS-52, pars. 32, 143) ___ ___ ___
   a. Disclosure for the rate change? ___ ___ ___
   b. The effects of rate changes on unsettled balances pertaining to foreign currency transactions? ___ ___ ___
   c. If the effects of rate changes cannot be determined, is that fact disclosed? ___ ___ ___
5. Are additional **optional** disclosures, such as the following, considered to supplement the required disclosures described above: (FAS-52, par. 144) ___ ___ ___
   a. Mathematical effects of translating revenue and expenses at rates that are different from those used in previous financial statements? ___ ___ ___
   b. Economic effects (such as selling prices, sales volume, and cost structures) of rate changes? ___ ___ ___

*Questions 6 through 10 apply if FAS-133 (Accounting for Derivative Instruments and Hedging Activities), as amended by FAS-138, has been adopted (**Note:** FAS-133 and FAS-138 are effective for all fiscal quarters of fiscal years beginning after June 15, 2000.)*

6. Are significant foreign operations disclosed, including foreign earnings reported in excess of amounts received in the United States? (ARB-43, Ch. 12, pars. 5–6) ___ ___ ___
7. Is the aggregate exchange transaction gain or loss disclosed as follows: (FAS-133, par. 45) ___ ___ ___
   a. For derivative instruments designated and qualifying as fair value hedging instruments, as well as nonderivative instruments that may give rise to foreign currency transaction gains or losses, and for the related hedged items, for

Yes No N/A

each reporting period for which a complete set of financial statements is presented: ___ ___ ___

(1) The net gain or loss recognized in earnings during the reporting period representing (a) the amount of the hedges' ineffectiveness and (b) the component of the derivative instruments' gain or loss, if any, excluded from the assessment of hedge effectiveness, and (c) a description of where the net gain or loss is reported in the statement of income or other statement of financial performance? ___ ___ ___

(2) The amount of net gain or loss recognized in earnings when a hedged firm commitment no longer qualifies as a fair value hedge? ___ ___ ___

b. For derivative instruments that have been designated and qualifying as cash flow hedging instruments and for the related hedged transactions: ___ ___ ___

(1) The net gain or loss recognized in earnings during the reporting period representing (a) the amount of the hedges' ineffectiveness, (b) the component of the derivative instruments' gain or loss, if any, excluded from the assessment of hedge effectiveness, and (c) a description of where the net gain or loss is reported in the statement of income or other statement of financial performance? ___ ___ ___

(2) A description of the transactions or other events that will result in the reclassification into earnings of gains and losses that are reported in accumulated other comprehensive income, and the estimated net amount of the existing gains or losses at the reporting date that is expected to be reclassified into earnings within the next 12 months? ___ ___ ___

(3) The maximum length of time over which the entity is hedging its exposure to the variability in future cash flows for forecasted transactions excluding those fore-

Yes No N/A

casted transactions related to the payment of variable interest on existing financial instruments? ___ ___ ___

(4) The amount of gains and losses reclassified into earnings as a result of the discontinuance of cash flow hedges because it is probable that the original forecasted transactions will not occur? ___ ___ ___

c. For derivative instruments designated and qualifying as hedging instruments for hedges of the foreign currency exposure of a net investment in a foreign operation (as well as for nonderivative instruments that may give rise to foreign currency transaction gains or losses): ___ ___ ___

(1) The net amount of gains or losses included in the cumulative translation adjustment during the reporting period? ___ ___ ___

8. Is there an analysis of the change in the cumulative translation adjustments (included as a component of accumulated other comprehensive income), and does the analysis include the following: (FAS-52, par. 31) ___ ___ ___

a. Beginning and ending amounts of cumulative translation adjustments? ___ ___ ___

b. The aggregate adjustment for the period resulting from translation adjustments and gains and losses from hedges of a net investment in a foreign entity and long-term intercompany balances? ___ ___ ___

c. The amount of income taxes for the period allocated to translation adjustments? ___ ___ ___

d. The amounts transferred from cumulative translation adjustments and included in determining net income for the period as a result of the sale or complete (or substantially complete) liquidation of an investment in a foreign entity? ___ ___ ___

9. Are the following disclosures made for rate changes that occur after the date of the client's financial statements: (FAS-52, pars. 32, 143) ___ ___ ___

	Yes	No	N/A
a. Disclosure for the rate change?	___	___	___
b. The effects of rate changes on unsettled balances pertaining to foreign currency transactions?	___	___	___
c. If the effects of rate changes cannot be determined, is that fact disclosed?	___	___	___
10. Are additional (**optional**) disclosures, such as the following, considered to supplement the required disclosures described above: (FAS-52, par. 144)	___	___	___
a. Mathematical effects of translating revenue and expenses at rates that are different from those used in previous financial statements?	___	___	___
b. Economic effects (such as selling prices, sales volume, and cost structures) of rate changes?	___	___	___

GOING-CONCERN DISCLOSURES

	Yes	No	N/A
1. If the auditor concludes, after considering management's plans, that there is substantial doubt about the entity's ability to continue as a going concern for a period of time not to exceed one year beyond the balance sheet date, do the financial statements include the following disclosures: (AU 341.10)	___	___	___
a. Pertinent conditions and events giving rise to the assessment of substantial doubt about the entity's ability to continue as a going concern for a period of time not to exceed one year beyond the balance sheet date?	___	___	___
b. The possible effects of such conditions and events?	___	___	___
c. Management's evaluation of the significance of those conditions and events and any mitigating factors?	___	___	___
d. Possible discontinuance of operations?	___	___	___
e. Management's plans (including relevant prospective financial information)?	___	___	___
f. Information about the recoverability or classification of recorded asset amounts or the amounts or classification of liabilities?	___	___	___

Yes No N/A

2. When, primarily because of the auditor's consideration of management's plans, the auditor concludes that substantial doubt about the entity's ability to continue as a going concern for a period of time not to exceed one year from the balance sheet date is alleviated, do the financial statements include the following disclosures: (AU 341.11) ___ ___ ___
   a. The principal conditions and events that initially caused the auditor to believe there was substantial doubt? ___ ___ ___
   b. The possible effects of such conditions and events, and any mitigating factors, including management's plans? ___ ___ ___

IMPAIRMENT OF CERTAIN LOANS

1. Have the following disclosures been made, either in the body of the financial statements or in the accompanying notes, about impaired loans as defined in paragraph 8 of FAS-114: (FAS-118, pars. 6 and 24) ___ ___ ___
   a. As of the date of each statement of financial position presented, the total recorded investment in the impaired loans at the end of each period and (1) the amount of that recorded investment for which there is a related allowance for credit losses and the amount of that allowance and (2) the amount of that recorded investment for which there is no related allowance for credit losses? ___ ___ ___
   b. The creditor's policy for recognizing interest income on impaired loans, including how cash receipts are recorded? ___ ___ ___
   c. For each period for which results of operations are presented: ___ ___ ___
      (1) The average recorded investment in the impaired loans during each period? ___ ___ ___
      (2) The related amount of interest income recognized during the time within that period that the loans were impaired? ___ ___ ___

Yes No N/A

(3) The amount of interest income recognized using a cash-basis method of accounting during the time within that period that the loans were impaired, unless not practicable?

d. For each period for which results of operations are presented, have disclosures been made of the activity in the total allowance for credit losses related to loans, including the following:

(1) The balance in the allowance at the beginning and end of each period?

(2) Additions charged to operations?

(3) Direct writedowns charged against the allowance?

(4) Recoveries of amounts previously charged off?

IMPAIRMENT OF LONG-LIVED ASSETS AND LONG-LIVED ASSETS TO BE DISPOSED OF

1. Have the following disclosures been made for impaired assets to be held and used: (FAS-121, par. 14)

   a. A description of the impaired assets and the facts and circumstances leading to the impairment?

   b. The amount of the impairment loss and how fair value was determined?

   c. The caption in the income statement in which the impairment loss is aggregated if that loss has not been presented as a separate caption or reported parenthetically on the face of the statement?

   d. If applicable, the business segment(s) affected?

2. Have the following disclosures been made for all assets to be disposed of for each period presented during which those assets are held: (FAS-121, par. 19):

	Yes	*No*	*N/A*
a. A description of the assets to be disposed of, the facts and circumstances leading to the expected disposal, the expected disposal date, and the carrying amount of those assets?	___	___	___
b. If applicable, the business segment(s) in which assets to be disposed of are held?	___	___	___
c. The loss, if any, resulting from writing down the assets to fair value less cost to sell?	___	___	___
d. The gain or loss, if any, resulting from changes in the carrying amounts of assets to be disposed of that arises from subsequent revisions in estimates of fair value less cost to sell?	___	___	___
e. The caption in the income statement in which the gains or losses in c. and d. are aggregated if those gains or losses have not been presented as a separate caption or reported parenthetically on the face of the statement?	___	___	___
f. The results of operations for assets to be disposed of to the extent that those results are included in the entity's results of operations for the period and can be identified?	___	___	___

INTEREST COST

1. Have the following disclosures been made with respect to interest costs:	___	___	___
a. For an accounting period in which no interest cost is capitalized, the amount of interest cost incurred and charged to expense during the period? (FAS-34, par. 21)	___	___	___
b. For an accounting period in which some interest cost is capitalized, the total amount of interest cost incurred during the period and the amount thereof that has been capitalized? (FAS-34, par. 21)	___	___	___
c. The amount of interest costs incurred in connection with product financing arrangements? (FAS-34, par. 21; FAS-49, par. 9)	___	___	___
d. For notes payable or receivable that require the imputation of interest, have disclosures included: (APB-21, par. 16)	___	___	___

Yes No N/A

(1) A description of the note? ___ ___ ___

(2) The effective interest rate? ___ ___ ___

(3) The face amount of the note? ___ ___ ___

(4) The amount of discount or premium resulting from present value determination? ___ ___ ___

(5) The amortization of the discount or premium to interest? ___ ___ ___

e. The amount of interest paid (net of amounts capitalized) for each period for which a statement of cash flows is presented? (FAS-95, par. 29) ___ ___ ___

INTERIM FINANCIAL REPORTING

1. If the company uses estimated gross profit rates to determine the cost of goods sold during interim periods or uses other methods different from those used at annual inventory dates, have the following disclosures been made: (APB-28, par. 14) ___ ___ ___

   a. The method used at the interim date? ___ ___ ___

   b. Any significant adjustments that result from reconciliations with the annual physical inventory? ___ ___ ___

2. When costs and expenses incurred in an interim period cannot be readily identified with the activities or benefits of other interim periods, have disclosures been made about the nature and amount of such costs? (Disclosure is not required if items of a comparable nature are included in both the current interim period and the corresponding interim period of the preceding year.) (APB-28, par. 15) ___ ___ ___

3. If revenues of the entity are subject to material seasonal variations, have the following disclosures been made to avoid the possibility that interim results may be taken as fairly indicative of the estimated results for a full fiscal year: (APB-28, par. 18) ___ ___ ___

	Yes	*No*	*N/A*
a. The seasonal nature of the business activities?	___	___	___
b. Information for 12-month periods ended at the interim date for the current and preceding years (**optional**)?	___	___	___
4. Have disclosures been made of the reasons for significant variations in the customary relationship between income tax expense and pretax accounting income, if they are not otherwise apparent from the financial statements or from the nature of the entity's business? (APB-28, par. 19)	___	___	___
5. Are extraordinary items, discontinued operations, unusual and infrequently occurring transactions, and events that are material to the operating results of the interim period reported separately and included in the determination of net income for the interim period in which they occur? (APB-28, par. 21)	___	___	___
6. Have disclosures been made about contingencies and other uncertainties that could be expected to affect the fairness of presentation of the interim financial information? (Such disclosures should be repeated in interim and annual reports until the contingencies have been removed or resolved or have become immaterial.) (APB-28, par. 22)	___	___	___
7. Have disclosures been made of any changes in accounting principles or practices from those applied in: (APB-28, par. 23)	___	___	___
a. The comparable interim period of the prior year?	___	___	___
b. The preceding interim periods in the current year?	___	___	___
c. The prior annual financial statements?	___	___	___
8. If there were changes in accounting principles that required retroactive restatement of previously issued financial statements, has the effect on all periods presented been disclosed? (APB-28, par. 25)	___	___	___
9. Has the effect of a change in accounting estimate, including a change in the estimated effective annual tax rate, been disclosed if material			

Yes No N/A

in relation to any period presented? (APB-28, par. 26) ___ ___ ___

10. Have the cumulative effects of an accounting change or correction of an error that are material to an interim period, but not material to the estimated income for the full fiscal year or to the trend of earnings, been disclosed separately in the interim period? (APB-28, par. 29) ___ ___ ___

11. Have the gross and net of tax effects of prior-period adjustments of net income been disclosed in the interim period in which the adjustments are made? (APB-9, par. 26) ___ ___ ___

12. Have the following disclosures been made in interim financial statements about an adjustment related to prior interim periods of the current fiscal year: (FAS-16, par. 15) ___ ___ ___

    a. The effect on income from continuing operations and net income for each prior interim period of the current fiscal year? ___ ___ ___

    b. Restated income from continuing operations and net income for each prior interim period? ___ ___ ___

13. Have the following disclosures about a cumulative effect-type accounting change, other than changes to LIFO, been made in interim financial reports: (FAS-3, par. 11) ___ ___ ___

    a. In financial reports for the interim period in which the new accounting principle is adopted, have disclosures been made of: ___ ___ ___

        (1) The nature of and justification for the change? ___ ___ ___

        (2) The effect of the change on income from continuing operations and net income (and related per share amounts for public companies) for the interim period in which the change is made? (If the change is made in a period other than the first interim period of a fiscal year, the effect of the change on income from continuing operations, net income, and related per share amounts for each prechange interim period of the fiscal year should be

Yes *No* *N/A*

disclosed. Also, the restated income from continuing operations, net income, and related per share amounts for each pre-change interim period of the fiscal year should be disclosed.) ___ ___ ___

(3) Income from continuing operations and net income (and related per share amounts for public companies) computed on a pro forma basis for (i) the interim period in which the change is made and (ii) any interim periods of prior fiscal years for which financial information is being presented? (If no financial information for interim periods of prior fiscal years is being presented, disclosure shall be made, in the period of change, of the actual and pro forma amounts of income from continuing operations, net income, and related per share amounts for the interim period of the immediately preceding fiscal year that corresponds to the interim period in which the changes are made.) ___ ___ ___

b. In year-to-date and last-12-months-to-date financial reports that include the interim period in which the new accounting principle is adopted, have disclosures been made of: ___ ___ ___

(1) The effect of the change on income from continuing operations and net income (and related per share amounts for public companies) for the interim period in which the change is made? ___ ___ ___

(2) Income from continuing operations and net income (and related per share amounts for public companies) computed on a pro forma basis for (i) the interim period in which the change is made and (ii) any interim periods of prior fiscal years for which financial information is being presented? (If no financial information for interim periods of prior fiscal years is being presented, disclosure should be made, in the period of change, of the actual and pro forma amounts of

Yes No N/A

income from continuing operations, net income, and related per share amounts for the interim period of the immediately preceding fiscal year that corresponds to the interim period in which the changes are made.)

c. In financial reports for subsequent (postchange) interim periods of the fiscal year in which the new accounting principle is adopted, have disclosures been made of the effect of the change on income from continuing operations and net income (and related per share amounts for public companies) for that postchange interim period?

14. For changes in accounting principles when neither the cumulative effect of the change nor the pro forma amounts can be computed (principally a change to the LIFO method of inventory pricing), have the following disclosures been made: (FAS-3, par. 12)

    a. An explanation of the reasons for omitting accounting for the cumulative effect of the change?

    b. An explanation of the reasons for omitting disclosure of pro forma amounts for prior years?

Items 15 and 16 are additional disclosures that are applicable only to publicly held companies

15. For publicly traded companies that report summarized financial information to their security holders at interim dates (including reports on fourth quarters), have the following items, at a minimum, been reported: (APB-28, par. 30)

    a. Sales or gross revenues?

    b. Provision for income taxes?

    c. Extraordinary items (including related income tax effects)?

    d. Cumulative effect of a change in accounting principles or practices?

    e. Net income?

    f. Comprehensive income?

	Yes	*No*	*N/A*
g. Basic and diluted earnings per share data for each period presented?	___	___	___
h. Seasonal revenue, costs, or expenses?	___	___	___
i. Significant changes in estimates or provisions for income taxes?	___	___	___
j. Disposal of a segment of a business and extraordinary, unusual or infrequently occurring items?	___	___	___
k. Contingent items?	___	___	___
l. Changes in accounting principles or estimates?	___	___	___
m. Significant changes in financial position?	___	___	___
n. The following information about reportable operating segments (including provisions related to restatement of segment information in previously issued financial statements):	___	___	___
(1) Revenues from external customers?	___	___	___
(2) Intersegment revenues?	___	___	___
(3) A measure of segment profit or loss?	___	___	___
(4) Total assets for which there has been a material change from the amount disclosed in the last annual report?	___	___	___
(5) A description of differences from the last annual report in the basis of segmentation or in the measurement of segment profit or loss?	___	___	___
(6) A reconciliation of the total of the reportable segments' measures of profit or loss to the enterprise's consolidated income before income taxes, extraordinary items, discontinued operations, and the cumulative effect of changes in accounting principles? (However, if, for example, an enterprise allocates items such as income taxes and extraordinary items to segments, the enterprise may choose to reconcile the total of the segments' measures of profit or loss to consolidated income after those items. Significant reconciling items shall be separately identified and described in that reconciliation.)	___	___	___

	Yes	*No*	*N/A*
16. If financial information is not separately reported for the fourth quarter, or that information is not presented in the annual report, have the following information about the fourth quarter been disclosed in a note to the annual financial statements: (FAS-3, par. 14)	___	___	___
(1) Disposal of a segment of a business?	___	___	___
(2) Extraordinary, unusual, or infrequent transactions or events?	___	___	___
(3) The aggregate effect of year-end adjustments that are material to the operating results of the fourth quarter?	___	___	___
(4) Accounting changes presented in the manner required for interim accounting changes?	___	___	___

LEASES—LESSEES

1. Is there a general description of leasing arrangements including, but not limited to, the following: (FAS-13, par. 16)	___	___	___
a. The basis on which contingent rental payments are determined?	___	___	___
b. The existence and terms of renewal or purchase options and escalation clauses?	___	___	___
c. Restrictions imposed by lease agreements such as those concerning dividends, additional debt, and further leasing?	___	___	___
2. Has the nature and extent of leasing transactions with related parties been disclosed? (FAS-13, par. 29)	___	___	___
3. Are the following disclosures made for capital leases: (FAS-13, pars. 13, 16)	___	___	___
a. The gross amount of assets recorded under capital leases as of the date of each balance sheet presented by major classes according to nature or function? (This information may be combined with the comparable information for owned assets.)	___	___	___
b. Capitalized lease obligations separately identified in the balance sheet and appropriately classified as current and noncurrent amounts?	___	___	___

	Yes	*No*	*N/A*
c. Future minimum lease payments as of the date of the latest balance sheet presented, in the aggregate and for each of the five succeeding fiscal years, with separate deductions from the total for the amount representing executory costs (including any profit thereon), that are included in the minimum lease payments, and for the amount of the imputed interest necessary to reduce the net minimum lease payments to present value?	___	___	___
d. The total of minimum sublease rentals to be received in the future under noncancelable subleases as of the date of the latest balance sheet presented?	___	___	___
e. Total contingent rentals actually incurred for each period for which an income statement is presented?	___	___	___
f. Amortization of capitalized leases separately reported on the income statement or presented in a note to the financial statements? (The amortization may be combined with depreciation expense, but that fact must be disclosed.)	___	___	___
4. Are the following disclosures made for operating leases having initial or remaining noncancelable lease terms in excess of one year: (FAS-13, par. 16)	___	___	___
a. Future minimum rental payments required as of the date of the latest balance sheet presented, in the aggregate and for each of the five succeeding fiscal years?	___	___	___
b. The total amount of minimum rentals to be received in the future under noncancelable subleases as of the date of the latest balance sheet presented?	___	___	___
5. Are the following disclosures made for all operating leases, except for rental payments under leases with terms of a month or less that were not renewed: (FAS-13, par. 16)	___	___	___
a. Rental expense for each period for which an income statement is presented?	___	___	___
b. Presentation of separate amounts for minimum rentals, contingent rentals, and sublease rental income?	___	___	___

Yes No N/A

6. For seller-lessee transactions, is there a description of the terms of the sale-leaseback transaction including future commitments, obligations, provisions, or circumstances that require or result in the seller-lessee's continuing involvement? (FAS-98, par. 17) ___ ___ ___
7. If a sale-leaseback transaction is accounted for by the deposit method or as a real estate financing arrangement, are the following disclosures made: (FAS-98, par. 18) ___ ___ ___
   a. The obligation for future minimum lease payments as of the date of the latest balance sheet presented in the aggregate and for each of the five succeeding fiscal years? ___ ___ ___
   b. The total of minimum sublease rentals, if any, to be received in the future under noncancelable subleases in the aggregate and for each of the five succeeding fiscal years? ___ ___ ___

LEASES—LESSORS

1. Is there a general description of the lessor's leasing arrangements? (FAS-13, par. 23) ___ ___ ___
2. Has the nature and extent of leasing transactions with related parties been disclosed? (FAS-13, par. 29) ___ ___ ___
3. For sales-type and direct-financing leases, are the following components of the net investment in sales-type and direct financing leases disclosed as of the date of each balance sheet presented: (FAS-13, par. 23; FAS-91, par. 25) ___ ___ ___
   a. Future minimum lease payments to be received with separate deductions for (1) amounts representing executory costs, including any profit thereon, included in the minimum lease payments and (2) the accumulated allowance for uncollectible minimum lease payments receivable? ___ ___ ___
   b. The unguaranteed residual values accruing to the benefit of the lessor? ___ ___ ___
   c. Initial direct costs for direct financing leases only? ___ ___ ___
   d. Unearned income? ___ ___ ___

Yes No N/A

4. Are the following disclosures made for sales-type and direct financing leases: (FAS-13, par. 23) ___ ___ ___
   a. Future minimum lease payments to be received for each of the five succeeding fiscal years as of the date of the latest balance sheet presented? ___ ___ ___
   b. Total contingent rentals included in income for each period for which an income statement is presented? ___ ___ ___
5. Are the following disclosures made for operating leases: (FAS-13, par. 23) ___ ___ ___
   a. The cost and carrying amount, if different, of property on lease or held for leasing, by major classes of property according to nature or function, and the amount of accumulated depreciation in total as of the date of the latest balance sheet presented? ___ ___ ___
   b. Minimum future rentals on noncancelable leases as of the date of the latest balance sheet presented, in the aggregate and for each of the five succeeding fiscal years? ___ ___ ___
   c. Total contingent rentals included in income for each period for which an income statement is presented? ___ ___ ___
6. Are the following disclosures made for leveraged leases: (FAS-13, par. 47) ___ ___ ___
   a. The amount of related deferred taxes presented separately from the remainder of the net income investment? ___ ___ ___
   b. Separate presentation (in the income statement or in related notes) of pretax income from the leveraged lease, the tax effect of pretax income, and the amount of investment tax credit recognized as income during the period? ___ ___ ___
7. If leveraged leasing is a significant part of the lessor's business activities in terms of revenue, net income, or assets, are the following components of the net investment in leveraged leases disclosed in notes to the financial statements: (FAS-13, par. 47) ___ ___ ___
   a. Rentals receivable, net of that portion of the rental applicable to principal and interest on the nonrecourse debt? ___ ___ ___

Yes No N/A

b. A receivable for the amount of the investment tax credit to be realized on the transaction? ___ ___ ___

c. The estimated residual value of the leased assets? (The estimated residual value should not exceed the amount estimated at the inception of the lease, except as provided in FAS-23.) ___ ___ ___

d. Unearned and deferred income consisting of (1) the estimated pretax lease income (or loss), after deducting initial direct costs, remaining to be allocated to income over the lease term and (2) the investment tax credit remaining to be allocated to income over the lease term? ___ ___ ___

8. For lessors that recognize contingent rental income, have disclosures been made of the following: (EITF 98-9) ___ ___ ___

   a. The accounting policy for recognizing contingent rental income? ___ ___ ___

   b. If contingent rental income is recognized (accrued) prior to achieving the specified target that triggers the contingent rents, the impact on net income of accruing such rents prior to achieving the specified target? ___ ___ ___

LEASES—TAX LEASES

1. If the entity is involved in the sale or purchase of tax benefits through tax leases, have disclosures been made of the following: (FTB 82-1, par. 4) ___ ___ ___

   a. The method of recognizing revenue? ___ ___ ___

   b. The method of allocating the income tax benefits and asset costs to current and future periods? ___ ___ ___

2. If unusual or infrequent, have disclosures been made of the nature and financial effects of sales or purchases of tax benefits through tax leases on the face of the income statement or in a note to the financial statements? (FTB 82-1, par. 6) ___ ___ ___

3. Have significant contingencies existing with respect to sales or purchases of tax benefits through tax leases been disclosed? (FTB 82-1, par. 7) ___ ___ ___

Yes No N/A

4. If comparative financial statements are presented, have disclosures been made of any changes in the method of accounting for sales or purchases of tax benefits through tax leases that significantly affect comparability? (FTB 82-1, par. 7) ___ ___ ___
5. If a significant variation in the customary relationship between income tax expense and pretax accounting income occurs as a result of sales or purchases of tax benefits through tax leases, has the estimated amount and nature of the variation been disclosed? (FAS-109, par. 288) ___ ___ ___

LENDING ACTIVITIES

1. If the company anticipates prepayments of loan balances, have disclosures been made regarding the policy and the significant assumptions underlying the prepayment estimates? (FAS-91, par. 19) ___ ___ ___

LIMITED LIABILITY COMPANIES OR PARTNERSHIPS (LLCs OR LLPs)

1. In addition to all the disclosures that typically apply to any other business entity, are the following additional disclosures made in the financial statements of an LLC or an LLP: (PB-14, pars. 15–16) ___ ___ ___
   a. A description of any limitation of the LLC or LLP members' liability? ___ ___ ___
   b. The different classes of members' interests and the respective rights, preferences, and privileges of each class? ___ ___ ___
   c. The amount of each class of members' equity either in the equity section of the balance sheet or in the notes to the financial statements? ___ ___ ___
   d. The date the LLC or LLP will cease to exist, if the entity has a finite life? ___ ___ ___
   e. In the year of formation for LLCs and LLPs formed by combining entities under common control or by conversion from another type of entity, the fact that the assets and liabilities

	Yes	*No*	*N/A*
were previously held by a predecessor entity or entities?	___	___	___

LONG-TERM CONTRACTS

	Yes	*No*	*N/A*
1. Have the following disclosures been made for long-term contracts:	___	___	___
a. The method used to account for long-term contracts (i.e., the percentage-of-completion method or the completed-contract method)? (ARB-45, par. 15)	___	___	___
b. Departure from the basic revenue recognition policy for a single contract or group of contracts? (SOP 81-1, pars. 25, 31)	___	___	___
c. The policies relating to combining and segmenting contracts, if applicable? (SOP 81-1, par. 21)	___	___	___
d. When the percentage-of-completion method of accounting is used, the method of measuring the extent of progress toward completion (e.g., cost-to-cost, direct labor)? (SOP 81-1, pars. 21, 45)	___	___	___
e. If the completed-contract method is used, the criteria used to determine substantial completion? (SOP 81-1, par. 52)	___	___	___
f. The amount of revenue from claims recognized in excess of the agreed contract price? (SOP 81-1, pars. 65–67)	___	___	___
g. If the contractor recognizes revenues from claims only when the amounts have been received or awarded, the amounts of such revenues recorded during the period? (SOP 81-1, par. 66)	___	___	___
h. The effect of significant revisions in contract estimates? (SOP 81-1, par. 84)	___	___	___
i. The amount of advances, if any, offset against cost-type contract receivables? (ARB-43, Ch. 11A, par. 22)	___	___	___
j. Provisions for losses on contracts separately shown as liabilities on the face of the balance sheet, if material? (SOP 81-1, par. 89)	___	___	___

Yes No N/A

k. Provisions for losses on contracts that are material, unusual, or infrequent shown as a separate component of construction costs on the face of the income statement? (SOP 81-1, par. 88) ___ ___ ___

l. The nature and amount of any large or unusual contract commitments? (FAS-5, par. 18) ___ ___ ___

m. Unbilled costs and fees under cost-type contracts shown separately from billed accounts receivable? (ARB-43, Ch. 11A, par. 21) ___ ___ ___

NONMONETARY TRANSACTIONS

1. Are the following disclosures made for nonmonetary transactions: (APB-29, par. 28) ___ ___ ___
   a. The nature of the transactions? ___ ___ ___
   b. The basis of accounting for the assets transferred? ___ ___ ___
   c. Gains or losses, if any, recognized on transfers? ___ ___ ___
2. Are gains and losses resulting from involuntary conversions of nonmonetary assets to monetary assets reported as either an extraordinary item or an unusual or infrequent item, as appropriate? (FIN-30, par. 4) ___ ___ ___

PENSION AND POSTRETIREMENT BENEFIT PLANS

Pension and Postretirement Defined Benefit Plans—Reduced Disclosure Requirements for Nonpublic Companies

1. Has the following information about the plan been disclosed, for each balance sheet presented: (FAS-132, par. 8) ___ ___ ___
   a. The benefit obligation? ___ ___ ___
   b. The fair value of plan assets? ___ ___ ___
   c. The funded status of the plan? ___ ___ ___
   d. Employer contributions? ___ ___ ___

	Yes	*No*	*N/A*
e. Participant contributions?	___	___	___
f. Benefits paid?	___	___	___
g. The amounts recognized in the balance sheet, including:	___	___	___
(1) The net pension prepaid assets or accrued liabilities?	___	___	___
(2) The amount of any intangible asset recognized? **(Applicable to pension plans only)**	___	___	___
(3) The amount of accumulated other comprehensive income recognized pursuant to FAS-87, paragraph 37, as amended? **(Applicable to pension plans only)**	___	___	___
2. Has the amount of net periodic benefit cost recognized and the amount included within other comprehensive income arising from a change in the minimum pension liability recognized pursuant to FAS-87, paragraph 37, as amended, been disclosed, for each income statement presented? (FAS-132, par. 8)	___	___	___
3. Have the following assumptions used in the accounting for the plan been disclosed, for each balance sheet presented: (FAS-132, par. 8)	___	___	___
a. The weighted average assumed discount rate?	___	___	___
b. The weighted average rate of compensation increase (for pay-related plans)?	___	___	___
c. The weighted average expected long-term rate of return on plan assets?	___	___	___
4. Has disclosure been made of the assumed healthcare cost trend rate(s) for the next year used to measure the expected cost of benefits covered by the plan (gross eligible charges) and a general description of the direction and pattern of change in the assumed trend rates thereafter, together with the ultimate trend rate(s) and when that rate is expected to be achieved? (FAS-132, par. 8) **(Applicable to healthcare postretirement benefit plans only)**	___	___	___
5. Have the following transactions and events been disclosed: (FAS-132, par. 8)	___	___	___

	Yes	*No*	*N/A*
a. The amounts and types of securities of the employer and related parties included in plan assets?	___	___	___
b. The approximate amount of future annual benefits of plan participants covered by insurance contracts issued by the employer or related parties?	___	___	___
c. Any significant transactions between the employer or related parties and the plan?	___	___	___
d. The nature and effect of significant nonroutine events, such as amendments, combinations, divestitures, curtailments, and settlements?	___	___	___
6. For employers with two or more defined benefit pension plans, if disclosures for plans that have *projected* benefit obligations in excess of plan assets and plans that have plan assets in excess of projected benefit obligations are presented on a combined basis, have the following disclosures been made separately with respect to plans that have projected benefit obligations in excess of plan assets: (FAS-132, par. 6)	___	___	___
a. The aggregate projected benefit obligations?	___	___	___
b. The aggregate fair value of plan assets?	___	___	___
7. For employers with two or more defined benefit pension plans, if disclosures for plans that have *accumulated* benefit obligations in excess of plan assets and plans that have plan assets in excess of accumulated benefit obligations are presented on a combined basis, have the following disclosures been made separately with respect to plans that have accumulated benefit obligations in excess of plan assets: (FAS-132, par. 6)	___	___	___
a. The aggregate accumulated benefit obligations?	___	___	___
b. The aggregate fair value of plan assets?	___	___	___
8. If two or more defined benefit pension plans are combined, have the amounts recognized as prepaid benefit costs and accrued benefit liabilities been disclosed separately? (FAS-132, par. 6)	___	___	___
9. Have domestic and foreign defined benefit pension plans been disclosed separately if the bene-			

Yes No N/A

fit obligations of the foreign plans are significant relative to the total benefit obligation and the plans use significantly different assumptions? (FAS-132, par. 7) ___ ___ ___

10. If a gain or loss from settlement or curtailment has not been recognized in the current year and the employer's financial position or results of operations would have been materially different had it been recognized, have appropriate disclosures been made? (FAS-88 Q&A, No. 28) ___ ___ ___

Pension and Postretirement Defined Benefit Plans—Public Companies (and Nonpublic Companies That Elect to Voluntarily Provide Additional Disclosures)

1. Has disclosure been made of the amount of net periodic cost recognized, for each income statement presented, showing separately the following: (FAS-132, par. 5) ___ ___ ___
   a. Service cost component? ___ ___ ___
   b. Interest cost component? ___ ___ ___
   c. Expected return on plan assets for the period? ___ ___ ___
   d. Amortization of the unrecognized transition obligation or asset? ___ ___ ___
   e. Amount of recognized gains or losses? ___ ___ ___
   f. Amount of prior service cost recognized? ___ ___ ___
   g. Amount of gain or loss recognized due to a settlement or curtailment? ___ ___ ___
2. Has disclosure been made of the funded status of the plan, amounts not recognized in the entity's balance sheet, and amounts recognized in the entity's balance sheet, including the following, for each balance sheet presented: (FAS-132, par. 5) ___ ___ ___
   a. Amount of any unamortized prior service cost? ___ ___ ___
   b. Amount of any unrecognized net gain or loss (including asset gains and losses not yet reflected in market-related value)? ___ ___ ___

	Yes	*No*	*N/A*
c. Amount of any remaining unamortized, unrecognized net obligation or net asset at the initial application of FAS-87 or FAS-106?	___	___	___
d. Amount of net pension asset or liability?	___	___	___
e. Any intangible asset and the amount of accumulated other comprehensive income? **(Applicable to pension plans only)**	___	___	___
3. Has a reconciliation of the beginning and ending balances of the benefit obligation been disclosed, for each balance sheet presented, with separate disclosure of the following: (FAS-132, par. 5)	___	___	___
a. Service cost?	___	___	___
b. Interest cost?	___	___	___
c. Contributions by plan participants?	___	___	___
d. Actuarial gains and losses?	___	___	___
e. Foreign currency exchange rate changes?	___	___	___
f. Benefits paid?	___	___	___
g. Plan amendments?	___	___	___
h. Business combinations?	___	___	___
i. Divestitures?	___	___	___
j. Curtailments?	___	___	___
k. Settlements?	___	___	___
l. Special termination benefits?	___	___	___
4. Has a reconciliation of the beginning and ending balances of the fair value of plan assets been disclosed, for each balance sheet presented, including the effects of the following: (FAS-132, par. 5)	___	___	___
a. Actual return on plan assets?	___	___	___
b. Foreign currency exchange rate changes?	___	___	___
c. Contributions by employer?	___	___	___
d. Contributions by plan participants?	___	___	___
e. Benefits paid?	___	___	___
f. Business combinations?	___	___	___
g. Divestitures?	___	___	___
h. Settlements?	___	___	___

	Yes	*No*	*N/A*
5. Has the amount included within other comprehensive income arising from a change in the additional minimum pension liability recognized been disclosed, for each income statement presented? (FAS-132, par. 5)	___	___	___
6. Have the following assumptions used in the accounting for the plan been disclosed, for each balance sheet presented: (FAS-132, par. 5)	___	___	___
a. The weighted average assumed discount rate?	___	___	___
b. The weighted average rate of compensation increase (for pay-related plans)?	___	___	___
c. The weighted average expected long-term rate of return on plan assets?	___	___	___
7. Has disclosure been made of the assumed healthcare cost trend rate(s) for the next year used to measure the expected cost of benefits covered by the plan (gross eligible charges) and a general description of the direction and pattern of change in the assumed trend rates thereafter, together with the ultimate trend rate(s) and when that rate is expected to be achieved? (FAS-132, par. 5) **(Applicable to healthcare postretirement benefit plans only)**	___	___	___
8. Has disclosure been made of the effect of a one-percentage-point increase and the effect of a one-percentage-point decrease in the assumed healthcare cost trend rates on: (FAS-132, par. 5) **(Applicable to healthcare postretirement benefit plans only)**	___	___	___
a. The aggregate of the service and interest cost components of net periodic postretirement healthcare benefit cost of the current period?	___	___	___
b. The accumulated postretirement benefit obligation for healthcare benefits as of the current balance sheet?	___	___	___
9. Have the following transactions and events been disclosed: (FAS-132, par. 5)	___	___	___
a. The amounts and types of securities of the employer and related parties included in plan assets?	___	___	___
b. The approximate amount of future annual benefits of plan participants covered by in-			

Yes *No* *N/A*

surance contracts issued by the employer or related parties? ___ ___ ___

c. Any significant transactions between the employer or related parties and the plan? ___ ___ ___

d. Any alternative amortization method used to amortize prior service costs or unrecognized net gains and losses? ___ ___ ___

e. Any substantive commitment, such as past practice or a history of regular benefit increases, used as the basis for accounting for the benefit obligation? ___ ___ ___

f. The cost of providing special or contractual termination benefits recognized during the period and a description of the nature of the event? ___ ___ ___

g. An explanation of any significant change in the benefit obligation or plan assets not otherwise apparent in the above disclosures? ___ ___ ___

10. For employers with two or more defined benefit pension plans, if disclosures for plans that have *projected* benefit obligations in excess of plan assets and plans that have plan assets in excess of projected benefit obligations are presented on a combined basis, have the following disclosures been made separately with respect to plans that have projected benefit obligations in excess of plan assets: (FAS-132, par. 6) ___ ___ ___

    a. The aggregate projected benefit obligations? ___ ___ ___

    b. The aggregate fair value of plan assets? ___ ___ ___

11. For employers with two or more defined benefit pension plans, if disclosures for plans that have *accumulated* benefit obligations in excess of plan assets and plans that have plan assets in excess of accumulated benefit obligations are presented on a combined basis, have the following disclosures been made separately with respect to plans that have accumulated benefit obligations in excess of plan assets: (FAS-132, par. 6) ___ ___ ___

    a. The aggregate accumulated benefit obligations? ___ ___ ___

    b. The aggregate fair value of plan assets? ___ ___ ___

12. If two or more defined benefit pension plans are combined, have the amounts recognized as pre-

Yes No N/A

paid benefit costs and accrued benefit liabilities been disclosed separately? (FAS-132, par. 6)

13. Have domestic and foreign defined benefit pension plans been disclosed separately if the benefit obligations of the foreign plans are significant relative to the total benefit obligation and the plans use significantly different assumptions? (FAS-132, par. 7) ___ ___ ___

14. If a gain or loss from settlement or curtailment has not been recognized in the current year and the employer's financial position or results of operations would have been materially different had it been recognized, have appropriate disclosures been made? (FAS-88 Q&A, No. 28) ___ ___ ___

Pension and Postretirement Defined Contribution Plans—All Companies

1. Is the following information about the entity's defined contribution pension plans disclosed separately from the entity's defined benefit pension plans: (FAS-132, par. 9) ___ ___ ___
   a. A brief description of the plan? ___ ___ ___
   b. The amount of cost recognized during the period? ___ ___ ___
   c. The nature and effect of significant matters affecting comparability of information for all periods presented such as a change in the rate of employer contributions, a business combination, or a divestiture? ___ ___ ___

Pension and Postretirement Multiemployer Plans—All Companies

1. For multiemployer plans, has the following been disclosed: (FAS-132, pars. 10–11) ___ ___ ___
   a. Amount of contributions to such plans during the period? (Total contributions to multiemployer plans may be disclosed without separating the amounts attributable to pensions and other postretirement benefits.) ___ ___ ___
   b. A description of the nature and effect of any changes affecting comparability (such as a

Yes No N/A

change in the rate of employer contributions, a business combination, or a divestiture)? ___ ___ ___

c. The information required by FAS-5, if it is either probable or reasonably possible that an employer would withdraw from a multiemployer plan under circumstances that would give rise to a withdrawal obligation? **(Applicable to pension plans only)** ___ ___ ___

d. The information required by FAS-5, if it is either probable or reasonably possible that (a) an employer would withdraw from a multiemployer postretirement benefit plan under circumstances that would give rise to a withdrawal obligation, or (b) an employer's contribution to a multiemployer postretirement benefit plan would be increased during the remainder of a contract period in order to maintain a negotiated level of benefit coverage (a "maintenance of benefits" clause)? **(Applicable to postretirement benefit plans only)** ___ ___ ___

POSTEMPLOYMENT BENEFITS

1. If the company has not accrued an obligation for postemployment benefits (e.g., salary continuation, supplemental unemployment benefits, severance benefits, disability related benefits, job training and counseling, and continuation of health and insurance coverage) provided to former or inactive employees, including their beneficiaries and covered dependents, after employment but before retirement, only because the amount cannot be reasonably estimated, has that fact been disclosed? (FAS-112, par. 7) ___ ___ ___

PRIOR-PERIOD ADJUSTMENTS (CORRECTION OF ERRORS)

1. Are the following disclosures made for errors discovered in previously issued financial statements (disclosures required only for the year in which the error is discovered): (APB-20, par. 37; APB-9, par. 26) ___ ___ ___

Yes *No* *N/A*

a. The nature of the error? ___ ___ ___

b. The effect of the correction of the error on income before extraordinary items and net income (and related per share amounts when presented) in the period of correction? ___ ___ ___

c. The amount of income tax applicable to each prior-period adjustment? ___ ___ ___

2. If the effect of an error is presented in single-period financial statements, is the effect (gross and net of tax) on the opening balance of retained earnings and on net income (and on related per share amounts when presented) of the preceding year disclosed? (APB-9, par. 26) ___ ___ ___

3. If the effect of an error is presented in comparative financial statements, is the effect presented as an adjustment to the opening balance of retained earnings and by restating prior periods' financial statements affected by the error? (APB-9, par. 18) ___ ___ ___

QUASI-REORGANIZATIONS AND REORGANIZATIONS UNDER THE BANKRUPTCY CODE

Quasi-Reorganizations

1. After a quasi-reorganization or corporate readjustment: (ARB-43, Ch. 7A, par. 10; ARB-46, par. 2) ___ ___ ___

   a. Was the offsetting adjustment charged to retained earnings? ___ ___ ___

   b. If the adjustment exceeds the balance in the retained earnings account, was the difference charged to additional paid-in capital? ___ ___ ___

   c. Has a new retained earnings account been established and dated to show that it runs from the effective date of the readjustment? (This dating should be disclosed in the financial statements until such time as the effective date is no longer deemed to possess any special significance, which is generally not more than ten years.) ___ ___ ___

Yes No N/A

2. Are assets carried forward as of the date of the readjustment at fair amounts? (ARB-43, Ch. 7A, par. 4) ___ ___ ___
3. If the fair value of any asset is not readily determinable and a conservative estimate was used: (ARB-43, Ch. 7A, par. 4) ___ ___ ___
   a. Was the amount described as an estimate? ___ ___ ___
   b. Was any material difference arising through realization, or otherwise, and not attributable to events occurring or circumstances arising after the readjustment date not carried to income or retained earnings? ___ ___ ___
4. For companies that recognize the tax benefits of prior deductible temporary differences and carryforwards in income rather than contributed capital (i.e., companies that have previously adopted FAS-96 and effected a quasi-reorganization that involved only the elimination of a deficit in retained earnings), have the following disclosures been made: (FAS-109, par. 39) ___ ___ ___
   a. The date of the quasi-reorganization? ___ ___ ___
   b. The manner of reporting the tax benefits and that it differs from present accounting requirements for other entities? ___ ___ ___
   c. The effect of those tax benefits on income from continuing operations, income before extraordinary items, and net income (and on related per share amounts, if applicable)? ___ ___ ___

Reorganizations under the Bankruptcy Code

1. Have the following disclosures been made for companies that have filed petitions with the Bankruptcy Court and that expect to reorganize as going concerns under Chapter 11: (SOP 90-7, pars. 23–31, 34) ___ ___ ___
   a. Prepetition liabilities, including claims that become known after a petition is filed, which are not subject to reasonable estimation? ___ ___ ___
   b. Principal categories of claims subject to compromise? ___ ___ ___
   c. The extent to which reported interest expense differs from stated contractual interest? ___ ___ ___

Yes No N/A

d. Details of operating cash receipts and payments resulting from the reorganization if the indirect method is used in the statement of cash flows? ___ ___ ___

e. In the earnings per share calculation whether it is probable that the plan will require the issuance of common stock or common stock equivalents, thereby diluting current equity interests? ___ ___ ___

2. Have the following disclosures been made in consolidated financial statements including one or more entities in reorganization under Chapter 11 and one or more entities not in reorganization proceedings: (SOP 90-7, pars. 32–33) ___ ___ ___

   a. Condensed combined financial statements of the entities in reorganization proceedings? ___ ___ ___

   b. Intercompany receivables and payables of entities in reorganization? ___ ___ ___

3. Have the following disclosures been made for companies that have emerged from Chapter 11 under confirmed plans that adopt fresh start reporting: (SOP 90-7, par. 39) ___ ___ ___

   a. Adjustments to the historical amounts of individual assets and liabilities? ___ ___ ___

   b. The amount of debt forgiveness? ___ ___ ___

   c. The amount of prior retained earnings or deficit eliminated? ___ ___ ___

   d. Significant matters relating to the determination of reorganization value such as: ___ ___ ___

      (1) The method or methods used to determine reorganization value and factors such as discount rates, tax rates, the number of years for which cash flows are projected and the method of determining terminal value? ___ ___ ___

      (2) Sensitive assumptions about which there is a reasonable possibility of the occurrence of a variation that would significantly affect the measurement of reorganization value? ___ ___ ___

      (3) Assumptions about anticipated conditions that are expected to be different

	Yes	*No*	*N/A*
from current conditions, unless otherwise apparent?	___	___	___
4. Has the following disclosure been made for companies that have emerged from Chapter 11 under confirmed plans that adopt fresh start reporting and have recorded an adjustment that resulted from a preconfirmation contingency: (PB-11, pars. 8–9)	___	___	___
a. The adjustment in income or loss from continuing operations of the emerged entity?	___	___	___

RELATED-PARTY TRANSACTIONS

1. Are the following disclosures made for material related-party transactions (other than compensation arrangements, expense allowances, and other similar items in the ordinary course of business): (FAS-57, par. 2)	___	___	___
a. The nature of the relationship of the parties involved?	___	___	___
b. A description of the transactions, including transactions to which no amounts or nominal amounts were ascribed, for each of the periods for which income statements are presented, and such other information deemed necessary to an understanding of the effects of the transactions on the financial statements?	___	___	___
c. The dollar amounts of transactions for each of the periods for which income statements are presented and the effects of any change in the method of establishing the terms from those used in the preceding period?	___	___	___
d. Amounts due from or to related parties as of the date of each balance sheet presented and, if not otherwise apparent, the terms and manner of settlement?	___	___	___
2. Are disclosures concerning related-party transactions worded in a manner that does not imply that the transactions were consummated on terms equivalent to those that prevail in arm's-length transactions, unless such representations can be substantiated? (FAS-57, par. 3)	___	___	___

	Yes	*No*	*N/A*
3. Is the nature of the control relationship disclosed, even though there are no related-party transactions, when the client and one or more other enterprises are under common ownership or management control and the existence of that control could result in operating results or financial position of the client significantly different from those that would have resulted if the client were autonomous? (FAS-57, par. 4)	___	___	___
4. Are notes or accounts receivable due from officers, employees, or affiliated enterprises shown separately and not included under a general heading, such as notes receivable or accounts receivable? (ARB-43, Ch. 1A, par. 5)	___	___	___

RESEARCH AND DEVELOPMENT

1. Are the following disclosures made for an entity that accounts for its obligations under a research and development arrangement as a contract to perform research and development for others: (FAS-68, par. 14)	___	___	___
a. The terms of significant agreements under the research and development arrangement (including royalty arrangements, purchase provisions, license agreement, and commitments to provide additional funding) as of the date of each balance sheet presented?	___	___	___
b. The amount of compensation earned and costs incurred under such contracts for each period for which an income statement is presented?	___	___	___
2. Is disclosure made of total research and development costs charged to expense in each period for which an income statement is presented? (FAS-2, par. 13)	___	___	___
3. For research and development assets acquired in a business combination accounted for as a purchase that have no alternative future use, has disclosure been made of the portion of the purchase price that has been allocated to research and development and charged to expense at the date of consummation of the business combination? (FIN-4, par. 5)	___	___	___

	Yes	No	N/A

SEGMENT INFORMATION

1. Have disclosures been made of the factors used to identify the entity's reportable segments, including the basis of organization, such as: (FAS-131, par. 26) ___ ___ ___
   a. Differences in products and services? ___ ___ ___
   b. Geographic areas? ___ ___ ___
   c. Regulatory environments? ___ ___ ___
   d. A combination of factors? ___ ___ ___
2. Have the types of products and services from which each reportable segment derives its revenues been disclosed? (FAS-131, par. 26) ___ ___ ___
3. Have the amount of profit or loss and total assets for each reportable segment been disclosed? (FAS-131, par. 27) ___ ___ ___
4. Have the following financial information been disclosed about each reportable segment, if the specified amounts are included in the determination of segment profit or loss reviewed by the chief operating decision maker: (FAS-131, par. 27) ___ ___ ___
   a. Revenues from external customers? ___ ___ ___
   b. Revenues from transactions with other operating segment? ___ ___ ___
   c. Interest revenue (this may be reported net of interest expense if a majority of the segment's revenues are from interest and the chief operating decision maker relies primarily on net interest revenue to assess performance)? ___ ___ ___
   d. Interest expense? ___ ___ ___
   e. Depreciation, depletion, and amortization? ___ ___ ___
   f. Unusual items, as described in APB Opinion No. 30? ___ ___ ___
   g. Equity in the net income of investees accounted for by the equity method? ___ ___ ___
   h. Income tax expense or benefit? ___ ___ ___
   i. Extraordinary items? ___ ___ ___
   j. Significant noncash items other than depreciation, depletion, and amortization? ___ ___ ___

	Yes	*No*	*N/A*
5. Have the following financial information been disclosed about each reportable segment, if the specified amounts are included in the determination of segment assets reviewed by the chief operating decision maker: (FAS-131, par. 28)	___	___	___
a. The amount of investment in equity-method investees?	___	___	___
b. Total expenditures for additions to long-lived assets (other than financial instruments, long-term customer relationships of a financial institution, mortgage and other servicing rights, deferred policy acquisition costs, and deferred tax assets)?	___	___	___
6. Have disclosures been made of the measurements used for segment profit or loss and segment assets for each reportable segment, including at a minimum the following information: (FAS-131, par. 31)	___	___	___
a. The basis of accounting for any transactions between reportable segments?	___	___	___
b. The nature of any differences between the measurements of the reportable segments' profit or loss and the entity's consolidated income before income taxes, extraordinary items, discontinued operations, and cumulative effect of changes in accounting principles?	___	___	___
c. The nature of any differences between the measurements of the reportable segments' assets and the entity's consolidated assets?	___	___	___
d. The nature of any changes from prior periods in the measurement methods used to determine reported segment profit or loss and the effect, if any, of those changes on the amount of segment profit or loss?	___	___	___
e. The nature and effect of any asymmetrical allocations to segments (for example, an entity might allocate depreciation expense to a segment without allocating the related depreciable assets to that segment)?	___	___	___
7. Have reconciliations of all of the following items been disclosed: (FAS-131, par. 32)	___	___	___

	Yes	No	N/A
a. The total of the reportable segments' revenues to the entity's consolidated revenues?	___	___	___
b. The total of the reportable segments' profit or loss to the entity's consolidated income before income taxes, extraordinary items, discontinued operations, and cumulative effect of changes in accounting principles? (However, if an entity allocates items such as income taxes and extraordinary items to segments, the entity may choose to reconcile the total of the segments' profit or loss to consolidated income after those items.)	___	___	___
c. The total of the reportable segments' assets to the entity's consolidated assets?	___	___	___
d. The total of the reportable segments' amounts for every other significant item of information disclosed to the corresponding consolidated amount (e.g., an entity may choose to disclose liabilities for its reportable segments, in which case the entity would reconcile the total of reportable segments' liabilities for each segment to the enterprise's consolidated liabilities if the segment liabilities are significant)?	___	___	___
8. Have the following items been disclosed on an "entity-wide" basis, unless they are disclosed as part of the information about reportable segments (*Note:* Entities that have a single reportable segment are also required to disclose this information.): (FAS-131, pars. 36–39)	___	___	___
a. Revenues from external customers for each product and service or each group of similar products and services, based on information used to produce the entity's general-purpose financial statements (unless it is impracticable to do so, in which case that fact should be disclosed)?	___	___	___
b. The following information about geographic areas, based on information used to produce the entity's general-purpose financial statements (unless it is impracticable to do so, in which case that fact should be disclosed):	___	___	___
(1) Revenues from external sources (a) attributed to the entity's country of domi-			

Yes No N/A

cile, and (b) attributed to all foreign countries in total from which the entity derives revenues? (If revenues from external customers attributed to an individual foreign country are material, those revenues should be disclosed separately; an entity should disclose the basis for attributing revenues from external customers to individual countries.) ___ ___ ___

(2) Long-lived assets (other than financial instruments, long-term customer relationships of a financial institution, mortgage and other servicing rights, deferred policy acquisition costs, and deferred tax assets) located in (a) the entity's country of domicile and (b) all foreign countries in total in which the entity holds assets? (If assets in an individual foreign country are material, those assets should be disclosed separately.) ___ ___ ___

c. The extent of the entity's reliance on a single external customer from which 10% or more of revenues are derived, the amount of revenues earned from each such single customer, and the operating segment reporting the revenue? ___ ___ ___

9. Has the following information been disclosed about each reportable segment in condensed financial statements of interim periods: (FAS-131, par. 33) ___ ___ ___

a. Revenues from external customers? ___ ___ ___

b. Intersegment revenues? ___ ___ ___

c. Segment profit or loss? ___ ___ ___

d. Total assets for which there has been a material change from the amount disclosed in the last annual report? ___ ___ ___

e. A description of differences from the last annual report in the basis of segmentation or in the basis of measurement of segment profit or loss? ___ ___ ___

f. A reconciliation of the total of the reportable segments' profit or loss to the entity's consolidated income before income taxes, extraordi-

Yes No N/A

nary items, discontinued operations, and cumulative effect of changes in accounting principles? (However, if an entity allocates items such as income taxes and extraordinary items to segments, the entity may choose to reconcile the total of the segments' profit or loss to consolidated income after those items). ___ ___ ___

10. If an entity changes the structure of its internal organization in a manner that causes the composition of its reportable segments to change, has the corresponding information for earlier periods, including interim periods, been restated, unless it is impracticable to do so? (*Note:* The entity should also disclose that it has restated the segment information for earlier periods. If the segment information for earlier periods, including interim periods, is not restated to reflect the change, the entity should disclose in the year in which the change occurs segment information for the current period under both the old basis and the new basis of segmentation, unless it is impracticable to do so.) (FAS-131, pars. 34–35) ___ ___ ___

STOCK-BASED COMPENSATION

In October 1995 the FASB issued FAS-123 (Accounting for Stock-Based Compensation) which is effective for financial statements for years beginning after December 15, 1995. Due to the controversy involving this FASB project, the *accounting requirements* for measuring compensation cost under FAS-123 need not be followed unless an entity elects to do so; however, the *disclosure requirements* of FAS-123 apply to all entities. Also, entities that continue to measure compensation cost under the old rules must make certain *pro forma* disclosures for all awards granted in fiscal years beginning after December 15, 1994. ___ ___ ___

1. Are the following disclosures made regarding the entity's stock-based compensation plans (and separately for each type of award granted to the extent separate disclosure would be useful) for all companies regardless of whether they measure compensation cost using FAS-123 or APB-25: (FAS-123, par. 46–48) ___ ___ ___

	Yes	No	N/A
a. A description of the plan, including the general terms of awards, such as vesting requirements, maximum term of options granted, and number of shares authorized for grants of options or other equity instruments?	___	___	___
b. The number and weighted-average exercise prices of options that were:	___	___	___
(1) Outstanding at the beginning of the year?	___	___	___
(2) Outstanding at the end of the year?	___	___	___
(3) Granted during the year?	___	___	___
(4) Exercised during the year?	___	___	___
(5) Exercisable at the end of the year?	___	___	___
(6) Forfeited during the year?	___	___	___
(7) Expired during the year?	___	___	___
c. Weighted-average fair value (as of grant date) of options granted during the year? (*Note:* If the exercise price of some options differs from the market price of the stock on the grant date, weighted-average exercise prices and weighted-average fair values of options should be disclosed separately for options whose exercise price (a) equals, (b) exceeds, or (c) is less than the market price of the stock on the date of grant.)	___	___	___
d. Number and weighted-average fair value (as of grant date) of equity instruments other than options (e.g., shares of nonvested stock) granted during the year?	___	___	___
e. A description of the method and significant assumptions used during the year to estimate the fair values of options, including the risk-free interest rate, expected life, expected volatility, and expected dividends?	___	___	___
f. Total compensation cost recognized in the financial statements?	___	___	___
g. The terms of significant modifications of outstanding awards?	___	___	___
h. The range of exercise prices, the weighted-average exercise price, and the weighted-average remaining contractual life for options outstanding as of the date of the latest balance sheet presented, and for each range:	___	___	___

Yes No N/A

(1) The number, weighted-average exercise price, and weighted-average remaining contractual life of options outstanding? ___ ___ ___

(2) The number and weighted-average exercise price of options currently exercisable? ___ ___ ___

2. If the entity is measuring stock-based compensation cost under the old rules, rather than FAS-123, have *pro forma* net income (and *pro forma* earnings per share, if earnings per share is presented) been disclosed, as if the fair value based method prescribed by FAS-123 had been applied? (FAS-123, par. 45) ___ ___ ___

SUBSEQUENT EVENTS

1. Are appropriate adjustments made to the financial statements based on information that became available prior to the issuance of the financial statements (the information provides evidence with respect to conditions that existed at the date of the balance sheet)? (AU 560.03–.04) ___ ___ ___
2. Are appropriate disclosures made in the financial statements based on information that became available prior to the issuance of the financial statements (although the information does not suggest that conditions existed at the date of the balance sheet, it is nonetheless necessary to disclose such conditions in order for the financial statements not to be misleading)? (FAS-5, par. 11; AU 560.05–.07; AU 560.09) ___ ___ ___

TERMINATION CLAIMS

1. If the total of the undeterminable parts of a termination claim is believed to be material, have the essential facts been disclosed? (ARB-43, Ch. 11C, par. 19) ___ ___ ___
2. Have material termination claims been separately disclosed in the balance sheet? (ARB-43, Ch. 11C, par. 21) ___ ___ ___
3. Has disclosure been made of the relationship between advances or other loans received on terminated contracts and the potential termination claim receivable? (ARB-43, Ch. 11C, par. 22) ___ ___ ___

Yes No N/A

4. If the amount of termination sales is material, has it been separately disclosed in the income statement? (ARB-43, Ch. 11C, par. 23) ___ ___ ___

TRANSFERS AND SERVICING OF FINANCIAL ASSETS

Transfers of Financial Assets

1. Have the following disclosures been made for transfers of financial assets (FAS-140, par. 17): ___ ___ ___

   a. If the entity has entered into repurchase agreements or securities lending transactions, has the policy for requiring collateral or other security been disclosed? ___ ___ ___

   b. If the entity has pledged any of its assets as collateral that are not reclassified and separately reported in the balance sheet, has disclosure been made of the carrying amount and classification of those assets as of the date of the latest balance sheet presented? ___ ___ ___

   c. If the entity has accepted collateral that it is permitted by contract or custom to sell or repledge, have the following disclosures been made as of the date of each balance sheet presented: ___ ___ ___

      (1) The fair value of the collateral? ___ ___ ___

      (2) The portion of that collateral that it has sold or repledged? ___ ___ ___

      (3) Information about the sources and uses of that collateral? ___ ___ ___

   d. If it is not practicable to estimate the fair value of certain assets obtained or liabilities incurred in transfers of financial assets during the period, has disclosure been made of those items and the reasons why it is not practicable to estimate their fair value? ___ ___ ___

   e. If the entity has securitized financial assets during any period presented and accounts for that transfer as a sale, have the following disclosures been made for each major asset type (e.g., credit card receivables, automobile loans, mortgage loans): ___ ___ ___

	Yes	*No*	*N/A*
(1) The accounting policies for initially measuring the retained interests, if any, including the methodology (whether quoted market price, prices based on sales of similar assets and liabilities, or prices based on valuation techniques) used in determining their fair value?	___	___	___
(2) The characteristics of securitizations (a description of the transferor's continuing involvement with the transferred assets, including, but not limited to: servicing; recourse; and restrictions on retained interests) and the gain or loss from sale of financial assets in securitizations?	___	___	___
(3) The key assumptions used in measuring the fair value of retained interests at the time of securitization, including, at a minimum: quantitative information about discount rates; expected prepayments including the expected weighted-average life of prepayable financial assets; and anticipated credit losses, if applicable?	___	___	___
(4) Cash flows between the securitization SPE (special purpose entity) and the transferor, unless reported separately elsewhere in the financial statements or notes, including: proceeds from new securitizations; proceeds from collections reinvested in revolving-period securitizations; purchases of delinquent or foreclosed loans; servicing fees; and cash flows received on interests retained?	___	___	___
f. If the entity has retained interests in securitized financial assets at the date of the latest balance sheet presented, have the following disclosures been made for each major asset type (e.g., credit card receivables, automobile loans, mortgage loans):	___	___	___
(1) The accounting policies for subsequently measuring those retained interests, including the methodology (whether quoted market price, prices based on sales of similar assets and liabil-			

Yes No N/A

ities, or prices based on valuation techniques) used in determining their fair value? ___ ___ ___

(2) The key assumptions used in subsequently measuring the fair value of those interests, including at a minimum: quantitative information about discount rates; expected prepayments including the expected weighted-average life of prepayable financial assets; and anticipated credit losses, including expected static pool losses if applicable? ___ ___ ___

(3) A sensitivity analysis or stress test showing the hypothetical effect on the fair value of those interests of two or more unfavorable variations from the expected levels for each key assumption that is reported under (2) above independently from any change in another key assumption, and a description of the objectives, methodology, and limitations of the sensitivity analysis or stress test? ___ ___ ___

(4) For the securitized assets and any other financial assets that it manages together with them: ___ ___ ___

(i) The total principal amount outstanding, the portion that has been derecognized, and the portion that continues to be recognized in each category reported in the balance sheet, at the end of the period? ___ ___ ___

(ii) Delinquencies at the end of the period? ___ ___ ___

(iii) Credit losses, net of recoveries, during the period? ___ ___ ___

(iv) Average balances during the period? (This disclosure item is encouraged, but not required.) ___ ___ ___

Servicing of Financial Assets and Liabilities

1. Have the following disclosures been made for all servicing assets and servicing liabilities (FAS-140, par. 17): ___ ___ ___

	Yes	No	N/A
a. The amounts of servicing assets or liabilities recognized and amortized during the period?	___	___	___
b. The fair value of recognized servicing assets and liabilities for which it is practicable to estimate that value, and the method and significant assumptions used to estimate the fair value?	___	___	___
c. The risk characteristics of the underlying financial assets used to stratify recognized servicing assets for purposes of measuring impairment in accordance with FAS-140?	___	___	___
d. The activity in any valuation allowance for impairment of recognized servicing assets for each period for which results of operations are presented, including:	___	___	___
(1) Beginning and ending balances?	___	___	___
(2) Aggregate additions charged to operations?	___	___	___
(3) Aggregate reductions credited to operations?	___	___	___
(4) Aggregate direct write-downs charged against the allowances?	___	___	___

TROUBLED DEBT RESTRUCTURING—CREDITORS

	Yes	No	N/A
1. Has the amount of commitments, if any, to lend additional funds to debtors owing receivables whose terms have been modified in troubled debt restructuring been disclosed as of the date of each balance sheet presented? (FAS-15, par. 40)	___	___	___
2. Have the following disclosures been made, either in the body of the financial statements or in the accompanying notes, about impaired loans as defined in paragraph 8 of FAS-114: (FAS-118, pars. 6 and 24)	___	___	___
a. As of the date of each statement of financial position presented, the total recorded investment in the impaired loans at the end of each period and (1) the amount of that recorded investment for which there is a related allowance for credit losses and the amount of			

Yes No N/A

that allowance and (2) the amount of that recorded investment for which there is no related allowance for credit losses? ___ ___ ___

b. The creditor's policy for recognizing interest income on impaired loans, including how cash receipts are recorded? ___ ___ ___

c. For each period for which results of operations are presented: ___ ___ ___

(1) The average recorded investment in the impaired loans during each period? ___ ___ ___

(2) The related amount of interest income recognized during the time within that period that the loans were impaired? ___ ___ ___

(3) The amount of interest income recognized using a cash-basis method of accounting during the time within that period that the loans were impaired, unless not practicable? ___ ___ ___

d. For each period for which results of operations are presented, have disclosures been made of the activity in the total allowance for credit losses related to loans, including the following: ___ ___ ___

(1) The balance in the allowance at the beginning and end of each period? ___ ___ ___

(2) Additions charged to operations? ___ ___ ___

(3) Direct writedowns charged against the allowance? ___ ___ ___

(4) Recoveries of amounts previously charged off? ___ ___ ___

TROUBLED DEBT RESTRUCTURING—DEBTORS

1. Are the following disclosures made (either in the body of the financial statements or in related notes) for the period in which the troubled debt is restructured: (FAS-15, par. 25) ___ ___ ___

   a. For each restructuring, a description of the principal changes in terms, the major features of settlement, or both? ___ ___ ___

	Yes	*No*	*N/A*
b. Aggregate gain on restructuring of payables and the related income tax effect?	___	___	___
c. Aggregate net gain or loss on transfers of assets recognized during the period?	___	___	___
d. If applicable, the per share amount of the aggregate gain on restructuring, net of related income tax effect?	___	___	___
2. Are the following disclosures made for periods subsequent to the period in which the debt was restructured: (FAS-15, par. 26)	___	___	___
a. The extent to which amounts contingently payable are included in the carrying amount of restructured payables?	___	___	___
b. Total amounts that are contingently payable on restructured payables and the conditions under which those amounts would become payable or would be forgiven when there is at least a reasonable possibility that a liability for contingent payments will be incurred?	___	___	___

Accounting Resources on the Web

The following World Wide Web addresses are just a few of the resources on the Internet that are available to practitioners. Because of the evolving nature of the Internet, some addresses may change. In such a case, refer to one of the many Internet search engines, such as Yahoo! (http://www.yahoo.com).

AICPA http://www.aicpa.org/

American Accounting Association http://www.rutgers.edu/Accounting/raw/aaa/

Aspen Publishers, Inc. http://www.aspenpublishers.com

FASB http://www.rutgers.edu:80//Accounting/raw/fasb/

Federal Tax Code Search http://www.tns.lcs.mit.edu:80/uscode/

Fedworld http://www.fedworld.gov

GASB http://www.rutgers.edu/Accounting/raw/gasb/gasbhome.html

General Accounting Office http://www.gao.gov/

House of Representatives http://www.house.gov/

IRS Digital Daily http://www.irs.ustreas.gov/prod/cover.html

Library of Congress http://lcweb.loc.gov/homepage/

Office of Management and Budget http://www.gpo.gov/omb/omb001.html

Securities and Exchange Commission http://www.sec.gov/

Thomas Legislative Research http://thomas.loc.gov/

Cross-Reference

ORIGINAL PRONOUNCEMENTS TO 2001–02 *MILLER GAAP FINANCIAL STATEMENT DISCLOSURES MANUAL* CHAPTERS

This locator provides instant cross-reference between an original pronouncement and the chapter(s) in this publication in which a pronouncement is covered. Original pronouncements are listed chronologically on the left and the chapter(s) in which they appear in the 2001–02 *Miller GAAP Financial Statement Disclosures Manual* on the right. When an original pronouncement has been superseded, cross-reference is made to the succeeding pronouncement.

ACCOUNTING RESEARCH BULLETINS (ARBs)

(Accounting Research Bulletins 1–42 were revised, restated, or withdrawn at the time ARB No. 43 was issued.)

ORIGINAL PRONOUNCEMENT	2001–02 *MILLER GAAP FINANCIAL STATEMENT DISCLOSURES MANUAL* REFERENCE
ARB No. 43 Restatement and Revision of Accounting Research Bulletins	
Chapter 1—Prior Opinions	
1-A: Rules Adopted by Membership	Portions amended by FAS-111. Assets and Liabilities: General, ch. **30** Consolidated and Combined Financial Statements, ch. **8** Revenues and Gains, ch. **43** Stockholders' Equity, ch. **42** Other Assets: Current and Noncurrent, ch. **38** Other Liabilities: Current and Noncurrent, ch. **41**
1-B: Opinion Issued by Predecessor Committee	Portions amended by APB-6. Stockholders' Equity, ch. **42**
Chapter 2—Form of Statements	
2-A: Comparative Financial Statements	Portions amended by APB-20. Consolidated and Combined Financial Statements, ch. **8**
2-B: Combined Statement of Income and Earned Surplus	Superseded by APB-9

Chapter 3—Working Capital	
3-A: Current Assets and Current Liabilities	Portions amended by APB-6, 21, FAS-6, 78, 111, and 115. Assets and Liabilities: General, ch. **30** Other Assets: Current and Noncurrent, ch. **38** Other Liabilities: Current and Noncurrent, ch. **41**
3-B: Application of United States Government Securities Against Liabilities for Federal Taxes on Income	Superseded by APB-10
Chapter 4	
Inventory Pricing	Inventory, ch. **33**
Chapter 5	
Intangible Assets	Superseded by APB-16 and APB-17
Chapter 6	
Contingency Reserves	Superseded by FAS-5
Chapter 7—Capital Accounts	
7-A: Quasi-Reorganization or Corporate Readjustment	Portions amended by FAS-111. Stockholders' Equity, ch. **42**
7-B: Stock Dividends and Stock Split-Ups	Portions amended by APB-6. Stockholders' Equity, ch. **42**
7-C: Business Combinations	Superseded by ARB-48
Chapter 8:	
Income and Earned Surplus	Superseded by APB-9
Chapter 9—Depreciation	
9-A: Depreciation and High Costs	Property, Plant, and Equipment, ch. **36**
9-B: Depreciation on Appreciation	Superseded by APB-6
9-C: Emergency Facilities—Depreciation, Amortization, and Income Taxes	Portions amended or superseded by APB-6 and 11, FAS-96 and 109. Property, Plant, and Equipment, ch. **36**
Chapter 10—Taxes	
10-A: Real and Personal Property Taxes	Portions amended by APB-9 and FAS-111.
10-B: Income Taxes	Superseded by APB-11, FAS-96 and 109.
Chapter 11—Government Contracts	
11-A: Cost-Plus-Fixed-Fee Contracts	Government Contracts, ch. **19**
11-B: Renegotiation	Portions amended or superseded by APB-9, 11, FAS-96, 109 and 111. Long-Term Contracts, ch. **19**
11-C: Terminated War and Defense Contracts	Long-Term Contracts, ch. **19**

Chapter 12 Foreign Operations and Foreign Exchange	Superseded by FAS-52 and 94
Chapter 13—Compensation **13-A:** Pension Plans—Annuity Costs Based on Past Service	Superseded by APB-8
13-B: Compensation Involved in Stock Option and Stock Purchase Plans	Portions amended by APB-25 and FAS-123. Stock-Based Compensation, Stock Option Plans, and Stock Purchase Plans, ch. **28**
Chapter 14 Disclosures of Long-Term Leases in Financial Statements of Lessees	Superseded by APB-5
Chapter 15 Unamortized Discount, Issue Cost, and Redemption Premium on Bonds Refunded	Superseded by APB-26
ARB No. 44 Declining-Balance Depreciation	Superseded by ARB-44 (Revised)
ARB No. 44 (Revised) Declining-Balance Depreciation	Superseded by FAS-96 and FAS-109
ARB No. 45 Long-Term Construction-Type Contracts	Long-Term Contracts, ch. **19**
ARB No. 46 Discontinuance of Dating Earned Surplus	Stockholders' Equity, ch. **42**
ARB No. 47 Accounting for Costs of Pension Plans	Superseded by APB-8
ARB No. 48 Business Combinations	Superseded by APB-16
ARB No. 49 Earnings per Share	Superseded by APB-9
ARB No. 50 Contingencies	Superseded by FAS-5
ARB No. 51 Consolidated Financial Statements	Portions amended or superseded by APB-10, 11, 16, 18, 23, FAS-58, 71, 94, 96, 109, and 111. Consolidated and Combined Financial Statements, ch. **8**

ACCOUNTING PRINCIPLES BOARD OPINIONS (APBs)

ORIGINAL PRONOUNCEMENT	2001–02 *MILLER GAAP FINANCIAL STATEMENT DISCLOSURES MANUAL* REFERENCE
APB Opinion No. 1 New Depreciation Guidelines and Rules	Superseded by FAS-96 and 109
APB Opinion No. 2 Accounting for the "Investment Credit"	Portions amended or superseded by APB-4, FAS-71 and 109. Income Taxes, ch. **39**
APB Opinion No. 2—Addendum Accounting Principles for Regulated Industries	Superseded by FAS-71
APB Opinion No. 3 The Statement of Source and Application of Funds	Superseded by APB-19
APB Opinion No. 4 Accounting for the "Investment Credit"	Income Taxes, ch. **39**
APB Opinion No. 5 Reporting of Leases in Financial Statements of Lessee	Superseded by FAS-13
APB Opinion No. 6 Status of Accounting Research Bulletins	Portions amended or superseded by APB-11, 16, 17, 26, 28, FAS-8, 52, 71, 96, 109, and 111. Property, Plant, and Equipment, ch. **36** Stockholders' Equity, ch. 42
APB Opinion No. 7 Accounting for Leases in Financial Statements of Lessors	Superseded by FAS-13
APB Opinion No. 8 Accounting for the Cost of Pension Plans	Superseded by FAS-87
APB Opinion No. 9 Reporting the Results of Operations	Portions amended or superseded by APB-13, 15, 20, 30, FAS-16 and 111 Expenses and Losses, ch. **44** Discontinued Operations, ch. **45** Extraordinary Items, ch. **46** Unusual or Infrequent Items, ch. **47** Comprehensive Income, ch. **48**

APB Opinion No. 10
Omnibus Opinion—1966

Portions amended or superseded by APB-12, 14, 16, 18, FAS-111 and 129.
Assets and Liabilities: General, ch. **30**
Other Assets: Current and Noncurrent, ch. **38**
Other Liabilities: Current and Noncurrent, ch. **41**
Income Taxes, ch. **39**
Revenues and Gains, ch. **43**

APB Opinion No. 11
Accounting for Income Taxes

Superseded by FAS-96 and FAS-109

APB Opinion No. 12
Omnibus Opinion—1967

Portions amended or superseded by APB-14, FAS-87, 106, and 111.
Deferred Compensation Arrangements, ch. **10**
Property, Plant, and Equipment, ch. 36
Postemployment Benefits, ch. 22
Postretirement Benefits Other Than Pensions, ch. **23**
Stockholders' Equity, ch. **42**

APB Opinion No. 13
Amending Paragraph 6 of APB Opinion No. 9,

Expenses and Losses, ch. **44**
Discontinued Operations, ch. **45**
Extraordinary Items, ch. **46**
Unusual or Infrequent Items, ch. **47**
Comprehensive Income, ch. **48**

APB Opinion No. 14
Accounting for Convertible Debt and Debt Issued with Stock Purchase Warrants

Debt Obligations and Credit Arrangements, ch. **40**
Stockholders' Equity, ch. **42**

APB Opinion No. 15
Earnings per Share

Superseded by FAS-128 for periods ending after December 15, 1997

APB Opinion No. 16
Business Combinations

Portions amended or superseded by FAS-10, 38, 71, 79, 87, 96, 106, 109, and 121.
Business Combinations, ch. **4**
Intangible Assets, ch. **37**

APB Opinion No. 17
Intangible Assets

Portions amended or superseded by APB-30, FAS-71, 72, 96, 109, and 121.
Business Combinations, ch. **4**
Intangible Assets, ch. **37**

APB Opinion No. 18
The Equity Method of Accounting for Investments in Common Stock

Portions amended or superseded by FAS-13, 23, 30, 58, 94, 115, 121, and 128.
Investments: Equity and Cost Methods, ch. 35

APB Opinion No. 19 Reporting Changes in Financial Position	Superseded by FAS-95
APB Opinion No. 20 Accounting Changes	Portions amended or superseded by FAS-16, 32, 58, 71, 73, 95, 111, and 128. Accounting Changes, ch. **1** Expenses and Losses, ch. **44** Discontinued Operations, ch. **45** Extraordinary Items, ch. **46** Unusual or Infrequent Items, ch. **47** Comprehensive Income, ch. **48**
APB Opinion No. 21 Interest on Receivables and Payables	Portions amended or superseded by FAS-34, 96, and 109. Interest Cost, ch. **16** Accounts and Notes Receivable, ch. **32**
APB Opinion No. 22 Disclosure of Accounting Policies	Portions amended by FAS-2, 8, 52, 95, and 111. Accounting Policies, ch. 2
APB Opinion No. 23 Accounting for Income Taxes—Special Areas	Portions amended or superseded by FAS-9, 60, 71, 96, and 109. Income Taxes, ch. **39**
APB Opinion No. 24 Accounting for Income Taxes—Investments in Common Stock Accounted for by the Equity Method (Other Than Subsidiaries and Corporate Joint Ventures)	Superseded by FAS-96 and 109
APB Opinion No. 25 Accounting for Stock Issued to Employees	Portions amended or superseded by FAS-96, 109, and 123. Stock-Based Compensation, Stock Option Plans, and Stock Purchase Plans, ch. **28**
APB Opinion No. 26 Early Extinguishment of Debt	Portions amended or superseded by APB-30, FAS-4, 13, 15, 71, 76, 84, and 125. Debt Obligations and Credit Arrangements, ch. **40**
APB Opinion No. 27 Accounting for Lease Transactions by Manufacturer or Dealer Lessors	Superseded by FAS-13
APB Opinion No. 28 Interim Financial Reporting	Portions amended or superseded by FAS-3, 95, 96, 109, and 128. Interim Financial Reporting, ch. **17** Inventory, ch. **33**

APB Opinion No. 29 Accounting for Nonmonetary Transactions	Portions amended or superseded by FAS-71, 96, 109, and 123. Nonmonetary Transactions, ch. **20**
APB Opinion No. 30 Reporting the Results of Operations—Reporting the Effects of Disposal of a Segment of a Business, and Extraordinary, Unusual, and Infrequently Occurring Events and Transactions	Portions amended or superseded by FAS-4, 16, 60, 83, 96, 97, 101, 109, and 128. Expenses and Losses, ch. **44** Discontinued Operations, ch. **45** Extraordinary Items, ch. **46** Unusual or Infrequent Items, ch. **47** Comprehensive Income, ch. **48**
APB Opinion No. 31 Disclosure of Lease Commitments by Lessees	Superseded by FAS-13

ACCOUNTING PRINCIPLES BOARD STATEMENTS

ORIGINAL PRONOUNCEMENT	2001–02 *MILLER GAAP FINANCIAL STATEMENT DISCLOSURES MANUAL* REFERENCE
APB Statement No. 3 Financial Statements Restated for General Price-Level Changes	Changing Prices, ch. **5**

FINANCIAL ACCOUNTING STANDARDS BOARD STATEMENTS (FASs)

ORIGINAL PRONOUNCEMENT	2001–02 *MILLER GAAP FINANCIAL STATEMENT DISCLOSURES MANUAL* REFERENCE
FASB Statement No. 1 Disclosure of Foreign Currency Translation Information	Superseded by FAS-8 and 52
FASB Statement No. 2 Accounting for Research and Development Costs	Portions amended or superseded by FAS-71 and 86. Inventory, ch. **33** Research and Development Costs, ch. **26**
FASB Statement No. 3 Reporting Accounting Changes in Interim Financial Statements	Accounting Changes, ch. **1**

FASB Statement No. 4 Reporting Gains and Losses from Extinguishment of Debt	Portions amended or superseded by FAS-71 and 64. Debt Obligations and Credit Arrangements, ch. **40**
FASB Statement No. 5 Accounting for Contingencies	Portions amended or superseded by FAS-11, 16, 60, 71, 87, 111, 112, 113, 114, and 123. Contingencies, Risks, Uncertainties, and Concentrations, ch. **9**
FASB Statement No. 6 Classification of Short-Term Obligations Expected to Be Refinanced	Assets and Liabilities: General, ch. **30** Debt Obligations and Credit Arrangements, ch. **40**
FASB Statement No. 7 Accounting and Reporting by Development Stage Enterprises	Portions amended or superseded by FAS-71 and 95. Development Stage Enterprises, ch. **11**
FASB Statement No. 8 Accounting for the Translation of Foreign Currency Transactions and Foreign Currency Financial Statements	Superseded by FAS-52
FASB Statement No. 9 Accounting for Income Taxes—Oil and Gas Producing Companies	Superseded by FAS-19
FASB Statement No. 10 Extension of "Grandfather" Provisions for Business Combinations	Business Combinations, ch. **4**
FASB Statement No. 11 Accounting for Contingencies—Transition Method	No longer relevant
FASB Statement No. 12 Accounting for Certain Marketable Securities	Superseded by FAS-115
FASB Statement No. 13 Accounting for Leases	Portions amended or superseded by FAS-17, 22, 23, 26, 27, 28, 29, 34, 71, 77, 91, 96, 98, 109, and 125. Leases, ch. **18**
FASB Statement No. 14 Financial Reporting for Segments of a Business Enterprise	Segment Information, ch. **27** (Superseded by FAS-131 for periods beginning after December 15, 1997)

FASB Statement No. 15 Accounting by Debtors and Creditors for Troubled Debt Restructurings	Portions amended or superseded by FAS-71, 111, 114, and 121. Debt Obligations and Credit Arrangements, ch. **40**
FASB Statement No. 16 Prior Period Adjustments	Portions amended or superseded by FAS-71, 96, and 109. Accounting Changes, ch. **1**
FASB Statement No. 17 Accounting for Leases—Initial Direct Costs	Superseded by FAS-91
FASB Statement No. 18 Financial Reporting for Segments of a Business Enterprise—Interim Financial Statements	Segment Information, ch. **27** (Superseded by FAS-131 for periods beginning after December 15, 1997)
FASB Statement No. 19 Financial Accounting and Reporting by Oil and Gas Producing Companies	Portions amended or superseded by FAS-25, 69, 71, 96, 109, and 121.
FASB Statement No. 20 Accounting for Forward Exchange Contracts	Superseded by FAS-52
FASB Statement No. 21 Suspension of the Reporting of Earnings per Share and Segment Information by Nonpublic Enterprises	Segment Information, ch. **27** (Superseded by FAS-131 for periods beginning after December 15, 1997)
FASB Statement No. 22 Changes in the Provisions of Lease Agreements Resulting from Refundings of Tax-Exempt Debt	Portions amended or superseded by FAS-71, 76, 95, 123, 125, and 128. Debt Obligations and Credit Arrangements, ch. **40** Leases, ch. **18**
FASB Statement No. 23 Inception of the Lease	Leases, ch. **18**
FASB Statement No. 24 Reporting Segment Information in Financial Statements That Are Presented in Another Enterprise's Financial Report	Segment Information, ch. **27** (Superseded by FAS-131 for periods beginning after December 15, 1997)
FASB Statement No. 25 Suspension of Certain Accounting Requirements for Oil and Gas Producing Companies	Superseded by FAS-111.

FASB Statement No. 26 Profit Recognition on Sales-Type Leases of Real Estate	Superseded by FAS-98
FASB Statement No. 27 Classification of Renewals or Extensions of Existing Sales-Type or Direct Financing Leases	Leases, ch. **18**
FASB Statement No. 28 Accounting for Sales with Leasebacks	Portions amended by FAS-66. Leases, ch. **18**
FASB Statement No. 29 Determining Contingent Rentals	Portions amended by FAS-98. Leases, ch. **18**
FASB Statement No. 30 Disclosure of Information About Major Customers	Segment Information, ch. **27** (Superseded by FAS-131 for periods beginning after December 15, 1997)
FASB Statement No. 31 Accounting for Tax Benefits Related to U.K. Tax Legislation Concerning Stock Relief	Superseded by FAS-96 and FAS-109
FASB Statement No. 32 Specialized Accounting and Reporting Principles and Practices in AICPA Statements of Position and Guides on Accounting and Auditing Matters	Superseded by FAS-111
FASB Statement No. 33 Financial Reporting and Changing Prices	Superseded by FAS-89
FASB Statement No. 34 Capitalization of Interest Cost	Portions amended or superseded by FAS-42, 58, 62, 71, 75, and 121. Interest Costs, ch. **16**
FASB Statement No. 35 Accounting and Reporting by Defined Benefit Pension Plans	Portions amended or superseded by FAS-59, 75, and 110.
FASB Statement No. 36 Disclosure of Pension Information	Superseded by FAS-87
FASB Statement No. 37 Balance Sheet Classification of Deferred Income Taxes	Superseded by FAS-109
FASB Statement No. 38 Accounting for Preacquisition Contingencies of Purchased Enterprises	Portions amended or superseded by FAS-96 and 109. Business Combinations, ch. **4** Contingencies, Risks, Uncertainties, and Concentrations, ch. **9**

FASB Statement No. 39 Financial Reporting and Changing Prices: Specialized Assets—Mining and Oil and Gas	Superseded by FAS-89
FASB Statement No. 40 Financial Reporting and Changing Prices: Specialized Assets—Timberlands and Growing Timber	Superseded by FAS-89
FASB Statement No. 41 Financial Reporting and Changing Prices: Specialized Assets—Income-Producing Real Estate	Superseded by FAS-89
FASB Statement No. 42 Determining Materiality for Capitalization of Interest Cost	Interest Costs, ch. **16**
FASB Statement No. 43 Accounting for Compensated Absences	Portions amended or superseded by FAS-71, 112, and 123. Compensated Absences, ch. **7**
FASB Statement No. 44 Accounting for Intangible Assets of Motor Carriers	Portions amended by FAS-96 and 109. Intangible Assets, ch. **37**
FASB Statement No. 45 Accounting for Franchise Fee Revenue	Accounting Policies, ch. **2** Revenues and Gains, ch. **43**
FASB Statement No. 46 Financial Reporting and Changing Prices: Motion Picture Films	Superseded by FAS-89
FASB Statement No. 47 Disclosure of Long-Term Obligations	Portions superseded by FAS-129. Debt Obligations and Credit Arrangements, ch. **40**
FASB Statement No. 48 Revenue Recognition When Right of Return Exists	Accounts and Notes Receivables, ch. **32** Revenues and Gains, ch. **43**
FASB Statement No. 49 Accounting for Product Financing Arrangements	Portions superseded by FAS-71. Commitments, ch. **6** Contingencies, Risks, Uncertainties, and Concentrations, ch. **9** Debt Obligations and Credit Arrangements, ch. **40**
FASB Statement No. 50 Financial Reporting in the Record and Music Industry	Accounting Policies, ch. **2** Revenues and Gains, ch. **43**

FASB Statement No. 51 Financial Reporting by Cable Television Companies	Portions superseded by FAS-71. Accounting Policies, ch. **2** Revenues and Gains, ch. **43**
FASB Statement No. 52 Foreign Currency Translation	Portions amended by FAS-96 and 109. Foreign Operations and Currency Translation, ch. **14**
FASB Statement No. 53 Financial Reporting by Producers and Distributors of Motion Picture Films	Rescinded by FAS-139
FASB Statement No. 54 Financial Reporting and Changing Prices: Investment Companies	Superseded by FAS-89
FASB Statement No. 55 Determining Whether a Convertible Security Is a Common Stock Equivalent	Superseded by FAS-111
FASB Statement No. 56 Designation of AICPA Guide and Statement of Position (SOP) 81-1 on Contractor Accounting and SOP 81-2 Concerning Hospital-Related Organizations as Preferable for Purposes of Applying APB Opinion 20	Superseded by FAS-111
FASB Statement No. 57 Related Party Disclosures	Portions amended by FAS-95, 96, and 109. Related Party Disclosures, ch. **25**
FASB Statement No. 58 Capitalization of Interest Cost in Financial Statements That Include Investments Accounted For by the Equity Method	Interest Cost, ch. **16**
FASB Statement No. 59 Deferral of the Effective Date of Certain Accounting Requirements for Pension Plans of State and Local Governmental Units	Superseded by FAS-75
FASB Statement No. 60 Accounting and Reporting by Insurance Enterprises	Portions amended or superseded by FAS-91, 96, 97, 109, 113, 114, 115, 120, 121, and 124. Accounting Policies, ch. **2** Revenues and Gains, ch. **43**
FASB Statement No. 61 Accounting for Title Plant	Portions amended by FAS-121. Accounting Policies, ch. **2** Revenues and Gains, ch. **43**

FASB Statement No. 62 Capitalization of Interest Cost in Situations Involving Certain Tax-Exempt Borrowings and Certain Gifts and Grants	Interest Cost, ch. **16**
FASB Statement No. 63 Financial Reporting by Broadcasters	Portions amended by FAS-139. Accounting Policies, ch. **2** Revenues and Gains, ch. **43**
FASB Statement No. 64 Extinguishments of Debt Made to Satisfy Sinking-Fund Requirements	Debt Obligations and Credit Arrangements, ch. **40**
FASB Statement No. 65 Accounting for Certain Mortgage Banking Activities	Portions amended or superseded by FAS-91, 115, 122, 124, and 125. Accounting Policies, ch. **2** Revenues and Gains, ch. **43**
FASB Statement No. 66 Accounting for Sales of Real Estate	Portions amended or superseded by FAS-98 and 121. Accounting Policies, ch. **2** Revenues and Gains, ch. **43**
FASB Statement No. 67 Accounting for Costs and Initial Rental Operations of Real Estate Projects	Accounting Policies, ch. **2** Revenues and Gains, ch. **43**
FASB Statement No. 68 Research and Development Arrangements	Research and Development Costs, ch. **26**
FASB Statement No. 69 Disclosures about Oil and Gas Producing Activities	Portions amended or superseded by FAS-89, 95, 96, 109, 111, and 121. Accounting Policies, ch. **2** Revenues and Gains, ch. **43**
FASB Statement No. 70 Financial Reporting and Changing Prices: Foreign Currency Translation	Superseded by FAS-89
FASB Statement No. 71 Accounting for the Effects of Certain Types of Regulation	Portions amended or superseded by FAS-90, 92, 86, 96, 109, and 121. Accounting Policies, ch. **2** Revenues and Gains, ch. **43**
FASB Statement No. 72 Accounting for Certain Acquisitions of Banking or Thrift Institutions	Accounting Policies, ch. **2** Business Combinations, ch. **4** Intangible Assets, ch. **23** Revenues and Gains, ch. **43**

FASB Statement No. 73 Reporting a Change in Accounting for Railroad Track Structures	Accounting Changes, ch. **1**
FASB Statement No. 74 Accounting for Special Termination Benefits Paid to Employees	Superseded by FAS-88
FASB Statement No. 75 Deferral of the Effective Date of Certain Accounting Requirements for Pension Plans of State and Local Governmental Units	Accounting Policies, ch. **2**
FASB Statement No. 76 Extinguishment of Debt	Superseded by FAS-125
FASB Statement No. 77 Reporting by Transferors for Transfers of Receivables with Recourse	Superseded by FAS-125
FASB Statement No. 78 Classification of Obligations That Are Callable by the Creditor	Assets and Liabilities, ch. **30** Debt Obligations and Credit Arrangements, ch. **40**
FASB Statement No. 79 Elimination of Certain Disclosures for Business Combinations by Nonpublic Enterprises	Business Combinations, ch. **4**
FASB Statement No. 80 Accounting for Futures Contracts	Superseded by FAS-133
FASB Statement No. 81 Disclosure of Postretirement Health Care and Life Insurance Benefits	Superseded by FAS-106
FASB Statement No. 82 Financial Reporting and Changing Prices: Elimination of Certain Disclosures	Superseded by FAS-89
FASB Statement No. 83 Designation of AICPA Guides and Statement of Position on Accounting by Brokers and Dealers in Securities, by Employee Benefit Plans, and by Banks as Preferable for Purposes of Applying APB Opinion 20	Rescinded by FAS-111
FASB Statement No. 84 Induced Conversions of Convertible Debt	Debt Obligations and Credit Arrangements, ch. **40** Stockholders' Equity, ch. **42**
FASB Statement No. 85 Yield Test for Determining whether a Convertible Security Is a Common Stock Equivalent	Superseded by FAS-128 for periods ending after December 15, 1997

FASB Statement No. 86	
Accounting for the Costs of Computer Software to Be Sold, Leased, or Otherwise Marketed	Research and Development Costs, ch. **26**
FASB Statement No. 87	
Employers' Accounting for Pensions	Portions amended or superseded by FAS-96, 106, and 109. Pension Plans, ch. **21**
FASB Statement No. 88	
Employers' Accounting for Settlements and Curtailments of Defined Benefit Pension Plans and for Termination Benefits	Pension Plans, ch. **21**
FASB Statement No. 89	
Financial Reporting and Changing Prices	Portions amended by FAS-96, 109, and FAS-139. Changing Prices, ch. **5**
FASB Statement No. 90	
Regulated Enterprises—Accounting for Abandonments and Disallowances of Plant Costs	Portions amended or superseded by FAS-92, 96, and 109. Accounting Policies, ch. **2**
FASB Statement No. 91	
Accounting for Nonrefundable Fees and Costs Associated with Originating or Acquiring Loans and Initial Direct Costs of Leases	Portions amended or superseded by FAS-98, 114, 115, and 124. Accounting Policies, ch. **2** Leases, ch. **18**
FASB Statement No. 92	
Regulated Enterprises—Accounting for Phase-in Plans	Accounting Policies, ch. **2**
FASB Statement No. 93	
Recognition of Depreciation by Not-for-Profit Organizations	Portions amended by FAS-99. Accounting Policies, ch. **2**
FASB Statement No. 94	
Consolidation of all Majority-Owned Subsidiaries	Consolidated and Combined Financial Statements, ch. **35**
FASB Statement No. 95	
Statement of Cash Flows	Portions amended by FAS-102, 104, and 117. Statement of Cash Flow, ch. **50**
FASB Statement No. 96	
Accounting for Income Taxes	Superseded by FAS-109
FASB Statement No. 97	
Accounting and Reporting by Insurance Enterprises for Certain Long-Duration Contracts and for Realized Gains and Losses from the Sale of Investments	Portions amended or superseded by FAS-113, 115, and 120. Accounting Policies, ch. **2**

FASB Statement No. 98

Accounting for Leases:

- Sale-Leaseback Transactions Involving Real Estate
- Sales-Type Leases of Real Estate
- Definition of the Lease Term
- Initial Direct Costs of Direct Financing Leases

Accounting Policies, ch. **2**

Leases, ch. **18**

FASB Statement No. 99

Deferral of the Effective Date of Recognition of Depreciation by Not-for-Profit Organizations

Accounting Policies, ch. **2**

FASB Statement No. 100

Accounting for Income Taxes—Deferral of the Effective Date of FASB Statement No. 96

Superseded by FAS-103, 108, and 109.

FASB Statement No. 101

Regulated Enterprises—Accounting for the Discontinuation of Application of FASB Statement No. 71

Portions amended by FAS-121.

Accounting Policies, ch. **2**

FASB Statement No. 102

Statement of Cash Flows—Exemption of Certain Enterprises and Classification of Cash Flows from Certain Securities Acquired for Resale

Portions amended by FAS-115.

Statement of Cash Flow, ch. **50**

FASB Statement No. 103

Accounting for Income Taxes—Deferral of the Effective Date of FASB Statement No. 96

Superseded by FAS-108 and 109.

FASB Statement No. 104

Statement of Cash Flows—Net Reporting of Certain Cash Receipts and Cash Payments and Classification of Cash Flows from Hedging Transactions

Statement of Cash Flow, ch. **50**

FASB Statement No. 105

Disclosure of Information About Financial Instruments with Off-Balance-Sheet Risk and Financial Instruments with Concentrations of Credit Risk

Portions amended or superseded by FAS-107, 111, 119, 123, and 125.

Financial Instruments, Derivatives, and Hedging Activities, ch. **12**

FASB Statement No. 106

Employers' Accounting for Postretirement Benefits Other Than Pensions

Deferred Compensation Arrangements, ch. **10**

Postemployment Plans, ch. **22**

Postretirement Benefits Other Than Pensions, ch. **23**

FASB Statement No. 107 Disclosures about Fair Value of Financial Instruments	Portions amended or superseded by FAS-112, 119, 123, 125, and 126. Financial Instruments, Derivatives, and Hedging Activities, ch. **12**
FASB Statement No. 108 Accounting for Income Taxes—Deferral of the Effective Date of FASB Statement No. 96	Superseded by FAS-109
FASB Statement No. 109 Accounting for Income Taxes	Portions amended by FAS-115 and 123. Income Taxes, ch. **39**
FASB Statement No. 110 Reporting by Defined Benefit Pension Plans of Investment Contracts	Accounting Policies, ch. **2**
FASB Statement No. 111 Rescission of FASB Statement No. 32 and Technical Corrections	Accounting Changes, ch. **1**
FASB Statement No. 112 Employers' Accounting for Postemployment Benefits	Portions amended by FAS-123. Postemployment Plans, ch. **22** Postretirement Benefits Other Than Pensions, ch. **23**
FASB Statement No. 113 Accounting and Reporting for Reinsurance of Short-Duration and Long-Duration Contracts	Portions amended by FAS-120. Accounting Policies, ch. **2**
FASB Statement No. 114 Accounting by Creditors for Impairment of a Loan	Portions amended or superseded by FAS-118. Property, Plant, and Equipment, ch. **36** Intangible Assets, ch. **37** Debt Obligations and Credit Arrangements, ch. **40**
FASB Statement No. 115 Accounting for Certain Investments in Debt and Equity Securities	Portions amended by FAS-124 and 125. Investments: Debt and Equity Securities, ch. **34**
FASB Statement No. 116 Accounting for Contributions Received and Contributions Made	Accounting Policies, ch. **2**
FASB Statement No. 117 Financial Statements of Not-for-Profit Organizations	Portions amended by FAS-124. Accounting Policies, ch. **2**

FASB Statement No. 118 Accounting by Creditors for Impairment of a Loan—Income Recognition and Disclosures	Accounts and Notes Receivable, ch. **32**
FASB Statement No. 119 Disclosure about Derivative Financial Instruments and Fair Value of Financial Instruments	Financial Instruments, Derivatives, and Hedging Activities, ch. **12**
FASB Statement No. 120 Accounting and Reporting by Mutual Life Insurance Enterprises and by Insurance Enterprises for Certain Long-Duration Participating Contracts	Accounting Policies, ch. **2**
FASB Statement No. 121 Accounting for the Impairment of Long-Lived Assets and for Long-Lived Assets to Be Disposed Of	Portions amended by FAS-139 Property, Plant, and Equipment, ch. **36** Intangible Assets, ch. **37**
FASB Statement No. 122 Accounting for Mortgage Servicing Rights	Superseded by FAS-125
FASB Statement No. 123 Accounting for Stock-Based Compensation	Portions amended or superseded by FAS-128. Stock-Based Compensation, Stock Option Plans, and Stock Purchase Plans, ch. **28**
FASB Statement No. 124 Accounting for Certain Investments Held by Not-for-Profit Organizations	Accounting Policies, ch. **2**
FASB Statement No. 125 Accounting for Transfers and Servicing of Financial Assets and Extinguishments of Liabilities	Replaced by FAS-140
FASB Statement No. 126 Exemption from Certain Required Disclosures about Financial Instruments for Certain Nonpublic Entities	Financial Instruments, Derivatives, and Hedging Activities, ch. **12**
FASB Statement No. 127 Deferral of the Effective Date of Certain Provisions of FASB Statement No. 125	Portions superseded by FAS-127 Financial Instruments, Derivatives, and Hedging Activities, ch. **12** Accounts and Notes Receivable, ch. **32** Debt Obligations and Credit Arrangements, ch. **40**

FASB Statement No. 128 Earnings per Share	Earnings per Share, ch. **49**
FASB Statement No. 129 Disclosure of Information about Capital Structure	Stockholders' Equity, ch. **42**
FASB Statement No. 130 Reporting Comprehensive Income	Comprehensive Income, ch. **48**
FASB Statement No. 131 Disclosures about Segments of an Enterprise and Related Information	Segment Information, ch. **27**
FASB Statement No. 132 Employers' Disclosures about Pensions and Other Postretirement Benefits	Pension Plans, ch. **21** Postemployment Benefits, ch. **22** Postretirement Benefits Other Than Pensions, ch. **23**
FASB Statement No. 133 Accounting for Derivative Instruments and Hedging Activities	Financial Instruments, Derivatives, and Hedging Activities, ch. **12**
FASB Statement No. 134 Accounting for Mortgage-Backed Securities Retained after the Securitization of Mortgage Loans Held for Sale by a Mortgage Banking Enterprise	Accounting Policies, ch. **2**
FASB Statement No. 135 Rescission of Statement No. 75 and Technical Corrections	Accounting Policies, ch. **2**
FASB Statement No. 136 Transfer of Assets to a Not-for-Profit Organization or Charitable Trust That Raises or Holds Contributions for Others	Accounting Policies, ch. **2**
FASB Statement No. 137 Deferral of the Effective Date of Statement No. 133	Financial Instruments, Derivatives, and Hedging Activities, ch. **12**
FASB Statement No. 138 Accounting for Certain Derivative Instruments and Certain Hedging Activities	Financial Instruments, Derivatives, and Hedging Activities, ch. **12**
FASB Statement No. 139 Rescission of FASB Statement No. 53 and amendments to FASB Statements No. 63, 89, and 121	Accounting Policies, ch. **2**
FASB Statement No. 139 Accounting for Transfers and Servicing of Financial Assets and Extinguishments of Liabilities	

FINANCIAL ACCOUNTING STANDARDS BOARD INTERPRETATIONS (FINs)

ORIGINAL PRONOUNCEMENT	2001–02 *MILLER GAAP FINANCIAL STATEMENT DISCLOSURES MANUAL* REFERENCE
FASB Interpretation No. 1 Accounting Changes Related to the Cost of Inventory	Accounting Changes, ch. **1** Inventory, ch. **33**
FASB Interpretation No. 2 Imputing Interest on Debt Arrangements Made under the Federal Bankruptcy Act	Superseded by FAS-15
FASB Interpretation No. 3 Accounting for the Cost of Pension Plans Subject to the Employee Retirement Income Security Act of 1974	Superseded by FAS-87
FASB Interpretation No. 4 Applicability of FASB Statement No. 2 to Business Combinations Accounted for by the Purchase Method	Research and Development Costs, ch. **26**
FASB Interpretation No. 5 Applicability of FASB Statement No. 2 to Development Stage Enterprises	Superseded by FAS-7
FASB Interpretation No. 6 Applicability of FASB Statement No. 2 to Computer Software	Portions amended or superseded by FAS-86. Research and Development Costs, ch. **26**
FASB Interpretation No. 7 Applying FASB Statement No. 7 in Financial Statements of Established Operating Enterprises	Development Stage Enterprises, ch. **11**
FASB Interpretation No. 8 Classification of a Short-Term Obligation Repaid prior to Being Replaced by a Long-Term Security	Assets and Liabilities: General, ch. **30** Debt Obligations and Credit Arrangements, ch. **40**
FASB Interpretation No. 9 Applying APB Opinions No. 16 and 17 When a Savings and Loan Association or a Similar Institution Is Acquired in a Business Combination Accounted for by the Purchase Method	Portions amended by FAS-72. Business Combinations, ch. **4** Intangible Assets, ch. **37**
FASB Interpretation No. 10 Application of FASB Statement No. 12 to Personal Financial Statements	Rescinded by FAS-83

FASB Interpretation No. 11 Changes in Market Value after the Balance Sheet Date	Superseded by FAS-115
FASB Interpretation No. 12 Accounting for Previously Established Allowance Accounts	Superseded by FAS-115
FASB Interpretation No. 13 Consolidation of a Parent and Its Subsidiaries Having Different Balance Sheet Dates	Superseded by FAS-115
FASB Interpretation No. 14 Reasonable Estimation of the Amount of a Loss	Contingencies, Risks, Uncertainties, and Concentrations, ch. **9**
FASB Interpretation No. 15 Translation of Unamortized Policy Acquisition Costs by a Stock Life Insurance Company	Superseded by FAS-52
FASB Interpretation No. 16 Clarification of Definitions and Accounting for Marketable Equity Securities That Become Nonmarketable	Superseded by FAS-115
FASB Interpretation No. 17 Applying the Lower of Cost or Market Rule in Translated Financial Statements	Superseded by FAS-52
FASB Interpretation No. 18 Accounting for Income Taxes in Interim Periods	Portions amended or superseded by FAS-71, 96, 109, and 111 Income Taxes, ch. **39**
FASB Interpretation No. 19 Lessee Guarantee of the Residual Value of Leased Property	Leases, ch. **18**
FASB Interpretation No. 20 Reporting Accounting Changes under AICPA Statements of Position	Portions amended by FAS-111. Accounting Changes, ch. **1**
FASB Interpretation No. 21 Accounting for Leases in a Business Combination	Leases, ch. **18**
FASB Interpretation No. 22 Applicability of Indefinite Reversal Criteria To Timing Differences	Superseded by FAS-109
FASB Interpretation No. 23 Leases of Certain Property Owned by a Governmental Unit or Authority	Leases, ch. **18**
FASB Interpretation No. 24 Leases Involving Only Part of a Building	Leases, ch. **18**

FASB Interpretation No. 25 Accounting for an Unused Investment Tax Credit	Superseded by FAS-96 and 109
FASB Interpretation No. 26 Accounting for Purchase of a Leased Asset by the Lessee during the Term of the Lease	Leases, ch. **18**
FASB Interpretation No. 27 Accounting for a Loss on a Sublease	Leases, ch. **18** Expenses and Losses, ch. **44** Unusual or Infrequent Items, ch. **47**
FASB Interpretation No. 28 Accounting for Stock Appreciation Rights and Other Variable Stock Option or Award Plans	Portions amended or superseded by FAS-123 and 128, FIN-31 Stock-Based Compensation, Stock Option Plans, and Stock Purchase Plans, ch. **28**
FASB Interpretation No. 29 Reporting Tax Benefits Realized on Disposition of Investments in Certain Subsidiaries and Other Investees	Superseded by FAS-96 and 109
FASB Interpretation No. 30 Accounting for Involuntary Conversions of Nonmonetary Assets to Monetary Assets	Portions amended by FAS-96, 109, and 125 Nonmonetary Transactions, ch. **20**
FASB Interpretation No. 31 Treatment of Stock Compensation Plans in EPS Computations	Superseded by FAS-128 for periods ending after December 15, 1997
FASB Interpretation No. 32 Application of Percentage Limitations in Recognizing Investment Tax Credit	Superseded by FAS-96 and 109
FASB Interpretation No. 33 Applying FASB Statement No. 34 to Oil and Gas Producing Operations Accounted for by the Full Cost Method	Interest Cost, ch. **16**
FASB Interpretation No. 34 Disclosure of Indirect Guarantees of Indebtedness of Others	Contingencies, Risks, Uncertainties, and Concentrations, ch. **9**
FASB Interpretation No. 35 Criteria for Applying the Equity Method of Accounting for Investments in Common Stock	Investments: Equity and Cost Methods, ch. **35**
FASB Interpretation No. 36 Accounting for Exploratory Wells in Progress at the End of a Period	Accounting Policies, ch. **2**

FASB Interpretation No. 37 Accounting for Translation Adjustments upon Sale of Part of an Investment in a Foreign Entity	Foreign Operations and Currency Translation, ch. **14**
FASB Interpretation No. 38 Determining the Measurement Date for Stock Option, Purchase, and Award Plans Involving Junior Stock	Portions amended or superseded by FAS-121 and 128. Stock-Based Compensation, Stock Option Plans, and Stock Purchase Plans, ch. **28**
FASB Interpretation No. 39 Offsetting of Amounts Related to Certain Contracts	Portions amended by FAS-113 Financial Instruments, Derivatives, and Hedging Activities, ch **12** Assets and Liabilities: General, ch. **30**
FASB Interpretation No. 40 Applicability of Generally Accepted Accounting Principles to Mutual Life Insurance and Other Enterprises	Portions amended by FAS-115 and 120. Accounting Policies, ch. **2**
FASB Interpretation No. 41 Offsetting of Amounts Related to Certain Repurchase and Reverse Repurchase Agreements	Financial Instruments, Derivatives, and Hedging Activities, ch **12** Assets and Liabilities: General, ch. **30**
FASB Interpretation No. 42 Accounting for Transfers of Assets in Which a Not-for-Profit Organization Is Granted Variance Power	Accounting Policies, ch. **2**
FASB Interpretation No. 43 Real Estate Sales	Accounting Policies, ch. **2**
FASB Interpretation No. 44 Accounting for Certain Transactions Involving Stock Compensation	Stock-Based Compensation, Stock Option Plans, and Stock Purchase Plans, ch. **28**

FASB TECHNICAL BULLETINS

ORIGINAL PRONOUNCEMENT	2001–02 *MILLER GAAP FINANCIAL STATEMENT DISCLOSURES MANUAL* REFERENCE
FTB 79-1 (R) Purpose and Scope of FASB Technical Bulletins and Procedures for Issuance	Accounting Policies, ch. **2**

FTB 79-3	
Subjective Acceleration Clauses in Long-Term Debt Agreements	Assets and Liabilities: General, ch. **30** Debt Obligations and Credit Arrangements, ch. **40**
FTB 79-4	
Segment Reporting of Puerto Rican Operations	Segment Information, ch. **27**
FTB 79-5	
Meaning of the Term "Customer" asIt Applies to Health Care Facilitiesunder FASB Statement No. 14	Segment Information, ch. **27**
FTB 79-8	
Applicability of FASB Statements 21 and33 to Certain Brokers and Dealers in Securities	Segment Information, ch. **27**
FTB 79-9	
Accounting for Interim Periods for Changes in Income Tax Rates	Interim Financial Reporting, ch. **17**
FTB 79-10	
Fiscal Funding Clauses in LeaseAgreements	Leases, ch. **18**
FTB 79-12	
Interest Rate Used in Calculating thePresent Value of Minimum Lease Payments	Leases, ch. **18**
FTB 79-13	
Applicability of FASB Statement No. 13 to Current Value Financial Statements	Changing Prices, ch. **5**
FTB 79-14	
Upward Adjustment of Guaranteed Residual Values	Leases, ch. **18**
FTB 79-15	
Accounting for Loss on a Sublease Not Involving the Disposal of a Segment	Leases, ch. **18**
FTB 79-16 (R)	
Effect of a Change in Income Tax Rate on the Accounting for Leveraged Leases	Leases, ch. **18**
FTB 79-17	
Reporting Cumulative Effect Adjustment from Retroactive Application of FASB Statement No. 13	Leases, ch. **18**
FTB 79-18	
Transition Requirement of Certain FASB Amendments and Interpretations of FASB Statement No. 13	Leases, ch. **18**
FTB 79-19	
Investor's Accounting for Unrealized Losses on Marketable Securities Owned by an Equity Method Investee	Investments: Equity and Cost Methods, ch. **35**

FTB 80-1 Early Extinguishment of Debt through Exchange for Common orPreferred Stock	Debt Obligations and Credit Arrangements, ch. **40**
FTB 80-2 Classification of Debt Restructurings by Debtors and Creditors	Debt Obligations and Credit Arrangements, ch. **40**
FTB 81-6 Applicability of Statement 15 to Debtors in Bankruptcy Situations	Quasi-Reorganizations and Reorganizations under the Bankruptcy Code, ch. **24** Debt Obligations and Credit Arrangements, ch. **40**
FTB 82-1 Disclosure of the Sale or Purchase of Tax Benefits through Tax Leases	Accounting Policies, ch. **2**
FTB 84-1 Accounting for Stock Issued to Acquire the Results of a Research and Development Arrangement	Research and Development Costs, ch. **26**
FTB 85-1 Accounting for the Receipt of Federal Home Loan Mortgage Corporation Participating Preferred Stock	Nonmonetary Transactions, ch. **20**
FTB 85-3 Accounting for Operating Leases with Scheduled Rent Increases	Leases, ch. **18**
FTB 85-4 Accounting for Purchases of Life Insurance	Assets and Liabilities: General, ch. **30** Other Assets: Current and Noncurrent, ch. **38**
FTB 85-5 Issues Relating to Accounting for Business Combinations	Business Combinations, ch. **4**
FTB 85-6 Accounting for a Purchase of Treasury Shares at a Price Significantly in Excess of the Current Market Price of the Shares and the Income Statement Classification of Costs Incurred in Defending against a Takeover Attempt	Stockholders' Equity, ch. **42**
FTB 86-2 Accounting for an Interest in the Residual Value of a Leased Asset	Leases, ch. **18**
FTB 88-1 Issues Related to Accounting for Leases	Leases, ch. **18**

FTB 90-1 Accounting for Separately Priced Extended Warranty and Product Maintenance Contracts	Accounting Policies, ch. **2** Revenues and Gains, ch. **43**
FTB 94-1 Application of Statement 115 to Debt Securities Restructured in a Troubled Debt Restructuring	Debt Obligations and Credit Arrangements, ch. **40**
FTB 97-1 Accounting under Statement 123 for Certain Employee Stock Purchase Plans with a Look-Back Option	Stock-Based Compensation, Stock Option Plans, and Stock Purchase Plans, ch. **28**

AICPA STATEMENTS OF POSITION

ORIGINAL PRONOUNCEMENT	2001–02 *MILLER GAAP FINANCIAL STATEMENT DISCLOSURES MANUAL* REFERENCE
SOP 76-3 Accounting Practices for Certain Employee Stock Ownership Plans	Stock-Based Compensation, Stock Option Plans, and Stock Purchase Plans, ch. **28**
SOP 81-1 Accounting for Performance of Construction-Type and Certain Production-Type Contracts	Long-Term Contracts, ch. **19**
SOP 82-1 Accounting and Financial Reporting for Personal Financial Statements	Accounting Policies, ch. **2**
SOP 90-3 Definition of the term *Substantially the Same for Holders of Debt Instruments*, as Used in Certain Audit Guides and a Statement of Position	Investments: Debt and Equity Securities, ch. **34**
SOP 90-7 Financial Reporting by Entities in Reorganization Under the Bankruptcy Code	Quasi-Reorganizations and Reorganizations under the Bankruptcy Code, ch. **24**
SOP 92-3 Accounting for Foreclosed Assets	Quasi-Reorganizations and Reorganizations under the Bankruptcy Code, ch. **24**
SOP 93-3 Rescission of Accounting Principles Board Statements	Accounting Policies, ch. **2**

SOP 93-4 Foreign Currency Accounting and Financial Statement Presentation for Investment Companies	Foreign Operations and Currency Translation, ch. **14**
SOP 93-6 Employers' Accounting for Employee Stock Ownership Plans	Stock-Based Compensation, Stock Option Plans, and Stock Purchase Plans, ch. **28**
SOP 93-7 Reporting on Advertising Costs	Advertising Costs, ch. **3**
SOP 94-6 Disclosure of Certain Significant Risks and Uncertainties	Contingencies, Risks, Uncertainties, and Concentrations, ch. **9**
SOP 96-1 Environmental Remediation Liabilities	Contingencies, Risks, Uncertainties, and Concentrations, ch. **9**
SOP 97-2 Software Revenue Recognition	Accounting Policies, ch. **2**
SOP 98-1 Accounting for Costs of Computer Software Developed or Obtained for Internal Use	Accounting Policies, ch. **2**
SOP 98-5 Reporting on the Costs of Start-Up Activities	Expenses and Losses, ch. **44**
SOP 98-9 Modification of SOP 97-2, Software Revenue Recognition, With Respect to Certain Transactions	Accounting Policies, ch. **2**

CONSENSUS POSITIONS OF THE EMERGING ISSUES TASK FORCE (EITF)

ORIGINAL PRONOUNCEMENT	2001–02 *MILLER GAAP FINANCIAL STATEMENT DISCLOSURES MANUAL* REFERENCE
84-7 Termination of Interest Rate Swaps	Financial Instruments, Derivatives, and Hedging Activities, ch. **12**
84-9 Deposit Float of Banks	Accounting Changes, ch. **1**
84-13 Purchase of Stock Options and Stock Appreciation Rights in a Leveraged Buyout	Stock-Based Compensation, Stock Option Plans, and Stock Purchase Plans, ch. **28**

84-14 Deferred Interest Rate Setting	Financial Instruments, Derivatives, and Hedging Activities, ch. **12**
84-17 Profit Recognition on Sales of Real Estate with Graduated Payment Mortgages or Insured Mortgages	Accounting Policies, ch. **2** Revenues and Gains, ch. **43**
84-18 Stock Option Pyramiding	Stock-Based Compensation, Stock Option Plans, and Stock Purchase Plans, ch. **28**
84-19 Mortgage Loan Payment Modifications	Financial Instruments, Derivatives, and Hedging Activities, ch. **12**
84-30 Sales of Loans to Special-Purpose Entities	Consolidated and Combined Financial Statements, ch. **8**
84-33 Acquisition of a Tax Loss Carryforward—Temporary Parent-Subsidiary Relationship	Investments: Equity and Cost Methods, ch. **35**
84-34 Permanent Discount Restricted Stock Purchase Plans	Stock-Based Compensation, Stock Option Plans, and Stock Purchase Plans, ch. **28**
84-36 Interest Rate Swap Transactions	Financial Instruments, Derivatives, and Hedging Activities, ch. **12**
84-40 Long-Term Debt Repayable by a Capital Stock Transaction	Assets and Liabilities: General, ch. **30** Debt Obligations and Credit Arrangements, ch. **40** Stockholders' Equity, ch. **42**
85-1 Classifying Notes Received for Capital Stock	Assets and Liabilities: General, ch. **30** Accounts and Notes Receivable, ch. **32** Stockholders' Equity, ch. **42**
85-9 Revenue Recognition on Options to Purchase Stock of Another Entity	Financial Instruments, Derivatives, and Hedging Activities, ch. **12** Investments: Equity and Cost Methods, ch. **35** Stockholders' Equity, ch. **42** Revenues and Gains, ch. **43**
85-12 Retention of Specialized Accounting for Investments in Consolidation	Consolidated and Combined Financial Statements, ch. **8**

85-13	
Sale of Mortgage Service Rights on Mortgages Owned by Others	Financial Instruments, Derivatives, and Hedging Activities, ch. **12** Accounts and Notes Receivable, ch. **32**
85-14	
Securities That Can Be Acquired for Cash in a Pooling of Interests	Business Combinations, ch. **4**
85-16	
Leveraged Leases: Real Estate Leases and Sale-Leaseback Transactions, Delayed Equity Contributions by Lessors	Leases, ch. **18**
85-17	
Accrued Interest upon Conversion of Convertible Debt	Debt Obligations and Credit Arrangements, ch. **40** Stockholders' Equity, ch. **42**
85-20	
Recognition of Fees for Guaranteeing a Loan	Contingencies, Risks, Uncertainties, and Concentrations, ch. **9**
85-21	
Changes of Ownership Resulting in a New Basis of Accounting	Business Combinations, ch. **4**
85-23	
Effect of a Redemption Agreement on Carrying Value of a Security	Investments: Debt and Equity Securities, ch. **34**
85-24	
Distribution Fees by Distributors of Mutual Funds That Do Not Have a Front-End Sales Charge	Accounting Policies, ch. **2** Revenues and Gains, ch. **43**
85-27	
Recognition of Receipts from Made-Up Rental Shortfalls	Accounting Policies, ch. **2** Revenues and Gains, ch. **43**
85-29	
Convertible Bonds with a "Premium Put"	Debt Obligations and Credit Arrangements, ch. **40** Stockholders' Equity, ch. **42**
85-36	
Discontinued Operations with Expected Gain and Interim Operating Losses	Revenues and Gains, ch. **43** Expenses and Losses, ch. **44**
85-39	
Implications of SEC Staff Accounting Bulletin No. 59 on Noncurrent Marketable Equity Securities	Investments: Debt and Equity Securities, ch. **34**

85-45 Business Combinations: Settlement of Stock Options and Awards	Stock-Based Compensation, Stock Option Plans, and Stock Purchase Plans, ch. **28**
86-5 Classifying Demand Notes with Repayment Terms	Assets and Liabilities: General, ch. **30** Debt Obligations and Credit Arrangements, ch. **40**
86-6 Antispeculation Clauses in Real Estate Sales Contracts	Accounting Policies, ch. **2** Revenues and Gains, ch. **43**
86-7 Recognition by Homebuilders of Profit from Sales of Land and Related Construction Contracts	Accounting Policies, ch. **2** Revenues and Gains, ch. **43**
86-8 Sale of Bad-Debt Recovery Rights	Financial Instruments, Derivatives, and Hedging Activities, ch. **12**
86-9 IRC Section 338 and Push-Down Accounting	Income Taxes, ch. **39** Also see Issue 94-10.
86-10 Pooling with 10 Percent Cash Payout Determined by Lottery	Business Combinations, ch. **4**
86-12 Accounting by Insureds for Claims-Made Insurance Policies	Contingencies, Risks, Uncertainties, and Concentrations, ch. **9**
86-13 Recognition of Inventory Market Declines at Interim Reporting Dates	Interim Financial Reporting, ch. **17**
86-15 Increasing-Rate Debt	Interest Cost, ch. **16** Assets and Liabilities: General, ch. **30** Accounts and Notes Receivable, ch. **32**
86-17 Deferred Profit on Sale-Leaseback Transaction with Lessee Guarantee of Residual Value	Leases, ch. **18**
86-18 Debtor's Accounting for a Modification of Debt Terms	Debt Obligations and Credit Arrangements, ch. **40**

Issue	Cross-Reference
86-21 Application of the AICPA Notice to Practitioners regarding Acquisition, Development, and Construction Arrangements to Acquisition of an Operating Property	Accounting Policies, ch. **2** Revenues and Gains, ch. **43**
86-24 Third-Party Establishment of Collateralized Mortgage Obligations	Financial Instruments, Derivatives, and Hedging Activities, ch. **12** Accounts and Notes Receivable, ch. **32**
86-25 Offsetting Foreign Currency Swaps	Foreign Operations and Currency Translation, ch. **14**
86-26 Using Forward Commitments as a Surrogate for Deferred Rate Setting	Financial Instruments, Derivatives, and Hedging Activities, ch. **12**
86-27 Measurement of Excess Contributions to a Defined Contribution Plan or Employee Stock Ownership Plan	Stock-Based Compensation, Stock Option Plans, and Stock Purchase Plans, ch. **28**
86-28 Accounting Implications of Indexed Debt Instruments	Financial Instruments, Derivatives, and Hedging Activities, ch. **12**
86-29 Nonmonetary Transactions: Magnitude of Boot and the Exceptions to the Use of Fair Value	Nonmonetary Transactions, ch. **20**
86-30 Classification of Obligations When a Violation Is Waived by the Creditor	Assets and Liabilities: General, ch. **30** Debt Obligations and Credit Arrangements, ch. **40**
86-31 Reporting the Tax Implications of a Pooling of a Bank and a Savings and Loan Association	Income Taxes, ch. **39**
86-32 Early Extinguishment of a Subsidiary's Mandatorily Redeemable Preferred Stock	Stockholders' Equity, ch. **42**
86-33 Tax Indemnifications in Lease Agreements	Leases, ch. **18**
86-34 Futures Contracts Used as Hedges of Anticipated Reverse Repurchase Transactions	Financial Instruments, Derivatives, and Hedging Activities, ch. **12**

86-43 Effect of a Change in Tax Law or Rates on Leveraged Leases	Leases, ch. **18**
86-44 Effect of a Change in Tax Law on Investments in Safe Harbor Leases	Leases, ch. **18**
86-46 Uniform Capitalization Rules for Inventory under the Tax Reform Act of 1986	Inventory, ch. **33**
87-2 Net Present Value Method of Valuing Speculative Foreign Exchange Contracts	Foreign Operations and Currency Translation, ch. **14**
87-4 Restructuring of Operations: Implications of SEC Staff Accounting Bulletin No. 67	Expenses and Losses, ch. **44** Discontinued Operations, ch. **45** Extraordinary Items, ch. **46** Unusual or Infrequent Items, ch. **47** Comprehensive Income, ch. **48**
87-6 Adjustments Relating to Stock Compensation Plans	Stock-Based Compensation, Stock Option Plans, and Stock Purchase Plans, ch. **28**
87-7 Sale of an Asset Subject to a Lease and Nonrecourse Financing: "Wrap Lease Transactions"	Leases, ch. **18**
87-8 Tax Reform Act of 1986: Issues Related to the Alternative Minimum Tax	Leases, ch. **18** Income Taxes, ch. **39**
87-9 Profit Recognition on Sales of Real Estate with Insured Mortgages or Surety Bonds	Accounting Policies, ch. **2** Revenues and Gains, ch. **43**
87-10 Revenue Recognition by Television "Barter" Syndicators	Accounting Policies, ch. **2** Revenues and Gains, ch. **43**
87-11 Allocation of Purchase Price to Assets to Be Sold	Business Combinations, ch. **4**
87-12 Foreign Debt-for-Equity Swaps	Foreign Operations and Currency Translation, ch. **14**

87-15 Effect of a Standstill Agreement on Pooling-of-Interests Accounting	Business Combinations, ch. **4**
87-16 Whether the 90 Percent Test for a Pooling of Interests Is Applied Separately to Each Company or on a Combined Basis	Business Combinations, ch. **4**
87-17 Spinoffs or Other Distributions of Loans Receivable to Shareholders	Nonmonetary Transactions, ch. **20**
87-18 Use of Zero Coupon Bonds in a Troubled Debt Restructuring	Debt Obligations and Credit Arrangements, ch. **40**
87-19 Substituted Debtors in a Troubled Debt Restructuring	Debt Obligations and Credit Arrangements, ch. **40**
87-21 Change of Accounting Basis in Master Limited Partnership Transactions	Business Combinations, ch. **4**
87-23 Book Value Stock Purchase Plans	Stock-Based Compensation, Stock Option Plans, and Stock Purchase Plans, ch. **28**
87-24 Allocation of Interest to Discontinued Operations	Interest Cost, ch. **16** Discontinued Operations, ch. **45**
87-26 Hedging of Foreign Currency Exposure with a Tandem Currency	Foreign Operations and Currency Translation, ch. **14**
87-27 Poolings of Companies That Do Not Have a Controlling Class of Common Stock	Business Combinations, ch. **4** Also see Issue 96-8.
87-29 Exchange of Real Estate Involving Boot	Nonmonetary Transactions, ch. **20**
87-30 Sale of a Short-Term Loan Made under a Long-Term Credit Commitment	Financial Instruments, Derivatives, and Hedging Activities, ch. **12** Accounts and Notes Receivable, ch. **32**
87-33 Stock Compensation Issues Related to Market Decline	Stock-Based Compensation, Stock Option Plans, and Stock Purchase Plans, ch. **28** Also see Issue 94-6.

88-1	
Determination of Vested Benefit Obligation for a Defined Benefit Pension Plan	Pension Plans, ch. **21**
88-4	
Classification of Payment Made to IRS to Retain Fiscal Year	Accounting Policies, ch. **2** Assets and Liabilities: General, ch. **30**
88-5	
Recognition of Insurance Death Benefits	Revenues and Gains, ch. **43** No consensus on Issue 2, but FAS-109 provides guidance.
88-6	
Book Value Stock Plans in an Initial Public Offering	Stock-Based Compensation, Stock Option Plans, and Stock Purchase Plans, ch. **28**
88-8	
Mortgage Swaps	Financial Instruments, Derivatives, and Hedging Activities, ch. **12**
88-9	
Put Warrants	Debt Obligations and Credit Arrangements, ch. **40** Stockholders' Equity, ch. **42**
88-10	
Costs Associated with Lease Modification or Termination	Leases, ch. **18**
88-11	
Allocation of Recorded Investment When a Loan or Part of a Loan Is Sold	Financial Instruments, Derivatives, and Hedging Activities, ch. **12** Accounts and Notes Receivable, ch. **32**
88-12	
Transfer of Ownership Interest as Part of Down Payment under FASB Statement No. 66	Accounting Policies, ch. **2** Revenues and Gains, ch. **43**
88-15	
Classification of Subsidiary's Loan Payable in Consolidated Balance Sheet When Subsidiary's and Parent's Fiscal Years Differ	Assets and Liabilities: General, ch. **30**

88-16 Basis in Leveraged Buyout Transactions	Business Combinations, ch. **4**
88-18 Sales of Future Revenues	Foreign Operations and Currency Translation, ch. **14** Assets and Liabilities: General, ch. **30** Revenues and Gains, ch. **43**
88-20 Difference between Initial Investment and Principal Amount of Loans in a Purchased Credit Card Portfolio	Intangible Assets, ch. **37**
88-21 Accounting for the Sale of Property Subject to the Seller's Preexisting Lease	Leases, ch. **18**
88-22 Securitization of Credit Card and Other Receivable Portfolios	Financial Instruments, Derivatives, and Hedging Activities, ch. **12** Accounts and Notes Receivable, ch. **32**
88-23 Lump-Sum Payments under Union Contracts	Accounting Policies, ch. **2** Assets and Labilities: General, ch. **30**
88-24 Effect of Various Forms of Financing under FASB Statement No. 66	Accounting Policies, ch. **2** Revenues and Gains, ch. **43**
88-26 Controlling Preferred Stock in a Pooling of Interests	Business Combinations, ch. **4**
88-27 Effect of Unlocated Shares in an Employee Stock Ownership Plan on Accounting for Business Combinations	Business Combinations, ch. **4**
89-4 Accounting for a Purchased Investment in a Collateralized Mortgage Obligation Instrument or in a Mortgage-Backed Interest-Only Certificate	Investments: Debt and Equity Securities, ch. **34**
89-7 Exchange of Assets or Interest in a Subsidiary for a Noncontrolling Equity Interest in a New Entity	Nonmonetary Transactions, ch. **20**
89-8 Expense Recognition for Employee Stock Ownership Plans	Stock-Based Compensation, Stock Option Plans, and Stock Purchase Plans, ch. **28**

EITF Issue	Chapter
89-11 Sponsor's Balance Sheet Classification of Capital Stock with a Put Option Held by an Employee Stock Ownership Plan	Stock-Based Compensation, Stock Option Plans, and Stock Purchase Plans, ch. **28** Assets and Liabilities: General, ch. **30** Stockholders' Equity, ch. **42**
89-12 Earnings-per-Share Issues Related to Convertible Preferred Stock Held by an Employee Stock Ownership Plan	Earnings per Share, ch. **49**
89-13 Accounting for the Cost of Asbestos Removal	Accounting Policies, ch. **2** Assets and Labilities: General, ch. **30** Expenses and Losses, ch. **44**
89-14 Valuation of Repossessed Real Estate	Accounting Policies, ch. **2** Revenues and Gains, ch. **43**
89-15 Accounting for a Modification of Debt Terms When the Debtor Is Experiencing Financial Difficulties	Debt Obligations and Credit Arrangements, ch. **40**
89-16 Consideration of Executory Costs in Sale-Leaseback Transactions	Leases, ch. **18**
89-19 Accounting for a Change in Goodwill Amortization for Business Combinations Initiated Prior to the Effective Date of FASB Statement No. 72	Accounting Changes, ch. **1**
89-20 Accounting for Cross Border Tax Benefit Leases	Leases, ch. **18**
90-3 Accounting for Employers' Obligations for Future Contributions to a Multiemployer Pension Plan	Pension Plans, ch. **21**
90-5 Exchanges of Ownership Interests between Entities under Common Control	Business Combinations, ch. **4**
90-6 Accounting for Certain Events Not Addressed in Issue No. 87-11 Relating to an Acquired Operating Unit to Be Sold	Business Combinations, ch. **4**
90-7 Accounting for a Reload Stock Option	Stock-Based Compensation, Stock Option Plans, and Stock Purchase Plans, ch. **28**

90-8 Capitalization of Costs to Treat Environmental Contamination	Accounting Policies, ch. **2** Contingencies, Risks, Uncertainties, and Concentrations, ch. **9** Assets and Liabililities: General, ch. **30**
90-9 Changes to Fixed Employee Stock Option Plans as a Result of Equity Restructuring	Stock-Based Compensation, Stock Option Plans, and Stock Purchase Plans, ch. **28**
90-12 Allocating Basis to Individual Assets and Liabilities for Transactions within the Scope of Issue No. 88-16	Business Combinations, ch. **4**
90-13 Accounting for Simultaneous Common Control Mergers	Business Combinations, ch. **4**
90-14 Unsecured Guarantee by Parent of Subsidiary's Lease Payments in a Sale-Leaseback Transaction	Leases, ch. **18**
90-15 Impact of Nonsubstantive Lessors, Residual Value Guarantees, and Other Provisions in Leasing Transactions	Leases, ch. **18**
90-16 Accounting for Discontinued Operations Subsequently Retained	Discontinued Operations, ch. **45**
90-17 Hedging Foreign Currency Risks with Purchased Options	Foreign Operations and Currency Translation, ch. **14**
90-18 Effect of a "Removal of Accounts" Provision on the Accounting for a Credit Card Securitization	Financial Instruments, Derivatives, and Hedging Activities, ch. **12** Accounts and Notes Receivable, ch. **32**
90-19 Convertible Bonds with Issuer Option to Settle for Cash upon Conversion	Debt Obligations and Credit Arrangements, ch. **40** Stockholders' Equity, ch. **42**
90-20 Impact of an Uncollateralized Irrevocable Letter of Credit on a Real Estate Sale-Leaseback Transaction	Leases, ch. **18**

90-21	
Balance Sheet Treatment of a Sale of Mortgage Servicing Rights with a Subservicing Agreement	Financial Instruments, Derivatives, and Hedging Activities, ch. **12** Accounts and Notes Receivable, ch. **32**
90-22	
Accounting for Gas-Balancing Arrangements	Accounting Policies, ch. **2** Revenues and Gains, ch. **43**
91-1	
Hedging Intercompany Foreign Currency Risks	Financial Instruments, Derivatives, and Hedging Activities, ch. **12** Foreign Operations and Currency Translation, ch. **14**
91-4	
Hedging Foreign Currency Risks with Complex Options and Similar Transactions	Financial Instruments, Derivatives, and Hedging Activities, ch. **12** Foreign Operations and Currency Translation, ch. **14**
91-5	
Nonmonetary Exchange of Cost-Method Investments	Business Combinations, ch. **4**
91-6	
Revenue Recognition of Long-Term Power Sales Contracts	Accounting Policies, ch. **2** Revenues and Gains, ch. **43**
91-7	
Accounting for Pension Benefits Paid by Employers after Insurance Companies Fail to Provide Annuity Benefits	Pension Plans, ch. **21**
91-8	
Application of FASB Statement No. 96 to a State Tax Based on the Greater of a Franchise Tax or an Income Tax	Income Taxes, ch. **39**
91-9	
Revenue and Expense Recognition for Freight Services in Process	Accounting Policies, ch. **2** Revenues and Gains, ch. **43**
91-10	
Accounting for Special Assessments and Tax Increment Financing Entities	Contingencies, Risks, Uncertainties, and Concentrations, ch. **9**
92-1	
Allocation of Residual Value or First-Loss Guarantee to Minimum Lease Payments in Leases Involving Land and Building(s)	Leases, ch. **18**

92-2

Measuring Loss Accruals by Transferors for Transfers of Receivables with Recourse

Financial Instruments, Derivatives, and Hedging Activities, ch. **12**

Accounts and Notes Receivable, ch. **32**

92-3

Earnings-per-Share Treatment of Tax Benefits for Dividends on Unlocated Stock Held by an Employee Stock Ownership Plan (Consideration of the Implications of FASB Statement No. 109 on Issue 2 of EITF Issue No. 90-4)

Stock-Based Compensation, Stock Option Plans, and Stock Purchase Plans, ch. **28**

Income Taxes, ch. **39**

Earnings per Share, ch. **49**

92-4

Accounting for a Change in Functional Currency When an Economy Ceases to Be Considered Highly Inflationary

Foreign Operations and Currency Translation, ch. **14**

92-5

Amortization Period for Net Deferred Credit Card Origination Costs

Financial Instruments, Derivatives, and Hedging Activities, ch. **12**

92-7

Accounting by Rate-Regulated Utilities for the Effects of Certain Alternative Revenue Programs

Accounting Policies, ch. **2**

Revenues and Gains, ch. **43**

92-8

Accounting for the Income Tax Effects under FASB Statement No. 109 of a Change in Functional Currency When an Economy Ceases to Be Considered Highly Inflationary

Foreign Operations and Currency Translation, ch. **14**

92-9

Accounting for the Present Value of Future Profits Resulting from the Acquisition of a Life Insurance Company

Intangible Assets, ch. **37**

92-12

Accounting for OPEB Costs by Rate-Regulated Enterprises

Postemployment Benefits, ch. **22**

Postretirement Benefits Other Than Pensions, ch. **23**

92-13

Accounting for Estimated Payments in Connection with the Coal Industry Retiree Health Benefit Act of 1992

Contingencies, Risks, Uncertainties, and Concentrations, ch. **9**

93-1

Accounting for Individual Credit Card Acquisitions

Financial Instruments, Derivatives, and Hedging Activities, ch. **12**

Issue	Cross-Reference
93-2 Effect of Acquisition of Employer Shares for/by an Employee Benefit Trust on Accounting for Business Combinations	Business Combinations, ch. **4**
93-3 Plan Assets under FASB Statement No. 106	Postemployment Benefits, ch. **22** Postretirement Benefits Other Than Pensions, ch. **23**
93-4 Accounting for Regulatory Assets	See discussion in Issue 92-12, Postemployment Benefits, ch. **22** Postretirement Benefits Other Than Pensions, ch. **23**
93-7 Uncertainties Related to Income Taxes in a Purchase Business Combination	Income Taxes, ch. **39**
93-8 Accounting for the Sale and Leaseback of an Asset That Is Leased to Another Party	Leases, ch. **18**
93-9 Application of FASB Statement No. 109 in Foreign Financial Statements Restated for General Price-Level Changes	Income Taxes, ch. **39**
93-10 Accounting for Dual Currency Bonds	No consensus. Resolved by the SEC staff. Foreign Operations and Currency Translation, ch. **14**
93-11 Accounting for Barter Transactions Involving Barter Credits	Nonmonetary Transactions, ch. **20**
93-12 Recognition and Measurement of the Tax Benefit of Excess Tax-Deductible Goodwill Resulting from a Retroactive Change in Tax Law	Income Taxes, ch. **39**
93-13 Effect of a Retroactive Change in Enacted Tax Rates That Is Included in Income from Continuing Operations	Income Taxes, ch. **39**
93-16 Application of FASB Statement No. 109 to Basis Differences within Foreign Subsidiaries That Meet the Indefinite Reversal Criterion of APB Opinion No. 23	Income Taxes, ch. **39**
93-17 Recognition of Deferred Tax Assets for a Parent Company's Excess Tax Basis in the Stock of a Subsidiary That Is Accounted for as a Discontinued Operation	Income Taxes, ch. **39**

93-18	
Recognition of Impairment for an Investment in a Collateralized Mortgage Obligation Instrument or in a Mortgage-Backed Interest-Only Certificate	Investments: Debt and Equity Securities, ch. **34**
94-1	
Accounting for Tax Benefits Resulting from Investments in Affordable Housing Projects	Accounting Policies, ch. **2** Income Taxes, ch. **39** Revenues and Gains, ch. **43**
94-2	
Treatment of Minority Interests in Certain Real Estate Investment Trusts	Stockholders' Equity, ch. **42**
94-3	
Liability Recognition for Certain Employee Termination Benefits and Other Costs to Exit an Activity (including Certain Costs Incurred in a Restructuring)	Expenses and Losses, ch. **44** Unusual or Infrequent Items, ch. **47**
94-6	
Accounting for the Buyout of Compensatory Stock Options Plans, and Stock Purchase Plans, ch. **28**	Stock-Based Compensation, Stock Option
94-7	
Accounting for Financial Instruments Indexed to, and Potentially Settled in, a Company's Own Stock	Incorporated in Issue 96-13, Financial Instruments, Derivatives, and Hedging Activities, ch. **12**
94-8	
Accounting for Conversion of a Loan into a Debt Security in a Debt Restructuring	Debt Obligations and Credit Arrangements, ch. **40**
94-10	
Accounting by a Company for the Income Tax Effects of Transactions among or with Its Shareholders under FASB Statement No. 109	Income Taxes, ch. **39**
95-1	
Revenue Recognition on Sales with a Guaranteed Minimum Resale Value	Accounting Policies, ch. **2** Revenues and Gains, ch. **43**
95-2	
Determination of What Constitutes a Firm Commitment for Foreign Currency Transactions Not Involving a Third Party	Foreign Operations and Currency Translation, ch. **14**
95-3	
Recognition of Liabilities in Connection with a Purchase Business Combination	Business Combinations, ch. **4**

95-4	
Revenue Recognition on Equipment Sold and Subsequently Repurchased Subject to an Operating Lease	Accounting Policies, ch. **2** Revenues and Gains, ch. **43**
95-5	
Determination of What Risks andRewards, If Any, Can Be Retained and Whether Any Unresolved Contingencies May Exist in a Sale of Mortgage Loan Servicing Rights	Financial Instruments, Derivatives, and Hedging Activities, ch. **12** Accounts and Notes Receivable, ch. **32**
95-6	
Accounting by a Real Estate Investment Trust for an Investment in a Service Corporation	Accounting Policies, ch. **2** Revenues and Gains, ch. **43**
95-7	
Implementation Issues Related to the Treatment of Minority Interests in Certain Real Estate Investment Trusts	Accounting Policies, ch. **2** Stockholders' Equity, ch. **42** Revenues and Gains, ch. **43**
95-8	
Accounting for Contingent Consideration Paid to the Shareholders of an Acquired Enterprise in a Purchase Business Combination	Business Combinations, ch. **4**
95-9	
Accounting for Tax Effects of Dividends in France in Accordance with FASB Statement No. 109	Income Taxes, ch. **39**
95-10	
Accounting for Tax Credits Related to Dividend Payments in Accordance with FASB Statement No. 109	Income Taxes, ch. **39**
95-11	
Accounting for Derivative Instruments Containing both a Written Option-Based Component and a Forward-Based Component	Financial Instruments, Derivatives, and Hedging Activities, ch. **12**
95-12	
Pooling of Interests with a Common Investment in a Joint Venture	Business Combinations, ch. **4**
95-13	
Classification of Debt Issue Costs in the Statement of Cash Flows	Statement of Cash Flows, ch. **50**
95-14	
Recognition of Liabilities in Anticipation of a Business Combination	Business Combinations, ch. **4**

95-16 Accounting for Stock Compensation Arrangements with Employer Loan Features under APB Opinion No. 25	Stock-Based Compensation, Stock Option Plans, and Stock Purchase Plans, ch. **28**
95-17 Accounting for Modifications to an Operating Lease That Do Not Change the Lease Classification	Leases, ch. **18**
95-18 Accounting and Reporting for a Discontinued Business Segment When the Measurement Date Occurs after the Balance Sheet Date but before the Issuance of Financial Statements	Discontinued Operations, ch. **45**
95-19 Determination of the Measurement Date for the Market Price of Securities Issued in a Purchase Business Combination	Business Combinations, ch. **4**
95-20 Measurement in the Consolidated Financial Statements of a Parent of the Tax Effects Related to the Operations of a Foreign Subsidiary That Receives Tax Credits Related to Dividend Payments	Income Taxes, ch. **39**
95-22 Balance Sheet Classification of Borrowings Outstanding under Revolving Credit Agreements That Include both a Subjective Acceleration Clause and a Lock-Box Arrangement	Assets and Liabilities: General, ch. **30** Debt Obligations and Credit Arrangements, ch. **40**
95-23 The Treatment of Certain Site Restoration/Environmental Exit Costs When Testing a Long-Lived Asset for Impairment	Property, Plant, and Equipment, ch. **36** Intangible Assets, ch. **37**
96-1 Sale of Put Options on Issuer's Stock That Require or Permit Cash Settlement	Incorporated in Issue 96-13, Financial Instruments, Derivatives, and Hedging Activities, ch. **12**
96-2 Impairment Recognition When a Nonmonetary Asset Is Exchanged or Is Distributed to Owners and Is Accounted for at the Asset's Recorded Amount	Property, Plant, and Equipment, ch. **36** Intangible Assets, ch. **37**
96-4 Accounting for Reorganizations Involving a Non–Pro Rata Split-off of Certain Nonmonetary Assets to Owners	Nonmonetary Transactions, ch. **20**

96-5 Recognition of Liabilities for Contractual Termination Benefits or Changing Benefit Plan Assumptions in Anticipation of a Business Combination	Business Combinations, ch. **4**
96-6 Accounting for the Film and Software Costs Associated with Developing Entertainment and Educational Software Products	Accounting Policies, ch. **2** Revenues and Gains, ch. **43** Expenses and Losses, ch. **44**
96-7 Accounting for Deferred Taxes on In-Process Research and Development Activities Acquired in a Purchase Business Combination	Business Combinations, ch. **4**
96-8 Accounting for a Business Combination When the Issuing Company Has Targeted Stock	Business Combinations, ch. **4**
96-9 Classification of Inventory Markdowns and Other Costs Associated with a Restructuring	Expenses and Losses, ch. **44** Unusual or Infrequent Items, ch. **47**
96-10 Impact of Certain Transactions on the Held-to-Maturity Classification under FASB Statement No. 115	Investments: Debt and Equity Securities, ch. **34**
96-11 Accounting for Forward Contracts and Purchased Options to Acquire Securities Covered by FASB Statement No. 115	Financial Instruments, Derivatives, and Hedging Activities, ch. **12**
96-12 Recognition of Interest Income and Balance Sheet Classification of Structured Notes	Financial Instruments, Derivatives, and Hedging Activities, ch. **12**
96-13 Accounting for Derivative Financial Instruments Indexed to, and Potentially Settled in, a Company's Own Stock	Financial Instruments, Derivatives, and Hedging Activities, ch. **12**
96-14 Accounting for the Costs Associated with Modifying Computer Software for the Year 2000	Accounting Policies, ch. **2** Contingencies, Risks, Uncertainties, and Concentrations, ch. **9** Assets and Liabililities: General, ch. **30** Expenses and Losses, ch. **44**

96-15

Accounting for the Effects of Changes in Foreign Currency Exchange Rates on Foreign-Currency-Denominated Available-for-Sale Debt Securities

Foreign Operations and Currency Translation, ch. **14**

96-16

Investor's Accounting for an Investee When the Investor Has a Majority of the Voting Interest but the Minority Shareholder or Shareholders Have Certain Approval or Veto Rights

Consolidated and Combined Financial Statements, ch. **8**

96-17

Revenue Recognition under Long-Term Power Sales Contracts That Contain both Fixed and Variable Pricing Terms

Accounting Policies, ch. **2**

Revenues and Gains, ch. **43**

96-18

Accounting for Equity Instruments That Are Issued to Other Than Employees for Acquiring, or in Conjunction with Selling, Goods or Services

Stock-Based Compensation, Stock Option Plans, and Stock Purchase Plans, ch. **28**

96-19

Debtor's Accounting for a Modification or Exchange of Debt Instruments

Debt Obligations and Credit Arrangements, ch. **40**

96-21

Implementation Issues in Accounting for Leasing Transactions Involving Special-Purpose Entities

Leases, ch. **18**

96-22

Applicability of the Disclosures Required by FASB Statement No. 114 When a Loan Is Restructured in a Troubled Debt Restructuring into Two (or More) Loans

Debt Obligations and Credit Arrangements, ch. **40**

97-1

Implementation Issues in Accounting for Lease Transactions, Including Those Involving Special-Purpose Entities

Leases, ch. **18**

97-2

Application of FASB Statement No. 94 and APB Opinion No. 16 to Physician Practice Management Entities and Certain Other Entities with Contractual Management Arrangements

Consolidated and Combined Financial Statements, ch. **8**

97-3

Accounting for Fees and Costs Associated with Loan Syndications and Loan Participations after the Issuance of FASB Statement No. 125

Financial Instruments, Derivatives, and Hedging Activities, ch. **12**

Accounts and Notes Receivable, ch. **32**

Issue	Cross-Reference
97-5 Accounting for the Delayed Receipt of Option Shares upon Exercise under APB Opinion No. 25	Stock-Based Compensation, Stock Option Plans, and Stock Purchase Plans, ch. **28**
97-6 Application of Issue No. 96-20 to Qualifying Special-Purpose Entities Receiving Transferred Financial Assets Prior to the Effective Date of FASB Statement No. 125	Consolidated and Combined Financial Statements, ch. **8**
97-7 Accounting for Hedges of the Foreign Currency Risk Inherent in an Available-for-Sale Marketable Equity Security	Foreign Operations and Currency Translation, ch. **14**
97-8 Accounting for Contingent Consideration Issued in a Purchase Business Combination	Business Combinations, ch. **4**
97-9 Effect on Pooling-of-Interests Accounting of Certain Contingently Exercisable Options or Other Equity Instruments	Business Combinations, ch. **4**
97-10 The Effect of Lessee Involvement in Asset Construction	Leases, ch. **18**
97-11 Accounting for Internal Costs Relating to Real Estate Property Acquisitions	Accounting Policies, ch. **2** Contingencies, Risks, Uncertainties, and Concentrations, ch. **9** Assets and Liabililities: General, ch. **30** Expenses and Losses, ch. **44**
97-12 Accounting for Increased Share Authorizations in an IRS Section 423 Employee Stock Purchase Plan under APB Opinion No. 25	Stock-Based Compensation, Stock Option Plans, and Stock Purchase Plans, ch. **28**
97-13 Accounting for Costs Incurred in Connection with a Consulting Contract or an Internal Project That Combines Business Process Reengineering and Information Technology Transformation	Accounting Policies, ch. **2** Contingencies, Risks, Uncertainties, and Concentrations, ch. **9** Assets and Liabililities: General, ch. **30** Expenses and Losses, ch. **44**
97-14 Accounting for Deferred Compensation Arrangements Where Amounts Earned Are Held in a Rabbi Trust and Invested	Consolidated and Combined Financial Statements, ch. **8**

97-15 Accounting for Contingency Arrangements Based on Security Prices in a Purchase Business Combination	Business Combinations, ch. **4**
98-1 Valuation of Debt Assumed in a Purchase Business Combination	Business Combinations, ch. **4**
98-2 Accounting by a Subsidiary or Joint Venture for an Investment in the Stock of Its Parent Company or Joint Venture Partner	Stockholder's Equity, ch. **42**
98-3 Determining Whether a Transaction Is an Exchange of Similar Productive Assets or a Business Combination	Nonmonetary Transactions, ch. **20**.
98-5 Accounting for Convertible Securities with Beneficial Conversion Features or Contingently Adjustable Conversion Ratios	Debt Obligations and Credit Arrangements, ch. **40** Stockholders' Equity, ch. **42**
98-7 Accounting for Exchanges of Similar Equity Method Investments	Nonmonetary Transactions, ch. **20**
98-8 Accounting for Transfers of Investments That Are in Substance Real Estate	Accounting Policies, ch. **2** Revenues and Gains, ch. **43** Expenses and Losses, ch. **44**
98-9 Accounting for Contingent Rent	Leases, ch. **18**
98-10 Accounting for Energy Trading and Risk Management Activities	Financial Instruments, Derivatives, and Hedging Activities, ch. **12**
98-11 Accounting for Acquired Temporary Differences in Certain Purchase Transactions That Are Not Accounted for as Business Combinations	Income Taxes, ch. **39**
98-12 Application of Issue No. 96-13 to Forward Equity Sales Transactions	Financial Instruments, Derivatives, and Hedging Activities, ch. **12**
98-13 Accounting by an Equity Method Investor for Investee Losses When the Investor Has Loans to and Investments in Other Securities of the Investee	Investments: Equity and Cost Methods, ch. **35**

98-14 Debtor's Accounting for Changes in Line-of-Credit or Revolving-Debt Arrangements	Debt Obligations and Credit Arrangements, ch. **40**
98-15 Structured Notes Acquired for a Specified Investment Strategy	Financial Instruments, Derivatives, and Hedging Activities, ch. **12**
99-1 Accounting for Debt Convertible into the Stock of a Consolidated Subsidiary	Debt Obligations and Credit Arrangements, ch. **40** Stockholders' Equity, ch. **42**
99-2 Accounting for Weather Derivatives	Financial Instruments, Derivatives, and Hedging Activities, ch. **12**
99-3 Application of Issue No. 96-13 to Derivative Instruments with Multiple Settlement Alternatives	Financial Instruments, Derivatives, and Hedging Activities, ch. **12**
99-4 Accounting for Stock Received from the Demutualization of a Mutual Insurance Company	Nonmonetary Transactions, ch. **20**
99-5 Accounting for Pre-Production Costs Related to Long-Term Supply Arrangements	Accounting Policies, ch. **2** Contingencies, Risks, Uncertainties, and Concentrations, ch. **9** Assets and Liabililities: General, ch. **30** Expenses and Losses, ch. **44**
99-6 Impact of Acceleration Provisions in Grants Made between Initiation and Consummation of a Pooling-of-Interests Business Combination	Business Combinations, ch. **4**
99-7 Accounting for an Accelerated Share Repurchase Program	Stockholder's Equity, ch. **42**
99-9 Effect of Derivative Gains and Losses on the Capitalization of Interest	Financial Instruments, Derivatives, and Hedging Activities, ch. **12**
99-11 Subsequent Events Caused by Year 2000	Subsequent Events, ch. **29**
99-12 Determination of the Measurement Date for the Market Price of Acquirer Securities Issued in a Purchase Business Combination	Business Combinations, ch. **4**

99-13	
Application of Issue No. 97-10 and FASB Interpretation No. 23 to Entities That Enter into Leases with Governmental Entities	Leases, ch. **18**
99-14	
Recognition of Losses on Firmly Committed Executory Contracts	Intangible Assets, ch. **37**
99-15	
Accounting for Decreases in Deferred Tax Asset Valuation Allowances Established in a Purchase Business Combination as a Result of a Change in Tax Regulations	Income Taxes, ch. **39**
99-16	
Accounting for Transactions with Elements of Research and Development Arrangements	Research and Development Costs, ch. **26**
99-17	
Accounting for Advertising Barter Transactions	Nonmonetary Transactions, ch. **20**
99-19	
Reporting Revenue Gross as a Principal versus Net as an Agent	Revenues and Gains, ch. **43**
99-20	
Recognition of Interest Income and Impairment on Certain Investments	Financial Instruments, Derivatives, and Hedging Activities, ch. **12** Accounts and Notes Receivable, ch. **32** Investments: Debt and Equity Securities, ch. **34**
00-1	
Balance Sheet and Income Statement Display under the Equity Method for Investments in Certain Partnerships and Other Unincorporated Noncontrolled Ventures	Investments: Equity and Cost Methods, ch. **35**
00-2	
Accounting for Web Site Development Costs Capitalization or Expense Recognition	Accounting Policies, ch. **2**
00-3	
Application of AICPA Statement of Position 97-2 to Arrangements That Include the Right to Use Software Stored on Another Entity's Hardware	Accounting Policies, ch. **2**
00-4	
Majority Owner's Accounting for the Minority Interest in a Subsidiary and a Derivative	Financial Instruments, Derivatives, and Hedging Activities, ch. **12**

00-5 Determining Whether a Nonmonetary Transaction Is an Exchange of Similar Productive Assets	Nonmonetary Transactions, ch. **20**
00-6 Accounting for Freestanding Derivative Financial Instruments Indexed to, and Potentially Settled in, the Stock of a Consolidated Subsidiary	Financial Instruments, Derivatives, and Hedging Activities, ch. **12**
00-7 Application of Issue No. 96-13 to Equity Derivative Transactions That Contain Certain Provisions That Require Net Cash Settlement if Certain Events Outside the Control of the Issuer Occur	Financial Instruments, Derivatives, and Hedging Activities, ch. **12**
00-8 Accounting by a Grantee for an Equity Instrument to Be Received in Conjunction with Providing Goods or Services	Stock-Based Compensation, Stock Option Plans, and Stock Purchase Plans, ch. **28**
00-9 Classification of a Gain or Loss from a Hedge of Debt That Is Extinguished	Debt Obligations and Credit Arrangements, ch. **40**
00-10 Accounting for Shipping and Handling Fees and Costs	Revenues and Gains, ch. **43**
00-11 Meeting the Ownership Transfer Requirements of FASB Statement No. 13 for Leases of Real Estate	Leases, ch. **18**
00-12 Accounting for Stock-Based Compensation Granted by an Investor to Employees of an Equity Method Investee	Stock-Based Compensation, Stock Option Plans, and Stock Purchase Plans, ch. **28**
00-13 Determining Whether Equipment Is "Integral Equipment" Subject to FASB Statements No. 66 and No. 98	Property, Plant, and Equipment, ch. **36**
00-14 Accounting for Coupons, Rebates, and Discounts	Accounting Policies, ch. **2** Revenues and Gains, ch. **43**

00-15	
Classification in the Statement of Cash Flows of the Income Tax Benefit Received by a Company upon Exercise of a Nonqualified Employee Stock Option	Income Taxes, ch. **39**
00-16	
Recognition and Measurement of Employer Payroll Taxes on Employee Stock-Based Compensation	Stock-Based Compensation, Stock Option Plans, and Stock Purchase Plans, ch. **28**
00-17	
Measuring the Fair Value of Energy-Related Contracts in Applying EITF Issue No. 98-10, *Accounting for Contracts Involved in Energy Trading and Risk Management Activities*	Financial Instruments, Derivatives, and Hedging Activities, ch. **12**
00-18	
Accounting Recognition for Certain Transactions Involving Equity Instruments Granted to Other Than Employees	Stock-Based Compensation, Stock Option Plans, and Stock Purchase Plans, ch. **28**
00-19	
Determination of Whether Share Settlement Is within the Control of the Company for Purposes of Applying EITF Issue No. 96-13, *Accounting for Derivative Financial Instruments Indexed to, and Potentially Settled in, a Company's Own Stock*	Financial Instruments, Derivatives, and Hedging Activities, ch. **12**
00-20	
Accounting for Costs Incurred to Acquire or Originate Information for Database Content and Other Collections of Information	Accounting Policies, ch. **2** Expenses and Losses, ch. **44**
00-21	
Accounting for Revenue Arrangements with Multiple Deliverables	Accounting Policies, ch. **2** Revenues and Gains, ch. **43**
00-22	
Accounting for "Points" and Certain Other Time-Based or Volume-Based Sales Incentive Offers, and Offers for Free Products or Services to Be Delivered in the Future	Accounting Policies, ch. **2** Revenues and Gains, ch. **43** Expenses and Losses, ch. **44**
00-23	
Issues Related to the Accounting for Stock Compensation under APB Opinion No. 25, *Accounting for Stock Issued to Employees,* and FASB Interpretation No. 44, *Accounting for Certain Transactions Involving Stock Compensation*	Stock-Based Compensation, Stock Option Plans, and Stock Purchase Plans, ch. **28**

00-24 Revenue Recognition: Sales Arrangements That Include Specified-Price Trade-In Rights	Accounting Policies, ch. **2** Revenues and Gains, ch. **43**
00-25 Vendor Income Statement Characterization of Consideration from a Vendor to a Retailer	Accounting Policies, ch. **2** Revenues and Gains, ch. **43**
00-26 Recognition by a Seller of Losses on Firmly Committed Executory Contracts	Intangible Assets, ch. **37**
00-27 Application of EITF Issue No. 98-5, *Accounting for Convertible Securities with Beneficial Conversion Features or Contingently Adjustable Conversion Ratios,* to Certain Convertible Instruments	Debt Obligations and Credit Arrangements, ch. **40** Stockholders' Equity, ch. **42**

PRACTICE BULLETINS OF THE AICPA ACCOUNTING STANDARDS DIVISION

ORIGINAL PRONOUNCEMENT	2001–02 *MILLER GAAP FINANCIAL STATEMENT DISCLOSURES MANUAL* REFERENCE
PB-1 Purpose and Scope of AcSEC Practice Bulletins and Procedures for Their Issuance	Accounting Policies, ch. **2**
PB-2 Elimination of Profits Resulting from Intercompany Transfers of LIFO Inventories	Inventory, ch. **33**
PB-4 Accounting for Foreign Debt/Equity Swaps	Financial Instruments, Derivatives, and Hedging Activities, ch. **12**
PB-5 Income Recognition on Loans to Financially Troubled Countries	Debt Obligations and Credit Arrangements, ch. **40**
PB-11 Accounting for Preconfirmation Contingencies in Fresh-Start Reporting	Quasi-Reorganizations and Reorginizations under the Bankruptcy Code, ch. **24**
PB-12 Reporting Separate Investment Fund Option Information of Defined-Contribution Pension Plans	Accounting Policies, ch. **2**

PB-13 Direct-Response Advertising and Probable Future Benefits	Advertising Costs, ch. **3**
PB-14 Accounting and Reporting by Limited Liability Companies and Limited Liability Partnerships	Stockholders' Equity, ch. **42**

AICPA ACCOUNTING INTERPRETATIONS

ORIGINAL PRONOUNCEMENT	2001–02 *MILLER GAAP FINANCIAL STATEMENT DISCLOSURES MANUAL* REFERENCE
AIN-APB 4 Accounting for the Investment Tax Credit: Accounting Interpretations of APB Opinion No. 4	Income Taxes, ch. **39**
AIN-APB-9 Reporting the Results of Operations: Unofficial Accounting Interpretations of APB Opinion No. 9	Expenses and Losses, ch. **44** Discontinued Operations, ch. **45** Extraordinary Items, ch. **46** Unusual or Infrequent Items, ch. **47**
AIN-APB 16 Business Combinations: Accounting Interpretations of APB Opinion No. 16	Business Combinations, ch. **4**
AIN-APB 17 Intangible Assets: Unofficial Accounting Interpretations of APB Opinion No. 17	Intangible Assets, ch. **37**
AIN-APB 18 The Equity Method of Accounting for Investments in Common Stock: Accounting Interpretations of APB Opinion No. 18	Investments: Equity and Cost Methods, ch. **35**
AIN-APB 21 Interest on Receivables and Payables: Accounting Interpretations of APB Opinion No. 21	Interest Cost, ch. **16** Accounts and Notes Receivable, ch. **32**
AIN-APB 25 Accounting for Stock Issued to Employees: Accounting Interpretations of APB Opinion No. 25	Stock-Based Compensation, Stock Option Plans, and Stock Purchase Plans, ch. **28**
AIN-APB 26 Early Extinguishment of Debt: Accounting Interpretations of APB Opinion No. 26	Debt Obligations and Credit Arrangements, ch. **40**

AIN-APB-30 Reporting the Results of Operations: Accounting Interpretations of APB Opinion No. 30	Expenses and Losses, ch. **44** Discontinued Operations, ch. **45** Extraordinary Items, ch. **46** Unusual or Infrequent Items, ch. **47**

FASB IMPLEMENTATION GUIDES

ORIGINAL PRONOUNCEMENT	2001–02 *MILLER GAAP FINANCIAL STATEMENT DISCLOSURES MANUAL* REFERENCE
FIG-FAS 87 A Guide to Implementation of Statement 87 on Employers' Accounting for Pensions	Pension Plans, ch. **21**
FIG-FAS 88 A Guide to Implementation of Statement 88 on Employers' Accounting for Settlements and Curtailments of Defined Benefit Pension Plans and for Termination Benefits	Pension Plans, ch. **21**
FIG-FAS 106 A Guide to Implementation of Statement 106 on Employers' Accounting for Postretirement Benefits Other Than Pensions	Postemployment Benefits, ch. **22** Postretirement Benefits Other Than Pensions, ch. **23**
FIG-FAS 109 A Guide to Implementation of Statement 109 on Accounting for Income Taxes	Income Taxes, ch. **39**
FIG-FAS 5, 114 Application of FASB Statements 5 and 114 to a Loan Portfolio	Debt Obligations and Credit Arrangements, ch. **40**
FIG-FAS 115 A Guide to Implementation of Statement 115 on Accounting for Certain Investments in Debt and Equity Securities	Investments: Debt and Equity Securities, ch. **34**
FIG-FAS 131 Guidance on Applying Statement 31	Segment Information, ch. **27**
FIG-FAS 140 A Guide to Implementation of Statement 140 on Accounting for Transfers and Servicing of Financial Assets and Extinguishments of Liabilities	Financial Instruments, Derivatives, and Hedging Activities, ch. **12** Debt Obligations and Credit Arrangements, ch. **40**

EITF/FASB/SEC STAFF ANNOUNCEMENTS

ORIGINAL PRONOUNCEMENT	2001–02 *MILLER GAAP FINANCIAL STATEMENT DISCLOSURES MANUAL* REFERENCE
D-1 Implications and Implementation of an EITF Consensus	Accounting Changes, ch. **1**
D-8 Accruing Bad-Debt Expense at Inception of a Lease	Leases, ch. **18**
D-10 Required Use of Interest Method in Recognizing Interest Income	Financial Instruments, Derivatives, and Hedging Activities, ch. **12**
D-11 Impact of Stock Market Decline	Investments: Debt and Equity Securities, ch. **34**
D-12 Foreign Currency Translation—Selection of Exchange Rate When Trading Is Temporarily Suspended	Foreign Operations and Currency Translation, ch. **14**
D-13 Transfers of Receivables in Which Risk of Foreign Currency Fluctuation Is Retained	Superseded by FAS-125.
D-14 Transactions Involving Special-Purpose Entities	Consolidated and Combined Financial Statements, ch. **8**
D-16 Hedging Foreign Currency Risks of Future Net Income, Revenues, or Costs	Foreign Operations and Currency Translation, ch. **14**
D-18 Accounting for Compensation Expense If Stock Appreciation Rights Are Cancelled	Stock-Based Compensation, Stock Option Plans, and Stock Purchase Plans, ch. **28**
D-19 Impact on Pooling-of-Interests Accounting of Treasury Shares Acquired to Satisfy Conversions in a Leveraged Preferred Stock ESOP	Business Combinations, ch. **4**
D-22 Questions Related to the Implementation of FASB Statement No. 105	Financial Instruments, Derivatives, and Hedging Activities, ch. **12**

D-23 Subjective Acceleration Clauses and Debt Classification	Assets and Liabilities: General, ch. **30** Debt Obligations and Credit Arrangements, ch. **40**
D-24 Sale-Leaseback Transactions with Continuing Involvement	Leases, ch. **18**
D-27 Accounting for the Transfer of Excess Pension Assets to a Retiree Health Care Benefits Account	Pension Plans, ch. **21**
D-30 Adjustment Due to Effect of a Change in Tax Laws or Rates	Income Taxes, ch. **39**
D-31 Temporary Differences Related to LIFO Inventory and Tax-to-Tax Differences	Income Taxes, ch. **39**
D-32 Intraperiod Tax Allocation of the Tax Effect of Pretax Income from Continuing Operations	Income Taxes, ch. **39**
D-33 Timing of Recognition of Tax Benefits for Pre-reorganization Temporary Differences and Carryforwards	Income Taxes, ch. **39**
D-36 Selection of Discount Rates Used for Measuring Defined Benefit Pension Obligations and Obligations of Postretirement Benefit Plans Other Than Pensions	Pension Plans, ch. **21**
D-39 Questions Related to the Implementation of FASB Statement No. 115	Investments: Debt and Equity Securities, ch. **34**
D-40 Planned Sale of Securities following a Business Combination Expected to Be Accounted for as a Pooling of Interests	Business Combinations, ch. **4**
D-41 Adjustments in Assets and Liabilities for Holding Gains and Losses as Related to the Implementation of FASB Statement No. 115	Investments: Debt and Equity Securities, ch. **34**
D-42 The Effect on the Calculation of Earnings per Share for the Redemption or Induced Conversion of Preferred Stock	Earnings per Share, ch. **49**

D-43	
Assurance That a Right of Setoff Is Enforceable in a Bankruptcy under FASB Interpretation No. 39	Quasi-Reorganizations and Reorganizations under the Bankruptcy Code, ch. **24**
D-44	
Recognition of Other-Than-Temporary Impairment upon the Planned Sale of a Security Whose Cost Exceeds Fair Value	Investments: Debt and Equity Securities, ch. **34**
D-45	
Implementation of FASB Statement No. 121 for Assets to Be Disposed Of	Property, Plant, and Equipment, ch. **36** Intangible Assets, ch. **37**
D-46	
Accounting for Limited Partnership Investments	Investments: Equity and Cost Methods, ch. **35**
D-50	
Classification of Gains and Losses from the Termination of an Interest Rate Swap Designated to Commercial Paper	Financial Instruments, Derivatives, and Hedging Activities, ch. **12**
D- 51	
The Applicability of FASB Statement No. 115 to Desecuritizations of Financial Assets	Investments: Debt and Equity Securities, ch. **34**
D-52	
Impact of FASB Statement No. 125 on EITF Issues	Financial Instruments, Derivatives, and Hedging Activities, ch. **12** Accounts and Notes Receivable, ch. **32**
D-53	
Computation of Earnings per Share for a Period That Includes a Redemption or an Induced Conversion of a Portion of a Class of Preferred Stock	Earnings per Share, ch. **49**
D-54	
Accounting by the Purchaser for a Seller's Guarantee of the Adequacy of Liabilities for Losses and Loss Adjustment Expenses of an Insurance Enterprise Acquired in a Purchase Business Combination	Business Combinations, ch. **4**
D-55	
Determining a Highly Inflationary Economy under FASB Statement No. 52	Foreign Operations and Currency Translation, ch. **14**
D-56	
Accounting for a Change in Functional Currency and Deferred Taxes When an Economy Becomes Highly Inflationary	Foreign Operations and Currency Translation, ch. **14**

D-59 Payment of a Termination Fee in Connection with a Subsequent Business Combination That Is Accounted for Using the Pooling-of-Interests Method	Business Combinations, ch. **4**
D-60 Accounting for the Issuance of Convertible Preferred Stock and Debt Securities with a Nondetachable Conversion Feature	Debt Obligations and Credit Arrangements, ch. **40** Stockholders' Equity, ch. **42**
D-61 Classification by the Issuer of Redeemable Instruments That Are Subject to Remarketing Agreements	Financial Instruments, Derivatives, and Hedging Activities, ch. **12** Assets and Liabilities: General, ch. **30** Stockholders' Equity, ch. **42**
D-62 Computing Year-to-Date Diluted Earnings per Share under FASB Statement No. 128	Earnings per Share, ch. **49**
D-63 Call Options "Embedded" in Beneficial Interests Issued by a Qualifying Special-Purpose Entity	Financial Instruments, Derivatives, and Hedging Activities, ch. **12** Stockholders' Equity, ch. **42**
D-64 Accounting for Derivatives Used to Hedge Interest Rate Risk	Financial Instruments, Derivatives, and Hedging Activities, ch. **12**
D-65 Maintaining Collateral in Repurchase Agreements and Similar Transactions under FASB Statement No. 125	Financial Instruments, Derivatives, and Hedging Activities, ch. **12**
D-66 Effect of a Special-Purpose Entity's Powers to Sell, Exchange, Repledge, or Distribute Transferred Financial Assets under FASB Statement No. 125	Financial Instruments, Derivatives, and Hedging Activities, ch. **12**
D-67 Isolation of Assets Transferred by Financial Institutions under FASB Statement No. 125	Financial Instruments, Derivatives, and Hedging Activities, ch. **12**
D-68 Accounting by an Equity Method Investor for Investee Losses When the Investor Has Loans to and Investments in Other Securities of an Investee	Investments: Equity and Cost Methods, ch. **35**

D-69 Gain Recognition on Transfers of Financial Assets under FASB Statement No. 125	Financial Instruments, Derivatives, and Hedging Activities, ch. **12**
D-70 Questions Related to the Implementation of FASB Statement No. 131	Segment Information, ch. **27**
D-71 Accounting Issues Relating to the Introduction of the European Economic and Monetary Union (EMU)	Foreign Operations and Currency Translation, ch. **14**
D-72 Effect of Contracts That May Be Settled in Stock or Cash on the Computation of Diluted Earnings per Share	Earnings per Share, ch. **49**
D-73 Reclassification and Subsequent Sales of Securities in Connection with the Adoption of FASB Statement No. 133	Financial Instruments, Derivatives, and Hedging Activities, ch. **12**
D-75 When to Recognize Gains and Losses on Assets Transferred to a Qualifying Special-Purpose Entity	Financial Instruments, Derivatives, and Hedging Activities, ch. **12** Accounts and Notes Receivable, ch. **32**
D-77 Accounting for Legal Costs Expected to Be Incurred in Connection with a Loss Contingency	Accounting Policies, ch. **2** Contingencies, Risks, Uncertainties, and Concentrations, ch. **9** Assets and Liabililities: General, ch. **30** Expenses and Losses, ch. **44**
D-79 Accounting for Retroactive Insurance Contracts Purchased by Entities Other Than Insurance Enterprises	Accounting Policies, ch. **2** Assets and Liabililities: General, ch. **30**
D-80 Application of FASB Statements No. 5 and No. 114 to a Loan Portfolio	Contingencies, Risks, Uncertainties, and Concentrations, ch. **9** Accounts and Notes Receivable, ch. **32** Debt Obligations and Credit Arrangements, ch. **40**
D-81 Accounting for the Aquisition of Consolidated Business	Nonmonetary Transactions, ch. **20**

D-82 Effect of Preferred Stock Dividends Payable in Common Shares on Computation of Income Available to Common Stockholders	Earnings per Share, ch. **49**
D-83 Accounting for Payroll Taxes Associated with Stock Option Exercises	Stock-Based Compensation, Stock Option Plans, and Stock Purchase Plans, ch. **28**
D-84 Accounting for Subsequent Investments in an Investee after Suspension of Equity Method Loss Recognition When an Investor Increases Its Ownership Interest from Significant Influence to Control through a Market Purchase of Voting Securities	Investments: Equity and Cost Methods, ch. **35**
D-85 Application of Certain Transition Provisions in SEC Staff Accounting Bulletin No. 101	Accounting Policies, ch. **2** Revenues and Gains, ch. **43**
D-86 Issuance of Financial Statements	Revenues and Gains, ch. **43** Expenses and Losses, ch. **44**
D-87 Determination of the Measurement Date for Consideration Given by the Acquirer in a Business Combination When That Consideration Is Securities Other Than Those Issued by the Acquirer	Business Combinations, ch. **4**
D-88 Planned Major Maintenance Activities	Property, Plant, and Equipment, ch. **36**
D-89 Accounting for Costs of Future Medicare Compliance Audits	Accounting Policies, ch. **2**

Index

A

B

C

D

E

F

G

H

J

L

M

Q

R

About the CD-ROM

SYSTEM REQUIREMENTS

- IBM PC or compatible computer with CD-ROM drive
- Windows 95 or higher
- Microsoft® Word 7.0 for Windows™ or compatible word processor
- 10 MB available on hard drive

The CD-ROM provided with the 2001-02 Miller *GAAP Financial Statement Disclosures Manual* contains electronic versions of the over 850 separate sample disclosures presented in the book. Disclosures are available as separate pages within files for each chapter. The CD-ROM also includes the complete financial statement disclosures checklist, covering all types of disclosures, including items for special financial statement topics, the balance sheet, the income statement, and the statement of cash flows. Questions addressed in the checklist are keyed to specific authoritative literature to identify their regulatory antecedents.

Subject to the conditions in the license agreement and the limited warranty, which are reproduced at the end of this book, you may duplicate the files on this disc, modify them as necessary, and create your own customized versions. Using the disc in any way indicates that you accept the terms of the license agreement.

USING THE CD-ROM

The data disc is intended for use with your word processing software. Each document is provided in Rich Text Format. These files can be read by all compatible word processors, including Microsoft Word for Windows and WordPerfect 7 or above. Check your owner's manual for information on the conversion of documents as required.

USING THE DOCUMENTS

The list of the Disc Contents is available on your disc in a file called _contents.rtf. You can open this file and view it on your screen and use it to link the documents you're interested in, or print a hard copy to use for reference.

1. Open the file _contents.rtf in your word processor.

2. Locate the file you wish to access, and click on the hyper-linked file name. Your word processor will then open the file.

3. You may copy files from the CD-ROM to your hard disk. To edit files you have copied, remember to clear the read-only attribute from the file. To do this, select the name of the file in My Computer, right-click the filename, then choose Properties, and clear the Read-only checkbox.

SOFTWARE SUPPORT

If you experience any difficulties installing or running the electronic files and cannot resolve the problem using the information presented here, call our toll-free software support hotline at (800) 486-9296. Hours of operation are 8 a.m. to 5 p.m., EST, Monday through Friday.

CD-ROM Contents

PART I—SPECIAL FINANCIAL STATEMENT TOPICS AND DISCLOSURES

Chapter 1: Accounting Changes

Chapter 2: Accounting Policies

2–14	General Policy for Accounting for Business Combinations, Allocation of Purchase Price, and Acquisition Contingencies
2–15	Pooling-of-Interests
2–16	Purchase Method
2–17	Capitalization of Interest Costs on Borrowings
2–18	Types of Cash Equivalents Specifically Identified
2–19	Types of Cash Equivalents Described in General Terms
2–20	Components of Other Comprehensive Income Disclosed
2–21	Consolidation Policy Specifically Described
2–22	Combined Financial Statements
2–23	General Accounting Policy for Contingencies
2–24	Amounts Billed in Advance
2–25	Basic and Diluted Net Earnings Per Share
2–26	Environmental Expenditures Expensed or Capitalized
2–27	Accruals for Environmental Matters Exclude Claims for Recoveries
2–28	General Note Regarding Estimates Inherent in the Financial Statements
2–29	Significant Estimates Relating to Specific Financial Statement Accounts and Transactions Are Identified
2–30	Fair Value of Financial Instruments Approximate Carrying Amount
2–31	Fair Value of Financial Instruments Is Based on Quoted Market Prices or Pricing Models
2–32	Fair Value of Financial Instruments Is Based on Management's Estimates
2–33	Fair Value of Long-Term Debt Is Estimated Based on Current Rates and Terms Offered to the Company
2–34	Fair Value of Notes Receivable Based on Discounted Cash Flows
2–35	Interest Rate Swap Agreements—Prior to Adoption of FASB Statement No. 133 (Accounting for Derivative Instruments and Hedging Activities)
2–36	Foreign Exchange Forward Contracts—Prior to Adoption of FAS-133
2–37	Commodity Futures Contracts—Prior to Adoption of FAS-133
2–38	Off-Balance Sheet Financial Instruments—Prior to Adoption of FAS-133

Chapter 3: Advertising Costs

Chapter 4: Business Combinations

Chapter 5: Changing Prices

Chapter 6: Commitments

Chapter 7: Compensated Absences

Chapter 8: Consolidated and Combined Financial Statements

Chapter 10: Deferred Compensation Arrangements

Chapter 11: Development Stage Enterprises

Chapter 12: Financial Instruments, Derivatives, and Hedging Activities

Chapter 13: Financial Instruments: Comparative

Chapter 14: Foreign Operations and Currency Translation

Chapter 15: Going Concern

Chapter 18: Leases

Chapter 19: Long-Term Contracts

Chapter 20: Nonmonetary Transactions

Chapter 21: Pension Plans

Chapter 22: Postemployment Benefits

Chapter 23: Postretirement Benefits Other Than Pensions

Chapter 24: Quasi-Reorganizations and Reorganizations under the Bankruptcy Code

Chapter 25: Related-Party Disclosures

Chapter 29: Subsequent Events

PART II—BALANCE SHEET

Chapter 31: Cash and Cash Equivalents

Chapter 32: Accounts and Notes Receivable

Chapter 33: Inventory

Chapter 34: Investments: Debt and Equity Securities

Chapter 35: Investments: Equity and Cost Methods

Chapter 36: Property, Plant, and Equipment

Chapter 37: Intangible Assets

Chapter 38: Other Assets: Current and Noncurrent

Chapter 39: Income Taxes

Chapter 40: Debt Obligations and Credit Arrangements

Chapter 41: Other Liabilities: Current and Noncurrent

Chapter 42: Stockholders' Equity

PART III—INCOME STATEMENT

Chapter 43: Revenues and Gains

Chapter 47: Unusual or Infrequent Items

Chapter 48: Comprehensive Income

Chapter 49: Earnings per Share

PART IV—STATEMENT OF CASH FLOWS

Chapter 50: Statement of Cash Flows

ASPEN LAW & BUSINESS SOFTWARE LICENSE AGREEMENT

READ THE TERMS AND CONDITIONS OF THIS LICENSE AGREEMENT CAREFULLY BEFORE INSTALLING THE SOFTWARE (THE "PROGRAM") TO ACCOMPANY 2001–02 MILLER GAAP FINANCIAL STATEMENT DISCLOSURES MANUAL (THE "BOOK"). THE PROGRAM IS COPYRIGHTED AND LICENSED (NOT SOLD). BY INSTALLING THE PROGRAM, YOU ARE ACCEPTING AND AGREEING TO THE TERMS OF THIS LICENSE AGREEMENT. IF YOU ARE NOT WILLING TO BE BOUND BY THE TERMS OF THIS LICENSE AGREEMENT, YOU SHOULD PROMPTLY RETURN THE PACKAGE IN RESELLABLE CONDITION AND YOU WILL RECEIVE A REFUND OF YOUR MONEY. THIS LICENSE AGREEMENT REPRESENTS THE ENTIRE AGREEMENT CONCERNING THE PROGRAM BETWEEN YOU AND ASPEN LAW & BUSINESS (REFERRED TO AS "LICENSOR"), AND IT SUPERSEDES ANY PRIOR PROPOSAL, REPRESENTATION, OR UNDERSTANDING BETWEEN THE PARTIES.

1. License Grant. Licensor hereby grants to you, and you accept, a nonexclusive license to use the Program CD-ROM and the computer programs contained therein in machine-readable, object code form only (collectively referred to as the "Software"), and the accompanying User Documentation, only as authorized in this License Agreement. The Software may be used only on a single computer owned, leased, or otherwise controlled by you; or in the event of the inoperability of that computer, on a backup computer selected by you. Neither concurrent use on two or more computers nor use in a local area network or other network is permitted without separate authorization and the possible payment of other license fees. You agree that you will not assign, sublease, transfer, pledge, lease, rent, or share your rights under the License Agreement. You agree that you may not reverse engineer, decompile, disassemble, or otherwise adapt, modify, or translate the Software.

Upon loading the Software into your computer, you may retain the Program CD-ROM for backup purposes. In addition, you may make one copy of the Software on a set of diskettes (or other storage medium) for the purpose of backup in the event the Program Diskettes are damaged or destroyed. You may make one copy of any additional User Documentation (such as the README.TXT file or the "About the Computer Disc" section of the Book) for backup purposes. Any such copies of the Software or the User Documentation shall include Licensor's copyright and other proprietary notices. Except as authorized under this paragraph, no copies of the program or any portions thereof may be made by you or any person under your authority or control.

2. Licensor's Rights. You acknowledge and agree that the Software and the User Documentation are proprietary products of Licensor protected under U.S. copyright law. You further acknowledge and agree that all right, title, and interest in and to the Program, including associated intellectual property rights, are and shall remain with Licensor. This License Agreement does not convey to you an interest in or to the Program, including associated intellectual property rights, which are and shall remain with Licensor. This License Agreement does not convey to you an interest in or to the Program, but only a limited right of use revocable in accordance with the terms of the License Agreement.

3. License Fees. The license fees paid by you are paid in consideration of the licenses granted under this License Agreement.

4. Term. This License Agreement is effective upon your installing this software and shall continue until terminated. You may terminate this License Agreement at any time by returning the Program and all copies thereof and extracts therefrom to Licensor. Licensor may terminate this License Agreement upon the breach by you of any term hereof. Upon such termination by Licensor, you agree to return to Licensor the Program and all copies and portions thereof.

5. Limited Warranty. Licensor warrants, for our benefit alone, for a period of 90 days from the date of commencement of this License Agreement (referred to as the "Warranty Period") that the Program CD-ROM in which the Software is contained is free from defects in material and workmanship. If during the Warranty Period, a defect appears in the Program diskettes, you may return the Program to Licensor for either replacement or, at Licensor's option, refund of amounts paid by you under this License Agreement. You agree that the foregoing constitutes your sole and exclusive remedy for breach by Licensor of any warranties made under this Agreement. EXCEPT FOR THE WARRANTIES SET FORTH ABOVE, THE PROGRAM, AND THE SOFTWARE CONTAINED THEREIN, ARE LICENSED "AS IS," AND LICENSOR DISCLAIMS ANY AND ALL OTHER WARRANTIES, WHETHER EXPRESS OR IMPLIED, INCLUDING, WITHOUT LIMITATION, ANY IMPLIED WARRANTIES OF MERCHANTABILITY OR FITNESS FOR A PARTICULAR PURPOSE.

6. Limitation of Liability. Licensor's cumulative liability to you or any other party for any loss or damages resulting from any claims, demands, or actions arising out of or relating to this Agreement shall not exceed the license fee paid to Licensor for the use of the Program. IN NO EVENT SHALL LICENSOR BE LIABLE FOR ANY INDIRECT, INCIDENTAL, CONSEQUENTIAL, SPECIAL, OR EXEMPLARY DAMAGES (INCLUDING, BUT NOT LIMITED TO, LOSS OF DATA, BUSINESS INTERRUPTION, OR LOST PROFITS) EVEN IF LICENSOR HAS BEEN ADVISED OF THE POSSIBILITY OF SUCH DAMAGES.

7. Miscellaneous. This License Agreement shall be construed and governed in accordance with the laws of the State of New York. Should any term of this License Agreement be declared void or unenforceable by any court of competent jurisdiction, such declaration shall have no effect on the remaining terms hereof. The failure of either party to enforce any rights granted hereunder or to take action against the other party in the event of any breach hereunder shall not be deemed a waiver by that party as to subsequent enforcement of rights or subsequent actions in the event of future breaches.